To Paul
with a lot
" GRAZIE "

Dona A...

# A Trip to Africa:

A Comic Opera
by Franz von Suppé

# *A Trip to Africa*:

## A Comic Opera
## by Franz von Suppé

Compiled and Researched by

Dario Salvi and Hannah Salvi

Cambridge
Scholars
Publishing

*A Trip to Africa*: A Comic Opera by Franz von Suppé

Compiled and Researched by Dario Salvi and Hannah Salvi

This book first published 2016

Cambridge Scholars Publishing

Lady Stephenson Library, Newcastle upon Tyne, NE6 2PA, UK

British Library Cataloguing in Publication Data
A catalogue record for this book is available from the British Library

ISBN (10): 1-4438-9094-4
ISBN (13): 978-1-4438-9094-6

*Dario:*
*To my dad, Bepi,*
*who I know would have been*
*proud of me for contributing to this research.*
*Thank you for sitting me down as a toddler in front of the TV*
*to watch the New Year's Concert from Vienna.*

*Hannah:*
*To all those who have encouraged me,*
*both musically and in life, to pursue my goals;*
*to my family; and especially to my husband,*
*whose passion for music inspires me every day.*

# DISCLAIMER

This document has been constructed for historical reference, and therefore the lyrics and stage directions have been printed as per the original libretto. Some derogatory references have been omitted so that the operetta may be performed publically, however some content may still be seen as offensive. It is important to note that the operetta is intended as light-entertainment, and therefore any such instances are merely satirical humour of the time, and are not the views of the editors or publisher.

# CONTENTS

# FOREWORD

"Vienna—17th March 1883. In the Theater an der Wien the 22nd operetta by Franz von Suppé receives its first performance." So reads the entry made by the composer in the handwritten list of his works as documented in the Vienna library. It is the last listing of a complete work; later entries only sketch out intentions.

With this first performance, Suppé had returned to the origins of his life as a composer of operettas. Twenty three years earlier, by staging the first performance of his one-act operetta *Das Pensionat*, he had helped found the Wiener Operette as a new artistic genre in its own right, trying to get away from the influence of Offenbach. Several attempts by various composers had preceded this attempt but it was Suppé who took the decisive steps. The success of the amusing one-act show was such that the Viennese audience showed more interest in it than in the new compositions of the internationally renowned Johann Strauss Jr., the 'Waltz King', which he had brought back from his guest performance in Pavlovsk, St. Petersburg.

In 1862, when it became clear that the directorship of Alois Pokorny was coming to an end due to his inability to pay the salaries, Suppé left the Theater an der Wien where he had both worked and resided, and, under the protection of the up and coming operetta theatre director Karl Treumann, he moved first to the Theatre on the Franz-Josef-Kai and later to the more traditional Carltheater in the Praterstraße.

Neither building exists today; the Kai-Theater burned down in 1863 and the Carltheater was bombed in 1944 and pulled down in 1951.

The Carltheater established Franz von Suppé as the most important composer of operettas beside Johann Strauss Jr. It was here that the first performances of his three successes *Fatinitza, Boccaccio* and *Donna Juanita* took place. As in the Theater an der Wien, Suppé took up lodgings on the fourth floor of the theatre until 1882.

In 1882 Franz von Suppé ended his contract with the Carltheater, leaving himself free to choose any venue for his first performances. Once again, with the performance of *Die Afrikareise,* the Theater an der Wien brought him success as it had done 23 years previously; there had been suggestions after his last creation for the Carltheater, the operetta *Herzblättchen,* that he had lost his creative drive.

This idea was not entirely unwarranted: the average lifespan in Vienna in the 1880s was around 60 years and Suppé, at 63, was considered to be an old man.

But his creative powers had not waned. In *Herzblättchen*, the confused libretto of Carl Albert Tetzlaff, a renowned director but amateur librettist, did not inspire Suppé greatly. He did not even consider the work worthy of a proper overture and took an overture from one of his one-act operettas, *Das Corps der Rache,* which 19 years earlier had flopped and sank out of sight after only 11 performances within three weeks.

This situation was to change significantly in the case of *Die Afrikareise* because the old master and expert among the Viennese librettists, Richard Genée, appeared on the scene once again. In collaboration with F. Zell he had prepared the ground for Suppé's greatest operetta successes.

To regard Genée only as a librettist is not to do him justice: he was also a very talented composer, valued even by Johann Strauss Jr. on account of his musical gifts; furthermore he was sensitive to the literary trends of his time and to the public's expectations.

For *Die Afrikareise* however, it was not Zell, the genial collaborator and inventor of stories, who helped Genée, but Moritz West, alias Dr. Moritz Nitzelberger. He was a school and university friend of the composer Carl Zeller and by profession the director of the Moravian–Silesian Central Railway. Zell had persuaded and taught him to write librettos.

During the writing of the plot, Genée employed a well tried strategy which he had invented for the Viennese operetta. Whereas Offenbach's Parisian operetta resorted to political parody and provocation by showing up the moral weaknesses of contemporary society, the Viennese operetta, within the confines of the strictly catholic and absolute Habsburg regime, had to dispense with parody and open eroticism.

The Viennese operetta replaced parody with musical sentimentality, enriched with folk music and Bel Canto opera, and the erotic element by introducing trouser roles showing off the legs of the ladies and by setting the scenes in places evocative of erotic sentiments such as Venice or the Middle East.

Whereas in Offenbach, such places served as ciphers for real historical situations, in the Viennese operetta they became codes for sexual innuendo, sometimes bordering on pornography. The names of far-away cities and countries, known only through literature, aroused feelings of longing for remote places and dreams of unsuspected erotic possibilities.

The choice of place for *Die Afrikareise*—Cairo and its surroundings—was indeed influenced by a current political event: the occupation of Egypt by the English in 1882. The occupation was a reaction to the nationalistic Urabi movement which opposed the international financial control of the country forced upon the Khedives and against the autocratic regime of the Khedives themselves. The movement was put down by British troops under Garnet Joseph Wolseley. This political event was not mentioned in the libretto as such but is an indication of the topicality of the operetta.

That the libretto alone provides the erotic attraction is supported by the fact that the music of *Die Afrikareise* never has recourse to African rhythms and African sounds but stays within the usual spectrum of the Viennese operetta. Suppé never leaves the "sound-world" which he himself, as quasi founder of the Viennese operetta, had created, a "sound-world" which does not go beyond the core countries of the Habsburg monarchy. Whereas the Strauss brothers, for example, were responsive to fresh musical events, such as Richard Wagner, Suppé, who was present at the first *Ring des Nibelungen* in Bayreuth, 1876, on account of his 'discovery' of Amalie Materna, who sang Brünnhilde, and heard the master pontificating in the intervals, was quite unaffected by the new musical language which electrified Europe and America.

In Suppé's *A Trip to Africa* you hear the triangle and tambourine—and the slaves happily indulge in polka dancing.

Suppé also stayed faithful to his musical compositional principles and ended the work, as he did with all his successful oeuvres, with a convincing march in E-major. An instrumental version, again successful, appeared under the title "Over mountains and Valleys"—hardly evocative of Cairo and its surroundings.

In spite of its historical links, *Die Afrikareise* introduced some changes. No longer can we speak about a libretto with a clear plot which evolves step by step. The action develops erratically and jumps from situation to situation as though to represent the fast pace of modern times. The wit has become more scanty too as documented by the use of far-fetched names and certain peculiarities such as dates grown to make you sneeze.

The plundering of literary sources, however, is as alive as ever; this time even 'borrowings' from Mozart's *The Abduction from the Seraglio* are evident. Clearly Suppé still felt the longing to write an opera which he had been wanting to do all his life, with little success. He no longer uses the short, fragmented style; musical numbers, traditionally divided by dialogues, are now combined into larger groupings.

The first performance of *Die Afrikareise* in the Theater an der Wien could rely on an excellent cast: Karl Blasel, Therese Schäfer, Joseph Josephi, Caroline Finaly—all stars of the Viennese operetta. The biggest name was Alexander Girardi in the role of Miradillo. One could read in the 'Wiener Zeitung' newspaper that he was "greater than the music, the text and everything else". He was to prove the accuracy of this statement in his later career.

The press did not agree in its judgement of this work. The magazine 'Lyra' praised it exceedingly whilst the 'Wiener Zeitung' accused the composer of being trivial. Whatever, *Die Afrikareise* does not deserve to have been forgotten. Perhaps our times, with a more relaxed understanding of what is possible on stage, are better suited to the charm of this story. Certainly, the music of Franz von Suppé more than deserves our appreciation.

HANS DIETER ROSER
Offical biographer of Franz von Suppé
Vienna, Austria, February 2016

# PREFACE

It all started one autumn afternoon in 2014 when I was looking for some new music to perform with my orchestra; the Imperial Vienna Orchestra—a group of talented musicians based in East Anglia, England, with a passion for Viennese music. Since its formation in 2012, we have brought well-known works as well as rare gems and even world premieres to an ever growing audience.

It was with this in mind that I was browsing the internet to find something typically Viennese, but with something different about it.

I came across a piece called 'A Trip to Africa Polka'. The title alone resonated with me; a Viennese piece with Oriental themes thrown into it. It made me curious to find out more about it. I started browsing through the orchestral parts I could find—sadly not a full set—and I quickly realised the beauty and originality of the work. This prompted me to create a full orchestral arrangement of the polka from the incomplete set and a piano score I had managed to obtain.

We started performing the polka soon after with the orchestra, and my taste for it kept growing. It really is an amazing piece of music.

Intrigued by this little snippet from the opera, I wanted to find out more about the work from which it was taken. I soon came across the German/Italian vocal score, and, flicking through its pages I decided that I would love to perform this amazing work in its entirety.

I began the painstaking process of sourcing the full orchestral set of the whole opera, however nothing was available anywhere. What next?

All I came across were piano pieces, or vocal and piano pieces, both in German and English, a print of the original German libretto and a reduction of the English libretto.

The titles of these works were as intriguing as the music. They included: 'Flower Duettino', 'Life Oriental, Occidental', 'Fanfani March', 'Titania Waltz', 'The Snuff Song' and 'Spring Tide'. I also came across a march called 'Uber Berg, Uber Tal', two selections from the operetta for orchestra and some potpourris arranged for piano. The music was unfolding before my eyes.

However something was very wrong. I could not find anything in the German score that even remotely sounded or looked like the 'Snuff Song' or 'Spring Tide'. A name I had never heard before was associated to these works: Adolf Neuendorff. Who was this musician?

Some research taught me that he was a composer himself; a contemporary of Suppé, who exported—or imported since he was living there—to the States many operas from German speaking countries as well as composing original works.

Neuendorff had composed these two works to modify Suppé's original music and libretto in order to suit the American stage. He replaced a song (No.8) and a couplet (No.11) from the original score with his two compositions. I studied the music and the text, and the style was nothing like Suppé's, with the lyrics moving away dramatically from Genée and West's libretto.

I was confronted with yet another obstacle. What should I do with these two pieces? Shall I include them in my work or should I maintain Suppé's original version? The answer was not an immediate one.

After months of research I managed to source all the orchestral parts from an American production. They were hidden in the archives of the University of Wisconsin-Madison Library. I had to get hold of them and see for myself what material was there for me to use and what had to be recreated.

Thanks to the amazing staff at the University, I managed to get hold of all the orchestral parts, some promptbooks, a stage manager's guide and a couple of different scripts for the acted parts in between the songs.

At the same time in Milan I managed to find the Italian copione (script) and in Bologna the Italian libretto. It took almost a year but at last I had all the words in English and Italian and all the lyrics to the songs in German too.

However, problems soon started to arise. First of all, I did not have English text for the two songs Neuendorff had removed from the American production. I had to create English lyrics that followed Suppé's storyline without changing the meaning of the songs themselves. After some months of trial and error, and the precious help of my wife Hannah, I managed to come up with lyrics for those songs which were satisfactory.

After months of waiting, the scanned parts arrived from America. Both the Neuendorff orchestration and Suppé's orginal songs were included in the parts. Sadly though, all the parts were handwritten. What I had to do next was a mammoth task: digitising all the music into Sibelius—a music engraving program—to check for mistakes in the original parts and to create a full orchestral score that included everything needed for future productions of the opera. The task took months. I first created a vocal score, with piano and all the vocal parts.

Once that was completed, all the orchestral parts were added. I came across so many mistakes that I was amazed they managed to perform the operetta at all using this material—but I guess they did.

The whole score was completed within three or four months. It was time to test some of the music.

I decided on three pieces from the operetta: the 'Flower Duettino' (No.9), 'Terzett' (No. 15) and the mysterious 'Couplet' (No.11).

We performed them with the Imperial Vienna Orchestra in three concerts. The music proved to be amazing, the singing parts wonderfully romantic—and sometimes very funny! —and the melodies very catchy and easy to remember. The story of the opera was unfolding before my eyes and the music was being performed for the first time in a century, and for the first time in English in the UK and Europe. *A Trip to Africa* was starting to come back to life.

I just could not get enough of the music. I had to find any available recordings out there with music from the opera. Apart from the easily accessible ones ('Titania-Walzer', 'Die Afrikareise Polka', 'Orientale Polka Mazurka' and 'Uber Berg, Uber Tal Marsch') I could not find anything else anywhere. I came across a recording of an Overture from *Die Afrikareise*, but it was a puzzling piece of work.

I had managed to get a manuscript of Suppé's Overture through the Johann Strauss Society of Great Britain, of which I am an Honorary Lifetime Member. However what had been recorded was not what I had in my hands. Luckily the Society sent me another piece called 'Overture from Die Afrikareise'. This one was arranged by the famous German composer Paul Lincke and was the piece I had found a recording of. Now I wanted to hear the Overture. Also, was it a stand-alone piece or was it meant to be performed before the opera, since a Prelude was already part of the score? We will never know this, but future performances should include the Overture as an opening piece. Johann Strauss, Jr.'s *Die Fledermaus* has taught us how an Overture can become a performance-within-a-performance and a stand-alone concert piece in itself.

While researching it I stumbled upon a problem. I had already heard of Lincke's potpourri Overture, but I was very surprised that I could not come across an Overture written by the 'King of Overtures' himself for one of his most successful operas. Thanks to the precious help of John Diamond, chairman of the Johann Strauss Society of Great Britain, I managed to get hold of all Suppé's handwritten orchestral parts for the Overture, which was not included in any edition of the opera I could find. And what a surprise it was! I studied the score and could recognise all of the melodies included in the work but one; the Andante section in 3/4 had a very similar feel to the 'Flower Duettino', but with a completely different melody. I was very lucky that recently I had conducted in a concert a song I had arranged for orchestra by Suppé called 'Das Vergissmeinnicht' (The Forget-me-not). This was the melody in the Overture, however it was missing from the operetta itself. I was intrigued and wanted to find out more about this song and its role in the operetta. First of all, the vocal/piano parts of the songs I managed to retrive from the USA were all dated 1883, the year Suppé composed *A Trip To Africa*. Secondly, the title is the name of a flower, just like a rose is the subject of the 'Flower Duettino'. Thirdly, both songs are in the same time signature—3/4—and in a very similar tempo; one is Andante (66 bpm) and the other is Moderato (70 bpm) and develop in a very similar way. The only difference I could find, apart from the lyrics and melody, was that 'The Forget-me-not' was composed for one singer whereas the Duettino is, of course, for two singers.

I can only speculate that Suppé composed the Overture when 'The Forget-me-not' was still part of the operetta, but for some unknown reason—his own decision, pressure from the producers to include a love duet or other—he substituted it in the final work. This is probably why the work was never staged with the Overture and only with the Prelude. The Overture assumes, in light of all this, an even more interesting connotation.

In my search for recordings from the operetta I came across a live recording of the Prelude, kindly sent to me by Uwe Eisenpreis from the Franz von Suppé website. The recording is very good quality even if the tempo of the performance differs from Suppé's metronome markings. The other recordings I could find were not of actual performances but came from concertina and celestina owners who had rolls from *Die Afrikareise*. I managed to obtain them and I store them dearly in my archive. The sound is really beautiful and the choice of motifs from the opera in each roll is fascinating. They helped me a lot in understanding the real spirit of the music. Even with such a primitive instrument the music does not seem to require more; it works perfectly already. This told me a lot about the quality of the composition—simple and catchy but yet very effective and beautifully put together.

The music was now complete, all the lyrics were in place, all the corrections were made and the opera was ready to be performed in its musical form. What we were missing was a plot that made full sense, since the songs from the score were missing all the links between them. Hannah and I managed to extract a plot that made sense from the promptbooks, stage manager's guide and script from the American version of the opera.

The big task was now to put it all together and create a storyline that would allow the work to make sense from the raising of the curtain after the Prelude to the closing of the same after the Finale of Act 3.

Hannah undertook the task of compiling the full libretto, a work that took her some months to complete because our sources were sometimes clashing with each other or not making much sense. Using all the available material, we managed to recreate the full storyline—not without some difficulty especially since we came across two different versions of the very last scenes before the very ending. The version we have decided to go for is actually a mix of the two, and forms a better logical conclusion to all the events happening in the last act.

Now that we had what we needed to enable a performance of the whole work in English, I decided it was time for me to concentrate more on everything else that could make this work even more significant in the world of opera.

A meeting with Dr. Robert Ignatius Letellier in his lovely Cambridge home fostered in me the desire to make the libretto more complete by adding a full transcription of the original German libretto as well as a full transcription of the Italian libretto and script (copione) a very rare finding in itself.

On top of that I researched every newspaper article in the world press that talked about the performances of the original runs of the opera in Austria, Germany, Sweden, Slovenia, Italy and the U.S.A. I have decided to include some of them in this book to give the reader an idea of how the opera was received by the public in the late 19th and early 20th centuries. The last recorded performance was in Parma, Italy, in 1922.

Next I wanted to give a face and a setting to the opera. I needed photos or drawings from the historical productions, which proved to be a very difficult task. I came across drawings of actors that were at some point involved in *A Trip to Africa*, but none of them were in costume, until I came across a colour postcard from a Viennese production depicting Alexander Girardi in full costume as Miradillo. Now I had a name and a starting point. Miradillo looked interesting but nothing exceptional or exotic as I had expected.

Further research on Alexander Girardi allowed me to find an antique book called *Girardi Album*, a pictorial collection of most of the roles Girardi covered in his extensive career. Sure enough a photo of the tenor in Miradillo's costume was inside the book. I had found further material, but I needed more.

After weeks of thorough research on the Internet, I came across eight trade cards from a production of the operetta which started on 12th May

1884 at Haverly's Theatre in Philadelphia, U.S.A. I was overwhelmed by this finding. Almost all of the characters were featured on the cards and they were in full colour. Now I knew what the characters looked like in the original run of the opera. Everything was starting to come together. During the same week I also managed to come across two colour marquee posters from the very same production. They were massive in size and in amazing quality for their age. Scenes taken from the opera were drawn in detail on them, as well as characters and scenes. I had everything I needed visually apart from some photos that could show me the actual stage, props and backdrops.

I did not have to wait too long. I managed to find a book on the history of the Bijou Theatre in New York, which contained photos of the three acts. There were no characters on stage but I could see the square outside the Hotel Pharone for Act 1, Fanfani's villa by the Nile with the barge floating upstage for Act 2 and the tents and the desert for Act 3. I had managed, with passion and will-power to collect most of material available in the world about *A Trip to Africa*. I did not want to keep it all to myself; I wanted to share it with all the opera and theatre lovers in the world. I wanted it published and to be made available to everyone.

That's why, alongside the musical side of it, I have worked hard, and, with the help of amazing music enthusiasts from all over the world and the generosity of archives and libraries, I have been able to create what I believe to be the most extensive collection of material in the world on *A Trip to Africa*, which is now available for everyone to see and use.

The title of the operetta itself is *Die Afrikareise* in its German version, *Un Viaggio in Africa* and *Voyage en Afrique* in the Italian and French translation respectively. The problem with the English title is the slight difference of meaning that we can get if we choose one or the other between the two available versions: *Journey through Africa* or *A Trip to Africa*. As one can see the former implies some sort of exploring or just travelling within or through Africa whereas the latter involves more going to, a trip to, Africa from somewhere else—in this case Italy. The plot reveals that the latter one is the more accurate translation and the one I have decided to adopt.

Working on this gigantic project has enriched me as a musician and researcher. I have come into contact with incredible people from the world of opera and Viennese music. I have learnt to love, appreciate and promote operetta. I have become involved in the wonderful music of Suppé, the fantastic libretto of West and Genée, two of the great librettists of Viennese operettas. Nowadays Genée is surely better known for his work as a lyricist and sadly not remembered for his musical talent. Interestingly his musical output is at par with his literary one. He is the composer of amazing operettas and instrumental works as well as of great and incredibly witty choral music, including the world famous 'Insalata Italiana' (Italian Salad). To better understand one of the men behind *A Trip to Africa* I had to learn about and understand his music too. I have therefore been lucky enough to conduct an orchestra and singers in some excerpts from his most famous operetta, *Nanon*. 'Anna's Song' and the 'Duet' from the operetta, which I arranged, are amazing pieces of classical music; Viennese to the core with an eye to the masters and to comic theatre. Genée is surely an interesting and intelligent composer and *Nanon* is a masterpiece of the genre. I am now working on resurrecting the Overture from it as well as making more of his music available for orchestras to perform e.g. *Nisida*, *Freund Felix* and hopefully more.

The next step is to perform the opera. At the time of writing, a venue has already been booked; the Maddermarket Theatre in Norwich, England, one of the most beautiful cities in Britain and in its most historic theatre. The date is set for 3$^{rd}$ December 2016; auditions have already taken place and a cast of singers has been selected.

Kevin Bell Music, a music publishing company, is now working on the score and parts ready for our performance in December and for public use thereafter.

We are sourcing costumes for the performance from all over the world. The plan is to stage it as a concert performance in costume, with singers, choir and orchestra on stage and a narrator to describe the acted parts. We are also hoping to organise a week-long run of performances in the coming year to allow more people to attend such an historical event.

*A Trip to Africa* has been for me "A Trip through the world of Operetta". A battle against time as the material and recorded memories became harder to find; a journey of self-discovery, of my surprisingly strong will power, which I knew nothing of before-hand! It has been a fantastic trip full of melodies, colours, little things that have immense value, large things that touch many; it has been a spiritual meeting with the composer, the librettists, the translators and the illustrators, who are far from being long–forgotten, and I feel are all sitting here next to me while I am working on this book, and will be on stage with me when I am conducting their creation. I hope that reading this collection of words will bring you immense joy and trigger in you a desire to dig deeper into the world of operetta; into the world of the classical music that was not the output of those few 10% of composers that make up 90% of the orchestral repertoire nowadays. There is more to classical music than the masters.

This is more than *A Trip to Africa*; let me take you on a Trip of Discovery to a new musical world.

DARIO SALVI
Norwich, England, January 2016

# ACKNOWLEDGEMENTS

My wife, Hannah Salvi, for her continuous support, patience, help, professionalism, constructive criticism, smiles and love; John Diamond, Chairman of the Johann Strauss Society of Great Britain; The Imperial Vienna Orchestra; Simon Ireson for his help in preparing the score; Dr. Robert Ignatius Letellier for his precious insight into the world of operetta; Dr. Kevin Clarke from the Operetta Research Centre; Uwe Aisenpreis, curator of the German Franz von Suppé website (www.f-v-s.de); Hans-Dieter Roser, Suppé's official biographer; Jeanette L. Casey, Head at Mills Music Library, UW-Madison Libraries; Natasha Veeser, Head of Communications at UW-Madison Libraries; Tams Witmark/Wisconsin Collection; Mills Music Library, University of Wisconsin-Madison; University of Wisconsin Digital Collections Center; Connie Davey for her help in translating the text from the original German; Paul Thompson and Kevin Bell from Kevin Bell Music who are publishing the piano, vocal and orchestral scores and parts and everyone else involved in the research for this book and performance of the Opera.

# INTRODUCTION

Franz von Suppé, the originator of the Viennese operetta, was baptized Francesco Ezechiele Ermenegildo Cavaliere Suppé-Demelli. He was born on 18th April 1819, a contemporary of Offenbach, in Spalato (Split) in the southern part of the Habsburg Monarchy, the son of an Austrian civil servant of Italian-Belgian parentage. His mother, Katharina Landovsky, came of Bohemian-Polish stock. Suppé was in fact related to the great Gaetano Donizetti of Bergamo, and a desire to compose showed itself early in Francesco Suppé-Demelli. As a boy, before beginning a cursory study of law, Suppé was taken to Vienna without knowing a word of German.

Vienna, before the 1848 Revolution, showed many Italian characteristics: the small, single-storey houses, the many palaces of the nobility and, in particular, the musical theater, the 'Royal Opera'. The Viennese, like the Italians, were keen theater-goers. Suppé became the pupil of the Viennese master of counterpoint Simon Sechter, but professionally soon worked as a kind of musical factotum for the Vienna stages. As conductor at the Theater an der Wien, as well as at the Theater in der Leopoldstadt, Suppé collaborated with the directors Pokorny and Treumann in providing incidental music for the various plays—most memorably for *Morning, Noon and Night in Vienna*, 1844, and *Poet and Peasant*, 1845—farces and satires that were so popular with the Viennese public. During the 1850s the vogue for Offenbach's music spread out from Paris. Vienna was enthralled. Suppé decided to try to emulate something of his German-born French contemporary. In 1860 he celebrated his debut with a modest little operetta, *Das Pensionat,* and in 1865 he had his first truly international hit with the burlesque operetta *Die schöne Galathee* (The Beautiful Galatea) a Greek travesty in the manner of Offenbach. The next two decades saw Suppé at the height of his Viennese and international popularity as a composer of musical comedy, with works like *Fatinitza* (1876), *Boccaccio* (1879), *Donna Juanita* (1880) and *Die Afrikareise* (1883).

Suppé died in his adopted city on 21st May 1895. He survived Offenbach by 14 years, and left a legacy at least as important: 31 operettas and 180 vaudevilles, as well as more serious compositions like a Mass, a symphony, and many chamber works and string quartets. The operettas— the first actual products of the new genre in the Imperial city—reflected varying degrees of success. The librettos of some were reworked often.

Suppé was a master of three styles; the Italian, the French and the German. He knew how to blend them irresistibly, assisted in the instrumentation by his rich experience as a theatre orchestra conductor, and with a sure symphonic technique deriving from his classical training. His overtures were a major feature of his stage work, some attaining immense popularity, and securing him an enduring fame in the concert hall. Many of his operettas from the 1870s, on the other hand, have short preludes or instrumental introductions, very much in the mode of Offenbach, like *Der Teufel auf Erden*, *Fatinitza*, *Donna Juanita*, *Die Afrikareise*, *Des Matrosen Heimkehr* and *Die Jagd nach dem Glück*.

Suppé's music moves briskly; it is sparse in diction, free of cloying sentimentality, and effervescent in its crisp intensity. It mediates as it were between Vienna, the French *opéra-comique* and the Italian *opera buffa*. The melodious charm of his overtures, their artistic instrumentation— often featuring extended solos—the rhythmic verve and their masterful vocal composition, have ensured their survival for more than a century. *Poet and Peasant* and *Light Cavalry* are among the most famous overtures ever written.

Suppé's work inevitably reflects the changing fortunes of his adopted home of the city of Vienna, and by implication the social effects of the great historical events of the age. Vienna was radically affected by the events of 1848, the Year of Revolutions, which saw upheavals in Prague, Vienna and Budapest. The restoration of the Monarchy by force of arms and the imposition of the autocracy during the 1850s saw the end of the Biedermeier Period, and an intensification of the desire for national expression on the part of the member nations of the Habsburg Empire; this yearning is expressed in the Hungarian music of *Die leichte Kavallerie*, 1866. These aspirations found greater expression after the great confrontation with Prussia during the 1860s. Bismarck launched successful wars of aggression against Denmark (1864), Austria (1866) and France (1870), with momentous consequences. In Austria the Habsburg defeat at Königsgrätz led to the Ausgleich—or political compromise with Hungary —resulting in the establishment of the Dual Monarchy.

The city of Vienna in the meantime was caught up in the extraordinary physical transformation following the demolition of the walls of the old city (1857), and the huge building projects that followed this—with immense aesthetic and cultural implications for the city which now entered a period of tremendous efflorescence that would having enduring influence on the whole of modern European culture.

The new opera house became symbolic of this resurgence of creativity, which expressed itself musically not only in the Second Viennese School of Brahms, Bruckner, Wolf and Mahler, but also in the emergence of the Golden Age of Viennese Operetta, distilled for all time in *Die Fledermaus* (1874) of Johann Strauss the Younger. Suppé's *Boccaccio* was his lasting contribution to this refashioning of operetta into a melodically more lyrical and formally more developed expression of the typical satirical and parodistic concerns of the genre established by Offenbach.

And it was indeed Offenbach who would help to channel other new elements of the age into the operetta ethos. The defeat of France in 1870 and the Paris Commune of 1871 had changed the country politically and culturally. France, now the home of radical scientific discovery—like those of Louis Pasteur and Marie Curie—and the new school of Impressionism, turned to a more overt form of political self-expression in the growing international trend to colonial expansion. In the rush for an empire, Britain, France and Germany especially would be caught up in a race for global influence and dominance. Already Napoleon's Egyptian Campaign (1798) and the Greek War of Independence (1821-30) had marked the growing decline of the Ottoman Empire. The Algerian adventure of 1835-48 had seen France expand its influence aggressively into Africa, with the colonization of Algeria. In the 1850s a new fashion for Orientalism had found growing musical expression in the works of Félicien David (*Le Désert*, 1844), and would soon find significant operatic expression in Bizet's *Les Pêcheurs des Perles* (1863), Meyerbeer's *L'Africaine* (1865) and Delibes's *Lakmé* (1883). But these trends were now intensified by the hugely popular and influential novels of Jules Verne (1828-1905), whose fictional explorations of space, the oceans, the subterranean and foreign land set a mark on the age that culminated in *Around the World in Eighty Days* (1873). Practically the travel industry had already been initiated by the enterprising Thomas Cook who expanded his English excursion in 1841 into tours to Europe in 1855, and to the United States in 1865 with scientific discovery, geographical exploration, political imperialism, and a new interest in recreational travel, Offenbach, always alert to these social manifestations, adapted several of Verne's novels for the operetta stage; *Le Voyage dans la Lune* in 1875, and *Le Docteur Ox* in 1877. The success of this trend had its effects on the Viennese theatre too.

Suppé, always alert to the trends set in Paris, the home of operetta, produced several works (revues, or *Ausstattungsstücke*) on Jules Verne's novels: *Die Reise um die Erde in Achtzig Tage* (1875); *Zum Mond und unterm Meer* (1876); *Der Courier des Czaren, oder M. Strogoff's Reise* (1877). But he would bring out his own successful operetta reflecting these trends a few years later; *Die Afrikareise* (*Operette in drei Aufzüge*, with librettists Richard Genée and M. West, and first performed in Vienna, at the Theater an der Wien, on 17$^{th}$ March 1883). The work ran for less than a month despite the presence of Alexander Girardi in the cast. While not in the same league as the other great Suppé successes, the work played profitably in European and American theatres, a success acknowledged in the publication of the score in Hamburg (Cranz, 1883) and a number of different productions in the US (New York, Boston).

The scenario reflects many of the interests and concerns of the age, with exploration, colonialism, touristic excursion, exoticism, and Orientalism in particular, finding a most sentimental-satirical persuasive expression in the generic terms of operetta. The fascination with Egypt and Lebanon, reflecting French political engagement, is bound up with curiosity about the diversities and religions of the Near East (Islam and Maronite Christianity), as well as the mystique of travel and cultural novelty. The story presents perceived prototypes not only from exotic lands, but in the collections of tourists from different countries—a parody of the European abroad—all enmeshed in the usual social intrigues and sentimental wish-fulfilment and social transformation that are the default positions of this theatrical genre. All is garbed of course in the musical language of Vienna, which in the process presents the most striking of Suppé's late works.

The measure of the wider success of the score can also be gauged by the number of arrangements made by the composer himself out of themes from the work: the 'Titania Waltz', the gallop 'Le Voyage dans l'Afrique', the march 'Über Berg, Über Tal', and later the pot-pourri overture arranged by the Berlin master of operetta, Paul Lincke. All these pieces use motifs and melodies that capture the spirits of enterprise, tourism, and romantic adventure that dominate the work. While the brief 'Titania-Walzer' lacks the delicacy of Shakespeare's fairy queen, it draws from the work as a suite of memorable tunes that represents the enchantment of the operetta genre itself captured in the central waltz themes: the principal one "Ach was kann man dafur" and the secondary "Von Allah's Thron". The first is elegant and brisk in Suppé's typical manner, the second slower and more reflective, a distinction captured beautifully in Linke's overture. But it is perhaps the march 'Über Berg, Über Tal'—which became very well-known—that distills the mystique of exotic tourism in *Die Afrikareise*; the main theme derives from the perky melody that serves as a motto for the Europeans abroad ("Ich seh' das Vaterland") is followed by the motif of intrepid exploration ("Über Berg, über Tal"), both taken from the climactic No.15 – 'Terzett'. The march trio is made up of the 'Tourist Song' itself

("Land, wo Feuer dem Vulkan entspricht") which, as 1b, begins the work, and provides the leading theme.

This operetta, written towards the end of the Golden Age of Viennese Operetta, captures something important about the time it was written. It provides a glimpse into the late work of Franz von Suppé, one of the great figures of operetta. In the overture arranged by Lincke it looks to the Berlin School, which would find its typical expression in this composer's *Frau Luna* (1899), another tribute to Verne's space travel. Beyond that, *Die Afrikareise* looks to another work that compares the clash of cultures and values in an Oriental setting; *Die Rose von Stamboul* (1916), Leo Fall's splendid work, and a masterpiece of the Silver Age of Viennese operetta.

DR. ROBERT IGNATIUS LETELLIER
Cambridge, England, January 2016

# A Trip to Africa
## or Die Afrikareise

COMIC OPERA IN THREE ACTS

BY

## Moritz West, Richard Genée, Dario Salvi and Hannah Salvi

ORCHESTRATED AND CORRECTED
BY

Dario Salvi

LIBRETTO COMPILED
BY

Hannah Salvi

MUSIC BY

## Franz von Suppé

# LIST OF CHARACTERS

MIRADILLO ........................................................ An impecunious European
Tenor

TITANIA FANFANI .................................................................. The Heiress
Soprano

FANFANI PASHA ............................................................... Uncle of Titania
Comedian

ANTARSID ............................................................. Prince of the Maronites
Tenor

TESSA ........................................................ A young milliner from Palermo
Mezzo Soprano (Soubrette)

BUCCAMETTA ................................................................... Mother of Tessa
Contralto (Character)

PERICLES ............................................................................ A hotel keeper
Basso

NAKID ......................................... A Coptic dealer in poisons and perfumes
Tenor (Comedian)

SEBIL ........................................................................ An Abyssinian slave
Contralto (Small part)

HOSH ............................................................... A servant in Pericles' hotel
Mute slave

MUEZZIN
Baritone

MAJORDOMO

FIRST SAIS

SECOND SAIS
CHORUS of Maronites, Hotel Servants, Guests of Fanfani Pasha, Slave
Traders, Muleteers, Dancers, Bedouins, Greek and Arabian People.

Time...........1883

Scenes.........Acts 1 and 2 – Cairo
                Act 3 – The Interior of Africa

# LIST OF MUSIC

# ACT 1

PRELUDE

1A. INTRODUCTION............................................. Sebil, Pericles and Chorus

1B. TOURIST SONG ............................ Miradillo, Sebil, Pericles and Chorus
"I sail over ev'ry ocean".................................. Miradillo, Sebil and Chorus

1C. APPEARANCE OF THE MUEZZIN ...... Miradillo, Pericles, Muezzin, Sebil,
Chorus and Servants

2. ENTRANCE OF THE PRINCE ......................... Sais, Servants and Maronites
"Like winds that lightly" ............................................ Antarsid and Chorus

3. ENTRANCE OF TITANIA.............. Titania, Sebil, Antarsid, Nakid, Pericles
and Chorus
"Tho' we were strangers hitherto .................................. Titania and Chorus

ANTARSID EXITS

4. QUARTETTE...................................................... Fanfani, Pericles, Titania
and Miradillo
"In proud Palermo, throbs the air"....................... Fanfani, Pericles, Titania
and Miradillo

5. TERZETT
"Big beard visage framing" ........................Fanfani, Tessa and Buccametta

6. FINALE (ACT 1) ..............................Titania, Antarsid, Tessa, Buccametta
Sebil, Miradillo and Chorus
"Oh what delight"............................Titania, Antarsid, Tessa, Buccametta,
Sebil, Miradillo, Fanfani, Pericles and Chorus

# ACT 2

# ACT 3

# COSTUME PLOT

TITANIA (Age 19) ..........Act 1 – Walking dress cut short, red most suitable, with parasol
Acts 2 and 3 – White flannel travelling suit

TESSA (Age 18)..............Act 1 – Flashy travelling dress with short skirt
Act 2 – Turkish harem dress
Act 3 – White suit

BUCCAMETTA (Age 45) .Act1 – Very loud modern street dress, somewhat gay
Act 2 – Turkish harem dress, very loud and ridiculous
Act 3 – Same dress with white gown and cap

MIRADILLO (Age 25) .....Modern white flannel tennis suit, negligee shirt with palm leaf hat

FANFANI (Age 50)..........Act 1 – Partly modern and partly Turkish as follows; light pants, patent leather shoes, Turkish jacket and fez, sash around waist, eyeglass, watch with chain, cane and dagger
Act 2 – Same as above with smoking gown
Act 3 – Very handsome Arab dress, white full trunks, white cloak, very handsome turban

ANTARSID (Age 25) .......Act 1 – Very handsome Arab dress, full pants, black silk turban, carries Yataghan
Acts 2 and 3 – If a change of dress is desired, same style with different colours, but same dress can be worn all through

PERICLES ........................A Turkish commoner dress

NAKID ...........................Turkish trousers, very long; long shirt sleeves, small turban. This character should be dressed very poorly, and rather slouchy.

SEBIL.............................Dressed as a slave; brown tights, brown jersey, Turkish drapery, wrist and ankle ornaments, amulets and anklets, chains from ankles and wrists to a metal girdle. She is made up dark and wears a long black wig.

HOSH.............................Acts 1 and 2 – Turkish servant's dress
Act 3 – Same as above with light yellow gown

FEMALE CHORUS............Act 1 – Turkish dresses of heavy material, no silks. Long bloomer trousers, and long sacks shaped to the figure, and a turban hat. Some change to Turkish wives, silk trousers to the knees, silk over-shirt, loose shirt fly and little hat, long veil attached.
Acts 2 and 3 – Some are dressed as nobles and wives and some as populace, as in Act 1.

MALE CHORUS ...............Act 1 - Ankle length, loose Chinese pants, smocks, white turbans; some of the gents to change to nobles, same style as Prince's dress but not so good; tunics
Act 2 - Chorus ladies and gents, some are dressed as nobles and wives and some as populace, as in Act 1.
Act 3 – Chorus men to change to Turks or Arabs. Bloomer pants.

PAGES ...........................Act 1 - Brown tights, jersey waists, turban, spangled fly. These are the date carriers. The waiter carriers, same style as slave of first act.

Promotional trade cards from the 1884 production of the operetta at the Haverley's Theatre, Broad Street, Philadelphia (USA). Dario Salvi collection.

TRIP TO AFRICA. Act I.

Act 1 backdrop – Cairo, outside the Hotel Pharone. Originally published in '*Historical review of the Boston Bijou Theatre: with the original casts of all the operas that have been produced at the Bijou.*' Skelton, Edward Oliver (1884). Dario Salvi Collection.

# PROPERTY PLOT

# ACT 1

Street in Cairo:
Backdrop representing city of Cairo
On R. an Egyptian hotel with piazza and steps
Gaudy coloured awnings
Houses with striped sun-shades etc
On L. a common/bamboo table and two chairs or bamboo stools
Drinking cups and bottles on table
Plate and knife on table

Character props:
Bags of money (Chorus ladies)
Cigar (Miradillo)
Pipe (Hosh)
Two long glasses with ice, lemon and straws to represent punch (Alpha)
Grasshopper in one glass of punch (Hosh)
Chibouk pipe (Alpha)
Knife (Miradillo)
Telegram (Fanfani)
Tray with shoulder strap containing small medicine phials and packet (Nakid)
Long bill made of muslin on roller (Pericles)
Two visiting cards (Fanfani)
Triangles, tambourines and tomtoms (Chorus)
Two trunks (Porter)

TRIP TO AFRICA. Act II.

Act 2 backdrop – Garden of Fanfani's villa on the banks of the River Nile. Originally published in '*Historical review of the Boston Bijou Theatre: with the original casts of all the operas that have been produced at the Bijou.*' Skelton, Edward Oliver (1884). Dario Salvi Collection.

# ACT 2

Garden of Fanfani's villa:
Backdrop represents the city of Cairo with the River Nile, who's tide must be distinctly seen at finale of act. Must have water transparency for using of Nile effect.
Large moveable boat with single coloured sail off stage L.
Steps leading to river
Oriental foliage, palms, cactus etc
Rugs and Turkish mats
Two kiosks, green and red, R. and L.
Two rustic settees to fit two persons alongside each kiosk

Character props:
Bamboo carpet beaters (Chorus)
Snake whip (Fanfani)
Pistol/revolver (Titania)
Red rose (Titania)
Tray with shoulder strap containing small medicine phials and packets, one of which must be a red and black box filled with dates (Nakid)
Ball drum for cannon sound
Four baskets of dates (Chorus)
Twelve golden drinking goblets
Spears (Supers)
Eight small curtains

TRIP TO AFRICA. Act III.

Act 3 backdrop – An oasis in the interior of Africa with a view of the Sahara Desert. Originally published in '*Historical review of the Boston Bijou Theatre: with the original casts of all the operas that have been produced at the Bijou.*' Skelton, Edward Oliver (1884). Dario Salvi Collection.

# ACT 3

Oasis in Sahara Desert:
Backdrop represents the interior of Africa, with a view of the Sahara.
Chapel mirage needed for Finale.
Two practical tents L. and R. with flap openings, guy ropes etc
Rugs in tents and at each entrance
Bamboo couch C. covered with tiger skins
Palm trees around stage
Spring board RUE. about four feet from the ground masked by a rock, or
high bank

Ready in tent R.:
Chibouk pipe (Hosh)
Small table
Two stools
Tray with dish of fruit
Two wine bottles
Two wine glasses

Character props:
Comb (Miradillo)
Cigar (Hosh)
Book (Hosh)
Long knives/yataghans (Bedouins)
Cigarette (Miradillo)
Coloured signal lantern and white umbrella (Fanfani)
Dagger (Fanfani)

# A TRIP TO AFRICA

# ACT 1

## Prelude

### No. 1a – Introduction

*Street in front of the Hotel Pharone in the city of Cairo. On R1. is the hotel with piazza and steps. L. at front of stage are an arbour and awning with table and two chairs; above that is the entrance to a rail-road and further upstage R3. is an entrance to a minaret. Large stone steps leading to street. Backdrop representing the city of Cairo. At rise of curtain some servants are watering plants. Hosh is leaning against hotel smoking a pipe. Mouleteers, Arabian people and slave traders dispersed over the stage at back. The men are walking to and fro selling their wares.*

CHORUS
We're awaiting at our stands,
Guests from European lands,
To our net they're welcome fish,
For they all pay us
(*On "Backshish" hold out first one hand then another as if begging.*)
Backshish, Backshish;
Backshish is our end and aim,
Backshish all of us exclaim,
Yes! Backshish here!
Backshish there!
All around,
O pleasant sound,

(*Ladies pass through the men to the front and form a semi-circle, men remaining at the rear.*)

Kling, kling, kling!

(*Ladies shake bags of money.*)

Backshish! Backshish!
That word all quickly learn.
Backshish! Backshish!
'Tis heard at every turn;

At the front and in the rear,
This word you can hear, Backshish,
All hold it dear, Backshish,
Yes! That is clear!
Backshish is a pleasant sound;

(*Chorus get over L. and form rough oblique line L1. to C. upstage. Men behind women.*)

Backshish is our end and aim,
Backshish all of us exclaim;

(*Pericles enters from hotel. He is in a bad humour. Sebil follows him.*)

Backshish there,
Backshish here,
Everywhere the word sounds clear.

PERICLES (*Taunting to Chorus*)
Backshish! Backshish!
There they stand and shout and yell all day!
(*Indicating his hotel*)
Not a soul comes here to stay,
Room there's for a hundred guests here,
But this season not one rests here.
Not a single room's engaged—

CHORUS
Ha ha ha, ha ha ha ha, ha!

(*Chorus all guy Pericles, pointing at him.*)

| PERICLES | CHORUS |
|---|---|
| And that's what makes me so enraged, | That bothers him, |
| Yes that's what makes me so enraged! | Ha ha ha, ha ha ha ha, ha! |
| | That bothers him! |

SEBIL (*Coming forward*)
You forget the Frankish man!

PERICLES
Miradillo makes one sick,
Lives here like a swell on tick!

SEBIL (*Hastily*)
Don't talk so!

PERICLES
He must go!

SEBIL
He will pay you when he can!

PERICLES
If his bill he does not pay,
I'll complain of him today!

SEBIL (*Pleading to Pericles*)
No, no, no!

PERICLES
He must go!

SEBIL (*Ironically defiant*)
Miradillo, he will buy me,
I'll baptized be, off will hie me;
Yes, yes that's so, from here I'll go,
For Miradillo told me so, you know!

PERICLES                               SEBIL
(*Keeping C. gesticulating angrily*)
He's a clever swindler truly,        Yes! That's so sir!
Doesn't own a single sou;            Quite soon I'll go—
Yet he makes the help unruly,        Miradillo—
Pretty slaves he's bringing too!     Said so, you know.

PERICLES
(*Turning to threaten them*)
Silence monkeys, asses, idiots!
Soon with laughter you will split.
Backshish, Backshish, ever yelling,

But to earn it you're not fit!

SEBIL *and* CHORUS
Ha ha, ha ha,
Ha ha, ha ha, ha.

CHORUS
Kling, kling, kling.

(*Sebil and Chorus hold out hands on "Backshish".*)

PERICLES
Yes, yes this very day!

His bill I'll make him pay.

The braggart, the swindler,
Always dressed, always airy,
Oh his cheek's extraordinary!
Yes his bill I'll surely make him
pay,
This very day.

Wait, you swindler, I'll teach
you,
That this sort of thing won't do.
Cheating there, cheating here,
This thing must be stopped,
That's clear!

SEBIL *and* CHORUS
Backshish, Backshish—
That word all quickly learn,
Backshish, Backshish—
'Tis heard at every turn;
At the front and in the rear,
That word you can hear,
Backshish,
All hold it dear, Backshish,
Yes that is clear, Backshish—
Is a pleasant sound.

Backshish is our end and aim,

Backshish all of us exclaim,
Backshish there, Backshish here,
Ev'rywhere the word sounds
clear!

PERICLES (*Cried*)
The scamp!

## No. 1b – Tourist Song

(*Miradillo enters L3E.*)

MIRADILLO
Who's talking here about me?

(*Sebil runs over to Miradillo and Pericles wanders slowly R.*)

SEBIL
O Sir, he is reviling you!

MIRADILLO (*Pointing to Pericles, who has gone R.*)
What? That Greek there?

SEBIL
He called you cheat and swindler too.

MIRADILLO
Oh, did he really?

SEBIL
He said you're living here on tick.

MIRADILLO
Oh indeed!

SEBIL
And many flaws,

MIRADILLO
That will do!

SEBIL
In you did pick!

MIRADILLO
Well that was rather cool—
Yet I don't mind the fool,
If he knew more of me—
He'd more respectful be!

(*He strolls angrily to C.*)

PERICLES
—Indeed,

MIRADILLO
The fact I now will state,

PERICLES
—Indeed,

MIRADILLO
That I am a Tourist great!

PERICLES
Dear Sir you may be what you will,
I only wish you'd pay your bill!

MIRADILLO (*Turning half to Chorus*)
—Hold on!
O, say no further, know what that is?

PERICLES, SEBIL *and* CHORUS (*Chorus take short step forward*)
—No!

MIRADILLO
A world's tourist?

PERICLES, SEBIL *and* CHORUS (*Chorus take short step forward*)
—No!

MIRADILLO
Then please lend me a most attentive ear,
I'll tell you all assembled here!

(*Chorus gather around in semicircle. They listen to song and testify their admiration by suitable gestures.*)

## Song

MIRADILLO
I sail over ev'ry ocean,
Except at times when storms raise dangerous commotion,
Of all peaks, the heights I measure,
Except the highest one where climbing is no pleasure;

In all lands I turn up frisky,
Where the trav'ling's not too risky;
I am great at mensuration,

Also at triangulation,
And with greatest ease compute I can,
Any hard meridian!

Yes—discov'ry is my great delight,
And modern science to advance I've travelled day and night.
'Tis Europe that does my expenses pay,
And that I am a salaried discov'rer I must say!

I'm well versed in—
(*Chorus count on fingers these three words*):
    Geography,
    Ethnography,
    Topography!

Amongst the Khoekhoe I've tarried
Many a pleasant hour,
And 'neath Spice Island trees high
Seasoned meals I did devour.

(*Chorus manifest increased admiration.*)

At several occasions
With Dahomey's king I've dined,
His wives I most amusing did find.

I'm much liked by the Basutos,
Know well Congo, Zanzibar,
And the Kafirs; the Ashantis,
With my face acquainted are.

In—
(*Step down towards R on "line"*)
My line I'm very able,
(*Step back to C on "tell"*)
And what I tell you is no fable,
(*Step towards L on "telegraph"*)
By Telegraph, by post, by cable,
(*Step back to C on "o'er"*)
My fame all o'er the world is spread.

MIRADILLO, SEBIL *and* CHORUS
(Yes! I'm/In his line he's) very able
(This/And what he tells us) is no fable.
(*Imitates writing a letter.*)
By Telegraph, by post, by cable,
(My/his) fame all o'er the world is spread!

PERICLES
Swindler!
Braggart!

The scamp,
Has not a red!

MIRADILLO
My great fame is not confined
To Afric's tribes alone—
E'en among the animals
I'm favourably known;

Quadruped and biped,
Ostrich tall and Zebra striped,
Parrots, vultures and magpies,
They all hail me with joyful cries.

When the Antelopes from far
My form approaching see,
All of them stand still and bow
So much they honour me.

All the Lions know me
And the tigers rev'rence show me,
Humbly wag their tails at me.
(*Imitating monkey, scratching himself etc.*)
And the charming little monkeys,
The gazelles, giraffes and donkeys,
Are delighted when they meet me,
And with fond caresses greet me;

E'en the elephants tremendous,
Love me with a love stupendous,
The Rhinoceroses lastly,
When they see me pleased are vastly.

There's no rock, no ravine or crater,
That I have not seen,
Yes that's an honest fact,
I know ev'ry cataract;

From highest mountain peaks
Down to the bottom of the sea,
For curious finds I search incessantly.

(*Chorus enumerate on fingers*):
    Minerals, stones, Crystallizations,
    Flowers, grasses, malformations,
    These I gather, choose, reject,
    And in cabinets I collect!

Yes!—
(*Step down towards R on "trade"*)
My trade is profitable,
(*Step back to C on "tell"*)
And what I tell you is no fable,
(*Step towards L on "telegraph"*)
By Telegraph, by post, by cable,
(*Step back to C on "o'er"*)
My fame all o'er the world is spread.

| MIRADILLO, SEBIL *and* CHORUS | PERICLES |
|---|---|
| (Yes!'Tis/In his trade he's) profitable | Swindler! |
| (This/And what he tells us) is no fable. | Braggart! |
| (*Imitates writing a letter.*) | |
| (By Telegraph) by Post, by Cable, | The scamp, |
| (My/his) fame all o'er the world is spread! | Has not a red! |

| MIRADILLO | SEBIL *and* CHORUS | PERICLES |
|---|---|---|
| I'm a tourist of renown, | Great his name, | —Swindler! |
| Know each country, ev'ry town, | Great his fame, | —Boaster! |
| There's no place I ween, | There's no place | |
| That I've not seen. | That he's not seen; | A precious scamp! |
| I'm a tourist of renown, | Great his name, | —Swindler! |
| Know each country, ev'ry town, | Great his fame, | —Boaster! |
| All of them I've seen. | All he's seen. | |

MIRADILLO, SEBIL *and* CHORUS
Ev'ry peak and ev'ry dale,
Also each cavern, lake and waterfall,
On this earthly ball,
(I know/he knows) them one and all!

PERICLES
I despise all his lies,
What he says I don't believe
at all,
For my confidence in him,
Is very small!

## No. 1c – Appearance of the Muezzin

(*Chorus retire up and gradually get over to oblique line R. ready for entrance of the Muezzin—take plenty of time.*)

MIRADILLO
Now I have the best I could,
Explained to you what tourists do.

PERICLES
Interesting 'twas I know—
But now pay me what you owe!

MIRADILLO
Some day you will get your money
But at present I can't pay!

PERICLES
Money somehow he must raise,
He can't leave here 'til he pays!

MIRADILLO (*Indicating Sebil*)
Put the slave upon my bill Sir,
For she greatly pleases me.

PERICLES
Always to your bill you're adding,
But your cash I never see.

MIRADILLO
Greek, how often must I tell you
That 'tis Europe pays my dues.

(*He seats himself at table L. Sebil crosses to R. near Pericles.*)

PERICLES
With that bank I'm not acquainted,
Patience very soon I'll lose!

PERICLES (*To Miradillo*): If you don't pay me immediately I'll have you arrested.

(*The Muezzin's rattle is heard.*)

MIRADILLO (*To Pericles*): You hear! The Muezzin is coming! Behave yourself at all events in the presence of Allah!

CHORUS: Hush! The Muezzin!

(*Muezzin enters L3. and stands C. half facing audience. As soon as he appears, Chorus in 2 lines, men behind women, bow their heads and cross hands on breast and sing chorus until "Allah".*)

MUEZZIN (*Arms lifted up to heaven*)
Ya rezzak! Ya kerim!
Ya fettah! Ya allim![1]

PERICLES, SEBIL *and* CHORUS
Ya rezzak! Ya kerim!
Ya fettah! Ya allim!

MUEZZIN
Muslim!
Soon Ramadan's last hour will pass away—
Acknowledge Allah!

PERICLES, SEBIL *and* CHORUS (*Chorus lift heads and stretch out arms to heaven, then resume previous attitudes*)
—Allah!

MUEZZIN
Muslim!
For Bayram's feast put on your best array—

---

[1] *A Muslim prayer or chant in Turkish which approximately translates to: "Oh provider of sustenance, Oh generous one, Oh holy one, Oh all-knowing one".*

O praise ye Allah!

PERICLES, SEBIL *and* CHORUS (*Chorus lift head and arms as before*)
—Allah!

MUEZZIN
Ya rezzak! Ya Kerim!
Ya fettah! Ya Allim!

PERICLES, SEBIL *and* CHORUS
Ya rezzak! Ya Kerim!
Ya fettah! Ya Allim!

(*Muezzin slowly stalks off L3. Chorus break line.*)

PERICLES
Ramadan will end today—

4 SERVANTS
—Hurrah! Hurrah!

PERICLES
Then comes Bayram's feast so gay!

4 SERVANTS
—Hurrah! Hurrah!

PERICLES
Mirthful sounds then fill the air—

4 SERVANTS
—But then,'tis true,

PERICLES
Dancing, feasting ev'rywhere.

4 SERVANTS
—There's much, to do.

PERICLES
There's a train that comes at four—

4 SERVANTS
—'Twill soon, be here!

PERICLES
Guests will bring us by the score—

4 SERVANTS *and* CHORUS
—That is just, what we wish,

PERICLES
Oh! That sudden zeal I know—

4 SERVANTS *and* CHORUS
Then we'll all get Backshish.

PERICLES
Thoughts of Backshish move them so.

O the pack of worthless idlers!
Worse they are than I myself—
Capable of any baseness,
So it brings them sordid pelf.

Hear them shouting!
Laughing, shrieking!
Not a moment do they quit,
"Backshish, Backshish" ever squeaking,
But to earn it you're not fit!

4 SERVANTS *and*
CHORUS
When comes—
The train?
Backshish—
We'll gain ha ha,

Ha ha,
Ha ha,
Ha ha, ha!

Klink, klink, kilnk.

4 SERVANTS *and* CHORUS (*Alternating right and left hands held
    out on "Backshish"*)
Backshish, Backshish,
Each one does quickly learn,
Backshish, Backshish,
'Tis heard at ev'ry turn;

At the front and in the rear,

This word you will hear,
Backshish, all hold it dear,
Backshish, yes it is clear,
Backshish has a pleasant sound;

Backshish is our end and aim,
Backshish all of us exclaim
Backshish there, Backshish here,
Evr'ywhere the word sounds clear!

(*Chorus all exit R. and L. Sebil bows to Miradillo and exits into hotel. Miradillo seated at table L. smoking cigar. Pericles C. Hosh still leaning against hotel smoking pipe.*)

PERICLES (*To Miradillo*): Why did I mistake you for a distinguished foreigner? Why did you not go to Australia, instead of coming here?

MIRADILLO (*At table*): Australia! Happy thought…after I've got through with Africa, I'll go to the fifth of the four quarters of the globe.

PERICLES (*Firmly*): You don't stir from Cairo until you have paid my bill.

MIRADILLO: My dear friend, I don't wish to stir. You mistake me entirely. Your hotel is so comfortable that…

PERICLES: You look here, Sir. There has got to be an end to this thing. I don't propose keeping you for nothing any longer. I need money and I intend to have some. I give you fair warning that unless you plant down before evening, you'll find yourself accommodated free of charge at a different kind of hotel.

MIRADILLO: Fellow! What do you mean?

PERICLES: I mean to have you locked up and I have taken measures to prevent your escape until I get money or satisfaction. Here, Hosh.

(*Hosh crosses to C.*)

PERICLES: This mute has orders not to let you out of his sight. He will follow you wherever you go. You can't get away by leaving. Hosh, attend to your duty. (*Going angrily*) This fellow orders Maraschino at midnight, and eats enough breakfast for a Regiment and when I ask him for money begs me to wait until the clouds roll by.

(*Pericles goes off R. in a fury.*)

MIRADILLO (*Calling after him*): Would you accept some shares in the New Sewage and Deodorising Company? (*Aside*) Ha! He doesn't hear me. Poor fellow, he is deaf to his own interests.

(*He starts to go down R. Hosh follows on his heels so closely that when Miradillo turns Hosh is upon his heels and almost falls against him. He crosses to L.*)

MIRADILLO: So you won't quit me?

(*Hosh nods.*)

MIRADILLO: Do you intend to share my siesta?

(*Hosh nods.*)

MIRADILLO: Oh, perhaps you've made up your mind to be present when I court my girl?

(*Hosh nods.*)

MIRADILLO: The devil you have.

(*Hosh nods.*)

MIRADILLO: Well, this is a nice fix. Say, can't I offer you…(*He puts his hands in his pocket and turns them out*) No, I have nothing to offer. I'll get him drunk. (*Calling*) Alpha, bring punch and a Chibouk.

(*'Alpha' enters from hotel with drink and pipe, places them on the table and exits R.*)

MIRADILLO: Sit down, scruffy Turk.

(*They sit at table L. Hosh sits down with gravity. Miradillo takes pipe.*)

MIRADILLO: Now drink. There's good luck to you and may you choke yourself.

(*They drink.*)

MIRADILLO: Now light this, you snake.

(*Miradillo hands pipe to Hosh, who lights it and hands it back.*)

MIRADILLO: Hallo, he seems to understand our language. I'll test him. (*Takes out knife from pocket*) Shall I cut your head off?

(*Hosh nods and looks pleased.*)

MIRADILLO: He does not understand. I can free my fluttering heart of its burden, without fear of betrayal! Oh the agony of being an explorer who daren't explore, a traveller who never travels. Oh to have the soul of a lion, and the spirit of a mouse. With my heart filled with the mighty aspirations of a Columbus, I left my native Palermo and my charming little milliner Tessa. Now that I am here, I dare not penetrate the country I have come to explore. They say it is so unsafe for travellers. Oh Tessa, why did I leave you when I knew that you loved me better than your bonnet frames. I am so annoyed with myself that I could punch that fellow's head.

(*Looks round at Hosh, who has just fished a grasshopper out of his punch and eats it.*)

MIRADILLO: There he sits, smiling, happy and unwashed, while I can scarcely contain my tears. Oh Tessa. Tessa. If you only knew with what passion I could embrace you. Ah!

(*Notices Hosh has fallen asleep.*)

MIRADILLO: Ah, my nasty guard, napping. I'll scoot. Pleasant dreams, dear boy. Ta ta.

(*He sneaks off on tip toe towards R1. Hosh wakens, gets up and sneaks quietly after him. Miradillo turns and Hosh stands perfectly still gazing straight out into the audience.*)

MIRADILLO: Oh, you've had sleep enough?

(*Hosh nods.*)

MIRADILLO: Nonsense! You look as though a snooze would do you good. Don't let me disturb you. Broke up your dreams perhaps? Go back and finish it, while I take a little exercise.

(*Hosh shakes his head and signifies that he will walk too.*)

MIRADILLO: You want exercise too. Perhaps you are a little fleshy. You want exercise? Well you shall have it!

(*He starts walking at a furious pace, making a circuit of the stage from R1. to L1., up and off back down, followed by Hosh, running to keep up with him. Both take long strides and exit behind hotel. Enter Fanfani Pasha L3., holding telegram.*)

FANFANI: Well, the telegram's come—(*Reading*) "Shall arrive at four o'clock with my husband. Titania." (*To audience*) Titania has done it. My niece has got a husband and I lose two millions. Two absolute, real, and undisputed millions, bequeathed to her by her father, and left in trust with me, her uncle. Oh the bane of being an uncle with a niece, who is so shortly to cast you two millions. Oh agony, agony! Is there no escape? Where is the landlord?

(*Enter Pericles running from hotel R. Bows very low.*)

PERICLES (*Entering hurriedly*): Oh, Your Excellency! I worship the ground you walk upon.

FANFANI: That's something at least! Has my niece arrived?

PERICLES: Not that I know of.

FANFANI: Nor her husband either? Oh those two millions. If I could only pay them in Turkish bonds. Do you know what it is to have to pay two millions?

PERICLES: I never tried, but why has your Excellency to pay two millions?

FANFANI: My Excellency hmm! I! Who has forty six wives to nourish, on all the delicacies of the season. Do you know what it takes to keep their forty six respective appearances? When they want gloves, I have to buy a whole tannery! Last week we had a rainy spell. The result was; I had to sell a man of war to supply them with gum shoes, waterproofs and rubber soles.

PERICLES: But why have you got to pay two millions?

FANFANI: Why? Because my late lamented brother, Titania's father, bequeathed them to her if she was married on her nineteenth birthday. Tomorrow is pay day. She is coming here with her husband, and will take possession of the money. (*Crosses to R.*) Do you think I can find a bank anywhere that will lend me anything on a railroad to Jerusalem?

PERICLES: I hardly think so!

FANFANI: Perhaps you can assist me. You are doing a thriving business here, and worth considerable property too!

(*He indicates the hotel.*)

PERICLES: Unfortunately my money is all tied up in Turkish paper.

FANFANI: Well can't you untie it? What's the use of money if it's all tied up? Now I'm floating a gigantic enterprise for stocking the Nile with codfish. I shall realise handsomely in a month or two; I'll make you private secretary to the codfish association if you'll assist me. How does that strike you?

PERICLES: Very forcibly, but…

FANFANI: At all accounts, you'll do me a personal favour.

PERICLES: Command me. I am your slave.

FANFANI: When my niece arrives, I wish her to be respected as if she were not my niece.

PERICLES: I lay my house, my entire house, at her feet.

FANFANI: It must be a pretty weak structure. But as for her husband, keep a close watch on him, shadow him, and report to me. Do you understand?

(*Exit Pericles into hotel R.*)

FANFANI: This marriage of Titania's seems to have been conducted with a great deal of mystery and a haste that is positively indecent, and I'm damned if I'm going to part with two millions until I'm sure the thing is all right, and there's no help for it. (*Aside*) If I pay up, I'd have to sell all my horses and let my cavalry go on foot.

(*Enter Nakid slowly from RC. to the side of Fanfani with a tray hanging from his neck. He speaks with a Hebrew accent.*)

NAKID (*Softly*): Won't your Excellency do a little business with me? (*Aside*) Something in the way of poisons for man and beast?

FANFANI: No thanks, I'm poisoned enough.

NAKID: Or a love potion? Odalisque drops?

FANFANI: Don't need any. My Odalisques can get on quite well enough without drops.

NAKID: But here's a magic fluid that compels everybody to speak the truth! I always drink it myself.

FANFANI: Take it away! Do you think I want to break my own heart by hearing what people think of me? But hold! If you should happen to discover a tincture that can erase all signatures utterly beyond restoration, or recognition, you can report at my office. (*Aside*) Then we will hang him in the neatest possible manner, but his invention we will adopt to console him.

NAKID: I may strike the combination. Who knows? But here's some water, which it don't take more than one swallow for every woman to forget everything, what was before of some importance.

FANFANI: What's that? She forgets everything?

NAKID: As sure as you live! Zordie, the eleventh wife of Mustapha Pasha, drank some and she forgot all about the old Pasha at once, and ran away with a young captain.

FANFANI (*Scornfully*): You're an ass!

(*Exit Fanfani behind hotel R1. Nakid follows talking all the time. Enter Miradillo from hotel, closely followed by Hosh, who limps and appears tired out, with Pericles at a distance.*)

MIRADILLO (*While entering*): What's this I hear? Titania, the rich heiress from Naples, is coming here?

PERICLES: Si Signor!

MIRADILLO (*Solemnly*): Then, my friend, congratulate yourself and me.

PERICLES: What for?

MIRADILLO: You can afford to be my magnanimous, and send this— (*Pointing to Hosh*)—away.

(*Pericles laughs sarcastically.*)

PERICLES: I'll get you another. That seems worn out.

MIRADILLO: This shadow dance must come to an end. The moment of solvency approaches.

PERICLES (*Doubtfully*): Dare I risk it?

MIRADILLO: Either that, or the payment of your bill.

PERICLES (*To Hosh*): Off with you! March down to the cellar!

(*Hosh crosses his arms and limps off into hotel R.*)

PERICLES: What are you intending to do? Build a railroad to the moon?

MIRADILLO: You will soon find out, my friend. Trust in me, and keep your own council.

(*Exit Miradillo into hotel R.*)

CHORUS (*O.S*): Hail Antarsid, the hero of Lebanon!

## No. 2 – Entrance of the Prince

(*Chorus of Egyptian Maronites and Servants enter from everywhere. Two Sais and Majordomo of Antarsid enter LUE.*)

FIRST SAIS
Prince Antarsid—
Now approaches,
Make way, make way,
Our master now is near!

MALE CHORUS (*Coming from all sides*)
Quickly, quickly,
Let us meet him,
Let us greet him,
With a loud resounding hearty—

CHORUS
Hurrah!

MALE CHORUS
Hurrah!

FEMALE CHORUS
Hurrah!

MALE CHORUS
Hurrah!

CHORUS
Hail to noble Antarsid!
All hail the Lord of Lebanon!

(*Majordomo and First Sais go down L. Four Pages, military attendants of Antarsid, enter LUE, head down stage and stand 2 on each side. Antarsid enters LUE. and comes down C. Chorus fall in behind. Sebil comes out of hotel.*)

We flit—
With pleasure keen thro' meadows green,
Now here—
Now there, we're ev'rywhere.

Our coursers fleet, we speed, we speed,
Let then come whatever may,
New attractions bring each day!

(*Chorus do not exit.*)

# Song

ANTARSID
Like winds that lightly,
When morn dawns brightly,
Blow o'er grassy lea—
My trusty steed,
Onward does speed,
While my men follow me;
Each heart is light and gay,
As we pursue our way.

Then downward glancing,
Vistas entrancing,
Before the eye appear—
And all around,
Echoes resound,
Over Lebanon clear!

CHORUS
—Yes! All around!

ANTARSID                              CHORUS
Halloh! Halloh! Halloh!               —Halloh!—Halloh!—Halloh!
The echoes sound, Halloh!             Echoes sound, Halloh!

Oft I sit
Losing myself in musings tender,
Love's pictures all endearing,
In mem'ry's glass appearing;

Love, I know,
Happier far my life would render,
Would but some Scheherazade,
Love tales to me relate;

Then ev'ry night,
I'd hear the maid bright,
And stories of tender import relate!
(*Hands out in front first to R. then to L.*)
Ah!—
Of that, of this,
Of grief, of bliss;

Most varied tales I'd hear forsooth,
The course of true love ne'er ran smooth.

CHORUS                           ANTARSID
(*Both hands to R. then L. then R. then L.*)
Of that, of this,                —Of that, of this,
Of grief, of bliss,              —Of grief, of bliss,
Such tales he'd hear forsooth,   Such tales I'd hear forsooth,
Love's course did ne'er—         Love's course did ne'er—
Run smooth!                      Run smooth!

(*Chorus divide and leave C. open.*)

ANTARSID
Distance comes nigher,
Phoebus mounts higher,
With flaming flag unfurled;
Sweet 'tis to be,
Happy and free, in this beauteous world;
O freedom, gift divine!
Honour and praise be thine!

Life I'd give gladly,
Rather than sadly,
In bondage pass my days;
Free let us be,
Therefore with me proclaim
Liberty's praise!

CHORUS
—Its praise proclaim,

ANTARSID                          CHORUS
Halloh! Halloh! Halloh!           —Halloh!—Halloh!—Halloh!
Its praise proclaim, Halloh!      Praise proclaim, Halloh!

But when dust
Hovers o'er earth on purple pinions,
When night her mantle's spreading,
And stars their light are shedding;

Then once more,
Fancy reverts to love's dominions,
Would but some Scheherazade,
Love tales to me relate;

Then ev'ry night,
I'd hear the maid bright,
And stories of tender import relate!
(*Hands out in front first to R. then to L.*)
Ah!—
Of that, of this,
Of grief, of bliss;
Most varied tales I'd hear forsooth,
The course of true love ne'er ran smooth.

CHORUS                            ANTARSID
(*Both hands to R. then L. then R. then L.*)
Of that, of this,
Of grief, of bliss,                —Of that, of this,
Such tales he'd hear forsooth,     —Of grief, of bliss,
Love's course did ne'er—          Such tales I'd hear forsooth,
Run smooth!                        Love's course did ne'er—
                                   Run smooth!

ANTARSID (*After Chorus, to Maronites*): Majordomo, order the host to lead the way to our apartments.

MAJORDOMO (*Crosses to Pericles*): Greek! His Highness engages your house.

PERICLES: Unfortunately, my humble hotel has already been taken by a lady.

ANTARSID: Who is the lady that requires a whole hotel to herself?

PERICLES: Titania Fanfani, Your Highness!

ANTARSID: Titania Fanfani?

(*Enter Second Sais running.*)

SECOND SAIS: Imshi! Imshi! Make way for the Swan of the Occident. Make way for the great Titania Fanfani.

## No. 3 – Entrance of Titania

(*During introduction Titania enters LUE.—she is dressed in bright coloured European travelling dress, carries a parasol and is followed by Porters carrying her baggage. She remains standing at the entrance with opened parasol looking at everyone present. As she appears Antarsid expresses his rapture and keeps his eyes fixed on her. Nakid comes on R1. for Quartette. Shouts of the populace in the wings.*)

TITANIA, SEBIL, ANTARSID, NAKID *and* PERICLES
Oh, what do I see?
'Tis wondrous quite,
The picture that now greets my sight!

CHORUS
—Wondrous sight.

| TITANIA, SEBIL *and* ANTARSID | NAKID *and* PERICLES | CHORUS |
|---|---|---|
| So bright, so strange, | So bright, so strange, | So bright, |
| So lovely, too— | So lovely too— | So strange, |
| So long its equal has | I ne'er before did | I ne'er did |
| not met my view! | view! | view! |

(*Titania comes down a little and turns to Pericles.*)

TITANIA
If I mistake not,
In you the host I see?

(*Pericles bows low.*)

PERICLES
—O'er my house command I pray!

TITANIA
Quite well! Then there is room for me?

PERICLES
Without delaying notice I did give
To all the guests here staying
E'en the Maronites' proud lord—
(*Indicating Antarsid*)
—I turned away!

ANTARSID (*Aside*)
—O face divinely fair!

TITANIA (*Aside*)
Why, that was most discourteous,
And grieves me sore!

ANTARSID
—My duty'twas no more!

(*Titania glances over at Antarsid.*)

| TITANIA | ANTARSID |
|---|---|
| Of his eyes the ardent glances, | —Of her eyes the ardent glances, |
| Fill me with a strange delight; | —Fill me with a new delight, |
| Ev'ry look my soul entrances, | —Ev'ry look my soul entrances |
| Of those flashing orbs so bright! | —Of those flashing orbs so bright! |
| Of his eyes the ardent glances, | —Of her eyes the ardent glances, |

Fill me with a strange delight;
Ev'ry look my soul entrances,
Of those flashing orbs so bright!

—Fill me with a new delight,
—Ev'ry look my soul entrances
—Of those flashing orbs so bright!

PERICLES
He seems embarrassed;
Mutely stands he there—
Since came the stranger fair!

TITANIA
Ah how handsome,
Ah how manly,

Is this stranger!

PERICLES
Your apartments are prepared,
And await your presence now!

SEBIL *and* NAKID
Quite pleased the lady seems to be!

TITANIA, SEBIL, ANTARSID, NAKID *and* PERICLES
Oh what do I see?
'Tis wondrous quite,
The picture that now greets my sight!

| TITANIA, SEBIL *and* ANTARSID | NAKID *and* PERICLES | CHORUS |
|---|---|---|
| So bright, so strange, | So bright, so strange, | So bright, |
| So lovely, too— | So lovely too— | So strange, |
| So long its equal has not met my view! | I ne'er before did view! | I ne'er did view! |

(*Antarsid is about to go upstage with his attendants.*)

TITANIA (*Stopping him*)
What my lord,
You would away?
One word I pray!—

With regret I've just received
The information that through me
You've been refused accommodation!

But Sir you may believe me,

To annoy you much would grieve me;
This house I pleasant find,
We'll share it, Sir, if you don't mind.

PERICLES
'Tis astonishing how courteously
She meets him—

ANTARSID (*Bowing low*)
—You're most gen'rous!

TITANIA (*Inquiringly*)
Well?

PERICLES                                    ANTARSID
And her offer he most surely will           —Well! Gladly I accept!
accept!

TITANIA
And I hope that this arrangement,
Will be quite to your taste;
I hope that this arrangement,
Will be quite to your taste!

ANTARSID
Ah how soon,
Doth love's sweet thrill,
My bosom fill!

## Song

TITANIA
Tho' we were strangers hitherto,
I hope we'll soon each other better know,
And henceforth we shall neighbours be;
By chance that was arranged quite prettily!

Stiff etiquette is my aversion,
It casts a gloom o'er all diversion,
And in each hour of recreation
It must have its sacrifice.

You'd often look, but you don't dare to,
You'd often speak, but don't quite care to,
You go where gladly you would station,
Because 'twould not be nice!

(*Slight waltz movement and Chorus come down into straight line.*)

I ask, why bashful be?
I ask, why bashful be?
For often by one word,
All's arranged pleasantly!

(*All sway with waltz movement—straight forward on R. foot.*)

CHORUS
Bravo!

TITANIA *and* CHORUS
(Why/don't) bashful be?

CHORUS
Bravo!

TITANIA *and* CHORUS
Don't bashful be!

| CHORUS | TITANIA |
|---|---|
| For often by one word— | Thus all's arranged— |
| All's arranged pleasantly! | Pleasantly! |

(*At end of Chorus to 2^{nd} verse. Break up line and leave C. open.*)

TITANIA
How pleasant 'tis at the Café,
To sit and chat, and smoke a Nargileh!
But with constraint one naught enjoys;
Its presence ev'ry hour of mirth alloys.

Now if you'll pay me strict attention,
Of Europe's women much I'll mention,
Tho' for that kind of information,

An Eastern may hardly care.

You'll then paint me a picture mental,
Of ways and customs oriental,
Tho' dangerous such recreation,
We can at least take care!

(*Slight waltz movement and Chorus come down into straight line.*)

Therefore, why bashful be?
Therefore, why bashful be?
For often by one word,
All's arranged pleasantly!

(*Everybody sways with waltz movement.*)

CHORUS
Bravo!

TITANIA *and* CHORUS
(Why/don't) bashful be?

CHORUS
Bravo!

TITANIA *and* CHORUS
Don't bashful be!

| CHORUS | TITANIA |
|---|---|
| For often by one word— | Thus all's arranged— |
| All's arranged pleasantly! | Pleasantly! |

ANTARSID (*Aside*): How beautiful she is. That is the Scheherazade I am seeking. (*Aloud*) The delights of Paradise beam from thine eyes, and chance the desert into the flowery meadows of Damascus.

TITANIA: What does he mean? (*To Pericles*) Does he accept my invitation?

PERICLES: He expressed his acceptance in the flowery language of the Orientals.

TITANIA (*To Antarsid*): Very well then. Half of the hotel for you, and half for me!

PERICLES: Excuse me. What will be left for your husband?

TITANIA (*Startled*): My husband? (*Aside*) I haven't any.

ANTARSID: What, Queen of the West! Dos't thou belong to the Harem of a mortal?

TITANIA (*Recovering herself*): Oh my husband, dear fellow, will be only too glad to be able to offer you so small a courtesy. (*Aside*) Considering he does not exist, there can be no doubt upon that point. (*Aloud*) Pray have no hesitation in accepting. When you meet my husband he will but repeat my offer!

(*She dismisses Antarsid.*)

## No. 3 1/2 – Antarsid Exits

(*For exit of Antarsid, Chorus go off RUE. and LUE. singing "Of that, of this". Sebil enters hotel. Antarsid crosses towards hotel—makes very low bow to Titania who gives him her hand to kiss. He exits into hotel. All others exit L. apart from Titania and Pericles. Titania crosses to table L. Pericles offers her a chair and she sits.*)

PERICLES: When may I expect the Signora's husband?

TITANIA (*Without noticing the question*): Is my uncle here?

PERICLES: His Excellency is here, and will be with you immediately!

TITANIA (*Aside*): Immediately. That's awkward. (*Aloud*) You can go!

PERICLES: Your apartments are ready!

TITANIA: Very well. I will await the Pasha here. It is too warm inside. Leave me.

PERICLES: As the Signora commands. (*Bows and speaks aside while exiting*) Her husband has not yet arrived. That's something to report to the Pasha.

(*Exit Pericles into hotel.*)

TITANIA (*Still seated at table*): Really, this is a most embarrassing situation. I must find a husband before tomorrow or let my inheritance go to that greedy old uncle of mine. I thought my telegram would be enough to convince him, but as he has hurried here at once, he evidently intends to see my husband before he hands over the money. What am I to do? This anxiety drives the blood to my head. (*Rings bell*) I say, servants! Slaves!

(*Enter Miradillo from hotel. He stands on top of hotel steps, hat in hand.*)

MIRADILLO: Gracious Lady.

TITANIA: Well. (*Recognising him, she rises and comes C.*) Why, Signor Miradillo!

MIRADILLO (*Aside*): Rapture. She recognises me. (*He comes towards C. to meet her*) (*Aloud*) I heard of your arrival, and came to offer my services as a guide.

TITANIA: Indeed! You see, I too have undertaken a trip to Africa. (*Slyly*) Have you explored the Interior yet?

MIRADILLO (*Embarassed*): Well, not entirely as yet. You see the…er…the…err…sun was so hot. Oh, the heat was incredible!

TITANIA (*Sarcastically*): I hope the heat here has not melted your exchequer with the same rapidity as it did in Naples.

MIRADILLO (*Inconsolable aside*): She even remembers that. (*Aloud*) Far more rapidly. The temperature is warmer here, and the dissolving process even more rapid.

(*He sighs and turns his trouser pockets inside out.*)

TITANIA: Ah, Signor Miradillo. I thought I had your promise of reformation, when that Napolitan difficulty was surmounted.

MIRADILLO: Well, you see…

TITANIA: That poor Tessa must wait longer. I suppose you are bankrupt again!

MIRADILLO: As the Signora takes so kind an interest in me, I may admit that I am entirely so!

TITANIA: And I have again turned up in the nick of time.

MIRADILLO: Yes Signora—history repeats itself.

TITANIA (*After a moment of thought*): Well I'll be the good fairy once more. But this time, Miradillo, I shall require a service of you.

MIRADILLO: Command me!

(*Pericles makes noise in hotel.*)

TITANIA: Someone is coming. I have no time for explanations, but agree in all I say, and show no surprise.

(*Enter Pericles from hotel.*)

PERICLES: His Excellency, the Pasha!

TITANIA (*Aside to Miradillo*): Remember! (*Aloud*) Ah, my uncle. Then I can at last introduce him to my husband.

(*She lays her hand on Miradillo's arm.*)

MIRADILLO: Husband! Phew! (*Aside to Pericles*) First payment on account this evening.

PERICLES: He, her husband? That's something to report to the Pasha.

(*Exit Pericles into hotel.*)

TITANIA (*Hurriedly*): Do you understand?

MIRADILLO (*Same tone*): Thoroughly. Legacy. Shabby uncle. Hoodwink him. Payment guaranteed!

TITANIA: Of course. Play your part well and you won't have to complain. Here is my uncle. Be careful!

(*Enter Fanfani and Pericles from hotel. Pericles, pointing to Titania and Miradillo, informs Fanfani of something.*)

# No. 4 – Quartette

FANFANI (*To Pericles*)
Well, that's astounding surely!

PERICLES
Perhaps I'll now be paid!

TITANIA (*To Miradillo*)
Now play your part demurely!

MIRADILLO
Deceit come to my aid!

FANFANI
He and she a married
Couple claim to be,
Well I'm suspicious quite
That ev'rything's not right!

TITANIA (*Parodically to Miradillo*)
Oh what joy to see you a again,
Best of men!

PERICLES
—Did you hear?

TITANIA
Best of men!

PERICLES
—Was I right?

(*Miradillo and Titania go down L. pretending to be very affectionate. Fanfani RC., watching them.*)

TITANIA
Blissful moments hath married life,
Now and then!
Now and then!

MIRADILLO (*To Titania*)
You to see once more I did pine,
Darling mine—
Darling mine—
And to me the world doubly gay—
Seems today—
Seems today.

FANFANI
Oh this is a blow severe,
And it makes me nervous quite,
Yes she has a husband,

That is bad for me!
—Very true!
—Very true!
—And ere long to me shall say;
—"Dearest uncle now please pay!"

TITANIA *and* MIRADILLO
When in thy arms I rest,
Then I feel truly blest,
(*Aside*)
Love I must simulate,

All doubts to dissipate.

PERICLES
Now it is evident,
And folly'twere to doubt it,

The lady is his wife,
(*Crosses to C. and bows low to Miradillo and Titania*)
I'll make my compliment alright!

FANFANI
Oh I'm quite beside myself with rage and spite,
I could kick and choke the fellow with delight,
Thro' him I must lose two million francs 'tis clear,
(*Crosses to R.*)
At two sous I'd call his carcass pretty dear.

PERICLES
Here stands the tender loving pair
The uncle fond stands over there!

TITANIA (*Crosses to C. and beckons Fanfani*)
Uncle dearest, uncle mine, to you
I'd introduce the man whom
I did choose, he is so brave
So kind, so good, so dear!

FANFANI
Perhaps I'd better put
Some Strychnine in his soup!

(*He reluctantly crosses to C.*)

MIRADILLO                                  FANFANI
Uncle dearest
(*Crosses to C. to meet Fanfani*)
Uncle mine, my wife                        O I thank you!
She loves me so that she'll be             Most obliging!
Glad I know, to pay some debts             And what now?
That I've contracted here.

(*Titania and Miradillo among themselves.*)

TITANIA (*Annoyed, to Miradillo*)
Ah to bleed me!

MIRADILLO (*Aside to Titania*)
Why that's in the part you're playing,

TITANIA
You would try Sir!

MIRADILLO
Bleeding you should call it not!

TITANIA
But your meanness,

MIRADILLO
'Tis a bad thing for the husband,

TITANIA
I defy Sir!

MIRADILLO
When his wife won't pay the scot!

TITANIA
I will not pay!

MIRADILLO
Then I'll stop playing!

TITANIA
Oh that is mean.

MIRADILLO
I find it paying.

TITANIA
It's robbery,

MIRADILLO
Don't trouble me!

FANFANI
Ah, it seems to me already
Quarrels have this youthful pair!

TITANIA *and* MIRADILLO          PERICLES
(*Almost screamed*)
When in thy arms I rest.
Then I feel truly blest;          —He seems disgusted greatly,
Love I must simulate,             —But yet in spite of all,
All doubts to dissipate!          —He must pay ultimately.

FANFANI
'Tis disgusting now anew they bill and coo,
In the deepest depths of hell I wish them two;
Thro' him I must lose two million francs 'tis clear,
At that price I find them both extremely dear!
Cursed luck that brought them here.

TITANIA
Darling mine!

PERICLES
—He with rage will burst I fear!

MIRADILLO
—Dearest wife!

FANFANI
Pleasant I with all must be.

TITANIA
—Darling mine!

PERICLES
—Something wrong there seems to be!

MIRADILLO
—Dearest wife!

(*While Miradillo and Titania sing this passage embracing, Fanfani and Pericles go upstage a little watching.*)

TITANIA *and* MIRADILLO
Little darling, you're my lovey,
You're my dovey,

TITANIA (*Aside*)                      MIRADILLO (*Aside*)
Worst of all I now must              Best of all she now must
Give the scamp a kiss!               Let me have a kiss!

TITANIA            MIRADILLO            FANFANI *and*
                                       PERICLES
Oh, the scamp!     Oh, what bliss!     He's a scamp!

(*Fanfani and Pericles come down angrily. Titania crosses to C. and sings to Pericles.*)

TITANIA
Very well then!

Now let us settle at once!
Host, bring your bill!

PERICLES
Why there was no special hurry,
For my pay I did not worry,
But as long as you command it,
(*He crosses to C.—takes out long bill on roller and throws it over
    towards L.*)
Here's the bill made out with care!

(*Titania reads bill, pointing at items with her parasol. Fanfani and
Miradillo also look down bill beginning at bottom. One on each side of
the bill, they come face to face at top.*)

TITANIA
Twelve thousand and four hundred francs,
Within less than two weeks?

FANFANI                               MIRADILLO
Twelve thousand four hundred?         Bagatelle! Bagatelle!
Oh ho!

TITANIA
Eight hundred francs for a supper
With girls from the Café Francais?

MIRADILLO
To music I incline,
And their performance was so fine.

FANFANI
Confound the Scoundrel!

TITANIA (*Aside*)
His cool way,

FANFANI
The gallows bird!

TITANIA
I rather like!

MIRADILLO
What I have always had at heart
Was to promote the cause of art!

TITANIA (*Reading bill again*)
Two thousand francs are charged, I see
For boarding Mamsell Sanssouci!

MIRADILLO
She was an orphan lonely,
Whom I helped a little only!

FANFANI
Roué!

TITANIA (*Reading bill again*)
Here a Slave too,
At six thousand francs is priced?

MIRADILLO
Yes, yes!
I first mean to convert her,
Afterwards have her baptised!

FANFANI (*In great rage*)
Ha! He's a swindler; that I see!

(*Pericles folds up bill and throws it in hotel.*)

TITANIA, MIRADILLO *and* PERICLES
What?

FANFANI
And is cheating you and me!

TITANIA, MIRADILLO *and* PERICLES
He?

FANFANI
Not a single word is true.

TITANIA, MIRADILLO *and* PERICLES
Ha!

FANFANI
Lying's all that he can do,

TITANIA, MIRADILLO *and* PERICLES
No!

FANFANI
And this very dubious Marriage,

TITANIA, MIRADILLO *and* PERICLES
Well?

FANFANI
I'm inclined much to disparage.

| TITANIA, MIRADILLO *and* PERICLES | FANFANI |
|---|---|
| That would be quite indecent, | She so easy, |
| For our life is pleasant, | He so fertile, |
| Therefore just at present, | She phlegmatic, |
| Doubt is out of place. | He so bold. |

| TITANIA *and* MIRADILLO | PERICLES | |
|---|---|---|
| (He is/I am) careless, | —Just be easy, | Oh to fool me won't be easy, |
| But good natured, | —Do keep cool Sir! | He is much too windy for me, |
| | —Calm your passion, | I don't like his ways erratic; |
| Somewhat mild, | —Won't | By their tricks he'll |
| Yet quite brave. | you please? | not be sold. |

(*Titania tries to soothe Fanfani, who is in a terrible rage.*)

| TITANIA, MIRADILLO *and* PERICLES | FANFANI |
|---|---|
| O pray, be mild, | That this boaster is your husband, |
| Don't act so wild! | You pretend, ma'am, it's too thin. |

TITANIA
O dearest uncle, you're unjust!
Against abuse my husband now defend I must;
His rage is dire, like Etna's fire,
O do not waken a Sicilian's ire!

(*During Titania's solo Miradillo, Fanfani and Pericles are all upstage. Miradillo is trying to reconcile Fanfani, who won't have anything to do with him.*)

## Song

TITANIA
In proud Palermo, throbs the air,
With Etna's lava glow,
And in the veins of all its sons,
The blood doth hotly flow;

There billows are surging,
And on the surf the ship is toss'd,
Engulfed in the vortex,
The gallant craft is lost.

Holla ho, holla ho!
Thou sunny land—
Where streams of fire from Etna rise,
Where loving hearts
With double rapture beat,

Yes!—
Palermo's meadows are
An earthly paradise,
How balmy are the zephyrs there!

(*At end of solo, Miradillo, Fanfani and Pericles all come down.*)

Ah, how sweet!

(*All four back upstage.*)

MIRADILLO, FANFANI *and* PERICLES
Thou sunny land—

(*All four march down in line C.*)

ALL
Where streams of fire from Etna rise,
Where loving hearts with double rapture beat,
Yes!—
Palermo's meadows are
On earth the paradise!

How balmy are the zephyrs there,
Ah, how sweet!

Where quakes the earth,
With mighty throes volcanic;
(*Stop*)
There heaves the heart,
With passion most Titanic;

Where from earth's depth,
The fiery lava streameth,

There fiery love,
Each breast doth move!
There fiery love,
Each breast doth move!

(*Take hands and back up very slowly on these three long notes. On "land"
then all down to C*)

Thou sunny land—
Where streams of fire from Etna rise,
Where loving hearts with double rapture beat,

Yes—
Palermo's meadows are,
On earth the Paradise!

How balmy are the zephyrs there,
Ah, how sweet!
O Palermo, so balmy, so glowing, so sweet!

(*Miradillo and Pericles exeunt into hotel.*)

FANFANI (*Looks after Miradillo, nodding head*): But I say, my niece…this husband? (*Looks at bill*) This hotel bill. Don't these extra expenses constrain you?

TITANIA (*Calmly*): Oh no.

FANFANI: If I were to live at this rate, I should be compelled to sell half a dozen fortresses to the enemy.

TITANIA: My husband may be…a little thoughtless!

FANFANI: Now, all this champagne. It is enough to make a full regiment fuller. I vote to have this marriage annulled, not that any petty considerations for a paltry two millions influences me…oh no…but that an uncle's experienced eye tells me you are unhappy.

TITANIA: But I am not. Contrariwise, I am very happy.

FANFANI: Your nights are spent in bitter tears.

TITANIA: Absurd!

(*She crosses to L.*)

FANFANI: You are losing flesh!

TITANIA: Why uncle?

FANFANI (*Emphatically*): In a word, you need a divorce.

TITANIA: Hush, here comes the Prince. (*Aside*) And most opportunely.

(*She crosses to C.*)

FANFANI (*Aside, crossing to L.*): I can't talk her out of those two millions!

(*Enter Antarsid R.*)

ANTARSID: Ah Signora! Again, I greet you.

FANFANI (*Stunned, looking at them both*): What weird things in uniform are coming in and out of your quarters?

TITANIA (*Introducing*): My Uncle, Fanfani Pasha! (*She crosses to L.*) Prince Antarsid!

FANFANI: Your Highness. I am overjoyed, delighted. (*Aside*) That is the way I talk to Highnesses even when I want to throttle them.

ANTARSID: Delighted, Pasha. We have met before, on a little matter of business. I furnished you with a thousand tiger skins in exchange for a dozen pretty slaves. Is it not so?

FANFANI: I understand the slaves didn't turn out to your satisfaction. (*Crosses to L. corner*) There were six elderly cooks among them.

ANTARSID: To tell the truth, the whole shipment was a little off.

FANFANI: That's a princely way of putting it. (*Aside*) That's because I didn't handle the goods personally. It's always that way.

TITANIA: Is it possible Prince, you still retain so barbarous a custom as slave dealing? How uncivilised!

ANTARSID: If you would only condescend to civilize me, I would try to improve.

TITANIA (*Coquettishly*): Well, what then?

ANTARSID (*Passionately*): Then I should not only become your eager pupil, but your devoted slave!

TITANIA: Bravo. That had quite a European ring to it. (*To Fanfani*) We shall meet again at dinner.

FANFANI: At dinner! We shall celebrate the feast of Bayram at my country seat.

TITANIA: Charming! Come Prince.

(*She starts to go, crossing R. towards hotel.*)

FANFANI: And your husband?

TITANIA: My husband? Oh, I had forgotten all about him. He'll be delighted to see that I am enjoying myself. Come Prince!

(*She enters hotel with Antarsid.*)

FANFANI: Come Prince! I wonder if she takes him for a poodle. Well, her husband has serio-comic relations with music-hall singers and she has her new Prince in tow. This is genuine Turkish delight. (*Starts to go but notices Tessa and Buccametta, who are entering*) Ah, a pair of pretty strangers.

(*Enter Tessa and Buccametta L., followed by a Porter with two trunks.*)

BUCCAMETTA (*To Tessa*): Disgusting place, this Cairo. Nothing but beggars and sharpers…but I shall make that Miradillo pay for it.

PORTER: Backshish.

TESSA: Mamma, what does he want with "black fish"?

BUCCAMETTA (*Fumbling in pockets*): This is the third time I've given him money, and he still keeps crying "Backshish". (*Notices Fanfani*) Ah, an interesting native. I'll approach him. Please Sir, what does this man want?

(*Fanfani kicks Porter off R1. Porter exits howling.*)

FANFANI: Imshi! Imshi! That's what he wants. That's the Arabian for "Vamoose". (*To Tessa*) Sweet creature!

(*He tries to pinch her cheek.*)

TESSA (*Boxing his ears*): Imshi!

FANFANI: Charming! You are quite an Arabian scholar!

(*He crosses to R.*)

BUCCAMETTA: We don't want any more of that, old Turk. (*Crosses to C.*) We don't belong to Cairo. Is that the Hotel?

FANFANI: It is; but may I inquire whom you are seeking for there?

BUCCAMETTA: A gentleman.

(*She crosses L.*)

FANFANI (*Puzzled*): Not looking for me evidently. (*Aside*) A gentleman? That sounds suspicious.

TESSA: And lodgings.

FANFANI: It's all full. You can't get lodgings there, but if you would like to come to my house…?

BUCCAMETTA: No thank you. I do not propose that darling Tessa and myself shall be mistaken for Turks. I mean Turkesses.

FANFANI: When you are in Turkey, do as the Turkeys do. (*He crosses L. between Tessa and Buccametta. He takes out a card in each hand and gives them to Tessa and Buccametta.*) However, I don't mind confessing to you that I am not a Turkey. Turk, I should say. Allow me to offer you a card.

BUCCAMETTA (*Reading*): Fanfani Pasha! Your Excellency!

FANFANI: Ah, you are dumbfounded aren't you? You see, when the Government wants hard tack, I turn them out their hard tack. (*Softly*) When the Sheik al Islam wants a fresh Circassian beauty, I furnish that also. Not too fresh, but fresh enough. I furnish the army with neckties and suspenders and ruthlessly am a private Turkish executioner and Oriental town-crier, Directory and Railroad time table. You don't seem to know the Orient yet? Oh, you'll be acquainted in time. It's a very easy place to understand!

## No. 5 – Terzett

(*During each solo, the other two upstage. During Fanfani's solo, Tessa and Buccametta go upstage and come down again in time for ensemble.*)

## Song

FANFANI
Big beard visage framing,
"Allah" oft exclaiming;
Twisted turban wearing,
Servant big fan bearing;

All exertion shirking,
Ne'er a thought of working;
From Nargilehs smoking,
Silence keep provoking;

On a divan sitting,
Ne'er excited getting;
Food with hand dividing,
On a camel riding;

Through the noon hours sleeping;
Pretty harem keeping,
Adding to it ever,
Without shame whatever;

And with Eunuchs trying,
To prevent all prying;
Purest Mocha drinking,
Very little thinking;

That's the fundamental,
That's the elemental,
Status Oriental,
Status Oriental!

ALL
That's the fundamental,
That's the elemental,
Status Oriental,
Yes that's what it is!

TESSA (*This line very slowly*)
Although these customs,

(*All make sort of Spanish step to L.*)

| TESSA | BUCCAMETTA | FANFANI |
|---|---|---|
| Are to morals detrimental, | Are to morals fundamental, | Oriental fundamental, |
| (*This line very slowly*) Yet they are customs, | | |

ALL (*Make sort of Spanish step to L.*)
Fundamental, Oriental.

TESSA (*This line very slowly*)
And consequently,

ALL
(*Across stage hand R. and L. so as to leave next soloist in C.*)
Tho' the customs (Occidental/Oriental),
Are to morals detrimental,
Yet they're picturesque!

(*During Tessa's solo, Fanfani and Buccametta are upstage, Buccametta trying to flirt with Fanfani, who tries to escape from her—running around table etc. Buccametta following him. Must regulate the business so as to be down stage in time for trio.*)

TESSA
What the Orientals
Do, the Occidentals
Very largely practise;
That indeed a fact is,

For in Europe surely,

Woman fares but poorly,
That's a fact, I know it,
And can clearly show it;

On one man attending,
Whimsical, unbending,
Always wait his leisure,
Surely is no pleasure;

With us married life, sir,
Hard is for the wife, sir;
Men are always lying,
To deceive us trying;

Vows eternal swearing,
Yet not for them caring;
They their cash invest in,
Amourettes clandestine;

Thus our fundamental,
Status Occidental,
Has a kinship mental,
With the Oriental!

ALL
Thus our fundamental,
Status Occidental,
Has a kinship mental,
With the Orient!

TESSA (*This line very slowly*)
Although these customs,

(*All make sort of Spanish step to L.*)

| TESSA | BUCCAMETTA | FANFANI |
|---|---|---|
| Are to morals | Are to morals | Oriental |
| detrimental, | fundamental, | fundamental, |
| (*This line very slowly*) | | |
| Yet they are customs, | | |

ALL (*Make sort of Spanish step to L.*)
Fundamental, Oriental.

TESSA (*This line very slowly*)
And consequently,

ALL
(*Across stage hand R. and L. so as to leave next soloist in C.*)
Tho' the customs (Occidental/Oriental),
Are to morals detrimental,
Yet they're picturesque!

(*During Buccametta's solo, Tessa goes upstage LC. Fanfani up RC. and tries to make love to her. At first she turns her back and puts open parasol over her shoulder. Fanfani gradually gets his arm round her and they kiss behind parasol, which Tessa holds so as to hide them from audience.*)

BUCCAMETTA
Yes, the modern West, as
Well as the Far East, has
Many tricks invented,
That seem most demented;

Therefore an example;
Women not too ample,
Likewise quite talented,
To be complimented;

So they innocently,
Pleasantly and gently,
Listen to each falsehood,
Utter'd by the male brood,

So these consequently,
Often insolently,
And impertinently,
Sometimes vehemently,

Try by impositions,
To impose conditions,
Most humiliating,

And exasperating;

Thus our fundamental,
Status Occidental,
Has a kinship mental,
With the Oriental!

ALL
Thus our fundamental,
Status Occidental,
Has a kinship mental,
With the Orient!

TESSA (*This line very slowly*)
Although these customs,

(*All make sort of Spanish step to L.*)

| TESSA | BUCCAMETTA | FANFANI |
|---|---|---|
| Are to morals | Are to morals | Oriental |
| detrimental, | fundamental, | fundamental, |
| (*This line very slowly*) | | |
| Yet they are customs, | | |

ALL (*Make sort of Spanish step to L.*)
Fundamental, Oriental.

TESSA (*This line very slowly*)
And consequently,

ALL
(*Across stage hand R. and L. so as to leave next soloist in C.*)
Tho' the customs (Occidental/Oriental),
Are to morals detrimental,
Yet they're picturesque!

FANFANI: Ladies, don't distress yourselves. I am a respectable married man. Will you do me the honour of being my guests?

TESSA: What is the name of her Highness, your wife?

FANFANI: Metta. Melinda. Melitta. Laraide. Fatima. Kessula. Julennia. Marinka. Teresetta!...

BUCCAMETTA (*Interrupts him*): Why Sir, your wife can't have so many names as that; or perhaps according to the Oriental fashion, you possess several wives?

FANFANI: At present only forty six. Choice specimens off in all parts of the world. May I hope that you ladies...

TESSA: We came to Cairo to find a young gentleman named Miradillo!

FANFANI: What, Signor Miradillo of Palermo?

TESSA: Yes.

BUCCAMETTA: The very one.

FANFANI: You are on his track, for he has married my niece and I am his uncle-in-law.

TESSA: What? Miradillo married? Oh!

BUCCAMETTA (*Perplexed*): The traitor. Oh, mio Dio! Traditore con amore!

FANFANI (*Aside*): Ah, he has evidently had an amourette with one of them. I think I ought to make some atonement for his faithlessness, especially to the younger.

TESSA: Sir, you are very kind. We will accept your invitation.

BUCCAMETTA: Seeing you are so entirely married, I don't object. (*To Tessa*) We will have revenge.

(*Enter Miradillo from hotel R. Tessa crosses to L.*)

TESSA: Ha! 'Tis he, the traitor!

BUCCAMETTA: Veil yourself. He must not recognise use.

(*Tessa and Buccametta lower their veils.*)

MIRADILLO: Ah Pasha, won't you come and dine with us at the hotel?

FANFANI: You are already engaged to me. Your wife promised to dine at my country house.

MIRADILLO: Indeed, that will be charming.

TESSA (*Aside to Buccametta*): He really has a wife. I'd like to run a dagger into his false heart.

BUCCAMETTA: Wait, my dear, and you will.

FANFANI: I have also invited these ladies. They have been confided to my protection by the Swedish Government. I'm something of an Old Swede myself.

(*Miradillo crosses towards L.*)

MIRADILLO: Charming strangers. I bid you welcome most heartedly.

TESSA (*Curtly*): Thank you.

(*Exit Tessa L1E.*)

BUCCAMETTA (*Imitating Tessa*): Thank you.

(*Exit Buccametta haughtily L1.*)

MIRADILLO (*Aside*): She chops me off very short, but she'll get tractable in time.

FANFANI: Ah, my travelling salesmen are coming this way with a choice assortment of new slaves.

(*Exeunt Miradillo and Fanfani L1.*)

# No. 6 – Finale (Act 1)

(*Chorus enter LUE. marching four abreast. Some of the women have tambourines, some have triangles—some of the men have tom-toms. March down C and divide up on sides leaving C. open. Accent first beat of bar with whatever instrument each carries. Four or six Dancers ready LUE.—oriental slave dress, like Turkish costume—they carry small brass cymbals.*)

CHORUS
Hoio! Hoio!
Let music sound! Holaro!
Hoio! Hoio!
With vigour pound! Holaro!

Those tones excite,
To mirth and glee each breast,
And with delight,
All bow to joy's behest;

Now let the Tarabuka well be shaken,
And from Kemenche's strings
Sweet music waken;

Derwish flutes so loud and shrill,
Now the air with piping fill;

(*Dancers enter LUE. and come down C. in straight line with springing dance step, striking cymbals on each bar.*)

MALE CHORUS
La la, la la,
The merry music all,
La la, la la,
To song and dance doth call;

CHORUS
La la, la la,
The merry music all,
La la, la la,
To song and dance doth call;

(*Triangles and cymbals double tempo. Four Slaves make slow pirouette, then reverse.*)

> Zizirin zin zin, zizirin zin zin,
> Zizirin zin zin, zin ha ho!
> Zizirin zin zin, zizirin zin zin,
> Zizirin zin zin, zin ha ho!
>
> La la, la la,
> La la la la la la la la,
>
> (*All instruments three beats quick on this*:)
> Holaro!

(*Fanfani enters L1. in a clumsy coarse manner. As he sings he examines slave girls, walking backwards and forwards across line.*)

> FANFANI (*In a clumsy, course manner*)
> In Tsad, in Tsad,
> There beauties can be had,
> They're delicate like chocolate,
> Of light and dark brown shade!
>
> The Pasha as I knew,
> Much likes that dusky hue,
> So for his special pleasure,
> I these buxom women here did buy,
> The very best that could be had,
> In Tsad, in Tsad!

(*He calls up the Slaves. The Slaves dance back upstage striking cymbals. Fanfani goes up and dances in front of them.*)

| CHORUS | FANFANI |
|---|---|
| In Tsad, in Tsad, | |
| There beauties can be had, | |
| (*Down stage again*) | Come forward, |
| In Tsad, in Tsad, | |
| Of light and dark brown shade; | In the dance you may, |
| La la la, | Your charms display! |
| La la la, | Indeed my choice, |
| | Is extra nice, |

CHORUS
Now Kemenche's Echoes wake,
La la la,
La la la,
And the Tarabuka shake!

FANFANI
The finest women I pick out;
So sweet their face,
So pure their race,
Of that there is no doubt!

(*Chorus' triangles and cymbals double tempo. Dancers pirouette as before.*)

FANFANI (*In a clumsy, course manner*)
In Tsad, in Tsad,
There beauties can be had,
They're delicate like chocolate,
Of light and dark brown shade!

The Pasha as I knew,
Much likes that dusky hue,
So for his special pleasure,
I these buxom women here did buy,
The very best that could be had,
In Tsad, in Tsad!

(*He calls up the Slaves. The Slaves dance back upstage striking cymbals. Fanfani goes up and dances in front of them.*)

CHORUS
In Tsad, in Tsad,
There beauties can be had,
(*Down stage again*)
In Tsad, in Tsad,
Of light and dark brown shade;

La la la,
La la la,
Now Kemenche's Echoes wake,
La la la,
La la la,
And the Tarabuka shake!

FANFANI

Come forward,

In the dance you may,
Your charms display!

Indeed my choice,
Is extra nice,
The finest women I pick out;
So sweet their face,
So pure their race,
Of that there is no doubt!

(*Chorus' triangles and cymbals double tempo. Dancers pirouette as before.*)

CHORUS
Zizirin zin zin, zizirin zin zin,
Zizirin zin zin, zin ha ho!
Zizirin zin zin, zizirin zin zin,
Zizirin zin zin, zin ha ho!

La la, la la,
La la la la la la la la!
(*Strike all instruments*)
Holaro!

FANFANI
In the slave trade there are
many,
But of all those I'm the best;
That I tell the truth, this lovely
Group of women will attest.
In Tsad, in Tsad,
I find them in Tsad!

Holaro!

(*Miradillo, Tessa and Buccametta all enter L1. At same time Sebil enters from hotel R. She is held by two Male Hotel Servants. Pericles follows, followed by Nakid and Hosh. Miradillo crosses over to Sebil.*)

SEBIL
Miradillo! Gracious master!
Here am I! Take thy slave, O Lord!

(*Tessa with Soprano, Fanfani with Tenor, Buccametta with Alto, Pericles with Bass.*)

CHORUS
Ha! Oh see that!
Whoever would believe that?
What ails her? What brings her?
What is she seeking here?

SEBIL
Bought I was by him!

CHORUS
Your story we can't credit!

SEBIL
And shall stay with him!

CHORUS
No! Get yourself from here!

SEBIL (*Trying to release herself*)
Let go!

CHORUS
Away now,

SEBIL
Let go!

CHORUS
Away!

SEBIL
He's bought me, I repeat to you,

CHORUS
—Off!

SEBIL
Ask him yourselves if that's not true!

CHORUS
—Away!

MIRADILLO
Yes, it's true!

(*As Miradillo sings, servants release Sebil who throws herself at his feet. Miradillo raises her. Tessa and Buccametta on L. appear very much shocked.*)

My slave she's really,
And so you see,
She'll stay with me!
For shining cash,
I bought the girl!

| BUCCAMETTA, FANFANI *and* MALE CHORUS | TESSA |
|---|---|
| He bought the girl, And paid in cash, | —O Heaven, this is dreadful, —He does not mind his wife, |

BUCCAMETTA, FANFANI *and*
MALE CHORUS
At private sale,
How very rash,
It's queer, and very rash!

TESSA
—A slave he buys coolly!

FANFANI *and* MALE CHORUS
What will the wife say to that?
Hm, hm, hm!

TESSA
Woe is me!

BUCCAMETTA
Reason's left,

MIRADILLO
Well the fun,

FANFANI *and* MALE CHORUS
I wonder what she'll say?
Hm hm hm!

TESSA
What a shame!

BUCCAMETTA
Him bereft.

MIRADILLO
Has begun.

FANFANI *and* MALE CHORUS
I fear there'll be a small row;
Hm hm hm!

(*Antarsid and Titania ready in hotel R.*)

TESSA
O dire disgrace—
That threatens now my name!
To think he could so soon
forget,
O would that we had never met!
I never can condone his doings!

BUCCAMETTA
He'll yet have disgrace and
shame!
What one not satisfied,

He buys a slave besides;
Very strange his doings are.

MIRADILLO
Through me she will win the
game!
Calmly I'll smile,

And wait a while;

SEBIL
—Thy Sebil faithfully doth love
thee,
While holds the thread of life,
None she'll esteem above thee;
In weal and woe thy slightest
word,

MIRADILLO

To watch their doings.

SEBIL
With joy obeying,
Ever watchful near thee staying;

FANFANI *and* MALE CHORUS
I wonder what she'll say,
I fear, I fear there'll be a row.
What will the wife say to that?
Hm hm hm,
I wonder what she'll say?
Hm hm hm!
I fear there'll be a small row.
(FANFANI) What will his wife say to that?
(MALE CHORUS) Shameful doings, ah.

SEBIL
And when at night thou'rt calmly sleeping,
Vigils o'er thee she'll be keeping,
Yes thy Sebil loves thee true!

TESSA *and* BUCCAMETTA
Here I will remain!

MIRADILLO
Here I'll remain!

FANFANI
So I will remain!

MALE CHORUS
So we will remain!

(*Fanfani sees Titania.*)

FANFANI
The wife I coming see;
How angry she will be!

(*Antarsid and Titania enter slowly arm in arm from hotel R. and come down C. without noticing the others present.*)

Act 1 scene: from L-R, Pericles on the steps of the Hotel Pharone, Fanfani, Miradillo, Sebil, Titania and Antarsid, surrounded by the poplace. From the original poster for the 1884 production of the opera at Haverly's Theatre, Broad Street, Philadelphia (USA). Dario Salvi Collection.

TITANIA
You need not mind,
Those whom here you find;

ANTARSID
I'll follow your counsel,
With delight,
Vision bright.

TITANIA
—I little care,
—What they may,
—Of us say,

FANFANI (*Aside*)
They're very familiar,
That seems quite peculiar,
Their love is apparent!

—I know you'll be,
—A friend to me,
—What e'er betide,

ANTARSID
As thy slave at thy side,
I will ever abide!

You'll remain,
At my side.

(*Fanfani crosses over to Titania and calls her attention to Miradillo and Sebil.*)

FANFANI (*Low to Titania*)
Dear niece, of your husband,
I'm grieved to relate,
That he's acting badly,
The scandal is great.

TITANIA (*Not at all suspicious or angry*)
—Really?

FANFANI
A slave for himself
He did lately procure;
You won't let your husband
Behave so, I'm sure!

TITANIA
Why should I prevent him,
He don't bother me;
If slaves can content him,
To buy them he's free!

FANFANI
—Really?

TITANIA
Leave him,
Alone,
And listen to my resolution.
(*Indicating Antarsid*)
The prince my companion,
I find very pleasant.

FANFANI
—You won't?
—Well then.

FANFANI
Well what's that to me?

TITANIA
And therefore I,
To be our guest,
I'd him invite.

ANTARSID
—Oh, how fine,
—That's too much.

(*Antarsid and Titania retire up a little. When they come down again Titania is R. and Antarsid is L.*)

FANFANI

As our guest, awake I hardly seem;
As our guest, why, is this a dream?
This is awful, this is dreadful,
Oh what cheek!

TESSA, BUCCAMETTA
*and* FEMALE CHORUS
Her guest?
Her guest?
Yes indeed, this is queer.
—The matter is not clear!

TESSA, BUCCAMETTA *and* FEMALE CHORUS
Their assurance,

FANFANI
Aff!

TESSA, BUCCAMETTA *and* FEMALE CHORUS
Is great,

FANFANI
Aff!

MALE CHORUS
Their assurance,

FANFANI
I'm dizzy,

MALE CHORUS
Is great.

FANFANI, TESSA, BUCCAMETTA *and* CHORUS
As guest to, invite him,
That's really, most queer!

(*Antarsid and Titania come down.*)

BUCCAMETTA *and* FEMALE CHORUS
What will your husband say now?
(*With closed lips*)
Hm, hm, hm,

| TITANIA | TESSA | SEBIL |
|---|---|---|
| Ha ha ha! | Madding thought, | To thee Lord, |
| | | |
| ANTARSID | MIRADILLO | FANFANI |
| Angel fair, | What a lark! | I'm amazed! |

BUCCAMETTA *and* FEMALE CHORUS
What will the husband say now?
Hm, hm, hm.

| TITANIA | TESSA | SEBIL |
|---|---|---|
| Shall I scream? | This to me! | I belong, |
| | | |
| ANTARSID | MIRADILLO | FANFANI |
| Vision rare, | What a lark! | I am dazed! |

| BUCCAMETTA *and* FEMALE CHORUS | SEBIL |
|---|---|
| What will the husband say now? | And thou alone, |
| Hm, hm hm. | Yes, alone |

| | |
|---|---|
| BUCCAMETTA *and* FEMALE CHORUS (His wife/for she) alone Will the victor be! | SEBIL Will my victor be! |
| TESSA I'd like to scream! Silence! Now will much better be! | TITANIA 'Course that would seem— It would foolish be! |
| ANTARSID O thou alone, Yes only thou alone, Will my victor be! | MIRADILLO And she alone, Yes only she alone, Will the victor be! |
| FANFANI For she alone, Yes only she alone, Will the victor be! | MALE CHORUS For she— For she alone Will the victor be! |

*(Chorus divide and leave C. open. All listen as trumpets sound fanfare.)*

CHORUS
The signal resoundeth!
The guests now assemble!

TITANIA (*Turns to Miradillo*)
Offer me your escort now,
With stately pomp and courteous bow!

MIRADILLO
I'm ready now!
(*He goes up and calls off L. and comes down again*)
Come one, you fellows,
Collect Titania's trunks,
Gaily escort her!
On to the river banks!

CHORUS
Hurrah! Hurrah!
We're ready for the fun,
Allah! Allah!

Bayram at last begun!

# Song

(*Chorus march down into straight line.*)

TITANIA *and* ANTARSID
Oh what delight,
When merry songs are sounding,
And set each heart,
With joy and pleasure bounding!

There love's sweet power,
Fills us with joy;
There perfect bliss reigneth
Without alloy!

(*Tessa with Soprano #1. Buccametta and Sebil with Soprano #2. Miradillo with Tenor #1. Fanfani with Tenor #2. Pericles with Bass.*)

CHORUS
Tarabuka,
Now with vigor let be shaken,

TITANIA
—To the blithesome repast!

CHORUS
—And Kemenche's
Strings to dulcet music waken.

TITANIA
Where mirth's cheerful sound doth rebound,
Where sparkles the wine, gift divine.
Where joy with new zest fills each breast,

CHORUS
Come shout with glee, lustily;
Now Ramadan is o'er,
Come shout with glee,
For the gladsome Bayram's at the door,
This is the day,
When the fasting's o'er and all are gay.

| TITANIA | CHORUS |
|---|---|
| Now come move along— | Hail to this day of pleasure, |
| With joyous song! | Hail to this day of pleasure! |

(*All back upstage in straight lines—short steps.*)

ALL
Oh what delight,
When merry songs are sounding,
And set each heart,
With joy and pleasure bounding;
(*All march downstage*)
There love's sweet power,
Fills us with joy;
There perfect bliss reigneth
Without alloy.

(*Chorus back into oblique line R1. to C. upstage. As Chorus go back into oblique line, Miradillo offers his arm to Titania and leads her up R. and over to LUE. Fanfani offers his arm to Tessa who does not notice him but crosses to Antarsid who leads her after Miradillo and Titania. Fanfani watches her in surprise when Buccametta grabs his arm and drags him after the others. Time it so that principals are just about LUE. at Curtain.*)

Tarabuka now with vigour pound,
For now Ramadan is done,
Young and old rejoice with joyful sound,
For now Bayram has begun;

Tarabuka pound with vigour,
For now Bayram has begun, hurrah!

# CURTAIN

# END OF ACT 1

# ACT 2

*Garden of Fanfani's villa on the banks of the River Nile. The backdrop represents the city of Cairo and the river. Two kiosks on R. and L. with a settee beside each entrance. Plants all over stage. At rise of curtain, Ladies of the Chorus (dressed as slaves) are discovered brushing rugs and carpets.*

## No. 7a - Entr'acte

## No. 7b – Chorus and Couplet

CHORUS (SOPRANO #1)
Feasting, dancing, mirth and revels gay,

CHORUS (SOPRANO #2)
—Feasting, mirth and revels gay,

CHORUS (SOPRANO #1)
In this house will reign today!

CHORUS (SOPRANO #2)
—Clean ev'rything!

CHORUS (SOPRANO #1)
Clean ev'rything!

CHORUS (SOPRANO #2)
For a young and dainty wife again,

CHORUS (SOPRANO #1)
—For a dainty wife again,

CHORUS (SOPRANO #2)
Our old Pasha did obtain.

CHORUS (SOPRANO P #1)
Soon her he'll bring.

CHORUS (SOPRANO #2)
Soon her he'll bring!

FEMALE CHORUS
Ah, how sweet it must be purely
In a lover's arms to rest,
And submit to it demurely
When he draws you to his breast.

(*The Male Servants get up and rouse up the women. All come down front. They take up Turkish rugs and small mats and do business of cleaning them.*)

MALE CHORUS
Come bestir yourselves, make haste,
For there is no time to waste,

ALL
Ev'ry closet, ev'ry chair,
Must be furbished up with care,
Ev'ry rug and carpet beat,
'Till they're wholly clean and neat!

(*They beat rugs with bamboo sticks on word "pound".*)

CHORUS (BASS)
Where mirth's cheerful sound doth rebound,
Where sparkles the wine, gift divine.
Where joy with new zest fills each breast,

Now come move along—
With joyous song!

CHORUS (TENOR)
Come shout with glee, lustily;
Now Ramadan is o'er,
Come shout with glee,
For the gladsome Bayram's at the door,
This is the day,
When the fasting's o'er and all are gay.
Hail to this day of pleasure,
Hail to this day of pleasure!

FEMALE CHORUS
Pound and beat, pound and beat,
'Till each carpet's clean and neat,
Otherwise his Highness will,
Give of beating us our fill!
Pound and beat, pound and beat,
'Till each carpet's clean and neat,
Otherwise his Highness will—
Give of beating us our fill.

CHORUS (SOPRANO #1)
Many guests of high and low degree,

CHORUS (SOPRANO #2)
—Guests of high and low degree!

CHORUS (SOPRANO #1)
In this house today we'll see,

CHORUS (SOPRANO #2)
Clean all with care!

CHORUS (SOPRANO #1)
Clean all with care!

CHORUS (SOPRANO #2)
Wonder if amongst them one will be,

CHORUS (SOPRANO #1)
—If amongst them one will be,

CHORUS (SOPRANO #2)
That might think of loving me,

CHORUS (SOPRANO #1)
They'll soon be here!

CHORUS (SOPRANO #2)
—They'll soon be here!

FEMALE CHORUS
Ah! How sweet it must be surely,
In a lover's arms to rest,
And submit to it demurely,
When he clasps you to his breast!

MALE CHORUS
O'er such nonsense do not brood,
'Twill not bring you clothes nor food.

ALL
Let us do our work with zeal,
Else the Pasha's whip we'll feel.
Ev'ry rug and carpet beat,
'Till they're wholly clean and neat!

CHORUS (BASS)
Yes pound them, and beat
them,
'Till dust clouds, up whirling,

Around you, are curling,
On carpets, and cushions,
Whack sounding,
percussions,

Yes pound them, and beat
them,
With vigour, until they,
Are wholly clean; quite
clean!

CHORUS (TENOR)
—Yes pound them, and beat
them,
—'Till dust clouds, up
whirling,
—Around you, are curling,
—On carpets, and cushions,
—Whack sounding,
percussions,
—Yes pound them, and beat
them,
—With vigour, until they,
—Are clean; quite clean!

FEMALE CHORUS
Pound and beat, pound and beat,
'Till each carpet's clean and neat,
Otherwise his Highness will,
Give of beating us our fill!
Pound and beat, pound and beat,
'Till each carpet's clean and neat,
Otherwise his Highness will—
Give of beating us our fill.

ALL
Pound them, pound them,
'Till they are clean!

(*At end of chorus they are lying down on rugs etc when Fanfani enters R1. cracking snake whip.*)

FANFANI
Kush! Kush! Kush!
Wake up you lazy duffers,
And quickly go to work!
No sooner is my back turned,
Then you begin to shirk;
Unless you show more zeal,
My trusty whip you'll feel!

CHORUS
Let us quickly go away,

FANFANI
I'm in earnest, you will find,

CHORUS
For he's very cross today,

FANFANI
If you do not quickly mind,
(*Moves forward to audience*)
Yes, like the English,
Yes, like the English,
Whip as my tool I will use,
To instruct proper manners to you!

FANFANI: Hurry up you rascals or you shall feel my whip.

(*He threatens Chorus with whip. Slaves all jump up and run off L3. or L4.*)

## Song

FANFANI
Such a barren land we live in,
Nothing here is sacred, safe or sound,
With the bandits creeping, stealthy,
Pilfering what treasure can be found.

Look at Tel-el-Kebir to show you just,
How the British keep the Empire,
Yes, they claim the Suez Canal, it's true,
Taking over all of Egypt's power;
There's no need now for conferences,
Embrace the consequences!

Oh yes this is the English manner,
This is the proper way to act!
Oh yes this is the English manner,
The British way, that is a fact!

If a maiden fair is gentle,
And her loveliness oft' she spreads wide,
She will not yet seem suspicious,
What a perfect lady for a bride!

Then the age will creep on her shoulders, sure!
And you'll find out that it's over,
So avoid this mess, be an Englishman,
She is not to be your wife or lover!
Choose a governess if you're wise,
She will not be in disguise.

Oh yes this is the English manner,
This is the proper way to act!
Oh yes this is the English manner,
The British way, that is a fact!

London's streets are swathed in darkness,
Yet electric light shines bright indoor;
Families are safe from danger,
But this luxury is not for the poor.

All o'er London town you can see new fads,
Steam propelled machines so hazy;
And when visitors come to call on you,
Door bells make the housemaid seem quite lazy!
But you must be able to pay,
As that is the English way!

Oh yes this is the English manner,
This is the proper way to act!
Oh yes this is the English manner,
The British way, that is a fact!

If one wants to avenge insult,
He should go to court and tell them so,
He wastes all his time and money,
So a futile effort it seems now!

But the English will always defend, yes!
Morning, afternoon and nightly,
Their honour to the bitter end,
Against those who do not treat them rightly;
To hear "Sorry" they are expecting,
So give up and stop objecting!

Oh yes this is the English manner,
This is the proper way to act!
Oh yes this is the English manner,
The British way, that is a fact!

(*He goes to entrance L. with his back turned on Miradillo, who enters R.*)

MIRADILLO *(Not seeing Fanfani)*: Charming Villa, lavishly decorated, and all Fanfani's. How is it the worst people always have the best things? For this, Mr Fanfani…

(*He sees Fanfani, who is still threatening with whip into wings.*)

MIRADILLO: Ah! There he is now! His movements are very suspicious.

(*He steps behind Fanfani.*)

FANFANI (*Speaking off to Slaves R2E.*): Do you understand, idiots? Their Excellencies, my wives number one to ten, are to vacate their rooms. Go to work, otherwise…

(*He raises his whip. Miradillo steps up behind Fanfani, who is looking off L3.*)

MIRADILLO (*Seizing whip, irritated*): What? Slave driving, with the eyes of Europe upon you!

FANFANI (*Turning around*): Who dares interfere? Let go of the whip.

MIRADILLO: Certainly not.

FANFANI: Will you let go of the whip?

MIRADILLO: No.

FANFANI: Then I'll let go myself.

(*Miradillo takes the whip.*)

MIRADILLO: It is confiscated. I shall add it to my collection of Oriental curiosities.

FANFANI: You would do well to preserve it, for it is all you will get from me.

MIRADILLO: Come, don't be so hard. How about the millions "unkey dear"?

FANFANI (*Shortly*): I need them myself.

MIRADILLO (*Aghast*): And will you have the nerve to refuse to pay your niece, armed as she is with the will and a husband?

FANFANI (*Sneering*): She's got the husband, it is true, but what kind of husband?

MIRADILLO (*Amazed*): The kind specified in the will, I presume, or she wouldn't have married me.

FANFANI: I have my doubts whether you are her husband at all.

MIRADILLO (*Raising and cracking whip*): I can give you striking proof.

(*Miradillo slashes whip at Fanfani's head. He ducks to avoid it. Miradillo then slashes at his legs and he jumps up.*)

FANFANI: Easy there! (*Pleasantly*) If you are really my niece's husband, you will listen to common sense.

MIRADILLO: What do I want with common sense? Hasn't my wife two millions?

FANFANI (*Persuasively*): Now, how nice it would be to come to an amicable settlement. What do you say to fifty percent? I'll give you a million down.

MIRADILLO: Two millions, or nothing.

FANFANI (*With supressed fury*): Very well, I'll pay when I have sufficient proof. (*Aside*) And I'll make him dance for that proof. (*Aloud*) But a truce to business. I have been making every arrangement for the comfort of my dear niece and her husband and have placed that kiosk— (*Points to kiosk L.*)—entirely at your disposal.

MIRADILLO: The deuce you have.

FANFANI (*Watching him*): It is a charming little retreat. In it you will be shut out from the world and able to bill and coo like two turtle doves without interruption.

MIRADILLO (*Crossing to L.*): A charming idea uncle, but not feasible.

FANFANI: And why not?

MIRADILLO (*Aside*): What will my alleged wife say to this?

FANFANI: Why this sudden wealth of thoughts and poverty of words? Why this lack of rapture over my arrangements? Why do you not overflow with ecstasy? I'm sure I have arranged everything to your heart's content.

MIRADILLO: I will seek Titania at once, and inform her of your thoughtful plans. I'd like to reward you for this kiosk scheme. Uncle, embrace your nephew!

(*He seizes Fanfani by the waist, lifts him off the ground, turns and throws him L. Fanfani lands on his feet.*)

FANFANI: Here, here! What do you think you're doing?

MIRADILLO: I must give bent to my feelings. Bye bye, dear uncle. (*Aside*) Scoundrel!

(*He shakes his fist covertly at Fanfani and exits R1E.*)

FANFANI (*Triumphantly*): He's baffled! That kiosk scheme was great! That two millions feels much safer. If they are man and wife I'll have to pay it, but we'll see…

(*He goes upstage C. Enter Tessa and Buccametta L1., veiled in Oriental style. They are both dressed as Turkish women.*)

TESSA (*To Buccametta, looking after Miradillo*): There he goes, the wretch. Oh, for revenge.

(*She lifts her veil.*)

BUCCAMETTA: Or a substitute. Ah, how sweet revenge and a substitute combined would be.

(*She raises her veil.*)

FANFANI (*Turning and perceiving them, walking down C. between Tessa and Buccametta*): Ah! Already in Turkish costume. Charming. Fascinating. Do you begin to feel a little more at home now?

(*He puts an arm around each of them.*)

TESSA: Everything is exquisite here.

(*Buccametta lays her head on Fanfani's shoulder.*)

BUCCAMETTA (*On his shoulder*): Dream-like, enchanting, fairy-land! Pardon this emotion if I drop a tear!

FANFANI (*Pushing her away*): No, drop it there!...(*To Tessa*) But now tell me, my veiled beauty—

(*Buccametta bows.*)

FANFANI: Not you, old lady. (*To Tessa*) You, whose Turkish feet are so deliciously encased. How do you like it, as far as it goes? And what were you murmuring with such soft murmurs as you murmured like a mermaid as you came in?

TESSA (*Feigning enthusiasm*): That I esteem and respect you.

FANFANI: Is that all? Don't you love me? Won't you become one of my wives?

TESSA (*Bashfully*): Oh Sir! (*Aside*) Anything to gain time.

(*Buccametta, who has been taking it all to herself, throws herself into his arms.*)

BUCCAMETTA: Yes! Any sacrifice. Take me, I am yours. Yes! Say no more.

FANFANI (*Aside*): What is the matter with that Chinese fairy?

BUCCAMETTA: Oh Pasha. I am so happy. You may kiss me.

FANFANI (*Pushing her away from him, throwing her off to L.*): My dear lady. I would gladly do so, but there is a law in Turkey which makes kissing a misdemeanour.

BUCCAMETTA: What a country!

(*She flounces off in a fury L1.*)

FANFANI (*To Tessa*): And now, my little rosebud, my dainty floret, what do you say? Speak the blissful word, "yes", and become Mrs Fanfani Number Forty Seven.

TESSA: I really think I am too young to decide for myself. You must ask Mama!

## No. 8 – Tessa's Song

(*During both verses, Tessa pretends to be very shy. As song progresses Fanfani gets more and more in love, and gives Tessa all his jewellery a piece at a time, ending with his watch and chain. She takes everything, but won't let him embrace her.*)

## Song

TESSA
Indeed, you're very kind Sir,
Your offer highly I esteem;
The honour great, I find, Sir,
Yet wrong some points about it seem.

For instance, six and forty wives,
At present you possess,
'Tis well known!
And that I never could endure
With patience I confess,
No indeed!

I know that you as Muslims
Find that sort of thing correct,
That sort of thing correct,
But that a European should,
You hardly can expect;
You hardly can expect!

When'tis too late, I fear,
Remorse might seize me,
If sharing your affection,
Fail'd to please me,
And so! And so!

I won't say Yes!
I won't say Nay!

I won't say Yes!
I won't say Nay!
Therefore—

(*Coquettish curtsey, as Fanfani tries to embrace her.*)

Speak with Mama first I pray!
Speak first with—

(*Coquettish curtsey, as Fanfani tries to embrace her.*)

Mama, I pray!
About the marriage state, Sir,
Their notions here are very free;
One wife alone, they hate, Sir,
And none take less than two or three!

To be content with one,
As Europeans mostly do,
That's absurd!
Why ev'n in Europe, some
Adopt the Oriental view.
Take my word!

But as regards the wholesale way
In which you wed your fair,
In which you wed your fair,
While it may be quite practical,
We're somewhat backward there,
We're somewhat backward there!

I know the ways and customs
Of each nation,
At present meet with perfect
Toleration!
And so! And so!

I won't say Yes!
I won't say Nay!

I won't say Yes!
I won't say Nay!
Therefore—

(*Coquettish curtsey, as Fanfani tries to embrace her.*)

Speak with Mama first I pray!
Speak first with—

(*Coquettish curtsey, as Fanfani tries to embrace her.*)

Mama, I pray!

(*She turns and makes her exit into green kiosk R. At same time Buccametta re-enters L1.*)

FANFANI (*After Tessa's exit*): My dear lady.

(*Buccametta comes down.*)

FANFANI: Circumstances have debarred me from calling you my blushing bride. Will you not fill the void thus made in my aching heart, by giving me your daughter?

BUCCAMETTA (*Snappishly*): My daughter aspires to something more Christian-like than a heathen.

FANFANI: Ah Madame, be not this hard on me. Is it my fault that you are older than the law allows for Pasha's wives?

BUCCAMETTA: Who says so?

FANFANI: I do. I should judge you had passed the rubicon by at least twenty Ramadans!

BUCCAMETTA: Pray, my dear Pasha, what is a Ramadam?

FANFANI: Allow me to explain. There are several kinds of dams; for instance, there is the mill dam, the cofferdam, Amsterdam and damsels, and some people don't care a...but a (*Stressing 'n' at end of 'Ramadan'*)

**Ramadan** is a feast in conjunction with the rising of the Nile, which occurs at very uncertain periods. For your sake I have counted short ones.

BUCCAMETTA: Well, indeed!

FANFANI: If you will listen to my prayer, you shall have a carriage and a pair of Arab steeds and a proscenium box at the Opera! You won't refuse me your daughter's hand, will you?

BUCCAMETTA: Listen to me, Pasha. As we are already somewhat inured to the customs of the Orient, even if you have forty seven or forty eight wives, why not take me for your newest love?

FANFANI: You are a trifle too ancient.

BUCCAMETTA: How do you know?

FANFANI: The matrimonial laws are very strict here. A Pasha is not allowed to marry a woman who is over twenty nine years old.

BUCCAMETTA: Then you must at least allow me to remain near my Tessa.

FANFANI: How near, for instance?

BUCCAMETTA: Close enough to watch your every movement.

FANFANI: You don't think I'd do anything wrong to her, do you?

BUCCAMETTA: Who knows? And now tell me, where will the bridal chambers be?

FANFANI (*Smacks with tongue, pointing L.*): In a kiosk.

BUCCAMETTA: In the red one?

FANFANI: No, no, in the green one. The red one belongs to Titania and her husband.

(*Buccametta crosses to R.*)

BUCCAMETTA: Very well then. In the green kiosk we will await you.

## No. 8 1/2 – Buccametta Exits

(*Buccametta exits coquettishly singing into the green kiosk R., trying to imitate Tessa's coy manner.*)

BUCCAMETTA
I thought you heard my Tessa say;
Speak with Mama first, I pray,
Speak first with—
(*She curtseys*)
Mama, I pray!

(*She exits with giddy walk in kiosk R.*)

FANFANI: There she goes, a good square meal for an alligator. Now Fanfani, brace up. (*Points to L. kiosk*) There are two millions—(*Points to R. kiosk*)—and there's a pearl beyond price.

(*Exit Fanfani R1E. Enter Titania and Antarsid from L3. Titania carries a rose.*)

ANTARSID: Your narratives are so fascinating that I could almost believe I had found my "Scheherazade" in you.

TITANIA: But I haven't found my Sultan yet. You don't seem to get tired of listening to me, while the Sultan was so impolite as to fall asleep.

ANTARSID: That was because his entertainer was his wife. But if I could only call you mine, you should never have to complain.

(*He puts his arm around Titania's waist.*)

TITANIA (*Confused*): But Prince, don't you know?

ANTARSID: What, you belong to another?

TITANIA: To another! (*Pausing a moment*) Oh! If I dare but trust you with a secret…(*Roguishly*) But no! What were you saying about flowers, just now?

ANTARSID: I was telling you of their beautiful language!

TITANIA (*Pointing to rose in her hand*): Ah yes, then let us speak the language of flowers.

ANTARSID: Willingly, if you will but tell me in it—if I may dare to hope.

TITANIA (*Coquettishly*): I will ask the question of this rose!

## No. 9 – Flower Duettino

## Song

TITANIA (*Holding the rose in her hand*)
A word of magic import,
Is hid in ev'ry flow'r,
To love's emotion only,
Appeals their magic pow'r.

The little blossoms, sweet and dainty,
They carry lover's vows around,
They're voicing, the message,
Of grieving, rejoicing,
Without sound, without sound!

The cornflow'r and the poppy,
That bloom among the grain,
The violet, the lily,
A meaning all contain.

I offer thee, above all others,
The rose, so thorny, here.
(*Holding out rose*)
It says: if thou wouldst pluck me,
The thorns thou must not fear;
It says: if thou wouldst pluck me,
The thorns thou must not fear!

(*Between verses switch positions.*)

Act 2 – Flower Duettino: Titania offering the rose to Prince Antarsid. From the original poster for the 1884 production of the opera at the Haverly's Theatre, Broad Street, Philadelphia (USA). Dario Salvi Collection.

ANTARSID
The rose shall not dismay me,
Its sense is clear to me,
It means that danger threatens
While I am near to thee.

Thro' fire I'll go to follow thee,
Tho' foes rise as the desert sand,
To shield thee, defend thee,
Forever, forever!
By thee I'll stand, by thee I'll stand!
(*He embraces Titania.*)
While life remains, I love thee,
With ardent quenchless flame,
And in my dying moment,
My lips shall breathe thy name!

To thee I'll stand, I'll stand forever,
Whate'er thy lot be here!
(*He takes rose from Titania*)
The rose I'll gladly pluck it,
(*He kisses it and puts it in his bosom*)
Thy thorns I do not fear,
The rose I'll gladly pluck it,
The thorns I do not fear!

BOTH
The rose (he'll/I'll) gladly pluck it,
The thorns (he does/I do) not fear, ah!
The rose (he'll/I'll) gladly pluck it,
The thorns (he does/I do) not fear!

(*At end of duet, Antarsid kisses Titania on the forehead and they walk over to L. At the same moment Fanfani enters R1. pulling Miradillo after him. Buccametta and Tessa enter from green kiosk R2., both veiled.*)

FANFANI (*To Miradillo, pointing triumphantly to Titania and Antarsid*):
There! Look over yonder and crawl out of your skin!

MIRADILLO (*Exasperated*): He kisses her on the forehead. What an insult!

(*He crosses to C. towards Antarsid.*)

FANFANI (*Aside*): Ah, he waxes.

ANTARSID (*Low to Titania*): We have been overheard.

TITANIA (*Indifferently*): What is the difference?

ANTARSID (*To Miradillo*): Well Sir, I am at your service.

MIRADILLO (*Sarcastically*): I see you are…but I don't know that I have any special use for you or your service. (*He crosses to Titania*) (*To Titania*) Madame, do you think it quite right to allow Princes to imprint kisses on your forehead?

TITANIA (*Feigning confusion*): Oh Sir, I was…I am…

ANTARSID (*Furiously*): Signor Miradillo, I expect you as a man of honour, to…

MIRADILLO: Not so hasty Prince. Moderate your tone a trifle. Wait, my friend, till I have killed you, then you can say all you wish. But for the present, allow me a few moments private conversation with my wife.

FANFANI (*Taking Antarsid's arm*): They want to have a row. Give them a chance.

(*All but Titania and Miradillo retire upstage and remain there.*)

## No. 10 – Ensemble

(*Tessa, Buccametta, Antarsid and Fanfani all step forward stealthily— one step in a bar.*)

> TESSA, BUCCAMETTA, ANTARSID *and* FANFANI
> Let us stay here,
> Where we may hear,
> Still to them not appear;
> (*Step back, same business*)
> We see clearly,
> That most queerly,

He does act, that's a fact.

(*Tessa, Buccametta, Fanfani and Antarsid all try to listen to what Miradillo and Titania are saying to one another.*)

TITANIA (*Low to Miradillo*)
They're listening, love.
So be on your guard!

MIRADILLO (*Low to Titania*)
You need have no fear,
I'll well play my part.

TESSA, BUCCAMETTA, ANTARSID *and* FANFANI
Listen we, secretly,

MIRADILLO (*Aloud, very tenderly, pointing to open kiosk over L.*)
See the Kiosk there, neat and dainty,
Where your good uncle wants us to stay.

TITANIA (*With intention for the others to hear*)
That we are most immensely happy,
To all the world I'm prepared to say.

(*Miradillo has his arm around Titania's waist. They sway slowly back and forth and sing more warmly.*)

TITANIA *and* MIRADILLO (*Intimately*)
Quite soon, quite soon,
Philomel sings with cadence mellow,
And all around,
Will its melodious tones resound!

TITANIA (*Low to Miradillo, looking over towards others*)
See there, they've not yet departed I see.

MIRADILLO (*Very softly and slyly to Titania*)
Then 'pon my life,
I think the best would be
To walk in carelessly as man and wife.

Act 2 scene: from L-R, Fanfani Pasha on the steps of Fanfani's villa, Tessa and Buccametta veiled, Miradillo and Titania. From the original poster for the 1884 production of the opera at Haverly's Theatre, Broad Street, Philadelphia (USA). Dario Salvi Collection.

TITANIA
—Never! Too risky by far that would be.

MIRADILLO
(*Trying to induce Titania to enter kiosk—she refuses*)
Since as a married couple we appear,
We'd better meet the danger without fear,
To the kiosk we will together go,
Of course you understand it's all for show;

Quite modest I will be,
For all I want, you see,
Is to perform my part all through apparently!

(*Triumphant indifference*)
It is only for show,
To deceive them you know,
Is it only for show?
(*Contrite*)
I'll be modest you know!

TITANIA (*Frightened*)

—Ha! I'm seized with,

—Sudden terror,

—He would profit by my error;

No, no, no,
(*Enraged*)
It cannot be, not e'en to make a show.

—I tell you, Sir take care,
—And do not enter there,
—Once more, I say, beware!

TESSA, BUCCAMETTA, ANTARSID *and* FANFANI
Yes, this young woman is a treasure,
A very lucky young dog is he,
For he is wasting a world of pleasure,
And in his place I would like to be!

(*Miradillo has his arm around Titania—swaying movement. They sing very tenderly as before.*)

TITANIA *and* MIRADILLO
Quite soon, quite soon,
Philomel sings with cadence mellow,
And all around,
Will its melodious tones resound!

TESSA, BUCCAMETTA, ANTARSID *and* FANFANI
Happy—
He must be!

(*Tessa, Buccametta, Antarsid and Fanfani retire stealthily, one step in a bar up R. Miradillo and Titania back slowly up towards kiosk L.*)

MIRADILLO
Who then could cruel be?
Sweet love be kind to me!
O come!
O come!

TITANIA
Who then could cruel be?
Just come, you soon shall see!
—I come!
—Ah yes!

TESSA, BUCCAMETTA, ANTARSID *and* FANFANI
A couple, indeed they appear,
The symptoms of marriage are clear!
Quite clear! Quite clear!
As a pair, they appear!

(*The others gradually retire off stage. Buccametta and Tessa exit into kiosk R. Antarsid exits off R3. Fanfani off R. but comes right back— arrange exit on R. according to the stage setting. Miradillo tries to draw Titania to red kiosk.*)

MIRADILLO: Why don't you come, love?

TITANIA (*Resisting*): Yes, I'm coming.

(*She throws him off and rushes to red kiosk. As she ascends the steps she sees Miradillo following her. She presents a revolver at his head.*)

TITANIA (*Mocking*): Come love!

(*She exits into kiosk.*)

MIRADILLO: Well, upon my word! She guards the door with a revolver. Well, I must make a flank movement.

(*He exits behind kiosk L. Enter Fanfani R3E.*)

FANFANI: The decisive moment has arrived. Either he is her husband, or he is not.

(*Enter Nakid L3E.*)

FANFANI: Hallo Nakid, old quack! Come here a moment. Have you any new stock on hand?

NAKID: You mean specialities!

FANFANI: Have you anything to lull a person to sleep for about twenty four hours? (*Softly with gestures*) Or perhaps years? I'm not particular which.

NAKID: I'm fresh out of lullers. Just my luck.

FANFANI: And mine. Haven't you got anything in that way, no matter how simple, if it's effectual? Not a small dose even?

NAKID: So help me Isaac[2], not a grain.

(*Enter Miradillo L3E.*)

MIRADILLO: I can't get in through the window either. (*Sees Fanfani and Nakid*) Ah! Uncle Pasha, negotiating with the licensed poison dealer. (*To Nakid*) Is he asking you how to dispose of a superfluous husband?

FANFANI: Nakid, a poison dealer? Nonsense. He's a nice, honest, patent medicine man.

NAKID (*Offended*): You do me injustice, Signor. My preparations have all been approved by the Board of Health. Here, for instance, is an excellent thing.

(*He takes a red and black box from the tray.*)

MIRADILLO *and* FANFANI: What is it?

NAKID: A little invention of my own, called Revenge Dates.

---

[2] *In reference to the Biblical Patriarch.*

MIRADILLO: Revenge Dates?

FANFANI: Any relation to Return Dates?

NAKID: They're marvellous things. Whoever eats one of the dates will sneeze whenever he tries to kiss.

FANFANI: What's that? Kiss at every sneeze?

NAKID: No! Sneeze at every kiss. So help me Moses, it's true as I live. They can't help sneezing every time they try to embrace. It's the best thing to get revenge on a rival. He becomes perfectly harmless. That's why I call 'em Revenge Dates. (*To Fanfani*) Won't your Highness try some? They are quite fresh and only prepared yesterday.

(*Miradillo picks up the whip he took from Fanfani at the beginning of Act and had thrown upstage.*)

FANFANI: Now let me understand. If I eat one of these things, and kiss you, should I sneeze?

NAKID: Sure!

FANFANI: Well I should do that without them, so get out of here you old fraud!

(*He exits angrily R.*)

NAKID (*To Miradillo*): Won't you try some, Sir?

MIRADILLO: Be off, you Egyptian scoundrel. Find some country yokels to practice your tricks on!

(*He strikes Nakid with whip.*)

NAKID (*Enraged*): Swindler! Scoundrel. Tricks. Ah my masters, you shall pay for this. I can prove what I say! (*Aside*) Tonight at the feast! Bayram. I'll teach you my power. I'll make you all sneeze till you burst your suspenders.

(*Exit Nakid R. hastily after Fanfani.*)

MIRADILLO: If it wasn't such an obvious swindle, I'd offer some to the gallant Prince. He seems bent upon a duel. My wife threatens me with a revolver and the Uncle Pasha insists upon a tender meeting; rather a discouraging situation. I think I'd better leave for brighter fields.

# No. 11 – Couplet

## Song

MIRADILLO
Happily I'd go to rendezvous,
But very suspicious this all seems to me;
Duel it will be, not interview,
Big holes in my jacket, injured in the knee.

But the woman sure is not bothered much,
If I lose a limb or two;
And with laughter she never cares as such,
If she finds I am stuck in a coup!

It's a dang'rous business really,
It bruises your ego dearly.
That's why I am leaving,
I cannot abide!
So goodnight to
My sweet-hearted child!

Exercising charity is nice,
Going to the market, buying merchandise;
Jewels, garments, clothes of any size,
Help me meeting ladies to familiarise.

The last time I met with a lady bright,
Full of smiles and lovely eyes,
She then delicately supplied for me,
A cigar that she'd made with her hands;

"Only twenty Francs", she told me,
Grinning beautifully at me.

"I thank you my dear,

But I don't smoke," I said;
So goodnight to,
My sweet-hearted child!

Ev'ry time the Pasha goes away,
Pacing back and forth, he plans it piece by piece;
Angry and upset this time he seems,
To prove my commitment to his lovely niece.

But this tourist great, he would like to know,
If good news he can bestow,
So I questioned him very cautiously,
To find out what his plan would then be.

So he said, "Oh my dear fellow!
Your enquiry has no value!"

Then all I have left,
Is to hope 'twill be well,
So goodnight to,
My sweet-hearted child!

(*Exit Miradillo R. Enter Antarsid R3.*)

ANTARSID: The uncle and husband have both retired from the field of action. So much the better. (*He cautiously approaches red kiosk L. and calls:*) Titania!

TITANIA (*Opening door cautiously*): Are we alone?

ANTARSID: Yes, my adored one!

TITANIA (*Comes down hurriedly*): Oh Prince, can I trust you? Will you not help me? I must get away from here. If you could only hide me for twenty four hours without leaving any trace whatsoever I should be safe.

ANTARSID (*Ardently*): Fly with me, my best beloved, and you shall be safe forever.

(*He tries to embrace her.*)

TITANIA (*With matter-of-fact air, pushing him away*): Hmm. That's not a bad idea. (*She crosses to R.*) Couldn't you abduct me, so that there would be a big scandal about it?

ANTARSID (*Aside*): Ah, I see. (*Aloud*) You love me and would free yourself from a detested husband!

TITANIA (*Same common sense tone*): Nonsense. I'm thinking of business, not love. Abduct me first, and after, when I've got time, I'll think about love.

(*She crosses to L.*)

ANTARSID: But Titania!

(*Tessa ready to enter from Kiosk R.*)

TITANIA: Someone is coming. I appeal to you for the last time. Will you abduct me? Oh that I could kidnap myself.

(*Tessa appears at door of kiosk.*)

ANTARSID (*Kissing her hand*): Your wish is my law. Your slave sleeps blindly. At the festival, then, tonight.

(*He bows and exits L3.*)

TITANIA (*Aside*): I am saved. Tomorrow the term expires, and if Antarsid loves me as he says he does, why, it may not be so very long before I do have a husband.

(*Tessa advances timidly and slowly from kiosk R. and comes down R3. She is closely veiled.*)

TESSA: Signora!

TITANIA (*Aside*): Ah. I think this is my uncle's latest bride. What can she have to say to me? (*To Tessa*) I believe you are Auntie Fanfani Number Forty Seven. As it seems, Signora, you want an interview with me. Do remove your veil. I am burning with curiosity to see your face.

You must not feel bashful, for we are girls among ourselves. Tell me, whatever induced you, a European, to become one of my uncle's wives?

(*Tessa throws back veil.*)

TESSA: My despair.

TITANIA: Your despair? Tell me all, Auntie Fanfani Number Forty Seven. I have a sympathetic nature.

TESSA (*Angrily*): Yes. I know that to my cost.

TITANIA: What do you mean?

TESSA: It is to your sympathetic nature that I owe the loss of my Miradillo.

TITANIA: Ah, he's your Miradillo.

TESSA: He was before he met you. I was to have become his wife…and now…

TITANIA: You are Auntie Fanfani Number Forty Seven and your lover has become your nephew-in-law, forty seven times removed, and your successful rival is your niece. A pretty complication truly!

(*Tessa laughs.*)

TESSA (*Sarcastically*): You seem extremely sympathetic.

TITANIA: Forgive me. I am indeed sorry for you, my dear Auntie Fanfani Number Forty Seven. If you had only been a little less precipitate in your adaption of Oriental customs, your Miradillo could still have been yours.

TESSA (*Excitedly*): What do you mean?

TITANIA: That you should have spoken to me sooner. Now that it is too late, I will confide to you a secret which I trust to your honour to keep. Miradillo is not my husband, never was my husband, and never will be. For certain reasons, he only pretends to be.

TESSA (*Doubtfully*): He plays his part well.

TITANIA: He does so for consideration, which if I mistake not, was to find its way to a certain Napolitan milliner named Tessa. (*Sees Miradillo coming L.*) He comes. Veil yourself.

(*Tessa veils herself.*)

TITANIA: Learn from his own lips where his heart lies, and when he knows you he will rue on his knees for pardon for his neglect.

(*Enter Miradillo L. Titania goes to him and Tessa goes to bench and seats herself. Miradillo sits down next to her. She moves away a little—he follows. Same again then she moves with a long sweep over to R. and he follows.*)

TITANIA: Ah, Miradillo! Auntie Fanfani Number Forty Seven wants to speak to you.

(*Exit Titania into kiosk L.*)

MIRADILLO (*Aside*): I wonder if Auntie Fanfani Number Forty Seven carries firearms too. (*To Tessa*) Good evening.

(*Tessa moves away from him. Miradillo is alarmed and appears in fear of a weapon being produced.*)

MIRADILLO: I'm sure I beg your pardon miss. Pray, determine the appropriate distance yourself. I was venturing to suggest that the evening was not unpleasant.

TESSA (*In disguised voice*): No!

MIRADILLO (*Aside*): I don't seem to be making much of an impression. (*Aloud*) I think the evening lovely. It looks as if it would storm!

(*Tessa turns quickly and stares at him. Miradillo is much frightened.*)

MIRADILLO: That is, if you wish it…anything to oblige a lady.

(*Tessa draws further away from him.*)

MIRADILLO (*Aside*): There, I'm not getting on at all. I'll talk of her husband. She's a bride, so that subject is sure to be a congenial one. (*Aloud*) The festival tonight promises to be a gorgeous affair. Your husband is doing wonders. Splendid fellow, the Pasha, don't you think so?

TESSA: No!

MIRADILLO (*Aside and astonished*): No? On the wrong track again! Ah, she wishes to speak to me. Can it be that she loves me? Miradillo, you dog, you've been at it again.

(*He looks at Tessa and puts his arm around her. She lays her head on his shoulder.*)

MIRADILLO: You don't think much of the Pasha then? Seen someone else you like better, eh? Poor little susceptible heart; there, there…(*Petting her*) Why did you throw yourself away on the Old Turk?

(*Tessa gets up and crosses to L. while still veiled.*)

TESSA: Because I could not marry the man I loved, and that man was…you!

MIRADILLO: Me?

## No. 12 – Duett and Terzett

(*Tessa is still veiled. Miradillo conceitedly poses as he sings his solo.*)

TESSA
Ah, I could not well conceal it,
I felt so deeply,
But I fear you'll now despise me,
Think much less of me!

MIRADILLO
Oh no! Oh no!
That is not at all surprising!

No one who has seen these features,

This small foot, this perfect hand,
Has this well-proportioned figure,
E'er been able to withstand;

Women are completely conquered,
When these winning charms they see;
To arouse their warm affection,
Is a common thing for me.

(*Tessa crosses to R. Miradillo crosses to L. Both sing aside, each making game of the other.*)

TESSA
Wait now!

MIRADILLO
Wait now!

TESSA
Your boasting I will make you rue!

MIRADILLO
—Wait now!

TESSA
Wait now!

MIRADILLO
Amusement I'll have out of you;

TESSA
—Wait now!

MIRADILLO
Wait now!

TESSA
By women's wiles you'll be undone;

(*Miradillo tries to put his arm around Tessa—she keeps away from him.*)

MIRADILLO
I'll kiss you darling just for fun,
Ha ha ha ha ha, I delight!
Do not fear that I'll betray you,
Trustful you may safely be,
To arouse the love of women,
Is a common thing for me!

TESSA
—You'll soon be paid you
shameless wight.

TESSA (*Almost speaking*)
Ah, were I but an Egyptian,
And an Oriental, you
Then'twould not be wrong to take me
With you as wife number two!
(*She approaches Miradillo and pretends to be very affectionate*)
Ah, love me do!

MIRADILLO
She's not slow her love to show!

TESSA
I beg of you!

MIRADILLO
But say dear, don't you forget,
That I am a husband yet!
Think of it,
(*Trying to tease her*)
Just a bit!

TESSA
Ah, yes!
Ah, I try, but in vain,
Love's hot flame, to contain;
When the heart doth wildly flutter,

MIRADILLO
—Oh, I see.

TESSA
Then the head is soft as butter;

MIRADILLO
—Yes, I see.

TESSA
For where love holds its sway,
Peace of mind steals away;
In an ardent seething flood,

MIRADILLO
—Cupid's dart,

TESSA
Hot and hotter flows the flood.

MIRADILLO
Pierc'd her heart!
O thou poor loving one,
Thy veil just raise a little,

TESSA
—No, no, no! That won't do!

MIRADILLO
And thy countenance show;
It must be lovely, I know!
Thy countenance let me see!

TESSA
No, no, no! That won't do!

MIRADILLO
—Tell me why?

TESSA
That would so immoral be Sir,

MIRADILLO
—It's all lies!

TESSA
Do insist no longer, please Sir!

TESSA
No, no, that cannot be
For a husband alone may my
countenance see!

*(Miradillo gradually becomes more and more importunate 'till 'Moderato'. Tessa teases him and works up the scene by keeping him away from her, holding her veil down etc.)*

MIRADILLO
Don't talk to me of morals spurious,

TESSA
—I beg Sir!

MIRADILLO
When I stand here imploring thee,

TESSA
—Desist,

MIRADILLO
'Tis only done to make me curious!

TESSA
—Leave off Sir,

MIRADILLO
Off with the veil now,

TESSA
—I pray!

MIRADILLO
That I may see,

TESSA
—I pray!

MIRADILLO
Away!

TESSA
Leave off!

MIRADILLO
Away!

TESSA
I pray!

MIRADILLO
—I'll have my way I say.

TESSA
Ah I try, but in vain,
Love's hot flame to contain;
When the heart doth wildly
flutter,
Then the head is soft as butter;

MIRADILLO
—With passion I'm frenzied,
—The veil must be lifted,

—Come to me!
—Come to me!

For where love holds its sway,
Peace of mind steals away;
—Quickly one forgets one's
duties all,
And the veil must fall.

—And if you're not willing
To do what I ask you,
Compelled I will be
To use force, don't you see?
And then the veil must fall.

(*Tessa suddenly unveils herself and Miradillo is dumfounded. Tessa laughs haughtily.*)

MIRADILLO
Tessa? You here?
Tessa? You here?
You would join the Pasha's harem?
As his wife?
That you're in earnest now I doubt it,
I really doubt it!

TESSA
And why? And why?
I see nothing wrong about it!

(*Tessa mimicking Miradillo's conceited manner when he sang the same strain. Miradillo very much taken down begs Tessa to forgive him.*)

No one who has seen these features,
This small foot, this perfect hand,
Has this well-proportioned figure,
E'er been able to withstand;

MIRADILLO
—Forgive me!

TESSA
And the men are quickly conquered,
When these winning charms they see,
To arouse warm affection,
Is a common thing for me!

(*She is about to retire to kiosk R. when Miradillo detains her.*)

MIRADILLO
No, no, you shall not go!

TESSA
Then give up Titania or I will do so!

MIRADILLO
No, no, that is not right!

TESSA
I'll do it to spite you,
You conscienceless wight.

MIRADILLO
I cannot!

TESSA
I go,

MIRADILLO
O listen,

TESSA
No, no!

MIRADILLO
Here see me laying at thy feet!

TESSA
O, traitor! Ah!

(*They embrace and walk over to L. Miradillo has his arm round Tessa. Enter Fanfani R1. after Duett.*)

FANFANI
I come just right, just see the wight;
The fellow would seduce my wife!

TESSA
—Ah!

MIRADILLO
—Oh, spare me Tessa dear,

TESSA *and* MIRADILLO
Ah, I try but in vain,
Love's wild flame to contain!
When the heart doth wildly flutter,
Then the head is soft as butter!

For where love holds its sway,
Peace of mind steals away,
Quickly one forgets one's duties all,
And the veil must fall;
Yes love will ever conquer all!

FANFANI
You seducer, good for nothing,
Base deceiver, liar, flatt'rer,
Such a swindler upon my life,
Could imperil an honest wife;

The idea, is outrageous,
This adventurer first tried to fleece me,
My wife then he e'en tried to kiss,
Swindler don't think that I'll
Stand such abuse!
Swindler, beggar, loafer, ah!

MIRADILLO (*To Fanfani*): This charming creature shall never become one of your wives. I'd rather become a Turk and make her my wife Number Two!

FANFANI: Wretch! Have you forgotten my niece?

MIRADILLO (*Kissing Tessa*): Sir, I am too faithful a husband to forget your niece. We understand one another. We are a modern...I should say, a model couple. You see, we humour each other's little whims.

(*Miradillo and Tessa go up and over to R. and sit. Enter Antarsid L3. comes down LC. slowly. Fanfani crosses over near him while Miradillo speaks, but does not notice him.*)

MIRADILLO: I indulge her fancy for Persian rugs and Persian carpets and Persian Princes, and she allows me unfounded liberty in gaslights, and electric lights, and wax lights.

FANFANI (*Aside furiously*): If I only could dispose of that fellow in a gentlemanly way. (*Notices Antarsid*) Ah, there's the Prince. I see light. (*Taking Antarsid aside*) Prince, you love my niece?

ANTARSID (*On the defensive*): I make no denial; I love your niece ardently.

FANFANI: It just occurred to me how much happier her life would be if she were rid of that scoundrel husband. The marriage tie is an insupportable burden to her. Don't you know a nice, reliable man who could lift it off her shoulders?

ANTARSID (*Fiercely*): Shall I kill him?

FANFANI (*Restraining him*): No, dear Prince, let him live till the spring. You see, any violence would be so against...all our principles. I thought perhaps you had a man amongst your retinue who would take him to a nice little country cottage where his friends would know he was safe. In fact, suppose we board him out for the summer in the Desert; we won't harm him, but we'll give him every chance of losing himself.

ANTARSID: That would be cruel.

FANFANI: Your Highness. I am pleading for his life. Besides, every African explorer ought to get lost; they ought to be used to it by now. Show him mercy, for Titania's sake.

ANTARSID: For Titania's sake it shall be done. Tomorrow she shall be free.

FANFANI: And tomorrow you shall have the most beautiful of my slaves.

(*Antarsid goes up L.*)

FANFANI (*Aside*): To save two millions, I would part with Mrs Fanfani Number Forty Seven.

(*Exit Fanfani behind kiosk L1.*)

TESSA (*Coming down*): Miradillo, confess this deceit at once, or else…

MIRADILLO (*Aside*): But I have given my word of honour as a gentleman, and my hotel bill is paid.

TESSA (*Determined*): Very well then. I shall become Mrs Fanfani Number Forty Seven.

(*She crosses to R. and exits R1.*)

MIRADILLO (*Despondently*): She's capable of it. How can I not confess, and save Tessa for myself? (*Notices Antarsid*) Ah, the Prince! I have an idea. (*To Antarsid*) My dear Prince. (*Takes him aside*) You love my wife.

ANTARSID (*Haughtily*): If the acknowledgement isn't unpleasant to you; yes.

MIRADILLO: That's right, quite right, my dear fellow. I'm with you entirely. (*Shakes his hand warmly*) I was going to ask you if you didn't know a nice reliable man.

ANTARSID: All right. I know the rest. Whom do you want me to abduct?

MIRADILLO (*Aside*): How reasonable he is! How quick! (*Aloud*) You see, Prince, I love Tessa!

ANTARSID: But she is destined for the Pasha's harem!

MIRADILLO: That's just the point. I need her for my own, and if you will only steal her away from the Pasha this very day, tomorrow Titania shall be yours.

ANTARSID (*Aside*): The scoundrel. Ah Titania, I will free you from him.

MIRADILLO (*Pleadingly*): You will do this for Titania's sake.

ANTARSID: I will.

MIRADILLO: It's a bargain then? Let's shake hands.

ANTARSID (*Refusing the hand*): The hand of your wife is honour enough.

MIRADILLO: Then I'll go, and shake you for the drinks.

(*Both exeunt L1.*)

## No. 13 – Finale (Act 2)

(*Chorus enter LUE. and RUE. and form oblique lines on sides. The Muezzin comes over terrace and stands on top of steps C. while he sings.*)

CHORUS
Bayram, the pleasant feast at last is here,
Bayram, thy joyful signs at last appear!

MUEZZIN
A new life now believing,
All injuries forgiving;
No soul should be with hatred fraught,
Thus hath the Prophet taught;

CHORUS
A new life now believing,

MUEZZIN
—Allah!

CHORUS
All injuries forgiving;
No soul should be with hatred fraught,

MUEZZIN
—Allah!

CHORUS
Thus hath the Prophet taught;

(*Muezzin exits over terrace to L. Principals enter. Buccametta and Tessa from R2. Fanfani, Miradillo, Antarsid, Pericles and Titania from L1. Miradillo and Fanfani shake hands as a token of forgiveness.*)

By an ancient custom bound,
Let us pass the dates around,
For'twas this the Prophet taught.

Bayram, that pleasant feast is here at last,
Bayram, and gloomy Ramadan is past;
In joy now ev'ry voice is raised,
On ev'ry hand is Allah praised!

(*During this number, three Slave Girls get three baskets of dates.*)

FANFANI
'Tis custom to give the dates
When comes this feast of beauty,
It hath a charm, to keep off harm,
Therefore to give it
To your friends is duty.

TITANIA, TESSA, BUCCAMETTA, ANTARSID, MIRADILLO, PERICLES, *and* CHORUS
The custom is pretty,
'Tis hardly a duty;
We'll therefore, with pleasure,
The dates pass around!

(*Three Slave Girls come down, one between Buccametta and Tessa, another between Miradillo and Fanfani, and the third between Fanfani and Antarsid. The Principals take a date each. The Slaves then retire and give dates to Chorus. Fanfani offers a date to Miradillo.*)

FANFANI (*To Miradillo*)
Won't you have a date with me
My youthful friend!

(*Miradillo accepts it and eats.*)

MIRADILLO
Many thanks!

(*Titania offers one to Antarsid.*)

TITANIA (*To Antarsid*)
Please accept the date
Which I to you extend.

(*Antarsid accepts it and eats.*)

ANTARSID
Many thanks!

(*Tessa takes a date from Buccametta.*)

TESSA (*To Buccametta*)
I will eat a date dear mother now with you.

BUCCAMETTA
That will do.

ANTARSID
Understood.

FANFANI
That is right.

BUCCAMETTA
That was good.

PERICLES *and* CHORUS
Lovely concord works this feast.

(*Miradillo gives date to Fanfani.*)

MIRADILLO (*To Fanfani*)
—But dear uncle take a date
Now please with me.

(*Fanfani accepts it.*)

FANFANI
Give to me!

(*Antarsid gives one to Titania.*)

ANTARSID (*To Titania*)
And this date, sweet lady,
I now offer thee.

(*Titania accepts it. All are eating dates throughout.*)

TITANIA
Thank you Sir!

BUCCAMETTA (*To Tessa*)
I've already eaten all excepting three.

TESSA
Not so bad!

TITANIA
That is right!

MIRADILLO
Very good!

BUCCAMETTA
Now it's ripe!

FANFANI (*Aside*)
He looks so merry.

MIRADILLO (*Aside*)
He seems so happy,

FANFANI
I hope they'll do you good Sir!

MIRADILLO
I thank you!

FANFANI
Quite welcome.

(*Sneeze on "Tshi!"*)

BUCCAMETTA *and* FANFANI
Tshi!

BUCCAMETTA *and* MIRADILLO
Tshi!

MIRADILLO *and* FANFANI
Confounded sneezing!

BUCCAMETTA *and* FANFANI
Tshi!

BUCCAMETTA *and* MIRADILLO
Tshi!

MIRADILLO *and* FANFANI
'Tis most displeasing.

TITANIA *and* BUCCAMETTA
Tshi!

FANFANI
Bless you!

ANTARSID *and* BUCCAMETTA
Tshi!

MIRADILLO
Bless you!

TITANIA *and* ANTARSID
Whence comes this sneezing?

TITANIA,      ANTARSID,      BUCCAMETTA,      MIRADILLO      *and*
FANFANI
Tshi!

PERICLES *and* CHORUS
Bless you!

TITANIA,      ANTARSID,      BUCCAMETTA,      MIRADILLO      *and*
FANFANI
Tshi!

PERICLES *and* CHORUS
Bless you!

TITANIA,      ANTARSID,      BUCCAMETTA,      MIRADILLO      *and*
FANFANI
I thank you kindly,

ALL
Tshi!

TESSA *and* BUCCAMETTA
I don't see,

PERICLES *and* CHORUS                 MIRADILLO *and* FANFANI
What ails us?                         Tshi!

TESSA *and* BUCCAMETTA
What ails me?

PERICLES *and* CHORUS                 TITANIA *and* ANTARSID
This sneezing,                        Tshi!

PERICLES *and* CHORUS

Unceasing,

TITANIA, TESSA,
BUCCAMETTA, MIRADILLO,
ANTARSID *and* FANFANI
Dear o dear,
Tshi!
This is queer!


TESSA *and* BUCCAMETTA
Tshi!
What a noise,

Is really,

MIRADILLO *and* FANFANI
Tshi!

Extremely,

TESSA *and* BUCCAMETTA
There is here!

PERICLES *and* CHORUS
Displeasing!

TITANIA *and* ANTARSID
Tshi!

TITANIA, TESSA,
BUCCAMETTA, MIRADILLO,
ANTARSID *and* FANFANI
I! Tshi!
He! Tshi!
The tshi!
Tsha!

Tshi!
Tshi!
Tshi!
Tsha!

TITANIA *and* ANTARSID
I cannot stand this!

MIRADILLO *and* FANFANI
I don't understand this!

TESSA *and* BUCCAMETTA
It's magic, I'm sure,

TITANIA, TESSA, BUCCAMETTA, MIRADILLO, ANTARSID *and*
FANFANI
Tshi! Tshi!

PERICLES *and* CHORUS
—Tshi!—Tshi!

TITANIA, TESSA, BUCCAMETTA, MIRADILLO, ANTARSID *and*
FANFANI
Confounded sneezing,

PERICLES *and* CHORUS
Bless you,

TITANIA, TESSA, BUCCAMETTA, MIRADILLO, ANTARSID,
FANFANI *and* CHORUS (SOPRANO *and* TENOR)
Tshi! Tshi!

PERICLES *and* CHORUS (BASS)
—Tshi! Tshi!

(*All sneeze very loud on last note.*)

ALL
It's magic; magic sure, Tsha!

(*Chorus and Principals divide and leave C. open. Bass drum for cannon off stage. All turn facing upstage and listen.*)

FANFANI
Hark! Did you hear
The signal sound at last?

CHORUS
List the river murmurs low!

(*Cannon sounds again.*)

FANFANI
The hour is come, the Nile is rising fast.

CHORUS
Moist and cool the Zephyrs blow.

(*Cannon sounds again.*)

FANFANI
The third shot does to us
The flood announce.

(*Water begins to rise on transparent background. All bend down facing water, hands stretched out in front. Raise them gradually imitating the rising of the water. At same time turning very slowly inwards and down stage.*)

CHORUS
With murmurs mysterious,
The waters rise,
Wild surges upheaving,
Now greet our eyes.
The waters outpour.

PRINCIPALS
—Of Egypt's friends the best,

CHORUS
With deep sounding roar!

PRINCIPALS
—O Nile be doubly blessed,

CHORUS
Now praise Allah's pow'r,

ALL
(*Hands lowered and raised on "power".*)
(Now) praise Allah's pow'r,
(*Hands lowered and raised on "shower".*)
Who doth the land with blessings show'r,
(*Rush down to apron with hands stretched out heavenwards on "hour".*)
And works the wonders of this hour!

(*Slaves bring golden goblets and hand them to Principals. Titania crosses Fanfani to C. Tessa crosses Miradillo to C. Pericles moves to Chorus and sings with Bass until the end of the act.*)

TITANIA
Pass the cup! Sing with me!

TESSA, BUCCAMETTA, ANTARSID, MIRADILLO, FANFANI *and*
CHORUS
A song of praise in place will be!

TITANIA
From Allah's throne,
Ever since this land was known,
Comes an angel on pearly wings,
And the Nile floods blessing brings!

With a cup in his hand,
By his master sent is he,
To the source, which to us mortals
E'er unknown will be!
And the waters first whisper low,
Rising, surging, mightily grow!

Show'ring blessings, o'er the land,
All its life renewing.

(*All raise cups in air on "To the", "waves we", "when with" and
"Egypt's".*)

| TITANIA | TESSA, BUCCAMETTA, ANTARSID, MIRADILLO, FANFANI *and* CHORUS |
|---|---|
| To the waves we send joyful greeting, | Mighty, |
| When with Egypt's parched soil they're meeting; | River. |
| More than wine | |
| Do we welcome thy flood divine! | Joyfully thy flood we praise! |

(*Chorus divide in C. and leave back open. Large boat with coloured sail comes out from L. to C. manned by four or five Super—or Chorus men if they can be—dressed as followers of Antarsid. All point to boat as it comes out.*)

TESSA, BUCCAMETTA, ANTARSID, MIRADILLO, FANFANI *and*
CHORUS
See there, the galley,
All decked out with colours bright,
Charming, entrancing
Indeed is this lovely sight! See!

TITANIA (*Not loud, to Tessa*)
The chains I'll now loosen,
The galley is here,

I'll save you my dearest,
Salvation is near;

The barque it will surely,
Set both of us free!
Once again, raise the glass,
Sing with me.

| TITANIA | TESSA, BUCCAMETTA, ANTARSID, MIRADILLO, FANFANI *and* CHORUS |
|---|---|
| Yes! | Let's sing with joyous glee! |

(*Same positions until Supers come down from boat.*)

ALL
From Allah's throne,
Ever since this land was known,
Comes an angel on pearly wings,
And the Nile floods blessing brings.

With a cup in his hand,
By his master sent is he!
To the source, which to us mortals
E'er unknown will be!

TESSA, BUCCAMETTA, ANTARSID, MIRADILLO, FANFANI *and*
CHORUS
And the waters whisper low,

TITANIA
—And the waters first whisper low,

TESSA, BUCCAMETTA, ANTARSID, MIRADILLO, FANFANI *and*
CHORUS
—Then they rise up!

TITANIA

—Rise, then surge, then mightily grow,
Show'ring blessings o'er the land;
All its life renewing! Ah!
All its life,
Truly more than wine,
Do we welcome thy flood divine.

TESSA, BUCCAMETTA, ANTARSID, MIRADILLO, FANFANI *and* CHORUS
They flood the country,
All its life renewing!
To thy waves we send joyful greeting,
When with Egypt's parched soil they're meeting;
More than wine,
Do we welcome thy flood divine.

(*Supers leave ship and come downstage behind Principals.*)

CHORUS
O see there, the scorpions,

(*They seize Titania, Tessa, Antarsid and Miradillo and drag them upstage towards boat. Fanfani is down L., puzzled.*)

In intricate mazes they turn.

FANFANI
What's going to happen,
What will we see now?

CHORUS
—Just see!
They're leading the women,
By force to the barque over there.

FANFANI
I've got my suspicion,
Deceit's in the air!

CHORUS
—Tis queer!

TITANIA
We're taking a ride!

MIRADILLO
'Tis to humour your bride!

FANFANI (*Shaking fist at Miradillo*)
You scoundrel, quite plainly
I see that's your trick.

CHORUS
Just see them, just see them,
They're making off quick.

(*Fanfani calling upon his Slaves—the Chorus men—who run down stage from each side and up C.*)

FANFANI
Come you fellows,

MALE CHORUS
Stop them quick,

FANFANI
Go pursue them,

MALE CHORUS
Foil the trick!

FANFANI
Stop them, do not let them go!

MALE CHORUS
Too late, the barque's afloat.

(*Chorus men run upstage and are stopped by Supers who stand in front of steps holding spears at charge.*)

FANFANI

With anger I'm almost
distracted,
My money and bride are
abstracted;

Knavery, trickery,
All have been playing me;

Surely I'm faring but poorly,
This shame this disgrace,
They are thrown in my face,
But just wait, soon or late I will
fix them.

TITANIA, ANTARSID, TESSA,
MIRADILLO, BUCCAMETTA
*and* CHORUS
Freedom, freedom,
For which we've striven,
Freedom, freedom,
To us is given;

Fare you well,

Yes and proclaim,
Allah's might,
Praise ye all Allah's might!

(*Miradillo, Tessa, Titania and Antarsid on boat. Supers threatening Fanfani's men with spears, Supers standing, Fanfani's men cowering on ground. Women in oblique line kneel. Fanfani attempts to get at boat but is held back by Buccametta who drags him back by his coat tail, turns him round and he slides down in front of her, falling onstage for curtain.*)

# CURTAIN

# END OF ACT 2

# ACT 3

*An oasis in the interior of Africa, with a view of the Sahara. Groups of palms all over stage. Tents R. and L. either side of stage. In C. is a couch covered with tiger skins with Antarsid laying on top. At rise of curtain, Chorus (dressed as slaves and followers) are in a rough oblique line R. Antarsid is asleep. Titania, Tessa and Nakid must be ready in tent L.*

## No. 14 – Entr'acte, Chorus and Romanza

MALE CHORUS
Now the morn anew is breaking,

FEMALE CHORUS
—Splendour bright.

MALE CHORUS
Brightly shining Phoebus rays.

FEMALE CHORUS
Proclaimeth Allah's might.

MALE CHORUS
In the distant East awaking, it awakes.

FEMALE CHORUS
—In the East, it awakes.

CHORUS
It awakes,
Burst on our admiring gaze.

(*Antarsid awakes and sits on couch.*)

ANTARSID
What a dream, I was so happy,
Sweet delight, my soul did fill,

Rose entrancing, thy thorn I did not dread,
Did I not kiss the lovely flower?

(*He stands up and looks around. Two Servants quickly take couch off stage.*)

But ah! In danger we are here,
From robber bands I fear,
The tents with care conceal,
This place they might reveal.
(*Going to entrance of tent L.*)
And thou, my darling,
Awake, awake.

CHORUS
Allah's might shields us here,
Allah!

ANTARSID
—Darling awake!

CHORUS (*Humming*)
Mmm mmm…

Now dawns the morn, the darkness goes,
On heavens bow stars paler grow;
On azure throne the sun brightly glows,
Wakes us from sweet repose;

Wake, maiden fair, cool is the air,
Open thine eyes, on me let them beam;
Then will my star, no more be far,
Lighter than Sol's bright gleam.

—Maiden fair, cool the air,
Awaken;

—Phoebus gleams, with golden beams—

CHORUS (SOPRANO *and* TENOR)
Awake, awake, sweet maid!
Awake, the day is fair.

Quickly awaken sweetest maiden,
Waken darling, open thine eyes!

| ANTARSID | CHORUS |
|---|---|
| Come, ah, come vision bright, | Come, ah, come and leave thy |
| And be my heart's delight! | dreaming, |
| | Past is the dawn; |
| O come, o come, | And bright is the morning. |
| Awake, awake. | Mmm. |

(*Chorus gradually back off R. upstage, leaving Antarstid alone. He goes to tent L. and lifts curtain.*)

ANTARSID: Titania, the day has dawned.

(*Titania rises, enters and embraces him.*)

TITANIA: The day of happiness.

ANTARSID: My own sweet love!

TESSA (*Sighing, following Titania from tent*): And have you taken me out to this lonely desert to look on at your caressing and kissing? (*Sarcastically*) I am very much obliged to you.

TITANIA: But my dear friend; have you forgotten that Miradillo is with us?

TESSA (*Discontentedly*): No, but you've got such a lot of pretty slaves too. How do I know he won't be flirting with them instead of talking to me?

ANTARSID: Let us test his love!

TESSA: Test him? How?

TITANIA: Conceal yourself. We will make him believe you are lost, observe his actions and ascertain the state of his feelings towards you.

TESSA: Capital idea! Tell him that Fanfani Pasha carried me off last night.

(*Miradillo's voice heard inside tent R.*)

ANTARSID (*To Tessa*): Quick, that is his voice. Hide yourself.

TESSA: Oh Miradillo. My beloved Miradillo.

(*She exits into tent L.*)

MIRADILLO (*Sticking head between curtains of tent, aside*): I thought I heard Tessa's voice.

(*He enters from tent. R, fastening necktie, as if in act of dressing. He is followed by Hosh, who carries a comb, brush and mirror.*)

ANTARSID (*To Titania*): Now let us tell him some plausible story and see what happens.

(*He crosses L.*)

MIRADILLO (*To Titania*): Ah, dearest spouse, good morning. Pardon my unfinished toilet and smile graciously upon me. (*To Antarsid*) Bonjour dear Prince. (*To Hosh*) Come here.

(*Miradillo takes comb and fixes hair while looking in glass. Hosh shrugs.*)

ANTARSID: We have something very important to tell you.

MIRADILLO (*Cool and polite*): One moment please. (*To Hosh*) Didn't you pack up some cosmetics?

(*Hosh shrugs.*)

MIRADILLO: You miserable slave. I'll have you flogged. Where is the whip?

(*Hosh shrugs.*)

MIRADILLO (*Angrily*): You have forgotten the whip too? That is a nice state of affairs. Out here in the desert without any of the comforts of life, without the most indispensable toilet articles? Without even the whip!

(*Hosh grins.*)

MIRADILLO: The fellow is laughing! Perhaps you have also forgotten my Chibouk?

(*Hosh grins and exits into tent R.*)

MIRADILLO: Don't grin but speak, you scoundrel! But what's the use of me getting angry? I forgot he can't speak. (*To Titania and Antarsid*) I'll tell you right here that if he hasn't brought the Chibouk, I'll kill him straight away. I'll stab him in the heart.

(*Hosh enters from tent R. with Chibouk and hands it to Miradillo.*)

HOSH (*In broad Irish accent*): Me no African man. Me Irishman.

MIRADILLO (*Astonished*): A black Irishman? (*Pleasantly to Titania*) He is an Irishman! (*To Hosh*) But how did that happen?

HOSH (*Takes out book*): Irish grammar. I learnt it secretly. I don't like African any more. African no good now. Irishman heaps better. Everyone likes Irishman, especially the English. They make so much noise and cause such a mighty din.

MIRADILLO: An Irishman! (*Ironical*) Take a smoke yourself, Mr. O'Flanagan. (*Hands Hosh the chibouk*) Make yourself at home.

HOSH: No Chibouk for dis chap. Me heightened. Me smoke cigars.

(*He offers a cigar to Miradillo, lights one himself, and exits into tent R.*)

MIRADILLO (*To Antarsid*): And now, your Highness, what is your programme for the day?

ANTARSID: First I shall marry Titania.

(*He embraces her.*)

MIRADILLO (*Haughtily*): You seem to forget, the lady is my wife.

ANTARSID: And you seem to forget our compact of last night. But don't look so nonplussed my friend. I know all, and there is no longer any necessity for you to assume a role which must be as obnoxious to you as it is to us.

TITANIA (*Crossing to R., laughing*): Yes, Signor Miradillo. I solemnly declare that I release you from your obligations. Your assistance can now be dispensed with.

MIRADILLO: I'm dismissed then?

ANTARSID: Unquestionably. Within an hour, Titania will be my wife. Fast horses are awaiting us, and in a short time we can reach a Coptic settlement. The Copts, like ourselves, are Christians, and once in their little Chapel, there will be no more obstacle to our getting married.

MIRADILLO (*Uneasily*): Pardon me one question please. Did I understand you to name a bank?

TITANIA: Don't be afraid. Your recompense is deposited at the Italian Consulate at Cairo.

MIRADILLO (*Delighted*): Let me congratulate you, Signora. (*He gives right hand to Titania.*) And you more, Prince. (*He gives left hand to Antarsid and passes Titania over to him, then starts to go R3.*) I will bid you a speedy adieu, as I have a little business to transact in Cairo.

TITANIA: At the Consulate? Oh by the way; I forgot to tell you, the money is deposited in Tessa's name.

MIRADILLO (*Returning, crestfallen*): Oh!

TITANIA: Yes, I thought it would be a nice little wedding portion for her, and as you have been so long engaged, I felt it was quite safe to entreat it to her keeping. Besides, you know, Signor Miradillo, in this hot climate, money melts so quickly.

MIRADILLO (*Sighing*): Bachelor days…goodbye! Goodbye to my dreams of greatness. Great explorer in embryo, bid a long farewell to the world's untrodden fields, and launch your little bank on the troubled sea of matrimony. (*He comes back C. between Titania and Antarsid.*) Where's Tessa?

ANTARSID *and* TITANIA (*Feigning confusion*): Tessa?

MIRADILLO: Yes. I'll look for her without delay.

ANTARSID: Let me send some of my men with you, and if you wait a moment I'll give you a letter of recommendation to the Sultan of Timbuctoo!

MIRADILLO: What for?

TITANIA: Alas, poor Miradillo.

MIRADILLO: Why, what's the matter?

TITANIA: Is it possible, you really don't know?

ANTARSID (*Tragically*): Tell him the sad tidings Titania. It takes a woman to do that in a tender and sparing way.

MIRADILLO (*Anxiously*): For heaven's sake, what is the matter?

TITANIA: Compose yourself Miradillo. (*She seizes Miradillo's hand and leads him down R. corner. She gives three long melodramatic breaths, all very mysteriously. Indicating that she has vanished*) Tessa... Tessa...Tessa has pht!

(*As in the business of pantomimes. Antarsid seizes Miradillo's other hand and takes him over to L. corner. Same business. Miradillo goes back to the centre and does same business! Himself puzzled.*)

ANTARSID: She has been abducted during the night by Fanfani Pasha!

MIRADILLO (*In despair, furiously*): Villain! Villain! Where has he taken her? Tell me that I may follow.

ANTARSID: Into the Interior of Africa!

MIRADILLO (*Collapsing*): Into the Interior? Then I'll have to explore this dashed country after all. Just my luck. With the whole world to choose from, he must go and hit upon the one spot I most particularly dislike, and all that good money be wasted! Oh Africa!

(*Titania and Antarsid shrug shoulders.*)

MIRADILLO: I immolate myself upon thy altar. Take another victim unto thy sandy bosom. "On Stanley, on!"[3] were the last words of Miradillo.

## No. 14 1/2 – Sortie

(*Miradillo starts to walk away towards R3., but keeps retreating scared. Looks back at Antarsid and Titania, who beckon him back. He returns and stands in between them.*)

## No. 15 – Terzett

(*Titania on one side and Antarsid on the other, both trying to scare Miradillo.*)

## Song

TITANIA
Africa is full of danger,

ANTARSID                                    MIRADILLO
For the unacquainted stranger,              Ha!

TITANIA
Firstly from wild beasts ferocious,         Ah!

ANTARSID
That cause have most atrocious,             Stuff!

TITANIA
From Equator's                              Well

ANTARSID
Alligators;                                 I

---

[3] *In reference to the reporter Henry Stanley, who was sent to the Interior of Africa in search of Dr. Livingstone after he went missing in 1864 while trying to discover the source of the Nile. Stanley found the doctor in 1871 in the village of Ujiji on Lake Tanganyika and upon greeting him, he reportedly said "Dr. Livingstone, I presume?"*

TITANIA
From the snakes that

MIRADILLO
Do

ANTARSID
Roll and toss;

Not care.

TITANIA
And from the Rhinoceros,

ANTARSID
Yes from the Rhinoceros.

MIRADILLO
For my darling Tessa's sake,
Most willingly my life I'll stake,

TITANIA
You must not foolhardy be,

ANTARSID
But consider carefully.

MIRADILLO
What's already done you see.

TITANIA
Then the Bedouins; O horror!

ANTARSID
Coolly kill the rash Explorer.

MIRADILLO
Pooh!

TITANIA
And among the fierce Ashantis,

Stuff.

ANTARSID
You'll find Cannibals in plenty.

Well

TITANIA
Weather torrid,

I

ANTARSID
Serpents horrid,

TITANIA
Tarantulas,

ANTARSID
Scorpions too,

TITANIA
Of all kinds will threaten you,

ANTARSID
Of all kinds will threaten you.

MIRADILLO
What you say does not dismay me,

ANTARSID
And much beside,

MIRADILLO
As I told you once before,

TITANIA
Now wakes his pride,

MIRADILLO
All your terrors cannot sway me,

ANTARSID
His blood now boils,

MIRADILLO
Ev'ry country I'll explore,

TITANIA
For her sake, he dreads no toils,

TITANIA *and* ANTARSID
Very far you must roam,

MIRADILLO
Do

Care

A snap.

MIRADILLO
'Till I Tessa see once more.

MIRADILLO
O'er the continent I'll roam.
TITANIA *and* ANTARSID
Go with us to your home,

MIRADILLO
With her only I'll go home.

TITANIA *and* ANTARSID
Come to your fatherland,

MIRADILLO
When I have found her,

TITANIA *and* ANTARSID
We offer you our hand!

MIRADILLO
But not before!
Yes Tessa, love, whom I adore,
For you I'll Africa explore.

## Song

MIRADILLO
Over hill, over dale,
'Till the moon shines on the vale,
I'll away, all alone,
Love will help me find my own,
Love will help me find my own.

TITANIA *and* ANTARSID
Over hill,

MIRADILLO
—Over hill,

TITANIA *and* ANTARSID
Over dale,

MIRADILLO
—Over dale,

TITANIA *and* ANTARSID
'Till the moon shines on the
vale,
He'll away all sole alone,
Love will help him find his
own.

MIRADILLO
And thro' the veil,
I'll away all sole alone,
Love will help me find my
own..

MIRADILLO
Should a tiger in my way I find,

TITANIA *and* ANTARSID
Gracious me!

MIRADILLO
Jackal, lynx or any other kind;
A Gorilla would not me dismay,
Without minding them I'd pass my way!
If I also should meet savage tribes,

TITANIA *and* ANTARSID
Savage tribes,

MIRADILLO
Such as Stanley in his book describes,
From their village I'll not run away,
Like a man I'll fight my way.

Whom true love doth inspire,

ALL
Boldly (he encounters/I encounter),
Peril, dread and dire.

MIRADILLO
When I've found her at last,

ALL
From these dark dominions,

Home (he'll/I'll) travel fast.
(He/I) with her, hand in hand,
See once more (his/my) native land.

MIRADILLO
With her my native land,
Once more I'll see,
Vedere Napoli,
E poi morire;

But there to live in joy
More pleases me;
Vedere Napoli e mai morir!

(*All three back upstage.*)

ALL
Together to that land,
Return then we,
Vedere Napoli e poi morire!
(*All march down. Miradillo heads to L. Antarsid heads back C. Titania heads towards tent L.*)
But there to live in joy
More pleases me;
Vedere Napoli e mai morir!

(*Titania enters tent L., beckoning Tessa to come out. Titania disappears and Tessa emerges gingerly from the tent unnoticed by Miradillo and Antarsid.*)

TESSA
Life once more gains new zest,
When true love pervades one's breast;
Like a charm to the heart,
Courage new it doth impart,
Courage new it doth impart.

ANTARSID *and* MIRADILLO
Life once more,

TESSA
—Life once more,

ANTARSID *and* MIRADILLO
Gains a zest,

TESSA
—Gains a zest,

ANTARSID *and* MIRADILLO                TESSA
When true love pervades one's breast,   —Stirs love the breast,

ALL
Like a charm to ev'ry heart,
Valour new it doth impart.

TESSA
Tho' dread perils you may have to brave,

ANTARSID *and* MIRADILLO
He'll be brave,

TESSA
Tho' the lightnings flash
And wild storms rave,
Still the tho't of her will lead you on,
You'll not flinch until the prize is won.

Tho' of hope there's but the faintest ray,

ANTARSID *and* MIRADILLO
That is good,

TESSA
All at least succumb to true love's sway,
When a loving heart would seek its mate,
Then no peril is too great.

Therefore do not despair,

Act 3 scene: Tessa and Miradillo. From the original poster for the 1884 production of the opera at Haverly's Theatre, Broad Street, Philadelphia (USA). Dario Salvi Collection.

ALL
Tho' the goal be far,
Love soon will bring you there.

TESSA
Potent is Cupid's might,

ALL
Maiden fair and lover,
Soon he will unite;
Then the pair, hand in hand,
Hie both to their native land!

TESSA
To that dear native land,
Return then we;
Vedere Napoli,
E poi morire;
But there to live in joy
More pleases me;
Vedere Napoli e mai morir!

ALL
To that dear native land,
Return then we,
Vedere Napoli,
E poi morire;
But there to live in joy
More pleases me;
Vedere Napoli e mai morir!

(*After Terzett, Miradillo exits R1. Antarsid exits LUE. Tessa and Nakid emerge fully and cautiously from tent L. and stand near entrance of it.*)

NAKID: What did I tell you? You see how faithful he is. He loves you so much that he will follow you into the Interior.

(*Enter Miradillo R3. without seeing them. He crosses stage to tent R. without perceiving Tessa. Nakid heads upstage looking off L.*)

MIRADILLO (*Speaks as he slowly crosses to tent R.*): They are hastening to the Chapel, while I have to go into the Interior. (*Appears very dejected*) Well I'll make my preparations with a view to safety rather than speed, and in the meanwhile my Tessa may be found by somebody else.

(*He is about to enter tent.*)

TESSA: Miradillo!

(*Miradillo comes back to C.*)

MIRADILLO: Tessa, you are here, not carried off! My dearest, I was hurrying after you.

TESSA: I saved myself through cunning and strategy, hurried back, and here I am.

MIRADILLO (*Aside*): How glad I am I didn't hurry. I might have been in the Interior by this time…ugh!

(*Nakid comes running down excited.*)

NAKID (*Humming excitedly*): Fanfani Pasha is on our track with a lot of howling Bedouins! We are all dead men!

MIRADILLO: Fanfani Pasha? Tessa, you must hide in the tent and we must delay the Pasha here until Titania and the Prince have reached the Chapel. Come into my tent quick, while we make our plans.

(*Miradillo, Tessa and Nakid all enter tent R.*)

## No. 16 – Bedouin Chorus

(*Male Chorus of Bedouins enter RUE. They run along spring board and jump one after another. Their sneaky business—all around stage, looking off R. and L. etc. All carry yataghans. Fanfani enters last, also in Bedouin dress. He carries coloured lantern—red or green—comes down C. Men dance round each other in pairs—grotesque step, one in a bar, knives flourished in air.*)

FANFANI                              MALE CHORUS
We Bedouins of the Nile,             —the Nile,
When a chap stirs our bile,          —our bile,
Without winking, without shrinking,  —winking, shrinking,
(*All jump on "vengeance", very loud.*)
Kill him off in good style;          Kill him with style;
Vengeance!                           Vengeance!
                                     (*Reverse     and     dance
                                     around the other way.*)
Always thirsting for gore,           —for gore,
Ev'ry nook we explore,               —explore,

ALL
And what falls into our clutches
Never squeaks anymore;
(*Jump as before*)
Vengeance!

FANFANI
Serpent-like we creep up to our man,

(*On these five notes, Chorus all take five very short and quick steps down stage.*)

MALE CHORUS
To our man;

FANFANI
From its sheath draw the sharp Yataghan,

MALE CHORUS (*Same again, five steps down.*)
Yataghan.

(*Sway L., R., L., R. in each bar—stop for "ha ha ha".*)

ALL
(In a circle) unerring,
The bright blade comes whirring;
(*Scornfully*)
A flash, ha ha ha ha!

(*Step upstage four times—once in each bar, starting on first "death". All jump on "vengeance".*)

FANFANI                                MALE CHORUS
Sure death puts a stop to his breath,  Sure death, death, death,
Off his head goes like lead;           Yes, death;
Vengeance!                             Vengeance!

(*During this strain, men do waltz movement to R. and L.—all to R. first. Make it very grotesque, holding cloaks out on each side.*)

FANFANI
Should deceiver gay,
Steal your wife away,
If the dame was old and grey,
Not a word you say;

But if au contraire,
She was young and fair,
An indignant outcry make,
For good morals' sake.

(*Chorus stop waltz movement.*)

Such crimes must be punished,
With powder and steel,

ALL (*Very loud, shaking knives*)
Make 'em feel!

(*Chorus two steps down with R. foot. Sneaky business, finger to lips on "peeping" and "creeping", and one step on each "death". All down stage by last one.*)

FANFANI                                MALE CHORUS
We Bedouins of the Nile,               Peeping,
When a chap stirs our bile,            Creeping,
Ha ha ha ha, sure death               With us the watchword is death,

Puts a stop to his breath,             Death, death,
Off his head goes like lead.           Sure death.

ALL
Vengeance!

FANFANI
Should deceiver gay,
Steal your wife away,
If the dame was old and grey,
Not a word you say;

But if au contraire,
She was young and fair,
An indignant outcry make,
For good morals sake.

(*Chorus stop waltz movement.*)

Such crimes must be punished,
With powder and steel,

ALL (*Very loud, shaking knives*)
Make 'em feel!

(*Chorus two steps down with R. foot. Sneaky business, finger to lips on "peeping" and "creeping", and one step on each "death". All down stage by last one.*)

FANFANI                          MALE CHORUS
We Bedouins of the Nile,         Peeping,
When a chap stirs our bile,      Creeping,
Ha ha ha ha, sure death          With us the watchword is death,
Puts a stop to his breath,       Death, death,
Off his head goes like lead.     Sure death.

ALL
Stealthily, creeping we,
(*Motion of seizing a person with L. hand. Knife held R.*)
Seize the chap by the nap,

Act 3 scene: Fanfani and Bedouins. From the original poster for the 1884 production of the opera at Haverly's Theatre, Broad Street, Philadelphia (USA). Dario Salvi Collection.

FANFANI
Then give him a rap,

ALL (*Hop up in air on each "ha ha"*)
Ha ha, ha ha, ha ha,
(*Back upstage towards entrances, one step in a bar*)
Ears cut off, nose cut off
(*Very loud and stand still on "all cut off"*)
Head cut off, all cut off!

FANFANI                                    MALE CHORUS
Yes the Yataghan makes short          Thus we kill off our man!
work of a man!

FANFANI: Sons of the desert! Followers of the Great Sahia…I mean Sahara! I think we are upon the track of the fugitives. Lay yourself in ambush. Don't let anybody pass. Seize them and their…

(*All back up again.*)

ALL
Ears cut off, nose cut off,
Head cut off,
(*Very loud, as before.*)
All cut off;
Yes the Yataghan makes short work of our man!

(*After Chorus, Bedouins disappear at upper entrances leaving Fanfani alone.*)

FANFANI: Now to search the tents. (*He raises curtain of tent. Starts back in surprise*) Ah, one of them already.

(*Enter Miradillo from tent R. making a cigarette.*)

MIRADILLO (*Feigning surprise*): Why by jove, Fanfani Pasha, why? This is agreeable of you. First, you have us parried off, and then follow to see how we are getting on.

FANFANI (*Angrily*): It was you, you scoundrel, who was to be kidnapped. I didn't anticipate the Prince's taking half of Cairo with him.

MIRADILLO: Antarsid does things in style, I can tell you. He thought it was a shame to break up such a nice little family-party, so he brought us all along.

FANFANI (*Furiously producing dagger*): How dare he take my Tessa from me?

MIRADILLO (*Afraid of weapon*): Oh, you'd better settle that with him when you see him.

FANFANI: Where is he? Where is the thief?

MIRADILLO: Out shooting wild donkeys. Don't spring yourself suddenly on him, or you'll get shot.

FANFANI: Idiot! Where is Tessa? Produce her instantly, or—(*About to strangle him*)—I'll strangle you.

(*Enter Tessa from tent R. carrying tray of food. Hosh follows with two bottles of wine, and a Slave brings on chair and table, on which Tessa puts tray. Hosh keeps himself busy pouring drinks and tidying etc.*)

FANFANI (*Charmed, looking at Tessa*): How beautiful she is.

TESSA (*To Miradillo*): Your wife sends you your breakfast, Signor. She will be with you presently.

(*Miradillo goes up round table, sits R. of it and starts eating. Hosh fills his glass.*)

TESSA (*Noticing Fanfani*): Ah, my dear Pasha! What a delightful surprise.

(*Fanfani takes Tessa's hand.*)

FANFANI: At last I see you again, lovely gazelle, but in—(*Half loud pointing at Miradillo*)—what company?

TESSA (*Tragically, half loud*): Hush, pity him, his days are numbered. I shall kill him!

(*She crosses to L.*)

FANFANI: The deuce. Why?

TESSA (*Gloomily*): I loved him, and he deceived me. I am a Sicilian. We never forgive a wrong. The bottle which Hosh has just uncorked contains a poisoned wine. He will drink it and…

FANFANI (*Anxiously*): But the other bottle, sweet dove, does that also contain a life shortening tincture?

TESSA: Oh no, that is pure, unadulterated wine. (*Burlesque melodrama*) But Fanfani, watch him, and when his eyes roll and his teeth chatter, and his frame is convulsed with the agony of Death, whisper in his ear: "Such is the revenge of a Sicilian!"

(*Exit Tessa into tent L. with long strides—burlesque tragedy style.*)

FANFANI (*Throwing kisses at her*): A girl fit for the Gods. She makes my flesh creep. Me-thinks she could make things warm for me.

(*Miradillo raises his glass, empties it and turns to Fanfani.*)

MIRADILLO: Well uncle, won't you drink with me? Let me fill a glass for you.

(*He reaches for bottle. Fanfani sits L. of table.*)

FANFANI (*Quickly*): No, no, much obliged. You keep that bottle. I'll drink from this. (*Aside*) I'm too young to die yet!

MIRADILLO: Just as you please, dear uncle. I'll keep my own bottle then.

(*He drinks. Hosh opens second bottle and pours into Fanfani's glass.*)

FANFANI (*Aside*): He'll drop dead in a minute. (*Aloud*) Well, nephew. How do you feel?

MIRADILLO: Never was better in my life. (*Holding up glass*) Here's to your good health.

FANFANI (*Holding up glass, and taking a sip*): Same to you. (*Aside*) He'll keel over in a few seconds.

(*He notices Miradillo rubbing his forehead.*)

FANFANI: Wine a little heady, dear boy?

MIRADILLO: Not at all. Never drank better. Uncle, you and I have been enemies long enough. Let us be friends.

FANFANI (*Aside*): He's getting affectionate. That's a very bad sign. Well, I'll humour him. It's his last request. (*Aloud*) All right. Here we go.

(*They rise and embrace violently in front of table.*)

FANFANI (*Aside*): I hope he won't stiffen around my neck.

(*Tessa enters from tent L.*)

TESSA: You gentlemen seem quite jolly!

MIRADILLO: Yes, we are so happy. We are reconciled.

(*Fanfani crosses over to Tessa.*)

FANFANI (*To Tessa*): It doesn't seem to affect him at all!

TESSA: I don't understand it. It's Nakid's best elixir. (*As if struck by a terrible thought*) Can it be possible? (*She crosses to C., hurries to the table, looks at both bottles and returns to Fanfani scared and tragic*) He has changed the bottles.

FANFANI (*Annihilated*): Ch…ch…changed the bottles. Saeed-El-Mahdi. I'm a mummy.

(*He begins to stagger.*)

TESSA: What's the matter?

FANFANI (*Screaming*): I'm poisoned. I drank from the other bottle. (*Falls and rolls about as if in fearful agony*) The antidote, quick. (*Seems to remember*) Nakid! Nakid! Help!

TESSA: Nakid!

ALL: Nakid! Nakid!

NAKID (*Running in from tent R.*): What's the matter? Who calls for help?

FANFANI (*Clinging to him*): Oh Nakid, an antidote for heaven's sake!

NAKID: Have you taken poison?

FANFANI: Yes, from this bottle.

(*Nakid goes to the table and gets the bottle.*)

NAKID: Wait a moment 'till I analyse it.

(*Nakid tastes the wine.*)

FANFANI: No! Cure me first, then analyse it.

NAKID: That is quite impossible.

FANFANI (*Stoll rolling about down C.*): Oh! Is there no one who can help me in my distress?

(*Enter Buccametta from tent L. with giddy dance step. Two Servants remove table and stools.*)

BUCCAMETTA: Yes, dear Pasha. I can!

FANFANI (*Puzzled*): The old crow. Oh Mahomet!

TESSA: Mama Buccametta!

MIRADILLO: My future mother-in-law. (*To Nakid*) Say Nakid, haven't you got an antidote for mothers-in-law?

NAKID: My poisons are effectual.

FANFANI: Hear him. Can no one preserve my life?

BUCCAMETTA: Will you marry me, if I cure you?

FANFANI: If it will save me, I will swallow the bitter pill.

## No. 17– Melodramatic Music

MIRADILLO (*Consoling Fanfani*): That's it! You will soon be better!

NAKID: It wasn't poison! It is only plain, common, ordinary cider!

BUCCAMETTA: Then rise, my love, and live by my side!

FANFANI (*Rising crestfallen*): Under these circumstances, I'll consider the marriage question. Oh, unlucky me!

(*A cloud appears on horizon at back. As Chorus sing behind scenes L., Miradillo goes up and down on extreme L.*)

CHORUS (O.S)
Mira, mira, Fata Morgana!

TESSA: What does this mean?

MIRADILLO: It is a mirage. An optical illusion frequently seen in deserts, by which remote objects are distinctly seen.

(*Cloud gradually becomes more and more transparent until it is seen as a Fata Morgana: A small chapel before which Titania and Antarsid are standing hand in hand. The Priest stands in the entrance giving them his blessing. Antarsid and Titania walk down C. embracing.*)

ANTARSID: Let me present to you my bride!

FANFANI: And Miradillo?

BUCCAMETTA: Oh, that was…

FANFANI (*Groaning*): More cider. Bang goes two millions.

BUCCAMETTA (*Throwing herself in his arms*): But dearest, you have me instead!

# Finale

*(Enter Chorus LUE. singing. They form two lines across the stage, women in front.)*

CHORUS
Hurrah, Bayram, let all be glad and gay,

MIRADILLO
Allah, Allah, vouch safes us joy
this day,
Allah! Vouch safes us joy this day,
Bayram! Let us be glad and gay!

MIRADILLO
Tribes from the desert,
rejoice with us today,

PRINCIPALS
Man doth propose,

CHORUS
—Allah hail!

PRINCIPALS
God does dispose,

CHORUS
—Bayram,

PRINCIPALS
And therefore we accede to his decree!

CHORUS
Hail hurrah! Hurrah!
Hail!

MIRADILLO
Our adventures are o'er,
And to Naples go we four,
And when there, happy we,
As in Paradise will be,
As in Paradise will be!

TESSA *and* BUCCAMETTA
Our adventures are o'er,
And to Naples go we four,
And when there, happy we,
As in Paradise will be.

MIRADILLO *and* FANFANI
Far away, from this land,
Now go we four,
(And when there) as happy we,
As in Paradise will be.

> CHORUS
> Far away, from this land go they!

(*All march upstage in three straight lines.*)

TESSA, BUCCAMETTA, MIRADILLO, NAKID *with* *Tenor*,
FANFANI *and* CHORUS
Together to that land,
(We/they) go with glee,
Vedere Napoli,
E poi morire;
(*All march down stage again*)
But there to live in joy,
More pleases me,
Vedere Napoli,
E mai morir.

(*Divide in C. Chorus back to sides. Principals divide a little for picture pointing upstage.*)

NAKID *and* CHORUS                    TESSA, BUCCAMETTA,
                                      MIRADILLO *and* FANFANI

May good luck attend you,             Away,
Heaven blessings send you,            Away,
Pleasant breezes waft you             To our
To your home, hurrah!                 Dear home, hurrah!

# CURTAIN

# GLOSSARY

| | |
|---|---|
| Ashantis | Ethnic group of the Ashanti Empire (1701-1957) located in what is now southern Ghana. |
| Backshish | A tip given in exchange for a service. It is also used generally throughout to mean "money". |
| Bagatelle | A game derived from billiards. |
| Barque | Archaic term for a sailing ship. |
| Basutos | A tribe based in South Africa, now called the "Sotho" people. |
| Bayram | A national or religious festival. In this case it is used in reference to a celebration at the end of Ramadan that coincides with the rising of the water of the River Nile. |
| Bedouins | An Arabic group descended from the nomads of the Arabian and Syrian deserts. |
| Chibouk | A Turkish pipe with a long stem. |
| Circassian | A member of the Sunni Muslim peoples of the North West Caucasus. |
| Cofferdam | A temporary enclosure built over water, which is then pumped out to create a dry working environment. |
| Coptic | A Christian group situated in modern Egypt, Sudan and Libya. |
| Dahomey | An African kingdom which lasted from c.1600-1894, until it was defeated by the French and became part of the French colonial empire. It was located close to present day Benin and was known for having an all-female military unit called the "Dahomey Amazons". |

Derwish flute — Instrument (also called the "ney") used during meditation practices in Turkey involving spinning and dancing.

Frankish man — Originally the Franks were a group of Germanic and also Gaul tribes who became the ancestors of the modern day French people. However the term is used in this instance, as it was at the time, as a synonym for "western European".

Imshi — From the Arabic "miši", meaning "go!"

Kafirs — An Arabic term used to describe a person who does not believe in God, however it was adopted in English and Dutch up until the early 20th century as a general term for Southern African people.

Kemenche — A group of stringed folk instruments from Greece, Iran and Turkey.

Khoekhoe — A tribe based in Southern Africa.

Kush — An ancient civilisation based in what is now the south of Egypt, and would today be referred to as "Nubian".

Maraschino — A Croatian liquer.

Mill dam — A dam that creates a pond providing energy to a watermill.

Muezzin — Muslim prayer-leader.

Nargileh — Turkish smoking instrument also called a "hookah".

Odalisque — A maid of a Turkish harem.

Philomel — The "princess of Athens" from Greek mythology. The story goes that the Gods turned her into a nightingale so that she could flee from her brother-in-law, who had attacked and raped her.

| | |
|---|---|
| Phoebus | Olympian God in Greek and Roman mythology, also known as Apollo. |
| Ramadan | A period of fasting during the ninth month of the Islamic calendar. |
| Roué | A womanizer. |
| Scheherazade | Arabic queen and storyteller of One Thousand and One Nights. |
| Spice Island | A small group of islands north-east of Indonesia that were once the largest producers of nutmeg, mace, pepper and cloves in the world. |
| Sou | Originally a French coin of low value, it is now used generally to infer a very small amount of money. |
| Strychnine | A poison commonly used as a pesticide. |
| Tarabuka | A drum used in the Middle East, North Africa, South Asia and Eastern Europe. |
| Tel-el-Kebir | A battle that was fought between the British and the Egyptians in 1882. Britain wanted to protect its financial and territorial interests within Egypt, especially the Suez Canal, during a rebellion of Egyptian officers. |
| Tsad | Arabic word for "Chad", which borders Egypt. |
| Yataghan | A long, sharp-bladed Ottoman knife. |

# SYNOPSIS

# ACT 1

Miradillo, an explorer with little money, leaves his home and fiancée, Tessa, in Palermo, Italy, in order to penetrate the recesses of Africa. He arrives in Cairo, Egypt, and takes lodgings in the Hotel Pharone, however he is not courageous enough to leave the city. Pericles, the hotel owner, soon becomes tired of Miradillo being unable to pay and threatens to have him sent to prison if he cannot pay is dues. Sebil, a servant, implores Pericles not to be so angry with Miradillo, as she is in love with him and he has promised to buy her and free her from the life of a slave.

Miradillo is about to be ejected from the hotel, after hearing of the imminent arrival of the rich heiress Titania, when Prince Antarsid appears on the scene. He wishes to take lodgings at the hotel, however they have all been booked in preparation for Titania's arrival. Titania soon arrives and it is immediately apparent that the two are attracted to each other. Titania offers to share the rooms equally between herself, Antarsid and their respective parties.

Titania, however, is in a quandary herself; her fortune of two million francs, which is in the keeping of her uncle, Fanfani Pasha, will be forfeited if she is not married before her 19<sup>th</sup> birthday. She had told the Pasha that she would be arriving with a husband, however she has none. With her birthday the following day, she must find a husband quickly before her uncle finds out. After recognising Miradillo from some business in Naples, they resolve to help each other; she will pay Miradillo's debts if he pretends to be her husband.

Fanfani becomes suspicious when he hears the news of the matrimony. He senses that all is not as it seems, and blames Miradillo for robbing him of the two million francs that he has already squandered. Titania reluctantly pays Miradillo's hefty hotel bill in the hope that all will soon be settled and she can return to Palermo.

Antarsid approaches Fanfani to buy some slaves, much to the disapproval of Titania. He vows that he will change his ways if they can be together.

Meanwhile, Tessa, Miradillo's fiancée from Palermo, and her mother, Buccametta, have followed the young explorer to Cairo and are not getting on well with the Egyptian way of life. They meet Fanfani, who seems to have taken a fancy to Tessa, but she only has eyes for her Miradillo. The Pasha reveals that he has 46 wives in his harem, and that Miradillo is staying at the Hotel Pharone with his 'wife', Titania. Tessa and Buccametta are distraught at the news, and Fanfani consoles them by inviting them to stay with him at his villa. When Miradillo appears, they veil themselves so as not to be recognised by him. In order to free Titania of Miradillo, and unaware of her attachment to Antarsid, Fanfani Pasha invites them to accompany him to dinner where he can further his plot.

While preparing for the party, Sebil insists that Miradillo has bought her, which he eventually admits, much to the shock and disapproval of the onlookers. They worry about what Titania will think of her 'husband' fraternising with the slave girl, however she seems too busy to notice, with her attention firmly on Antarsid. She invites him to be her guest at the feast, and the act closes with their departure.

# ACT 2

The act opens in the garden of Fanfani's villa. He is whipping his slaves into shape when Miradillo appears and tries to stop him from his cruel behaviour. Fanfani accuses Miradillo of not being Titania's real husband and tries to offer him a share of the inheritance if he admits to the deceit, however he declines. Fanfani decides to continue with his original plan; he has reserved a kiosk for Miradillo and Titania to share, which they would not agree to if they were indeed not married. Miradillo, much to Fanfani's surprise, goes along with the plan and leaves to tell Titania of the 'good news'.

Tessa and Buccametta, meanwhile, appear to have taken to Egyptian life quite nicely. They are plotting revenge on the scoundrel Miradillo when Fanfani proposes that Tessa become his 47th wife. She deliberates the idea, to exact revenge on Miradillo, however her mother appears to have fallen for the Pasha in this short time. Fanfani refuses her overt advances, and she eventually agrees that her daughter should marry him.

Titania and Antarsid are falling more in love with each moment, and with Antarsid unaware of the fake marriage, they begin to lose all discretion. They are witnessed sharing an intimate moment, and Miradillo informs Antarsid that this behaviour is inappropriate, which makes him think that Miradillo is in love with Titania. With everyone having seen this interaction, they become increasingly suspicious as Miradillo and Titania share a whispered conversation. Miradillo wishes to go ahead with the Pasha's plan to share a kiosk so as to appear as a real married couple, however Titania is horrified at the idea. She threatens him with a gun, and he eventually accepts her decision. He realises he is in a tricky situation; his 'wife' has threatened him, Antarsid seems intent on a duel as he thinks that Miradillo wants to be with Titania, and the Pasha is trying to bribe him into admitting the false marriage. He decides it would be best for him to leave unnoticed.

Meanwhile, Fanfani has met with Nakid, the local poison dealer, who attempts to sell him Revenge Dates, which make the eater sneeze every time they try to kiss somebody. Fanfani threatens him and accuses him of being a con. Nakid is enraged and vows revenge, which he plans to take at the feast that evening.

Titania implores Antarsid to abduct her in order to avoid the 'advances' of Miradillo. He agrees to 'abduct' her at the feast, as long as they can leave together. Titania becomes hopeful that Antarsid may marry her before the term expires, meaning that she would be entitled to the inheritance after all.

Tessa appears and reveals her identity and despair to Titania for having 'stolen' her fiancée. Titania explains the marriage is a farce, and that if she had been more patient she could have had Miradillo after all. Miradillo appears, and Tessa veils herself again in order to get a confession from him. Not realising that she is in fact his fiancée, he flirts with her after she confesses his love for him, and begins to fancy himself as somewhat of a ladies' man. Tessa becomes upset and eventually gives up her identity. Miradillo is shocked and begs her forgiveness for his unfaithfulness, however she threatens to go back to join the Pasha's harem unless he drops the façade with Titania. He refuses, and Fanfani arrives on the scene with the belief that Miradillo is trying to seduce Tessa. Miradillo refuses to accept that Tessa could marry the Pasha, and they share a kiss. In order to continue the deceit, he reveals that he and Titania allow each other to do as they please, and that it is an 'open' marriage. Fanfani wants more than ever to get rid of Miradillo for good, having stolen the affections of his latest wife and his money, and enlists the help of Antarsid to have him abducted. Tessa joins the Pasha's harem, as Miradillo cannot break off the deal with Titania. He also asks the Prince to abduct Tessa so that they can be together, and so Antarsid can be with Titania; an offer which he agrees to also.

The feast begins, and the slaves pass around the dates, which Nakid has laced with his poison. Soon all of the guests begin sneezing, much to Nakid's delight. The flood arrives, marking the end of Ramadan, and the boat appears with Antarsid's men, who seize Titania (under her own instruction), Miradillo (under Fanfani's instruction) and Tessa (under Miradillo's instruction). They all board the boat, while Fanfani watches on in a state of confusion. He orders his men to stop them, however they are thwarted by Antarsid's followers.

# ACT 3

The act opens in a desert oasis. Antarsid is in a dreamlike state having taken his love and rescued Miradillo and Tessa. Tessa, however, doubts Miradillo's fidelity and suspects him of flirting with the slave girls. Antarsid hatches a plan to test his faithfulness and instructs Tessa to hide in one of the tents so that they can tell Miradillo that she has been kidnapped and needs to be rescued. Antarsid informs Miradillo that he wishes to marry Titania that very day, however Miradillo objects to keep up appearances of the false marriage between himself and Titania. Antarsid reveals that he knows of the plot, and Titania releases Miradillo from his obligations. She informs him that his share of the money has been deposited in the bank under Tessa's name. Miradillo accepts that he will no longer be a travelling bachelor, and instead will marry Tessa. He asks after her, and Antarsid and Titania inform him that she has been kidnapped in the night by Fanfani, and taken to the Interior of Africa. Miradillo decides that he will have to buck up the courage to explore the country after all in order that he finds his future wife. Titania and Miradillo try their best to scare him so that he does not go, and will instead go back to Naples with them, however he displays the required courage by saying that he will not go unless he has Tessa by his side.

Tessa is elated that Miradillo really does love her, and reveals her hiding place stating that she managed to escape. However it is not long before the Pasha actually is hot on their heels. Titania and Antarsid flee the camp and head for the nearest chapel so that they can marry. The others hatch a plan to delay Fanfani until the deed is done to ensure that he does not retain the money that is rightfully Titania's. The Bedouins storm the camp under the command of Fanfani and search the tents. He finds Miradillo, and exclaims his disbelief that Antarsid duped him by taking all of them away. He demands that Tessa appear before him, and she soon enters with a tray of drinks. She greets Fanfani, and tells him that she has a plan to kill Miradillo because of his deceit, which Fanfani welcomes heartily. She reveals that the bottle of wine that Miradillo is drinking from contains poison, and encourages the Pasha to share a drink with him from the other bottle. He agrees, and Miradillo makes a show of making friends with the Pasha again. Fanfani humours him, believing that he will die soon, until Tessa rushes in, feigning horror, stating that the bottles must have been switched and that Fanfani is actually drinking the poison. He rolls around on the floor, calling for Nakid, who says he cannot help, until Buccametta appears, having once again followed the party to the desert, and says she will save the Pasha if he will take her as his wife. Fanfani hastily agrees, before Nakid reveals that there was never any poison at all!

Amidst the din, a mirage appears showing Titania and Antarsid getting married. They have wed on her 19th birthday, meaning that Fanfani must give up the inheritance after all. Miradillo and Tessa are free to be together, and the four declare that they will leave for Naples after an eventful trip to Africa, with Buccametta staying in Cairo to join the Pasha's harem.

# HISTORICAL REVIEWS

## Austrian Reviews

Suppé is a Southerner—he needs a deep blue sky, warm, fragrant air, hot-blooded people, vibrant colours, glowing sunshine and moonlight and magical nights to decorate his musical sensations. He found it all in "A Trip To Africa"! – *Morgen Post, 18ᵗʰ March 1883*

Suppé's latest opera "A Trip to Africa" will help the composer's popularity to increase, because the majority of the marches, waltzes, solos and ensemble pieces included in the Operetta will so easily please the ears of the crowds. Through the medium of military bands and street organs we soon expect those melodies to become property of our youths and people on the streets. – *Neue Freie Press, 18ᵗʰ March 1883*

So we travel back to Africa! Suppé is at his best since "Fatinitza" and "Boccaccio". He is cheerful, lively, witty, he brings fresh, joyful melodies and adds on top of that a pair of intimate love songs. – *Wiener Salonblatt, 18ᵗʰ March 1883*

A newcomer in the theatre would say it was an unheard of success; we add, a shouting and noise that you almost forfeited the hearing! Everything and everyone were applauded, cheered; you just distinguish the forte of the Opera under the fortissimo of the public! – *Wiener Zeitung, 19ᵗʰ March 1883*

A light, funny—something that was previously almost unthinkable—quite decent libretto (by Richard Genée and Moritz West) and a peculiar, mostly characteristic, often downright brilliant music, rich in lovely vocal numbers characterise "A Trip to Africa". – *Lyra, Vienna, 1ˢᵗ April 1883*

Suppé always achieves instrumental efficacy, as in general the nature of its instrumentation has a very peculiar charm. Even if it is what we consider familiar it has a new guise. And he really knows how to dress it nicely with pleasant successful couplets, sparkling dance rhythms and finely composed ensemble sets. – *Salzburger Volksblatt, 20ᵗʰ October 1885*

## American and European Reviews

This is a most amusing comic opera, produced with splendid scenic effects, and the music is delightfully enchanting. – *Cambridge Chronicle, Massachusetts, 22nd March 1884*

This charming opera has had a long run, but not longer than it deserves. The music is pleasing, the singing excellent, the acting spirited, the scenery beautiful, the costumes gorgeous and the stage setting very artistic. – *Cambridge Chronicle, Massachusetts, 26th April 1884*

The immediate production of Suppé's tuneful and amusing comic opera "A Trip to Africa" is promising, having music and fun enough in it to keep it on the boards an indefinite period. – *Daily Alta California, 30th March 1884*

"A Trip to Africa" is a piquant opera, and that is what all the papers, both German and English, write about it; and we do not hesitate to endorse their opinion...– *Chigagoer Arbeiter Zeitung, 2nd June 1884*

The music is said to be bright, sparkling, vivacious, and catchy. – *The Argonaut, N.15, Jan-Jun 1884*

The music is inventive and witty...– *Svensk Musiktidning, Sweden, 1st March 1885*

The piece is certainly well done and a visit to it will result in satisfying both the eye and the ear. – *New York Dramatic Mirror, 1884-1886*

"A Trip to Africa" is, in short, one of the brightest and most musical of modern light opera. – *Sacramento Daily Union, 15th October 1892*

One of von Suppé's operas that is both pretty and rich. It contains more refreshing music than several of his other works combined, and in the matter of ensembles, rich choruses, fine orchestration, beautiful numbers, there are but few works that can equal it. It is full of spirit and brilliancy, and the scenic equipment is superb. – *Philadelphia Inquirer 29th August 1897*

The music is very tuneful and in quality above the average, while the story is amply amusing. – *Brooklyn Life from Brooklyn, 24th September 1898*

The melodies run into tuneful success in a drinking song, a sneezing chorus, and some clever dance music. – *New York Times, 27th September 189*

(Overleaf) 1887 production playbill – 3 page playbill advertising the operetta's run in Philadelphia in 1887. Pictured are Lilian Russell as Titania Fanfani, Vernona Jarbeau as Tessa, Zelda Seguin as Buccametta, Harry S. Hilliard as Antarsid and J.H.Ryley as Fanfani Pasha. Interestingly Hilliard and Seguin are pictured in their costumes, whereas the others are in normal clothes. Performing Arts (1887) reported on the success of one of Vernona Jarbeau's performances. The writer states that 3,000 people crowded into Philadelphia's Academy of Music to hear the Duff Opera Company perform Von Suppe's "A Trip to Africa". The cast was described as "strong" and included Lillian Russell and Jarbeau. Dario Salvi Collection.

# EXTRA!

## AMERICAN ⁛ ACADEMY ⁛ OF ⁛ MUSIC.

### A COMIC OPERA FESTIVAL.

A bright opera, mirthful in every word and musical in every line, a chorus both pretty and tuneful, a cast of stars who fit their parts like a glove the hand, costumes bright, pleasing and tasteful, scenery actually new and strikingly beautiful, and an orchestra that interprets the melody without drowning it, made Monday night charming and render the week brilliant with promise at the Opera House. Of Franz Von Suppé's opera "A Trip to Africa," the assertion can be truthfully and confidently made that it is one of the most inspiring of the productions of the composer of "Fatinitza." It is as light as champagne and as sparkling.—*Chicago Times.*

## *Monday Evening, February 7th.*

### ONE WEEK ONLY.

## GRAND SPECTACULAR PRODUCTION

OF

# "A TRIP TO AFRICA"

BY THE

## J. C. DUFF

## COMIC OPERA COMPANY,

## 150 PEOPLE.

### Artists, Chorus and Grand Orchestra,

FORMING AN ENSEMBLE OF

### *UNRIVALLED MAGNITUDE AND MERIT!*

(SEE LIST OF ARTISTS, NEXT PAGE.)

*Tuesday Evening Feby 8th 1887*

## MONDAY EVENING, FEBRUARY 7th.

(ONE WEEK ONLY.)

EMINENT ARTISTS ENGAGED:

# MISS LILLIAN RUSSELL,

*(HER FIRST APPEARANCE IN SPECTACULAR OPERA.)*

"A revelation, even to her admirers."—*Chicago Tribune.*

| MISS VERNONA JARBEAU, | MRS. ZELDA SEGUIN, |
|---|---|
| MISS MADELINE LUCETTE, | MISS HORTENSE CLEVELAND, |
| MR. HARRY HILLIARD, | MR. J. H. RYLEY, |
| MR. CHAS. DUNGAN, | MR. FRANKLIN BOUDINOT, |

and other Prominent Artists.

**A CHORUS OF SIXTY.**

**AN INCREASED ORCHESTRA.**

**SUPERB SPECTACULAR SCENERY.**

(Exhibited for the first time in Philadelphia.)

# J. C. DUFF'S

# Comic Opera Co.

IN VON SUPPE'S OPERA IN THREE ACTS, ENTITLED

# "A TRIP TO AFRICA,"

WITH THE FOLLOWING

## UNAPPROACHABLE CAST OF LYRIC ARTISTS.

| | |
|---|---|
| TITANIA FANFANI | LILLIAN RUSSELL |
| FANFANI PASHA, her Uncle | J. H. RYLEY |
| ANTARSIA, Prince of the Mironites | HARRY S. HILLIARD |
| MIRADILLO, a European Traveler | C. W. DUNGAN |
| PERICLES, Hotel Keeper | JOHN E. NASH |
| SIBIL, a Slave | HORTENSE CLEVELAND |
| HASH, Hotel Servant | J. E. FOX |
| TESSA, a French Milliner | VERNONA JARBEAU |
| BUCCAMETTA, her Aunt | ZELDA SEGUIN |
| A MUEZZEIN | FRANKLIN BOUDINOT |
| A MIRONITE | EDWARD E. WEBB |
| FIRST SAIS | ARTHUR UNDERWOOD |
| SECOND SAIS | A. W. McDOWELL |

SYNOPSIS OF SCENERY.

ACT I.—PUBLIC SQUARE, CAIRO, EGYPT.

ACT II.—BANKS OF THE RIVER NILE. (THE RISING OF THE WATERS)

ACT III.—AN OASIS IN THE GREAT DESERT.

*Only Matinee, Saturday, February 12th, at 2.*

TEXT DER GESÄNGE:

# DIE AFRIKAREISE.

OPERETTE IN 3 ACTEN

VON

M. WEST UND RICHARD GENÉE.

MUSIK VON FR. V. SUPPÉ

VERLAG VON AUG. CRANZ IN HAMBURG.
WIEN, C. A. SPINA, VERLAGS UND KUNSTHANDLUNG
(ALWIN CRANZ).

BRÜSSEL A. CRANZ.

1883

# PERSONNEN

MIRADILLO ................................................................. ein Europäer

TITANIA FANFANI

FANFANI PASHA ........................................................... ihr Oheim

ANTARSID .............................................................ein Maronitenfürst

TESSA................................................... Putzmacherin aus Palermo

BUCCAMETTA ........................................................... ihre Mutter

PERIKLES.......................................................... Hotelier in Cairo

NAKID .......................................................ein koptischer Gifthändler

SEBIL...............................................eine abessynische Sklavin

HOSH.............................................Hausknecht bei Perikles

EIN MUEZZIN

EIN MARONITE

EIN LASTTRÄGER

ERSTER SAIS (VORLÄUFER)

ZWEITER SAIS (VORLÄUFER)

Maroniten, Hoteldiener, Gäste bei Fanfani-Pascha, Sklavenhändler, Sklaven, Tänzerinnen, Arabisches Volk.

Ort der Handlung:    Act I: Im "Hotel Pharaone" in Cairo
                             Act II: Auf Fanfani-Pascha's Landsitz am Nil
                             Act III: In der Wüste
                             Zeit:                          Gegenwart

# DIE AFRIKAREISE

## ERSTER ACT

## No. 1 – Introduction

CHOR
Sehnsuchsvoll erwarten wir
Gäste aus Europa hier,
Wenn sie angekommen frisch,
Da zahlen sie uns Backschisch!

Backschisch! Backschisch,
Ist die Hauptsach' hier!
Backschisch rufen Alle wir!
Ja, Backschisch da—
Backschisch dort—
Immer fort
Ein schönes Wort!

Kling! kling! kling!
Backschisch! Backschisch
Lernt Jeder schnell versteh'n!
Backschisch, Backschisch
Wo man mag immer steh'n!

Backschisch vorn und Backschisch hinten
Ueberall ertönt!
Backschisch Jeder kennt,
Backschisch, Mordelement!

Backschisch ist ein schönes Wort,
Backschisch ist die Hauptsach' hier;
Backschisch rufen Alle wir!
Backschisch da, Backschisch dort,
Tönt es immer fort und fort!

PERIKLES
Backschisch! Backschisch!
Schreit doch nicht so albern,'s ist ein Graus!
Hol' der Teufel solch' ein Haus!
Im Hotel "zum Pharaonen"
Könnten hundert Gäste wohnen;
Doch dies Jahr bleibt Alles aus!

CHOR
Das ärgert ihn! Hahaha!

SEBIL
Ihr vergeßt den Frankenmann!

PERIKLES
Miradillo, dieser Lump,
Der lebt nobel hier auf Pump!

SEBIL
Schmäht ihn nicht!

PERIKLES
's ist ein Wicht!

SEBIL
Er wird zahlen, wenn er kann!

PERIKLES
Wenn er heut' gezahlt nicht hat,
Muß er mit auf's Consulat!

SEBIL
Nein—nein—nein!

PERIKLES
So soll's sein!

SEBIL
Miradillo wird mich kaufen—
Laß mich taufen,
Will entlaufen!

Ja–ja, so ist's,
Bald zieh' ich fort,
Sehr weit von hier—
Er hat's versprochen mir!
Miradillo gab mir sein Wort!

PERIKLES
Ha! das nenn' ich einen Schwindel!
Hat im Sack nicht einen Sou,
Macht rebellisch das Gesindel,
Kauft noch Sklavinnen dazu!

CHOR
Haha, haha, haha!

PERIKLES
Still Ihr Laffen!
Papageien!
Wie die Affen
Lachen sie!

Backschisch! Backschisch könnt Ihr schreien,
Doch verdienen könnt Jhr's nie!

SEBIL UND CHOR
Kling! kling! kling!
Backschisch! Backschisch
Lernt Jeder schnell versteh'n!
*Etc.*

PERIKLES (*zugleich*)
Jetzt hab' ich's endlich satt!
Er muß auf's Consulat!
Der Prahler—der Schwindler!
Immer nobel thun und pumpen
Das ist Brauch bei jedem Lumpen!
Ja, er muß—
Jetzt hab' ich's endlich satt—
Auf's Consulat!

Warte nur, ich zeige Dir

Unsere Landessitte hier!
Pumpen da—pumpen dort
Soll vergeh'n Dir sofort!
Der Lump!!

MIRADILLO
Ist hier von mir die Rede?

SEBIL
Er schmähet Dich ganz offenbar!

MIRADILLO
Wie? Helene?

SEBIL
Und nannte Dich'nen Schwindler gar!

MIRADILLO
Was muß ich hören?

SEBIL
Er sagt, Du lebtest hier auf Pump;
Mit einem Wort, Du sei'st ein Lump!

MIRADILLO
Das ist stark! Schon genug!—
Du Thor, der das gewagt,
Der sich darob beklagt;—
Mir pumpen—ist vielmehr
Für Dich die größte Ehr'!

PERIKLES
So—so?

MIRADILLO
Respekt vor mir und wißt—
Ich bin ein Welt-Tourist!

PERIKLES
Von mir aus seid Ihr was Ihr wollt;
Zahlt mir die Rechnung wie Ihr sollt!

MIRADILLO
Halt ein!
O sprich nicht weiter!
Wißt, was das ist:
Ein Welt-Tourist?!

ALLE
Nein! Nein!

MIRADILLO
Nun denn! Erfahren sollt Ihr es sogleich
—Paßt Alle auf, ich sag' es Euch!

I.
Ich durchschiffe alle Seen
Wenn gerade keine Stürme,
Keine Stürme wehen;
Ich berechne alle Höhen,—
Nur die zu hoch sind,
Die zu hoch sind laß' ich gehen!

Ich durchstreife alle Zonen,
Wo nicht böse Menschen wohnen;
Ich bin groß in Nivellirung,
Kenne auch Triangulirung;
Den rabiat'sten Meridian
Den pack' ich mit dem Nonius an!

Nur Entdecken ist mir Leidenschaft!—
D'rum reise ich zu Zwecken
Der modernen Wissenschaft!
Europa giebt Moneten
Für die Expedition—
Entdecker mit Diäten
Bin ich von Profession!

Man preiset mich als Geograf,
Als Kosmo-Ethno-Topograf;

Mit Hottentotten Hab' ich mir
Die Zeit gar oft verkürzt!

Dann an der Pfefferküste
Die Mahlzeit mir gewürzt.

Beim König von Dahome
Hab' soupirt ich, oft dinirt—
Und im Serail mich amüsirt!
Bin beliebt bei den Basuto's,
Kenne Congo, Zanzibar;
Auch die Kaffern, die Aschanti,
Die besuch' ich jedes Jahr!

Ja, das Geschäft ist profitabel,
Mein Renomee ganz formidabel,
Der Telegraf, die Post, das Kabel
Verkünden meinen Ruhm der Welt! Ja!

CHOR
Das Geschäft ist profitabel!
*Etc.*

PERIKLES
Schwindler! Prahler! Filou!
Hat doch kein Geld!

II
MIRADILLO
Nicht nur bei den Völkern
Afrika's werd' ich genannt,
Selbst auch in der Thierwelt
Bin ich ringsherum bekannt!

Alle mich begrüßen,
Ob auf zwei, ob auf vier Füßen!
Casuar, Strauß und Papagei'n
Fangen freudig an zu schrei'n;

Antilopen, wenn sie mich
Von Weitem kommen seh'n
Bleiben gleich mit ehrfurchtsvollem
Nicken vor mir steh'n!

Löwen kenn' gewöhnlich,
Sowie Tiger ich persönlich,
Grüß' sie im Vorübergeh'n!
Und die lieben, kleinen Affen,
Die Gazellen, die Giraffen
Eilen alle mir entgegen,
Sich zu Füßen mir zu legen!

Selbst die größten Elefanten
Zähle ich zu den Bekannten;
Hab' auch mit Rhinozerossen
Warme Freundschaft schon geschlossen!

Kein Fels und keine Schlucht,
Ja selbst kein Krater bleibt intakt,
Von Allem nehm' ich Akt,
Dring' in jedem Katarakt:

Vom höchsten Gipfel bis hinab
Zum tiefen Meeresgrund
Bemüh' ich mich um einen selt'nen Fund!

Petrefakten, Mineralien,
Blumen, Pflanzen, Naturalien,
Alles wird durchsucht, zerhackt—
Schließlich sorgsam eingepackt!

Ja das Geschäft ist profitable
*Etc.*

*Dann:*
Bin der größte Geograf,
Kosmo-Ethno-Topograf!
Kenn' ganz Afrika,
Jeder Berg—auch jedes Thal—
Selbst all' die Grotten,
Schluchten ohne Zahl,
Auf dem Erdenball,
Da war ich überall!

PERIKLES
Prahler! Schwindler! Ein Erz-Filou!
Alles Lug, Alles Trug!
Schwindeleien sind es ohne Zahl,
Und auf jeden Fall
Kennt man ihn überall!

CHOR
Geograf! Topograph!
Alles liegt ja vor ihm da!
Geograf! Topograf!
Ja, er kennt jeden Berg,
Auch jedes Thal;

Selbst all' die Schluchten,
Grotten ohne Zahl;
Auf dem Erdenball,
Da war er überall!

MIRADILLO
Nun hast Du's genau vernommen,
Was das ist: Ein Welt-Tourist!

PERIKLES
Hab's begriffen ganz und gar;
Doch nun zahlt auch blank und baar!

MIRADILLO
Einst wirst Du Dein Geld bekommen,
Wenn's nicht augenblicklich ist!

PERIKLES
Das klingt wahrlich sehr kurios!
Ohne Geld kommt er nicht los!

MIRADILLO
Auch diese Sklavin setz' auf Rechnung,
Da die Kleine mir gefällt!

PERIKLES
Lauter Rechnung und Berechnung,

Immer kaufen ohne Geld!

MIRADILLO
Hast Du nicht gehört. Helene,
Daß Europa für mich zahlt?

PERIKLES
Diese Zahlstell' ich nicht kenne—
Die Geduld verlier' ich bald!
Der Muezzin!—Still!

MUEZZIN
Ya rezzak!
Ya kerim!
Ya fellah!
Ya alim!

PERICLES UND CHOR
Ya rezzak!
Ya kerim!
Ya fellah!
Ya alim!

MUEZZIN
Moslim!
Bald ist vorbei der letzte Ramadan!
Erkennet Allah!

CHOR
Allah!

MUEZZIN
Moslim!
Zum Beiramfeste kleidet neu Euch an
Und preiset Allah!
CHOR
Allah!

MUEZZIN
Ya rezzak! Ya kerim!
Ya fellah! Ya alim!

CHOR (*repetiert*)

PERIKLES
Bald vorbei ist Ramadan,
Beiramfest kommt gleich heran!
Freude dann in jedem Haus—
Nacht für Nacht bei Tanz und Schmaus!
Eilt! Der Zug kommt an um Vier!
Fremde dann bekommen wir.

DIE HOTELDIENER
Juchhe! Famos!
Dann geht es los!
Ja wohl!—Doch nun
Gibt's auch zu thun!
Er ist bald hier!
Sputet Euch, flink und frisch!

PERIKLES
Diesen Eifer kenn ich schon!

DIE HOTELDIENER
Bald schon winkt uns Backschisch!

PERIKLES
Ach, Backschisch, du Zauberton!
Ja, das ist ein Raubgesindel,
Schlimmer noch als ich schon bin!
Nichts als Geldgier, Trug und Schwindel;

Bringt es ihnen nur Gewinn!
Wie sie jubeln und sich freuen!
Schreien, lärmen können sie!
Backschisch, Backschisch!
Könnt ihr schreien,
Doch verdienen könnt Ihr's nie!

CHOR
Vorwärts zur Bahn!
Backschisch giebt's dann!
Hahaha! Hahaha!

Kling! Kling! Kling!
Backschisch!Backschisch
Lernt Jeder schnell versteh'n—
*Etc.*

## No. 2 – Lied mit Chor

SAIS
Platz dem Prinzen Antarsid!
Heil ihm! Heil ihm!
Der dieses Haus beglückt!

CHOR
Schnelle, schnelle
Klinge Helle
Ihm entgegen
Rings herum
Ein frohes kräftiges Hurrah!
Heil dem Prinzen Antarsid,
Heil ihm dem Falken Libanon's!

DIE PAGEN
Mit Lust ziehen wir dahin
Durch Wiesengrün
Bald hier, bald dort,
Von Ort zu Ort,

Wie Morgenwind,
Geschwind, geschwind!
Was auch immer kommen mag,
Neues bringt uns jeder Tag!

I.
ANTARSID
Wie die Gazelle
Munter und schnelle
Dahin fliegt leicht beschwingt:
Flieget mein Roß
Folget mein Troß
Meinem Wink unbedingt!

Mit Lust und Frohgefühl
Nah'n wir uns dem Ziel!

Blühende Gefilde
Zeiget im Bilde
Der Libanon in Pracht;
Rings überall
Des Echo's Schall
In den Bergen erwacht!

Halloh! Halloh! Halloh!
Auf Berg und Thal Halloh!

CHOR
Das Echo schallt, Halloh!
Die Freiheit hoch, Halloh!
Berg und Thal, halloh!
Freiheit, hoch, Halloh!

ANTARSID
Einsamkeit hat mir zu denken dann gegeben
An tausend gold'ne Märchen
Von zärtlich trauten Pärchen.
Liebesglück würde versüßen mir mein Leben;

Wollt' eine Scheherazade
Mir auch etwas erzählen,
Gern würd' ich hören,
Niemals sie stören,
Kein andres Glück mir jemals erwählen, Ach!

Bald dies—bald das.
Bald Ernst—bald Spaß,—

So hätt' den Märchen ich gelauscht!
Bis Liebesglück mich satt berauscht!

ALLE
Bald dies—bald das—
Bald Ernst—bald Spaß—
Stets hätt er so gelauscht

Von Lieb' berauscht!

II.
ANTARSID
Ferne rückt näher,
Sonne steigt höher
Am blauen Himmelszelt!
Wonniges Sein
Frei und allein
In der herrlichen Welt!
hebt sich frei die Brust –
Freiheit ist Mannes Lust!

Möchte das Leben
Mancher doch geben
Für Freiheit nur allein!
Frei laßt uns sein;
,stimmet ein;
Um ein Hoch ihr zu weih'n!

CHOR
|: Die Freiheit, hoch, Halloh!:|

ANTARSID
Doch wenn Dämmerung
 Auf die Fluren wallet nieder,
Die mächt'gen Schatten sinken,
Nur Sterne schimmernd blinken.—

Denkt man sinnend
Der süßen Märchen wieder!
Wollt' eine Scheherazade
Mir auch etwas erzählen,
*Etc.*

## No. 3 – Auftritt Titania's

ALLE
Welch seltnes Bild—
Fast wunderbar—
Stellt sich dem Blick

Hier plötzlich dar!

SEBIL UND NAKID
So bunt—so fremd—
So fesselnd schön
Hab ich so bald noch nichts geseh'n!

CHOR
Wunderbar—
So fremd—so schön—
Noch nichts geseh'n!

TITANIA
Wenn ich nicht irr,
Seh' ich den Wirth vor mir?

PERIKLES
Ganz zu Diensten steht mein Haus!

TITANIA
Sehr gut!
So find ich Aufnahm' hier?

PERIKLES
Ganz ohne Schonung
Werf ich alle andern Gäste aus der Wohnung,
Wies sogar den Maronitenfürsten aus!

ANTARSID
O Gott, wie ist sie schön!

TITANIA
Das wäre ja unhöflich und thät mir leid!

ANTARSID
Es wär' nur Schuldigkeit!

TITANIA UND ANTARSID
Dieser Blicke Feuerstrahlen
Mächtig ziehen sie mich an!
Ja, das wär' ein Bild zum Malen,

Schade nur, daß ich's nicht kann!

PERIKLES
Er scheint verlegen, wortlos steht er da,
Seit er die Fremde sah!

TITANIA
Charmant! Charmant!

PERIKLES
Die Gemächer steh'n bereit,
Wenn's gefällig, jederzeit!

TITANIA
's ist nicht pressant!

SEBIL UND NAKID
Sie scheint so froh und hochentzückt!

TITANIA
Ach wie reizend!

ALLE
Welch seltnes Bild,
Fast wunderbar,
*Etc.*

TITANIA
Wie, mein Herr, Sie wollen fort?
Ich bitt'—ein Wort!—

Mit Bedauern hab' soeben ich vernommen,
Daß durch mich Sie um Ihr Obdach sollen kommen!

Doch ferne lag es mir,
Zu verdrängen Jemand hier!
Dies Haus scheint mir bequem;
Wir können theilen, wenn's genehm!

PERIKLES
Überraschend freundlich kommt

Sie ihm entgegen!

ANTARSID
Viel zu gütig!

TITANIA
Nun?

ANTARSID
Nun, gern ist's acceptirt!

PERIKLES
Ueberlegen wird er kaum—er acceptirt!

TITANIA
Doch—vorausgesetzt—ich bitte,
Daß Euch das nicht genirt!

ANTARSID
Ach, wie warm regt Sympathie
Sich schon für sie!

I.
TITANIA
Wenn fremd wir auch bisher uns sind,
Auf Reisen wird man ja bekannt geschwind.
Wir werden jetzt hier Nachbar'n! sein,
Der Zufall richtet das recht artig ein!

Ich hasse steife Etikette—
Sie drückt gleich einer schweren Kette:
Sie macht das Leben gar nicht heiter;
Verstimmet und quält uns sehr!

Was gern man sieht, darf man nicht sehen,
Was gern man sagte—nicht gestehen,
Wo gern man bliebe, da heißt's "weiter!"
Weil das "genannt" sonst wär'!

|: Ich sag': nur nicht genir'n!:|
Oft läßt sich durch ein Wort

Alles leicht arrangir'n!

CHOR
Bravo! Bravo!

TITANIA UND CHOR
|: Nur nicht genir'n!:|

TITANIA
Es läßt sich leicht arrangir'n!

II.
Auf dem Balkon und beim Caffee
Da rauchen wir vereint das Nargileh!
Ich seh', Sie sind ein Cavalier,
Dem ich gestatten darf, zu huld'gen mir.

Sie werden mich erheitern müssen,
Sie dürfen auch die Hand mir küssen,
Galant für duft'ge Blumen sorgen,
Wenn's g'rade sich so macht!

Sie dürfen plaudern, scherzen, lachen,
Kurz—was man sagt—den Hof mir machen;
Sie wünschen stets mir "guten Morgen,"
Ich Ihnen "gute Nacht."—

|: Ich frag': warum genir'n?:|
Frei muß man diskuriren.
Will man sich orientiren!

## No. 4 – Quartett

FANFANI
Nein das ist nicht möglich!

PERIKLES
Da stehen sie alle Zwei!

TITANIA
Nun spielen Sie erträglich!

MIRADILLO
Verstellung—steh' mir bei!

FANFANI
Er und sie—und sie und er
Ein Ehepaar—
Wer weiß, ob das auch wahr—
Mir ist es noch nicht klar!

TITANIA
Daß ich endlich dich wiederseh',
Theurer Mann!

PERIKLES
Haben Sie's gehört? Hab' ich recht?

TITANIA
Wonnestunden schafft doch die Eh'
Dann und wann!

FANFANI
Die Entdeckung mich empört,
Aus der Haut man fahren möcht';
Einen Gatten hat sie, das ist sehr fatal!

MIRADILLO
Daß ich endlich dich wiederseh',
Süße Frau!

PERIKLES
Offenbar ihr Gemahl!

MIRADILLO
Nun scheint mir die Welt nicht mehr grau—
Himmelblau!

FANFANI
Es ist richtig—ja—fürwahr—
Und jetzt heißt es: Onkel, zahl'!

PERIKLES
Nun ist es evident!

TITANIA UND MIRADILLO
Ruh' ich in deinem Arm,
Wird mir so wohl so warm!

TITANIA
Ich muß ja zärtlich sein,
Die Zweifel zu zerstreu'n!

MIRADILLO
Warum nicht zärtlich sein!
Es bringt ja Geld mir ein!

FANFANI
Zwei Millionen kostet er mich! Unerhört!
Dieser Kerl ist wahrlich keinen Groschen werth!

PERIKLES
Die Wahl, die macht ihm Ehre!
Hier steht das Paar voll Zärtlichkeit
Und hier der Onkel hoch erfreut!

TITANIA
Onkel, liebes Onkelchen,
Hier stelle ich dir vor
Den Mann den ich erkor!
Er ist so lieb, so brav,
So fromm, so gut!

FANFANI
Am liebsten gäbe ich ihm Cyankali ein!

MIRADILLO
Onkel, liebes Onkelchen,
Mein Weib ist excellent!
Jetzt will sie justament
Die Schulden zahl'n für mich,
Das süße Blut!

FANFANI
O, ich danke!
Viel zu gütig!
Was denn nun?

TITANIA
Welch' ein Unsinn, mich zu zwingen!
Doch die Frechheit soll mißlingen!
Ich zahle nicht—
Das ist gemein,
Ist Prellerei!

MIRADILLO
Das gehört ja zur Komödie,
Ist natürlich und gerecht!
Für den Gatten wär's Tragödie
Wenn die Frau nicht für ihn blecht!

Ich spiel' nicht weiter,
Als Ihr Begleiter,
Mir einerlei!

FANFANI
Ach, mir scheint, daß sie schon straiten,
Dieses junge Ehepaar!
Schon beginnen sie auf's Neu'
Die Winselei!

TITANIA UND MIRADILLO
Ruh' ich in deinem Arm,
Wird mir so wohl, so warm!

PERIKLES
Er schaut ganz wild, verdrießlich!

FANFANI
In der Hölle wünsche ich sie alle Zwei;

PERIKLES
Die Eh' scheint ihm nicht recht!

TITANIA UND MIRADILLO
Ich muß ja ⌉ zärtlich sein!
Warum nicht⌋

TITANIA
Die Zweifel zu zerstreu'n!

MIRADILLO
Das bringt ja Geld mir ein!

TITANIA
Lieber Mann!

MIRADILLO
Liebes Weib!

FANFANI
Zwei Millionen muß ich zahlen! Unerhört!
So viel Geld sind alle Beide gar nicht werth
Ja, die Galle bringt mich um,
Muß dabei noch freundlich sein!

PERIKLES
Sich fügen muß er schließlich—
Doch ihm geht's im Kopf herum;
Nicht ganz richtig scheint's zu sein.

TITANIA
Süßes Männchen,
Bist mein Täubchen,
Bist mein Leben!
O Genuß!

Jetzt muß ich ihm gar noch geben
Einen Kuß!
Diesem Lump.

MIRADILLO
Süßes Weibchen,
Bist mein Täubchen,
Bist mein Leben,

O Genuß!

Jetzt mußt du geben
Einen Kuß,—
Nicht auf Pump!

FANFANI
Haderlump!

PERIKLES
s' ist ein Lump!

TITANIA
Nun wohlan den,
Ich will bezahlen!
Herr Wirth—die Rechnung her!

PERIKLES
Ei, das hat ja keine Eile!
Hätte Zeit noch eine Weile!
Doch, da Sie es so befehlen,
Hier die Rechnung—bitte sehr!

TITANIA
Zwölftausend und vierhundert Francs
Für vierzehn Tage nur?

MIRADILLO
Kleinigkeit!

FANFANI
Zwölftausend vierhundert? Ich danke!

TITANIA
Elfhundert Francs für ein Souper
Mit Damen vom Caffee francais?

MIRADILLO
Ich liebe die Musik
Die Leute sangen magnifique!

FANFANI
O, der Hallunke, Galgenstrick!

TITANIA
Sonderbar! Originell!
Ja, ja—das Hab' ich schon in mir,
Daß gern die Kunst ich protegir'!
Zweitausend Francs für das Logis,
Von Fräulein Olga Sanssoucis!

MIRADILLO
Das war'ne arme Waise
Brauchte Geld zur Weiterreise!

FANFANI
Wüstling!

TITANIA
Eine Sklavin für 6000 Francs gekauft!

MIRADILLO
Ja, ja: die will ich erst bekehren—
Schließlich wird sie dann getauft!

FANFANI
Ha solchen Schwindler sah man nie!

TITANIA, MIRADILLO UND PERIKLES
Wie?

FANFANI
Er beschwindelt mich und sie!

DIE DREI
Nie!

FANFANI
Nicht ein einzig Wort ist wahr!

DIE DREI
Ha!

FANFANI
Alles Lüge, das ist klar!

DIE DREI
Nein!

FANFANI
Darum möcht' ich mir diese Ehe—

DIE DREI
Nun?

FANFANI
Erst besehen in der Nähe!

DIE DREI
Das wäre gar nicht schicklich,
Denn (wir/sie) leben glücklich;
Drum hat augenblicklich
Zweifel keinen Zweck!

FANFANI
Sie gelassen—er so findig—
Sie phlegmatisch—er so keck!

Foppen will ich mich nicht lassen,
Er ist mir zu leicht, zu windig!
Sein Gesicht mir antipatisch.
Mich zu täuschen ist der Zweck!

TITANIA UND MIRADILLO
(Er ist/Ich bin) leicht, aber gut,
Etwas wild, doch voll Muth!
O seid nur mild,
Nicht hart—nicht wild!

FANFANI
Dieser Prahler,
Schlechte Zahler
Wär' dein Gatte?
Solch ein Lump?!

PERIKLES
Nur gelassen,
Nicht so kräftig,
Nicht so heftig
Rasch vom Fleck!
O seid doch mild,
Nicht hart—nicht wild!

TITANIA
Ach, lieber Onkel, meine Pflicht
Befiehlt mir dann,
Daß ich vertheid'ge meinen Mann,

Des Aetna's Glut
Erhitzt sein Blut;
Ein Sicilianer Kommt gar leicht in Wuth:

Palermo's Lüfte sind erfüllt
Von Aetna's Lavagluth;
Wer dort gelebt, dem rollet wild
Und feurig stets das Blut!

Dort brausen die Wellen—
Mit wilder Brandung kämpft das Schiff
Im Strudel zerschellen
Sieht man's am Felsenriff!

O la ho! O la ho!
Du sonnig Land,
Wo Feuer dem Vulkan entsprüht,
Wo doppelt heiß
Das Herz in Lieb' erglüht! Ja!

Palermo's Auen
Sind der Erde Paradies
Wie weht die Luft balsamisch da—
Ach, wie süß!

ALLE
Du sonnig Land,
Wo Feuer dem Vulkan entsprüht,

Wo doppelt heiß
Das Herz in Lieb' erglüht! Ja!

Palermo's Auen
Sind der Erde Paradies,
Wie weht die Luft balsamisch da—
Ach, wie süß!

Wo vom Vulkan die Erde rings erbebet,
Bebt auch das Herz
Von Liebesgluth belebet,
Strömt die Lava aus der Erde Tiefen,

Sprüht auch die Brust!
Flammende Lust!

Ja, Feuer glüht in jeder Brust!
Palermo's Lüste sind erfüllt
Von Aetna's Lavagluth,
*Etc. bis.*

Ach wie süß!
Palermo, so gluthvoll,
Balsamisch und süß!

## No. 5 – Terzett

FANFANI
Großen Vollbart tragen,
Häufig „Allah" sagen,
Turban auf dem Schädel,
Mohr mit Pfauenwedel;—

Stets in Morgenschuhen,
Niemals etwas thuen,—
Lange Pfeifen rauchen,
Keine Stühle brauchen.

Auf dem Teppich sitzen,
Niemals sich erhitzen,
Ohne Gabel speisen,

Per Kamel nur reisen.

Große Pracht entfalten,
Einen Harem halten,
Ohne sich zu schämen,
Viele Weiber nehmen,—

Und sie durch Eunuchen
Streng zu hüten suchen!
Nichts als Mocca trinken—
Weder Wein noch Schinken.

Das ist zwar vandalisch,
Aber orientalisch!

ALLE DREI
Das ist zwar vandalisch,
Aber orientalisch!

BUCCAMETTA
Höchst unmoralisch!

ALLE DREI
Orientalisch!—Unmoralisch!

BUCCAMETTA
Fast infernalisch!

ALLE DREI
Orientalisch! Unmoralisch!

BUCCAMETTA
Und theatralisch!

ALLE DREI
Manches ist zwar theatralisch,
Unmoralisch—
Hier zu Land
Jedoch höchst interessant!

II.
TESSA
Oriental'sche Sitten
Sind wohl unbestritten
Auch bei uns zu finden—
Gleich werd' ich's begründen!

Daß in unsern Zonen
Frei die Frauen wohnen,
Sind nur Illusionen,—
Sag' ich ohne Schonen!

Schön geputzt erscheinen
Immer nur für Einen,—
Seinem Wink sich fügen,
Ist zwar kein Vergnügen—

Aber, ach, man sehe
Nur bei uns die Ehe,
Wo die Männer lügen;—
Nur um zu betrügen,

Einer Einz'gen schwören,
Doch sich dann nicht stören
Und getrost daneben
Wie die Türken leben:

's ist nicht orientalisch,
Doch höchst unmoralisch!

ALLE DREI
's ist nicht orientalisch,
Doch höchst unmoralisch!

BUCCAMETTA
Höchst unmoralisch!

ALLE
Orientalisch—unmoralisch!

BUCCAMETTA
Recht infernalisch!

ALLE
Unmoralisch—orientalisch!

BUCCAMETTA
Fast schon vandalisch!

ALLE
Manches ist gar theatralisch—
Unmoralisch
Hier zu Land—
Jedoch höchst int'ressant!

III
BUCCAMETTA
Auch im Occidente
Wie im Oriente
Giebt es Elemente,
Daß man meinen könnte!

Recht intelligente
Und ganz excellente,
Nicht so indolente
Frauen von Talente!

Auch nicht corpulente
Wie im Oriente,
Sind durch Complimente
Machtlos im Momente—

Und durch consequente
Höchst impertinente
Männerregimente
Und Experimente,

Dann auch durch Präsente
Und durch vehemente
Oft recht insolente
Schlechte Argumente,

Unterdrückt moralisch,
Das ist kannibalisch!

ALLE
Unterdrückt moralisch,
Das ist kannibalisch!
Kannibalisch sehr!

BUCCAMETTA
Höchst kannibalisch!

ALLE
Kannibalisch! Unmoralisch!

BUCCAMETTA
Recht infernalisch!

ALLE
Unmoralisch! Kannibalisch!

BUCCAMETTA
Fast schon vandalisch'

ALLE
Manches ist gar
Theatralisch—unmoralisch—
Hier zu Land;
Jedoch höchst int'ressant!

## No. 6 – Finale

CHOR
Hoio! Hoio!
Spielt lustig auf!
Hollaho! Haho!
Schlagt kräftig drauf! Holaho!

Das klingt!
Das schafft im Herzen
Frohe Lust!
Das zwingt mit Kraft zu Sang

Aus voller Brust!

Die Tarabuka, laßt sie lustig schwingen,
Und der Kemenghe Saiten laßt erklingen,
Derwischflöten auch dabei
Blasen hell die Melodei!
La—la—la—
Das stimmt rings im Kranz,
La—la—la—
Zu Sang und frohem Tanz!

|: Zinzirin, zin, zin,
Zin, ha ho!:|

La—la—la—
Holaro.

FANFANI
Am Tsad! Am Tsad!—
Da kriegt man schöne Frauen;
Sind delicat wie Chocolad';
Bald hell, bald dunkelbraun!

Der Pascha ist gar sehr
Entzückt von der Couleur;
D'rum kaufte ich für ihn speciell
Die schönsten Weiber hier zur Stell';
Wie sie zu Markte kamen grad'

Am Tsad! Am Tsad!
Avanti!

Zeigt nun im Tanz
Der Reize Glanz!
Ja, meine Wahl
Ist colossal!
Die schönsten Weiber
Hab' nur ich—Sie sind so fein,
Die Race rein,
Das weiß man sicherlich!

CHOR
Die Kemenghe stimmet an
La, la, la,
Tarabuka schlage d'rein,
La, la, la.

II.
FANFANI
Am Kur! Am Kur!
Wer Mädchen dort geseh'n,
Macht immer nur dahin die Tour,
Um auf den Markt zu geh'n!

Sie sind durchaus nicht schlank;
Den Pascha,—Allah dank!—
Den int'ressirt nicht das Gesicht,
Wenn das Gewicht!
Ihm nur cntspricht!
Die schwersten Frau'n gedeihen nur
Am Kur! am Kur!

CHOR
Am Kur! Am Kur!
Wer Mädchen dort geseh'n.
Am Kur, am Kur,
Wird auch zum Markt hingeh'n,
La la la la
Die Kemenghe stimmet an
*Etc.*

FANFANI
Avanti!
Zeigt nun im Tanz
Der Reize Glanz;
Ja, meine Wahl
Ist colossal!

Die schönsten Weiber hab nur!
Sie sind so fein.
Die Race rein,
Das weis man sicherlich!

Sklavenhändler gibt's nur Einen,
Und der Eine, der bin ich!
Den Geschmack, den edlen, feinen,
Hab' nur ich ganz sicherlich!

Am Tsad! Am Kur!
*Etc.*

SEBIL
Miradillo! Deine Sklavin—
Hier bin ich! Nimm mich hin, o Herr!

ALLE
Ha! seht doch—
Wie darf sie sich erlauben—?
Was hat sie? Was will sie?
Was sucht die Sklavin hier?

SEBIL
Bin seine Sklavin!

ALLE
Das können wir nicht glauben!

SEBIL
Und bleibe bei ihm!

ALLE
Nein! Nein! Hinweg mit ihr!

SEBIL
Laßt ab!

ALLE
Entferne dich!

SEBIL
Laßt ab!

ALLE
Hinaus!

SEBIL
Gekauft hat er mich blank und baar!

ALLE
Fort!

SEBIL
O, fragt ihn selbst, ob das nicht wahr!

ALLE
Hinaus!

MIRADILLO
Ja—so ist's! dies meine Sklavin—
Drum vor der Hand
Bleibt sie auch hier!
Ich kaufte sie privatim mir!

ALLE
Er kaufte sie—bezahlte baar
Am Sklavenmarkt? Höchst sonderbar!
Curios, höchst sonderbar!

TESSA
Mein Gott was mußt' ich hören?
Der Gattin denkt er nicht,
Kauft hier sich die Sklavin!

FANFANI UND CHOR
Was wird dazu die Frau sag'n?
Hm! Hm! Hm!

TESSA
Weh mir!

BUCCAMETTA
Der Verstand
In ihm schwand!

MIRADILLO
Amüsant!

Interessant!

TESSA
Welche Schand!
Mir drohet Schmach,
An diesem fremden Strand!
Vergaß er mich
Denn so geschwind?
Hab' ich dies Loos
Um ihn verdient?

Nicht zu verzeihen
Ist dies Treiben!
Welche bitt're Qual!

BUCCAMETTA
Er erlebt noch Schmach und Schand'!
Siebst dem Ehestand
Eine Sklavin noch!
Bei dem tollen Treiben, ach,
Wo bleibt die Moral?!

SEBIL
Ja, Sebil bleibt Dir treu ergeben
Zu jeder Zeit!
Sie will Dir weihen ganz ihr Leben
In Leid und Freud'!
Sie wird sich dankbar stets bezeigen,
Wie ein Hündchen bei Dir bleiben:
Des Nachts bewachen Deine Ruh',
Bei Tag Dir lächeln,
Kühlung fächeln—
Ach, Sebil ist ein Bijou!

MIRADILLO
So erlebt man allerhand!
Warten mit Ruh',
Lachen dazu—
In solchem Treiben
Steckt viel Moral!

FANFANI
Was wird dazu die Frau sag'n?
Hm! Hm! Hm!
Bei dem Treiben gieb'ts Skandal!
Schändlich Treiben, ach,
Ja, da giebt's Skandal!

Da kommt die Frau schon her—
Jetzt gibt es ein Malheur!

TITANIA
Nur ungenirt!
Ganz ungenirt!

ANTARSID
Gern folge ich der Lehre—

TITANIA
Ich rede frei;
Wer dabei—einerlei!

ANTARSID
Sie entzückt und beglückt!

FANFANI
Die thut recht vertraulich!

TITANIA
Sie sind ein Freund—

FANFANI
Das klingt erbaulich!

TITANIA
Der treu es meint;—

FANFANI
Ist äußerst anschaulich!

TITANIA
Der meinem Dienst

Sich allein nur wird weih'n!

ANTARSID
Ja, Dein Sklave allein
Will ich ewig Dir sein!

FANFANI
Doch sieh', liebe Nichte,
Dort steht der Gemahl—
'Ne schöne Geschichte—
Es ist ein Skandal!

TITANIA
Was denn?

FANFANI
Er kaufte—'s ist gräulich—
'Ne Sklavin sich an,
Das find' ich abscheulich—
Er ist doch Dein Mann!

TITANIA
Warum sich geniren?
Ich bin tolerant!
Er mag aequiriren
Was ihm int'ressant!

Laßt ihm die Freud'.
Hört lieber, was ich nun beschlossen!

FANFANI
Aber—doch wenn—höre—

TITANIA
Der Prinz, mein Begleiter,
Stimmt froh mich und heiter,

FANFANI
Was soll ich mit ihm?
TITANIA
Ich lud ihn ein—

ANTARSID
O wie fein!

TITANIA
Mein Gast—

ANTARSID
Ach—zu viel!

TITANIA
Heut' zu sein!

FANFANI
Unser Gast?
Das war noch nicht da!
Unser Gast—

Schreit ganz Afrika!
Ist es möglich?
Ist's erträglich?
O Skandal!
Uff! Uff! Mir schwindelt

TESSA, BUCCAMETTA UND DIE UEBRIGEN
Ihr Gast? Ihr Gast?
Ja fürwahr
Sonderbar—
Die Sache scheint nicht klar.'
Die Keckheit ist groß!

CHOR
Als Gast ihn zu laden
Bleibt immer curios!
Was wird dazu der Mann sag'n
Hm! Hm! Hm!

TITANIA
Ha—ha—ha! Soll ich schreien?

TESSA
Der Vampyr! So'was mir!

SEBIL
Dir, o Herr
Ich gehör'!

ANTARSID
Engel, Du; lächle zu!

MIRADILLO
Amüsant!
Jnt'ressant!

FANFANI
Ich bin stumm; bin ganz dumm!

CHOR
Was wird dazu der Mann sag'n?
Hm! Hm! Hm!

BUCCAMETTA, PERIKLES UND DAMEN-CHOR
Was wird dazu der Mann sag'n?
Hm! Hm! Hm!

(Sein/das) Weib allein
Muß (doch/stets) Sieger sein!

MÄNNER-CHOR
Das Weib, das Weib allein
Muß stets Sieger sein!

TITANIA
Das wär' nicht fein,
Ich will klüger sein!

TESSA
O dürft' ich schrei'n!
Schweigen wird jetzt noch klüger sein!

SEBIL
Du allein—ja allein!
Sollst mein Sieger sein!

FANFANI, MIRADILLO UND ANTARSID
Das Weib allein,
Muß stets Sieger sein!

CHOR
Das Zeichen zum Feste
Versammelt die Gäste!

TITANIA
Geben Sie voll Höflichkeit
Mit Glanz und Pomp mir jetzt Geleit!

MIRADILLO
Bin schon bereit!
Herbei, Ihr Leute
Erhebt den Palankin!
Jubel geleite
Zum Fest die Gattin hin!

CHOR
Hurrah! Hurrah!
Zur Lust sind wir bereit!
Allah! Allah!
Beiram, du Freudenzeit!

TITANIA UND ANTARSID
Herrliches Bild,
Wo Lied und Becher klingen,
Wo lusterfüllt
Die Herzen auf sich schwingen!
Dorthin, wo Liebe selig uns macht,
Dort, wo das Glück,
Wo holde Freiheit lacht!

ALLE
Tarabuka lasset lustig nun erklingen,
Auch Kemenghe soll mit Kraft die Saiten schwingen,
Auf! jubelt d'rein voller Lust
Vorbei ist Ramadan!
Ruft hell und laut aus der Brust
Der Beiram bricht nun an.

Das ist der Tag,
Der von Fastenzwang uns frei gemacht,
Hoch sei dem Tag,
Ein dreimal Hoch gebracht!

O, welch' ein herrliches Bild
Bei Lied und Becherklingen,
Wo lusterfüllt
Die Herzen auf sich schwingen.

Dorthin, wo Liebe selig uns macht,
Dort, wo das Glück, wo holde Freiheit lacht!
Tarabuka schlage kräftig d'rein,
Denn vorbei ist Ramadan;
Jung und alt soll jubeln, lustig sein,
Denn das Beiramfest bricht an!
Hurrah!
pound with vigour,
For now Bayram has begun, hurrah!

## ENDE DES ERSTEN ACTES

# ZWEITER ACT

## No. 7 – Introduction

CHOR (SOPRANI)
Lustbarkeit, Gesang mit Tanz und Schmaus
Gibt es heute hier im Haus!
Macht alles rein!
Eine hübsche, niedlich'—junge Frau
Nimmt der Pascha sich ganz schlau—
Bald zieht sie ein!

Ach, wie sehr ist zu beneiden
Solch' ein glücklich' Liebespaar;
Dem voll Paradieses Freuden
Winkt die Zukunft licht und klar!

SKLAVEN
Rasch behende—nicht zerstreut—
Denn schon ist's die höchste Zeit!

ALLE
Jedes Möbel, jeder Schrank,
Muß erglänzen spiegelblank!
Klopfet frisch vom ganzen Haus
Jeden Teppich sorgsam aus!

SKLAVINNEN
Klopfet, ja klopft Alles aus,
Jeden Teppich hier im Haus,
Sonst mit Wucht und Vehemenz
Klopft uns seine Excellenz!

SKLAVEN
Klopfet, ja klopfet
Vom Staube ein Nebel
Aus Teppich und Möbel
Aus Divan und Stühle
Die Motten umwühle
Ja klopfet und klopfet

Recht heñig und kräftig!
Ja, Alles rein
Muß sein!

II.
SKLAVINNEN
Viele Gäste—alt' und junge Herr'n
Kommen her von nah und fern!
Macht Alles rein!
Möcht' wohl wissen, wer sie Alle sind,
Was sie herführt so geschwind.

Bald zieh'n sie ein!
Ach, wie sehr ist zu beneiden.
*Etc.*

SKLAVEN
Laßt doch solche Schwärmerei,
Die bringt Euch nur bitt're Reu'!

ALLE
Denken wir an uns're Pflicht,
And'res ziemt den Sklaven nicht!
Klopfet frisch vom ganzen Haus
*Etc.*

FANFANI
Kusch! kusch! kusch!
Ihr elendes Gesindel,
Zur Arbeit marsch sogleich!
Nur Faulenzen und Schwindel,
Das ist das Liebste Euch!

Der Peitsche nur allein
Könnt Ihr gehorsam sein!

CHOR
Schlecht gelaunt ist unser Herr!

FANFANI
Wollt Ihr nicht gleich pariren—

CHOR
Ziehen wir fort, sonst gibt's Malheur!

FANFANI
Werd' ich englisch Euch kuriren!
Ach ja, nur Englisch,
Das ist das Beste, das Einzige hier,
Ist die richtige Manier!

I.
In Egypten wird gestohlen
Oben, unten, kreuz und quer!
Keinem bleibt mehr was zu holen,
Selbst für England blieb nichts mehr:

Doch der Brite unverdrossen
Handelt immer kurz entschlossen—
Während andre conferenzen
Zieht er seine Consequenzen
Schießt zusammen, was im Weg ihm,
Schlägt dann bei Tel-et-Kebir!

Ach ja, dies Englisch,
Nur dies Englisch,
Das ist die richtige Manier!

II.
And're Staaten annexiren
Länder, wo es gar nichts gibt;
Und nur Gesindel existiren
Und das Schweindl stehl'n beliebt;

Doch der Brite nimmt sich Indien,
Wo sie die Brillanten finden
Und wo man anstatt Gotschebern
Dutzendweis' begegnet Naböbern,
Denen man so gentlemanisch
Steuern auflad't mehr als hier—

Ach ja, dies Englisch
*Etc.*

## No. 8 – Lied der Tessa

I
TESSA
Mein Herr, Sie sind sehr gütig,
Ich leg' aus Ihren Antrag Werth;
Bin gar nicht übermüthig,
Ich fühle mich sogar geehrt!

Doch haben Sie der Frauen mehr
Bereits in Ihrem Haus—
Und ich gesteh', daß ich nur schwer
Darüber könnt hinaus!

Sie sehen das als Muselmann
Als ganz natürlich an—
Doch ich als Europäerin
Nehm's nicht so ruhig hin;

Wer weiß ob mich nicht später Reu' ergriffe,
Wenn ich zu früh verbrenne meine Schiffe;
Darum, darum:

Ich sag' nicht "nein"—
Ich sag' nicht "ja"—
Aber—reden Sie mit der Mama!

II.
Man denkt in solchen Dingen
Hier sehr gemüthlich, scheinet mir!
Die Menge muß es bringen,
So lautet die Parole hier!

Daß man in Einer sucht sein Heil,
Wie's sonst Europa macht,—
Wird auch bei uns als Vorurtheil
Schon mehr und mehr verlacht,

Doch, daß ein Mann wie Ihr' en gros
Probirt der Ehe Glück—

Ich finde das ganz praktisch so,
Wir sind darin zurück!

Und nationale Eigenthümlichkeiten
Sind vollberechtigt in den jetz'gen Zeiten—
Darum—darum:

Ich sag' nicht "nein"—
Ich sag' nicht "ja"—
Aber—reden Sie mit der Mama!

## No. 9 – Blumen-Duett

TITANIA
Es spricht aus jeder Blume
Ein Räthselwörtchen leis',
Für jenen nur verständlich,
Der es zu deuten weiß.

Die holden Blüthen fragen,
Und geben Antwort traut—
Sie warnen, mahnen, klagen,
Sie jubeln ohne Laut!

Das Veilchen, die Narcisse,
Der duftende Jasmin,
Die Nelke, die Cypresse,
Sie alle haben Sinn,

Ich biete Dir, ja Dir von Allem
Die Rose, die Dich sticht!
Sie sagt: Willst du mich pflücken,
So scheu! die Dornen nicht!

ANTARSID
Die Rose soll mich schrecken,
Den Sinn errath' ich schon;
Sie warnt, daß mir Gefahren
In deiner Nähe droh'n!
Durch's Feuer geh', ich folge,
Ich folge in Wüstensand!

Sei zornig, stoß' mich von Dir,
Ich bleibe an dich gebannt!

Für dich nur will ich leben,
In Liebe für und für
Und sollt' ich sterben müssen
So sei's aus Lieb' zu dir!

An dich bleib' ich gefesselt
Was auch dein Selam spricht!
Die Rose will ich pflücken—
Die Dornen fürcht' ich nicht!

BEIDE
Die Rose will (er/ich) pflücken
Die Dornen (scheut er/fürcht'ich) nicht.

## No. 10 – Ensemble

TESSA, ANTARSID, FANFANI UND BUCCAMETTA
Laßt zum Scheine
Sie alleine,
Aber lauscht im Vereine!
Sein Betragen,
Heimlich Zagen
Weckt Verdacht, gebet Acht!

TITANIA
Man lauschet—d'rum still
Und seid aus der Hut!

MIRADILLO
Nur ruhig, ich spiel'
Natürlich und gut!

DIE VIER
Lauschen wir heimlich hier!

MIRADILLO
Sieh den Kiosk dort traulich winken,
Wo uns der Pascha heut einlogirt!

TITANIA
Daß wir ganz ungeheuer glücklich
Soll Jeder hören, den's int'ressirt!

MIRADILLO UND TITANIA
Ach bald, ach bald
Tönt der Gesang der Nachtigallen
Mit süßem Klang
Lockt uns voll Wonne ihr Liebessang!

TITANIA
Seht nur, sie halten noch immer dort Wacht!

MIRADILLO
D'rum sei'n wir schlau:
Das Best' ist ungenirt
In den Kiosk spaziert
Als Mann und Frau!

TITANIA
Niemals! Das wär' mir denn doch zu gewagt!

MIRADILLO
Daß wir schon gelten nun als Ehepaar,
Begegnen wir am Besten der Gefahr
Geh'n wir zusammen heute still hinein
In den Kiosk, natürlich nur zum Schein!
Bescheiden will ich sein
Begehre ja allein
Ganz im Charakter meiner Rolle nur zu sein!
Es geschieht nur zum Schein,
Will bescheiden ja sein!

TITANIA
Ha! Mich fasset plötzlich Grauen!
Wollt' mißbrauchen mein Vertrauen? Nein!
's kann nicht sein,
Auch nicht einmal zum Schein!
Wagt Ihr's und dringt hinein—
So werdet Ihr's bereu'n!
Ich weiß mich zu befrei'n.

DIE VIER
Dieser Mann ist wohl zu beneiden
Ihm winkt ein süßes Stelldichein;
Ja, diese Nacht winkt ihm voll Freuden
An seiner Stelle möcht' ich sein!

MIRADILLO UND TESSA
Ach bald, ach bald
Tönt der Gesang der Nachtigallen
Mit süßem Klang
Lockt uns voll Wonne ihr Liebessang!

DIE VIER
Selig muß er sein!
Sie sind, ja ich sehe, ein Paar
Die Zeichen der Ehe sind klar!

TITANIA
Wer kann da widersteh'n?
Ja, komm. Du sollst schon seh'n!
Ich komm! Ach ja!

MIRADILLO
Kannst Du noch widersteh'n?
Erhör' mein liebend Fleh'n!
So komm! So komm!

## No. 11 – Couplet

I
MIRADILLO
Gerne geh' ich sonst zum Stelldichein,
Aber sehr verdächtig scheint mir dies zu sein!
Wenn ich komme gibt es ein Duell—
Ihr Verehrer schießt mir Löcher in das Fell!

Ja, die Weiber machen sich Nichts draus,
Wenn man Schläge kriegt für sie,
Lachen obend'rein den Dummkopf aus,
Der sich gab so viele Müh'!

Die Geschichte ist gefährlich
Und mir danken wird sie's schwerlich—

D'rum wär's sehr gescheidt,
Ich fahr' ab und verschwind'
Gute Nacht, du mein herziges Kind!

II
Wenn bei uns man übt Wohlthätigkeit
Ist auch ein Bazar sogleich dazu bereit;
Da verkaufen Damen allerlei—
Damen vom Theater hat man gern dabei!

Kürzlich trat ich an'nen solchen Stand
Zu'nem Fräulein hold und schön;
Ein Cigarrl' bot sie mit zarter Hand,
Ließ dazu ein Lächeln seh'n!

Als ich fragte nach dem Preise,
Lispelt sie „Zehn Gulden" leise.—

"Dein Lächeln wohl süß, aber theuer ich find' –
"Gute Nacht, Du mein herziges Kind!"

III
Einer, der den Schlaf verloren hat
Will von seinem Doctor einen guten Rath;
Der verordnet ihm Chloral hydrat,
Gibt ihm gar Morphin und Opium-Präparat—

Doch vergeblich!—Was er auch nimmt ein,
Ach! er findet keinen Schlaf!
Selbst der Doctor leidet Qual und Pein,
Daß er nie das Rechte traf.—

Endlich läßt nach langem Quälen
Als Gemeinde-Rath er sich wählen!

Jetzt schläft er in offener Sitzung geschwind—
Gute Nacht, Du mein herziges Kind!

# No. 12 – Terzett

TESSA
Ach ich mußte es gestehen, es drängt mich;
Nun werden schlecht Sie von mir denken—
Kaum Mitleid schenken!

MIRADILLO
Warum? Warum?
Find' die Sache ganz natürlich!

Wer dies Antlitz, diese Blicke,
Dies Ensemble hat gesehen,
Diese Nase zum Entzücken,
Konnte selten widerstehen!

Wenn sie so viel Reiz betrachten
Sind die Herzen leicht gerührt!
Daß die Weiber nach mir schmachten,
Ist mir hundertmal passirt!

TESSA
Wart' nur!
Du sollst es theuer noch bereuen!
Wart' nur! Wart' nur!
Du unterliegst der Weiber List,
Die Strafe folgt Dir auf dem Fuß!

MIRADILLO
Wart' nur! Wart' nur!
Dein Schwärmen soll mich noch erfreuen!
Wart' nur!
Du wirst zum Zeitvertreib geküßt!
Ha, ha, ha, ha, o Genuß!

Fürchte gar nicht mein Verachten,
Rede nur ganz ungenirt—
Daß die Weiber nach mir schmachten
Ist mir tausendmal passirt!

TESSA
Warum bin ich nicht Mulattin
Und ein Muselmann nicht Du—
Nähmst vielleicht nebst Deiner Gattin
Mich als zweite Frau dazu!
Ach, liebe mich!

MIRADILLO
Teufel nein,
Die geht scharf d'rein!

TESSA
Ich bitte Dich!

MIRADILLO
Ja, das geht doch nicht so schnell,
Bin als Gatte ein Juwel!
Dann zumal—
Die Moral?!

TESSA
Ja so!—
Ach, was kann man dafür,
Wühlt die Lieb' drinnen hier;
Pocht das Herz mit wilden Schlägen,
Hilft kein Widerstand dagegen!

Wenn die Ruh' dann entfloh,
Flammt es auf, lichterloh,
Heiß und heißer rollt das Blut,
Es verzehrt mich Liebesglut!
Nein, nein, nein.
Das geht nicht!
Nein, das darf nicht gescheh'n!

MIRADILLO
Ach  herrje—
Ich versteh'!
Diese Hast—
Schnell erfaßt!
Armes, fühlendes Weib,

Laß' mich den Schleier lüften.
Laß' dein Antlitz mich seh'n;
Ich bin gewiß, es ist schön!
Ach laß' mich Dein Antlitz seh'n!

TESSA
Ohne Schleier mich seh'n,
Darf ein Gatte allein!

MIRADILLO
Und warum?

TESSA
Nein, nein,'s darf nicht sein!

MIRADILLO
Lächerlich!

TESSA
Das wäre gegen uns're Sitte
D'rum laßt ab, ich bitte, bitte!
Ich bitte, laßt ab!
Laßt ab, nein, nein—
Laßt ab!

Ach, was kann man dafür
*Etc. bis:*

Flammt es auf lichterloh,
Man vergißt die Pflicht, die ganze Welt,
Und der Schleier fällt!

MIRADILLO
Red' nicht von Sitte,'s ist zum Lachen,
Wenn ich hier flehend vor Dir steh'!
Neugierig willst Du mich nur machen.—
Fort mit dem Schleier,
Daß ich Dich seh'!

Nur fort! Schnell fort!
Dich zwing' ich durch Gewalt!

Mein Blut ist im Wallen—
Der Schleier muß fallen—
Komm zu mir! Komm zu mir!
Und lüftest nicht willig den lästigen Schleier,
Dann werd' ich noch freier
Und brauche Gewalt,

MIRADILLO
Tessa! bist Du's?
Tessa! Du hier?!
Du willst in des Pascha's Harem
Als seine Frau?
Dieser Schritt wär' ungebührlich
Und unnatürlich!

TESSA
Warum? Warum?
Find' die Sache ganz natürlich!

Wer dies Antlitz, diese Blicke,
Dies Ensemble hat geseh'n—
Diese Nase, zum Entzücken,—
Der kann selten widersteh'n!

Wenn sie so viel Reiz betrachten,
Sind die Herzen leicht gerührt—
Daß die Männer nach mir schmachten
Ist mir tausendmal passirt!

MIRADILLO
Nein—nein—Du darfst nicht fort!

TESSA
Entsage Titania, sonst halt' ich mein Wort!

MIRADILLO
Nein—nein—das thust Du nicht!

TESSA
Ich thu' es zum Trotze, Du treuloser Wicht!

MIRADILLO
Ich kann nicht!

TESSA
Ich geh'!

MIRADILLO
O höre!

TESSA
Nein, nein! Verräther! Ach!

MIRADILLO
Sieh mich zu Deinen Füßen hier!

FANFANI
Komm' grad' zurecht! Sieh' da, schau, schau,
Der Kerl verführt gar meine Frau!

MIRADILLO
Ach, Tessa, schone mich!

BEIDE
Ach, was kann man dafür,
Wühlt die Lieb' drinnen hier—
*Etc.*

FANFANI
Du Verführer, Leut'anschmierer!
O Du Heuchler, Lügner, Schmeichler,
Solch' ein Schwindler, ein Landstreicher gar,
Bringt'ne ehrsame Frau in Gefahr!

Für den Frechen Soll ich blechen,
Soll mein blut'ges Geld
Ich verschwenden, versenden
Hinaus in die Welt!

Schwindler, ich wollt',
Daß dich der Teufel holt!
Schwindler, Schnorrer, Gauner, ha!

# No. 13 – Finale II

**CHOR**
Beiram, das schönste Fest, rückt heran;
Beiram, die Weihestunde, endlich kam!

**MUEZZIN**
Beginnet neu das Leben,
Die Unbill sei vergeben!
Nicht Haß, noch Feindschaft mehr besteht—
So lehret der Profet.

**CHOR**
Beginnet neu das Leben,
Die Unbill sei vergeben!
Nicht Haß noch Feindschaft mehr besteht.

So lehret der Profct!
Wie's in alten Zeiten war,
Reichet Euch die Datteln dar—
So befiehlt es der Profet!

Beiram, das schönste Fest, es rückt heran!
Beiram, die Weihestunde, endlich kam.—
Laßt schallen
Und hallen
Von Fern und Nah':
Gepriesen sei Allah!

**FANFANI**
Die Dattel nach Landessitte
Ist der Wohlfahrt Zeichen;
Sie bringt Glück,
Bannt Mißgeschick,
D'rum ist es Pflicht,
Den Freunden sie zu reichen!

**ALLE**
Die Dattel zu nehmen
Muß man sich bequemen,

Den Freunden sie reichen
Ist Sitte und Pflicht!

FANFANI
Ist gefällig eine Dattel, bester Freund?

MIRADILLO
Halte mit!

TITANIA
Ist gefällig eine Dattel gutgemeint?

ANTARSID
O, ich bitt'!

TESSA
Wir verzehren diese Datteln hier vereint!

BUCCAMETTA
Warum nicht?

ANTARSID
Wohlgemuth!

FANFANI
's ist ja Pflicht!

BUCCAMETTA
Die war gut!

CHOR
Eintracht schmückt das schöne Fest!

MIRADILLO
Doch nun nehmet diese Dattel auch von mir

FANFANI
Gebet her!

ANTARSID
Wenn ich bitten darf, nehmt diese Eine hier!

TITANIA
Bitte sehr!

BUCCAMETTA
Ich verzehrte sie schon alle bis auf vier!

TESSA
Gar nicht schlecht!

TITANIA
So ist's recht'

MIRADILLO
Wunderbar!

BUCCAMETTA
Jetzt ist's gar!

FANFANI
Sein Blick ist fröhlich!

MIRADILLO
Er schaut so selig!

FANFANI
Mag wohl es Euch bekommen!

MIRADILLO
Ich danke!

MIRADILLO UND FANFANI
Haha! Haha! Haha!

FANFANI UND MIRADILLO
FANFANI
Pschi!

MIRADILLO
Pschi!

BEIDE
Verdammtes Niesen!

FANFANI
Pschi!

MIRADILLO
Pschi!

BEIDE
's ist zum verdrießen!

FANFANI
Helf Gott!

MIRADILLO
Helf Gott!

TITANIA
Ptschi! Woher dies Nießen? Ptschi! Ptschi!

ANTARSID
Ptschi! Woher dies Nießen? Ptschi! Ptschi!
Schön Dank von Alle! Ptscbi! Ptschi!
Wunderbar ist's fürwahr! Ptschi!
Ich—Ptschi! Der—Ptschi! Die—Ptschi! Ptschi!
Kann's nicht bezwingen—Ptschi! Ptschi!
Verdammtes Nießen—Ptschi! Ptschi
' sist Zauberei—Ptscha!

BUCCAMETTA UND TESSA
Ptschi! Ptschi! Ptschi! Ptschi!
Schön Dank an Alle Ptschi!
Ja, woher dies Malheur'?
Wunderbar ist's fürwahr!

Höchst fatal der Skandal!
Ich—Ptschi! Der—Ptschi! Die—Ptschi! Ptschi!
Ein Zauber ist das Ptschi!
Verdammtes Nießen, Ptschi! s ist Zauberei—Ptscha!

TITANIA
Kann's nicht bezwingen! Ptschi!

FANFANI
Ich muß zerspringen! Ptschi!
Verdammtes Nießen! Ptschi!
's ist Zauberei! Ptscha!

CHOR
Helf Gott! Ptschi!
Der Schnupfen, das Nießen
Muß Jeden verdrießen!
Es rasen die Nasen! Ptschi!
Helf Gott! Ptschi!
's ist Zauberei! Ptscha!

FANFANI
Vernehmet Ihr, das war das erste Zeichen!
Die Stund' ist da, der Nil beginnt zu steigen!
Der dritte Schuß verkündet uns die Fluth!

CHOR
Hört, o hört und lauschet still,
Lüfte wehen schwer und kühl!
Es rauschen die Wellen so geisterhaft,
Die Wässer, sie schwellen mit Zauberkraft!

Gesegnet sei der Nil—
Bald ist erreicht das Ziel!
Wie brausend es hallt,
Wie schäumend es wallt!

Nun preiset Allah's Macht,
Der uns mit Segen reich bedacht,
Der dieses Wunder hat vollbracht!

TITANIA
Reicht den Becher—stimmet ein!
Von Allah's Thron
Seit uralten Zeiten schon,

Kommt ein Engel jedes Jahr,
Bringt der Nilfluth Segen dar!

Er war gesandt
Eine Schale in der Hand
Zu dem Quell, der uns Menschen
Bleibt ewig unbekannt!

Und die Wellen flüstern dann sacht,
Wachsen, wogen, steigen mit Macht,
Spenden Segen rings dem Land,
Geben neues Leben!

Seine Welle
Grüßen wir Alle,
Rein und Helle
Gleich dem Crystalle!
Mehr als Wein
Soll Dein Naß uns willkommen sein!

ALLE
Seht dort die Barke,
Wie prachtvoll und bunt geschmückt!
Ach, wie ihr Anblick
Ergötzet und hochentzückt! Seht!

TITANIA
Ich löse die Ketten,
Die Hilfe ist da;
Du wirst mich erretten—
Erlösung ist nah'!
Die Barke wird sicher uns Beide befrei'n
Noch einmal hebt das Glas, stimmt mit ein!

ALLE
Von Allah's Thron
*Etc.*

CHOR
O, sehet doch Skorpione
Im ringelnden Tanze sich dreh'n!

FANFANI
Was wird da begonnen?
Was werden wir seh'n?

CHOR
Seht! seht! Sie führen die Frauen
Gewaltsam auf's harrende Schiff!

FANFANI
Dem ist nicht zu trauen—
Das scheinet mir ein Kniff!

CHOR
Curios!

TITANIA
Wir fahren spazieren!

MIRADILLO
Das soll keinen geniren!

FANFANI
Verführer, ich merk' es schon,
Das ist Dein Werk!

CHOR
Ha, seht nur; ha, seht nur.
Was ist da im Werk?

FANFANI
Auf, Ihr Leute! Schnell behende
Hindert diese Frevelthat!

CHOR
Schnell, nur schnell
Eilt zur Stell';
Zu spät, das Schiff ist flott!

FANFANI
Ach, schändlich, mich so dupiren!
Das Geld und die Braut mir entführen!

Bubenstreich!
Gaunerstreich
Sondergleich!
Nie dagewesen—
Ich bin auserlesen
Zum Spott und zum Hohn!
Aber wartet Betrüger,
Ich bleibe doch Sieger;
Es kommt schon!

ALLE ÄNDERN
Freiheit, Freiheit gibt neues Leben;
Freiheit, Freiheit ist uns gegeben.
Lebet wohl!

Ja, preiset hoch Allah's Macht!

## ENDE DES ZWEITEN ACTES

# DRITTER ACT

## No. 14 – Chor und Romanze

MÄNNER-CHOR
Schon bricht an der neue Morgen—

FRAUEN-CHOR
Allah's Macht—

MÄNNER-CHOR
Sonnenlicht taucht rasch empor.—

FRAUEN-CHOR
Zeigt sich in gold'ner Pracht!

MÄNNER-CHOR
Aus dem Schlummer, tief verborgen—

FRAUEN-CHOR
Hoch empor

ALLE
Wacht es auf und kommt hervor!

ANTARSID
Welch' ein Traum?
Ich war so selig, so entzückt,
So hoch beglückt!
Meine Rose—
Die Dornen scheut' ich nicht—
Ich küßte sie die holde Blume!
Doch ach, hier drohet uns Gefahr
Von wilder Räuberschaar!
Verbergt die Zelte nur,
Leicht kommt mau auf die Spur!
Und Du, mein Liebchen,
Wach' auf! Wach' auf!

CHOR
Allah's Macht
Uns bewacht!
Allah!

ANTARSID
Liebchen, wach auf!—
Schon weicht die Nacht dem Morgengrau,
Sternendamast
Schwindend erblaßt—
Heiterer Himmel, sonnig und blau,
Weckt uns aus süßer Rast!

Liebliche Maid,
Schon ist es Zeit;
Oeffne Dein Äuge
Strahlend und rein.
Dann ist mein Stern
Mir nicht mehr fern,
Heller als Sonnenschein!

Schnell erwache, süßes' Täubchen,
Girre, lache hold mir zu!
Ja—ach komm'—herzige Maid,
Sei meine Seligkeit!
O komm'! O komm'!
Wach' auf! Wach' auf!

CHOR
Holde Maid—Es ist Zeit—
Erwache!
Hell und rein
Winkt Sonnenschein!

Der Tag bricht an—
Wach' auf, lieb' Kind!
Wach' auf, es ist schon Zeit.—
Ach komm', ach komm'—
Laß' das Träumen;
Mußt Dich erheben
Zu neuem Leben!

# No. 15 – Terzett

TITANIA
Afrika ist sehr gefährlich!

ANTARSID
Ja, der Tod droht unaufhörlich!

MIRADILLO
Ha, gut!

TITANIA
Erstlich von den wilden Thiereu,

ANTARSID
Die dort frei herumspazieren

MIRADILLO
Spaß!—Schön!

TITANIA
Von den vielen

ANTARSID
Krokodilen;

MIRADILLO
Mir ganz—egal!

TITANIA
Von den Schlangen—

ANTARSID
Riesengroß!

TITANIA
Und von dem Rhinozeros!

ANTARSID
Ja, von dem Rhinozeros!

MIRADILLO
Tessa ist mein einzig' Ziel—
Das Leben setz' ich gern auf's Spiel!

TITANIA
Nur nicht tollkühn—unbedacht!

ANTARSID
Nehmt behutsam Euch in Acht!

MIRADILLO
Habe Alles schon durchdacht!

TITANIA
Da gibt's Beduinenhorden,

ANTARSID
Die den Fremden tückisch morden!

MIRADILLO
Gut!—Bravo!

TITANIA
Weiter d'runten kommt's noch besser

ANTARSID
Da bedroh' Euch Menschenfresser!

MIRADILLO
Spaß!—Schön!

TITANIA
Schlangengrotten, Berbern, Kaffern –

ANTARSID
Hottentotten und noch mehr!

MIRADILLO
Mir ganz—egal!

TITANIA UND ANTARSID
Wie leicht geschieht da ein Malheur!

MIRADILLO
Sollen drohen, wie sie wollen—

ANTARSID
Nehmt Euch in Acht!

MIRADILLO
Mein Entschluß ist felsenfest!

TITANIA
Sein Stolz erwacht!

MIRADILLO
Wenn auch Blitz und Donner rollen—

ANTARSID
Es rollt sein Blut!

MIRADILLO
Ich durchkreuze Ost und West,
Bis sich Tessa finden läßt!

TITANIA
Ihn erfaßt Heldenmut!

TITANIA UND ANTARSID
Doch der Weg ist gar weit!

MIRADILLO
Wenig mach' ich mir daraus!

TITANIA UND ANTARSID
Kommt nach Haus—seid gescheidt!

MIRADILLO
Nur mit ihr geh ich nach Haus!

TITANIA UND ANTARSID
O, kommt in's Heimatland!

MIRADILLO
Bis sie gefunden—

TITANIA UND ANTARSID
Wir bieten Euch die Hand!

MIRADILLO
Doch früher nicht!!
Ja! Tessa ist mein Losungswort—
Um sie zu suchen, eil' ich fort!

I.
Ueber Berg, über Thal,
Ueber Feld bei Mondenstrahl
Zieh' ich fort ganz allein—
Amor soll mein Führer sein!

ALLE DREI
Ueber Berg, über Thal,
Ueber Feld bei Mondenstrahl
Zieht (er/ich) fort so ganz allein,
Amor wird (sein/mein) Führer sein!

MIRADILLO
Käm' ein Tiger mir auch in die Quer—
Schakal, Panther und dergleichen mehr,
Ein Gorilla brächt' mich auch nicht um;
Ich geh' ruhig immer weiter d'rum!

Treff' ich endlich am Aeguator gar
Auch auf manche wilde, schwarze Schaar,
Auf die Farbe kommt mir's gar nicht an—
Kämpfen will ich wie ein Mann!

Wenn man liebt treu und wahr.

ALLE DREI
Geht man kühn entgegen jeglicher Gefahr!

MIRADILLO
Ist der Sieg endlich mein—

ALLE DREI
(Eilt er /eile ich) rasch auf Schwingen
Ueber Stock und Stein
Und mit ihr Hand in Hand
(Zieht er/ziehe ich) fort ins Heimatland!

MIRADILLO
Ich seh' das Vaterland zugleich mit ihr.
Vedere Napoli e poi morire!
Doch froh zu leben dort
Scheint bester mir—
Vedere Napoli e mai morir!

ALLE DREI
In's theure Vaterland vereint zieh'n wir,
Vedere Napoli e poi morire,
Doch froh zu leben dort
Scheint besser mir—
Vedere Napoli e mai morir!

TITANIA
Schnell erwacht Lebenslust,
Wenn die Lieb' durchglüht die Brust;
Sie gibt Muth in Gefahr,
Stärkt das Herz ganz wunderbar!

ALLE
Schnell erwacht Lebenslust
*Etc.*

TITANIA
Was auch immer mag entgegensteh'n—
Ob die Brandung tobt, ob Stürme weh'n—
Locket ihn ein süßer Zauberblick,
Hält den Helden vor Gefahr zurück!
Ob auch ferne nur die Hoffnung lacht,
Sieget endlich treuer Liebe Macht!

Wo das Herz sich zu dem Herzen fand,
Endet jeder Widerstand!
Amor kommt schnell an's Ziel—

ALLE DREI
Ob es fern auch scheint, bald wird es doch erreicht:
Ihm ist Alles nur Spiel
Und zum Glück vereinet
Er die Herzen leicht,
Und das Paar, Hand in Hand,
Zieht dann fort in's Heimatsland!

In's theure Vaterland vereint ziehn' wir,
*Etc.*

## No. 16 – Bedouinen-Entree

FANFANI UND CHOR
Wir Egypter am Nil—
Wird uns etwas zu viel,
Morden grausam
Ohne Grauen
Keine Spur von Gefühl! Rache!

Schleicht voll Blutdurst herum,
Was im Weg ist—bringt um!
Was wir halten in den Klauen
Wird vernichtet! Punktum! Punktum!

Schlangen gleich schleicht herum
Um den Mann—
Euren Yatagan
Schwinget sodann!

Kommt die Klinge im Bogen
Blank sausend geflogen—
Ein Blitz—Hahaha! Nur Mord!

Eh er spricht
Noch ein Wort

Fliegt sein Kopf
Ab sofort! Rache!

FANFANI
Stiehlt man eine Frau,
Ueberlegt genau:
War die Dame alt und grau
Laßt sie laufen schlau!

War sie jung und schön,
Lieblich anzuseh'n—
Macht entrüstet Mordskandal—
Rettet die Moral!

Bestraft solchen Frevel
Mit Feuer und Stahl!
Radical! Radical!
Wir Egypter am Nil
*Etc.*

Wer sein Geld uns leiht,
Dann voll Heiterkeit
Nicht mehr d'rauf zu denken scheint,
Der ist unser Freund!

Wenn er aber zählt
Und verlangt sein Geld,
Dann ist's auch mit ihm schon Rest—
Diesen Kerl packet fest!
Bestraft solchen Frevel
*Etc.*

Leise dann
Schleicht heran—
Packet an
Euren Mann
Und skalpirt ihn dann!
Haha! Haha! Haha!

Ohren ab—Nase ab—
Schädel ab—Alles ab—

Mit dem Yatagan!
Darauf kommt's uns nicht an!

## No. 17 – Finale

CHOR (*hinter der Scene*)
Mira, mira! Fata morgana!

CHOR
Hurrah! Hurrah!
Zur Lust sind wir bereit!
Allah! Allah! Beiram, Du Freudenzeit!
Allah! Allah! Zur Lust sind wir bereit!

MIRADILLO
Völker der Wüste bejubeln unser Glück!

ALLE SOLI
Was Gott gefügt,
Uns stets beglückt;
D'rum fügen mir uns dem,
Was er geschickt

MIRADILLO
|: Frohen Muth's ziehen wir
Nach Neapel alle Vier,
Wollen dort im Verein
Wie im Paradiese sein!:|

ALLE
In's theure Vaterland vereint (ziehen wir/zieht ihr),
Vedere Napoli e poi morire,
Doch froh zu leben dort scheint besser mir—
Vedere Napoli e mai morire!

CHOR
Zieht beglückt von dannen
hin zu Euren Ahnen,
Nehmt den Abschiedsgruß aus Afrika!
Hurrah!

MIRADILLO
Nun fort—nun fort aus Afrika!
Hurrah!

# ENDE

Die Afrikareise
Girardi als Miradillo

Von M. West und Rich. Genee      Musik von Franz v. Suppé

1934 postcard by Druck J. Gerstmayer, Wien, XIV,; Series IV. 17. On reverse: 'Dein Lächeln wohl süß, Aber teuer ich find – Gute Nacht, du mein herziges Kind!' Dario Salvi Collection.

# Un Viaggio in Africa

Operetta cominca in tre atti

di

## M. West e Riccardo Genée

Riduzione Italiana

Di

Italo Celesti e Dario Salvi


Musica del Maestro

## Cav. Francesco De-Suppé


25 Marzo 1886
al Teatro Arena Nazionale – Firenze

Compagnia P. Franceschini

# PERSONAGGI

TITANIA FANFANI

FANFANI PASCIÁ .........................................................................Di lei zio

MIRADILLO ...............................................................Giovane palermitano

ELDA .............................................................. Modista, di lui fidanzata

BUCCAMETTA ...................................................................Die lei madre

ANTARSI...................................................................Principe maronita

SEBIL............................................................................Schiava abissina

PERICLE.....................................Greco, proprietario dell'Hotel dei Faraoni

HOSCH.............................................................. Schiavo di Pericle

NACHI ............................................................... Mercante girovago

FIDIA .......................................................................... Cameriere Greco

UN MUEZZINO

JUCHI........................................................................ Capo degli Schiavi

PRIMO SAIS

SECONDO SAIS

UN FACCHINO

Paggi, Maroniti, Facchini, Schive, Schiavi, Popolo.

La scena ha luogo in Egitto.
Epoca presente.

Atto Primo – Nell'Hotel dei Faraoni in Cairo

Atto Secondo – Sulle sponde del Nilo, nella Villa di Fanfani Pasciá

Atto Terzo – Nel deserto.

# ATTO PRIMO

**L'azione si svolge all' Hotel dei Faraoni in Cairo.**

*Cortile dell'Hotel. A destra, posta in altura a guisa di terrazzo, si vede la porta d'ingresso dell'Hotel; a sinistra forma il fondo del cortile una macchia fantastica. A destra, in fondo, parimenti in altura, v'é il piazzale d'un minareto chiuso con una balaustrata in pietra.*

## SCENA I
### Pericle, Sebil, Hosch, Schiavi e Popolo.

## N. 1 – Introduzione

CORO DI TUTTI
Aspettiam con ansietà
Ospiti d'Europa qua;
Quando essi arriveranno
Ci pagheranno. Baxis!
    Baxis!
Baxis! gridan tutti qua;
Baxis! chiaman tutti là;
Sì, Baxis qua—Baxis là!
Che bel suon—amico suon!
    Tin, tin, tin!
    Baxis! Baxis!
Capisce anche un bambin!
    Baxis! Baxis!
Si grida ovunque alfin;
Baxis sopra—Baxis sotto;
    Si griderà: Baxis!
    Si chiamerà: Baxis!
    Si adorerà: Baxis!
Quell'amico suon!
Baxis! gridan tutti qua;
Baxis! chiaman tutti là;

Baxis qua! Baxis là!
È pur bello in verità.

PERICLE
Baxis! Baxis!
Sempre grida, urli da lontano!
Maledetto sia il baccano!
Nell'Hotel dei Faraoni
Si facevan affaroni;
Ma quest'anno non c'é un can!
Sia maledetto quel baccan!

CORO
Ah, ah, ah! Ah, ah, ah!
Ciò non gli va! ciò non gli va!

SEBIL
Non ricordi il forestiere?

PERICLE
Miradillo? quel briccone!
Fa il signor, ed è un scroccone.

SEBIL
È un signore.

PERICLE
Truffatore.

SEBIL
Pagherà quando potrà.

PERICLE
Se oggi pagato non mi avrà.
Chiamerò l'Autorità.

SEBIL
No, no, no!

PERICLE
Lo faro!

SEBIL
Miradillo vuol comprarmi,
    Battezzarmi,
    Via portarmi;
    La é cosi!
Presto men vo'—lungi da qui;
Me l'ha promesso, si!

PERICLE
Questa poi é da canaglia!
Non ha in tasca un soldo sol,
Mi ribella la marmaglia
E le schiave inoltre vuol.

CORO
Ah, ah, ah! ah, ah, ah!

PERICLE
O marmotte—pappagalli,
Bei scimmiotti—siete, qui!
Baxis! Baxis!—gridacchiate,
Sempre oziosi—schiamazzar.

SEBIL E CORO
Tin, tin, tin!
Baxis! Baxis!
Capisce anche un bambin, (ecc.)

PERICLE
Son proprio stanco già!
Verrà l'Autorità.'
    Furfante!
    Briccone!
Fa il signor ed é un scroccone;
L'é già un uso da imbroglione.
    Si, si, si,
Bentosto lo saprà
    L'Autorità.

Caro aspetta, aspetta un po',
Viver io t'insegnerò!

Lo vedrai,—lo vedrai!
Truffator,—ti pentirai!
Birbon!

## SCENA II

PERICLE: Ebbene Signor Miradillo?

MIRADILLO: Ebbene mio caro Pericle?

PERICLE: Quando pensa di saldarmi il di lei conto?

MIRADILLO: Subito che mi avranno mandato i denari; scrissi già in proposito e da un giorno all'altro...

PERICLE: Signore, io non posso andare più innanzi in questo modo, se lei non mi paga fra 24 ore io la denuncio al consolato italiano.

MIRADILLO: Faresti molto male!

PERICLE: Ma, perché ha scelto proprio il mio Hotel?...

MIRADILLO: Perché è il migliore del Cairo...

PERICLE: Grazie tante!

MIRADILLO: Un momento, ascoltate!

PERICLE: Non ascolto nulla!

MIRADILLO: Greco, usuraio!

PERICLE (*ad Hosch*): Non perdere di vista costui!

MIRADILLO: Non mi mancava altro che questo per angelo custode!

(*Hosch accenna di sì.*)

MIRADILLO: Ti avrò sempre al mio fianco come l'ombra di Bacco?

(*Hosch come sopra.*)

MIRADILLO: Si eh! Mummia egiziana! Alfa, portami la bottiglia del Rum.

ALFA SERVO: Subito Signore.

MIRADILLO (*che avrà fatta una sigaretta*): Dammi fuoco, bestia del Nilo.

(*Hosch eseguisce.*)

MIRADILLO: Io domando a me stesso come farò a pagare il mio albergatore; non ho l'ombra d'un soldo nelle mie tasche e nemmeno la più lontana idea d'averne...Infamia eterna ai miei creditori che mi fecero abbandonare la mia magica Palermo, la mia bella Italia, la mia cara modistina, che mi amava quasi più del suo canarino, povera Elsa; chi sa cosa sarà accaduto di te...Come schiaffeggerei volentieri questa marmotta! Ma tu sorridi, eh? Canaglia africana; ma, se dorme...si sarà sognato. Bella la guardia di sicurezza...si è addormentata....se approfittassi...(*p. p. Hosch, si alza*). Ah, sei sveglio, maledetto, vieni angelica creatura, vieni mio rinoceronte; e ride veh, andiamo a fare una passeggiata...(*viano*).

## SCENA III
### Miradillo e detti.

MIRADILLO
Di me si parla forse?

SEBIL
T'offende troppo, per mia fè.

MIRADILLO
Che! davvero?

SEBIL
Ti fa parer un imbroglione.

MIRADILLO
Che sento mai?

SEBIL
Aggiunge infin che sei un briccone,
E poi scroccon e furfantone.

MIRADILLO
Proprio ver? Basta già?
É sciocco chi ardì
Si gran temerità.
Qual uom alberga qui
Ei no no no, non sa!

PERICLE
Ah, ah!

MIRADILLO
Turista, per mia fé,
Maggior di me non v'è.

PERICLE
Chi siate voi non vo saper.
Ma il mio denaro io voglio aver.

MIRADILLO
Olà! Io son turista!
Capite voi?

TUTTI
No!

MIRADILLO
Attenti! tutto chiaro vi dirò;
Sì, tutto ben vi spiegherò.

## Couplet

I.
Tutti i mari ho attraversato
Quando ogni vento burrascoso era cessato.
Tutti i monti ho misurati,
Solo quelli alti e perigliosi ho trascurati.
    Io viaggio ogni paese,
      Dove il popolo é cortese;
      Son famoso in livellare,
      E stupendo in triangolare;
      Il più astruso meridiano

Misuro io col nonio in mano;
Far scoperte è mia passione..
Come illustre viaggiatore
Conosciuto ovunque son,
L'Europa paga la missione,
Ma io faccio per onore,
Questa mia profession.
Geografo son io pur,
Etnografo più che sicur;
Cogli Ottentotti son
Famigliar come fratello;
Laggiù poi, in Guinea
Stimato da gioiello.
Dal prence di Dahome
Ho pranzato spesso assai,
E nel serraglio—mi trastullai.
Noto sono in terra, in mare,
Ed al Congo e al Zanzibar;
Cafri, Arabi ed Ascianti,
Li conosco tutti quanti.
Si, codesto é un buon affare,
Perché si può ben guadagnare;
Eppoi dovunque in terra e in mare
Il gran turista ammireran.

CORO
Si, nodoso é un buon affare, (*ecc.*)

FANFANI
Fiabe! Bombe! Buffon!
O fanfaron!

II.
MIRADILLO
Non dei popol solo
Io vi posso raccontar;
Ma persin da belve
Mi feci riamar.
Mi salutan tutti.
Ed i belli ed i brutti;
Orsi, lupi e leoni,

Tutti sento giubilar.
E le tigri stesse—se mi vedon da lontano,
Corron giulive—e mi bacian la mano.
I somari, poi,
Li conosco come voi,
Li saluto nel passar.
Ed i piccoli scimmiotti
Avvoltoi e passerotti,
Vengon tutti a me contenti
Sol per farmi complimenti;
E gli stessi elefanti
Li conosco tutti quanti;
E persin rinoceronti,
E giraffe e mastodonti.
Nè grotte, nè deserto,
Monte, lago, valle c'è,
Nemmeno v'ha una fossa
Che ignota sia a me.
Dall'apice del monte
Sin al fondo dell'alto mare
Vo franco un gioiello per trovar.
Petrefatti, minerali,
Fiori, piante ed animali,
Tutto investigato fu,
Tutto investigato fu.
Si codesto è un buon affar, (*ecc.*)

CORO
Si, codesto è un buon affar, (*ecc.*)

MIRADILLO
Hai capito dunque chiaro,
Un turista che sia mai?

PERICLE
L'ho capito più che ben;
Paghi sol quel che mi vien.

MIRADILLO
Sta tranquillo, amico caro,
Il denaro tuo l'avrai.

PERICLE
Si la è bella in verità:
Chi non paga, via non va.

MIRADILLO
Metti in conto anche la schiava,
Chè Sebil meco verrà.

PERICLE
Natural! Lo immaginava!
Nuove spese!...Pagherà!

MIRADILLO
Pericle, t'è dunque ignoto
Che l'Europa mi mandò?

PERICLE
Il cassiere non m' è noto;
La pazienza perderò!

## SCENA IV

FANFANI (*leggendo un telegramma*): Arrivo oggi, ore 4, con mio marito...

PERICLE: Ah! É lei eccellenza...le bacio...

FANFANI: Cosa mi vuoi baciare animale?

PERICLE: Mi voglia scusare, Eccellenza, l'avevo presa per la sua signora.

FANFANI (*interrompendolo*): È arrivata mia nipote?

PERICLE: Nipote? Non saprei...

FANFANI: E neppure suo marito? Un marito che mi costa due milioni in tante obbligazioni inglesi? Fossero almeno turche!

PERICLE: Come, Vostra Eccellenza deve pagare?

FANFANI: Ti spiego subito come stanno le cose. Morto mio fratello mi lasciò 4 milioni, due esclusivamente per me, dei quali non esiste più nemmeno un parte, e due da consegnare a sua figlia Titania il giorno che si presenterà maritata. Sono già tre anni ch'essa se ne vive in Italia da sola; e non mi fece mai concepire la più piccola idea di matrimonio; io me ne viveva tranquillo col frutto dei due milioni, dicevo fra me: Ecco una donna che sa il fatto suo, essa non vuole la schiavitù d'un marito e fa bene: quando questa settimana ricevo questo fatale telegramma; "Arrivo oggi, ore 4, con mio marito;" Con Suo marito; comprendi Pericle?

PERICLE: Eh! Comprendo benissimo, Eccellenza...

FANFANI: Io venni qui perché ho bisogno di te.

PERICLE: Sono a vostra disposizione; Eccellenza;

FANFANI: Mia nipote alloggerà nel tuo Hotel...Questo matrimonio improvviso non mi persuade..; dubito che essa abbia preso a prestito questo marito per avere i due milioni...Tu li sorveglierai e mi farai nota del più piccolo sospetto, mi hai capito?

PERICLE: Perfettamente, Eccellenza...,

FANFANI: Ora vattene...(*Pericle parte*)

## SCENA V
### Nachi e detti.

NACHI: Eccellenza, abbisogna di filtri amorosi, di gocciole per Odalische?

FANFANI: Va al diavolo! Ci vorrebbe una gocciola per il marito di mia nipote.

NACHI: Ho qui un'acqua miracolosa, una sola goccia, data ad una donna le fa dimenticare tutto il passato.

FANFANI: Come?

NACHI: Ecco, veda un esempio: Zobaide, la moglie di Salomone il gioielliere, ne ha bevuto una sola goccia e dimenticò subito suo marito per fuggire con un bel giovinetto.

FANFANI: Sborsare due milioni! Mi è impossibile, altrimenti la cavalleria diverrebbe fanteria.

NACHI: Eccellenza, dei datteri della vendetta.

FANFANI: Va al diavolo te ed i tuoi datteri.

NACHI: Sono d'un potere meraviglioso...per accertarsi se una persona diede un bacio, basta dargli da mangiare uno di questi...

NACHI: Datteri che starnuta subito.

FANFANI: Mi lasci in pace?

NACHI: E tanti baci diede, tanti starnuti fa...è l'unica maniera per sapere se l'amante o la moglie vi sia fedele.

FANFANI: Ti levi dai piedi, imbecille? (*via*).

NACHI: Vi farò vedere se sono un imbecille, questa sera; alla festa del Beiram. Voglio farvi starnutare finche scoppiate (*musica*).

## SCENA VI
### Il Muezzino e detti.

MUEZZINO
Ya rezzak! Ya Kerim!
Ya fellah! Ya alim!

PERICLE E CORO
Ya rezzak, (*ecc.*)

MUEZZINO
Moslin! Siam quasi alla fin del Ramadan;
Sia gloria ad Allah!

CORO
Allah!

MUEZZINO
Vestitevi pel santo Beiram;
Onore ad Allah!

CORO
Allah!

MUEZZINO
Ya rezzak, (*ecc.*)

CORO
Ya rezzak, (*ecc.*)

PERICLE
Passa presto il Ramadan,
Tosto viene il Beiram,
Ed ognun giubilerà,
Lieto, allegro danzerà!
Ora il treno arriverà,
Passeggeri avremo quo.

SEBIL (*dall'Hotel*)
Olà! Olà!
Uno vien, uno va,
Chi meno, chi più,
Chi su, chi giù,
Regalerà.
Ed ognun—che verrà
Il Baxis—ci darà.

PERICLE
Oh! Capisco questo suon!
Oh Baxis, amico suon!
Tu sei pure incantatore
Quanto mai si può pensar!
Porti gioie tutte l'ore
E guadagni sai portar.

CORO
Presto di là Baxis verrà;
Ah, ah, ah! ah, ah, ah!

Tin! tin! tin!
Baxis! Baxis!
Capisce anche un bambin, (*ecc.*)

## SCENA VII
**Pericle, un Sais, dei Maroniti, Antarsi e Popolo.**

# N. 2 – Canzone e Coro di Maroniti e Paggi

SAIS
Posto al prence Antarsi!
Onor, onor!
A lui che ci onorò.

CORO
Presti, presti,
Lesti, lesti,
Su corriamo presto a lui gridando: viva!
Viva, viva!
Gloria al prence Antarsi!
La stella egli é del Libano!

PAGGI
Corriam, su, su, corriam
Al verde pian;
Or qua, or là
Si volerà.
Rapidità—non mancherà!
Nasca quel che sa,
Abbiam sempre novità!

I.
ANTARSI
Già spicca il volo
Ad un cenno solo
Lo snello mio destrier.
Come balen
Lieto, seren,
Io solcavo i verdi campi rapido,
Col dolce mio pensier;
E vidi quadri

Belli leggiadri
Per l'ampio Libano;
E l'eco qua—risuona già
Su nei monti—già nel piano:
Olà! olà!
Al monte! al pian!

CORO
E l'eco qua, (*ecc.*)

ANTARSI
Nel pensier sempre sognando di donzelle
 Di fate, d'un bel fiore,
 A me gioisce il core
Voluttà sempre m'inspiran le storielle
 D'incanti e di magie
 E di bei sogni d'or!
 V'ascolterei—v'ammirerei,
 Felicità—mi dona l'amor!
 Vorrei sentir,
  Spiar, gioir,
Finche nel cor un fremito
D'umor si desti fulgido!

CORO
Vorrei sentir, (*ecc.*)

II.
ANTARSI
 L'azzurro cielo
 Si spoglia il velo
 Se vien degli astri il re.
 Si, anche il sol libero vuol
Aver ampio il firmamento splendido
 Sempre intorno a sé!
 La vita fiori
 Dona ed amori,
 La sola libertà
Liberi fa! Noi tutti assiem
Sempre, Si, griderem:

    Viva! Viva!
    La libertà!

CORO
    La libertà, si, viva!
    Viva! Viva!
    La libertà, si, viva!

ANTARSI
Ma se in ciel tutte le mille e mille stelle
    La chiara notte svela
    E il sol i raggi cela;
Voluttà sempre m'ispiran le storielle, *ecc.*

## SCENA VIII

ANTARSI: Greco, il tuo Hotel é disponibile?

PERICLE: No, Altezza. È occupato da una signora.

ANTARSI: Come, tutto l'Hotel?

PERICLE: Sì, Altezza.

ANTARSI: E chi è questa signora che le abbisogna tutto l'Hotel?

PERICLE: La signorina Titania Fanfani.

## SCENA IX
**Titania e detti.**

# N. 3 – Entrata di Titania

SAIS (*servo*): Iuschi! Iuschi! Largo alla bella Titania! Largo alla stella d'Occidente! (*musica*)

    TITANIA
    Che quadro amen,
    Sì, sì, davver,
    Si stende or qui
    Dinnanzi a me!

Sì fulgida,
Sì splendida
Veduta tal
No, no, non v'è!

(CORO *ripete*)

TITANIA
Se non mi sbaglio
Il locandiere voi...

PERICLE
Per servirla sono qua.

TITANIA
Va ben. Avete camere?

PERICLE
Senza riguardo
Caccio tutti gli altri, senza alcun ritardo,
Caccerò lo stesso prence fuor di qua.

ANTARSI (*fra sé*)
Che angelica beltà!

TITANIA
No, ciò m'apporterebbe del dispiacere.

ANTARSI
Codesto è suo dovere.

TITANIA E ANTARSI (*ognuno fra sé*)
Quegli sguardi tutto amore
Come fanno delirar!
Oh, perché non son pittore
Per potermeli ritrar!

PERICLE (*fra sé*)
È imbarazzato, muto se ne sta,
Da che la vide qua!
(*forte*)

Sgombre son le stanze già,
Ne approfitti a volontà.

TITANIA
Si, si; or, ora:
C'é tempo ancora.

SEBIL E NACHI
Oh che diletto provar de'!

TITANIA (*osservando il paese*)
Attraente!

TUTTI
Che quadro ameno, (*ecc.*)

TITANIA
Ma...signor! Pria di partire,
Mi voglia udire:
Rilevai con mio sommo dispiacere
Che sgarbato fu con lei il locandiere.
    La casa grande é già,
    Se crede, noi farem metà.

ANTARSI
Troppo buona!

PERICLE (*fra sé*)
Amichevol tanto essa gli si mostra;
Non è più imbarazzato; resterà.

TITANIA
E?

ANTARSI
Tutta sua bontà!

TITANIA
E voglio ben sperare.
Non le rincrescerà.

ANTARSI (*fra sé*)
Fervido amor
Sento nel cor!

# Couplet

I.
TITANIA
Se ignoti l'uno all'altro siam,
Col tempo amici pur noi diventiam.
Vicini or or si parlerà,
Il rimanente poi il ciel farà.
Qui l'etichetta non è amena,
Pesante è più di una catena,
    Ci fa la vita più penosa,
Ci annoia, ci molesta ancor;
E c'impedisce di parlare,
Talvolta pur di guardare;
Formalità così noiosa
Possiam lasciar per or.
    Perché sottilizzar?
    La vita ben passar!
    Una parola sola
    Tutto può aggiustar.

CORO
Perché sottilizzar? (*ecc.*)

II.
TITANIA
All'albeggiare col narghilè
Gustando assieme un buon caffè;
Lui tratterà da cavaliere;
A me il chiacchierar farà piacere!
Un fiorellin, che vago sia,
Mi porgerà con cortesia,
Ed io allor per adornarmi
Al sen lo fermerò.
Cortese lui e con rispetto
A' piedi miei in dolce affetto,
Volendo la man baciarmi,

Io lo permetterò.
Perché sottilizzar? (*ecc.*)

CORO
Bene, bene, *ecc.*

## SCENA X

TITANIA: Dunque resta stabilito; una metà dell'Hotel per lei; l'altra per me.

PERICLE: Scusi, e che cosa rimarrà per il di lei marito!

TITANIA: Per mio marito? (È necessario prima che lo trovi!)

ANTARSI: Maritata?

TITANIA: Mio marito non farà che approvare quello che io feci; al mio posto avrebbe fatto altrettanto. Prenda, dunque possesso senza riguardo, prego!

ANTARSI (*entrando*): Com'é bella! (*musica*).

PERICLE: E il di lei marito, non è arrivato?

TITANIA: Mio zio è forse nell'Hotel?

PERICLE: No, signora, Sua Eccellenza sarà qui fra poco.

TITANIA: Ma come, non farsi trovare...

PERICLE: Fra tanto può accomodarsi, l'appartamento è pronto.

TITANIA: No, no, lo attenderò qui fuori, là dentro fa troppo caldo, andate!

PERICLE: Come comanda! (Il marito non è arrivato con lei, ecco una buona notizia per Sua Eccellenza il Pascià (*via*).

TITANIA: La mia posizione è alquanto imbrogliata per ottenere l'eredità di due milioni, devo avere un marito! Per due milioni si può fare un tal sacrificio...ma dove pescarlo? Eppure lo devo trovare a qualunque costo!

## SCENA XI
### Miradillo, Hosch e detti.

MIRADILLO: Ma dunque non mi lascerai un solo istante?

(*Hosch accenna di no.*)

TITANIA: Non m'inganno, signor Miradillo?

MIRADILLO: Chi mi vuole? Chi vedo! Voi qui, signorina Titania?

TITANIA: Quale meraviglia? L'Egitto è la mia patria! Ditemi voi piuttosto come mai vi trovate da queste parti, perché avete lasciata la vostra bella Italia?

MIRADILLO: Ho voluto fare un viaggio di piacere; era un pezzo che bramavo di visitare l'Africa! (*soggetto*).

TITANIA: Bravissimo, e quello schiavo sarà la vostra guida, m'immagino...

MIRADILLO: Sicuro...è la mia guida...oh! Non mi lascerà mai...è fidatissimo, mi viene dietro come un cane (*maledetto*).

TITANIA: Siete stato a visitare il centro di questo paese?

MIRADILLO: No, non ancora...fa troppo caldo!

TITANIA: Specialmente in questa stagione!...Infatti, se non ero qui chiamata da un forte interesse, me ne sarei andata volentieri a Livorno.

MIRADILLO: Ah! Livorno! Lei si rammenta quelle belle serate che si passavano. All'Ardenza fu precisamente là ch'ebbi la fortuna di conoscerla per la prima volta.

TITANIA: E fu dove imparai a conoscere il vostro spirito e le vostre scappataggini...

MIRADILLO: E allora potevo farle! Ora invece....

TITANIA: Siete divenuto un uomo serio?
MIRADILLO: Questo poi no! Ciò non potrà mai succedere, non è il mio naturale.

TITANIA: Allora, se non vi rincresce, voglio approfittare di un poco del vostro spirito.

MIRADILLO: Approfitti pure...sarò fortunatissimo...cosa devo fare?

TITANIA: Sostenere in faccia a mio zio una parte alquanto comica.

MIRADILLO: Fosse almeno quella dell'amoroso! Eh! Quella sì che la sosterrei volentieri!

TITANIA: No, vi si adatta di più il brillante.

## SCENA XII
### Pericle e detti.

PERICLE: Viene Sua Eccellenza vostro zio...vado incontro per avvisarlo del vostro arrivo.

TITANIA: Benissimo! Prima però voglio presentarvi mio marito.

MIRADILLO: Marito?!

PERICLE: Marito?!

TITANIA: Quale meraviglia?

MIRADILLO: Ma già, qual meraviglia? Marito né più né meno, suo marito.

PERICLE: Scusate!...ma...la sorpresa.

MIRADILLO: Ora spero che vorrai levarmi dai piedi quella brutta faccia? (*indicando Hosch*)

PERICLE: Ma subito, signore...anzi, scusate...

MIRADILLO: Nulla, nulla, licenziate la mia guida.

PERICLE: Subito, Signore! (*Hosch via*). Corro ad avvisare Sua Eccellenza!

TITANIA: Ha capito?

MIRADILLO: Non del tutto...ma quasi...

TITANIA: Per ottenere un'eredità di due milioni devo avere un marito.

MIRADILLO: Ed io devo passare per tale.

TITANIA: Precisamente.

MIRADILLO: In tutte le sue funzioni?

TITANIA: Ah! questo poi no.

(*Musica*).

SCENA XIII
**Titania, Pericle, Fanfani e Miradillo.**

## N. 4 – Quartetto

FANFANI
Ti dico sei stordito!

PERICLE
È pura verità!

TITANIA (*a Miradillo*)
Or fingasi marito.

MIRADILLO (*a Titania*)
Il ciel m'aiuterà!

FANFANI
Ma che sia quella coppia anche legal!
Il vero qui d'investigar la pena val.

TITANIA
Or ti posso alfin riveder
Mio tesoro, mio tesor!
Che diletto! che piacer
Nel mio cor! nel mio cor!

MIRADILLO
Posso alfine te ammirar,
Dolce ben! dolce ben!
Or il limpido ciel m'appar
Più seren più seren.

PERICLE
Ehi, signor! Ho ragion?

FANFANI
Qui si deve sorvegliare;
Un intrigo questo pare...
Egli è il caso da impazzar!
Sono sposi, già lo so,
E pagare ora dovrò.

PERICLE
Or dubbi più non ha;
Sarebbe una sciocchezza...
E festa gli farà
Con tutta gentilezza.

TITANIA E MIRADILLO
Posato sul tuo cor
M'infiamma un dolce amor!
 (Gentil si dee mostrar,
I dubbi a dileguar).

FANFANI (*fra sé*)
Se potessi il manigoldo avvelenar,
Fracassarlo, strangolarlo, massacrar!
Ei mi costa due milion, quell'animal,
E nemmeno due centesimi non val.

PERICLE
Insigne coppia, grata a noi
Lo zio or qui presento a voi.

TITANIA
Oh bel zio amabile,
E sì trattabile,
Sempre placabile,
Lo sposo mio ti voglio presentar.

FANFANI (*fra sé*)
Oh, se potessi,quattro
schiaffi gli darei!

MIRADILLO
Oh, bel zio amabile,
Mia moglie è affabile,
Più che adorabile.
Persino i debiti mi vuol pagar.

FANFANI
Mille grazie!
Oh che cara!
Oh gioiel!

TITANIA
Questa é troppa pretensione,
(*a Miradillo*) È maniera da briccone!
Non pagherò! Codesta è già
        Trivialità!

MIRADILLO
Cosi vuole la commedia;
(*a Titania*) Ciò é più che naturale...
Altrimenti una tragedia
Noi avremo in carnevale.
        Vi lascio in bianco,
        Non sto più a fianco;
        Così sarà.

FANFANI
Già incomincian le baruffe...
Spero almen si accopperan!

TITANIA E MIRADILLO
Posato sul tuo cuor
M'infiamma un dolce amor!
Gentil si dee mostrare
I dubbi a dileguare.

FANFANI
Rincomincian le moine. O che affar!
All'inferno tutti due vorrei mandar!
Ei mi costa due milioni, quel maiale,
E nemmeno due centesimi non vale
          Dalla bile scoppio già;
          Sento il sangue infiammar

PERICLE
Mi sembra un po' turbato,
Per parentela tale,
Furente ed irritato;
Egli é matto, in verità!
Qui convien all'erta star.

TITANIA
Mio tesor! mio tesor!

MIRADILLO
Dolce ben! Dolce ben!

TITANIA E MIRADILLO
Sei l'amore
Del mio cuore!
Il mio tutto!

PERICLE
Che briccon!

TITANIA
Su, finiamo! Or vo' pagare.

Orsù! il conto a me.

PERICLE
Oh, la prego...non c'è fretta;
Ma se pur ciò la diletta
E pagare vuole tosto,
Ecco il conto; è pronto già.

TITANIA (*legge*)
Cinquantamila franchi...e tre!
Per venti giorni sol!

MIRADILLO
Modico!...modico!..
Cinquanta...e mille...e tre!...

TITANIA (*legge*)
"Tre mila franchi un souper
Con cantatrici al Grand Café..."

MIRADILLO
La musica io l'amo assai,
E là del canto m'inebriai.

FANFANI (*fra sé*)
Oh che furfante! Che mariolone!

TITANIA
Si, davvero, originale!

MIRADILLO
Sì, sì; lo calcolo un onore
Esser dell'arte il protettore.

TITANIA (*legge*)
"Duemila franchi la pigion
Di damigella De Nanon..."

MIRADILLO
Questa era un'orfanella,
Una povera zitella.

FANFANI (*fra sé*)
Volpe!

TITANIA (*legge*)
"Una schiava per seimila franchi ancor?"

MIRADILLO
Sì, sì; al ciel volea serbarla
E poi farla battezzare!

FANFANI
Oh! tal furfante, per mia fé,
Non ha visto ancora, veh!
Un cotale mentitor
Non si trova a prova a peso d'or
Quindi voglio lo sposino
Studiar meglio da vicino

TITANIA, MIRADILLO E PERICLE
No, non é il momento
Turbare tal contento;
Dubbio qui al presente
Esser non vi de.

FANFANI
Essa queta—egli ardito.
Loro meta—è ingannar!
Ma giuntarmi non mi lascio
Da un simile bandito,
Che d'ogn'erba ha fatto un fascio!
Loro scopo è d'imbrogliar!

TITANIA E MIRADILLO
Ma perché—tal rumore?
Ma perché—tanto furore?
Oh deh!—zio buono,
Bontà!—perdono!

PERICLE
Mio signore—meno bile!
Più gentile—sia con lor;

Oh, deh!—zio buono,
Bontà!—perdono!

FANFANI
Tal briccone—fanfarone
Tuo marito—esser può?

TITANIA
Da moglie tenera e prudente é mio dovere
Schivar qualunque dispiacere.
 Di fuoco ardor
 Gli riempie il cuor.
Un siciliano presto va in furor.
 Nel siciliano etere
 Dell'Etna il fuoco v'ha;
 Chi là si porta a vivere
 Di fuoco fremerà!
 Là bollon le onde,
Col mare là lotta il vascel;
 Il vortice fende
Con l'acque spesso il ciel!
 Oh bel suol! Oh bel suol!
Diletto suol! Colà vi bolle con furor
 Il fuoco; là si freme per d'amor!
 Un paradiso di Palermo é il terren,
 Il cielo é sempre splendido, seren!

TUTTI
Diletto suol, (ecc.)
Sempre colà scuote Vulcano il suolo,
Quivi l'amor non é congiunto a duolo;
Sgorga la lava dai profondi abissi,
 E spira il cor
 Fervido amor!
Di fiamme sentesi l'ardor!
Nel siciliano etere, (ecc.)

## SCENA XIV
### Titania e Fanfani.

FANFANI: Senti, cara nipote, hai un certo marito che non mi garba affatto! Tu sei una donna infelicissima!

TITANIA: Ma vi dico di no!

FANFANI: Tu piangi giorno e notte.

TITANIA: Io?

FANFANI: Vedo che hai bisogno del divorzio.

TITANIA: Ah! Ecco il principe. (Viene a tempo per levarmi d'impaccio).

FANFANI: È testarda veh! Vuole a tutti i costi i due milioni.

## SCENA XV
### Antarsi e detti.

ANTARSI: Signora!

TITANIA: Mio zio Fanfani, Pascià, il principe Antarsi!

FANFANI: Altezza!

ANTARSI: Noi ci conosciamo...

FANFANI: Si, per corrispondenza.

ANTARSI: Si fece qualche affare; io gli mandai mille pelli di tigre!

FANFANI: Ed io vi spedii in cambio 20 schiave, anzi udii che non foste troppo contento del cambio?

ANTARSI: Ciò dipende da non far gli affari in persona...

FANFANI: (Gli spedii fra le 20 schiave sei vecchie cuoche).

TITANIA: Come, principe, anche voi avete il barbaro costume di comperare e vendere le schiave? Ciò è da selvaggi!

ANTARSI: Voi che siete tanto gentile, dovreste cercare di civilizzarmi, e allora.....non solo sarei il vostro diligente scolaro, ma anche il vostro devotissimo servo.

TITANIA: E perché no? Proveremo. Ci rivedremo a pranzo, caro zio?

FANFANI: Sicuro, festeggeremo il Beiram nella mia villa.

TITANIA: Benissimo, venite Principe?

FANFANI: E tuo marito?

TITANIA: (Ma già me n'ero scordata) Oh! Mio marito sarà felice che mi diverto.

FANFANI: Il marito si diverte da una parte, la moglie dall'altra... benissimo, si vede subito che mia nipote fu educata all'europea!

## SCENA XVI
### Elda, Buccametta, Fanfani ed un facchino.

BUCCAMETTA (di dentro): E un'ora che ci fai girare per questo maledetto albergo!

ELDA: Abbi pazienza, mamma!

FANFANI: Chi saranno queste forestiere?

FACCHINO: Per di qui...! Baxis! Baxis!

BUCCAMETTA: Baxis! Ma com'è? Se è già là terza volta che ti do denaro! Non ne sei ancora content?

FACCHINO: Baxis!

FANFANI (dando un calcio al facchino): Rù...

FACCHINO: Ahi! Scusi Eccellenza (via)

ELDA: Ma perché?

FANFANI: Non meravigliatevi, signorina, è l'usanza del paese; quando qualcuno ci annoia, un calcio e Rù...! Siete sicuri di non esser più annoiati.

BUCCAMETTA: Bella maniera! È bene saperlo!

FANFANI: Gentile fanciulla! Italiana, non è vero? A me piacciono tanto le italiane (*toccando il mento ad Elda*).

ELDA (*battendogli con sgarbo la mano*): Rù...!

FANFANI: Ah! Come impara subito l'arabo!

BUCCAMETTA: Oh! mia figlia è d'una intelligenza unica.

FANFANI: Si vede e si sente anche!

BUCCAMETTA: Ma in quest' Hotel non c'è nessuno?

FANFANI: Credo non c'è più una stanza disponibile!

ELDA: Come? Non c'è' più posto?

BUCCAMETTA: E quella bestia ci conduce proprio qui!

ELDA: Ora bisogna andare in cerca d'un altro albergo.

BUCCAMETTA: Quanti fastidi e tutto a causa di quel mastro! Ma se lo trovo...

ELDA: Pazienza mamma, andiamo.

FANFANI: Ma sarà cosa difficile che possiate trovare posto in qualche Hotel con tanta affluenza di forestieri. Se volessero approfittare del mio alloggio, mi chiamerei ben fortunato!

BUCCAMETTA: E perché no?

ELDA: Mamma, che dici? Non ci mancherebbe altro che andassimo ad alloggiare in casa d'un turco!

FANFANI: E cosa c'è di male? In casa mia ho ricevuto tanti ospiti! Ora vi voglio dare un'idea dei nostri costumi. (*Musica*)

SCENA XVII
**Elda, Buccametta e Fanfani.**

## N. 5 – Terzetto

FANFANI
Una barba piena,
Una lauta cena,
Un turbante in testa,
Esser sempre in festa,
Senza mai lavoro,
Sempre al fianco un moro,
Sempre un pipone,
Niente seggiolone;
Non abbisognare
Né stufe né caldare,
E nemmen forchetta;
Mai non aver fretta.
Lussi strombazzati,
Harem ben ornati,
E che in tasca il mondo
Hassi, dirlo tondo;
I viaggi, quelli,
Farli su cammelli;
Ber del Moka puro,
È il più sicuro.
Questo sarà male,
Ma é da orientale.

A 3
Questo è più che male,
Ma è da orientale.

ELDA
Usi d'oriente,

Vero è certamente,
Sonvi anche da noi;
Ma lo dico a voi,
Senza alcun rispetto,
Ve lo dico schietto:
Nelle nostre zone
Libertà è illusone!
Esser ben ornate,
Ad uno destinate,
Ubbidir dovere,
No, non é un piacere!
E le nozze poi
Studiansi da noi!
L'uomo sempre mente,
Giura poi per niente;
Giura sempre amore
E ride nel suo cuore;
Hanno tutti quanti
Centomila amanti!
No, non é orientale,
Mi bensì immorale!

A 3
No, non é orientale,
Ma bensì immorale!

BUCCAMETTA
Sì, nell'occidente
Come nell'oriente,
V'han degli elementi
Molto intelligenti;
Donne eccellenti
Piene di talenti,
E non corpulenti
Como nell'oriente;
Ma son tormentate,
Sempre maltrattate
Dai mariti sciocchi
Che spalancano gli occhi.
Sempre complimenti
Fanno a tutti i venti;

E così insolenti
Sono ed indolenti,
Causa i loro sposi
Imbecilli, odiosi!
Vita disgraziata
Fanno e bistrattata.
Schiave son! È male,
Peggio che orientale!

A 3
Schiave son! è male,
Peggio che orientale!

## SCENA XVIII

FANFANI: In casa mia potete stare tranquille, là vi sono le mie mogli.

ELDA: Mogli?

BUCCAMETTA: Mogli?

FANFANI: Precisamente. Nel mio Harem non vi sono che 46 pezzi e vorrei sperare di...

BUCCAMETTA: D'arrivare ai 48?

FANFANI: No, quando mai, ai 47!

BUCCAMETTA: (Turco screanzato!) E tutto a causa di quel maledetto Miradillo!

FANFANI: Miradillo?

ELDA: Lo conosce forse?

FANFANI: Un giovane italiano?

BUCCAMETTA: Sì, palermitano...

FANFANI: Per Maometto! Il marito di mia nipote!

ELDA: Maritato?

BUCCAMETTA: Ah! traditore, furfante! Ti dissi di portare una boccetta di vetriolo!

ELDA: Calmatevi mamma, bisogna prima vedere, bisogna sentire....

BUCCAMETTA: Cosa vuoi vedere, cosa vuoi sentire di più?

FANFANI: Sembra che quel briccone ne abbia fatta una delle sue!

ELDA: Senta, signore; giacché è tanto gentile, accettiamo il di lei alloggio.

FANFANI: Benissimo!

BUCCAMETTA: Brava! E ci vendicheremo. Ha della dinamite in casa?

FANFANI: Non ci mancherebbe altro!

## SCENA XIX
**Miradillo, Nachi, Pericle, Hosch e detti.**

MIRADILLO (*da dentro*): Vado a sentire se lo zio pranza da noi.

ELDA: Ah! eccolo l'infame!

BUCCAMETTA: E non avere del vetriolo! Qui, qui il velo, altrimenti ci conosce!

MIRADILLO: Ebbene zio, pranzate da noi?

FANFANI: No, pranziamo tutti in compagnia nella mia villa, lo dissi a vostra moglie!

MIRADILLO: Troppo gentile!

FANFANI: Faranno parte della tavola queste due gentili signore che mi furono raccomandate dal loro console Svedese.

MIRADILLO: Sarà una fortuna la nostra, signore!

(*Elda le volta le spalle*).

BUCCAMETTA: Crepa mostro!

MIRADILLO: Come?

FANFANI: Sono parole svedesi, non comprendono l'Italiano...Ah! Ecco i miei schiavi.

SCENA XX
**Elda, Buccametta, Fanfani, Miradillo,
Nachi, Pericle, Hosch,
Musicanti, Schiave, Schiavi, Popolo.**

# N. 6 – Finale I

CORO
La, la! La, la!
    Orsù suoniam!
La, la! la, la!
    Orsù cantiam!
La, la! Si, si!
A noi destà del piacer
Da noi caccia ogni pensieri
La tarabuka già sonora vibra,
Ed il kemenghen scuote qualunque fibra;
    Melodia splendida,
    Anche il flauto ci darà!
    La, la, la!
    Balliamo in circolo,
    La, la, la!
    Un ballo rapido.

FANFANI
Al Tsad! al Tsad!
Si compran Veneri,
Son belle, tonde fulgide,
Invitano all'amor!
Il pascià è davver
Già ebbro dal piacer!

A peso sempre le comprai,
Dal Nord al Sud io le cercai,
Pagando tutte a peso d'or!
Al Tsad! al Tsad!

CORO
Al Tsad! al Tsad!
Si comperan veneri!
Al Tsad! al Tsad!
Invitano all'amor!

FANFANI
Avanti! Il piè, la man....
Mostrate qua;
In verità—nessun avrà
Cosi vezzose Veneri!
In verità—altre non v'ha
Che belle sian così!

(CORO *ripete.*)

FANFANI
Al Kur! al Kur!
Giunoni trovansi
Di forza pari ad Ercole,
Di cento chili almen!
Non è la qualità
Di grande agilità,
Ma pur dell'anitre al par,
Si vendon sempre dondolar
Col viso rubicondo e pien!
Al Kur! Al Kur!

(CORO *ripete.*)

FANFANI
Un mercante tanto fino
Non é facile trovar:
Ho un buon gusto sì divino
Quando schiave vò a comprar!

## SCENA XXI
**Sebil e detti.**

SEBIL
Miradillo, la tua schiava;
Ai tuoi comandi pronta sono.

TUTTI
Ma, vedete!
Che vuol qui questa donna?
Ha persa la quiete
E non si sa perché.

SEBIL
Io son sua schiava.

TUTTI
Sfacciata!

SEBIL
Restare vo' qua!

TUTTI
No, no, va tosto fuor!

SEBIL
No, no!

TUTTI
Va via di qua!

SEBIL
No, no!

TUTTI
Va fuor!

SEBIL
Comprata ei m'ha, è mio padron;
Restare qui ho ben ragion!

TUTTI
Va fuor!

MIRADILLO
Si, é vero essa è mia schiava,
Ed è per ciò che resterà!
Comprata l'ho, é verità.

BUCCAMETTA E CORO
La comperò—e la pagò
A peso d'or!—Original!
Davver, originai!

FANFANI E CORO
Or che dirà la moglie?

ELDA
Oh ciel che sento mai?!
A me non pensa più;
Si compra una schiava!
Dovevo qui in straniero suol
Sopportare un simil duol,
Ed incontrar un tale oltraggio!
    O sorte crudel!

MIRADILLO
Singolar! Non c'é mal!
Fatto egli é da carnevali
    Un quid pro quo
    Ora vedrò;
    Una risata
    Io ci darò!

BUCCAMETTA
Singolar! Caso tal
Fatto egli è per noi fatal!
Una moglie aver
E schiave poi tener!
Scandalo simile, ah!
Si, si, raro vi ha!

SEBIL
Si, Sebil dona pur la vita
    Al suo signor;
E presteragli sempre aita
    Con grato amor.
Ed esser vuole veramente
Sempre a lui riconoscente,
I sonni suoi tuttor vegliar,
    E sempre in viso
    Col sorriso
Al fianco suo sempre star!

TUTTI
Ma che dirà la moglie?...

FANFANI
La moglie, eccola qua!
(Vedrem che nascerà!)

Scena XXII<br>**Antarsi, Titania e detti.**

TITANIA
Timidità—qui non ci sta;
Franco parlar—non curar mai nessun;
Lei ha bel cuor—che sente amor,
E se vorrà—lei potrà
    Me servir.

ANTARSI
A tale consiglio
Ci starò!—seguirò!
Vostro schiavo signora—sarò con piacer!

FANFANI
Han già confidenza,
Secondo apparenza....
È anzi evidenza.
Nipote mia, vedi (*piano a Titania*)
Tuo sposo che fa?
E tu lo concedi!

Ma che si dirà?
Ei compra una schiava...
Ben fatto ti par?
No non meritava
Titania sposar!

TITANIA
Comprar una schiava!
Che male qui c'é?...
Se ciò gli garbava
Ben fatto, in mia fé!
Si, si! fa ben!
Sentite piuttosto un mio piano!

FANFANI
Ah ma...ma se...dico!...

TITANIA
Il prence, qui allato,
Sì, tanto garbato,
Vorrei pregar
Seco noi di pranzar!

ANTARSI
Che gentil!...troppo onor!

FANFANI
Io mi sento abbrividir!
Che vergogna degg'io soffrir!
Una coppia singolar! Quale orror!...

ELDA, BUCCAMETTA E ALTRI
Ma che sia vero?
Singolar! Singolar!
È proprio singolar!
È grande l'ardir...
Un caso simile
È raro sentir.

FANFANI, PERICLE E CORO
Ma che dirà il marito?

ELDA (*fra sé*)
Si, si, mi tradì!

SEBIL (*a Miradillo*)
Tua son—mio padron!

ANTARSI (*fra sé*)
Si farò, si l'andrà!

MIRADILLO
Singolar! non c'é mal!

FANFANI
Chi lo sa—come andrà?...

CORO
La donna sola sempre vincerà,
    Sì, trionferà!
A festa gradita
Lo squillo c'invita!

TITANIA (*a Miradillo*)
Fate che or mi si accompagni
Con gran pompa e con onor.

MIRADILLO
Farò, farò!
Orsù, avanti;
Alzate il baldacchini
Pompa festosa
Titania colmi ognor!

CORO
Viva! viva!
Noi pronti siam già.
    Allah! Allah!
Il Beiram è qua!

TITANIA E ANTARSI
O che piacer!
Il canto scote il cuore;

Ridestano all'amore!
Si, là si sente la libertà...
Trepido il cor fremi di voluttà!

TUTTI
Tarabuke scuoton l'aria qui d'intorno,
E kemenghe strillan ora tutto il giorno;
        Sì, or possiam banchettar,
        È scorso il Ramadan!
        Sì, noi possiam giubilar;
        È giunto il Beiram!
Quest'è il dì che affin ogni digiun troncò!
Viva il Beiram! Viva la bella festa!

TITANIA
Su lieti corriam,
Corriam, su corriam a banchettar!
Andiam: là c'é il vin,
Il divin!
Sì, là danzerem—canterem!
Andiam, su di voi
Ove splende il sol.

TUTTI
O che piacer!
Il canto scuote il cuore!
Colà i bicchier
Ridestano all'amore;
Sì, là si sente la libertà...
Trepido il cor freme di voluttà!
Tarabuka batti forte...giù!
        È passato il Ramadan!
Vecchi e giovani, allegri, su!
        Giunto é il Beiram!

# FINE DEL PRIMO ATTO

# ATTO SECONDO

**L'azione ha luogo nella villa di Fanfani Pascià sul Nilo.**

*Giardino nella villa di Fanfani; a destra un chiosco rosso, a sinistra uno verde. Vicino ai chioschi, panche di bronzo dorato; a destra ed a sinistra porte d'entrata. Il fondo vien formato dal Nilo; al di là della riva, prospetto del Cairo.*

## SCENA I
**Schiavi di Fanfani, indi Fanfani.**

## N. 7 – Coro

SOPRANI
È giorno di gioia! Si, al lavor Oggi andiam con amor!
Oggi andiam con amor!
    Su, lesti qua!
Una bella fata assai gentil
Sposa il Pascià, egli è sottil!
    Or ora verrà!
Oh che coppia! è un sorriso...
Sol vederla fa gioir.
Sì, di gioie un paradiso
Loro serba l'avvenir.

TENORI E BASSI
Su, veloci corriamo
Ed il tempo non perdiam.

TUTTI
E l'armadio e il tavolin
Lucidi farem persin;

SOPRANI
I tappeti sul balcon
Batteremo con passion.
Altrimenti se vien qua
Il padron noi batterà,

TENORI E BASSI
Su lesti, su lesti,
Puliamo divani,
Poniamo le mani
A sedie, a tappeti,
A tavoli, a letti;
Su lesti, su lesti,
Andiamo, corriamo
Lavoriamo, battiam.

SOPRANI
Ora molti ospiti verran
Da vicino e da lontan.
      Su lesti qua!
Chi essi son, noto a tutti è,
Tutto pulito esser quindi de.
      Li avrem or qua.
O che coppia! è un sorriso, (*ecc.*)

TENORI E BASSI
Via, lasciate il chiacchierar,
E tornate a lavorar.

TUTTI
I tappeti sul balcon, (*ecc.*)

FANFANI
Via, misera canaglia!
Su, tosto a lavorar!
Sapete sol, canaglia,
Qui sempre schiamazzar!
Ma ben vi frusterò,
Così vi educherò.

CORO
Ha la luna il padron!

FANFANI
Io saltare vi farò!

CORO
Via scappiamo dal bastoni

FANFANI
Sì, da inglese li tratterò!
Sì, sì, all'inglese, all'inglese!
La frusta sempre...è l'unica
Frustar la gente stupida!

## Couplet

I.
Nell'Egitto ruban tutto,
Niente quivi è sicuri
Il forziere è già asciutto,
Un quattrin non v'ha neppur:
Ma l'inglese che ha un naso fino
Ne trova sempre in un cantoncino.
Fa l'Europa conferenze,
Egli trae le conseguenze;
Parla sempre coi cannoni
E si fa ben rispettar.
        Ah sì! all'inglese, all'inglese
        Bisogna sempre ovunque agir!

II.
L'Inghilterra fa canali,
—Così vuol la civiltà;—
Costruisce pur fanali
Per cacciar l'oscurità;
Natural poi che pagare
Deve chi vuol navigare.
Chiede ciò con gentilezza,
Ma a pagar ci vuol prestezza,
Altrimenti...quattro bombe,
E nessuno ha nulla a dir!
        Ah sì! all'inglese, all'inglese
        Bisogna sempre ovunque agir!

III.

Se qualcun riceve offese,
Qui va tosto al tribunal,
Ci rimette tempo e spese
Che la pena poi non val!
Ma gl'inglesi a tutte l'ore
San difendere l'onore;
A chi fa lor qualche ingiuria,
Dan due calci senza furia;
Gli offron poi una bistecca,
Dopo fattolo pentir!
            Ah sì! all'inglese, all'inglese
            Bisogna sempre ovunque agir!

IV.

L'Inghilterra ha la missione
I selvaggi a illuminar,
E va sempre col cannone
La cultura a seminar;
Così fanno anch'altri Stati,
Ma aspettano i mandati;
L'Inghilterra fa da sola
E spalanca la sua gola;
Colle pugna innanzi al muso
Fa la scienza digerir!
            Ah sì! all'inglese, all'inglese
            Bisogna sempre ovunque agir!

V.

Se le donne son zitelle
Sono tutte un amorin;
Quando poi son vecchierelle,
Oh, é meglio un diavolin!
La più bella riesce odiosa
E pettegola noiosa!
Ma l' Inglese non la guarda,
Lascia in pace la maliarda;
Scegliesi una governante
La vecchiotta per supplir!
            Ah sì! all'inglese, all'inglese
            Bisogna sempre ovunque agir!

VI.
Per le nostre signorine,
Se tradite, c'é il carbon;
Ma invece le inglesine
Per lo sposo han un baston!
Si, le nostre damigelle
Studian romanze e novelle,
Il francese ed il tedesco,
E...non sanno un fico fresco!
Ed invece le milady
L'Alpi corrono a salir!
    Ah sì! all'inglese, all'inglese
    Bisogna sempre ovunque agir!

## SCENA II
### Miradillo e Fanfani.

MIRADILLO: Splendida questa villa! Un vero soggiorno di fate! Sembra impossibile, a questo mondo, le persone più goffe possiedono le cose migliori!...Questo signor Fanfani...Ah! Eccolo là! Che fa la pantomima ....con chi l'avrà?

FANFANI: Badate veh furfanti! Avrete a che fare col mio staffile.

MIRADILLO (*trattenendo lo staffile*): Vergogna, alla mia presenza, dinanzi agli occhi dell'Europa!

FANFANI: Come?

MIRADILLO: Durante il mio soggiorno in Europa, in Egitto, la pena dello scudiscio dev'essere abolita. Frattanto, carissimo zio, v'invito a sborsare i due milioni appartenenti a vostra nipote Titania, mia moglie...

FANFANI: Per questo c'è tempo!

MIRADILLO: Non mi sembra; il testamento parla chiaro: "Lascio a mia figlia Titania due milioni di franchi. Detta somma le verrà sborsata il giorno che compirà il suo 20° anno e che si presenti al fianco d'un marito legale". Dunque il testamento è qui, Titania è là, il marito è qua...e i due milioni devono esser qua...

FANFANI: Qua, qua i due milioni per ora non sono qua, ma bensì sono...

MIRADILLO: Dove?

FANFANI: Là!...

MIRADILLO: Vuol dire che avremo l'incomodità di andare là a prenderli.

FANFANI: Non prima di domani, giorno che mia nipote compirà il suo 20° anno e che mi sia       accertato che voi siete un marito legittimo.

MIRADILLO: Come, ne dubitereste?

FANFANI: Certamente, chi mi assicura che non siate un marito posticcio?

MIRADILLO: Un marito posticcio? (*minacciandolo*)...

FANFANI: Ehi! quieto!...

FANFANI: Ehi! quietò!...Voi avrete i due milioni, ma prima voglio delle prove che voi siete il vero marito di mia nipote.

MIRADILLO: L'affare si fa più serio di quello che credevo. Bene, si spieghi, quali prove esige?

FANFANI: Vedete questo chiosco?

MIRADILLO: Lo vedo.

FANFANI: Esso è composto d'una camera da letto, quello che appunto ci vuole per due giovani sposi...voi andrete ad abitarlo con vostra moglie...

MIRADILLO: (Ah! Furbo d'un egiziano!)

FANFANI: Cosa avete?

MIRADILLO: Io? Nulla.

FANFANI: Avreste forse della difficoltà?

MIRADILLO: Io, nessuna! Figuratevi, anzi, non mi sembra, vero. È lei...

FANFANI: (Spero con questo mezzo di pormi al sicuro).

MIRADILLO: (È necessario vada ad avvisare Titania). E così, caro zio, dico che fu una bella idea quella del chiosco, tanto é vero che corro a partecipare a vostra nipote, mia moglie.

FANFANI: Bravo!...

MIRADILLO: Sono certo che ne sarà felicissima! (*via*).

FANFANI: Pare che non gli piace troppo l'idea del chiosco! Io conosco troppo bene i libati costumi di mia nipote, di qui non si scappa! O dormono insieme e allora domani devo vendere due   caserme...o   no,   e allora i due milioni sono risparmiati...Ah! Ecco le belle Italiane!

## SCENA III
### Elda, Buccametta e detto.

BUCCAMETTA: Eccoci pronte!

FANFANI: Già in costume orientale! Belle! Seriamente! E come trovate questa mia villa?

BUCCAMETTA: Stupenda!

ELDA: Sembra un luogo fatato!

FANFANI: Del quale potrete disporre a vostro talento se vi decidete...

ELDA: A che?

FANFANI: A divenire mia moglie, come già vi dissi.

ELDA: Ah! Signore! (Bisogna guadagnar tempo, altrimenti...)

FANFANI: Coraggio, dunque, rendetemi felice, dite un bel sì...(*Musica*).

SCENA IV
**Elda, Buccametta e Fanfani.**

## N. 8 – Cabaletta di Elda

I.
ELDA
Codesta è seria cosa,
  Ci voglio sopra un po' pensar!
Non sono orgogliosa,
La debbo anzi ringraziar;
  Ma lei ha donne in quantità,
  Non è poi un mister...
    Noto è!
E a me, per dir la verità
Ciò no, non fa piacer,
  No, davver!
Per lei, ch'è turco, è natural,
Lei non lo crede un mal;
Ma io, se debbo il vero dir,
Non posso ciò soffrir.
Potrei più tardi forse aver dolore,
Se subito donassi a lei il mio cuore;
  Perciò...perciò...
  Non dico: no,
  Non dico: sì,
Pure...parli prima con mammà.


II.
Io credo che si pensi
Con molta pratica da voi;
Non siete almen melensi,
Purtroppo! come son da noi!
  Davver, l'accerto por mia fè,
  Ognuna ragion vi dà!
    Fate ben!
L'Europa stessa, creda a me,
Così la penserà nel futur!
E vi potete poi vantare...
Da voi non nascon guai.

É certo, debbo confessar,
Noi siamo indietro assai!
Ma pur da noi c'è ancora il pregiudizio,
Chiamar codesto agire—un grande vizio!
    Perciò...perciò...
    Non dico: no,
    Non dico: sì,
Pure...parli prima con mammà!

## SCENA V
### Fanfani e Buccametta.

FANFANI: Sentite, se mi fate sposare vostra figlia, la vostra fortuna è assicurata, voi non avrete più nulla a desiderare, palazzo, carrozze, palco al teatro, schiavi al vostro comando, infine, tutto.....

BUCCAMETTA: Sì, tutte queste cose sono bellissime cose, ma io vorrei, se fosse possibile, combinare diversamente...

FANFANI: Come?

BUCCAMETTA: Ecco qui! Lei dice che ha 46 mogli, non è vero?

FANFANI: Verissimo, ma vostra figlia sarà la favorita!

BUCCAMETTA: Non dico questo, 46 mogli...con mia figlia sarebbero 47...E così, sposate anche me, e saremo 48, così il numero resta pari!

FANFANI: No, no, preferisco che rimanga dispari in eterno!

BUCCAMETTA: Come, sarebbe a dire?

FANFANI: Non è possibile, voi avete già trascorsa l'età legale per il matrimonio.

BUCCAMETTA: Lo dice lei!

FANFANI: E lo sostengo. Voi l'avete passata almeno di 30 anni l'età matrimoniale; le leggi sono molto rigorose da noi.

BUCCAMETTA: Va bene; frattanto io non mi staccherò un sol momento da mia figlia.

FANFANI: (Maledetta).

BUCCAMETTA: Ed effettuandosi il matrimonio, dove resterebbe la camera matrimoniale?

FANFANI: Là in quel chiosco.

BUCCAMETTA: In questo?

FANFANI: No, quello è di mia nipote e suo marito in questo qui.

BUCCAMETTA: Ah! va bene, noi vi aspetteremo là nel chiosco.

FANFANI: Ma dunque?

BUCCAMETTA: Non ha udito? Lei da Elda ha inteso già. Parli prima, con mammà...(*via*).

FANFANI: Vecchia megera! Hai di buono d'essere la madre di tua figlia, altrimenti a quest'ora ti avrei fatta sposare con un coccodrillo.

## Scena VI
### Titania e Antarsi.

ANTARSI: Voi siete Zoraide, la bella Odalisca delle mille e una notte!

TITANIA: Sì, ma fortunatamente, voi non siete quel sultano che si addormentava ai racconti della sua  bella...Dunque restiamo al linguaggio dei fiori?

ANTARSI: Per forza! Ma almeno ditemi nel linguaggio dei fiori, se potrò meritare la speranza di conquistare il vostro bel cuore?

TITANIA: Ascoltate!

(*Musica*).

# N. 9 – Duetto dei Fiori

**TITANIA**
Un dolce bel linguaggio
Parlare sa ogni fior;
Capirli sa quel saggio,
Che chiedelo al suo cor!
   Domande fanno i fiorellini,
   E dan risposte con piacer;
   Confidan segreti carini
   D'amore col tacer—col tacer!
Garofani, narcisi
Linguaggio han singolar;
Begonie, fiordalisi,
Sì, tutti san parlar!
   Ed oggi a te, per oggi intanto,
   La viola vo' donar;
   Vuoi cogliere la rosa,
   Le spine non curar!

**ANTARSI**
Il fiore da te colto
Mi vuole intimorir;
M'avvisa che pur molto
Dovrò per te soffrir!
   Con te nel fondo d'alto mar,
   Andrei diletta con piacer;
   M'inebbria il sol pensar
   Te cara, te cara—ognor veder!
Con te la vita é bella,
Ornata dal tuo amor;
E te, vezzosa stella,
Donato ho già il mio cor!
   E qui ti resto accanto,
   Te chino ad adorar;
   Vo' cogliere la rosa.
   Le spine non curar.

**TITANIA E ANTARSI**
Vo' cogliere la rosa,
Le spine non curar!

SCENA VII
**Detti, Fanfani, Miradillo, Elda e Buccametta.**

FANFANI: Come potete soffrire di simili cose?

MIRADILLO: Ah! disgraziata! Un bacio in fronte!...e voi osaste?

ANTARSI: Signore, sono a vostra disposizione.

MIRADILLO: Grazie tanto! Saprò approfittare delle sue buone qualità...stia pure qui per ora...(quando avrò bisogno di qualche galoppino saprò dove rivolgermi). In quanto a lei, signora, credo che sia inutile il dire che la di lei condotta...

ANTARSI: Signor Miradillo, io la tengo per un uomo d'onore e le ripeto che sono a sua disposizione...

MIRADILLO: Ho inteso...non sono già sordo; me lo avete detto un' altra volta; più tardi cercherò di occuparmi in qualche faccenda. Ora ho bisogno di stare alcuni momenti solo con mia moglie.

FANFANI: È giusto, lasciamoli in libertà.

(*Musica.*)

SCENA VIII
**Titania, Elda, Buccametta, Antarsi,
Miradillo e Fanfani.**

## N. 10 – Concertato

FANFANI, ANTARSID, ELDA E BUCCAMETTA (*origliando*)
Qui nascosti ed attenti
Spiamo i loro accenti;
Il suo fare, quel parlare
Ci dà molto da pensar.

TITANIA (*piano a Miradillo.*)
Nascosti là son...
Ci vuol attenzion!

MIRADILLO (*piano a Titania*)
Coraggio ed ardir
Fàranci riuscir!

I QUATTRO
Ascoltiam che diran!

MIRADILLO
In quel chioschetto vieni, vieni;
(*forte*) Egli c'invita dolce ad amar!

TITANIA (*piano a Miradillo*)
A te fan duopo freni freni,
Nella passione, per non traviar!

TITANIA E MIRADILLO
Or sì—or sì!
Dell'usignolo il flebil canto
        Giù scenderà!
Oh com'è pieno di voluttà!

TITANIA (*piano*)
Vedi? continuan sempre a spiar.

MIRADILLO (*piano*)
Se è cosi,
Allor con giubilo—nel chiosco subito
Dovrem andar.

TITANIA
Scaltro! Sarebbe un po' troppo azzardar!

MIRADILLO
Giacché ci tengono sposati già,
Facciam da coniugi, in verità!
Sprezziamo scrupoli e malignità,
E il piano splendido ci riuscirà.

TITANIA
Che cosa dite!? Quale ardire!
Che mai devo da voi sentire!

MIRADILLO
Si fidi pur di me;
S'intende già da se
Che sol per apparenza
Fare ciò si de.
Perché tanto rigor?
Sempre queto starò!
Perché tal furor?
Modesto sarò!

TITANIA
No, no! Mai! Giammai!
Con voi là non ci andrò!
Se dentro vi vedrò
Difender mi saprò!
Pentire vi farò!

I QUATTRO
Là dentro assieme queti, queti,
La bella notte vi passeran!
E sorridendo lieti, lieti,
Gioie d'amore vi goderan!

MIRADILLO E TITANIA
Or sì—or sì!
Dell'usignolo il canto
          Giù scenderà!
Oh com'è pieno di voluttà!
Resister chi mai può?
D'amor palpiterò!

I QUATTRO
È ver, sposi son!
Un dubbio più ora non v'ha!
Felice l'aurora sarà
Per lor!—felice sì sarà!

MIRADILLO
Su vien!

TITANIA
Si, si!

MIRADILLO
Andiam!

TITANIA
Andiam!

## SCENA IX
### Miradillo.

MIRADILLO: Se vogliono la mia posizione non è bella! La mia sposa minaccia di prendermi a colpi di rivoltella; il principe pretende di battersi con me e dice ch'è a mia disposizione...per conto mio resterà per un bel pezzo...(*Musica*)

## N. 11 – Couplet

I.

MIRADILLO
Ho per il duello una passione,
Ma sol la forchetta è l'arma adatta a me;
So pugnar coi polli e coi capponi
E periglio certo qui non v'è.
Se le diamo ci puniscono,
Ride ognuno se le buschiam:
Ma in duello fatto a tavola,
Vincitori sempre siam.
A pugnar altri ci vada
Col moschetto o colla spada,
    Io no non ho cor...
    Ti saluto, mio dolce tesor!


II.

Il beneficar è una finzion,
Spingonci le donne a far la carità,
Perché più belle allora son,
E l'amante dee passar di là.
Mi diressi ad una Venere
 Che dei sigari mi offrì;

Mi faceva le luci tenere
E guardandomi così: "Quanto costan?"
"Cinque scudi!" "Ah lasciate che ci studi...
    No, no; non per or!"
    Ti saluto, mio dolce tesor!

III.
Oggi una baruffa scoppierà,
E correr tutto il mondo vedi a curiosar;
Per suonar ciascuno corre là,
Ma suonato spesso dee tornar.
In fra due che si contendono,
Gode il terzo, già si sa;
Dice bene quel proverbio,
Chi ha prudenza l'userà.
A divider altri vada
Chi si batte per la strada,
    Io non ho cor...
    Ti saluto, mio dolce tesor!

## SCENA X
### Titania e Antarsi.

ANTARSI: Fanfani mi ha tolta l'occasione di battermi con Miradillo, tanto meglio per ora...Titania?

TITANIA: Ascoltatemi Principe...Io ho bisogno di sparire da questo luogo per 24 ore...S'è vero che voi m'amate, dovete rapirmi alla presenza di tutti.

ANTARSI: Ma questo sarebbe un'atto di violenza!

TITANIA: Qualcuno viene...decidetevi...

ANTARSI: Giacche lo volete.

TITANIA: Ma non più tardi di questa sera, durante la festa.

ANTARSI: Avete la mia parola (*baciandole la mano; via*)

TITANIA: Ora sono salva! Domani avrò un marito legittimo...e voi caro zio, sborserete i due milioni!

## SCENA XI
### Titania e Elda.

ELDA: Un momento signora, vorrei parlarvi.

TITANIA: Ah! Se non m'inganno voi siete la nuova sposa di mio zio...vi ascolto, ma desidero che vi leviate quel velo.

ELDA: Volentieri!

TITANIA: Ma come, voi giovane e bella volete divenire una...delle tante mogli di mio zio? Ma che v'induce a ciò?

ELDA: La disperazione!

TITANIA: Disperazione, e di che?

ELDA: Di avermi veduto rapire l'uomo che doveva essere mio!

TITANIA: E da chi?

ELDA: Da voi, signora!

TITANIA: Da me?

ELDA: Colui ch'io amava è Miradillo, vostro marito....

TITANIA: Ah! ora comprendo, poverina! Rassicuratevi, mia cara, voglio avere della confidenza in  voi e spero non ne abuserete...

ELDA: Vi pare?

TITANIA: Or bene, sappiate dunque che il signore Miradillo non è mai stato, non è e non sarà mai mio marito.

ELDA: Che dite?

TITANIA: Egli finge d'esserlo onde secondarmi in un certo affare che per ora non posso palesarvi.

ELDA: Finge! Ma finge, così bene!

TITANIA: Ah! Sì, e anche troppo! Ah! Eccolo, rimettete il velo, tentate il di lui cuore, sono certa che non vi avrà dimenticata!

### Scena XII
**Miradillo e detti.**

MIRADILLO: Eccomi qui...signora!

TITANIA: Un momento! La mia futura zia desidera avere un colloquio con voi. Vi lascio in libertà; arrivederci, coraggio! (*via nel chiosco*)

MIRADILLO: Sua zia! Ah! comprendo. La 47a moglie di Fanfani....chi sa che cerotto sarà...signora...

ELDA: Signore...

MIRADILLO: Signore, fa molto caldo quest'oggi...

ELDA: Sì...

MIRADILLO: Questa sera speriamo d'aver un poco di fresco così riuscirà più bella la festa che ci offre il di lei gentile sposo. Caro uomo quel Fanfani! Gentile, simpatico!

ELDA: Eh! Così...così...

MIRADILLO: Come così? (Ah! ho capito; deve essere innamorata di me) Forse ama il di lei futuro marito?

ELDA: Non troppo.

MIRADILLO: E perché lo sposa allora?

ELDA: Perché non mi fu dato di sposare l'uomo che veramente amo!

MIRADILLO: Poverina! (Eppure deve essere carina!) E quell' uomo è?

ELDA: É lei.

MIRADILLO: Io? (*Musica*).

## SCENA XIII
**Elda e Miradillo.**

## N. 12 – Duetto

ELDA
Lo dovevo confessare, perché poi no?
Lei mi dirà che son sfacciata
E spensierata...

MIRADILLO
Perché? Perché?
La è una cosa naturale!
Il mio naso, il mio viso
Fa all'istante innamorar!
Il mio sguardo, tal sorriso,
Fa d'amore palpitar.
Al mio tutto lusinghiero
Ogni donna ceder dò.
Alla fine poi davvero,
All'inferno van per me!

ELDA (*fra sé*)
Vedrai!
Assai cara la pagherai!
Vedrai! vedrai!
Esposto sei al mio furor,
La pena poi ti è dietro già!

MIRADILLO
(Vedrai! vedrai!
Con me ben ti divertirai!
Vedrai!
Per passatempo un bacio ancor
Ti vò dar!—Voluttà!)
Io con tè sarò sincero

E riguardi avrò per te.
Ogni donna, sì davvero,
Va all'inferno pur per me!

ELDA
Si, perbacco, infame sorte
Che tu non sia mussulman;
Forse allora qual consorte
Mi daresti la tua man!
Deh, amami!

MIRADILLO
Santi dei!—Che fretta ha lei!

ELDA
Amami!

MIRADILLO
Sì, ma aspetta, mio gioiel:
Io marito son fedel...
Poi che vai:—e la moral?!

ELDA
Così?
Ma che mai or farò
Se il mio ben mi sprezzò?
Il mio core è in tempesta,
Sento grave già la testa;
La mia quiete fuggì,
E la febbre ho qui;
Il mio sangue è tutto ardor,
Mi divora febbre d'amor!

MIRADILLO
Vedo ben! vedo ben!
E un amor tutto arder!
Cara alma gentil!
Ma getta via quel velo,
Lasciati almen veder,
La faccia tua mirar!
Deh lasciati almen veder!

ELDA
No, no, no, non farò;
No, non permetterò!
Senza velo non vò
Mi si veda, mai no!
No, no, no, non lo vo'!

MIRADILLO
E perché?...Strano è!

ELDA
Codesto non permetto mai;
Nascer potrian dei guai!
Non voglio mai, no!
Non vò, no, no, non vò!
Ma che mai or farò
Se il mio ben mi sprezzò?
Il mio core è in tempesta,
Sento grave già la festa;
La mia quiete fuggì,
E la febbre ho qui;
Si dimentica la terra, il ciel!...
Leverò, sì, il vel!

MIRADILLO
Via, lascia i guai...è noioso!
E lasciati da me veder!
Rendere mi vuoi tu curioso;
Butta via il vel, fammi piacer.
Orsù! orsù!
Se no lo strapperò!
Il sangue mi bolle,
L'amor mi fa folle!
Vieni a me!...vieni a me!...
Se sola non togli tu il velo,
Lo giuro pel cielo,
Io lo strapperò,
Allora ti vedrò!
(*Elda si toglie il velo*)
      Elda, sei tu!
      Elda, tu qui!

Tu vuoi nell'harem del Pascià entrar?
Questo poi è immorale!
È molto male!
Elda, perdono!

ELDA (*parodiandolo*)
Perché? Perché?
La è una cosa naturale!
Il mio naso, il mio viso,
Fa all'istante innamorar!
Il mio sguardo, il sorriso
Fa d'amore palpitar.
Al mio tutto lusinghiero
Ogni uomo ceder dè!
Ogni uomo, si davvero,
(*p.p.*)
Va all'inferno anche per me!

MIRADILLO (*trattenendola*)
No, no! non far ciò!

ELDA
Rinunzia Titania, se no lo farò!

MIRADILLO
No, no! ciò non farai!

ELDA
Farò per dispetto! tra poco il vedrai.

MIRADILLO
Deh, Elda, m'ascolta!

ELDA
Non vo' no, traditore! Ah!

MIRADILLO
A' piedi tuoi prostrato son!

## Scena XIV
**Miradillo, Fanfani ed Elda.**

FANFANI: E tu osi sedurre la mia futura moglie?

MIRADILLO: Elda vostra moglie? Preferisco farmi turco e la prendo come moglie N. 2!

FANFANI: Miserabile! E mia nipote?

MIRADILLO: Vostra nipote sarà il numero 1 e poi essa non è gelosa come io non sono geloso di lei, in questa materia andiamo perfettamente d'accordo.

FANFANI: Ma voi signora, non dite nulla?

ELDA: E cosa devo dire?

MIRADILLO: Essa approva le mie intenzioni, non è vero?

FANFANI: Ah! questo è troppo!

## Scena XV
**Antarsi e detti.**

FANFANI: (Ah! un'idea) Altezza, io so che lei ama mia nipote...

ANTARSI: Ebbene?

FANFANI: Ebbene, quest'uomo la rende infelice! Fate del bene alla povera Titania, liberatela da questo infame!

ANTARSI: E come devo fare?

FANFANI: Fatelo rapire dalla vostra gente, confinatelo all'interno dell'Africa.

ANTARSI: Bene! Procurerò di contentarvi...

FANFANI: Bravo! In compenso vi manderò una dozzina di schiave...

ELDA: Ora è tempo di finirla questa brutta commedia, non voglio che ci creda che tu sei suo marito!

MIRADILLO: Ma come fare? Diedi la mia parola!

ELDA: Bene, se tu non lo puoi, io diverrò la moglie del Pascià. Pensaci, perché sono risoluta.

MIRADILLO: E come fare? Ah! Un'idea! Altezza, una parola.

ANTARSI: Che volete?

MIRADILLO: Lei ama mia moglie?

ANTARSI: Avreste nulla a dire?

MIRADILLO: Io, nulla, si figuri; anzi ne sono contentissimo, perché io amo Elsa.

ANTARSI: La promessa sposa del Pascià?

MIRADILLO: Nè più nè meno, così va il mondo! Mi faccia un favore lei che ha molta gente al suo  comando, faccia rapire Elda.

ANTARSI: E per conto di chi la devo rapire?

MIRADILLO: Per me! Così domani io le consegno mia moglie e lei mi restituisce Elda; è un favore che fa anche a Titania!

ANTARSI: Sta bene!

MIRADILLO: Obbligato, Altezza!

## Scena XVI
**Antarsi, Elda, Miradillo, Titania, Fanfani
Buccametta, Pericle, Muezzin e Coro.**

## N. 13 – Finale Secondo

CORO
Beiram, il giorno sacro già arrivò!

MUEZZIN
A festa sì gradita,
Lo squillo ora c'invita!
Ogni odio deve terminar,
Si deve perdonar! Allah! Allah!

CORO
A festa gradita,
Lo squillo ora c'invita!
Ogni odio deve terminar,
Si deve perdonar!
Come fu una volta ancor,
Datteri offritevi or!
Maometto comandò!
Beiram alfine ci liberò!
Beiram il giorno sacro già arrivò!
Gridate—cantate
Or tutti là:—Onore ad Allah!

FANFANI
La legge del gran Corano vuol che sian felici!
I datteri, é noto a voi, si devono scambiare fra gli amici!

TUTTI
Bisogna accettarli,
Quindi mangiarli;
Offrirli agli amici
È sacro dover!

FANFANI (*a Miradillo*)
Posso offre, caro amico, un dattero?

MIRADILLO
Lei è buon!

TITANIA (*ad Antarsi*)
Posso offrirle, caro prence, un dattero?

ANTARSI
Grato son!

PERICLE (*a Buccametta*)
Noi mangiamo pur assieme un dattero?

BUCCAMETTA
Volentier!

ANTARSI
Che sapor!

FANFANI
Sì davver!

BUCCAMETTA
Che odor!

CORO
Si, la festa fa l'union!

MIRADILLO (*a Fanfani*)
Questo dattero prendete voi ancor?

FANFANI
Volentier!

ANTARSI (*a Titania*)
Prenda un dattero anche lei per mio amor!

TITANIA
Con piacer!

BUCCAMETTA (*a Elda*)
Quattro datteri mangiai già fin'or!

ELDA
Non c'è mal!

TITANIA
Ben davver!

MIRADILLO
Più che ben!

BUCCAMETTA E FANFANI
Più che ben! Sì davver!

FANFANI
Com' è sereno!

MIRADILLO
Che viso ameno!

FANFANI (*a Miradillo*)
Felicità vi auguro!

MIRADILLO
O grazie!

FANFANI
O prego!

MIRADILLO E FANFANI
Ah, ah, ah! Ah, ah, ah!

FANFANI
Psì!

MIRADILLO
Psì!

MIRADILLO E FANFANI
Sto a starnutare....

FANFANI
Psì!

MIRADILLO
Psì!

MIRADILLO E FANFANI
Ci fa crepare!

FANFANI
Buon ciel...

MIRADILLO
Buon ciel...

MIRADILLO E FANFANI
Psì! Psì!
O grazie a tutti!
        Psì! Psì!
È un affare singolar!
Io....psì! che...psì! ma...psì! psì!
La è da scoppiare
Psì! psì!
Col starnutare!
        Psì! psì!
Al diavolo!

TITANIA
Che vuol dir ciò? Psì! psì!

ANTARSI
Che vuol dir ciò? Psì! psì!
        O grazie a tutti!
        Psì! psì!
È un affare singolar!
Io...psì! che...psì! ma...psì!
O ciel che affare.
Psì! Psì!
Sto a starnutare
        Psì! Psì!
Al diavolo!

ELDA E BUCCAMETTA
Da che mai questi guai?

È un affare singolar!
È un orrore, è un orrore
Io...psì! che...psì! ma...psì!
Magia qui v'è!
Psì! Psì!
Lo starnutare...
          Psì! Psì!
Al diavolo!

CORO
O ciel! buon ciel...psì!
Codesto starnuto
È strano saluto! psì!
Che casi...I nasi...psì! psì!
O ciel! Psì!
Al diavolo!

FANFANI
Sentite voi?

CORO
Quest'era il segno primo;
Fra poco poi il Nilo ascender deve;
Il terzo colpo il flusso annunzierà.
Or sì, or ascenderà
Ed i campi inonderà!
Spumeggian le onde
Con impeto,
E l'acqua rifonde
Con strepito;
Un vortice par
Che turbini il mar!

TUTTI
O Nilo incantator,
Di beni apportator!
Onore sia ad Allah
Che il Nilo a noi donato ha,
Sorgente di felicità!

TITANIA
Su, brindiamo coi bicchier!
Dai primi dì
Un divin messo apparì,
Ed appare pur tutt'or;
È del Nilo il protettor!
E si portò
Una coppa nella man
Alle tetre sorgenti,
E là ei la versò.
Le acque tosto sussurreggiar,
Lente a crescere incominciar;
Lente salgon da lontano,
E destan tutto a festa.
Onde care, vi salutiamo...
Onde chiare, noi vi adoriamo!
Fulgido voi splendete
Al sol magiche.

CORO
V'e' là un burchiello
Screziato a bei color;
Oh, come è bello!
Esalta, inebbria il cor!

TITANIA (*a Antarsi*)
Finiscono i guai—l'aiuto verrà;
Or mi salverai—poi si fuggirà;
Or ora il burchiello—ci libererà.
     Ancora su i bicchier!
     Su brindiamo,
     Ed Allah ancor lodiamo!

TUTTI
Dai primi dì, (*ecc.*)

CORO
Ve'! ve'! Conducon le donne
Per forza nel fermo battel!

FANFANI
Ci vuol attenzione!
M'aiuti or il ciel!

CORO
Ve'! ve'!

TITANIA
Andiamo a passeggiare!

MIRADILLO
Nessun ci può turbare.

FANFANI
Briccone! Vedo già
Ch'ei me la fa!

CORO
Ma che c'è? Che mai egli ha?

FANFANI
Su, voi tutti accorrete
E fermate quel briccon!

CORO
Su corriam, là voliaml...
Ahimè! che tardi è già!

FANFANI
Infamia! Così ingannarmi!
La sposa e il denaro truffarmi!
Tu, briccon! imbroglioni fannulloni!
Sei stato svelto;
Io son proprio scelto
Per farmi giuntar!
Ma vedrete, furfanti,
Farò a tutti quanti il fio pagar!

CORO E GLI ALTRI
Viva, viva! Liberi siamo....
Viva, viva! Vi salutiamo...

State ben!
Sì, voi lodate or Allah,
Si, voi cantate or Allah!

# FINE DEL SECONDO ATTO

# ATTO TERZO

**L'azione si svolge nel mezzo di un deserto.**

*Oasi colla veduta del deserto; da ambe le parti gruppi di palme. A destra una sontuosa tenda, in cui sonnecchiano Titania ed Elda. A sinistra una tenda semplice da cui esce più tardi Miradillo. Nel mezzo della scena Antarsi è coperto da una pelle di tigre. Intorno a lui sono raggruppati i Maroniti. Schiave agli ingressi delle tende.*

## SCENA I
**Maroniti ed Antarsi.**

## N. 14 – Coro

CORO UOMINI
Fulgido risplende il sole,
Della notte squarcia il sen;
Vita nuova han le aiuole,
Terra e ciel è già seren.

CORO DONNE
Viva Allah!
Or tutto rivivrà...
Tutto è amen.

ANTARSI
Che sia ver?...
Io era lieto, ebbro d'amor;
La mia rosa—
Le spine non curai—
Io la baciai, la bella rosa!—
Ma su, pericolo qui v'ha...
Fuggiamo via di qua!
Le tende tosto su,
Non dimoriam qui più.
E tu, mia stella,
Ridestati, su!

CORO
Noi Allah guarderà! Allah!

ANTARSI
Sorgi, mio amor!

CORO ED ANTARSI
Fuggono già le tenebre,
E le stelle impallidir;
Ultima resta Venere,
Che deve pur sparir.
     Bella del cor—svogliati su!
     Apri i tuoi occhi limpidi,
      E chiari allor—saran di più
I cieli limpidi.
Su ti desta, mio tesoro;
Ridi, scherza, vien con me!
Sì, sì, vien! sorgi di là!
Mia dolce voluttà!

CORO
Splendida deità, ti desta;
È un gioiel già tutto il ciel!
Or sorge il dì: su, su,
Ti sveglia, bel tesor!
Orsù, ti desta ormai,
Su vien, su vien! scorda i guai:
A nuova vita il ciel t'invita!

## Scena II
### Titania, Miradillo, Elda, e Schiava.

TITANIA: È già giorno?

ANTARSI: Sì, mia diletta, e giorno di felicità!

ELDA: E Miradillo?

ANTARSI: Dorme ancora il poltrone!

TITANIA: Bisogna castigarlo della sua poltroneria; nasconditi nella tenda, gli diremo che fosti rapita nella notte da Fanfani.

ELDA: Benissimo! Così vedrò poi dove arriva il suo amore.

MIRADILLO (*da dentro*): Lo specchio, bestia! Non vedi ch'è già giorno? (*sortendo aspramente*) Buon giorno, madama; buon giorno principe! Si può sapere che cosa avete intenzione di fare quest'oggi?

ANTARSI: Sposare Titania...

MIRADILLO: Come? Sposare mia moglie?

TITANIA: Non inquietatevi, amico mio, vi esonero fin da questo momento della vostra carica di marito.

MIRADILLO: Peccato! Ci avevo preso gusto!

TITANIA: Fra poco il principe sarà mio sposo legittimo e così lo zio dovrà sborsare i due milioni.

MIRADILLO: Eh! l'è piaciuto il principino Maronita; e dove si faranno le nozze?

TITANIA: Il principe ha pensato a tutto!

ANTARSI: Poco lungi di qui vi è un sacerdote che ci unirà in matrimonio.

MIRADILLO: Bravissimi! Ed Elda dov'è?

ANTARSI: Ecco...Elda!

TITANIA: Non disperatevi perché si potrà rimediare almeno, speriamo...

MIRADILLO: Rimediare? Ma che cosa l'è successo?

ANTARSI: Il pascià Fanfani...

TITANIA: La fece rapire durante la notte!

MIRADILLO: Rapita?!
ANTARSI: La fece condurre nell'internò dell'Africa.

MIRADILLO: Ah! Turco ladro! Povera Elda! A qualunque costo bisogna che vado in cerca di lei...(*Musica*).

SCENA III
**Titania, Antarsi e Miradillo.**

TITANIA
L'Africa è pericolosa...

ANTARSI
È una terra dolorosa...

MIRADILLO
Ah! ben!

TITANIA
Prima sonvi gli animali.

ANTARSI
I terribili cignali...

MIRADILLO
Puh! poi?

TITANIA
Sonvi tanti...

ANTARSI
Elefanti...

MIRADILLO
E ciò che fa?

TITANIA
E serpenti...

ANTARSI
Avidi...

TITANIA
Orsi poi terribili...

ANTARSI
Lupi pur famelici...

MIRADILLO
Elda vogl'io trovar!
La vita per essa rischiar!

TITANIA
Solo vuolsi attenzion.

ANTARSI
Adoprate precauzion.

MIRADILLO
Conosco la region!

TITANIA
Là ci sono beduini...

ANTARSI
Son peggio che assassini!

MIRADILLO
Puh! ben!

TITANIA
E negli intimi paraggi...

ANTARSI
Antropofagi selvaggi...

MIRADILLO
Puh! Poi?

TITANIA
E Barberi, Ottentotti

ANTARSI
Masnadieri altri ancor...

MIRADILLO
E ciò che fa?

TITANIA
Pensarci solo fa terror!

MIRADILLO
Io di quelli son sicuro.

ANTARSI
Solo attenzion!

MIRADILLO
Voglio andare impavido.

TITANIA
Ci pensi ancor!

MIRADILLO
Lampi e folgori non curo.

ANTARSI
Gli freme il cor...

MIRADILLO
Vo' girare intrepido.

TITANIA
Terra e ciel vuol sfidar.

MIRADILLO
La mia Elda vò trovar!

TITANIA ED ANTARSI
Corresi rischio assai...

MIRADILLO
Non m'importa nulla ciò.

TITANIA ED ANTARSI
Resti qui...Schivi guai...

MIRADILLO
Sol con Elda; solo mai!

TITANIA ED ANTARSI
Andiam rimpatriare.

MIRADILLO
L'Elda mia trovare io vò!

TITANIA ED ANTARSI
Andiamolo aiutar.

MIRADILLO
Sì, Elda noi ricercherem,
E lei presto ritroverem!

I.
MIRADILLO
Girerò monti e pian,
Spingerommi giù lontan,
Sprezzerò il timor,
Condurrà me sol l'amor.

(*I tre ripetono*)

MIRADILLO
Io non temo né terra né ciel!

TITANIA ED ANTARSI
Dice il ver!

MIRADILLO
Orsi, Iene, tutto sfiderò,
Né gorilla mi spaventerà!
Sempre avanti io m'inoltrerò,
Finché all'Equator si giungerà.

TITANIA ED ANTARSI
Sì davver!

MIRADILLO
Né i selvaggi mi spaventeran,
Rossi o neri non m'importa poi;
Imitare vo' gli eroi
Se l'Amor mi dà la man.

A 3
Cercar vo' Elda,
Anche in fondo al mar;
Sorridendo con essa
Nella patria mia tornar!

MIRADILLO
I patri cantici alfin sentire,
Vedere Napoli e poi morire!
Risveglia rapido il gran desire,
Vedere Napoli e mai morire!
I patri cantici alfin sentire, (*ecc.*)

II.
TITANIA
Vivere bramasi
Se l'amor riscalda il cor!
Fremere sentesi
Dentro al cor—sacro furor!

A 3
Vivere bramasi, (*ecc.*)

TITANIA
Nasca pur quel che nascer vuol!

ANTARSI E MIRADILLO
Sempre ardir!

TITANIA
Densa nube pur nasconda il sol!
Ma l'eroe ciò non spaventerà;

Ogni cosa egli sprezzerà,
Se la speme un sorriso gli dà!

ANTARSI E MIRADILLO
Sempre ardir!

TITANIA
Sì, l'amore pure trionferà!
Alla meta giungere si dè,
E timore poi non v'è,
Se l'Amore ne guiderà!

A 3
Giugerem al fin,
Basta sol perseverar!
Ché l'amore non fa
Che sia mai paura nè difficoltà!
Elda noi cercherem—ed alfin
La troverem!
I patri cantici alfin sentire, (*ecc.*)

## SCENA IV
### Elda e detti.

MIRADILLO: Titania ed il Principe sono andati a sposarsi, io bisogna che vada a cercare la sposa nel centro dell'Africa. Ah! cane d'un Fanfani! (*fa per entrare nelle tende e vede Elda*).

MIRADILLO: Elda! ma come! non fosti rapita?

ELDA: Sì, ma il mio coraggio mi salvò.

MIRADILLO: Ah! moderna Pulzella d'Orleans!

## SCENA IV
**Miradillo, Fanfani, Elda ed un Popolano.**

SERVO: Presto, presto è qui il Pascià coi beduini!

MIRADILLO: Fanfani! Bisogna cercar di trattenerlo fin che sia compiuto il matrimonio; vi dirò cosa dobbiamo fare (*via*).
(*Musica*)

## SCENA VI
**Fanfani e beduini.**

# N. 15 – Coro

I.
CORO
Egiziani noi siam,
Ogni cosa bruciam;
E feroci, inumani
Tutto noi distruggiam. Morte!
Dove quote v'è ancor
Noi portiam terror;
Quel che vienci nelle mani
Saccheggiamo. Morte!

II.
Quai serpenti noi pur strisciam,
E col Yatagan tutto assaliam!
Noi al rapitore
Spaccar il cuore
Vogliam! se ancor
Vuol parlar—noi allor
Lo vogliamo divorar. Morte!

FANFANI
Se una moglie poi
Rubano a voi;
Era quella orrida,
Vada al diavolo;
Era fulgida
Come un angelo,

Allor devesi cercar,
Tosto liberar;
Ardir tal, punir
Col fuoco, col ferro,
Si davver! si davver!
Egiziani noi siam,
Ogni cosa bruciam;
Ah ah ah—se ancor
Vuol parlar—noi allor
Lo vogliam divorar. Morte!

CORO
Si! Fuoco, ferro,
Ovunque portiam!
Si, si, si!
Ferro, fuoco!

FANFANI
Chi presta denar,
Per tosto scordar.
Colui solo, in verità,
Amici ci avrà
Se il denaro sol
Riavere vuol,
Si deve allor punir,
Pagar deve l'ardire!
Col fuoco, col ferro! (ecc.)
Allor pian—nostre man
Coglieran—quel marran,
E lo legheran. Ah ah aah!
Pasteran—feriran,
Taglieran—tutto assiem;
Noi col Yatagan
Faremo gran baccan!

## Scena VII
**Fanfani, Elda e Miradillo.**

FANFANI: Ora farò una perquisizione ai rispettivi domicili.

MIRADILLO: Che succede?

FANFANI: Ah! Ti ho colto, furfante!

MIRADILLO: Oh! carissimo zio...ma questa è una gran sorpresa!

FANFANI: Te ne accorgerai! Dov'è Elda? Dov'è la donna che mi hai rapita?

MIRADILLO: Del resto pigliatevela col principe che sono certo che la vuol sposare...

FANFANI: Come, vuol sposare Elda? Me la pagherà. Dov'è quel briccone?

MIRADILLO: È andato a caccia perché vuole che al pranzo di nozze vi sia della selvaggina. Volete far parte anche voi della selvaggina?

FANFANI: Io ti strozzo se non mi dici dove si trova Elda!

MIRADILLO: Ehi! Qui le mani! volete commettere un nipoticidio?

FANFANI: Ti farò scannare! Dov'è Elda?

ELDA: Signor Miradillo, la di lei signora sposa manda intanto la colazione...ella verrà fra poco...Oh! chi vedo? lei qui, signor Pascià?

FANFANI: Finalmente ti ritrovo! Ma non possa vederti sempre con costui!...

ELDA: Silenzio; le sue ore sono contate...

FANFANI: Come?

ELDA: Egli fra poco morrà, e per mia mano.

FANFANI: E perché?

ELDA: Io lo amavo ed egli mi ha ingannata, il vino che versa da quella bottiglia è avvelenato! Io m'allontano...Quando starà per spirare gli direte che muore per mano d'una siciliana (*via*).

FANFANI: È un tesoro di bontà questa ragazza!

MIRADILLO: Venite caro zio, voi sarete stanco, fatemi compagnia; volete bere?

FANFANI: No, no grazie; berrò questo di mia nipote.

MIRADILLO: Come volete!

FANFANI: E come vi sentite?

MIRADILLO: Io, benissimo! E perché una tale domanda?

FANFANI: Nulla, domandavo così.

MIRADILLO: Ahi forse voi sperate ch'io stia male, che muoia forse per non pagare i due milioni a vostra nipote? Ma v'ingannate perché sto benissimo, anzi, non sono mai stato tante bene come in questo momento, caro zio!

ELDA: Come siete allegro, signor Miradillo!

MIRADILLO: E come non dovrei esserlo? Oggi è il giorno fissato per riscuotere i due milioni di mia moglie.

FANFANI: Sembra che il veleno non agisca!

ELDA: Impossibile Nachi m'assicurò ch'è infallibile forse...che...ah!...

FANFANI: Cosa c'è?

ELDA: Furono scambiate le bottiglie!

FANFANI: Scam....biate le botti...glie! Ah! presto un contro-veleno, olà....aiuto...ma non c'è dunque un filtro per salvarmi?

SCENA VIII
**Buccametta, Beduini, Tutti.**

BUCCAMETTA: Eccomi, io sono il filtro, io sono il contro-veleno.

FANFANI: Se fossi sicuro di vivere, ignorerei anche questa medicina.

(*Musica*)

FANFANI: Cos'è questo?

MIRADILLO: Fatevi coraggio, voi non siete avvelenato!

FANFANI: Ah! respiro!

MIRADILLO: Ma sborserete i due milioni al principe Antarsi, legittimo marito di vostra nipote.

FANFANI: Sono rovinato! E voi?

ELDA: Ritorno in Italia per sposare Miradillo.

FANFANI: Anche la sposa!

BUCCAMETTA: Ebbene, sposate me!

FANFANI: Sposati con un pesce cane!

TUTTI: Viva il Principe.

SCENA ULTIMA

## N. 16 – Finale

CORO
Viva! viva!
Noi lieti siamo qua
Allah! Allah!
Beiram felicità
A noi ci porterà!
E noi si goderà!

TUTTI
Il ciel ci dà felicità
E noi profittem con voluttà!

MIRADILLO
Alla patria corriam!
Su, a Napoli voliam!
E colà noi vivrem
Lieti sempre assiem!

TUTTI
I patri cantici alfin sentire, (*ecc.*)

MIRADILLO
Su, via dall'Africa corriam!

CORO
Ritornate, cari,
Ai paterni lari!
Noi vi salutiam dall'Africa!
Viva!

# FINE

# BIBLIOGRAPHY

Castle Square Opera Company. *"500 Times": Monday, October 16, 1899.* CreateSpace Independent Publishing Platform, 2013. (Reprint of 1899 original).

Drinklow, John. *The Vintage Operetta Book.* Osprey Publishing Limited, Reading, 1972.

Hughes, Gervase. *Composers of Operetta.* Macmillan & Co. Ltd., London, 1962.

Letellier, Robert I. *Operetta – A Sourcebook, Vol. 1 & 2.* Cambridge Scholars Publishing, Newcastle-upon-Tyne, 2015.

Skelton, Edward O. *Historical Review of the Boston Bijou Theatre: with the original casts of all the operas that have been produced at the Bijou.* ULAN Press, 2012. (Reprint of 1884 original).

Traubner, Richard. *Operetta – A Theatrical History.* Victor Gollancz Ltd, London, 1984.

# Theophrastus

Enquiry into plants and minor works
on odours and weather signs
In Two Parts (Volume I)

Translator
Arthur Hort

**Alpha Editions**

This edition published in 2020

ISBN : 9789354157066 (Hardback)
ISBN : 9789354159251 (Paperback)

Design and Setting By
**Alpha Editions**
www.alphaedis.com
email - alphaedis@gmail.com

# PREFACE

Tins is, I believe, the first attempt at an English
translation of the 'Enquiry into Plants.' That it
should be found entirely satisfactory is not to be
expected, since the translator is not, as he should be,
a botanist; moreover, in the present state at least
of the text, the Greek of Theophrastus is sometimes
singularly elusive. I should never have undertaken
such a responsibility without the encouragement of
that veteran student of plant-lore the Rev. Canon
Ellacombe, who first suggested that I should make
the attempt and introduced me to the book. It is a
great grief that he did not live to see the completion
of the work which he set me. If I had thought
it essential that a translator of Theophrastus should
himself grapple with the difficulties of identifying
the plants which he mentions, I must have declined
a task which has otherwise proved quite onerous
enough. However the kindness and the expert
knowledge of Sir William Thiselton-Dyer came to
my rescue; to him I not only owe gratitude for
constant help throughout; the identifications in the
Index of Plants are entirely his work, compared
with which the compilation of the Index itself was

v

## PREFACE

but mechanical labour. And he has greatly increased
my debt and the reader's by reading the proofs of
my translation and of the Index. This is perhaps
the place to add a note on the translation of the
plant-names in the text:—where possible, I have
given an English equivalent, though I am conscious
that such names as 'Christ's thorn,' 'Michaelmas
daisy' must read oddly in a translation of a work
written 300 years before Christ ; to print Linnean
binary names would have been at least equally
incongruous. Where an English name was not
obvious, although the plant is British or known in
British gardens, I have usually consulted Britten
and Holland's Dictionary of Plant-names. Where
no English equivalent could be found, *i.e.* chiefly
where the plant is not either British or familiar in
this country, I have either transliterated the Greek
name (as *arakhidna*) or given a literal rendering of it
in inverted commas (as 'foxbrush' for ἀλωπέκουρος) ;
but the derivation of Greek plant-names being often
obscure, I have not used this device unless the
meaning seemed to be beyond question. In some
cases it has been necessary to preserve the Greek
name and to give the English name after it in
brackets. This seemed desirable wherever the author
has apparently used more than one name for the
same plant, the explanation doubtless being that he
was drawing on different local authorities; thus κέρασος
and λακάρη both probably represent 'bird-cherry,'
the latter being the Macedonian name for the tree.

vi

## PREFACE

Apart from this reason, in a few places (as 3.8.2 ; 3.10.3.) it seemed necessary to give both the Greek and the English name in order to bring out some particular point. On the other hand one Greek name often covers several plants, e.g. λωτός ; in such cases I hope that a reference to the Index will make all clear. Inverted commas indicate that the rendering is a literal translation of the Greek word ; the identification of the plant will be found in the Index. Thus φελλόδρυς is rendered 'cork-oak,' though 'holm-oak' would be the correct rendering,—cork-oak (quercus Suber) being what Theophrastus calls φελλός, which is accordingly rendered cork-oak without commas. As to the spelling of proper names, consistency without pedantry seems unattainable. One cannot write names such as Arcadia or Alexander otherwise than as they are commonly written ; but I cannot bring myself to Latinise a Greek name if it can be helped, wherefore I have simply transliterated the less familiar names ; the line drawn must of course be arbitrary.

The text printed is in the main that of Wimmer's second edition (see Introd. p. xiv). The textual notes are not intended as a complete apparatus criticus ; to provide a satisfactory apparatus it would probably be necessary to collate the manuscripts afresh. I have had to be content with giving Wimmer's statements as to MS. authority ; this I have done wherever any question of interpretation depended on the reading ; but I have not thought it necessary to record mere

variations of spelling. Where the textual notes go
beyond bare citation of the readings of the MSS., Ald.,
Gaza, and Pliny, it is usually because I have there
departed from Wimmer's text. The references to
Pliny will, I hope, be found fairly complete. I am
indebted for most of them to Schneider, but I have
verified these and all other references.

I venture to hope that this translation, with its
references and Index of Plants, may assist some
competent scholar-botanist to produce an edition
worthy of the author.

Besides those already mentioned I have to thank
also my friends Professor D'Arcy Thompson, C.B.,
Litt.D. of Dundee, Mr. A. W. Hill of Kew, Mr. E. A.
Bowles for help of various kinds, and the Rev. F. W.
Galpin for his learned exposition of a passage which
otherwise would have been dark indeed to me—the
description of the manufacture of the reed mouthpieces of wood-wind instruments in Book IV. Sir John
Sandys, Public Orator of Cambridge University, was
good enough to give me valuable help in matters of
bibliography.

# INTRODUCTION

## I.—Bibliography and Abbreviations used

### A. *Textual Authorities*

Wimmer divides the authorities on which the text of the περὶ φυτῶν ἱστορία is based into three classes:—

*First Class :*

> U. Codex Urbinas : in the Vatican. Collated by Bekker and Amati ; far the best extant MS., but evidently founded on a much corrupted copy. See note on 9. 8. 1.

> P₂. Codex Parisiensis : at Paris. Contains considerable excerpts ; evidently founded on a good MS. ; considered by Wimmer second only in authority to U.

> (Of other collections of excerpts may be mentioned one at Munich, called after Pletho.)

*Second Class :*

> M (M₁, M₂). Codices Medicei : at Florence. Agree so closely that they may be regarded as a single MS. ; considered by Wimmer much inferior to U, but of higher authority than Ald.

P. Codex Parisiensis : at Paris. Considered by Wimmer somewhat inferior to M and V, and more on a level with Ald.

mP. Margin of the above. A note in the MS. states that the marginal notes are not *scholia*, but *variae lectiones aut emendationes*.

V. Codex Vindobonensis : at Vienna. Contains the first five books and two chapters of the sixth ; closely resembles M in style and readings.

*Third Class :*

Ald. Editio Aldina : the *editio princeps*, printed at Venice 1495–8. Believed by Wimmer to be founded on a single MS., and that an inferior one to those enumerated above, and also to that used by Gaza. Its readings seem often to show signs of a deliberate attempt to produce a smooth text : hence the value of this edition as witness to an independent MS. authority is much impaired.

(Bas. Editio Basiliensis : printed at Bâle, 1541. A careful copy of Ald., in which a number of printer's errors are corrected and a few new ones introduced (Wimmer).

Cam. Editio Camotiana (or Aldina minor, altera) : printed at Venice, 1552. Also copied from Ald., but less carefully corrected than Bas.; the editor Camotius, in a few passages, altered the text to accord with Gaza's version.)

G. The Latin version of Theodore Gaza,[1] the Greek refugee : first printed at Treviso (Tarvisium) in 1483. A wonderful work for the time at which it appeared. Its present value is due to the fact that the translation was made from a different MS. to any now known. Unfortunately however this does not seem to have been a better text than that on which the Aldine edition was based. Moreover Gaza did not stick to his authority, but adopted freely Pliny's versions of Theophrastus, emending where he could not follow Pliny. There are several editions of Gaza's work : thus

G.Par.G.Bas. indicate respectively editions published at Paris in 1529 and at Bâle in 1534 and 1550. Wimmer has no doubt that the Tarvisian is the earliest edition, and he gives its readings, whereas Schneider often took those of G.Bas.

---

Vin.Vo.Cod.Cas. indicate readings which Schneider believed to have MS. authority, but which are really anonymous emendations from the margins of MSS. used by his predecessors, and all, in Wimmer's opinion

[1] See Sandys, *History of Classical Scholarship*, ii. p. 62, etc.

# INTRODUCTION

traceable to Gaza's version. Schneider's
so-called Codex Casauboni he knew, according to Wimmer, only from Hofmann's
edition.

## B. *Editions*

H.  Editio Heinsii, printed at Leyden, 1613 : founded
    on Cam. and very carelessly printed, repeating
    the misprints of that edition and adding many
    others.   In the preface Daniel Heins[1] pretends
    to have had access to a critical edition and to a
    Heidelberg MS.; this claim appears to be en-
    tirely fictitious.   The book indeed contains what
    Wimmer calls a *farrago emendationum*; he remarks
    that 'all the good things in it Heinsius owed
    to the wit of others, while all its faults and
    follies we owe to Heinsius.'   Schneider calls it
    *editio omnium pessima*.

Bod.  Editio Bodaei (viz. of Joannes Bodaeus à
      Stapel), printed at Amsterdam, 1644.   The text
      of Heinsius is closely followed ; the margin con-
      tains a number of emendations taken from the
      margin of Bas. and from Scaliger, Robertus Con-
      stantinus, and Salmasius, with a few due to the
      editor himself.   The commentary, according to
      Sir William Thiselton-Dyer, is 'botanically
      monumental and fundamental.'

[1] See Sandys, *op. cit.* p. 313 etc.

St. Stackhouse, Oxford, 1813: a prettily printed
edition with some illustrations: text founded on
Ald. The editor seems to have been a fair
botanist, but an indifferent scholar, though occasionally he hits on a certain emendation. The
notes are short and generally of slight value.
The book is however of interest, as being apparently the only work on the 'Enquiry' hitherto
published in England.

Sch. J. G. Schneider (and Linck), Leipzig : vols.
i.–iv. published in 1818, vol. v. in 1821 ; contains
also the περὶ αἰτιῶν and the fragments, and a reprint of Gaza's version (corrected). The fifth,
or supplementary, volume, written during the
author's last illness, takes account of the Codex
Urbinas, which, unfortunately for Schneider,
did not become known till his edition was
finished. It is remarkable in how many places
he anticipated by acute emendation the readings
of U. The fifth volume also gives an account of
criticisms of the earlier volumes by the eminent
Greek Adamantios Koraës [1] and Kurt Sprengel.
This is a monumental edition, despite the ver-
bosity of the notes, somewhat careless references
and reproduction of the MSS. readings, and an
imperfect comprehension of the compressed
style of Theophrastus, which leads to a good
deal of wild emendation or rewriting of the
text. For the first time we find an attempt at

[1] See Sandys, *op. cit.* iii. pp. 361 foll.

INTRODUCTION

providing a critical text, founded not on the
Aldine edition, but on comparison of the manuscripts then known ; the Medicean and Viennese
had been collated a few years before by J. Th.
Schneider. We find also full use made of the
ancient authors, Athenaeus, Plutarch, Pliny,
Dioscorides, Nicander, Galen, etc., who quoted or
adapted passages of Theophrastus, and copious
references, often illuminating, to those who
illustrate him, as Varro, Columella, Palladius,
Aelian, the *Geoponica*.

Spr. Kurt Sprengel, Halle, 1822. This is not an
edition of the text, but a copious commentary
with German translation. Sprengel was a better
botanist than scholar; Wimmer speaks dis-
paragingly of his knowledge of Greek and of
the translation. (See note prefixed to the
Index of Plants.)

W. Fr. Wimmer : (1) An edition with introduction,
analysis, critical notes, and Sprengel's identifications of the plant-names ; Breslau, 1842.
(2) A further revised text with new Latin
translation, apparatus criticus, and full indices ;
the Index Plantarum gives the identifications of
Sprengel and Fraas; Didot Library, Paris, n.d.
(3) A reprint of this text in Teubner's series,
1854.

These three books are an indispensable supplement
to Schneider's great work. The notes in the edition of

xiv

## INTRODUCTION

1842 are in the main critical, but the editor's remarks
on the interpretation of thorny passages are often
extremely acute, and always worth attention. The
mass of material collected by Schneider is put into
an accessible form. Wimmer is far more conservative
in textual criticism than Schneider, and has a better
appreciation of Theophrastus' elliptical and somewhat peculiar idiom, though some of his emendations
appear to rest on little basis. A collation of the
Paris MSS. (P and P₂) was made for Wimmer; for
the readings of U and M he relied on Schneider,
who, in his fifth volume, had compared U with
Bodaeus' edition. A fresh collation of the rather
exiguous manuscript authorities is perhaps required
before anything like a definitive text can be provided. Wimmer's Latin translation is not very
helpful, since it slurs the difficulties: the Didot
edition, in which it appears, is disfigured with
numerous misprints.

(Sandys' *History of Classical Scholarship* (ii. p. 380)
mentions translations into Latin and Italian by
Bandini ; of this work I know nothing.)

### C. *Other Commentators*

Scal.  J. C. Scaliger : *Commentarii et animadversiones* on
the περὶ φυτῶν ἱστορία posthumously published
by his son Sylvius at Leyden, 1584. (He also
wrote a commentary on the περὶ αἰτιῶν, which
was edited by Robertus Constantinus and pub-

lished at Geneva in 1566.) The most accurate and brilliant scholar who has contributed to the elucidation of Theophrastus.

R.Const. Robertus Constantinus (see above). Added notes of his own, many of them valuable, which are given with Scaliger's in Bodaeus' edition.

Salm. Salmasius (Claude de Saumaise). Made many happy corrections of Theophrastus' text in his *Exercitationes Plinianae.*

Palm. Jacobus Palmerius (Jacques de Paulmier). His *Exercitationes in optimos auctores Graecos* (Leyden, 1668) contain a certain number of acute emendations; Wimmer considers that he had a good understanding of Theophrastus' style.

Meurs. Johannes Meursius (Jan de Meurs). Author of some critical notes on Theophrastus published at Leyden in 1640; also of a book on Crete.

Dalec. Jean Jacques D'Aléchamps: the botanist. Author of *Historia plantarum universalis*, Lyons, 1587, and editor of Pliny's *Natural History.*

Mold. J. J. P. Moldenhauer. Author of *Tentamen in Historiam plantarum Theophrasti*, Hamburg, 1791. This book, which I have not been able to see and know only from Wimmer's citations, contains, according to him, very valuable notes on the extremely difficult Introduction to the 'Historia' (Book I. chaps. i.–ii.).

## II.—THEOPHRASTUS' LIFE AND WORKS

Such information as we possess concerning the life of Theophrastus comes mainly from Diogenes Laertius' *Lives of the Philosophers*, compiled at least four hundred years after Theophrastus' death; it is given therefore here for what it may be worth; there is no intrinsic improbability in most of what Diogenes records.

He was born in 370 B.C. at Eresos in Lesbos; at an early age he went to Athens and there became a pupil of Plato. It may be surmised that it was from him that he first learnt the importance of that principle of classification which runs through all his extant works, including even the brochure known as the 'Characters' (if it is rightly ascribed to him), and which is ordinarily considered as characteristic of the teaching of his second master Aristotle. But in Plato's own later speculations classification had a very important place, since it was by grouping things in their 'natural kinds' that, according to his later metaphysic, men were to arrive at an adumbration of the 'ideal forms' of which these kinds are the phenomenal counterpart, and which constitute the world of reality. Whether Theophrastus gathered the principle of classification from Plato or from his fellow-pupil Aristotle, it appears in his hands to have been for the first time systematically applied to the vegetable world. Throughout his botanical

works the constant implied question is ' What is its
*difference?* ', 'What is its essential nature?', viz. 'What
are the characteristic features in virtue of which a
plant may be distinguished from other plants, and
which make up its own 'nature' or essential
character ?

Theophrastus appears to have been only Aristotle's
junior by fifteen years. On Plato's death he became
Aristotle's pupil, but, the difference in age not being
very great, he and his second master appear to have
been on practically equal terms. We are assured
that Aristotle was deeply attached to his friend;
while as earnest of an equally deep attachment on
the other side Theophrastus took Aristotle's son
under his particular care after his father's death.
Aristotle died at the age of sixty-three, leaving to
his favourite pupil his books, including the auto-
graphs of his own works, and his garden in the
grounds of the Lyceum. The first of these bequests,
if the information is correct, is of great historical
importance ; it may well be that we owe to
Theophrastus the publication of some at least of
his master's voluminous works. And as to the
garden it is evident that it was here that the first
systematic botanist made many of the observations
which are recorded in his botanical works. Diogenes
has preserved his will, and there is nothing in the
terms of this interesting document to suggest that
it is not authentic. Of special interest is the
provision made for the maintenance of the garden ;

# INTRODUCTION

it is bequeathed to certain specified friends and to
those who will spend their time with them in learn-
ing and philosophy; the testator is to be buried
in it without extravagant expense, a custodian is
appointed, and provision is made for the emancipa-
tion of various gardeners, so soon as they have
earned their freedom by long enough service.

According to Diogenes Theophrastus died at the
age of eighty-five. He is made indeed to say in the
probably spurious Preface to the 'Characters' that he
is writing in his ninety-ninth year; while St. Jerome's
Chronicle asserts that he lived to the age of 107.
Accepting Diogenes' date, we may take it that he
died about 285 B.C.; it is said that he complained
that "we die just when we are beginning to live."
His life must indeed have been a remarkably full
and interesting one, when we consider that he
enjoyed the personal friendship of two such men as
Plato and Aristotle, and that he had witnessed the
whole of the careers of Philip and Alexander of
Macedon. To Alexander indeed he was directly
indebted; the great conqueror had not been for
nothing the pupil of the encyclopaedic Aristotle.
He took with him to the East scientifically trained
observers, the results of whose observations were at
Theophrastus' disposal. Hence it is that his descriptions of plants are not limited to the flora of
Greece and the Levant; to the reports of Alexander's
followers he owed his accounts of such plants as the
cotton-plant, banyan, pepper, cinnamon, myrrh and

INTRODUCTION

frankincense. It has been a subject of some controversy whence he derived his accounts of plants whose habitat was nearer home. Kirchner, in an able tract, combats the contention of Sprengel that his observations even of the Greek flora were not made at first hand. Now at this period the Peripatetic School must have been a very important educational institution; Diogenes says that under Theophrastus it numbered two thousand pupils. Moreover we may fairly assume that Alexander, from his connexion with Aristotle, was interested in it, while we are told that at a later time Demetrius Phalereus assisted it financially. May we not hazard and guess that a number of the students were appropriately employed in the collection of facts and observations? The assumption that a number of 'travelling students' were so employed would at all events explain certain references in Theophrastus' botanical works. He says constantly 'The Macedonians say,' 'The men of Mount Ida say' and so forth. Now it seems hardly probable that he is quoting from written treatises by Macedonian or Idaean writers. It is at least a plausible suggestion that in such references he is referring to reports of the districts in question contributed by students of the school. In that case 'The Macedonians say' would mean 'This is what our representative was told in Macedonia.' It is further noticeable that the tense used is sometimes past, *e.g.* 'The men of Mount Ida *said*'; an obvious explanation of this is

INTRODUCTION

supplied by the above conjecture. It is even possible
that in one place (3. 12. 4.) the name of one of these
students has been preserved.

Theophrastus, like his master, was a very voluminous writer; Diogenes gives a list of 227 treatises
from his pen, covering most topics of human interest,
as Religion, Politics, Ethics, Education, Rhetoric,
Mathematics, Astronomy, Logic, Meteorology and
other natural sciences. His oratorical works enjoyed
a high reputation in antiquity. Diogenes attributes
to him ten works on Rhetoric, of which one On Style
was known to Cicero, who adopted from it the
classification of styles into the 'grand,' the 'plain,'
and the 'intermediate.'[1]  Of one or two other lost
works we have some knowledge. Thus the substance
of an essay on Piety is preserved in Porphyry *de
Abstinentia.*[2] The principal works still extant are
the nine books of the Enquiry into Plants, and the
six books on the Causes of Plants ; these seem to be
complete. We have also considerable fragments of
treatises entitled :—of Sense-perception and objects
of Sense, of Stones, of Fire, of Odours, of Winds, of
Weather-Signs, of Weariness, of Dizziness, of Sweat,
Metaphysics, besides a number of unassigned excerpts.
The style of these works, as of the botanical books,
suggests that, as in the case of Aristotle, what we
possess consists of notes for lectures or notes taken
of lectures. There is no literary charm ; the sen-

[1] Sandys, i. p. 99.
[2] Bernays, Theophrastus, 1866.

tences are mostly compressed and highly elliptical,
to the point sometimes of obscurity. It follows that
translation, as with Aristotle, must be to some extent
paraphrase. The thirty sketches of 'Characters'
ascribed to Theophrastus, which have found many
imitators, and which are well known in this country
through Sir R. Jebb's brilliant translation, stand on
a quite different footing; the object of this curious
and amusing work is discussed in Sir R. Jebb's
Introduction and in the more recent edition of
Edmonds and Austen. Well may Aristotle, as we
are assured, have commended his pupil's diligence.
It is said that, when he retired from the headship of
the school, he handed it over to Theophrastus. We
are further told that the latter was once prosecuted
for impiety, but the attack failed; also that he was
once banished from Athens for a year, it does not
appear under what circumstances. He was considered an attractive and lively lecturer. Diogenes'
sketch ends with the quotation of some sayings
attributed to him, of which the most noteworthy
are 'Nothing costs us so dear as the waste of time,'
'One had better trust an unbridled horse than
an undigested harangue.' He was followed to
his grave, which we may hope was, in accordance
with his own wish, in some peaceful corner of the
Lyceum garden, by a great assemblage of his fellow
townsmen.

xxii

# INTRODUCTION

The principal references in the notes are to the following ancient authors :—

| | |
|---|---|
| Apollon. | Apollonius, *Historia Miraculorum*. |
| Arist. | Aristotle. Bekker, Berlin, 1831. |
| Arr. | Arrian. Hercher (Teubner). |
| Athen. | Athenaeus. Dindorf, Leipzig, 1827. |
| Col. | Columella, *de re rustica*. Schneider, Leipzig, 1794. |
| Diod. | Diodorus. |
| Diosc. | Pedanius Dioscurides, *de materia medica*. Wellmann, Berlin, 1907. |
| Geop. | *Geoponica*. Beckh (Teubner), 1895. |
| Nic. | Nicander, *Theriaca*. Schneider, Leipzig, 1816. |
| Pall. | Palladius, *de re rustica*. Schneider, Leipzig, 1795. |
| Paus. | Pausanias. Schubart (Teubner), Leipzig, 1881. |
| Plin. | Plinius, *Naturalis Historia*. Mayhoff (Teubner), 1887. (Reference by book and section.) |
| Plut. | Plutarch. Hercher (Teubner), Leipzig, 1872. |
| Scyl. | Scylax, *Periplus*. Vossius, Amsterdam, 1639. |

# CONTENTS

# CONTENTS

# CONTENTS

## BOOK IV

### OF THE TREES AND PLANTS SPECIAL TO PARTICULAR DISTRICTS AND POSITIONS

# CONTENTS

## BOOK V

# THEOPHRASTUS

## ENQUIRY INTO PLANTS

### BOOK I

# ΘΕΟΦΡΑΣΤΟΥ
## ΠΕΡΙ ΦΥΤΩΝ ΙΣΤΟΡΙΑΣ

### Λ

I. Τῶν φυτῶν τὰς διαφορὰς καὶ τὴν ἄλλην φύσιν ληπτέον κατά τε τὰ μέρη καὶ τὰ πάθη καὶ τὰς γενέσεις καὶ τοὺς βίους· ἤθη γὰρ καὶ πρά[ξεις οὐκ ἔχουσιν ὥσπερ τὰ ζῷα. εἰσὶ δ' αἱ μὲν κατὰ τὴν γένεσιν καὶ τὰ πάθη καὶ τοὺς βίους εὐθεωρητότεραι καὶ ῥᾴους, αἱ δὲ κατὰ τὰ μέρη πλείους ἔχουσι[1] ποικιλίας. αὐτὸ γὰρ τοῦτο πρῶτον οὐχ ἱκανῶς ἀφώρισται τὰ ποῖα δεῖ μέρη καὶ μὴ μέρη καλεῖν, ἀλλ' ἔχει τινὰ ἀπορίαν.

2 Τὸ μὲν οὖν μέρος ἅτε ἐκ τῆς ἰδίας φύσεως ὂν ἀεὶ δοκεῖ διαμένειν ἢ ἁπλῶς ἢ ὅταν γένηται, καθάπερ ἐν τοῖς ζῴοις τὰ ὕστερον γενησόμενα, πλὴν εἴ τι

---

[1] τὰ ins. Sch., om. Ald.H.
[2] πάθη, a more general word than δυνάμεις, 'virtues': cf. 1. 5. 4 ; 8. 4. 2 ; it seems to mean here something like 'behaviour,' in relation to environment. Instances of πάθη are given 4. 2. 11 ; 4. 14. 6.
[3] ἔχουσι conj. H.; ἔχουσαι W. with Ald.

2

# THEOPHRASTUS

## ENQUIRY INTO PLANTS

## BOOK I

OF THE PARTS OF PLANTS AND THEIR COMPOSITION.
OF CLASSIFICATION.

*Introductory: How plants are to be classified; difficulty
of defining what are the essential 'parts' of a plant
especially if plants are assumed to correspond to animals.*

I. IN considering the distinctive characters of
plants and their nature generally one must take
into account their [1] parts, their qualities,[2] the
ways in which their life originates, and the course
which it follows in each case : (conduct and activities
we do not find in them, as we do in animals).
Now
the differences in the way in which their life originates, in their qualities and in their life-history are comparatively easy to observe and are simpler, while
those shewn [3] in their 'parts' present more com-
plexity. Indeed it has not even been satisfactorily
determined what ought and what ought not to be
called 'parts,' and some difficulty is involved in
making the distinction.

Now it appears that by a 'part,' seeing that it is
something which belongs to the plant's characteristic
nature, we mean something which is permanent either
absolutely or when once it has appeared (like those
parts of animals which remain for a time undeveloped)

3

B 2

διὰ νόσον ἢ γῆρας ἢ πήρωσιν ἀποβάλλεται. τῶν
δ' ἐν τοῖς φυτοῖς ἔνια τοιαῦτ' ἐστὶν ὥστ' ἐπέτειον
ἔχειν τὴν οὐσίαν, οἷον ἄνθος βρύον φύλλον
καρπός, ἁπλῶς ὅσα πρὸ τῶν καρπῶν ἢ ἅμα
γίνεται τοῖς καρποῖς· ἔτι δὲ αὐτὸς ὁ βλαστός·
αἰεὶ γὰρ ἐπίφυσιν λαμβάνει τὰ δένδρα κατ'
ἐνιαυτὸν ὁμοίως ἔν τε τοῖς ἄνω καὶ ἐν τοῖς περὶ
τὰς ῥίζας· ὥστε, εἰ μέν τις ταῦτα θήσει μέρη, τό
τε πλῆθος ἀόριστον ἔσται καὶ οὐδέποτε τὸ αὐτὸ
τῶν μορίων· εἰ δ' αὖ μὴ μέρη, συμβήσεται, δι' ὧν
τέλεια γίνεται καὶ φαίνεται, ταῦτα μὴ εἶναι μέρη·
βλαστάνοντα γὰρ καὶ θάλλοντα καὶ καρπὸν
ἔχοντα πάντα καλλίω καὶ τελειότερα καὶ δοκεῖ
καὶ ἔστιν. αἱ μὲν οὖν ἀπορίαι σχεδόν εἰσιν
αὗται.

3 Τάχα δὲ οὐχ ὁμοίως ἅπαντα ζητητέον οὔτε
ἐν τοῖς ἄλλοις οὔθ' ὅσα πρὸς τὴν γένεσιν,
αὐτά τε τὰ γεννώμενα μέρη θετέον οἷον τοὺς
καρπούς. οὐδὲ γὰρ τὰ ἔμβρυα τῶν ζώων. εἰ
δὲ ἐν τῇ ὥρᾳ ὄψει τοῦτό γε κάλλιστον,

---

[1] i.e. the male inflorescence of some trees ; the term is
of course wider than 'catkin.'
[2] i.e. flower, catkin, leaf, fruit, shoot.

4

—permanent, that is, unless it be lost by disease, age
or mutilation. However some of the parts of plants
are such that their existence is limited to a year, for
instance, flower, 'catkin,'[1] leaf, fruit, in fact all
those parts which are antecedent to the fruit or else
appear along with it. Also the new shoot itself must
be included with these; for trees always make fresh
growth every year alike in the parts above ground
and in those which pertain to the roots. So that if
one sets these[2] down as 'parts,' the number of parts
will be indeterminate and constantly changing;
if on the other hand these are not to be called
'parts,' the result will be that things which are
essential if the plant is to reach its perfection, and
which are its conspicuous features, are nevertheless
not 'parts'; for any plant always appears to be, as
indeed it is, more comely and more perfect when it
makes new growth, blooms, and bears fruit. Such,
we may say, are the difficulties involved in defining
a 'part.'

But perhaps we should not expect to find in
plants a complete correspondence with animals
in regard to those things which concern reproduction any more than in other respects; and so
we should reckon as 'parts' even those things
to which the plant gives birth, for instance their
fruits, although[3] we do not so reckon the unborn
young of animals. (However, if such[4] a product seems
fairest to the eye, because the plant is then in its
prime, we can draw no inference from this in

[3] οὐδὲ γάρ: οὐδὲ seems to mean no more than οὐ (cf. neque
enim = non enim); γάρ refers back to the beginning of the §.
[4] ἐν τῇ ὥρᾳ ὄψει τοῦτό γε I conj.: τῇ ὥρᾳ ὄψει τό γε vulg.
W.; τοῦτο, i.e. flower or fruit.

5

οὐδὲν σημεῖον, ἐπεὶ καὶ τῶν ζώων εὐθενεῖ τὰ
κύοντα.

Πολλὰ δὲ καὶ τὰ μέρη κατ᾽ ἐνιαυτὸν ἀποβάλλει, καθάπερ οἵ τε ἔλαφοι τὰ κέρατα καὶ
τὰ φωλεύοντα τὰ πτερὰ καὶ τρίχας τετράποδα·
ὥστ᾽ οὐδὲν ἄτοπον ἄλλως τε καὶ ὅμοιον ὂν τῷ
φυλλοβολεῖν τὸ πάθος.

Ὡσαύτως δ᾽ οὐδὲ τὰ πρὸς τὴν γένεσιν· ἐπεὶ καὶ
ἐν τοῖς ζώοις τὰ μὲν συνεκτίκτεται τὰ δ᾽ ἀπο-
καθαίρεται καθάπερ ἀλλότρια τῆς φύσεως. ἔοικε
δὲ παραπλησίως καὶ τὰ περὶ τὴν βλάστησιν
ἔχειν. ἡ γάρ τοι βλάστησις γενέσεως χάριν ἐστὶ
τῆς τελείας.

Ὅλως δὲ καθάπερ εἴπομεν οὐδὲ πάντα
ὁμοίως καὶ ἐπὶ τῶν ζώων ληπτέον. δι᾽ ὃ καὶ ὁ
ἀριθμὸς ἀόριστος· πανταχῇ γὰρ βλαστητικὸν
ἅτε καὶ πανταχῇ ζῶν. ὥστε ταῦτα μὲν οὕτως
ὑποληπτέον οὐ μόνον εἰς τὰ νῦν ἀλλὰ καὶ τῶν
μελλόντων χάριν· ὅσα γὰρ μὴ οἷόν τε ἀφο-
μοιοῦν περίεργον τὸ γλίχεσθαι πάντως, ἵνα μὴ
καὶ τὴν οἰκείαν ἀποβάλλωμεν θεωρίαν. ἡ δὲ
ἱστορία τῶν φυτῶν ἐστιν ὡς ἁπλῶς εἰπεῖν ἢ κατὰ

<hr/>

1 εὐθενεῖ conj. Sch., εὐθετεῖ UMVAld. i.e. we do not
argue from the fact that animals are at their handsomest
in the breeding season that the young is therefore 'part' of
the animal.
2 Lit. 'which are in holes,' in allusion to the well-known
belief that animals (especially birds) which are out of sight
in the winter are hiding in holes ; the text is supported by
[Arist.] de plantis 1. 3, the author of which had evidently
read this passage : but possibly some such words as τάς τε
φολίδας καὶ have dropped out after φωλεύοντα.

6

support of our argument, since even among animals those that are with young are at their best.[1])

Again many plants shed their parts every year, even as stags shed their horns, birds which hibernate[2] their feathers, four-footed beasts their hair: so that it is not strange that the parts of plants should not be permanent, especially as what thus occurs in animals and the shedding of leaves in plants are analogous processes.

In like manner the parts concerned with reproduction are not permanent in plants: for even in animals there are things which are separated from the parent when the young is born, and there are other things[3] which are cleansed away, as though neither of these belonged to the animal's essential nature. And so too it appears to be with the growth of plants; for of course growth leads up to reproduction as the completion of the process.[4]

And in general, as we have said, we must not assume that in all respects there is complete correspondence between plants and animals. And that is why the number also of parts is indeterminate; for a plant has the power of growth in all its parts, inasmuch as it has life in all its parts. Wherefore we should assume the truth to be as I have said, not only in regard to the matters now before us, but in view also of those which will come before us presently; for it is waste of time to take great pains to make comparisons where that is impossible, and in so doing we may lose sight also of our proper subject of enquiry. The enquiry into plants, to put it generally, may

[3] i.e. the embryo is not the only thing derived from the parent animal which is not a 'part' of it; there is also the food-supply produced with the young, and the after-birth.
[4] cf. C.P. 1. 11. s.

τὰ ἔξω μόρια καὶ τὴν ὅλην μορφὴν ἢ κατὰ τὰ
ἐντός, ὥσπερ ἐπὶ τῶν ζώων τὰ ἐκ τῶν ἀνατομῶν.

5 Ληπτέον δ' ἐν αὐτοῖς ποῖά τε πᾶσιν ὑπάρχει
ταὐτὰ καὶ ποῖα ἴδια καθ' ἕκαστον γένος, ἔτι δὲ
τῶν αὐτῶν ποῖα ὅμοια· λέγω δ' οἷον φύλλον ῥίζα
φλοιός. οὐ δεῖ δὲ οὐδὲ τοῦτο λανθάνειν εἴ τι κατ'
ἀναλογίαν θεωρητέον, ὥσπερ ἐπὶ τῶν ζώων, τὴν
ἀναφορὰν ποιουμένους δῆλον ὅτι πρὸς τὰ ἐμ-
φερέστατα καὶ τελειότατα. καὶ ἁπλῶς δὲ ὅσα
τῶν ἐν φυτοῖς ἀφομοιωτέον τῷ ἐν τοῖς ζώοις, ὡς
ἄν τίς τῷ γ' ἀνάλογον ἀφομοιοῖ. ταῦτα μὲν οὖν
διωρίσθω τὸν τρόπον τοῦτον.

6 Αἱ δὲ τῶν μερῶν διαφοραὶ σχεδὸν ὡς τύπῳ
λαβεῖν εἰσιν ἐν τρισίν, ἢ τῷ τὰ μὲν ἔχειν
τὰ δὲ μή, καθάπερ φύλλα καὶ καρπόν, ἢ τῷ
μὴ ὅμοια μηδὲ ἴσα, ἢ τρίτον τῷ μὴ ὁμοίως.
τούτων δὲ ἡ μὲν ἀνομοιότης ὁρίζεται σχήματι
χρώματι πυκνότητι μανότητι τραχύτητι λειότητι
καὶ τοῖς ἄλλοις πάθεσιν, ἔτι δὲ ὅσαι διαφοραὶ
τῶν χυλῶν. ἡ δὲ ἀνισότης ὑπεροχῇ καὶ ἐλλείψει
κατὰ πλῆθος ἢ μέγεθος. ὡς δ' εἰπεῖν τύπῳ

---

¹ A very obscure sentence ; so W. renders the MSS. text.
² *i.e.* 'inequality' might include ' unlikeness.'

8

either take account of the external parts and the form of the plant generally, or else of their internal parts : the latter method corresponds to the study of animals by dissection.

Further we must consider which parts belong to all plants alike, which are peculiar to some one kind, and which of those which belong to all alike are themselves alike in all cases ; for instance, leaves roots bark. And again, if in some cases analogy ought to be considered (for instance, an analogy presented by animals), we must keep this also in view ; and in that case we must of course make the closest resemblances and the most perfectly developed examples our standard ; [1] and, finally, the ways in which the parts of plants are affected must be compared to the corresponding effects in the case of animals, so far as one can in any given case find an analogy for comparison. So let these definitions stand.

*The essential parts of plants, and the materials of which they are made.*

Now the differences in regard to parts, to take a general view, are of three kinds : either one plant may possess them and another not (for instance, leaves and fruit), or in one plant they may be unlike in appearance or size to those of another, or, thirdly, they may be differently arranged. Now the unlikeness between them is seen in form, colour, closeness of arrangement or its opposite, roughness or its opposite, and the other qualities ; and again there are the various differences of flavour. The inequality is seen in excess or defect as to number or size, or, to speak generally, [2] all the above-mentioned differences too

9

κἀκεῖνα πάντα καθ᾽ ὑπεροχὴν καὶ ἔλλειψιν· τὸ
7 γὰρ μᾶλλον καὶ ἧττον ὑπεροχὴ καὶ ἔλλειψις· τὸ
δὲ μὴ ὁμοίως τῇ θέσει διαφέρει· λέγω δ᾽ οἷον τὸ
τοὺς καρποὺς τὰ μὲν ἐπάνω τὰ δ᾽ ὑποκάτω τῶν
φύλλων ἔχειν καὶ αὐτοῦ τοῦ δένδρου τὰ μὲν ἐξ
ἄκρου τὰ δὲ ἐκ τῶν πλαγίων, ἔνια δὲ καὶ ἐκ τοῦ
στελέχους, οἷον ἡ Αἰγυπτία συκάμινος, καὶ ὅσα δὴ
καὶ ὑπὸ γῆς φέρει καρπόν, οἷον ἥ τε ἀραχίδνα καὶ
τὸ ἐν Αἰγύπτῳ καλούμενον οὔιγγον, καὶ εἰ τὰ μὲν
ἔχει μίσχον τὰ δὲ μή. καὶ ἐπὶ τῶν ἀνθέων ὁμοίως·
τὰ μὲν γὰρ περὶ αὐτὸν τὸν καρπὸν τὰ δὲ ἄλλως.
ὅλως δὲ τὸ τῆς θέσεως ἐν τούτοις καὶ τοῖς φύλλοις
καὶ ἐν τοῖς βλαστοῖς ληπτέον.

8 Διαφέρει δὲ ἔνια καὶ τῇ τάξει· τὰ μὲν ὡς
ἔτυχε, τῆς δ᾽ ἐλάτης οἱ κλῶνες κατ᾽ ἀλλήλους
ἑκατέρωθεν· τῶν δὲ καὶ οἱ ὄζοι δι᾽ ἴσου τε καὶ
κατ᾽ ἀριθμὸν ἴσοι, καθάπερ τῶν τριόζων.
Ὥστε τὰς μὲν διαφορὰς ἐκ τούτων ληπτέον ἐξ
ὧν καὶ ἡ ὅλη μορφὴ συνδηλοῦται καθ᾽ ἕκαστον.

9 Αὐτὰ δὲ τὰ μέρη διαριθμησαμένους πειρατέον
περὶ ἑκάστου λέγειν. ἔστι δὲ πρῶτα μὲν καὶ
μέγιστα καὶ κοινὰ τῶν πλείστων τάδε, ῥίζα
καυλὸς ἀκρεμὼν κλάδος, εἰς ἃ διέλοιτ᾽ ἄν τις

---

¹ cf. C.P. 5. 1. 9.
² cf. 1. 6. 11. T. extends the term καρπός so as to
include any succulent edible part of a plant.
³ T. does not consider that καρπός was necessarily ante-
ceded by a flower.

are included under excess and defect: for the 'more' and the 'less' are the same thing as excess and defect, whereas 'differently arranged' implies a difference of position; for instance, the fruit may be above or below the leaves,[1] and, as to position on the tree itself, the fruit may grow on the apex of it or on the side branches, and in some cases even on the trunk, as in the sycamore; while some plants again even bear their fruit underground, for instance *arakhidna*[2] and the plant called in Egypt *uingon*; again in some plants the fruit has a stalk, in some it has none. There is a like difference in the floral organs: in some cases they actually surround the fruit, in others they are differently placed[3]: in fact it is in regard to the fruit, the leaves, and the shoots that the question of position has to be considered.

Or again there are differences as to symmetry[4]: in some cases the arrangement is irregular, while the branches of the silver-fir are arranged opposite one another; and in some cases the branches are at equal distances apart, and correspond in number, as where they are in three rows.[5]

Wherefore the differences between plants must be observed in these particulars, since taken together they shew forth the general character of each plant.

But, before we attempt to speak about each, we must make a list of the parts themselves. Now the primary and most important parts, which are also common to most, are these—root, stem, branch, twig; these are the parts into which we might divide the plant, regarding them as members,[6] corresponding to

---

[1] Plin. 16. 122.    [3] *i.e.* ternate.
[5] *i.e.* if we wished to make an anatomical division. μέλη conj. Sch. *cf.* 1. 2. 7; μέρη Ald.

THEOPHRASTUS

ὥσπερ εἰς μέλη, καθάπερ ἐπὶ τῶν ζώων. ἕκαστόν τε γὰρ ἀνόμοιον καὶ ἐξ ἁπάντων τούτων τὰ ὅλα. Ἔστι δὲ ῥίζα μὲν δι᾽ οὗ τὴν τροφὴν ἐπάγεται, καυλὸς δὲ εἰς ὃ φέρεται. καυλὸν δὲ λέγω τὸ ὑπὲρ γῆς πεφυκὸς ἐφ᾽ ἕν· τοῦτο γὰρ κοινότατον ὁμοίως ἐπετείοις καὶ χρονίοις, ὃ ἐπὶ τῶν δένδρων καλεῖται στέλεχος· ἀκρεμόνας δὲ τοὺς ἀπὸ τούτου σχιζομένους, οὓς ἔνιοι καλοῦσιν ὄζους. κλάδον δὲ τὸ βλάστημα τὸ ἐκ τούτων ἐφ᾽ ἕν, οἷον μάλιστα τὸ ἐπέτειον.

Καὶ ταῦτα μὲν οἰκειότερα τῶν δένδρων. 10 ὁ δὲ καυλός, ὥσπερ εἴρηται, κοινότερος· ἔχει δὲ οὐ πάντα οὐδὲ τοῦτον, οἷον ἔνια τῶν ποιωδῶν. τὰ δ᾽ ἔχει μὲν οὐκ ἀεὶ δὲ ἀλλ᾽ ἐπέτειον, καὶ ὅσα χρονιώτερα ταῖς ῥίζαις. ὅλως δὲ πολύχουν τὸ φυτὸν καὶ ποικίλον καὶ χαλεπὸν εἰπεῖν καθόλου· σημεῖον δὲ τὸ μηδὲν εἶναι κοινὸν λαβεῖν ὃ πᾶσιν ὑπάρχει, καθάπερ τοῖς ζώοις 11 στόμα καὶ κοιλία. τὰ δὲ ἀναλογίᾳ ταὐτὰ τὰ δ᾽ ἄλλον τρόπον. οὔτε γὰρ ῥίζαν πάντ᾽ ἔχει οὔτε καυλὸν οὔτε ἀκρεμόνα οὔτε κλάδον οὔτε φύλλον οὔτε ἄνθος οὔτε καρπὸν οὔτ᾽ αὖ φλοιὸν ἢ μήτραν ἢ ἶνας ἢ φλέβας, οἷον μύκης ὕδνον· ἐν τούτοις δὲ ἡ οὐσία καὶ ἐν τοῖς τοιούτοις· ἀλλὰ μάλιστα ταῦτα

---

¹ *i.e.* before it begins to divide.    ² Or ‘knots.’
³ ἐφ᾽ conj. W.; ὑφ᾽ P₂P₃Ald.
⁴ χρονιώτερα conj. Sch.; χρονιώτερον Ald.H.
⁵ ἀναλογίᾳ conj. Sch.; ἀναλογία UAld.H.

12

the members of animals: for each of these is distinct in character from the rest, and together they make up the whole.

The root is that by which the plant draws its nourishment, the stem that to which it is conducted. And by the 'stem' I mean that part which grows above ground and is single[1]; for that is the part which occurs most generally both in annuals and in long-lived plants; and in the case of trees it is called the 'trunk.' By 'branches' I mean the parts which split off from the stem and are called by some 'boughs.'[2] By 'twig' I mean the growth which springs from the branch regarded as a single whole,[3] and especially such an annual growth.

Now these parts belong more particularly to trees. The stem however, as has been said, is more general, though not all plants possess even this, for instance, some herbaceous plants are stemless; others again have it, not permanently, but as an annual growth, including some whose roots live beyond the year.[4] In fact your plant is a thing various and manifold, and so it is difficult to describe in general terms: in proof whereof we have the fact that we cannot here seize on any universal character which is common to all, as a mouth and a stomach are common to all animals; whereas in plants some characters are the same in all, merely in the sense that all have analogous[5] characters, while others correspond otherwise. For not all plants have root, stem, branch, twig, leaf, flower or fruit, or again bark, core, fibres or veins; for instance, fungi and truffles; and yet these and such like characters belong to a plant's essential nature. However, as has been said, these

ὑπάρχει, καθάπερ εἴρηται, τοῖς δένδροις κἀκείνων οἰκειότερος ὁ μερισμός· πρὸς ἃ καὶ τὴν ἀναφορὰν τῶν ἄλλων ποιεῖσθαι δίκαιον.

12 Σχεδὸν δὲ καὶ τὰς ἄλλας μορφὰς ἑκάστων ταῦτα διασημαίνει. διαφέρουσι γὰρ πλήθει τῷ τούτων καὶ ὀλιγότητι καὶ πυκνότητι καὶ μανότητι καὶ τῷ ἐφ᾽ ἓν ἢ εἰς πλείω σχίζεσθαι καὶ τοῖς ἄλλοις τοῖς ὁμοίοις. ἔστι δὲ ἕκαστον τῶν εἰρημένων οὐχ ὁμοιομερές· λέγω δὲ οὐχ ὁμοιο-μερὲς ὅτι ἐκ τῶν αὐτῶν μὲν ὁτιοῦν μέρος σύγ-κειται τῆς ῥίζης καὶ τοῦ στελέχους, ἀλλ᾽ οὐ λέγεται στέλεχος τὸ ληφθὲν ἀλλὰ μόριον, ὡς ἐν τοῖς τῶν ζῴων μέλεσίν ἐστιν. ἐκ τῶν αὐτῶν μὲν γὰρ ὁτιοῦν τῆς κνήμης ἢ τοῦ ἀγκῶνος, οὐχ ὁμώνυμον δὲ καθάπερ σὰρξ καὶ ὀστοῦν, ἀλλ᾽ ἀνώνυμον· οὐδὲ δὴ τῶν ἄλλων οὐδενὸς ὅσα μονο-ειδῆ τῶν ὀργανικῶν· ἁπάντων γὰρ τῶν τοιούτων ἀνώνυμα τὰ μέρη. τῶν δὲ πολυειδῶν ὠνομασμένα καθάπερ ποδὸς χειρὸς κεφαλῆς, οἷον δάκτυλος ῥὶς ὀφθαλμός. καὶ τὰ μὲν μέγιστα μέρη σχεδὸν ταῦτά ἐστιν.

II. Ἄλλα δὲ ἐξ ὧν ταῦτα φλοιὸς ξύλον μήτρα, ὅσα ἔχει μήτραν. πάντα δ᾽ ὁμοιομερῆ. καὶ τὰ τούτων δὲ ἔτι πρότερα καὶ ἐξ ὧν ταῦτα, ὑγρὸν ἲς

---

¹ There is no exact English equivalent for ὁμοιομερές, which denotes a whole composed of parts, each of which is, as it were, a miniature of the whole. *cf.* Arist. *H.A.* 1. 1.
² *i.e.* any part taken of flesh or bone may be called ' flesh ' or ' bone.'
³ *e.g.* bark ; *cf.* 1. 2. 1.     ⁴ *e.g.* fruit.

characters belong especially to trees, and our
classification of characters belongs more particularly
to these ; and it is right to make these the standard
in treating of the others.

Trees moreover shew forth fairly well the other
features also which distinguish plants; for they exhibit
differences in the number or fewness of these which
they possess, as to the closeness or openness of their
growth, as to their being single or divided, and in
other like respects. Moreover each of the characters
mentioned is not ‘composed of like parts’[1]; by
which I mean that though any given part of the root
or trunk is composed of the same elements as the
whole, yet the part so taken is not itself called
‘trunk,’ but ‘a portion of a trunk.’ The case is the
same with the members of an animal's body ; to
wit, any part of the leg or arm is composed of the
same elements as the whole, yet it does not bear the
same name (as it does in the case of flesh or bone[2]);
it has no special name. Nor again have subdivisions
of any of those other organic parts[3] which are uniform
special names, subdivisions of all such being nameless.
But the subdivisions of those parts[4] which are
compound have names, as have those of the foot,
hand, and head, for instance, toe, finger, nose or eye.
Such then are the largest[5] parts of the plant.

II. Again there are the things of which such parts
are composed, namely bark, wood, and core (in the
case of those plants which have it[6]), and these are
all ‘composed of like parts.’ Further there are
the things which are even prior to these, from which

[5] *i.e.* the ‘compound’ parts.
[6] ξύλον μήτρα conj. W. from G. μήτρα ξύλον MSS. ;
ξ ίλον, ὅσα conj. W. ; ξύλα, ἢ ὅσα Ald.H.

THEOPHRASTUS

φλὲψ σάρξ· ἀρχαὶ γὰρ αὗται· πλὴν εἴ τις λέγοι
τὰς τῶν στοιχείων δυνάμεις, αὗται δὲ κοιναὶ πάντων. ἡ μὲν οὖν οὐσία καὶ ἡ ὅλη φύσις ἐν τούτοις.

Ἄλλα δ᾽ ἐστὶν ὥσπερ ἐπέτεια μέρη τὰ πρὸς
τὴν καρποτοκίαν, οἷον φύλλον ἄνθος μίσχος·
τοῦτο δ᾽ ἐστὶν ᾧ συνήρτηται πρὸς τὸ φυτὸν τὸ
φύλλον καὶ ὁ καρπός· ἔτι δὲ [ἕλιξ] βρύον, οἷς
ὑπάρχει, καὶ ἐπὶ πᾶσι σπέρμα τὸ τοῦ καρποῦ·
καρπὸς δ᾽ ἐστὶ τὸ συγκείμενον σπέρμα μετὰ τοῦ
περικαρπίου. παρὰ δὲ ταῦτα ἐνίων ἴδια ἄττα,
καθάπερ ἡ κηκὶς δρυὸς καὶ ἡ ἕλιξ ἀμπέλου.

2 Καὶ τοῖς μὲν δένδρεσιν ἔστιν οὕτως διαλαβεῖν.
τοῖς δ᾽ ἐπετείοις δῆλον ὡς ἅπαντα ἐπέτεια·
μέχρι γὰρ τῶν καρπῶν ἡ φύσις. ὅσα δὴ ἐπετειό-
καρπα καὶ ὅσα διετίζει, καθάπερ σέλινον καὶ ἄλλ᾽
ἄττα, καὶ ὅσα δὲ πλείω χρόνον ἔχει, τούτοις
ἅπασι καὶ ὁ καυλὸς ἀκολουθήσει κατὰ λόγον·
ὅταν γὰρ σπερμοφορεῖν μέλλωσι, τότε ἐκκαυλοῦ-
σιν, ὡς ἕνεκα τοῦ σπέρματος ὄντων τῶν καυλῶν.
Ταῦτα μὲν οὖν ταύτῃ διῃρήσθω. τῶν δὲ ἄρτι
εἰρημένων μερῶν πειρατέον ἕκαστον εἰπεῖν τί
ἐστιν ὡς ἐν τύπῳ λέγοντας.

3 Τὸ μὲν οὖν ὑγρὸν φανερόν· ὃ δὴ καλοῦσί τινες
ἁπλῶς ἐν ἅπασιν ὀπόν, ὥσπερ καὶ Μενέστωρ, οἱ

---

¹ οὐσία conj. Sch. (but he retracted it); συνουσία MSS. (?)
Ald.
² This definition is quoted by Hesych. s.v. μίσχος.
³ ? om. ἕλιξ, which is mentioned below.
⁴ τὸ συγκείμενον σπέρμα, lit. 'the compound seed,' i.e. as
many seeds as are contained in one περικάρπιον.

16

they are derived—sap, fibre, veins, flesh: for these are elementary substances—unless one should prefer to call them the active principles of the elements; and they are common to all the parts of the plant. Thus the essence[1] and entire material of plants consist in these.

Again there are other as it were annual parts, which help towards the production of the fruit, as leaf, flower, stalk (that is, the part by which the leaf and the fruit are attached to the plant),[2] and again tendril,[3] 'catkin' (in those plants that have them). And in all cases there is the seed which belongs to the fruit : by 'fruit' is meant the seed or seeds,[4] together with the seed-vessel. Besides these there are in some cases peculiar parts, such as the gall in the oak, or the tendril in the vine.

In the case of trees we may thus distinguish the annual parts, while it is plain that in annual plants *all* the parts are annual : for the end of their being is attained when the fruit is produced. And with those plants which bear fruit annually, those which take two years (such as celery and certain others[5]) and those which have fruit on them for a longer time —with all these the stem will correspond to the plant's length of life : for plants develop a stem at whatever time they are about to bear seed, seeing that the stem exists for the sake of the seed.

Let this suffice for the definition of these parts : and now we must endeavour to say what each of the parts just mentioned is, giving a general and typical description.

The sap is obvious : some call it simply in all cases 'juice,' as does Menestor[6] among others : others, in

[5] *cf.* 7.1.2 and 3.    [6] A Pythagorean philosopher of Sybaris.

17

THEOPHRASTUS

δ' ἐν μὲν τοῖς ἄλλοις ἀνωνύμως ἐν δέ τισιν ὀπὸν
καὶ ἐν ἄλλοις δάκρυον. ἶνες δὲ καὶ φλέβες καθ'
αὑτὰ μὲν ἀνώνυμα τῇ δὲ ὁμοιότητι μεταλαμβά-
νουσι τῶν ἐν τοῖς ζώοις μορίων. ἔχει δὲ ἴσως
καὶ ἄλλας διαφορὰς καὶ ταῦτα καὶ ὅλως τὸ τῶν
φυτῶν γένος· πολύχουν γὰρ ὥσπερ εἰρήκαμεν.
ἀλλ' ἐπεὶ διὰ τῶν γνωριμωτέρων μεταδιώκειν δεῖ
τὰ ἀγνώριστα, γνωριμώτερα δὲ τὰ μείζω καὶ ἐμ-
φανῆ τῇ αἰσθήσει, δῆλον ὅτι καθάπερ ὑφήγηται
1 περὶ τούτων λεκτέον· ἐπαναφορὰν γὰρ ἔξομεν
τῶν ἄλλων πρὸς ταῦτα μέχρι πόσου καὶ πῶς
ἕκαστα μετέχει τῆς ὁμοιότητος. εἰλημμένων δὲ
τῶν μερῶν μετὰ ταῦτα ληπτέον τὰς τούτων
διαφοράς· οὕτως γὰρ ἅμα καὶ ἡ οὐσία φανερὰ
καὶ ἡ ὅλη τῶν γενῶν πρὸς ἄλληλα διάστασις.
Ἡ μὲν οὖν τῶν μεγίστων σχεδὸν εἴρηται· λέγω
δ' οἷον ῥίζης καυλοῦ τῶν ἄλλων· αἱ γὰρ δυνάμεις
καὶ ὧν χάριν ἕκαστον ὕστερον ῥηθήσονται. ἐξ
ὧν γὰρ καὶ ταῦτα καὶ τὰ ἄλλα σύγκειται
πειρατέον εἰπεῖν ἀρξαμένους ἀπὸ τῶν πρώτων.
Πρῶτα δέ ἐστι τὸ ὑγρὸν καὶ θερμόν· ἅπαν γὰρ
φυτὸν ἔχει τινὰ ὑγρότητα καὶ θερμότητα σύμφυτον ὥσπερ καὶ ζῷον, ὧν ὑπολειπόντων γίνεται
γῆρας καὶ φθίσις, τελείως δὲ ὑπολιπόντων θάνα-
5 τος καὶ αὔανσις. ἐν μὲν οὖν τοῖς πλείστοις ἀνώ-

---

¹ Lit. 'muscles and veins.'
² i.e. the analogy with animals is probably imperfect, but
is useful so far as it goes.
³ I. I. 10.    ⁴ e.g. the root, as such.
⁵ e.g. the different forms which roots assume.

18

the case of some plants give it no special name, while in some they call it 'juice,' and in others 'gum.' Fibre and 'veins'[1] have no special names in relation to plants, but, because of the resemblance, borrow the names of the corresponding parts of animals. [2] It may be however that, not only these things, but the world of plants generally, exhibits also other differences as compared with animals: for, as we have said,[3] the world of plants is manifold. However, since it is by the help of the better known that we must pursue the unknown, and better known are the things which are larger and plainer to our senses, it is clear that it is right to speak of these things in the way indicated: for then in dealing with the less known things we shall be making these better known things our standard, and shall ask how far and in what manner comparison is possible in each case. And when we have taken the parts,[4] we must next take the differences which they exhibit,[5] for thus will their essential nature become plain, and at the same time the general differences between one kind of plant and another.

Now the nature of the most important parts has been indicated already, that is, such parts as the root, the stem, and the rest: their functions and the reasons for which each of them exists will be set forth presently. For we must endeavour to state of what these, as well as the rest, are composed, starting from their elementary constituents.

First come moisture and warmth: for every plant, like every animal, has a certain amount of moisture and warmth which essentially belong to it; and, if these fall short, age and decay, while, if they fail altogether, death and withering ensue. Now in

19

νυμος ἡ ὑγρότης, ἐν ἐνίοις δὲ ὠνομασμένη καθάπερ
εἴρηται. τὸ αὐτὸ δὲ καὶ ἐπὶ τῶν ζώων ὑπάρχει·
μόνη γὰρ ἡ τῶν ἐναίμων ὑγρότης ὠνόμασται, δι᾽
ὃ καὶ διήρηται πρὸς τοῦτο στερήσει· τὰ μὲν γὰρ
ἄναιμα τὰ δ᾽ ἔναιμα λέγεται. ἔν τι μὲν οὖν τοῦτο
τὸ μέρος καὶ τὸ τούτῳ συνηρτημένον θερμόν.
Ἄλλα δ᾽ ἤδη ἕτερα τῶν ἐντός, ἃ καθ᾽ ἑαυτὰ μέν
ἐστιν ἀνώνυμα, διὰ δὲ τὴν ὁμοιότητα ἀπεικάζεται
τοῖς τῶν ζώων μορίοις. ἔχουσι γὰρ ὥσπερ ἶνας·
ὅ ἐστι συνεχὲς καὶ σχιστὸν καὶ ἐπίμηκες, ἀπαράβλαστον δὲ καὶ ἄβλαστον. ἔτι δὲ φλέβας. αὗται
δὲ τὰ μὲν ἄλλα εἰσὶν ὅμοιαι τῇ ἰνί, μείζους δὲ καὶ
παχύτεραι καὶ παραβλάστας ἔχουσαι καὶ ὑγρότητα. ἔτι ξύλον καὶ σάρξ. τὰ μὲν γὰρ ἔχει
σάρκα τὰ δὲ ξύλον. ἔστι δὲ τὸ μὲν ξύλον σχισ-
τόν, ἡ δὲ σὰρξ πάντῃ διαιρεῖται ὥσπερ γῆ καὶ
ὅσα γῆς· μεταξὺ δὲ γίνεται ἰνὸς καὶ φλεβός·
φανερὰ δὲ ἡ φύσις αὐτῆς ἐν ἄλλοις τε καὶ ἐν τοῖς
τῶν περικαρπίων δέρμασι. φλοιὸς δὲ καὶ μήτρα
κυρίως μὲν λέγεται, δεῖ δὲ αὐτὰ καὶ τῷ λόγῳ
διορίσαι. φλοιὸς μὲν οὖν ἐστι τὸ ἔσχατον καὶ
χωριστὸν τοῦ ὑποκειμένου σώματος. μήτρα δὲ
τὸ μεταξὺ τοῦ ξύλου, τρίτον ἀπὸ τοῦ φλοιοῦ οἷον
ἐν τοῖς ὀστοῖς μυελός. καλοῦσι δέ τινες τοῦτο

---

¹ πλείστοις conj. Mold.; πρώτοις Ald. H.   ² 1. 1. 3.
³ ἀπαράβλαστον conj. R. Const.; ἀπαράβλητον UMVAld.
⁴ ἔτι δὲ conj. W.; ἔχον Ald.   ⁵ Fibre.
⁶ i.e. can be split in one direction.
⁷ e.g. an unripe walnut.

most [1] plants the moisture has no special name, but
in some it has such a name, as has been said [2] : and
this also holds good of animals : for it is only the
moisture of those which have blood which has
received a name ; wherefore we distinguish animals
by the presence or absence of blood, calling some
'animals with blood,' others 'bloodless.' Moisture
then is one essential 'part,' and so is warmth, which
is closely connected with it.

There are also other internal characters, which in
themselves have no special name, but, because of
their resemblance, have names analogous to those of
the parts of animals. Thus plants have what
corresponds to muscle ; and this quasi-muscle is
continuous, fissile, long : moreover no other growth
starts from it either branching from the side [3] or
in continuation of it. Again [4] plants have veins :
these in other respects resemble the 'muscle,' [5] but
they are longer and thicker, and have side-growths
and contain moisture. Then there are wood and
flesh : for some plants have flesh, some wood. Wood
is fissile, [6] while flesh can be broken up in any
direction, like earth and things made of earth : it is
intermediate between fibre and veins, its nature being
clearly seen especially in the outer covering [7] of
seed-vessels. Bark and core are properly so called, [8]
yet they too must be defined. Bark then is the
outside, and is separable from the substance which it
covers. Core is that which forms the middle of the
wood, being third [9] in order from the bark, and
corresponding to the marrow in bones. Some call this
part the 'heart,' others call it 'heart-wood' : some

[8] i.e. not by analogy with animals, like 'muscle,' 'veins,'
flesh.'  [9] Reckoning inclusively.

21

καρδίαν, οἱ δ' ἐντεριώνην· ἔνιοι δὲ τὸ ἐντὸς τῆς
μήτρας αὐτῆς καρδίαν, οἱ δὲ μυελόν.

7 Τὰ μὲν οὖν μόρια σχεδόν ἐστι τοσαῦτα. σύγκειται δὲ τὰ ὕστερον ἐκ τῶν προτέρων· ξύλον
μὲν ἐξ ἰνὸς καὶ ὑγροῦ, καὶ ἔνια σαρκός· ξυλοῦται
γὰρ σκληρυννομένη, οἷον ἐν τοῖς φοίνιξι καὶ νάρ-
θηξι καὶ εἴ τι ἄλλο ἐκξυλοῦται, ὥσπερ αἱ τῶν
ῥαφανίδων ῥίζαι· μήτρα δὲ ἐξ ὑγροῦ καὶ σαρκός·
φλοιὸς δὲ ὁ μέν τις ἐκ πάντων τῶν τριῶν, οἷον ὁ
τῆς δρυὸς καὶ αἰγείρου καὶ ἀπίου· ὁ δὲ τῆς ἀμπέλου ἐξ ὑγροῦ καὶ ἰνός· ὁ δὲ τοῦ φελλοῦ¹ ἐκ
σαρκὸς καὶ ὑγροῦ. πάλιν δὲ ἐκ τούτων σύνθετα
τὰ μέγιστα καὶ πρῶτα ῥηθέντα καθαπερανεὶ
μέλη, πλὴν οὐκ ἐκ τῶν αὐτῶν πάντα οὐδὲ ὡσαύτως ἀλλὰ διαφόρως.

Εἰλημμένων δὲ πάντων τῶν μορίων ὡς εἰπεῖν
τὰς τούτων διαφορὰς πειρατέον ἀποδιδόναι καὶ
τὰς ὅλων τῶν δένδρων καὶ φυτῶν οὐσίας.

III. Ἐπεὶ δὲ συμβαίνει σαφεστέραν² εἶναι τὴν
μάθησιν διαιρουμένων κατὰ εἴδη,³ καλῶς ἔχει
τοῦτο ποιεῖν ἐφ' ὧν ἐνδέχεται. πρῶτα δέ ἐστι
καὶ μέγιστα καὶ σχεδὸν ὑφ' ὧν πάντ'⁴ ἢ τὰ
πλεῖστα περιέχεται τάδε, δένδρον θάμνος φρύγανον πόα.

Δένδρον μὲν οὖν ἐστι τὸ ἀπὸ ῥίζης μονοστέλεχες

¹ φελλοῦ conj. H.; φύλλον UVP₂P₃Ald.; φυλλοῦ M.
² i.e. root, stem, branch, twig : cf. 1. 1. 9.
³ σαφεστέραν conj. W. ; σαφέστερον Ald.
⁴ εἴδη here = γένη ; cf. 6. 1. 2. n.
⁵ πάντ' ἢ conj. Sch. after G ; πάντη UMVAld.

22

again call only the inner part of the core itself
the 'heart,' while others distinguish this as the
'marrow.'

Here then we have a fairly complete list of the
'parts,' and those last named are composed of the first
'parts'; wood is made of fibre and sap, and in some
cases of flesh also; for the flesh hardens and turns to
wood, for instance in palms ferula and in other
plants in which a turning to wood takes place, as in
the roots of radishes. Core is made of moisture and
flesh: bark in some cases of all three constituents,
as in the oak black poplar and pear; while the
bark of the vine is made of sap and fibre, and that
of the cork-oak [1] of flesh and sap. Moreover out of
these constituents are made the most important
parts,[2] those which I mentioned first, and which may
be called 'members': however not all of them are
made of the same constituents, nor in the same
proportion, but the constituents are combined in
various ways.

Having now, we may say, taken all the parts, we
must endeavour to give the differences between them
and the essential characters of trees and plants taken
as wholes.

*Definitions of the various classes into which plants may be
divided.*

III. Now since our study becomes more illuminating [3] if we distinguish different kinds,[4] it is well to
follow this plan where it is possible. The first and
most important classes, those which comprise all
or nearly all [5] plants, are tree, shrub, under-shrub,
herb.

A tree is a thing which springs from the root with

23

THEOPHRASTUS

πολύκλαδον ὀζωτὸν οὐκ εὐαπόλυτον, οἷον ἐλάα
συκῇ ἄμπελος· θάμνος δὲ τὸ ἀπὸ ῥίζης πολύκλαδον, οἷον βάτος παλίουρος. φρύγανον δὲ τὸ
ἀπὸ ῥίζης πολυστέλεχες καὶ πολύκλαδον οἷον
καὶ θύμβρα καὶ πήγανον. πόα δὲ τὸ ἀπὸ ῥίζης
φυλλοφόρον προϊὸν ἀστέλεχες, οὗ ὁ καυλὸς σπερ-
μοφόρος, οἷον ὁ σῖτος καὶ τὰ λάχανα.

2 Δεῖ δὲ τοὺς ὅρους οὕτως ἀποδέχεσθαι καὶ λαμβάνειν ὡς τύπῳ καὶ ἐπὶ τὸ πᾶν λεγομένους· ἔνια
γὰρ ἴσως ἐπαλλάττειν δόξειε, τὰ δὲ καὶ παρὰ τὴν
ἀγωγὴν ἀλλοιότερα γίνεσθαι καὶ ἐκβαίνειν τῆς
φύσεως, οἷον μαλάχη τε εἰς ὕψος ἀναγομένη
καὶ ἀποδενδρουμένη· συμβαίνει γὰρ τοῦτο καὶ
οὐκ ἐν πολλῷ χρόνῳ ἀλλ᾽ ἐν ἓξ ἢ ἑπτὰ μησὶν,
ὥστε μῆκος καὶ πάχος δορατιαῖον γίνεσθαι, δι᾽ ὃ
καὶ βακτηρίαις αὐταῖς χρῶνται, πλείονος δὲ χρόνου γινομένου κατὰ λόγον ἡ ἀπόδοσις· ὁμοίως
δὲ καὶ ἐπὶ τῶν τεύτλων· καὶ γὰρ ταῦτα λαμβάνει
μέγεθος· ἔτι δὲ μᾶλλον ἄγνοι καὶ ὁ παλίουρος
καὶ ὁ κιττός, ὥσθ᾽ ὁμολογουμένως ταῦτα γίνεται
3 δένδρα· καί τοι θαμνώδη γέ ἐστιν. ὁ δὲ μύρρινος
μὴ ἀνακαθαιρόμενος ἐκθαμνοῦται καὶ ἡ ἡρακλεωτικὴ καρύα. δοκεῖ δὲ αὕτη γε καὶ τὸν καρπὸν
βελτίω καὶ πλείω φέρειν ἐὰν ῥάβδους τις ἐᾷ

¹ θάμνος . . . πήγανον. W.'s text transposes, without
alteration, the definitions of θάμνος and φρύγανον as given
in U. φρύγανον δὲ τὸ ἀπὸ ῥίζης καὶ πολυστέλεχες καὶ πολύκλαδον
οἷον βάτος παλίουρος, Ald. So also M, but with a lacuna
marked before φρύγανον and a note that the definition of
θάμνος is wanting. φρύγανον δὲ τὸ ἀπὸ ῥίζης καὶ πολυστέλεχες
καὶ πολύκλαδον οἷον καὶ γάμβρη καὶ πήγανον. θάμνος δὲ ἀπὸ ῥίζης
πολύκλαδον οἷον βάτος παλίουρος U. So also very nearly P₁P₂.
G gives to θάμνος (frutex) the definition assigned in U to
φρύγανον (suffrutex) and the other definition is wanting.

24

a single stem, having knots and several branches, and it cannot easily be uprooted; for instance, olive fig vine. [1]A shrub is a thing which rises from the root with many branches: for instance, bramble Christ's thorn. An under-shrub is a thing which rises from the root with many stems as well as many branches; for instance, savory [2] rue. A herb is a thing which comes up from the root with its leaves and has no main stem, and the seed is borne on the stem; for instance, corn and pot-herbs.

These definitions however must be taken and accepted as applying generally and on the whole. For in the case of some plants it might seem that our definitions overlap; and some under cultivation appear to become different and depart from their essential nature, for instance, mallow [3] when it grows tall and becomes tree-like. For this comes to pass in no long time, not more than six or seven months, so that in length and thickness the plant becomes as great as a spear, and men accordingly use it as a walking-stick, and after a longer period the result of cultivation is proportionately greater. So too is it with the beets; they also increase in stature under cultivation, and so still more do chaste-tree Christ's thorn ivy, so that, as is generally admitted, these become trees, and yet they belong to the class of shrubs. On the other hand the myrtle, unless it is pruned, turns into a shrub, and so does filbert [4]: indeed this last appears to bear better and more abundant fruit, if one leaves

Note that W.'s transposition gives καὶ ... καὶ the proper force: § 4 shews that the *typical* φρύγανον in T.'s view was πιλυστέλεχές.

[2] θύμβρα conj. W.; γάμβρη MSS. But the first καὶ being meaningless, W. also suggests σισύμβριον for καὶ γάμβρη.

[3] *cf.* Plin. 19. 62.    [4] *cf.* 3. 15. 1.

πλείους ὡς τῆς φύσεως θαμνώδους οὔσης. οὐ
μονοστέλεχες δ᾽ ἂν δόξειεν οὐδ᾽ ἡ μηλέα οὐδ᾽ ἡ
ῥοιὰ οὐδ᾽ ἡ ἄπιος εἶναι, οὐδ᾽ ὅλως ὅσα παραβλαστητικὰ ἀπὸ τῶν ῥιζῶν ἀλλὰ τῇ ἀγωγῇ τοιαῦτα
παραιρουμένων τῶν ἄλλων. ἔνια δὲ καὶ ἐῶσι
πολυστελέχη διὰ λεπτότητα, καθάπερ ῥόαν
μηλέαν· ἐῶσι δὲ καὶ τὰς ἐλάας κοπάδας καὶ τὰς
συκᾶς.
4 Τάχα δ᾽ ἄν τις φαίη καὶ ὅλως μεγέθει καὶ μικρότητι διαιρετέον εἶναι, τὰ δὲ ἰσχύϊ καὶ ἀσθενείᾳ
καὶ πολυχρονιότητι καὶ ὀλιγοχρονιότητι. τῶν τε
γὰρ φρυγανωδῶν καὶ λαχανωδῶν ἔνια μονοστελέχη καὶ οἷον δένδρου φύσιν ἔχοντα γίνεται,
καθάπερ ῥάφανος πήγανον, ὅθεν καὶ καλοῦσί
τινες τὰ τοιαῦτα δενδρολάχανα, τά τε λαχανώδη
πάντα ἢ τὰ πλεῖστα ὅταν ἐγκαταμείνῃ λαμβάνει
τινὰς ὥσπερ ἀκρεμόνας καὶ γίνεται τὸ ὅλον ἐν
σχήματι δενδρώδει πλὴν ὀλιγοχρονιώτερα.
5 Διὰ δὴ ταῦτα ὥσπερ λέγομεν οὐκ ἀκριβολογη-
τέον τῷ ὅρῳ ἀλλὰ τῷ τύπῳ ληπτέον τοὺς
ἀφορισμούς· ἐπεὶ καὶ τὰς διαιρέσεις ὁμοίως, οἷον
ἡμέρων ἀγρίων, καρποφόρων ἀκάρπων, ἀνθοφόρων
ἀνανθῶν, ἀειφύλλων φυλλοβόλων. τὰ μὲν γὰρ
ἄγρια καὶ ἥμερα παρὰ τὴν ἀγωγὴν εἶναι δοκεῖ·
πᾶν γὰρ καὶ ἄγριον καὶ ἥμερόν φησιν Ἵππων
γίνεσθαι τυγχάνον ἢ μὴ τυγχάνον θεραπείας.

---

[1] *i.e.* so that the tree comes to look like a shrub from the
growth of fresh shoots after cutting. *cf.* 2 6. 12 ; 2. 7. 2.
[2] ῥάφανος conj. Bod. from G ; ῥαφανὶς Ald.
[3] *cf.* 3. 2. 2. The Ionian philosopher. See Zeller, *Pre-
Socratic Philosophy* (Eng. trans.), 1. 281 f.
[4] καὶ add. W.; so G.
[5] ἦ conj. Sch.; καὶ U Ald. Cam. Bas. H.

a good many of its branches untouched, since it is by
nature like a shrub. Again neither the apple nor the
pomegranate nor the pear would seem to be a tree of
a single stem, nor indeed any of the trees which have
side stems from the roots, but they acquire the character of a tree when the other stems are removed.
However some trees men even leave with their
numerous stems because of their slenderness, for instance, the pomegranate and the apple, and they
leave the stems of the olive and the fig cut short.[1]

*Exact classification impracticable: other possible bases of*
*classification.*

Indeed it might be suggested that we should
classify in some cases simply by size, and in some
cases by comparative robustness or length of life.
For of under-shrubs and those of the pot-herb
class some have only one stem and come as it were
to have the character of a tree, such as cabbage[2]
and rue : wherefore some call these 'tree-herbs'; and
in fact all or most of the pot-herb class, when
they have been long in the ground, acquire a sort
of branches, and the whole plant comes to have a
tree-like shape, though it is shorter lived than a tree.

For these reasons then, as we are saying, one
must not make a too precise definition : we should
make our definitions typical. For we must make
our distinctions too on the same principle, as
those between wild and cultivated plants, fruit-
bearing and fruitless, flowering and flowerless,
evergreen and deciduous. Thus the distinction
between wild and cultivated seems to be due
simply to cultivation, since, as Hippon[3] remarks,
any plant may be either[4] wild or cultivated according as it receives or[5] does not receive attention.

27

ἄκαρπα δὲ καὶ κάρπιμα καὶ ἀνθοφόρα καὶ ἀνανθῆ
παρὰ τοὺς τόπους καὶ τὸν ἀέρα τὸν περιέχοντα·
τὸν αὐτὸν δὲ τρόπον καὶ φυλλοβόλα καὶ ἀείφυλλα. περὶ γὰρ Ἐλεφαντίνην οὐδὲ τὰς ἀμπέλους
οὐδὲ τὰς συκᾶς φασι φυλλοβολεῖν.

6    Ἀλλ᾿ ὅμως τοιαῦτα διαιρετέον· ἔχει γάρ τι τῆς
φύσεως κοινὸν ὁμοίως ἐν δένδροις καὶ θάμνοις καὶ
τοῖς φρυγανικοῖς καὶ ποιώδεσιν· ὑπὲρ ὧν καὶ τὰς
αἰτίας ὅταν τις λέγῃ περὶ πάντων κοινῇ δῆλον ὅτι
λεκτέον οὐχ ὁρίζοντα καθ᾿ ἕκαστον· εὔλογον δὲ
καὶ ταύτας κοινὰς εἶναι πάντων. ἅμα δὲ καὶ
φαίνεταί τινα ἔχειν φυσικὴν διαφορὰν εὐθὺς ἐπὶ
τῶν ἀγρίων καὶ τῶν ἡμέρων, εἴπερ ἔνια μὴ δύναται ζῆν ὥσπερ τὰ γεωργούμενα μηδ᾿ ὅλως δέχεται
θεραπείαν ἀλλὰ χείρω γίνεται, καθάπερ ἐλάτη
πεύκη κήλαστρον καὶ ἁπλῶς ὅσα ψυχροὺς τόπους
φιλεῖ καὶ χιονώδεις, ὡσαύτως δὲ καὶ τῶν φρυγανικῶν καὶ ποιωδῶν, οἷον κάππαρις καὶ θέρμος.
ἥμερον δὲ καὶ ἄγριον δίκαιον καλεῖν ἀναφέροντα
πρός τε ταῦτα καὶ ὅλως πρὸς τὸ ἡμερώτατον· [ὁ
δ᾿ ἄνθρωπος ἢ μόνον ἢ μάλιστα ἥμερον.]

IV.   Φανεραὶ δὲ καὶ κατ᾿ αὐτὰς τὰς μορφὰς αἱ
διαφοραὶ τῶν ὅλων τε καὶ μορίων, οἷον λέγω

---

¹ ἀνθόφορα καὶ ἀνανθῆ conj. Sch. from G : καρπόφορα ἄνθη
P₂Ald.    ² cf. 1. 9. 5 ; Plin. 16. 81.
³ τοιαῦτα conj. W.: διαιρετέον conj. Sch.: τοῖς αὐτοῖς
αἱρετέον Ald.    The sense seems to be : Though these
'secondary' distinctions are not entirely satisfactory, yet
(if we look to the *causes* of different characters), they are
indispensable, since they are due to causes which affect all
the four classes of our 'primary' distinction.
⁴ *i.e.* we must take the *extreme* cases.
⁵ *i.e.* plants which entirely refuse cultivation.

Again the distinctions between fruitless and fruit-bearing,[1] flowering and flowerless, seem to be due to position and the climate of the district. And so too with the distinction between deciduous and evergreen. [2] Thus they say that in the district of Elephantine neither vines nor figs lose their leaves.

Nevertheless we are bound to use such distinctions.[3] For there is a certain common character alike in trees, shrubs, under-shrubs, and herbs. Wherefore, when one mentions the causes also, one must take account of all alike, not giving separate definitions for each class, it being reasonable to suppose that the causes too are common to all. And in fact there seems to be some natural difference from the first in the case of wild and cultivated, seeing that some plants cannot live under the conditions of those grown in cultivated ground, and do not submit to cultivation at all, but deteriorate under it; for instance, silver-fir fir holly, and in general those which affect cold snowy country; and the same is also true of some of the under-shrubs and herbs, such as caper and lupin. Now in using the terms 'cultivated' and 'wild'[4] we must make these[5] on the one hand our standard, and on the other that which is in the truest sense[6] 'cultivated.'  [7] Now Man, if he is not the only thing to which this name is strictly appropriate, is at least that to which it most applies.

*Differences as to appearance and habitat.*

IV. Again the differences, both between the plants as wholes and between their parts, may be seen in

[6] ὅλως πρὸς τὸ. ? πρὸς τὸ ὅλως conj. St.
[7] ὁ δ' ἄνθρωπος . . . ἥμερον.  I have bracketed this clause, which seems to be an irrelevant gloss.

μέγεθος καὶ μικρότης, σκληρότης μαλακότης,
λειότης τραχύτης, φλοιοῦ φύλλων τῶν ἄλλων,
ἁπλῶς εὐμορφία καὶ δυσμορφία τις, ἔτι δὲ καὶ
καλλικαρπία καὶ κακοκαρπία. πλείω μὲν γὰρ
δοκεῖ τὰ ἄγρια φέρειν, ὥσπερ ἀχρὰς κότινος, καλλίω δὲ τὰ ἥμερα καὶ τοὺς χυλοὺς δὲ αὐτοὺς
γλυκυτέρους καὶ ἡδίους καὶ τὸ ὅλον ὡς εἰπεῖν
εὐκράτους μᾶλλον.

2  Αὗταί τε δὴ φυσικαί τινες ὥσπερ εἴρηται διαφοραί, καὶ ἔτι δὴ μᾶλλον τῶν ἀκάρπων καὶ καρποφόρων καὶ φυλλοβόλων καὶ ἀειφύλλων καὶ ὅσα
ἄλλα τοιαῦτα. πάντων δὲ ληπτέον ἀεὶ καὶ τὰς
κατὰ τοὺς τόπους· οὐ γὰρ οὐδ᾽ οἷόν τε ἴσως
ἄλλως. αἱ δὲ τοιαῦται δόξαιεν ἂν γενικόν τινα
ποιεῖν χωρισμόν, οἷον ἐνύδρων καὶ χερσαίων, ὥσπερ
ἐπὶ τῶν ζῴων. ἔστι γὰρ ἔνια τῶν φυτῶν ἃ οὐ
δύναται μὴ ἐν ὑγρῷ ζῆν· διῄρηται δὲ ἄλλο κατ᾽
ἄλλο γένος τῶν ὑγρῶν, ὥστε τὰ μὲν ἐν τέλμασι
τὰ δὲ ἐν λίμναις τὰ δ᾽ ἐν ποταμοῖς τὰ δὲ καὶ ἐν
αὐτῇ τῇ θαλάττῃ φύεσθαι, τὰ μὲν ἐλάττω καὶ ἐν
τῇ παρ᾽ ἡμῖν τὰ δὲ μείζω περὶ τὴν ἐρυθράν. ἔνια
δὲ ὡσπερεὶ κάθυγρα καὶ ἕλεια, καθάπερ ἰτέα καὶ
πλάτανος, τὰ δὲ οὐκ ἐν ὕδατι δυνάμενα ζῆν οὐδ᾽
ὅλως ἀλλὰ διώκοντα τοὺς ξηροὺς τόπους· τῶν δ᾽
ἐλαττόνων ἔστιν ἃ καὶ τοὺς αἰγιαλούς.

---

¹ κατ᾽ αὐτὰς τὰς conj. Sch. ; καὶ τά τ᾽ αὐτὰς τὰς U ; κατὰ
ταύτας τὰς MVAld.
² πάντων . . . τόπους, text perhaps defective.
³ i.e. as to locality.    ⁴ cf. 4. 7. 1.

the appearance itself[1] of the plant. I mean differences such as those in size, hardness, smoothness or their opposites, as seen in bark, leaves, and the other parts; also, in general, differences as to comeliness or its opposite and as to the production of good or of inferior fruit. For the wild kinds appear to bear more fruit, for instance, the wild pear and wild olive, but the cultivated plants better fruit, having even flavours which are sweeter and pleasanter and in general better blended, if one may so say.

These then as has been said, are differences of natural character, as it were, and still more so are those between fruitless and fruitful, deciduous and evergreen plants, and the like. But with all the differences in all these cases we must take into account the locality,[2] and indeed it is hardly possible to do otherwise. Such [3] differences would seem to give us a kind of division into classes, for instance, between that of aquatic plants and that of plants of the dry land, corresponding to the division which we make in the case of animals. For there are some plants which cannot live except in wet; and again these are distinguished from one another by their fondness for different kinds of wetness; so that some grow in marshes, others in lakes, others in rivers, others even in the sea, smaller ones in our own sea, larger ones in the Red Sea.[4] Some again, one may say, are lovers of very wet places,[5] or plants of the marshes, such as the willow and the plane. Others again cannot live at all [6] in water, but seek out dry places; and of the smaller sorts there are some that prefer the shore.

[5] *i.e.* though not actually living *in* water.
[6] οὐδ' ὅλως conj. W.; ἐν τούτοις Ald.H. *Minime* G.

# THEOPHRASTUS

3 Οὐ μὴν ἀλλὰ καὶ τούτων εἴ τις ἀκριβολο-
γεῖσθαι θέλοι, τὰ μὲν ἂν εὕροι κοινὰ καὶ ὥσπερ
ἀμφίβια, καθάπερ μυρίκην ἰτέαν κλήθραν, τὰ δὲ
καὶ τῶν ὁμολογουμένων χερσαίων πεφυκότα ποτὲ
ἐν τῇ θαλάττῃ βιοῦν, φοίνικα σκίλλαν ἀνθέρικον.
ἀλλὰ τὰ τοιαῦτα καὶ ὅλως τὸ οὕτω σκοπεῖν οὐκ
οἰκείως ἐστὶ σκοπεῖν· οὐδὲ γὰρ οὐδ' ἡ φύσις οὕτως οὐδ' ἐν τοῖς τοιούτοις ἔχει τὸ ἀναγκαῖον. τὰς
μὲν οὖν διαιρέσεις καὶ ὅλως τὴν ἱστορίαν τῶν φυτῶν οὕτω ληπτέον. [ἅπαντα δ' οὖν καὶ ταῦτα καὶ
τὰ ἄλλα διοίσει καθάπερ εἴρηται ταῖς τε τῶν
ὅλων μορφαῖς καὶ ταῖς τῶν μορίων διαφοραῖς, ἢ
τῷ ἔχειν τὰ δὲ μὴ ἔχειν, ἢ τῷ πλείω τὰ δ'
ἐλάττω, ἢ τῷ ἀνομοίως ἢ ὅσοι τρόποι διήρηνται
4 πρότερον. οἰκεῖον δὲ ἴσως καὶ τοὺς τόπους συμ-
παραλαμβάνειν ἐν οἷς ἕκαστα πέφυκεν ἢ μὴ
πέφυκε γίνεσθαι. μεγάλη γὰρ καὶ αὕτη διαφορὰ
καὶ οὐχ ἥκιστα οἰκεία τῶν φυτῶν διὰ τὸ συνηρ-
τῆσθαι τῇ γῇ καὶ μὴ ἀπολελύσθαι καθάπερ
τὰ ζῶα.]
V. Πειρατέον δ' εἰπεῖν τὰς κατὰ μέρος διαφορὰς ὡς ἂν καθόλου λέγοντας πρῶτον καὶ κοινῶς,

---

1 θέλοι conj. Sch.; θέλει Ald. H.
2 εὕροι conj. Sch.; εὕρη Ald. ; εὕρῃ H.
3 Presumably as being sometimes found on the shore below
high-water mark.
4 ἅπαντα . . . ζῶα. This passage seems not to belong
here (W.).
5 τρόποι conj. Sch. ; τόποι UMVAld.

However, if one should wish [1] to be precise, one would find [2] that even of these some are impartial and as it were amphibious, such as tamarisk willow alder, and that others even of those which are admitted to be plants of the dry land sometimes live in the sea,[3] as palm squill asphodel. But to consider all these exceptions and, in general, to consider in such a manner is not the right way to proceed. For in such matters too nature certainly does not thus go by any hard and fast law. Our distinctions therefore and the study of plants in general must be understood accordingly. [4] To return—these plants as well as all others will be found to differ, as has been said, both in the shape of the whole and in the differences between the parts, either as to having or not having certain parts, or as to having a greater or less number of parts, or as to having them differently arranged, or because of other differences [5] such as we have already mentioned. And it is perhaps also proper to take into account the situation in which each plant naturally grows or does not grow. For this is an important distinction, and specially characteristic of plants, because they are united to the ground and not free from it like animals.

*Characteristic differences in the parts of plants, whether general, special, or seen in qualities and properties.*

V. Next we must try to give the differences as to particular parts, in the first instance speaking broadly of those of a general character,[6] and then

[6] *i.e.* those which divide plants into large classes (*e.g.* evergreen and deciduous).

33

εἶτα καθ᾽ ἕκαστον, ὕστερον ἐπὶ πλεῖον ὥσπερ
ἀναθεωροῦντας.

Ἔστι δὲ τὰ μὲν ὀρθοφυῆ καὶ μακροστελέχη
καθάπερ ἐλάτη πεύκη κυπάριττος, τὰ δὲ σκολιώτερα καὶ βραχυστελέχη οἷον ἰτέα συκῆ ῥοιά,
καὶ κατὰ πάχος δὲ καὶ λεπτότητα ὁμοίως.
καὶ πάλιν τὰ μὲν μονοστελέχη τὰ δὲ πολυ-
στελέχη· τοῦτο δὲ ταὐτὸ τρόπον τινὰ καὶ τῷ
παραβλαστητικὰ ἢ ἀπαράβλαστα εἶναι· καὶ
πολυκλαδῆ καὶ ὀλιγόκλαδα καθάπερ ὁ φοῖνιξ,
καὶ ἐν αὐτοῖς τούτοις ἔτι κατὰ ἰσχὺν ἢ πάχος ἢ
2 τὰς τοιαύτας διαφοράς. πάλιν τὰ μὲν λεπτό-
φλοια, καθάπερ δάφνη φίλυρα, τὰ δὲ παχύφλοια,
καθάπερ δρῦς. ἔτι τὰ μὲν λειόφλοια, καθάπερ
μηλέα συκῆ, τὰ δὲ τραχύφλοια, καθάπερ ἀγρία
δρῦς φελλὸς φοῖνιξ. πάντα δὲ νέα μὲν ὄντα
λειοφλοιότερα, ἀπογηράσκοντα δὲ τραχυφλοιότερα, ἔνια δὲ καὶ ῥηξίφλοια, καθάπερ ἄμπελος, τὰ
δὲ καὶ ὡς περιπίπτειν, οἷον ἀνδράχλη μηλέα
κόμαρος. ἔστι δὲ καὶ τῶν μὲν σαρκώδης ὁ φλοιός,
οἷον φελλοῦ δρυὸς αἰγείρου· τῶν δὲ ἰνώδης καὶ
ἄσαρκος ὁμοίως δένδρων καὶ θάμνων καὶ ἐπετείων,
οἷον ἀμπέλου καλάμου πυροῦ. καὶ τῶν μὲν
πολύλοπος, οἷον φιλύρας ἐλάτης ἀμπέλου λινο-
σπάρτου κρομύων, τῶν δὲ μονόλοπος, οἷον συκῆς

---

[1] *i.e.* taking account of differences in qualities, etc. See
§ 4, but the order in which the three kinds of ' differences '
are discussed is not that which is here given ; the second is
taken first and resumed at 6. 1, the third begins at 5. 4, the
first at 14. 4.
[2] ταὐτὸ conj. Sch.; αὐτὸ UMVPAld.
[3] τραχυφλοιότερα conj. H. from G ; παχυφ. UMAld.
*cf.* Plin. 16. 126.

of special differences between individual kinds; and
after that we must take a wider range, making as it
were a fresh survey.[1]

Some plants grow straight up and have tall stems,
as silver-fir fir cypress; some are by comparison
crooked and have short stems, as willow fig pomegranate; and there are like differences as to degree
of thickness. Again some have a single stem, others
many stems; and this difference corresponds[2] more
or less to that between those which have side-
growths and those which have none, or that between
those which have many branches and those which
have few, such as the date-palm. And in these
very instances we have also differences in strength
thickness and the like. Again some have thin
bark, such as bay and lime; others have a thick
bark, such as the oak. And again some have
smooth bark, as apple and fig; others rough bark,
as 'wild oak' (Valonia oak) cork-oak and date-palm.
However all plants when young have smoother
bark, which gets rougher[3] as they get older; and
some have cracked bark,[4] as the vine; and in some
cases it readily drops off, as in andrachne apple[5]
and arbutus. And again of some the bark is fleshy,
as in cork-oak oak poplar; while in others it is
fibrous and not fleshy; and this applies alike to trees
shrubs and annual plants, for instance to vines
reeds and wheat. Again in some the bark has more
than one layer, as in lime silver-fir vine Spanish
broom[6] onions[7]; while in some it consists of only

[4] ῥηξίφλοια conj. St.; ῥιζίφοια (?) U; ῥιζίφλοια P.; ῥιζό-
φλοια P₂Ald. cf. 4. 15. 2, Plin. l.c.
[5] μηλέα conj. H. Steph., etc.; νηλεια UMPAld.; νήλεια
P₂V. cf. Plin. l.c.
[6] G appears to have read λίνου, σπάρτου.    [7] cf. 5. 1, 6.

35

καλάμου αὔρας. κατὰ μὲν δὴ τοὺς φλοιοὺς ἐν
τούτοις αἱ διαφοραί.

3 Τῶν δὲ ξύλων αὐτῶν καὶ ὅλως τῶν καυλῶν οἱ
μέν εἰσι σαρκώδεις, οἷον δρυὸς συκῆς, καὶ τῶν
ἐλαττόνων ῥάμνου τεύτλου κωνείου· οἱ δὲ ἄσαρκοι,
καθάπερ κέδρου λωτοῦ κυπαρίττου. καὶ οἱ μὲν
ἰνώδεις· τὰ γὰρ τῆς ἐλάτης καὶ τοῦ φοίνικος ξύλα
τοιαῦτα· τὰ δὲ ἄϊνα, καθάπερ τῆς συκῆς. ὡσαύτως δὲ καὶ τὰ μὲν φλεβώδη τὰ δ' ἄφλεβα. περὶ
δὲ τὰ φρυγανικὰ καὶ θαμνώδη καὶ ὅλως τὰ ὑλήματα καὶ ἄλλας τις ἂν λάβοι διαφοράς· ὁ μὲν
γὰρ κάλαμος γονατῶδες, ὁ δὲ βάτος καὶ ὁ
παλίουρος ἀκανθώδη. ἡ δὲ τύφη καὶ ἔνια τῶν
ἑλείων ἢ λιμναίων ὁμοίως ἀδιάφρακτα καὶ ὁμαλῆ,
καθάπερ σχοῖνος. ὁ δὲ τοῦ κυπείρου καὶ βουτόμου καυλὸς ὁμαλότητά τινα ἔχει παρὰ τούτους·
ἔτι δὲ μᾶλλον ἴσως ὁ τοῦ μύκητος.

4 Λύται μὲν δὴ δόξαιεν ἂν ἐξ ὧν ἡ σύνθεσις. αἱ
δὲ κατὰ τὰ πάθη καὶ τὰς δυνάμεις οἷον σκληρότης μαλακότης γλισχρότης κραυρότης <πυκνό-
της> μανότης κουφότης βαρύτης καὶ ὅσα ἄλλα
τοιαῦτα· ἡ μὲν γὰρ ἰτέα καὶ χλωρὸν εὐθὺ κοῦφον,
ὥσπερ ὁ φελλός, ἡ δὲ πύξος καὶ ἡ ἔβενος οὐδὲ
αὐανθέντα. καὶ τὰ μὲν σχίζεται, καθάπερ τὰ τῆς

---

¹ ῥάμνου conj. W.: θάμνου P₂; βαλάνου Ald.H.
² κωνείου conj. Sch.; κωνίου Ald.U (corrected to κωνείου).
cf. 7. 6. 4.
³ δὲ ἄϊνα conj. Sca from G.; δὲ βῖνα U; δὲ μανά Ald.;
δὲ . . . να M.
⁴ ὑλήματα conj. Sch. (a general term including shrubs,
under-shrubs, etc. cf. 1. 6. 7 ; 1. 10. 6) ; κλήματα, Ald.

36

one coat, as in fig reed darnel.    Such are the
respects in which bark differs.

Next of the woods themselves and of stems
generally some are fleshy, as in oak and fig, and,
among lesser plants, in buckthorn [1] beet hemlock [2];
while some are not fleshy, for instance, prickly cedar
nettle-tree cypress.   Again some are fibrous, for of
this character is the wood of the silver-fir and the
date-palm; while some are not fibrous,[3] as in the
fig.   In like manner some are full of 'veins,' others
veinless.   Further in shrubby plants and under-
shrubs and in woody plants [4] in general one might
find other differences: thus the reed is jointed,
while the bramble and Christ's thorn have thorns on
the wood.   Bulrush and some of the marsh or pond
plants are in like manner [5] without joints and smooth,
like the rush; and the stem of galingale and sedge
has a certain smoothness beyond those just mentioned; and still more perhaps has that of the
mushroom.

*Differences as to qualities and properties.*

These then would seem to be the differences in
the parts which make up the plant.   Those which
belong to the qualities [6] and properties are such as
hardness or softness, toughness or brittleness, closeness or openness of texture, lightness or heaviness,
and the like.   For willow-wood is light from the
first, even when it is green, and so is that of the
cork-oak; but box and ebony are not light even
when dried.   Some woods again can be split,[7] such

[5] ὁμοίως, sense doubtful; ὁμωνύμων conj. W.
[6] πάθη, cf. 1. 1. 1 n.
[7] σχίζεται conj. W.; σχισθέντα UMVAld.; σχιστά H.;
fissiles G.

THEOPHRASTUS

ἐλάτης, τὰ δὲ εὔθραυστα μᾶλλον, οἷον τὰ τῆς ἐλάας. καὶ τὰ μὲν ἄοζα, οἷον τὰ τῆς ἀκτῆς, τὰ δὲ ὀζώδη, οἷον τὰ τῆς πεύκης καὶ ἐλάτης.

5 Δεῖ δὲ καὶ τὰς τοιαύτας ὑπολαμβάνειν τῆς φύσεως. εὔσχιστον μὲν γὰρ ἡ ἐλάτη τῷ εὐθυπορεῖν, εὔθραυστον δὲ ἡ ἐλάα διὰ τὸ σκολιὸν καὶ σκληρόν. εὔκαμπτον δὲ ἡ φίλυρα καὶ ὅσα ἄλλα διὰ τὸ γλίσχραν ἔχειν τὴν ὑγρότητα. βαρὺ δὲ ἡ μὲν πύξος καὶ ἡ ἔβενος ὅτι πυκνά, ἡ δὲ δρῦς ὅτι γεῶδες. ὡσαύτως δὲ καὶ τὰ ἄλλα πάντα πρὸς τὴν φύσιν πως ἀνάγεται.

VI. Διαφέρουσι δὲ καὶ ταῖς μήτραις· πρῶτον μὲν εἰ ἔνια ἔχει ἢ μὴ ἔχει, καθάπερ τινές φασιν ἄλλα τε καὶ τὴν ἀκτήν· ἔπειτα καὶ ἐν αὐτοῖς τοῖς ἔχουσι· τῶν μὲν γάρ ἐστι σαρκώδης τῶν δὲ ξυλώδης τῶν δὲ ὑμενώδης. καὶ σαρκώδης μὲν οἷον ἀμπέλου συκῆς μηλέας ῥοιᾶς ἀκτῆς νάρθηκι. ξυλώδης δὲ πίτυος ἐλάτης πεύκης, καὶ μάλιστα αὕτη διὰ τὸ ἔνδαδος εἶναι. τούτων δ' ἔτι σκληρότεραι καὶ πυκνότεραι κρανείας πρίνου δρυὸς κυτίσου συκαμίνου ἐβένου λωτοῦ.

2 Διαφέρουσι δὲ αὐταὶ καὶ τοῖς χρώμασι· μέλαιναι γὰρ τῆς ἐβένου καὶ τῆς δρυός, ἣν καλοῦσι μελάνδρυον. ἅπασαι δὲ σκληρότεραι καὶ κραυρό-

---

[1] i.e. break across the grain. εὔθραυστα mP ; ἄθραυστα UPAld.; *fragilis* G. *cf.* 5. 5, Plin. 16. 186.
[2] ἄοζα conj. Palm. from G ; λοξά UPAld.
[3] i.e. across the grain. [4] *cf.* 5. 6. 2. [5] *cf.* 5. 1. 4.
[6] T. appears not to agree as to elder : see below.

38

as that of the silver-fir, while others are rather break-able,[1] such as the wood of the olive. Again some are without knots,[2] as the stems of elder, others have knots, as those of fir and silver-fir.

Now such differences also must be ascribed to the essential character of the plant: for the reason why the wood of silver-fir is easily split is that the grain is straight, while the reason why olive-wood is easily broken[3] is that it is crooked and hard. Lime-wood and some other woods on the other hand are easily bent because their sap is viscid.[4] Boxwood and ebony are heavy because the grain is close, and oak because it contains mineral matter.[5] In like manner the other peculiarities too can in some way be referred to the essential character.

*Further 'special' differences.*

VI. Again there are differences in the 'core': in the first place according as plants have any or have none, as some say[6] is the case with elder among other things; and in the second place there are differences between those which have it, since in different plants it is respectively fleshy, woody, or membranous; fleshy, as in vine fig apple pomegranate elder ferula; woody, as in Aleppo pine silver-fir fir; in the last-named[7] especially so, because it is resinous. Harder again and closer than these is the core of dog-wood kermes-oak oak laburnum mulberry ebony nettle-tree.

The cores in themselves also differ in colour; for that of ebony and oak is black, and in fact in the oak it is called 'oak-black'; and in all these the core is harder and more brittle than the ordinary

[7] αὕτη conj. Sch.; αὐτὴ UAld.; αὐτῇ MV; αὐτῆς P₂.

τεραι τῶν ξύλων· δι' ὃ καὶ οὐχ ὑπομένουσι
καμπήν. μανότεραι δὲ αἱ μὲν αἱ δ' οὔ. ὑμενώ-
δεις δ' ἐν μὲν τοῖς δένδροις οὐκ εἰσὶν ἢ σπάνιοι,
ἐν δὲ τοῖς θαμνώδεσι καὶ ὅλως τοῖς ὑλήμασιν
οἷον καλάμῳ τε καὶ νάρθηκι καὶ τοῖς τοιούτοις
εἰσίν. ἔχει δὲ τὴν μήτραν τὰ μὲν μεγάλην καὶ
φανεράν, ὡς πρῖνος δρῦς καὶ τἆλλα προειρημένα, τὰ δ' ἀφανεστέραν, οἷον ἐλάα πύξος· οὐ
γὰρ ἔστιν ἀφωρισμένην οὕτω λαβεῖν, ἀλλὰ καί
φασί τινες οὐ κατὰ τὸ μέσον ἀλλὰ κατὰ τὸ πᾶν
ἔχειν· ὥστε μὴ εἶναι τόπον ὡρισμένον· δι' ὃ καὶ
ἔνια οὐδ' ἂν δόξειεν ὅλως ἔχειν· ἐπεὶ καὶ τοῦ
φοίνικος οὐδεμία φαίνεται διαφορὰ κατ' οὐδέν.

3 Διαφέρουσι δὲ καὶ ταῖς ῥίζαις. τὰ μὲν γὰρ
πολύρριζα καὶ μακρόρριζα, καθάπερ συκῆ δρῦς
πλάτανος· ἐὰν γὰρ ἔχωσι τόπον, ἐφ' ὁσονοῦν
προέρχονται. τὰ δὲ ὀλιγόρριζα, καθάπερ ῥοιὰ
μηλέα· τὰ δὲ μονόρριζα, καθάπερ ἐλάτη πεύκη·
μονόρριζα δὲ οὕτως, ὅτι μίαν μεγάλην τὴν εἰς
βάθος ἔχει μικρὰς δὲ ἀπὸ ταύτης πλείους. ἔχουσι
δὲ καὶ τῶν μὴ μονορρίζων ἔνια τὴν ἐκ τοῦ μέσου
μεγίστην καὶ κατὰ βάθους, ὥσπερ ἀμυγδαλῆ·
ἐλάα δὲ μικρὰν ταύτην τὰς δὲ ἄλλας μείζους καὶ
ὡς κεκαρκινωμένας. ἔτι δὲ τῶν μὲν παχεῖαι
μᾶλλον τῶν δὲ ἀνωμαλεῖς, καθάπερ δάφνης ἐλάας·
4 τῶν δὲ πᾶσαι λεπταί, καθάπερ ἀμπέλου. διαφέρουσι δὲ καὶ λειότητι καὶ τραχύτητι καὶ πυκνότητι. πάντων γὰρ αἱ ῥίζαι μανότεραι τῶν ἄνω,

---

[1] μανότεραι . . . οὔ: text can hardly be sound, but sense is
clear.  [2] i.e. homogeneous.  [4] Plin. 16. 127.
[4] 3. 6, 4 seems to give a different account.
[5] cf. C.P. 3. 23. 5, and καρκινώδης C.P. 1. 12. 3 ; 3. 21. 5.

wood; and for this reason the core of these trees can
not be bent. Again the core differs in closeness
of texture.[1] A membranous core is not common
in trees, if indeed it is found at all; but it is found
in shrubby plants and woody plants generally, as in
reed ferula and the like. Again in some the core is
large and conspicuous, as in kermes-oak oak and
the other trees mentioned above; while in others it
is less conspicuous, as in olive and box. For in these
trees one cannot find it isolated, but, as some say, it
is not found in the middle of the stem, being diffused
throughout, so that it has no separate place; and for
this reason some trees might be thought to have no
core at all; in fact in the date-palm the wood is
alike throughout.[2]

*Differences in root.*

[3] Again plants differ in their roots, some having
many long roots, as fig oak plane; for the roots of
these, if they have room, run to any length. Others
again have few roots, as pomegranate and apple,
others a single root, as silver-fir and fir; these have
a single root in the sense that they have one long
one[4] which runs deep, and a number of small ones
branching from this. Even in some of those which
have more than a single root the middle root is the
largest and goes deep, for instance, in the almond;
in the olive this central root is small, while the
others are larger and, as it were, spread out crab-
wise.[5] Again the roots of some are mostly stout, of
some of various degrees of stoutness, as those of
bay and olive; and of some they are all slender,
as those of the vine. Roots also differ in degree
of smoothness and in density. For the roots of all

41

πυκνότεραι δὲ ἄλλαι ἄλλων καὶ ξυλωδέστεραι·
καὶ αἱ μὲν ἰνώδεις, ὡς αἱ τῆς ἐλάτης, αἱ δὲ σαρκώδεις μᾶλλον, ὥσπερ αἱ τῆς δρυός, αἱ δὲ οἷον
ὀζώδεις καὶ θυσανώδεις, ὥσπερ αἱ τῆς ἐλάας·
τοῦτο δὲ ὅτι τὰς λεπτὰς καὶ μικρὰς πολλὰς
ἔχουσι καὶ ἀθρόας· ἐπεὶ πᾶσαί γε καὶ ταύτας
ἀποφύουσιν ἀπὸ τῶν μεγάλων ἀλλ᾽ οὐχ ὁμοίως
ἀθρόας καὶ πολλάς.

Ἔστι δὲ καὶ τὰ μὲν βαθύρριζα, καθάπερ δρῦς,
τὰ δ᾽ ἐπιπολαιόρριζα, καθάπερ ἐλάα ῥοιὰ μηλέα
κυπάριττος. ἔτι δὲ αἱ μὲν εὐθεῖαι καὶ ὁμαλεῖς,
αἱ δὲ σκολιαὶ καὶ παραλλάττουσαι· τοῦτο γὰρ
οὐ μόνον συμβαίνει διὰ τοὺς τόπους τῷ μὴ
εὐοδεῖν ἀλλὰ καὶ τῆς φύσεως αὐτῆς ἐστιν, ὥσπερ
ἐπὶ τῆς δάφνης καὶ τῆς ἐλάας· ἡ δὲ συκῆ καὶ τὰ
τοιαῦτα σκολιοῦται διὰ τὸ μὴ εὐοδεῖν.

5 Ἅπασαι δ᾽ ἔμμητροι καθάπερ καὶ τὰ στελέχη
καὶ οἱ ἀκρεμόνες· καὶ εὔλογον ἀπὸ τῆς ἀρχῆς.
εἰσὶ δὲ καὶ αἱ μὲν παραβλαστητικαὶ εἰς τὸ ἄνω,
καθάπερ ἀμπέλου ῥόας, αἱ δὲ ἀπαράβλαστοι,
καθάπερ ἐλάτης κυπαρίττου πεύκης. αἱ αὐταὶ
δὲ διαφοραὶ καὶ τῶν φρυγανικῶν καὶ τῶν ποιωδῶν
καὶ τῶν ἄλλων· πλὴν εἰ ὅλως ἔνια μὴ ἔχει,
καθάπερ ὕδνον μύκης πέζις κεραύνιον. τὰ μὲν
πολύρριζα καθάπερ πυρός τίφη κριθή, πᾶν τὸ
τοιοῦτο, καθάπερ εἰκαζούσαις· τὰ δ᾽ ὀλιγόρριζα
6 καθάπερ τὰ χεδροπά. σχεδὸν δὲ καὶ τῶν λαχανωδῶν τὰ πλεῖστα μονόρριζα, οἷον ῥάφανος

¹ πέζις κεραύνιον : πύξος κράνιον UMVAld. ; πέζις conj. Sch.
from Athen. 2. 59 ; κεραύνιον conj. W. cf. Plin. 3. 36 and 37,
Juv. 5. 117. ² εἰκαζούσαις : word corrupt ; so UMVAld.
³ Plin. 19. 98.

42

plants are less dense than the parts above ground,
but the density varies in different kinds, as also does
the woodiness. Some are fibrous, as those of the
silver-fir, some fleshier, as those of the oak, some are
as it were branched and tassel-like, as those of the
olive ; and this is because they have a large number
of fine small roots close together ; for all in fact produce these from their large roots, but they are not
so closely matted nor so numerous in some cases as
in others.

Again some plants are deep-rooting, as the oak,
and some have surface roots, as olive pomegranate
apple cypress. Again some roots are straight and
uniform, others crooked and crossing one another.
For this comes to pass not merely on account of the
situation because they cannot find a straight course :
it may also belong to the natural character of the
plant, as in the bay and the olive ; while the fig and
such like become crooked because they can not find
a straight course.

All roots have core, just as the stems and branches
do, which is to be expected, as all these parts are
made of the same materials. Some roots again have
side-growths shooting upwards, as those of the vine
and pomegranate, while some have no side-growth,
as those of silver-fir cypress and fir. The same
differences are found in under-shrubs and herbaceous
plants and the rest, except that some have no roots
at all, as truffle mushroom bullfist [1] 'thunder-truffle.'
Others have numerous roots, as wheat one-seeded
wheat barley and all plants of like nature, for
instance,[2] . . . . Some have few roots, as leguminous plants. [3] And in general most of the pot-
herbs have single roots, as cabbage beet celery

43

τεῦτλον σέλινον λάπαθος· πλὴν ἔνια καὶ ἀπο-
φυάδας ἔχει μεγάλας, οἷον τὸ σέλινον καὶ τὸ
τεῦτλον· καὶ ὡς ἂν κατὰ λόγον ταῦτα βαθυρριζότερα τῶν δένδρων. εἰσὶ δὲ τῶν μὲν σαρκώδεις,
καθάπερ ῥαφανίδος γογγυλίδος ἄρου κρόκου·
τῶν δὲ ξυλώδεις, οἷον εὐζώμου ὠκίμου· καὶ τῶν
ἀγρίων δὲ τῶν πλείστων, ὅσων μὴ εὐθὺς πλείους
καὶ σχιζόμεναι, καθάπερ πυροῦ κριθῆς καὶ τῆς
καλουμένης πόας. αὕτη γὰρ ἐν τοῖς ἐπετείοις καὶ
ἐν τοῖς ποιώδεσιν ἡ διαφορὰ τῶν ῥιζῶν ὥστε τὰς
μὲν εὐθὺς σχίζεσθαι πλείους οὔσας καὶ ὁμαλεῖς,
τῶν δὲ ἄλλων μίαν ἢ δύο τὰς μεγίστας καὶ ἄλλας
ἀπὸ τούτων.

7 Ὅλως δὲ πλείους αἱ διαφοραὶ τῶν ῥιζῶν ἐν
τοῖς ὑλήμασι καὶ λαχανώδεσιν· εἰσὶ γὰρ αἱ μὲν
ξυλώδεις, ὥσπερ αἱ τοῦ ὠκίμου· αἱ δὲ σαρκώδεις,
ὥσπερ αἱ τοῦ τεύτλου καὶ ἔτι δὴ μᾶλλον τοῦ
ἄρου καὶ ἀσφοδέλου καὶ κρόκου· αἱ δὲ ὥσπερ
ἐκ φλοιοῦ καὶ σαρκός, ὥσπερ αἱ τῶν ῥαφανίδων καὶ
γογγυλίδων· αἱ δὲ γονατώδεις, ὥσπερ αἱ τῶν καλάμων καὶ ἀγρώστεων καὶ εἴ τι καλαμῶδες, καὶ μόναι
δὴ αὗται ἡ μάλισθ᾽ ὅμοιαι τοῖς ὑπὲρ γῆς· ὥσπερ
γὰρ κάλαμοί εἰσιν ἐρριζωμένοι ταῖς λεπταῖς. αἱ
δὲ λεπυρώδεις ἢ φλοιώδεις, οἷον αἵ τε τῆς σκίλλης
καὶ τοῦ βολβοῦ καὶ ἔτι κρομύου καὶ τῶν τούτοις
ὁμοίων. αἰεὶ γὰρ ἔστι περιαιρεῖν αὐτῶν.

8 Πάντα δὲ τὰ τοιαῦτα δοκεῖ καθάπερ δύο γένη
ῥιζῶν ἔχειν· τοῖς δὲ καὶ ὅλως τὰ κεφαλοβαρῆ
καὶ κατάρριζα πάντα· τήν τε σαρκώδη ταύτην

---

[1] The same term being applied to 'herbaceous' plants in
general.    [2] Plin. 19. 98.

monk's rhubarb; but some have large side-roots, as celery and beet, and in proportion to their size these root deeper than trees. Again of some the roots are fleshy, as in radish turnip cuckoo-pint crocus; of some they are woody, as in rocket and basil. And so with most wild plants, except those whose roots are to start with numerous and much divided, as those of wheat barley and the plant specially[1] called 'grass.' For in annual and herbaceous plants this is the difference between the roots:—Some are more numerous and uniform and much divided to start with, but the others have one or two specially large roots and others springing from them.

To speak generally, the differences in roots are more numerous in shrubby plants and pot-herbs; [2] for some are woody, as those of basil, some fleshy, as those of beet, and still more those of cuckoo-pint asphodel and crocus; some again are made, as it were, of bark and flesh, as those of radishes and turnips; some have joints, as those of reeds and dog's tooth grass and of anything of a reedy character; and these roots alone, or more than any others, resemble the parts above ground; they are in fact like[3] reeds fastened in the ground by their fine roots. Some again have scales or a kind of bark, as those of squill and purse-tassels, and also of onion and things like these. In all these it is possible to strip off a coat.

Now all such plants, seem, as it were, to have two kinds of root; and so, in the opinion of some, this is true generally of all plants which have a solid 'head'[4] and send out roots from it downwards. These have,

---

[2] i.e. the main root is a sort of repetition of the part above ground.   [4] i.e. bulb, corm, rhizome, etc.

καὶ φλοιώδη, καθάπερ ἡ σκίλλα, καὶ τὰς ἀπὸ
ταύτης ἀποπεφυκυίας· οὐ γὰρ λεπτότητι καὶ παχύτητι διαφέρουσι μόνον, ὥσπερ αἱ τῶν δένδρων καὶ
τῶν λαχάνων, ἀλλ᾽ ἀλλοῖον ἔχουσι τὸ γένος.
ἐκφανεστάτη δ᾽ ἤδη ἥ τε τοῦ ἄρου καὶ ἡ τοῦ κυ-
πείρου· ἡ μὲν γὰρ παχεῖα καὶ λεία καὶ σαρκώδης,
ἡ δὲ λεπτὴ καὶ ἰνώδης. διόπερ ἀπορήσειεν ἄν
τις εἰ ῥίζας τὰς τοιαύτας θετέον· ᾗ μὲν γὰρ κατὰ
γῆς δόξαιεν ἄν, ᾗ δὲ ὑπεναντίως ἔχουσι ταῖς
ἄλλαις οὐκ ἂν δόξαιεν. ἡ μὲν γὰρ ῥίζα λεπτοτέρα πρὸς τὸ πόρρω καὶ ἀεὶ σύνοξυς· ἡ δὲ τῶν
σκιλλῶν καὶ τῶν βολβῶν καὶ τῶν ἄρων ἀνάπαλιν.

9 Ἔτι δ᾽ αἱ μὲν ἄλλαι κατὰ τὸ πλάγιον ἀφιᾶσι
ῥίζας, αἱ δὲ τῶν σκιλλῶν καὶ τῶν βολβῶν οὐκ
ἀφιᾶσιν· οὐδὲ τῶν σκορόδων καὶ τῶν κρομύων.
ὅλως δέ γε ἐν ταύταις αἱ κατὰ μέσον ἐκ τῆς
κεφαλῆς ἠρτημέναι φαίνονται ῥίζαι καὶ τρέφονται. τοῦτο δ᾽ ὥσπερ κῦμα ἢ καρπός, ὅθεν καὶ οἱ
ἐγγεοτόκα λέγοντες οὐ κακῶς· ἐπὶ δὲ τῶν ἄλλων
τοιοῦτο μὲν οὐδέν ἐστιν· ἐπεὶ δὲ πλεῖον ἡ φύσις
ἡ κατὰ ῥίζαν ταύτῃ ἀπορίαν ἔχει. τὸ γὰρ δὴ
πᾶν λέγειν τὸ κατὰ γῆς ῥίζαν οὐκ ὀρθόν· καὶ γὰρ
ἂν ὁ καυλὸς τοῦ βολβοῦ καὶ ὁ τοῦ γηθύου καὶ

---

[1] τὰς conj. Sch.; τῆς Ald.H.; τὴν . . . ἀποπεφυκυῖαν P.
[2] ἀλλ᾽ ἀλλοῖον ἔχουσι conj. St.; ἀλλὰ λεῖον ἔχοντες PMV
Ald.; ἀλλοῖον ἐχ. mBas.mP from G ; ἀλλ᾽ ἀλλοῖον ἔχουσαι
conj. Scal.    [3] cf. 4. 10. 5.
[4] καὶ ἀεὶ Ald. ; ἀεὶ καὶ conj. W.    [5] Plin. 19. 99.
[6] cf. the definition of 'root,' 1. 1. 9.
[7] ἐγγεότοκα λέγοντες conj. W.; cf. ἡ τῶν ἐγγεοτόκων
τούτων γένεσις in Athenaeus' citation of this passage (2. 60) ;

that is to say, this fleshy or bark-like root, like squill,
as well as the [1] roots which grow from this. For
these roots not only differ in degree of stoutness,
like those of trees and pot-herbs; they are of quite
distinct classes.[2] This is at once quite evident in
cuckoo-pint and galingale,[3] the root being in the one
case thick smooth and fleshy, in the other thin and
fibrous. Wherefore we might question if such roots
should be called 'roots'; inasmuch as they are under
ground they would seem to be roots, but, inasmuch
as they are of opposite character to other roots, they
would not. For your root gets slenderer as it gets
longer and tapers continuously [4] to a point: but the
so-called root of squill purse-tassels and cuckoo-pint
does just the opposite.

Again, while the others send out roots at the
sides, this is not the case [5] with squill and purse-
tassels, nor yet with garlic and onion. In general
in these plants the roots which are attached to
the 'head' in the middle appear to be real roots
and receive nourishment,[6] and this 'head' is, as
it were, an embryo or fruit; wherefore those who
call such plants 'plants which reproduce themselves underground' [7] give a fair account of them.
In other kinds of plants there is nothing of this
sort.[8] But a difficult question is raised, since here
the 'root' has a character which goes beyond what
one associates with roots. For it is not right to call
a l that which is underground 'root,' since in that
case the stalk [9] of purse-tassels and that of long
onion and in general any part which is under-

ει τεοσ οισαλεγοντες U; ἐν τε τοῖς ὀστοῖς ἀλέγοντες MV (omitting τε) Ald. (omitting τοῖς).
[5] τοιοῦτο μέν οὐδέν conj. W.; τοῦτο μὲν MSS.
[9] ἂν ὁ καυλός conj. St.; ἀνάκαυλος Ald.

ὅλως ὅσα κατὰ βάθους ἐστὶν εἴησαν ἂν ῥίζαι,
καὶ τὸ ὕδνον δὲ καὶ ὃ καλοῦσί τινες ἀσχίον καὶ
τὸ οὔϊγγον καὶ εἴ τι ἄλλο ὑπόγειόν ἐστιν· ὧν
οὐδέν ἐστι ῥίζα· δυνάμει γὰρ δεῖ φυσικῇ διαιρεῖν
καὶ οὐ τόπῳ.

10  Τάχα δὲ τοῦτο μὲν ὀρθῶς λέγεται, ῥίζα δὲ οὐδὲν
ἧττόν ἐστιν· ἀλλὰ διαφορά τις αὕτη τῶν ῥιζῶν,
ὥστε τὴν μέν τινα τοιαύτην εἶναι τὴν δὲ τοιαύτην
καὶ τρέφεσθαι τὴν ἑτέραν ὑπὸ τῆς ἑτέρας. καίτοι
καὶ αὐταὶ αἱ σαρκώδεις ἐοίκασιν ἕλκειν. τὰς
γοῦν τῶν ἄρων πρὸ τοῦ βλαστάνειν στρέφουσι
καὶ γίγνονται μείζους κωλυόμεναι διαβῆναι πρὸς
τὴν βλάστησιν. ἐπεὶ ὅτι γε πάντων τῶν τοιούτων ἡ φύσις ἐπὶ τὸ κάτω μᾶλλον ῥέπει φανερόν·
οἱ μὲν γὰρ καυλοὶ καὶ ὅλως τὰ ἄνω βραχέα καὶ
ἀσθενῆ, τὰ δὲ κάτω μεγάλα καὶ πολλὰ καὶ
ἰσχυρὰ οὐ μόνον ἐπὶ τῶν εἰρημένων ἀλλὰ καὶ ἐπὶ
καλάμου καὶ ἀγρώστιδος καὶ ὅλως ὅσα καλαμώδη
καὶ τούτοις ὅμοια. καὶ ὅσα δὴ ναρθηκώδη, καὶ
τούτων ῥίζαι μεγάλαι καὶ σαρκώδεις.

11  Πολλὰ δὲ καὶ τῶν ποιωδῶν ἔχει τοιαύτας ῥίζας,
οἷον σπάλαξ κρόκος καὶ τὸ περδίκιον καλούμενον·
καὶ γὰρ τοῦτο παχείας τε καὶ πλείους ἔχει τὰς
ῥίζας ἢ φύλλα· καλεῖται δὲ περδίκιον διὰ τὸ τοὺς
πέρδικας ἐγκυλίεσθαι καὶ ὀρύττειν. ὁμοίως δὲ

---

¹ βάθους conj. Sch.; βάθος Ald.
² καὶ ὃ W. after U: καὶ om. Ald.; G omits also τὸ before
οὔϊγγον, making the three plants synonymous. The passage
is cited by Athen., *l.c.*, with considerable variation.
³ τοιαύτην conj. St.; τοσαύτην MSS.
⁴ *i.e.* the fleshy root (tuber, etc.).
⁵ *i.e.* the fibrous root (root proper).

ground[1] would be a root, and so would the truffle, the plant which[2] some call puff-ball, the *uingon*, and all other underground plants. Whereas none of these is a root; for we must base our definition on natural function and not on position.

However it may be that this is a true account and yet that such things are roots no less; but in that case we distinguish two different kinds of root, one being of this character[3] and the other of the other, and the one[4] getting its nourishment from the other[5]; though the fleshy roots too themselves seem to draw nourishment. At all events men invert[6] the roots of cuckoo-pint before it shoots, and so they become larger by being prevented from pushing[7] through to make a shoot. For it is evident that the nature of all such plants is to turn downwards for choice; for the stems and the upper parts generally are short and weak, while the underground parts are large numerous and strong, and that, not only in the instances given, but in reeds dog's-tooth grass and in general in all plants of a reedy character and those like them. Those too which resemble ferula[8] have large fleshy roots.

[9]Many herbaceous plants likewise have such roots, as colchicum[10] crocus and the plant called 'partridge-plant'; for this too has thick roots which are more numerous than its leaves. [11](It is called the 'partridge-plant' because partridges roll in it and grub it up.) So too with the plant called in Egypt

---

[6] στρέφουσι conj. Sch.; τρέφουσι MVAld.; cf. 7. 12. 2.
[7] διαβῆναι conj. W.; διαθεῖναι UMV.
[8] i.e. have a hollow stem (umbelliferous plants, more or less). [9] Plin. 19. 99.
[10] σπάλαξ UMV; ἀσπάλαξ mBas.: perhaps corrupt.
[11] Plin. 21. 102.

49

καὶ τὸ ἐν Αἰγύπτῳ καλούμενον οὔϊγγον· τὰ μὲν
γὰρ φύλλα μεγάλα καὶ ὁ βλαστὸς αὐτοῦ βραχύς,
ἡ δὲ ῥίζα μακρὰ καί ἐστιν ὥσπερ ὁ καρπός.
διαφέρει τε καὶ ἐσθίεται, καὶ συλλέγουσι δὲ ὅταν
12 ὁ ποταμὸς ἀποβῇ στρέφοντες τὰς βώλους. φανερώτατα δὲ καὶ πλείστην ἔχοντα πρὸς τὰ ἄλλα
διαφορὰν τὸ σίλφιον καὶ ἡ καλουμένη μαγύδαρις·
ἀμφοτέρων γὰρ τούτων καὶ ἁπάντων τῶν τοιούτων
ἐν ταῖς ῥίζαις μᾶλλον ἡ φύσις. ταῦτα μὲν οὖν
ταύτῃ ληπτέα.

Ἔνιαι δὲ τῶν ῥιζῶν πλείω δόξαιεν ἂν ἔχειν
διαφορὰν παρὰ τὰς εἰρημένας· οἷον αἵ τε τῆς ἀρα-
χίδνης καὶ τοῦ ὁμοίου τῷ ἀράκῳ· φέρουσι γὰρ
ἀμφότεραι καρπὸν οὐκ ἐλάττω τοῦ ἄνω· καὶ μίαν
μὲν ῥίζαν τὸ ἀρακῶδες τοῦτο παχεῖαν ἔχει τὴν
κατὰ βάθους, τὰς δ᾽ ἄλλας ἐφ᾽ ὧν ὁ καρπὸς
λεπτοτέρας καὶ ἐπ᾽ ἄκρῳ [καὶ] σχιζομένας πολ-
λαχῇ· φιλεῖ δὲ μάλιστα χωρία τὰ ὕφαμμα· φύλλον δὲ οὐδέτερον ἔχει τούτων οὐδ᾽ ὅμοια τοῖς
φύλλοις, ἀλλ᾽ ὥσπερ ἀμφίκαρπα μᾶλλόν ἐστιν· ὃ
καὶ φαίνεται θαυμάσιον. αἱ μὲν οὖν φύσεις
καὶ δυνάμεις τοσαύτας ἔχουσι διαφοράς.

VII. Αὐξάνεσθαι δὲ πάντων δοκοῦσιν αἱ ῥίζαι
πρότερον τῶν ἄνω· καὶ γὰρ φύεται εἰς βάθος·
οὐδεμία δὲ καθήκει πλέον ἢ ὅσον ὁ ἥλιος ἐφικνεῖ-
ται· τὸ γὰρ θερμὸν τὸ γεννῶν· οὐ μὴν ἀλλὰ

---

¹ οὔϊγγον mBas.H.; οὔϊτον MV; ουϊτον Ald.; cf. 1. 1. 7;
Plin. 21. 88 (oetum).
² μεγάλα : text doubtful (W.).
³ διαφέρει : text doubtful (Sch.).
⁴ στρέφοντες τὰς βώλους conj. Coraës ; στέφοντες βωμούς
UMVAld.     ⁵ ἐν ins. Sch.

*ningon*[1]; for its leaves are large[2] and its shoots short, while the root is long and is, as it were, the fruit. It is an excellent thing[3] and is eaten; men gather it when the river goes down by turning the clods.[4] But the plants which afford the most conspicuous instances and shew the greatest difference as compared with others are silphium and the plant called *magydaris*; the character of both of these and of all such plants is especially shewn in[5] their roots. Such is the account to be given of these plants.

Again some roots would seem to shew a greater difference[6] than those mentioned, for instance, those of *arakhidna*,[7] and of a plant[8] which resembles *arakos*. For both of these bear a fruit underground which is as large as the fruit above ground, and this *arakos*-like[9] plant has one thick root, namely, the one which runs deep, while the others which bear the 'fruit' are slenderer and branch[10] in many directions at the tip. It is specially fond of sandy ground. Neither of these plants has a leaf nor anything resembling a leaf, but they bear, as it were, two kinds of fruit instead, which seems surprising. So many then are the differences shewn in the characters and functions of roots.

VII. The roots of all plants seem to grow earlier than the parts above ground (for growth does take place downwards[11]). But no root goes down further than the sun reaches, since it is the heat which induces growth. Nevertheless the nature of the soil,

[6] *i.e.* to be even more abnormal: διαφορὰν conj. Sch.; διαφοραὶ Ald.    [7] Plin. 21. 89.
[8] tine-tare. See Index, App. (1).
[9] ἀρακώδεs conj. Sch.; σαρκώδεs Ald.G.
[10] καὶ before σχιζ. om. Sch. from G.
[11] *cf. C.P.* 1. 12. 7. (cited by Varro, 1. 45. 3); 3. 3. 1.

# THEOPHRASTUS

ταῦτα μεγάλα συμβάλλεται πρὸς βαθυρριζίαν καὶ ἔτι μᾶλλον πρὸς μακρορριζίαν, ἡ τῆς χώρας φύσις ἐὰν ᾖ κούφη καὶ μανὴ καὶ εὐδίοδος· ἐν γὰρ ταῖς τοιαύταις πορρωτέρω καὶ μείζους αἱ αὐξήσεις. φανερὸν δὲ ἐπὶ τῶν ἡμερωμάτων· ἔχοντα γὰρ ὕδωρ ὁπουοῦν δίεισιν ὡς εἰπεῖν, ἐπειδὰν ὁ τόπος ᾖ κενὸς καὶ μηδὲν τὸ ἀντιστατοῦν. ἤγουν ἐν τῷ Λυκείῳ ἡ πλάτανος ἡ κατὰ τὸν ὀχετὸν ἔτι νέα οὖσα ἐπὶ τρεῖς καὶ τριάκοντα πήχεις ἀφῆκεν ἔχουσα τόπον τε ἅμα καὶ τροφήν.

2 Δόξειε δὲ ὡς εἰπεῖν ἡ συκῆ μακρορριζότατον εἶναι καὶ ὅλως δὲ μᾶλλον τὰ μανὰ καὶ εὐθύρριζα. πάντα δὲ τὰ νεώτερα τῶν παλαιῶν, ἐὰν εἰς ἀκμὴν ἥκωσιν, ἤδη βαθυρριζότερα καὶ μακρορριζότερα. συμφθίνουσι γὰρ καὶ αἱ ῥίζαι τῷ ἄλλῳ σώματι. πάντων δὲ ὁμοίως οἱ χυλοὶ τοῖς φυτοῖς δεινότεροι, τοῖς δὲ ὡς ἐπίπαν· δι' ὃ καὶ ἐνίων πικραὶ ὧν οἱ καρποὶ γλυκεῖς· αἱ δὲ καὶ φαρμακώδεις· ἔνιαι δ' εὐώδεις, ὥσπερ αἱ τῆς ἴριδος.

3 Ἰδία δὲ ῥίζης φύσις καὶ δύναμις ἡ τῆς Ἰνδικῆς συκῆς· ἀπὸ γὰρ τῶν βλαστῶν ἀφίησι, μέχρι οὗ ἂν συνάψῃ τῇ γῇ καὶ ῥιζωθῇ, καὶ γίνεται περὶ τὸ δένδρον κύκλῳ συνεχὲς τὸ τῶν ῥιζῶν οὐχ ἁπτόμενον τοῦ στελέχους ἀλλ' ἀφεστηκός.

---

¹ ταῦτα before μέγαλα om. W.
² ἡμερωμάτων conj. Sch.; ἡμερωτάτων UP₂Ald.; cf. C.P. 5. 6. 8.
³ ὁπουοῦν MSS.; ὁποσονοῦν conj. W. from G, in quantum libent.    ⁴ ἐπειδὰν conj. Sch.; ἐπεὶ κἂν UMVPAld.
⁵ Quoted by Varro, 1. 37. 5.
⁶ ἐπὶ conj. Sch.; παρὰ P₂; περὶ Ald.
⁷ συμφθίνουσι : συμφωνοῦσι conj. St.

52

if it is light open and porous, contributes greatly[1] to deep rooting, and still more to the formation of long roots; for in such soils growth goes further and is more vigorous. This is evident in cultivated plants.[2] For, provided that they have water, they run on, one may say, wherever it may be,[3] whenever[4] the ground is unoccupied and there is no obstacle. [5] For instance the plane-tree by the watercourse in the Lyceum when it was still young sent out its roots a distance of[6] thirty-three cubits, having both room and nourishment.

The fig would seem, one may say, to have the longest roots, and in general plants which have wood of loose texture and straight roots would seem to have these longer. Also young plants, provided that they have reached their prime, root deeper and have longer roots than old ones; for the roots decay along with[7] the rest of the plant's body. And in all cases alike the juices of plants[8] are more powerful in the roots than in other parts, while in some cases they are extremely powerful; wherefore the roots are bitter in some plants whose fruits are sweet; some roots again are medicinal, and some are fragrant, as those of the iris.

The character and function of the roots of the 'Indian fig' (banyan) are peculiar, for this plant sends out roots from the shoots till it has a hold on the ground[9] and roots again; and so there comes to be a continuous circle of roots round the tree, not connected with the main stem but at a distance from it.

---

[8] τοῖς φυτοῖς Ald.; ταῖς ῥίζαις conj. W. from G; text probably defective.

[9] τῇ γῇ conj. Scal. from G; συκῇ U; τῇ συκῇ P₂Ald.

Παραπλήσιον δὲ τούτῳ μᾶλλον δὲ τρόπον τινὰ
θαυμασιώτερον εἴ τι ἐκ τῶν φύλλων ἀφίησι ῥίζαν,
οἷόν φασι περὶ 'Οποῦντα ποιάριον εἶναι, ὃ καὶ
ἐσθίεσθαί ἐστιν ἡδύ. τὸ γὰρ αὖ τῶν θέρμων
θαυμαστὸν ἧττον, ὅτι ἂν ἐν ὕλῃ βαθείᾳ σπαρῇ
διείρει τὴν ῥίζαν πρὸς τὴν γῆν καὶ βλαστάνει διὰ
τὴν ἰσχύν. ἀλλὰ δὴ τὰς μὲν τῶν ῥιζῶν διαφορὰς ἐκ τούτων θεωρητέον.

VIII. Τῶν δένδρων τὰς τοιαύτας ἄν τις λάβοι
διαφοράς. ἔστι γὰρ τὰ μὲν ὀζώδη τὰ δ' ἄνοζα
καὶ φύσει καὶ τόπῳ κατὰ τὸ μᾶλλον καὶ ἧττον.
ἄνοζα δὲ λέγω οὐχ ὥστε μὴ ἔχειν ὅλως—οὐδὲν
γὰρ τοιοῦτο δένδρον, ἀλλ' εἴπερ, ἐπὶ τῶν ἄλλων
οἷον σχοῖνος τύφη κύπειρος ὅλως ἐπὶ τῶν λιμνωδῶν—ἀλλ' ὥστε ὀλίγους ἔχειν. φύσει μὲν οἷον
ἀκτὴ δάφνη συκῆ ὅλως πάντα τὰ λειόφλοια καὶ
ὅσα κοῖλα καὶ μανά. ὀζῶδες δὲ ἐλάα πεύκη
κότινος· τούτων δὲ τὰ μὲν ἐν παλισκίοις καὶ
νηνέμοις καὶ ἐφύδροις, τὰ δὲ ἐν εὐηλίοις καὶ χει-
μερίοις καὶ πνευματώδεσι καὶ λεπτοῖς καὶ ξηροῖς·
τὰ μὲν γὰρ ἀνοζότερα, τὰ δὲ ὀζωδέστερα τῶν

---

[1] τι conj. W.; τις MSS.  [2] Plin. 21. 104.
[3] cf. 8. 11. 8; Plin. 18. 133 and 134.
[4] διείρει conj. Sch.; διαιρεῖ P₂Ald.; cf. C.P. 2. 17. 7.
[5] ὄζος is the knot and the bough starting from it: cf.
Arist. de inv. et sen. 3.
[6] ἐπὶ τῶν conj. Coraës; ἡ τῶν UM; ἧττον (erased) P (ἐκ
τῶν marg.) ἧττον Ald.

54

Something similar to this, but even more surprising, occurs in those plants which[1] emit roots from their leaves, as they say does a certain herb[2] which grows about Opus, which is also sweet to taste. The peculiarity again of lupins[3] is less surprising, namely that, if the seed is dropped where the ground is thickly overgrown, it pushes[4] its root through to the earth and germinates because of its vigour. But we have said enough for study of the differences between roots.

*Of trees (principally) and their characteristic special differences: as to knots.*

VIII. One may take it that the following are the differences between trees :—Some have knots,[5] more or less, others are more or less without them, whether from their natural character or because of their position. But, when I say 'without knots,' I do not mean that they have no knots at all (there is no tree like that, but, if it is true of any plants, it is only of[6] other kinds, such as rush bulrush[7] galingale and plants of the lake side[8] generally) but that they have few knots. Now this is the natural character of elder bay fig and all smooth-barked trees, and in general of those whose wood is hollow or of a loose texture. Olive fir and wild olive have knots; and some of these grow in thickly shaded windless and wet places, some in sunny positions exposed to storms and winds,[9] where the soil is light and dry; for the number of knots varies between trees of the

[7] τύφη conj. Bod.; τίφη UAld.H.: cf. 1. 5. 3.
[8] ἐπὶ τῶν conj. W.; εἴ τι ἐπὶ τῶν Ald.
[9] πνευματώδεσι conj. Scal.; πυματώδεσι U; πυγματώδεσι MVAld.

ὁμογενῶν. ὅλως δὲ ὀζωδέστερα τὰ ὀρεινὰ τῶν πεδεινῶν καὶ τὰ ξηρὰ τῶν ἑλείων.

2 Ἔτι δὲ κατὰ τὴν φυτείαν τὰ μὲν πυκνὰ ἄνοζα καὶ ὀρθά, τὰ δὲ μανὰ ὀζωδέστερα καὶ σκολιώτερα· συμβαίνει γὰρ ὥστε τὰ μὲν ἐν παλισκίῳ εἶναι τὰ δὲ ἐν εὐηλίῳ. καὶ τὰ ἄρρενα δὲ τῶν θηλειῶν ὀζωδέστερα ἐν οἷς ἐστιν ἄμφω, οἷον κυπάριττος ἐλάτη ὀστρυῒς κρανεία· καλοῦσι γὰρ γένος τι θηλυκρανείαν· καὶ τὰ ἄγρια δὲ τῶν ἡμέρων, καὶ ἁπλῶς καὶ τὰ ὑπὸ ταὐτὸ γένος, οἷον κότινος ἐλάας καὶ ἐρινεὸς συκῆς καὶ ἀχρὰς ἀπίου. πάντα γὰρ ταῦτα ὀζωδέστερα· καὶ ὡς ἐπὶ τὸ πολὺ πάντα τὰ πυκνὰ τῶν μανῶν· καὶ γὰρ τὰ ἄρρενα πυκνότερα καὶ τὰ ἄγρια· πλὴν εἴ τι διὰ πυκνότητα παντελῶς ἄνοζον ἢ ὀλίγοζον, οἷον πύξος λωτός.

3 Εἰσὶ δὲ τῶν μὲν ἄτακτοι καὶ ὡς ἔτυχεν οἱ ὄζοι, τῶν δὲ τεταγμένοι καὶ τῷ διαστήματι καὶ τῷ πλήθει καθάπερ εἴρηται· δι' ὃ καὶ ταξιόζωτα ταῦτα καλοῦσιν. τῶν μὲν γὰρ οἷον δι' ἴσου τῶν δὲ μεῖζον αἰεὶ τὸ πρὸς τῷ πάχει. καὶ τοῦτο κατὰ λόγον. ὅπερ μάλιστα ἔνδηλον καὶ ἐν τοῖς κοτίνοις καὶ ἐν τοῖς καλάμοις· τὸ γὰρ γόνυ καθάπερ ὄζος. καὶ οἱ μὲν κατ' ἀλλήλους, ὥσπερ οἱ τῶν

---

¹ Plin. 16. 125.    ² 1. 8. 1.
³ ταξιόζωτα conj. W.; ἀξιολογώτατα Ald.; cf. ταξίφυλλος, 1. 10. 8.    ⁴ Plin. 16. 122.

56

same kind. And in general mountain trees have
more knots than those of the plain, and those that
grow in dry spots than those that grow in marshes.
Again the way in which they are planted makes a
difference in this respect: those trees that grow close
together are knotless and erect, those that grow far
apart have more knots and a more crooked growth;
for it happens that the one class are in shade, the
others in full sun. Again the 'male' trees have
more knots than the 'female' in those trees in which
both forms are found, as cypress silver-fir hop-hornbeam cornelian cherry—for there is a kind called
'female cornelian cherry' (cornel)—and wild trees
have more knots than trees in cultivation: this is
true both in general and when we compare those of
the same kind, as the wild and cultivated forms of
olive fig and pear. All these have more knots in the
wild state; and in general those of closer growth
have this character more than those of open growth;
for in fact the 'male' plants are of closer growth,
and so are the wild ones; except that in some cases,
as in box and nettle-tree, owing to the closer growth
there are no knots at all, or only a few.

[1] Again the knots of some trees are irregular and
set at haphazard, while those of others are regular,
alike in their distance apart and in their number, as
has been said[2]; wherefore also they are called 'trees
with regular knots.'[3] [4] For of some the knots are,
as it were, at even distances, while in others the
distance between them is greater at the thick end of
the stem. And this proportion holds throughout.
This is especially evident in the wild olive and in
reeds—in which the joint corresponds to the knot in
trees. Again some knots are opposite one another,

κοτίνων, οἱ δ' ὡς ἔτυχεν. ἔστι δὲ τὰ μὲν δίοζα, τὰ
δὲ τρίοζα, τὰ δὲ πλείους ἔχοντα· ἔνια δὲ πεντάοζά
ἐστι. καὶ τῆς μὲν ἐλάτης ὀρθοὶ καὶ οἱ ὄζοι καὶ οἱ
4 κλάδοι ὥσπερ ἐμπεπηγότες, τῶν δὲ ἄλλων οὔ. δι'
ὃ καὶ ἰσχυρὸν ἡ ἐλάτη. ἰδιώτατοι δὲ οἱ τῆς
μηλέας· ὅμοιοι γὰρ θηρίων προσώποις, εἷς μὲν ὁ
μέγιστος ἄλλοι δὲ περὶ αὐτὸν μικροὶ πλείους.
εἰσὶ δὲ τῶν ὄζων οἱ μὲν τυφλοί, οἱ δὲ γόνιμοι.
λέγω δὲ τυφλοὺς ἀφ' ὧν μηδεὶς βλαστός. οὗτοι
δὲ καὶ φύσει καὶ πηρώσει γίνονται, ὅταν ἢ μὴ
λυθῇ καὶ ἐκβιάζηται ἢ καὶ ἀποκοπῇ καὶ οἷον
ἐπικαυθεὶς πηρωθῇ· γίνονται δὲ μᾶλλον ἐν τοῖς
παχέσι τῶν ἀκρεμόνων, ἐνίων δὲ καὶ ἐν τοῖς
στελέχεσιν. ὅλως δὲ καὶ τοῦ στελέχους καὶ τοῦ
κλάδου καθ' ὃ ἂν ἐπικόψῃ ἢ ἐπιτέμῃ τις, ὄζος
γίνεται καθαπερανεὶ διαιρῶν τὸ ἓν καὶ ποιῶν
ἑτέραν ἀρχήν, εἴτε διὰ τὴν πήρωσιν εἴτε δι' ἄλλην
αἰτίαν· οὐ γὰρ δὴ κατὰ φύσιν τὸ ὑπὸ τῆς
πληγῆς.
5 Ἀεὶ δὲ ἐν ἅπασιν οἱ κλάδοι φαίνονται πολυο-
ζότεροι διὰ τὸ μήπω τἀνὰ μέσον προσηυξῆσθαι,
καθάπερ καὶ τῆς συκῆς οἱ νεόβλαστοι τραχύ-
τατοι καὶ τῆς ἀμπέλου τὰ ἄκρα τῶν κλημάτων.
ὡς γὰρ ὄζος ἐν τοῖς ἄλλοις οὕτω καὶ ὀφθαλμὸς

---

[1] cf. 4. 4. 12.    [2] Plin. 16. 122.
[3] i.e. primary and secondary branches.
[4] cf. 5. 2. 2.    [5] Plin. 16. 124.
[6] cf. Arist. de inr. et sen. 3 ; Plin. 16. 125.
[7] ὅταν . . . πηρωθῇ conj. W. ; ἢ ὅταν ἢ μὴ λυθῇ καὶ ἐκβιάζηται
καὶ ἡ ἀποκοπὴ καὶ U ; ὅταν ἡ μὴ λυθῇ καὶ ἐκβιάζηται ἢ ἀποκοπῇ
P ; ἢ ὅταν λυθῇ καὶ ἐκβιάζηται ἢ ἀποκοπὴ καὶ οὐ P₂ ; ὅταν ἢ
μὴ λυθῇ καὶ ἐκβιάζηται καὶ ἢ ἀποκοπῇ καὶ Ald.H. ; G differs
widely.

as those of the wild olive, while others are set at
random. Again some trees have double knots, some
treble,[1] some more at the same point; some have as
many as five. [2] In the silver-fir both the knots and
the smaller branches[3] are set at right angles, as if
they were stuck in, but in other trees they are not
so. And that is why the silver-fir is such a strong
tree.[4] Most peculiar[5] are the knots of the apple, for
they are like the faces of wild animals; there is one
large knot, and a number of small ones round it.
Again some knots are blind,[6] others productive; by
'blind' I mean those from which there is no growth.
These come to be so either by nature or by mutilation,
according as either the knot[7] is not free and so the
shoot does not make its way out, or, a bough having
been cut off, the place is mutilated, for example by
burning. Such knots occur more commonly in the
thicker boughs, and in some cases in the stem also.
And in general, wherever one chops or cuts part of
the stem or bough, a knot is formed, as though one
thing were made thereby into two and a fresh
growing point produced, the cause being the mutilation or some other such reason; for the effect of such
a blow cannot of course be ascribed to nature.

Again in all trees the branches always seem to
have more knots, because the intermediate parts[8]
have not yet developed, just as the newly formed
branches of the fig are the roughest,[9] and in the
vine the highest[10] shoots. [11] (For to the knot in other

[8] i.e. the internodes; till the branch is fully grown its
knots are closer together, and so seem more numerous: μήπω
τὰνὰ μέσον προσηυξῆσθαι conj. Sch.; μήπω τὰνὰ μέσον προσκυ-
ξῆθαι U; μήτ' ἀνὰ μέσον προσκυζεῖσθαι MAld.; μήποτ' ἀνάμεσον
ρροσηυξῆσθαι P₂. [9] i.e. have most knots.
[10] i.e. youngest. [11] Plin. 16. 125.

ἐν ἀμπέλῳ καὶ ἐν καλάμῳ γόνυ ... ἐνίοις δὲ
καὶ οἷον κράδαι γίνονται, καθάπερ πτελέα καὶ
δρυῒ καὶ μάλιστα ἐν πλατάνῳ· ἐὰν δὲ ἐν τραχέσι
καὶ ἀνύδροις καὶ πνευματώδεσι καὶ παντελῶς.
πάντως δὲ πρὸς τῇ γῇ καὶ οἷον τῇ κεφαλῇ τοῦ
στελέχους ἀπογηρασκόντων τὸ πάθος τοῦτο
γίνεται.

6    Ἔνια δὲ καὶ ἴσχει τοὺς καλουμένους ὑπό τινων
ἢ γόγγρους ἢ τὸ ἀνάλογον, οἷον ἡ ἐλάα· κυριώ-
τατον γὰρ ἐπὶ ταύτης τοῦτο τοὔνομα καὶ πάσχειν
δοκεῖ μάλιστα τὸ εἰρημένον· καλοῦσι δ᾽ ἔνιοι
τοῦτο πρέμνον οἱ δὲ κροτώνην οἱ δὲ ἄλλο ὄνομα.
τοῖς δὲ εὐθέσι καὶ μονορρίζοις καὶ ἀπαραβλά-
στοις οὐ γίνεται τοῦθ᾽ ὅλως ἢ ἧττον· [φοῖνιξ δὲ
παραβλαστητικόν] ἡ δὲ ἐλάα καὶ ὁ κότινος
καὶ τὰς οὐλότητας ἰδίας ἔχουσι τὰς ἐν τοῖς
στελέχεσι.

IX. Ἔστι μὲν οὖν τὰ μὲν ὡς εἰς μῆκος αὐξη-
τικὰ μάλιστ᾽ ἢ μόνον, οἷον ἐλάτη φοῖνιξ κυπάριττος καὶ ὅλως τὰ μονοστελέχη καὶ ὅσα μὴ
πολύρριζα μηδὲ πολύκλαδα· <ἡ δὲ φοῖνιξ ἀπαρα-
βλαστητικόν.> τὰ δὲ ὅμοια τούτοις ἀνὰ λόγον
καὶ εἰς βάθος. ἔνια δ᾽ εὐθὺς σχίζεται, οἷον ἡ

---

[1] The opening of the description of the diseases of trees
seems to have been lost.     [2] κράδαι; cf. C.P. 5. 1. 3.
[3] πάντως ... γίνεται conj. W.; πάντως δὲ ὁ πρὸς τῇ γῇ καὶ
οἷον τ. κ. στ. ἀπογηράσκων τῶν παχυτέρων γίνεται Ald.; so U
except παχύτερον, and M except παχύτερος.
[4] γόγγρους; cf. Hesych., s.vv. γόγγρος, κροτώνη.
[5] The word is otherwise unknown.
[6] ἧττον· ἡ δὲ ἐλάα conj. W.; ἧττον· ἡ δὲ φοῖνιξ πάραβλασ-
ητικόν· ἡ δὲ ἐλάα U ; so Ald. except παραβλαστικόν.   The

60

trees correspond the 'eye' in the vine, the joint in the reed). . . . .[1] In some trees again there occurs, as it were, a diseased formation of small shoots,[2] as in elm oak and especially in the plane; and this is universal if they grow in rough waterless or windy spots. Apart from any such cause [3] this affection occurs near the ground in what one may call the 'head' of the trunk, when the tree is getting old.

Some trees again have what are called by some 'excrescences'[4] (or something corresponding), as the olive; for this name belongs most properly to that tree, and it seems most liable to the affection; and some call it 'stump,' some *krotone*,[5] others have a different name for it. It does not occur, or only occurs to a less extent, in straight young trees, which have a single root and no side-growths. To the olive[6] also, both wild and cultivated, are peculiar certain thickenings [7] in the stem.

*As to habit.*

IX. [8] Now those trees which grow chiefly or only [9] in the direction of their height are such as silver-fir date-palm cypress, and in general those which have a single stem and not many roots or branches (the date-palm, it may be added, has no side-growths at all[10]). And trees like [11] these have also similar growth downwards. Some however divide from the first,

note about the palm (φοῖνιξ δὲ παραβλαστητικόν) I have omitted as untrue as well as irrelevant; possibly with ἀπαραβα. for παραβα. it belongs to the next section.

[7] οὐλότητας conj. W.; κοιλότητας MSS. (?) Ald.

[2] Plin. 16. 125.

[9] μάλιστ' ἤ μόνον conj. W.; μάλιστα μανὰ Ald. H.

[10] See 3. 8. 6. n.

[11] ὅμοια conj. Sch.; ὁμοίως MSS. Sense hardly satisfactory.

μηλέα· τὰ δὲ πολύκλαδα καὶ μείζω τὸν ὄγκον
ἔχει τὸν ἄνω, καθάπερ ῥόα· οὐ μὴν ἀλλ' οὖν
μέγιστά γε συμβάλλεται πρὸς ἕκαστον ἡ ἀγωγὴ
καὶ ὁ τόπος καὶ ἡ τροφή. σημεῖον δ' ὅτι ταὐτὰ
πυκνὰ μὲν ὄντα μακρὰ καὶ λεπτὰ γίνεται, μανὰ
δὲ παχύτερα καὶ βραχύτερα· καὶ ἐὰν μὲν εὐθύς
τις ἀφιῇ τοὺς ὄζους βραχέα, ἐὰν δὲ ἀνακαθαίρῃ
μακρά, καθάπερ ἡ ἄμπελος.

2    Ἱκανὸν δὲ κἀκεῖνο πρὸς πίστιν ὅτι καὶ τῶν
λαχάνων ἔνια λαμβάνει δένδρου σχῆμα, καθάπερ
εἴπομεν τὴν μαλάχην καὶ τὸ τεῦτλον· ἅπαντα
δ' ἐν τοῖς οἰκείοις τόποις εὐαυξῆ . . . καὶ τὸ αὐτὸ
κάλλιστον. ἐπεὶ καὶ τῶν ὁμογενῶν ἀνοζότερα
καὶ μείζω καὶ καλλίω τὰ ἐν τοῖς οἰκείοις, οἷον
ἐλάτη ἡ Μακεδονικὴ τῆς Παρνασίας καὶ τῶν ἄλλων. ἅπαντα δὲ ταῦτα καὶ ὅλως ἡ ὕλη ἡ ἀγρία
καλλίων καὶ πλείων τοῦ ὄρους ἐν τοῖς προσβορείοις ἢ ἐν τοῖς πρὸς μεσημβρίαν.

3    Ἔστι δὲ τὰ μὲν ἀείφυλλα τὰ δὲ φυλλοβόλα. τῶν μὲν ἡμέρων ἀείφυλλα ἐλάα φοῖνιξ
δάφνη μύρρινος πεύκης τι γένος κυπάριττος· τῶν
δ' ἀγρίων ἐλάτη πεύκη ἄρκευθος μίλος θυία καὶ
ἣν Ἀρκάδες καλοῦσι φελλόδρυν φιλυρέα κέδρος
πίτυς ἀγρία μυρίκη πύξος πρῖνος κήλαστρον
φιλύκη ὀξυάκανθος ἀφάρκη, ταῦτα δὲ φύεται
περὶ τὸν Ὄλυμπον, ἀνδράχλη κόμαρος τέρμινθος

---

[1] οὖν marked as doubtful in U.    [2] 1. 3. 2.
[3] καὶ τὸ αὐτὸ κάλλιστον. The first part of the sentence to
which these words belong is apparently lost (W.).
[4] i.e. the fir and other trees mentioned in the lost words.
[5] Plin. 16. 80.
[6] μίλος conj. Sch.; σμίλαξ P₂Ald.; cf. 3. 3. 3.

such as apple; some have many branches, and their
greater mass of growth high up, as the pomegranate:
however [1] training position and cultivation chiefly
contribute to all of these characters. In proof of
which we have the fact that the same trees which,
when growing close together, are tall and slender,
when grown farther apart become stouter and
shorter; and if we from the first let the branches
grow freely, the tree becomes short, whereas, if we
prune them, it becomes tall,—for instance, the vine.

This too is enough for proof that even some pot-
herbs acquire the form of a tree, as we said [2] of
mallow and beet. Indeed all things grow well in
congenial places. . . .[3] For even among those of the
same kind those which grow in congenial places have
less knots, and are taller and more comely: thus the
silver-fir in Macedon is superior to other silver-firs,
such as that of Parnassus. Not only is this true of
all these,[4] but in general the wild woodland is more
beautiful and vigorous on the north side of the
mountain than on the south.

*As to shedding of leaves.*

Again some [5] trees are evergreen, some deciduous.
Of cultivated trees, olive date-palm bay myrtle a
kind of fir and cypress are evergreen, and among
wild trees silver-fir fir Phoenician cedar yew [6] odorous
cedar the tree which the Arcadians call 'cork-oak'
(holm-oak) mock-privet prickly cedar 'wild [7] pine'
tamarisk box kermes-oak holly alaternus cotoneaster
hybrid arbutus [8] (all of which grow about Olympus)

[7] ἀγρία after πίτυς conj. Sch.; after πρῖνος UPAld.: *cf.*
3. 3. 3.

[8] κόμαρος conj. Bod.; σύναρος UMV; οὔναρος Ald.; σύναρος P₂.

ἀγρία δάφνη. δοκεῖ δ' ἡ ἀνδράχλη καὶ ὁ κόμαρος
τὰ μὲν κάτω φυλλοβολεῖν τὰ δὲ ἔσχατα τῶν
ἀκρεμόνων ἀείφυλλα ἔχειν, ἐπιφύειν δὲ ἀεὶ τοὺς
ἀκρεμόνας.

4 Τῶν μὲν οὖν δένδρων ταῦτα. τῶν δὲ θαμνωδῶν κιττὸς βάτος ῥάμνος κάλαμος κεδρίς· ἔστι
γάρ τι μικρὸν ὃ οὐ δενδροῦται. τῶν δὲ φρυγανικῶν
καὶ ποιωδῶν πήγανον ῥάφανος ῥοδωνία ἰωνία
ἀβρότονον ἀμάρακον ἔρπυλλος ὀρίγανον σέλινον
ἱπποσέλινον μήκων καὶ τῶν ἀγρίων εἴδη πλείω.
διαμένει δὲ καὶ τούτων ἔνια τοῖς ἄκροις τὰ δὲ
ἄλλα ἀποβάλλει οἷον ὀρίγανον σέλινον . . . ἐπεὶ
καὶ τὸ πήγανον κακοῦται καὶ ἀλλάττεται.

5 Πάντα δὲ καὶ τῶν ἄλλων τὰ ἀείφυλλα στενο-
φυλλότερα καὶ ἔχοντά τινα λιπαρότητα καὶ
εὐωδίαν. ἔνια δ' οὐκ ὄντα τῇ φύσει παρὰ τὸν
τόπον ἐστὶν ἀείφυλλα, καθάπερ ἐλέχθη περὶ τῶν
ἐν Ἐλεφαντίνῃ καὶ Μέμφει· κατωτέρω δ' ἐν τῷ
Δέλτα μικρὸν πάνυ χρόνον διαλείπει τοῦ μὴ ἀεὶ
βλαστάνειν. ἐν Κρήτῃ δὲ λέγεται πλάτανόν
τινα εἶναι ἐν τῇ Γορτυναίᾳ πρὸς πηγῇ τινι ἣ οὐ
φυλλοβολεῖ· μυθολογοῦσι δὲ ὡς ὑπὸ ταύτῃ
ἐμίγη τῇ Εὐρώπῃ ὁ Ζεύς· τὰς δὲ πλησίας πάσας
φυλλοβολεῖν. ἐν δὲ Συβάρει δρῦς ἐστιν εὐ-
σύνοπτος ἐκ τῆς πόλεως ἣ οὐ φυλλοβολεῖ· φασὶ

---

[1] Plin. 16. 80.
[2] Some words probably missing (W.) which would explain
the next two clauses. [3] Plin. 16. 82. [4] 1. 3. 5.
[5] Plin. 12. 11 ; Varro, 1. 7.

andrachne arbutus terebinth 'wild bay' (oleander).
Andrachne and arbutus seem to cast their lower
leaves, but to keep those at the end of the twigs
perennially, and to be always adding leafy twigs.
These are the trees which are evergreen.

[1] Of shrubby plants these are evergreen :—ivy
bramble buckthorn reed *kedris* (juniper)—for there
is a small kind of *kedros* so called which does not
grow into a tree. Among under-shrubs and herbaceous plants there are rue cabbage rose gilliflower
southernwood sweet marjoram tufted thyme marjoram celery alexanders poppy, and a good many
more kinds of wild plants. However some of these
too, while evergreen as to their top growths, shed
their other leaves, as marjoram and celery . . . . . .[2]
for rue too is injuriously affected and changes its
character.

[3] And all the evergreen plants in the other classes
too have narrower leaves and a certain glossiness and
fragrance. Some moreover which are not evergreen
by nature become so because of their position, as
was said[4] about the plants at Elephantine and
Memphis, while lower down the Nile in the Delta
there is but a very short period in which they are not
making new leaves. It is said that in Crete[5] in the
district of Gortyna there is a plane near a certain
spring[6] which does not lose its leaves : (indeed the
story is that it was under[7] this tree that Zeus lay
with Europa), while all the other plants in the
neighbourhood shed their leaves. [8] At Sybaris there
is an oak within sight of the city which does not shed

[6] πηγῇ conj. H. from G ; σκηνῇ UMVAld.; κηνῇ P₂; κρηνῇ
nBas.
[7] ὑπὸ conj. Hemsterhuis ; ἐπὶ Ald.      [8] Plin. 16. 81.

THEOPHRASTUS

δὲ οὐ βλαστάνειν αὐτὴν ἅμα ταῖς ἄλλαις ἀλλὰ μετὰ Κύνα. λέγεται δὲ καὶ ἐν Κύπρῳ πλάτανος εἶναι τοιαύτη.

6 Φυλλοβολεῖ δὲ πάντα τοῦ μετοπώρου καὶ μετὰ τὸ μετόπωρον, πλὴν τὸ μὲν θᾶττον τὸ δὲ βραδύτερον ὥστε καὶ τοῦ χειμῶνος ἐπιλαμβάνειν. οὐκ ἀνάλογοι δὲ αἱ φυλλοβολίαι ταῖς βλαστήσεσιν, ὥστε τὰ πρότερον βλαστήσαντα πρότερον φυλλοβολεῖν, ἀλλ' ἔνια πρωϊβλαστεῖ μὲν οὐδὲν δὲ προτερεῖ τῶν ἄλλων, ἀλλά τινων καὶ ὑστερεῖ, καθάπερ ἡ ἀμυγδαλῆ.

7 Τὰ δὲ ὀψιβλαστεῖ μὲν οὐδὲν δὲ ὡς εἰπεῖν ὑστερεῖ τῶν ἄλλων, ὥσπερ ἡ συκάμινος. δοκεῖ δὲ καὶ ἡ χώρα συμβάλλεσθαι καὶ ὁ τόπος ὁ ἔνικμος πρὸς τὸ διαμένειν. τὰ γὰρ ἐν τοῖς ξηροῖς καὶ ὅλως λεπτογείοις πρότερα φυλλοβολεῖ καὶ τὰ πρεσβύτερα δὲ τῶν νέων. ἔνια δὲ καὶ πρὸ τοῦ πεπᾶναι τὸν καρπὸν ἀποβάλλει τὰ φύλλα, καθάπερ αἱ ὄψιαι συκαῖ καὶ ἀχράδες.

Τῶν δ' ἀειφύλλων ἡ ἀποβολὴ καὶ ἡ αὔανσις κατὰ μέρος· οὐ γὰρ δὴ ταὐτὰ αἰεὶ διαμένει, ἀλλὰ τὰ μὲν ἐπιβλαστάνει τὰ δ' ἀφαναίνεται. τοῦτο δὲ περὶ τροπὰς μάλιστα γίνεται θερινάς. εἰ δέ τινων καὶ μετ' Ἀρκτοῦρον ἢ καὶ κατ' ἄλλην ὥραν ἐπισκεπτέον. καὶ τὰ μὲν περὶ τὴν φυλλοβολίαν οὕτως ἔχει.

<hr>

[1] Plin. 16. 82 and 83.

66

its leaves, and they say that it does not come into leaf along with the others, but only after the rising of the dog-star. It is said that in Cyprus too there is a plane which has the same peculiarity.

[1] The fall of the leaves in all cases takes place in autumn or later, but it occurs later in some trees than in others, and even extends into the winter. However the fall of the leaf does not correspond to the growth of new leaves (in which case those that come into leaf earlier would lose their leaves earlier), but some (such as the almond) which are early in coming into leaf are not earlier than the rest in losing their leaves, but are even comparatively late.[2]

[3] Others again, such as the mulberry, come into leaf late, but are hardly at all later than the others in shedding their leaves. It appears also that position and a moist situation conduce to keeping the leaves late; for those which grow in dry places, and in general where the soil is light, shed their leaves earlier, and the older trees earlier than young ones. Some even cast their leaves before the fruit is ripe, as the late kinds of fig and pear.

In those which are evergreen the shedding and withering of leaves take place by degrees; for it is not the same [4] leaves which always persist, but fresh ones are growing while the old ones wither away. This happens chiefly about the summer solstice. Whether in some cases it occurs even after the rising of Arcturus or at a quite different season is matter for enquiry. So much for the shedding of leaves.

[2] ὑστερεῖ conj. H.; ὕστερον UMVP Ald.

[3] Plin. 16. 84.

[4] ταὐτὰ conj. Sch.; ταῦτα Ald.

THEOPHRASTUS

X. Τὰ δὲ φύλλα τῶν μὲν ἄλλων δένδρων ὅμοια
πάντων αὐτὰ ἑαυτοῖς, τῆς δὲ λεύκης καὶ τοῦ
κιττοῦ καὶ τοῦ καλουμένου κρότωνος ἀνόμοια καὶ
ἑτεροσχήμονα· τὰ μὲν γὰρ νέα περιφερῆ τὰ δὲ
παλαιότερα γωνοειδῆ, καὶ εἰς τοῦτο ἡ μετάστασις
πάντων. τοῦ δὲ κιττοῦ ἀνάπαλιν νέου μὲν ὄντος
ἐγγωνιώτερα πρεσβυτέρου δὲ περιφερέστερα· μεταβάλλει γὰρ καὶ οὗτος. ἴδιον δὲ καὶ τὸ τῇ ἐλάᾳ καὶ
τῇ φιλύρᾳ καὶ τῇ πτελέᾳ καὶ τῇ λεύκῃ συμβαῖνον·
στρέφειν γὰρ δοκοῦσιν τὰ ὕπτια μετὰ τροπὰς θερινάς, καὶ τούτῳ γνωρίζουσιν ὅτι γεγένηνται τροπαί.
2 πάντα δὲ τὰ φύλλα διαφέρει κατὰ τὰ ὕπτια καὶ τὰ
πρανῆ. καὶ τῶν μὲν ἄλλων τὰ ὕπτια ποιωδέστερα
καὶ λειότερα· τὰς γὰρ ἶνας καὶ τὰς φλέβας ἐν
τοῖς πρανέσιν ἔχουσιν, ὥσπερ ἡ χεὶρ <τὰ ἄρθρα>·
τῆς δ᾽ ἐλάας λευκότερα καὶ ἧττον λεῖα ἐνίοτε
καὶ τὰ ὕπτια. πάντα δὴ ἡ τά γε πλεῖστα ἐκφανῆ
ἔχει τὰ ὕπτια καὶ ταῦτα γίνεται τῷ ἡλίῳ φανερά.
καὶ στρέφεται τὰ πολλὰ πρὸς τὸν ἥλιον· δι᾽ ὃ καὶ
οὐ ῥάδιον εἰπεῖν ὁπότερον πρὸς τῷ κλῶνι μᾶλλόν
ἐστιν· ἡ μὲν γὰρ ὑπτιότης μᾶλλον δοκεῖ ποιεῖν τὸ
πρανές, ἡ δὲ φύσις οὐχ ἧττον βούλεται τὸ ὕπτιον,
ἄλλως τε καὶ ἡ ἀνάκλασις διὰ τὸν ἥλιον· ἴδοι δ᾽

¹ Plin. 16. 85.
² καὶ τοῦ κιττοῦ καὶ τοῦ MSS. cf. Plin. l.c.; Diosc. 4. 164.
καὶ τοῦ κικίου τοῦ καὶ conj. W.; Galen, Lex. Hipp., gives
κίκιον as a name for the root of κρότων. cf. C.P. 2. 16. 4.
³ i.e. not 'entire.' 'Young leaves' = leaves of the young tree.
⁴ This seems to contradict what has just been said.
⁵ τὰ ἄρθρα add. Sch. from Plin. 16. 88, incisuras. cf. Arist.
H.A. 1. 15, where Plin. (11. 274) renders ἄρθρα incisuras.
68

*Differences in leaves.*

X. [1] Now, while the leaves of all other trees are all alike in each tree, those of the abele ivy [2] and of the plant called *kroton* (castor-oil plant) are unlike one another and of different forms. The young leaves in these are round, the old ones angular,[3] and eventually all the leaves assume that form. On the other hand [4] in the ivy, when it is young, the leaves are somewhat angular, but when it is older, they become rounder: for in this plant too a change of form takes place. There is a peculiarity special to the olive lime elm and abele: their leaves appear to invert the upper surface after the summer solstice, and by this men know that the solstice is past. Now all leaves differ as to their upper and under surfaces; and in most trees the upper surfaces are greener and smoother, as they have the fibres and veins in the under surfaces, even as the human hand has its 'lines,'[5] but even the upper surface of the leaf of the olive is sometimes whiter and less smooth.[6] So all or most leaves display their upper surfaces, and it is these surfaces which are exposed to the light.[7] Again most leaves turn towards the sun; wherefore also it is not easy to say which surface is next to the twig[8]; for, while the way in which the upper surface is presented seems rather to make the under surface closer to it, yet nature desires equally that the upper surface should be the nearer, and this is specially seen in the turning back [9] of the leaf towards the sun. One

[6] ἐνίοτε καὶ τὰ ὕπτια conj. W.; λεῖα δὲ καὶ τὰ τοῦ κιττοῦ MSS. A makeshift correction of an obscure passage.
[7] *cf.* Plin. *l.c.*    [8] i.e. is the under one.
[9] Whereby the under surface is exposed to it: see above.

THEOPHRASTUS

ἄν τις ὅσα πυκνὰ καὶ κατ᾽ ἄλληλα, καθάπερ τὰ τῶν μυρρίνων.

3 Οἴονται δέ τινες καὶ τὴν τροφὴν τῷ ὑπτίῳ διὰ τοῦ πρανοῦς εἶναι, διὰ τὸ ἔνικμον ἀεὶ τοῦτο καὶ χνοῶδες εἶναι, οὐ καλῶς λέγοντες. ἀλλὰ τοῦτο μὲν ἴσως συμβαίνει χωρὶς τῆς ἰδίας φύσεως καὶ διὰ τὸ μὴ ὁμοίως ἡλιοῦσθαι, ἡ δὲ τροφὴ διὰ τῶν φλεβῶν ἢ ἰνῶν ὁμοίως ἀμφοτέροις· ἐκ θατέρου δ᾽ εἰς θάτερον οὐκ εὔλογον μὴ ἔχουσι πόρους μηδὲ βάθος δι᾽ οὗ· ἀλλὰ περὶ μὲν τροφῆς διὰ τίνων ἕτερος λόγος.

4 Διαφέρουσι δὲ καὶ τὰ φύλλα πλείοσι διαφοραῖς· τὰ μὲν γάρ ἐστι πλατύφυλλα, καθάπερ ἄμπελος συκῆ πλάτανος, τὰ δὲ στενόφυλλα, καθάπερ ἐλάα ῥόα μύρρινος· τὰ δ᾽ ὥσπερ ἀκανθόφυλλα, καθάπερ πεύκη πίτυς κέδρος· τὰ δ᾽ οἷον σαρκόφυλλα· τοῦτο δ᾽ ὅτι σαρκῶδες ἔχουσι τὸ φύλλον, οἷον κυπάριττος μυρίκη μηλέα, τῶν δὲ φρυγανικῶν κνέωρος στοιβὴ καὶ ποιωδῶν ἀείζωον πόλιον· [τοῦτο δὲ καὶ πρὸς τοὺς σῆτας τοὺς ἐν τοῖς ἱματίοις ἀγαθόν·] τὰ γὰρ αὖ τῶν τευτλίων ἢ ῥαφάνων ἄλλον τρόπον σαρκώδη καὶ τὰ τῶν πηγανίων καλουμένων· ἐν πλάτει γὰρ καὶ οὐκ ἐν στρογγυλότητι τὸ σαρκῶδες. καὶ τῶν θαμνωδῶν
5 δὲ ἡ μυρίκη σαρκῶδες τὸ φύλλον ἔχει. ἔνια δὲ

---

[1] cf. 1. 8. 3 ; 1. 10. 8 ; Plin. 16. 92.
[2] ἐκ θατέρου δ᾽ εἰς conj. Sch. from G ; δὲ ἐκ θατέρου εἰς with stop at ἰνῶν Ald.    [3] δι᾽ οὗ I conj.; δι᾽ ὧν U.
[4] ἀκανθόφυλλα conj. W. ; σπανόφυλλα UMAld.; ἀνόφυλλα P₂; cf. 3. 9. 5, whence Sch. conj. τριχόφυλλα: Plin. l.c. has capillata pino cedro.
[5] μηλέα probably corrupt ; omitted by Plin. l.c.

70

may observe this in trees whose leaves are crowded and opposite,[1] such as those of myrtle.

Some think that the nourishment too is conveyed to the upper surface through the under surface, because this surface always contains moisture and is downy, but they are mistaken. It may be that this is not due to the trees' special character, but to their not getting an equal amount of sunshine, though the nourishment conveyed through the veins or fibres is the same in both cases. That it should be conveyed from one side to the other[2] is improbable, when there are no passages for it nor thickness for it to pass through.[3] However it belongs to another part of the enquiry to discuss the means by which nourishment is conveyed

Again there are various other differences between leaves; some trees are broad-leaved, as vine fig and plane, some narrow-leaved, as olive pomegranate myrtle. Some have, as it were, spinous[4] leaves, as fir Aleppo pine prickly cedar: some, as it were, fleshy leaves; and this is because their leaves are of fleshy substance, as cypress tamarisk apple,[5] among under-shrubs *kueoros* and *stoibe*, and among herbaceous plants house-leek and hulwort. [6] This plant is good against moth in clothes. For the leaves of beet and cabbage are fleshy in another way, as are those of the various plants called rue: for their fleshy character is seen in the flat instead of in the round.[7] Among shrubby plants the tamarisk[8] has fleshy

[6] Probably a gloss.

[7] Or 'solid,' such leaves being regarded as having, so to speak, three, and not two dimensions. στρόγγυλος = 'thickset' in Arist. *H.A.* 9. 44.

[8] μυρίκη probably corrupt: u. was mentioned just above, among *trees*; ἐρείκη conj. Dalec.

καὶ καλαμόφυλλα, καθάπερ ὁ φοῖνιξ καὶ ὁ κόιξ
καὶ ὅσα τοιαῦτα· ταῦτα δὲ ὡς καθ᾽ ὅλου εἰπεῖν
γωνιόφυλλα· καὶ γὰρ ὁ κάλαμος καὶ ὁ κύπειρος
καὶ ὁ βούτομος καὶ τἆλλα δὲ τῶν λιμνωδῶν
τοιαῦτα· πάντα δὲ ὥσπερ ἐκ δυοῖν σύνθετα καὶ
τὸ μέσον οἷον τρόπις, οὗ ἐν τοῖς ἄλλοις μέγας
πόρος ὁ μέσος. διαφέρουσι δὲ καὶ τοῖς σχήμασι·
τὰ μὲν γὰρ περιφερῆ, καθάπερ τὰ τῆς ἀπίου, τὰ
δὲ προμηκέστερα, καθάπερ τὰ τῆς μηλέας· τὰ δὲ
εἰς ὀξὺ προήκοντα καὶ παρακανθίζοντα, καθάπερ
τὰ τοῦ μίλακος. καὶ ταῦτα μὲν ἄσχιστα· <τὰ δὲ
σχιστὰ> καὶ οἷον πριονώδη, καθάπερ τὰ τῆς
ἐλάτης καὶ τὰ τῆς πτερίδος· τρόπον δέ τινα
σχιστὰ καὶ τὰ τῆς ἀμπέλου, καὶ τὰ τῆς συκῆς
6 δὲ ὥσπερ ἂν εἴποι τις κορωνοποδώδη. ἔνια δὲ
καὶ ἐντομὰς ἔχοντα, καθάπερ τὰ τῆς πτελέας καὶ
τὰ τῆς Ἡρακλεωτικῆς καὶ τὰ τῆς δρυός. τὰ δὲ
καὶ παρακανθίζοντα καὶ ἐκ τοῦ ἄκρου καὶ ἐκ τῶν
πλαγίων, οἷον τὰ τῆς πρίνου καὶ τὰ τῆς δρυὸς
καὶ μίλακος καὶ βάτου καὶ παλιούρου καὶ τὰ τῶν
ἄλλων. ἀκανθώδες δὲ ἐκ τῶν ἄκρων καὶ τὸ τῆς
πεύκης καὶ πίτυος καὶ ἐλάτης ἔτι δὲ κέδρου καὶ
κεδρίδος. φυλλάκανθον δὲ ὅλως ἐν μὲν τοῖς
δένδροις οὐκ ἔστιν οὐδὲν ὧν ἡμεῖς ἴσμεν, ἐν δὲ
τοῖς ἄλλοις ὑλήμασίν ἐστιν, οἷον ἥ τε ἄκορνα καὶ
ἡ δρυπὶς καὶ ὁ ἄκανος καὶ σχεδὸν ἅπαν τὸ τῶν
ἀκανωδῶν γένος· ὥσπερ γὰρ φύλλον ἐστὶν ἡ
ἄκανθα πᾶσιν· εἰ δὲ μὴ φύλλα τις ταῦτα θήσει,

---

¹ Plin. l.c. and 13. 30.  ² οὗ ἐν conj. W.; ὅθεν Ald. H.
³ παρακανθίζοντα conj. Sch.; παραγωνίζοντα UMV Ald.
⁴ τὰ δὲ σχιστὰ add. W.

leaves. Some again have reedy leaves, as date-palm
doum-palm and such like. But, generally speaking,
the leaves of these end in a point; for reeds galingale sedge and the leaves of other marsh plants are
of this character. [1] The leaves of all these are com-
pounded of two parts, and the middle is like a keel,
placed where in [2] other leaves is a large passage
dividing the two halves. Leaves differ also in their
shapes; some are round, as those of pear, some
rather oblong, as those of the apple; some come to a
sharp point and have spinous projections [3] at the
side, as those of smilax. So far I have spoken of
undivided leaves; but some are divided [4] and like
a saw, as those of silver-fir and of fern. To a
certain extent those of the vine are also divided,
while those of the fig one might compare to a crow's
foot. [5] [6] Some leaves again have notches, as those of
elm filbert and oak, others have spinous projections
both at the tip and at the edges, as those of kermes-
oak oak smilax bramble Christ's thorn and others.
The leaf of fir Aleppo pine silver-fir and also of prickly
cedar and *kedris* (juniper) [7] has a spinous point at
the tip. Among other trees there is none that we
know which has spines for leaves altogether, but it
is so with other woody plants, as *akorna drypis* pine-
thistle and almost all the plants which belong to
that class. [8] For in all these spines, as it were, take
the place of leaves, and, if one is not to reckon these

---

[5] κορωνοποδώδη conj. Gesner. The fig-leaf is compared to a
crow's foot, Plut. *de defect. orac.* 3: σκολοπώδη Ald., which
word is applied to thorns by Diosc. [6] Plin. 16. 90.
[7] κεδρίδος conj. Dalec.; κεδρίας MSS. cf. Plin. *l.c.*, who
seems to have read ἀγρίας.
[8] ἀκανωδῶν conj. W., cf. 1. 13. 3: ἀκανθωδῶν MSS.; ἀκανθῶν P₂.

συμβαίνοι ἂν ὅλως ἄφυλλα εἶναι, ἐνίοις δὲ ἄκανθαν μὲν εἶναι φύλλον δὲ ὅλως οὐκ ἔχειν, καθάπερ ὁ ἀσφάραγος.

7 Πάλιν δ' ὅτι τὰ μὲν ἄμισχα, καθάπερ τὰ τῆς σκίλλης καὶ τοῦ βολβοῦ, τὰ δ' ἔχοντα μίσχον. καὶ τὰ μὲν μακρόν, οἷον ἡ ἄμπελος καὶ ὁ κιττός, τὰ δὲ βραχὺν καὶ οἷον ἐμπεφυκότα, καθάπερ ἐλάα καὶ οὐχ ὥσπερ ἐπὶ τῆς πλατάνου καὶ ἀμπέλου προσηρτημένον. διαφορὰ δὲ καὶ τὸ μὴ ἐκ τῶν αὐτῶν εἶναι τὴν πρόσφυσιν, ἀλλὰ τοῖς μὲν πλείστοις ἐκ τῶν κλάδων τοῖς δὲ καὶ ἐκ τῶν ἀκρεμόνων, τῆς δρυὸς δὲ καὶ ἐκ τοῦ στελέχους, τῶν δὲ λαχανωδῶν τοῖς πολλοῖς εὐθὺς ἐκ τῆς ῥίζης, οἷον κρομύου σκόρδου κιχορίου, ἔτι δὲ ἀσφοδέλου σκίλλης βολβοῦ σισυριγχίου καὶ ὅλως τῶν βολβωδῶν· καὶ τούτων δὲ οὐχ ἡ πρώτη μόνον ἔκφυσις ἀλλὰ καὶ ὅλος ὁ καυλὸς ἄφυλλον. ἐνίων δ' ὅταν γένηται, φύλλα εἰκός, οἷον θριδακίνης ὠκίμου σελίνου καὶ τῶν σιτηρῶν ὁμοίως. ἔχει δ' ἔνια τούτων καὶ τὸν καυλὸν εἶτ' ἀκανθίζοντα, ὡς ἡ θριδακίνη καὶ τὰ φυλλάκανθα πάντα καὶ τῶν θαμνωδῶν δὲ καὶ ἔτι μᾶλλον, οἷον βάτος παλίουρος.

8 Κοινὴ δὲ διαφορὰ πάντων ὁμοίως δένδρων καὶ τῶν ἄλλων ὅτι τὰ μὲν πολύφυλλα τὰ δ' ὀλιγόφυλλα. ὡς δ' ἐπὶ τὸ πᾶν τὰ πλατύφυλλα ταξίφυλλα, καθάπερ μύρρινος, τὰ δ' ἄτακτα καὶ ὡς ἔτυχε, καθάπερ σχεδὸν τὰ πλεῖστα τῶν ἄλλων

---

[1] Plin. 16. 91.  [2] ἐπὶ conj. W.; ἡ Ald.H.
[3] ἐνίων . . . εἰκός. So Sch. explains : text probably defective.

74

as leaves, they would be entirely leafless, and some
would have spines but no leaves at all, as asparagus.

[1] Again there is the difference that some leaves
have no leaf-stalk, as those of squill and purse-
tassels, while others have a leaf-stalk. And some
of the latter have a long leaf-stalk, as vine
and ivy, some, as olive, a short one which grows, as
it were, into the stem and is not simply attached to
it, as it is in [2] plane and vine. Another difference is
that the leaves do not in all cases grow from the
same part, but, whereas in most trees they grow from
the branches, in some they grow also from the twigs,
and in the oak from the stem as well; in most
pot-herbs they grow directly from the root, as in
onion garlic chicory, and also in asphodel squill
purse-tassels Barbary-nut, and generally in plants
of the same class as purse-tassels; and in these
not merely the original growth but the whole
stalk is leafless. In some, when the stalk is produced, the leaves may be expected to grow,[3] as in
lettuce basil celery, and in like manner in cereals.
In some of these the stalk presently becomes spinous,
as in lettuce and the whole class of plants with
spinous leaves, and still more in shrubby plants, as
bramble and Christ's thorn.

[4] Another difference which is found in all trees
alike and in other plants as well is that some have
many, some few leaves. And in general those that
have flat leaves[5] have them in a regular series, as
myrtle, while in other instances the leaves are in no
particular order, but set at random, as in most other

[4] Plin. 16. 92.
[5] πλατύφυλλα UVP; πολύφυλλα conj. W.; but πλατύτης is
one of the 'differences' given in the summary below.

THEOPHRASTUS

[ἦν]. ἴδιον δὲ ἐπὶ τῶν λαχανωδῶν, οἶον κρομύου γητείου, τὸ κοιλόφυλλον.

Ἁπλῶς δ' αἱ διαφοραὶ τῶν φύλλων ἢ μεγέθει ἢ πλήθει ἢ σχήματι ἢ πλατύτητι ἢ στενότητι ἢ κοιλότητι ἢ τραχύτητι ἢ λειότητι καὶ τῷ παρακανθίζειν ἢ μή. ἔτι δὲ κατὰ τὴν πρόσφυσιν ὅθεν ἢ δι' οὗ· τὸ μὲν ὅθεν, ἀπὸ ῥίζης ἢ κλάδου ἢ καυλοῦ ἢ ἀκρεμόνος· τὸ δὲ δι' οὗ, ἢ διὰ μίσχου ἢ δι' αὐτοῦ καὶ εἰ δὴ πολλὰ ἐκ τοῦ αὐτοῦ. καὶ ἔνια καρποφόρα, μεταξὺ περιειληφότα τὸν καρπόν, ὥσπερ ἡ Ἀλεξανδρεία δάφνη ἐπιφυλλόκαρπος. Αἱ μὲν οὖν διαφοραὶ τῶν φύλλων κοινοτέρως πᾶσαι εἴρηνται καὶ σχεδόν εἰσιν ἐν τούτοις.

(Σύγκειται δὲ τὰ μὲν ἐξ ἰνὸς καὶ φλοιοῦ καὶ σαρκός, οἶον τὰ τῆς συκῆς καὶ τῆς ἀμπέλου, τὰ δὲ ὥσπερ ἐξ ἰνὸς μόνον, οἶον τοῦ καλάμου καὶ σίτου. τὸ δὲ ὑγρὸν ἁπάντων κοινόν· ἅπασι γὰρ ἐνυπάρχει καὶ τούτοις καὶ τοῖς ἄλλοις τοῖς ἐπετείοις [μίσχος ἄνθος καρπὸς εἴ τι ἄλλο]· μᾶλλον δὲ καὶ τοῖς μὴ ἐπετείοις· οὐδὲν γὰρ ἄνευ τούτου. δοκεῖ δὲ καὶ τῶν μίσχων τὰ μὲν ἐξ ἰνῶν μόνον συγκεῖσθαι, καθάπερ τὰ τοῦ σίτου καὶ τοῦ καλάμου, τὰ δ' ἐκ τῶν αὐτῶν, ὥσπερ οἱ καυλοί.

---

¹ τῶν ἄλλων ἦν MSS.; τῶν ποιωδῶν conj. W. ἦν, at all events, cannot be right.   ² Plin. 19. 100.
³ ἢ στενότητι ἢ κοιλότητι: so G; ἢ κοιλότητι ἢ στενότητι MSS.   ⁴ i.e. petiolate.   ⁵ i.e. sessile.
⁶ i.e. compound: εἰ δὴ conj. W.: εἴδη UMVAld.
⁷ The passage from here to the end of the chapter is a digression.

76

plants.[1]  [2] It is peculiar to pot-herbs to have hollow leaves, as in onion and horn-onion.

To sum up, the differences between leaves are shewn in size, number, shape, hollowness, in breadth,[3] roughness and their opposites, and in the presence or absence of spinous projections; also as to their attachment, according to the part from which they spring or the means by which they are attached; the part from which they spring being the root or a branch or the stalk or a twig, while the means by which they are attached may be a leaf-stalk,[4] or they may be attached directly;[5] and there may be[6] several leaves attached by the same leaf-stalk. Further some leaves are fruit-bearing, enclosing the fruit between them, as the Alexandrian laurel, which has its fruit attached to the leaves.

These are all the differences in leaves stated somewhat generally, and this is a fairly complete list of examples.

*Composition of the various parts of a plant.*

[7] (Leaves are composed some of fibre bark and flesh, as those of the fig and vine, some, as it were, of fibre alone, as those of reeds and corn. But moisture is common to all, for it is found both in leaves and in the other annual parts,[8] leaf-stalk, flower, fruit and so forth but more especially in the parts which are not annual[9]; in fact no part is without it. Again it appears that some leaf-stalks are composed only of fibre, as those of corn and reeds, some of the same materials as the stalks.

[8] μίσχος . . . ἄλλο has no construction; probably a (correct) gloss, taken from 1, 2. 1.
[9] i.e. while these are young, W.

10 Τῶν δ' ἀνθῶν τὰ μὲν ἐκ φλοιοῦ καὶ φλεβὸς καὶ
σαρκός, <τὰ δ' ἐκ σαρκὸς> μόνον, οἷον τὰ ἐν μέσῳ
τῶν ἄρων.

Ὁμοίως δὲ καὶ ἐπὶ τῶν καρπῶν· οἱ μὲν γὰρ ἐκ
σαρκὸς καὶ ἰνός, οἱ δὲ ἐκ σαρκὸς μόνον, οἱ δὲ καὶ
ἐκ δέρματος σύγκεινται· τὸ δὲ ὑγρὸν ἀκολουθεῖ
καὶ τούτοις. ἐκ σαρκὸς μὲν καὶ ἰνὸς ὁ τῶν
κοκκυμήλων καὶ σικύων, ἐξ ἰνὸς δὲ καὶ δέρματος
ὁ τῶν συκαμίνων καὶ τῆς ῥόας. ἄλλοι δὲ κατ'
ἄλλον τρόπον μεμερισμένοι. πάντων δὲ ὡς
εἰπεῖν τὸ μὲν ἔξω φλοιὸς τὸ δ' ἐντὸς σὰρξ τῶν δὲ
καὶ πυρήν.)

XI. Ἔσχατον δ' ἐν ἅπασι τὸ σπέρμα. τοῦτο
δὲ ἔχον ἐν ἑαυτῷ σύμφυτον ὑγρὸν καὶ θερμόν, ὧν
ἐκλιπόντων ἄγονα, καθάπερ τὰ ᾠά. καὶ τῶν μὲν
εὐθὺ τὸ σπέρμα μετὰ τὸ περιέχον, οἷον φοίνικος
καρύου ἀμυγδάλης, πλείω δὲ τούτων τὰ ἐμπερι-
έχοντα, ὡς τὰ τοῦ φοίνικος. τῶν δὲ μεταξὺ σὰρξ
καὶ πυρήν, ὥσπερ ἐλάας καὶ κοκκυμηλέας καὶ
ἑτέρων. ἔνια δὲ καὶ ἐν λοβῷ, τὰ δ' ἐν ὑμένι, τὰ
δ' ἐν ἀγγείῳ, τὰ δὲ καὶ γυμνόσπερμα τελείως.

2 Ἐν λοβῷ μὲν οὐ μόνον τὰ ἐπέτεια, καθάπερ τὰ
χεδροπὰ καὶ ἕτερα πλείω τῶν ἀγρίων, ἀλλὰ καὶ
τῶν δένδρων ἔνια, καθάπερ ἥ τε κερωνία, ἥν τινες
καλοῦσι συκῆν Αἰγυπτίαν, καὶ ἡ κερκὶς καὶ ἡ
κολοιτία περὶ Λιπάραν· ἐν ὑμένι δ' ἔνια τῶν

---

¹ τὰ U ; τὸ Ald.
² τὰ δ' ἐκ σαρκὸς preserved only in mBas.; om. UMVP₂.
Sch. reads τὸ.
² ἄρων conj. W.; αἰρῶν MSS.    ⁴ i.e. rind.
⁵ Plin. 18. 53.    ⁶ οὐ conj. Sch.; οὖν Ald.H.

Of flowers some [1] are composed of bark veins and flesh, some of flesh only,[2] as those in the middle of cuckoo-pint.[3]

So too with fruits ; some are made of flesh and fibre, some of flesh alone, and some of skin [4] also. And moisture is necessarily found in these also. The fruit of plums and cucumbers is made of flesh and fibre, that of mulberries and pomegranates of fibre and skin. The materials are differently distributed in different fruits, but of nearly all the outside is bark, the inside flesh, and this in some cases includes a stone.)

*Differences in seeds.*

XI. Last in all plants comes the seed. This possesses in itself natural moisture and warmth, and, if these fail, the seeds are sterile, like eggs in the like case. In some plants the seed comes immediately inside the envelope, as in date filbert almond (however, as in the case of the date, there may be more than one covering). In some cases again there is flesh and a stone between the envelope and the seed, as in olive plum and other fruits. Some seeds again are enclosed in a pod, some in a husk, some in a vessel, and some are completely naked.

[5] Enclosed in a pod are not [6] only the seeds of annual plants, as leguminous plants, and of considerable numbers of wild plants, but also those of certain trees, as the carob-tree (which some [7] call the 'Egyptian fig'), Judas-tree,[8] and the *koloitia* [9] of the Liparae islands. In a husk are enclosed the

[7] ἤν τινες conj. St. from G ; ἤντινα Ald. H.
[8] Clearly not the κερκίς (aspen) described 3. 14. 2.
[9] κολοιτία MSS. ; κολουτέα conj. St., *cf.* 3. 17. 2 n.

ἐπετείων, ὥσπερ ὁ πυρὸς καὶ ὁ κέγχρος· ὡσαύτως
δὲ καὶ ἐναγγειοσπέρματα καὶ γυμνοσπέρματα.
ἐναγγειοσπέρματα μὲν οἷον ἥ τε μήκων καὶ ὅσα
μηκωνικά· τὸ γὰρ σήσαμον ἰδιωτέρως· γυμνοσπέρματα δὲ τῶν τε λαχάνων πολλά, καθάπερ
ἄνηθον κορίαννον ἄννησον κύμινον μάραθον καὶ
3 ἕτερα πλείω. τῶν δὲ δένδρων οὐδὲν γυμνόσπερμον
ἀλλ' ἡ σαρξὶ περιεχόμενον ἡ κελύφεσιν, τὰ μὲν
δερματικοῖς, ὥσπερ ἡ βάλανος καὶ τὸ Εὐβοϊκόν,
τὰ δὲ ξυλώδεσιν, ὥσπερ ἡ ἀμυγδάλη καὶ τὸ
κάρυον. οὐδὲν δὲ ἐναγγειόσπερμον, εἰ μή τις τὸν
κῶνον ἀγγεῖον θήσει διὰ τὸ χωρίζεσθαι τῶν
καρπῶν.
Αὐτὰ δὲ τὰ σπέρματα τῶν μὲν εὐθὺ σαρκώδη,
καθάπερ ὅσα καρυηρὰ καὶ βαλανηρά· τῶν δὲ ἐν
πυρῆνι τὸ σαρκῶδες ἔχεται, καθάπερ ἐλάας καὶ
δαφνίδος καὶ ἄλλων. τῶν δ' ἐμπύρηνα μόνον ἡ
πυρηνώδη γε καὶ ὥσπερ ξηρά, καθάπερ τὰ
κνηκώδη καὶ κεγχραμιδώδη καὶ πολλὰ τῶν
λαχανηρῶν. ἐμφανέστατα δὲ τὰ τοῦ φοίνικος·
οὐδὲ γὰρ κοιλότητα ἔχει τοῦτο οὐδεμίαν ἀλλ'
ὅλον ξηρόν· οὐ μὴν ἀλλ' ὑγρότης δή τις καὶ
θερμότης ὑπάρχει δῆλον ὅτι καὶ τούτῳ, καθάπερ
εἴπομεν.

---

¹ μηκωνικὰ . . . τὸ γὰρ conj. W. from G ; μήκωνι κατὰ γὰρ
UMVAld.
² κορίαννον ἄννησον conj. Sch.; κορίαννησον UMAld.; κο-
ράννησον V ; cf. Plin. 19. 119.
³ ἡ κελύφεσιν conj. Sch., cf. C.P. 4. 1. 2 ; ἡ δὲ κύμασιν U ;
Plin. 15. 112, crusta teguntur glandes.        ⁴ Plin. 15. 113.

seeds of some annuals, as wheat and millet; and in like manner some plants have their seeds in a vessel, some have them naked. In a vessel are those of the poppy and plants of the poppy kind;[1] (the case of sesame however is somewhat peculiar), while many pot-herbs have their seeds naked, as dill coriander[2] anise cummin fennel and many others. No tree has naked seeds, but either they are enclosed in flesh or in shells,[3] which are sometimes of leathery nature, as the acorn and the sweet chestnut, sometimes woody, as almond and nut. Moreover no tree has its seeds in a vessel, unless one reckons a cone as a vessel, because it can be separated from the fruits.

The actual seeds are in some cases fleshy in themselves, as all those which resemble nuts or acorns;[4] in some cases the fleshy part is contained in a stone, as in olive bay and others. The seeds in some plants again merely consist of a stone,[5] or at least are of stone-like character, and are, as it were,[6] dry; for instance those of plants like safflower millet and many pot-herbs. Most obviously of this character are those of the date,[7] for they contain no cavity, but are throughout dry[8];—not but what there must be even in them some moisture and warmth, as we have said.[9]

[5] ἐμπύρηνα μόνον ἢ πυρηνώδη conj. Sch.; ἐν πυρῆνι μόνον ἢ πυρηνώδει Ald. (P has πυρηνώδη .

[6] i.e. no seed can really be without moisture; cf. 1. 11. 1.

[7] cf. C.P. 5. 18. 4.

[8] ξηρὸν I conj., as required by the next clause; ἔξορθον PAld.; ἔξορρον W. from Sch. conj. The germ in the date-stone is so small as to be undiscoverable, whence the stone seems to be homogeneous throughout, with no cavity for the germ.

[9] 1. 10. 9.

4 Διαφέρουσι δὲ καὶ τῷ τὰ μὲν ἀθρόα μετ'
ἀλλήλων εἶναι, τὰ δὲ διεστῶτα καὶ στοιχηδόν,
ὥσπερ τὰ τῆς κολοκύντης καὶ σικύας καὶ τῶν
δένδρων, ὡς Περσικῆς μηλέας. καὶ τῶν ἀθρόων
τὰ μὲν ἑνί τινι περιέχεσθαι, καθάπερ τὰ τῆς ῥόας
καὶ τῆς ἀπίου καὶ μηλέας καὶ τῆς ἀμπέλου καὶ
συκῆς· τὰ δὲ μετ' ἀλλήλων μὲν εἶναι, μὴ περιέχεσθαι δὲ ὑφ' ἑνός, ὥσπερ τὰ σταχυηρὰ τῶν
ἐπετείων, εἰ μή τις θείη τὸν στάχυν ὡς περιέχον·
οὕτω δ' ἔσται καὶ ὁ βότρυς καὶ τἆλλα τὰ
βοτρυώδη καὶ ὅσα δὴ φέρει δι' εὐβοσίαν καὶ
χώρας ἀρετὴν ἀθρύους τοὺς καρπούς, ὥσπερ ἐν
Συρίᾳ φασὶ καὶ ἄλλοθι τὰς ἐλάας.

5 Ἀλλὰ καὶ αὕτη δοκεῖ τις εἶναι διαφορὰ τὸ τὰ
μὲν ἀφ' ἑνὸς μίσχου καὶ μιᾶς προσφύσεως
ἀθρόα γίνεσθαι, καθάπερ ἐπί τε τῶν βοτρυηρῶν
καὶ σταχυηρῶν εἴρηται μὴ περιεχόμενα κοινῷ
τινι γίνεσθαι· τὰ δὲ μὴ γίνεσθαι. ἐπεὶ καθ'
ἕκαστόν γε λαμβάνοντι τῶν σπερμάτων ἢ τῶν
περιεχόντων ἰδίαν ἀρχὴν ἔχει τῆς προσφύσεως,
οἷον ἥ τε ῥὰξ καὶ ἡ ῥόα καὶ πάλιν ὁ πυρὸς καὶ ἡ
κριθή. ἥκιστα δ' ἂν δόξειεν τὰ τῶν μήλων καὶ
τὰ τῶν ἀπίων, ὅτι συμψαύει τε καὶ περιείληπται
καθάπερ ὑμένι τινι δερματικῷ περὶ ὃν τὸ περι-
6 κάρπιον· ἀλλ' ὅμως καὶ τούτων ἕκαστον ἰδίαν
ἀρχὴν ἔχει καὶ φύσιν· φανερώτατα δὲ τῷ

---

¹ στοιχηδόν conj. W.; σχεδὸν Ald.
² ἑνί τινι conj. Sch.; ἐν τινι Ald.      ³ cf. Plin. 15. 15.
⁴ αὕτη conj. Sch.; αὐτὴ Ald.      ⁵ τὸ conj. W.; τῷ Ald.

Further seeds differ in that in some cases they are massed together, in others they are separated and arranged in rows,[1] as those of the gourd and bottle-gourd, and of some trees, such as the citron. Again of those that are massed together some differ in being contained in a single[2] case, as those of pomegranate pear apple vine and fig; others in being closely associated together, yet not contained in a single case, as, among annuals, those which are in an ear—unless one regards the ear as a case. In that case the grape-cluster and other clustering fruits will come under the description, as well as all those plants which on account of good feeding or excellence of soil bear their fruits massed together,[3] as they say the olive does in Syria and elsewhere.

But this[4] too seems to be a point of difference, that[5] some grow massed together from a single stalk and a single attachment, as has been said in the case of plants with clusters or ears whose seeds do not grow contained in one common case; while others grow otherwise. For in these instances, if one takes each seed or case separately, it has its own special point of attachment, for instance each grape or pomegranate,[6] or again each grain of wheat or barley. This would seem to be least of all the case with the seeds of apples and pears, since[7] these touch one another[8] and are enclosed in a sort of skin-like membrane, outside which is the fruit-case.[9] However each of these too has its own peculiar point of attachment and character; this is most

---

[6] ἥ τε ... ῥόα.: text perhaps defective; ἥ τε ῥὰξ βότρυας καὶ τῆς ῥόας ὁ πυρήν conj. Bod.

[7] ὅτι conj. Sch.: ὅτε U; ὅποι PMAld.

[8] cf. 8. 5. 2.    [9] i.e. pulp.

κεχωρίσθαι τὰ τῆς ῥόας· ὁ γὰρ πυρὴν ἑκάστῳ
προσπέφυκεν, οὐχ ὥσπερ τῶν συκῶν ἄδηλα διὰ
τὴν ὑγρότητα. καὶ γὰρ τούτῳ ἔχουσι διαφορὰν
καίπερ ἀμφότερα περιεχόμενα σαρκώδει τινὶ καὶ τῷ
τοῦτο περιειληφότι μετὰ τῶν ἄλλων· τὰ μὲν γὰρ
περὶ ἕκαστον ἔχει πυρῆνα τὸ σαρκῶδες τοῦτο τὸ
ὑγρόν, αἱ δὲ κεγχραμίδες ὥσπερ κοινόν τι πᾶσαι,
καθάπερ καὶ τὸ γίγαρτον καὶ ὅσα τὸν αὐτὸν ἔχει
τρόπον. ἀλλὰ τὰς μὲν τοιαύτας διαφορὰς τάχ᾽
ἄν τις λάβοι πλείους· ὧν δεῖ τὰς κυριωτάτας καὶ
μάλιστα τῆς φύσεως μὴ ἀγνοεῖν.

XII. Αἱ δὲ κατὰ τοὺς χυλοὺς καὶ τὰ σχήματα
καὶ τὰς ὅλας μορφὰς σχεδὸν φανεραὶ πᾶσιν, ὥστε
μὴ δεῖσθαι λόγου· πλὴν τοσοῦτόν γ᾽ ὅτι σχῆμα
οὐδὲν περικάρπιον εὐθύγραμμον οὐδὲ γωνίας ἔχει.
τῶν δὲ χυλῶν οἱ μέν εἰσιν οἰνώδεις, ὥσπερ ἀμπέλου συκαμίνου μύρτου· οἱ δ᾽ ἐλαώδεις, ὥσπερ
ἐλάας δάφνης καρύας ἀμυγδαλῆς πεύκης πίτυος
ἐλάτης· οἱ δὲ μελιτώδεις, οἷον σύκου φοίνικος
διοσβαλάνου· οἱ δὲ δριμεῖς, οἷον ὀριγάνου θύμβρας
καρδάμου νάπυος· οἱ δὲ πικροί, ὥσπερ ἀψινθίου
κενταυρίου. διαφέρουσι δὲ καὶ ταῖς εὐωδίαις,
οἷον ἀννήσου κεδρίδος· ἐνίων δὲ ὑδαρεῖς ἂν δόξαιεν,
οἷον οἱ τῶν κοκκυμηλέων· οἱ δὲ ὀξεῖς, ὥσπερ ῥοῶν

¹ i.e. of the pulp.　² τούτῳ conj. Sch.; τοῦτο Ald.
³ τὸν om. St.: i.e. the seeds are arranged in compartments
of the pulp.

84

obvious in the separation of the pomegranate seeds,
for the stone is attached to each, and the connexion
is not, as in figs, obscured by the moisture.[1] For
here[2] too there is a difference, although in both
cases the seeds are enclosed in a sort of fleshy
substance, as well as in the case which encloses this
and the other parts of the fruit. For in the pomegranate the stones have this moist fleshy substance
enclosing each[3] separate stone; but in the case of
fig-seeds, as well as in that of grape-stones and other
plants which have the same arrangement, the same
pulp is common to all.[4] However one might find
more such differences, and one should not ignore the
most important of them, namely those which specially
belong to the plant's natural character.

*Differences in taste.*

XII. The differences in taste, shape, and form as
a whole are tolerably evident to all, so that they do
not need explanation; except that it should be
stated that[5] the case containing the fruit is never
right-lined in shape and never has angles. [6] Of
tastes some are like wine, as those of vine mulberry and myrtle; some are like olive-oil, as, besides
olive itself, bay hazel almond fir Aleppo pine silver-
fir; some like honey, as fig date chestnut; some are
pungent, as marjoram savory cress mustard; some
are bitter, as wormwood centaury. Some also are
remarkably fragrant, as anise and juniper[7]; of
some the smell would seem to be insipid,[8] as in
plums; of others sharp, as in pomegranates and

---

[4] *i.e.* the fruit is not divided into compartments.
[5] πλὴν ἢ τοσοῦτον conj. W.: πλὴν τοσοῦτον ἢ UMAld.
[6] Plin. 19. 186; 15. 109.   [7] *cf.* 1. 9. 4.   [8] Lit. watery.

καὶ ἐνίων μήλων. ἁπάντων δὲ οἰνώδεις καὶ τοὺς
ἐν τούτῳ τῷ γένει θετέον· ἄλλοι δὲ ἐν ἄλλοις
εἴδεσιν· ὑπὲρ ὧν ἁπάντων ἀκριβέστερον ἐν τοῖς
περὶ χυλῶν ῥητέον, αὐτάς τε τὰς ἰδέας διαριθμου-
μένους ὁπόσαι καὶ τὰς πρὸς ἀλλήλους διαφορὰς
καὶ τίς ἡ ἑκάστου φύσις καὶ δύναμις.

2 Ἔχει δὲ καὶ ἡ τῶν δένδρων αὐτῶν ὑγρότης,
ὥσπερ ἐλέχθη, διάφορα εἴδη· ἡ μὲν γάρ ἐστιν
ὀπώδης, ὥσπερ ἡ τῆς συκῆς καὶ τῆς μήκωνος· ἡ
δὲ πιττώδης, οἷον ἐλάτης πεύκης τῶν κωνοφόρων·
ἄλλη δ᾽ ὑδαρής, οἷον ἀμπέλου ἀπίου μηλέας, καὶ
τῶν λαχανωδῶν δέ, οἷον σικύου κολοκύντης θριδα-
κίνης· αἱ δὲ [ἤδη] δριμύτητά τινα ἔχουσι, καθάπερ
ἡ τοῦ θύμου καὶ θύμβρας· αἱ δὲ καὶ εὐωδίαν,
ὥσπερ αἱ τοῦ σελίνου ἀνήθου μαράθου καὶ τῶν
τοιούτων. ὡς δ᾽ ἁπλῶς εἰπεῖν ἅπασαι κατὰ τὴν
ἰδίαν φύσιν ἑκάστου δένδρου καὶ ὡς καθ᾽ ὅλου
εἰπεῖν φυτοῦ· πᾶν γὰρ ἔχει κρᾶσίν τινα καὶ μίξιν
ἰδίαν, ἥπερ οἰκεία δῆλον ὅτι τυγχάνει τοῖς ὑπο-
κειμένοις καρποῖς· ὧν τοῖς πλείστοις συνεμφαίνε-
ταί τις ὁμοιότης οὐκ ἀκριβὴς οὐδὲ σαφής· ἀλλ᾽
ἐν τοῖς περικαρπίοις· διὸ μᾶλλον κατεργασίαν
λαμβάνει καὶ πέψιν καθαρὰν καὶ εἰλικρινῆ ἡ τοῦ

---

[1] cf. C.P. 6. 6. 4.
[2] T. is said to have written a treatise περὶ χυμῶν.
[3] ὀπώδης. ὀπός is used specially of the juice of the fig itself.
[4] μήκωνος probably corrupt : it should be a tree.

some kinds of apples. [1] But the smells even of those in this class must in all cases be called wine-like, though they differ in different kinds, on which matter we must speak more precisely, when we come to speak of flavours,[2] reckoning up the different kinds themselves, and stating what differences there are between them, and what is the natural character and property of each.

Now the sap of the trees themselves assumes different kinds of tastes as was said; sometimes it is milky,[3] as that of the fig and poppy,[4] sometimes like pitch, as in silver-fir fir and the conifers; sometimes it is insipid, as in vine pear and apple, as well as such pot-herbs as cucumber gourd lettuce; while others[5] again have a certain pungency, such as the juice of thyme and savory; others have a fragrance, such as the juices of celery dill fennel and the like. To speak generally, all saps correspond to the special character of the several trees, one might almost add, to that of each plant. For every plant has a certain temperament and composition of its own, which[6] plainly belongs in a special sense to the fruits of each. And in most of these is seen a sort of correspondence with the character of the plant as a whole, which is not however exact nor obvious; it is chiefly[7] in the fruit-cases[8] that it is seen, and that is why it is the character of the flavour which becomes more complete and matures into something separate and

---

[5] I have bracketed ἤδη : ? a dittography of αἱ δέ.

[6] ᾗπερ mBas.H ; εἴπερ MAld.

[7] ἀλλ᾽ ἐν . . . μᾶλλον MSS. (?) Ald.H ; γὰρ for διὸ conj. W., omitting stop before it.

[8] i.e. the pulp : so G.  cf. 1. 11. 6.

χυλοῦ φύσις· δεῖ γὰρ ὥσπερ τὸ μὲν ὕλην ὑπο-
λαβεῖν τὸ δὲ εἶδος καὶ μορφήν.

3 Ἔχει δὲ αὐτὰ τὰ σπέρματα καὶ οἱ χιτῶνες οἱ
περὶ αὐτὰ διαφορὰν τῶν χυλῶν. ὡς δ᾽ ἁπλῶς
εἰπεῖν ἅπαντα τὰ μόρια τῶν δένδρων καὶ φυτῶν,
οἷον ῥίζα καυλὸς ἀκρεμὼν φύλλον καρπός, ἔχει
τινὰ οἰκειότητα πρὸς τὴν ὅλην φύσιν, εἰ καὶ
παραλλάττει κατά τε τὰς ὀσμὰς καὶ τοὺς χυλούς,
ὡς τὰ μὲν εὔοσμα καὶ εὐώδη τὰ δ᾽ ἄοσμα καὶ
ἄχυλα παντελῶς εἶναι τῶν τοῦ αὐτοῦ μορίων.

4 Ἐνίων γὰρ εὔοσμα τὰ ἄνθη μᾶλλον ἢ τὰ
φύλλα, τῶν δὲ ἀνάπαλιν τὰ φύλλα μᾶλλον καὶ
οἱ κλῶνες, ὥσπερ τῶν στεφανωματικῶν· τῶν δὲ οἱ
καρποί· τῶν δ᾽ οὐδέτερον· ἐνίων δ᾽ αἱ ῥίζαι· τῶν
δέ τι μέρος. ὁμοίως δὲ καὶ κατὰ τοὺς χυλούς· τὰ
μὲν γὰρ βρωτὰ τὰ δ᾽ ἄβρωτα τυγχάνει καὶ ἐν
φύλλοις καὶ περικαρπίοις. ἰδιώτατον δὲ τὸ ἐπὶ
τῆς φιλύρας· ταύτης γὰρ τὰ μὲν φύλλα γλυκέα
καὶ πολλὰ τῶν ζώων ἐσθίει, ὁ δὲ καρπὸς οὐδενὶ
βρωτός· ἐπεὶ τό γε ἀνάπαλιν οὐδὲν θαυμαστόν,
ὥστε τὰ μὲν φύλλα μὴ ἐσθίεσθαι τοὺς δὲ καρποὺς
οὐ μόνον ὑφ᾽ ἡμῶν ἀλλὰ καὶ ὑπὸ τῶν ἄλλων
ζώων. ἀλλὰ καὶ περὶ τούτου καὶ τῶν ἄλλων
τῶν τοιούτων ὕστερον πειρατέον θεωρεῖν τὰς
αἰτίας.

XIII. Νῦν δὲ τοσοῦτον ἔστω δῆλον, ὅτι κατὰ
πάντα τὰ μέρη πλείους εἰσὶ διαφοραὶ πολλαχῶς·

---

[1] *i.e.* the pulp.　　[2] *i.e.* the flavour.

[3] Sense : Every tree has a characteristic juice of its own,
which is however specially recognisable in its fruit ; in the
tree as a whole its character is not always apparent.　Hence
the importance of the flavour (which is seen in the fruit-
pulp), since it is this which determines the specific character,

distinct; in fact we must consider the one[1] as 'matter,' the other[2] as 'form' or specific character.[3]

Again the seeds themselves and the coats containing them have different flavours. And, to speak generally, all parts of trees and plants, as root stem branch leaf fruit, have a certain relationship to the character of the whole, even if[4] there is variation in scents and tastes, so that of the parts of the same plant some are fragrant and sweet to the taste, while others are entirely scentless and tasteless.

For in some plants the flowers are more fragrant than the leaves, in others on the contrary it is rather the leaves and twigs which are fragrant, as in those used for garlands. In others again it is the fruits; in others it is neither[5] of these parts, but, in some few cases, the root or some part of it. And so too with the flavours. Some leaves and some fruit-pulps are, and some are not good for food. [6] Most peculiar is the case of the lime: the leaves of this are sweet, and many animals eat them, but the fruit no creature eats, (for, as to the contrary case, it would not be at all surprising that the leaves should not be eaten, while the fruits were eaten not only by us but by other animals). But concerning this and other such matters we must endeavour to consider the causes on some other occasion.

### Differences in flowers.

XIII. For the present let so much be clear, that in all the parts of plants there are numerous differ-

the pulp of fruit in general being, in Aristotelian language, the 'matter,' while the flavour is 'form.' cf. C.P. 6. 6. 6.
[4] εἰ καὶ conj. Sch.; ἢ δὲ U; εἰ δὲ MVAld.
[5] οὐδέτερον seems inaccurately used, as four parts have been mentioned. [6] cf. 3 10. 5; Plin 16. 65.

THEOPHRASTUS

ἐπεὶ καὶ τῶν ἀνθῶν τὰ μέν ἐστι χνοώδη, καθάπερ
τὸ τῆς ἀμπέλου καὶ συκαμίνου καὶ τοῦ κιττοῦ·
τὰ δὲ φυλλώδη, καθάπερ ἀμυγδαλῆς μηλέας
ἀπίου κοκκυμηλέας. καὶ τὰ μὲν μέγεθος ἔχει,
τὸ δὲ τῆς ἐλάας φυλλῶδες ὂν ἀμέγεθες. ὁμοίως
δὲ καὶ ἐν τοῖς ἐπετείοις καὶ ποιώδεσι τὰ μὲν
φυλλώδη τὰ δὲ χνοώδη. πάντων δὲ τὰ μὲν δίχροα
τὰ δὲ μονόχροα. τὰ μὲν τῶν δένδρων τά γε
πολλὰ μονόχροα καὶ λευκανθῆ· μόνον γὰρ ὡς
εἰπεῖν τὸ τῆς ῥόας φοινικοῦν καὶ ἀμυγδαλῶν
τινων ὑπέρυθρον· ἄλλου δὲ οὐδενὸς τῶν ἡμέρων
οὔτε ἀνθῶδες οὔτε δίχρουν, ἀλλ᾽ εἴ τινος τῶν
ἀγρίων, οἷον τὸ τῆς ἐλάτης· κρόκινον γὰρ τὸ
ταύτης ἄνθος· καὶ ὅσα δή φασιν ἐν τῇ ἔξω θαλάττῃ ῥόδων ἔχειν τὴν χρόαν.
2 Ἐν δὲ τοῖς ἐπετείοις σχεδὸν τά γε πλείω
τοιαῦτα καὶ δίχροα καὶ διανθῆ. λέγω δὲ διανθὲς
ὅτι ἕτερον ἄνθος ἐν τῷ ἄνθει ἔχει κατὰ μέσον,
ὥσπερ τὸ ῥόδον καὶ τὸ κρίνον καὶ τὸ ἴον τὸ μέλαν.
ἔνια δὲ καὶ μονόφυλλα φύεται διαγραφὴν ἔχοντα
μόνον τῶν πλειόνων, ὥσπερ τὸ τῆς ἰασιώνης· οὐ
γὰρ κεχώρισται ταύτης ἐν τῷ ἄνθει τὸ φύλλον
ἕκαστον· οὐδὲ δὴ τοῦ λειρίου τὸ κάτω μέρος, ἀλλὰ
ἐκ τῶν ἄκρων ἀποφύσεις γωνιώδεις. σχεδὸν δὲ
καὶ τὸ τῆς ἐλάας τοιοῦτόν ἐστιν.
3 Διαφέρει δὲ καὶ κατὰ τὴν ἔκφυσιν καὶ θέσιν·
τὰ μὲν γὰρ ἔχει περὶ αὐτὸν τὸν καρπόν, οἷον ἄμ-

¹ i.e. petaloid.
² ἀγρίων Ald.; αἰτίων U; ἀντιῶν MV; ποντίων conj. W.
³ i.e. corolla and stamens, etc.
⁴ i.e. are gamopetalous (or gamosepalous).
90

ences shewn in a variety of ways. Thus of flowers
some are downy, as that of the vine mulberry and
ivy, some are 'leafy,'[1] as in almond apple pear
plum. Again some of these flowers are conspicuous,
while that of the olive, though it is 'leafy,' is incon-
spicuous. Again it is in annual and herbaceous
plants alike that we find some leafy, some downy.
All plants again have flowers either of two colours or
of one; most of the flowers of trees are of one colour
and white, that of the pomegranate being almost the
only one which is red, while that of some almonds is
reddish. The flower of no other cultivated trees is
gay nor of two colours, though it may be so with
some uncultivated[2] trees, as with the flower of silver-
fir, for its flower is of saffron colour; and so with
the flowers of those trees by the ocean which have,
they say, the colour of roses.

However, among annuals, most are of this character—their flowers are two-coloured and twofold.[3]  I
mean by 'twofold' that the plant has another
flower inside the flower, in the middle, as with rose
lily violet. Some flowers again consist of a single
'leaf,'[4] having merely an indication of more, as that
of bindweed.[5] For in the flower of this the separate
'leaves' are not distinct; nor is it so in the lower
part of the narcissus,[6] but there are angular projections[7] from the edges. And the flower of the olive
is nearly of the same character.

But there are also differences in the way of growth
and the position of the flower; some plants have it

[5] cf. C.P. 2. 18. 2 and 3; Plin. 21. 65.
[6] λειρίου conj. Sch., i.e. narcissus, cf. 6. 6. 9; χειρίου MSS.
[7] i.e. something resembling separate 'leaves' (petals or
sepals).

THEOPHRASTUS

πελος ἐλάα· ἧς καὶ ἀποπίπτοντα διατετρημένα
φαίνεται, καὶ τοῦτο σημεῖον λαμβάνουσιν εἰ
καλῶς ἀπήνθηκεν· ἐὰν γὰρ συγκαυθῇ ἢ βρεχθῇ,
συναποβάλλει τὸν καρπὸν καὶ οὐ τετρημένον
γίγνεται· σχεδὸν δὲ καὶ τὰ πολλὰ τῶν <ἀνθῶν>
ἐν μέσῳ τὸ περικάρπιον ἔχει, τάχα δὲ καὶ ἐπ'
αὐτοῦ τοῦ περικαρπίου, καθάπερ ῥόα μελέα ἄπιος
κοκκυμηλεα μύρρινος, καὶ τῶν γε φρυγανικῶν
ῥοδωνία καὶ τὰ πολλὰ τῶν στεφανωτικῶν· κάτω
γὰρ ὑπὸ τὸ ἄνθος ἔχει τὰ σπέρματα· φανερώτατον δὲ ἐπὶ τοῦ ῥόδου διὰ τὸν ὄγκον. ἔνια δὲ
καὶ ἐπ' αὐτῶν τῶν σπερμάτων, ὥσπερ ὁ ἄκανος
καὶ ὁ κνῆκος καὶ πάντα τὰ ἀκανώδη· καθ' ἕκαστον γὰρ ἔχει τὸ ἄνθος. ὁμοίως δὲ καὶ τῶν
ποιωδῶν ἔνια, καθάπερ τὸ ἄνθεμον· ἐν δὲ τοῖς
λαχανηροῖς ὅ τε σίκυος καὶ ἡ κολοκύντη καὶ ἡ
σικύα· πάντα γὰρ ἐπὶ τῶν καρπῶν ἔχει καὶ
προσαυξανομένων ἐπιμένει τὰ ἄνθη πολὺν χρόνον.
Ἄλλα δὲ ἰδιωτέρως, οἷον ὁ κιττὸς καὶ ἡ συκά-
μινος· ἐν αὐτοῖς μὲν γὰρ ἔχει τοῖς ὅλοις περικαρπίοις, οὐ μὴν οὔτε ἐπ' ἄκροις οὔτ' ἐπὶ
περιειληφόσι καθ' ἕκαστον, ἀλλ' ἐν τοῖς ἀνὰ
μέσον· εἰ μὴ ἄρα οὐ σύνδηλα διὰ τὸ χνοῶδες.
Ἔστι δὲ καὶ ἄγονα τῶν ἀνθῶν ἔνια, καθάπερ
ἐπὶ τῶν σικύων ἃ ἐκ τῶν ἄκρων φύεται τοῦ κλή-

¹ cf. 3. 16. 4.  ² Lacuna in text ; ἀνθῶν I conj.
³ τάχα Ald.; τινα W. after Sch. conj.
⁴ ἄπιος conj. Bod. ; ἄγνος Ald.H.
⁵ i.e. composites.
⁶ σπερμάτων conj. Dalec. from G ; στομάτων Ald.
⁷ ἄκανος conj. W.; ἄκαρος UV.
⁸ ἀκανώδη conj. W.; ἀνθώδη Ald.H.  cf. 1. 10. 6 ; 6. 4. 4.

close above the fruit, as vine and olive; in the latter,
when the flowers drop off, they are seen to have a
hole through them,[1] and this men take for a sign
whether the tree has blossomed well; for if the
flower is burnt up or sodden, it sheds the fruit along
with itself, and so there is no hole through it.  The
majority of flowers[2] have the fruit-case in the middle
of them, or, it may be,[3] the flower is on the top of
the fruit-case, as in pomegranate apple pear[4] plum
and myrtle, and among under-shrubs, in the rose
and in many of the coronary plants.  For these have
their seeds below, beneath the flower, and this is
most obvious in the rose because of the size of the
seed-vessel.  In some cases[5] again the flower is on
top of the actual seeds,[6] as in pine-thistle[7] safflower
and all thistle-like[8] plants; for these have a flower
attached to each seed.  So too with some herbaceous plants, as *anthemon*, and among pot-herbs, with
cucumber[9] gourd and bottle-gourd; all these have
their flowers attached on top of the fruits,[10] and the
flowers persist for a long time while the fruits are
developing.

In some other plants the attachment is peculiar,
as in ivy and mulberry; in these the flower is closely
attached to the whole[11] fruit-case; it is not however
set above it, nor in a seed-vessel that envelops each[12]
separately, but it occurs in the middle part of the
structure—except that in some cases it is not easily
recognised because it is downy.

[13] Again some flowers are sterile, as in cucumbers
those which grow at the ends of the shoot, and that

---

[9] ὅ τε σίκυος conj. W.; ὅπερ σίκυος UM; ὁ περσίκυος Ald.
[10] καρπᾶν conj. Sch.; ἄκρων Ald.H.
[11] *i.e.* compound.    [12] οὔτ' ἐπὶ I conj. for οὔτε.
[13] *cf.* Arist. *Probl.* 20. 3.

ματος, δι' ὃ καὶ ἀφαιροῦσιν αὐτά· κωλύει γὰρ τὴν
τοῦ σικύου βλάστησιν. φασὶ δὲ καὶ τῆς μηλέας
τῆς Μηδικῆς ὅσα μὲν ἔχει τῶν ἀνθῶν ὥσπερ
ἠλακάτην τινὰ πεφυκυῖαν ἐκ μέσου ταῦτ' εἶναι
γόνιμα, ὅσα δὲ μὴ ἔχει ταῦτ' ἄγονα. εἰ δὲ καὶ ἐπ'
ἄλλου τινὸς ταῦτα συμβαίνει τῶν ἀνθοφόρων
ὥστε ἄγονον ἄνθος φύειν εἴτε κεχωρισμένον εἴτε
μή, σκεπτέον. ἐπεὶ γένη γε ἔνια καὶ ἀμπέλου καὶ
ῥόας ἀδυνατεῖ τελεοκαρπεῖν, ἀλλὰ μέχρι τοῦ
ἄνθους ἡ γένεσις.

5 (Γίνεται δὲ καὶ τό γε τῆς ῥόας ἄνθος πολὺ καὶ
πυκνὸν καὶ ὅλως ὁ ὄγκος πλατὺς ὥσπερ ὁ τῶν
ῥόδων· κάτωθεν δ' ἑτεροῖος· οἷος δίωτος μικρὸς
ὥσπερ ἐκτετραμμένος ὁ κύτινος ἔχων τὰ χείλη
μυχώδη.)

Φασὶ δέ τινες καὶ τῶν ὁμογενῶν τὰ μὲν ἀνθεῖν
τὰ δ' οὔ, καθάπερ τῶν φοινίκων τὸν μὲν ἄρρενα
ἀνθεῖν τὸν δὲ θῆλυν οὐκ ἀνθεῖν ἀλλ' εὐθὺ προ-
φαίνειν τὸν καρπόν.

Τὰ μὲν οὖν τῷ γένει ταὐτὰ τοιαύτην τὴν δια-

---

1 i.e. the pistil.
2 i.e. as seen from above: καὶ ὅλων . . . ῥόδων describes the
corolla, κάτωθεν . . . μυχώδη the undeveloped ovary, including
the adherent calyx.
3 ῥόδων conj. Bod.; ῥοῶν Ald.
4 κάτωθεν . . . μυχώδη I conj.; δ' ἕτεροι δι' ὧν ὡς μικρὸν
ὥσπερ ἐκτετραμμένος κύτινος ἔχων τὰ χείλη μυχώδη UMVAld.
(except that Ald. has ἄνω for χείλη and ἐκτετραμμένον: so
also P, but ἐκτετραμμένος). The sentence explains incidentally
why the pomegranate flower was called κύτινος (cf. 2. 6. 12;
C.P. 1. 14. 4; 2. 9. 3; 2. 9. 9; Diosc. 1. 110; Plin. 23. 110

94

is why men pluck them off, for they hinder the growth of the cucumber. And they say that in the citron those flowers which have a kind of distaff[1] growing in the middle are fruitful, but those that have it not are sterile. And we must consider whether it occurs also in any other flowering plants that they produce sterile flowers, whether apart from the fertile flowers or not. For some kinds of vine and pomegranate certainly are unable to mature their fruit, and do not produce anything beyond the flower.

(The flower of the pomegranate is produced abundantly and is solid[2]: in general appearance it is a substantial structure with a flat top, like the flower of the rose[3]; but,[4] as seen from below, the interior part of the flower is different-looking, being like a little two-eared jar turned on one side and having its rim indented.)

Some say that even of plants of the same kind[5] some specimens flower while others do not; for instance that the 'male' date-palm flowers but the 'female' does not, but exhibits its fruit without any antecedent flower.

Such[6] is the difference which we find between

and 111), i.e. because it resembled a κέτος (see LS. s.v.). T. chooses the particular form of jar called δῖπτος, because the indentations between the sepals suggest this : ᗑ. This is called ἐκτετραμμένος, because the weight of the developing fruit causes it to take up at one stage a horizontal position, like a jar lying on its side; χείλη refers to the jar (for the plural cf. the use of ἄντυγες), μυχώδη to the indentations in the calyx (a jar having ordinarily an unindented rim).

[5] ὁμογενῶν conj. Sch.: ὁμοιογενῶν Ald.

[6] ταὐτὰ τοιαύτην I conj. from G : τοιαῦτα τὴν UM : τοιαύτην P.

THEOPHRASTUS

φορὰν ἔχει, καθάπερ ὅλως ὅσα μὴ δύναται τελεοκαρπεῖν. ἡ δὲ τοῦ ἄνθους φύσις ὅτι πλείους ἔχει
διαφορὰς φανερὸν ἐκ τῶν προειρημένων.

XIV. Διαφέρει δὲ τὰ δένδρα καὶ τοῖς τοιούτοις
κατὰ τὴν καρποτοκίαν· τὰ μὲν γὰρ ἐκ τῶν νέων
βλαστῶν φέρει τὰ δ' ἐκ τῶν ἔνων τὰ δ' ἐξ ἀμφοτέρων. ἐκ μὲν τῶν νέων συκῆ ἄμπελος· ἐκ δὲ τῶν
ἔνων ἐλάα ῥόα μηλέα ἀμυγδαλῆ ἄπιος μύρρινος
καὶ σχεδὸν τὰ τοιαῦτα πάντα·¹ ἐκ δὲ τῶν νέων
ἐὰν ἄρα τι συμβῇ κυῆσαι καὶ ἀνθῆσαι (γίνεται
γὰρ καὶ ταῦτ' ἐνίοις, ὥσπερ καὶ τῷ μυρρίνῳ καὶ
μάλισθ' ὡς εἰπεῖν περὶ τὰς βλαστήσεις τὰς μετ'
Ἀρκτοῦρον) οὐ δύναται τελεοῦν ἀλλ' ἡμιγενῆ
φθείρεται· ἐξ ἀμφοτέρων δὲ καὶ τῶν ἔνων καὶ τῶν
νέων εἴ τινες ἄρα μηλέαι τῶν διφόρων⁴ ἢ εἴ τι
ἄλλο κάρπιμον· ἔτι δὲ ὁ ὄλυνθος ἐκπέττων καὶ
σῦκα φέρων ἐκ τῶν νέων.

2    Ἰδιωτάτη δὲ ἡ ἐκ τοῦ στελέχους ἔκφυσις,
ὥσπερ τῆς ἐν Αἰγύπτῳ συκαμίνου· ταύτην γάρ
φασι φέρειν ἐκ τοῦ στελέχους· οἱ δὲ ταύτῃ τε καὶ
ἐκ τῶν ἀκρεμόνων, ὥσπερ τὴν κερωνίαν· αὕτη γὰρ
καὶ ἐκ τούτων φέρει πλὴν οὐ πολύν· καλοῦσι δὲ
κερωνίαν ἀφ' ἧς τὰ σῦκα τὰ Αἰγύπτια καλούμενα.

---

¹ ? i.e. that, like the 'female' date-palm, they have no
flower.
² τοιαῦτα πάντα· ἐκ δὲ τῶν νέων ἐὰν ἄρα τι conj. W. ; τοιαῦτα·
πάντα γὰρ ἐκ τῶν ἔνων· ἐὰν δὲ ἄρα τι MSS.
³ cf. 3. 5. 4.
⁴ διφόρων conj. Sch. from G ; διαφόρων UAld.

96

plants of the same kind ; and the like may be said [1]
in general of those which cannot mature their fruit.
And it is plain from what has been said that flowers
shew many differences of character.

### Differences in fruits.

XIV. Again as to the production of fruit trees
differ in the following respects. Some bear on their
new shoots, some on last year's wood, some on both.
Fig and vine bear on their new shoots : on last year's
wood olive pomegranate apple almond pear myrtle
and almost all such trees. And, if any of these does [2]
happen to conceive and to produce flowers on its new
shoots, (for this does occur in some cases, as with
myrtle, and especially, one may say, in the growth
which is made after the rising of Arcturus) [3] it can
not bring them to perfection, but they perish half-
formed. Some apples again of the twice-bearing [4]
kinds and certain other fruit-trees bear both on last
year's wood and on the new shoots ; and so does the
*olynthos*,[5] which ripens its fruit as well as bearing figs
on the new shoots.

Most peculiar is the growth of fruit direct from
the stem, as in the sycamore ; for this, they say,
bears fruit on the stem. Others say that it bears
both in this way and [6] also on the branches, like the
carob ; for the latter bears on the branches too,
though not abundantly : (the name carob is given to
the tree which produces what are called 'Egyptian

[5] ὄλυνθος is not elsewhere used for a kind of fig : ἔτι δὲ
συκῆ τους ὀλύνθους ἐκπέττουσα καὶ σῦκα φέρουσα conj. Sch.
somewhat drastically.

[6] ταύτῃ τε καὶ ἐκ conj. W.; ταύτης μὲν ἐκ UMVAld. cf.
4. 2. 4.

## THEOPHRASTUS

ἔστι δὲ καὶ τὰ μὲν ἀκρόκαρπα τῶν δένδρων καὶ ὅλως τῶν φυτῶν τὰ δὲ πλαγιόκαρπα τὰ δ' ἀμφοτέρως. πλείω δ' ἀκρόκαρπα τῶν ἄλλων ἢ τῶν δένδρων, οἷον τῶν τε σιτηρῶν τὰ σταχυώδη καὶ τῶν θαμνωδῶν ἐρείκη καὶ σπειραία καὶ ἄγνος καὶ ἀλλ' ἄττα καὶ τῶν λαχανωδῶν τὰ κεφαλόρριζα. ἐξ ἀμφοτέρων δὲ καὶ τῶν δένδρων ἔνια καὶ τῶν λαχανωδῶν, οἷον βλίτον ἀδράφαξυς ῥάφανος· ἐπεὶ καὶ ἐλάα ποιεῖ πως τοῦτο,¹ καί φασιν ὅταν ἄκρον ἐνέγκῃ σημεῖον εὐφορίας εἶναι. ἀκρόκαρπος δέ πως καὶ ὁ φοῖνιξ· πλὴν τοῦτό² γε καὶ ἀκρόφυλλον καὶ ἀκρόβλαστον· ὅλως γὰρ ἐν τῷ ἄνω πᾶν τὸ ζωτικόν.   τὰς μὲν οὖν κατὰ <τὰ>³ μέρη διαφορὰς πειρατέον ἐκ τούτων θεωρεῖν.

3   Αἱ δὲ τοιαῦται τῆς ὅλης οὐσίας φαίνονται· δῆλον ὅτι τὰ μὲν ἥμερα τὰ δ' ἄγρια· καὶ τὰ μὲν κάρπιμα τὰ δ' ἄκαρπα· καὶ ἀείφυλλα καὶ φυλλοβόλα, καθάπερ ἐλέχθη, τὰ δ' ὅλως ἄφυλλα· καὶ τὰ μὲν ἀνθητικὰ τὰ δ' ἀνανθῆ· καὶ πρωϊβλαστῆ δὲ καὶ πρωΐκαρπα τὰ δὲ ὀψιβλαστῆ καὶ ὀψίκαρπα· ὡσαύτως δὲ καὶ ὅσα παραπλήσια τούτοις. καί πως τά γε τοιαῦτα ἐν τοῖς μέρεσιν ἢ οὐκ ἄνευ τῶν μερῶν ἐστιν. ἀλλ' ἐκείνη ἰδιωτάτη καὶ τρόπον τινὰ μεγίστη διάστασις, ἥπερ καὶ ἐπὶ τῶν ζῴων, ὅτι τὰ μὲν ἔνυδρα τὰ δὲ χερσαῖα· καὶ γὰρ τῶν φυτῶν

---

¹ Plin. 16. 112.
² τοῦτο conj. Sch.; τούτου UAld. ; τοῦτον M.
³ τὰ add. W.; cf. 1. 13. 1.

98

figs '). [1] Again some trees, and some plants in general, produce fruit at the top, others at the sides, others in both ways. But bearing fruit at the top is less common in trees than in other plants, as among grains in those which have an ear, among shrubby plants in heath privet chaste tree and certain others, and among pot-herbs in those with a bulbous root. Among plants which bear both on the top and at the sides are certain trees and certain pot-herbs, as blite orach cabbage. I say trees, since the olive does this too in a way, and they say that, when it bears at the top, it is a sign of fruitfulness. The date-palm too bears at the top, in a sense, but this [2] tree also has its leaves and shoots at the top; indeed it is in the top that its whole activity is seen. Thus we must endeavour to study in the light of the instances mentioned the differences seen in the [3] various parts of the plant.

*General differences (affecting the whole plant).*

But there appear to be the following differences which affect the plant's whole being : some are cultivated, some wild ; some fruitful, some barren ; some evergreen, some deciduous, as was said, while some again have no leaves at all ; some are flowering plants, some flowerless; some are early, some late in producing their shoots and fruits; and there are other differences similar to these. Now it may be said that [4] such differences are seen in the parts, or at least that particular parts are concerned in them. But the special, and in a way the most important distinction is one which may be seen in animals too, namely, that some are of the water, some of the land. For

[4] καί πως τά γε τοιαῦτα conj. Sch. ; καί πᾶν τά γε ταῦτα U ; καί τά γε τοιαῦτα Ald.

ἔστι τι τοιοῦτον γένος ὃ οὐ δύναται φύεσθαι <μὴ>
ἐν ὑγρῷ· τὰ δὲ φύεται μέν, οὐχ ὅμοια δὲ ἀλλὰ
χείρω. πάντων δὲ τῶν δένδρων ὡς ἁπλῶς εἰπεῖν
καὶ τῶν φυτῶν εἴδη πλείω τυγχάνει καθ᾽ ἕκαστον
4 γένος· σχεδὸν γὰρ οὐδέν ἐστιν ἁπλοῦν· ἀλλ᾽ ὅσα
μὲν ἥμερα καὶ ἄγρια λέγεται ταύτην ἐμφανε-
στάτην καὶ μεγίστην ἔχει διαφοράν, οἷον συκῆ
ἐρινεός, ἐλάα κότινος, ἄπιος ἀχράς· ὅσα δ᾽ ἐν
ἑκατέρῳ τούτων τοῖς καρποῖς τε καὶ φύλλοις καὶ
ταῖς ἄλλαις μορφαῖς τε καὶ τοῖς μορίοις. ἀλλὰ
τῶν μὲν ἀγρίων ἀνώνυμα τὰ πλεῖστα καὶ ἔμπειροι
ὀλίγοι· τῶν δὲ ἡμέρων καὶ ὠνομασμένα τὰ πλείω
καὶ ἡ αἴσθησις κοινοτέρα· λέγω δ᾽ οἷον ἀμπέλου
συκῆς ῥόας μηλέας ἀπίου δάφνης μυρρίνης τῶν
ἄλλων· ἡ γὰρ χρῆσις οὖσα κοινὴ συνθεωρεῖν
ποιεῖ τὰς διαφοράς.
5 Ἴδιον δὲ καὶ τοῦτ᾽ ἐφ᾽ ἑκατέρων· τὰ μὲν γὰρ
ἄγρια τῷ ἄρρενι καὶ τῷ θήλει ἢ μόνοις ἢ μάλιστα
διαιροῦσι, τὰ δὲ ἥμερα πλείοσιν ἰδέαις. ἔστι δὲ
τῶν μὲν ῥᾷον λαβεῖν καὶ διαριθμῆσαι τὰ εἴδη,
τῶν δὲ χαλεπώτερον διὰ τὴν πολυχοΐαν.
Ἀλλὰ δὴ τὰς μὲν τῶν μορίων διαφορὰς καὶ τῶν
ἄλλων οὐσιῶν ἐκ τούτων πειρατέον θεωρεῖν. περὶ
δὲ τῶν γενέσεων μετὰ ταῦτα λεκτέον· τοῦτο γὰρ
ὥσπερ ἐφεξῆς τοῖς εἰρημένοις ἐστίν.

of plants too there is a class which cannot grow except [1] in moisture, while others will indeed grow on dry land, but they lose their character and are inferior. Again of all trees, one might almost say, and of all plants there are several forms to each kind; for hardly any kind contains but a single form. But the plants which are called respectively cultivated and wild shew this difference in the clearest and most emphatic way, for instance the cultivated and wild forms of fig olive and pear. In each of these pairs there are differences in fruit and leaves, and in their forms and parts generally. But most of the wild kinds have no names and few know about them, while most of the cultivated kinds have received names [2] and they are more commonly observed; I mean such plants as vine fig pomegranate apple pear bay myrtle and so forth; for, as many people make use of them, they are led also to study the differences.

But there is this peculiarity as to the two classes respectively; in the wild kinds men find only or chiefly the distinction of 'male' and 'female,' while in the cultivated sorts they recognise a number of distinguishing features. In the former case it is easy to mark and count up the different forms, in the latter it is harder because the points of difference are numerous.

However we have said enough for study of the differences between parts and between general characters. We must now speak of the methods of growth, for this subject comes naturally after what has been said.

[1] μὴ add. W.
[2] ὠνομασμένα τὰ πλείω conj. Sch.; ὠνομασμένων πλείω Ald.

BOOK II

# B

I. Αἱ γενέσεις τῶν δένδρων καὶ ὅλως τῶν
φυτῶν ἢ αὐτόμαται ἢ ἀπὸ σπέρματος ἢ ἀπὸ
ῥίζης ἢ ἀπὸ παρασπάδος ἢ ἀπὸ ἀκρεμόνος ἢ
ἀπὸ κλωνὸς ἢ ἀπ' αὐτοῦ τοῦ στελέχους εἰσίν, ἢ
ἔτι τοῦ ξύλου κατακοπέντος εἰς μικρά· καὶ γὰρ
οὕτως ἔνια φύεται.¹ τούτων δὲ ἡ μὲν αὐτόματος
πρώτη τις, αἱ δὲ ἀπὸ σπέρματος καὶ ῥίζης φυσι-
κώταται δόξαιεν ἄν· ὥσπερ γὰρ αὐτόμαται καὶ
αὐταί· δι' ὃ καὶ τοῖς ἀγρίοις ὑπάρχουσιν· αἱ δὲ
ἄλλαι τέχνης ἢ δὴ προαιρέσεως.

2 Ἅπαντα δὲ βλαστάνει κατά τινα τῶν τρόπων
τούτων, τὰ δὲ πολλὰ κατὰ πλείους· ἐλάα μὲν
γὰρ πάντως φύεται πλὴν ἀπὸ τοῦ κλωνός· οὐ
γὰρ δύναται καταπηγνυμένη, καθάπερ ἡ συκῆ
τῆς κράδης καὶ ἡ ῥόα τῆς ῥάβδου. καίτοι φασί
γέ τινες ἤδη καὶ χάρακος παγείσης καὶ πρὸς τὸν
κιττὸν συμβιῶσαι καὶ γενέσθαι δένδρον· ἀλλὰ
σπάνιόν τι τὸ τοιοῦτον· θάτερα δὲ τὰ πολλὰ τῆς
φύσεως. συκῆ δὲ τοὺς μὲν ἄλλους τρόπους

¹ ἔνια φύεται conj. Sch.; ἀναφύεται Ald.

# BOOK II

*Of the ways in which trees and plants originate. Instances of
degeneration from seed.*

I. The ways in which trees and plants in general
originate are these :—spontaneous growth, growth
from seed, from a root, from a piece torn off, from a
branch or twig, from the trunk itself; or again from
small pieces into which the wood is cut up (for some
trees can be produced [1] even in this manner). Of
these methods spontaneous growth comes first, one
may say, but growth from seed or root would seem
most natural; indeed these methods too may be
called spontaneous: wherefore they are found even
in wild kinds, while the remaining methods depend
on human skill or at least on human choice.

However all plants start in one or other of these
ways, and most of them in more than one. Thus the
olive is grown in all the ways mentioned, except
from a twig; for an olive-twig will not grow if it is
set in the ground, as a fig or pomegranate will grow
from their young shoots. Not but what some say
that cases have been known in which, when a stake
of olive-wood was planted to support ivy, it actually
lived along with it and became a tree ; but such
an instance is a rare exception, while the other
methods of growth are in most cases the natural
ones. The fig grows in all the ways mentioned,

105

φύεται πάντας, ἀπὸ δὲ τῶν πρέμνων καὶ τῶν
ξύλων οὐ φύεται· μηλέα δὲ καὶ ἄπιος καὶ ἀπὸ
τῶν ἀκρεμόνων σπανίως. οὐ μὴν ἀλλὰ τά γε
πολλὰ ἢ πάνθ᾽ ὡς εἰπεῖν ἐνδέχεσθαι δοκεῖ καὶ
ἀπὸ τούτων, ἐὰν λεῖοι καὶ νέοι καὶ εὐαυξεῖς ὦσιν.
ἀλλὰ φυσικώτεραί πως ἐκεῖναι· τὸ δὲ ἐνδεχόμενον
ὡς δυνατὸν ληπτέον.

3    Ὅλως γὰρ ὀλίγα τὰ ἀπὸ τῶν ἄνω μᾶλλον
βλαστάνοντα καὶ γεννώμενα, καθάπερ ἄμπελος
ἀπὸ τῶν κλημάτων· αὕτη γὰρ οὐκ ἀπὸ τῆς
πρώρας ἀλλ᾽ ἀπὸ τοῦ κλήματος φύεται, καὶ εἰ δή
τι τοιοῦτον ἕτερον ἢ δένδρον ἢ φρυγανῶδες, ὥσπερ
δοκεῖ τό τε πήγανον καὶ ἡ ἰωνία καὶ τὸ σισύμβριον καὶ ὁ ἕρπυλλος καὶ τὸ ἐλένιον. κοινοτάτη
μὲν οὖν ἐστι πᾶσιν ἥ τε ἀπὸ τῆς παρασπάδος καὶ
ἀπὸ σπέρματος. ἅπαντα γὰρ ὅσα ἔχει σπέρματα
καὶ ἀπὸ σπέρματος γίνεται· ἀπὸ δὲ παρασπάδος
καὶ τὴν δάφνην φασίν, ἐάν τις τὰ ἔρνη παρελὼν
φυτεύσῃ. δεῖ δὲ ὑπόρριζον εἶναι μάλιστά γε τὸ
παρασπώμενον ἢ ὑπόπρεμνον. οὐ μὴν ἀλλὰ καὶ
ἄνευ τούτου θέλει βλαστάνειν καὶ ῥόα καὶ μηλέα
ἐαρινή· βλαστάνει δὲ καὶ ἀμυγδαλῆ φυτευομένη.

4    κατὰ πλείστους δὲ τρόπους ὡς εἰπεῖν ἡ ἐλάα
βλαστάνει· καὶ γὰρ ἀπὸ τοῦ στελέχους καὶ ἀπὸ
τοῦ πρέμνου κατακοπτομένου καὶ ἀπὸ τῆς ῥίζης
[καὶ ἀπὸ τοῦ ξύλου] καὶ ἀπὸ ῥάβδου καὶ χάρακος
ὥσπερ εἴρηται. τῶν δ᾽ ἄλλων ὁ μύρρινος· καὶ
γὰρ οὗτος ἀπὸ τῶν ξύλων καὶ τῶν πρέμνων

---

¹ τά γε πολλὰ πάνθ᾽ conj. Sch.; ἢ before πάνθ᾽ ins. St.; τά
τε πολλὰ πάνθ᾽ Ald.
² εὐαυξεῖς conj. H; αὐξεῖς UMVAld.
³ οὐκ I conj.; οὐδ᾽ MSS.

except from root-stock and cleft wood; apple and
pear grow also from branches, but rarely. However
it appears that most, if not practically all,[1] trees may
grow from branches, if these are smooth young and
vigorous.[2] But the other methods, one may say, are
more natural, and we must reckon what may
occasionally occur as a mere possibility.

In fact there are quite few plants which grow and
are brought into being more easily from the upper
parts, as the vine is grown from branches; for this,
though it cannot[3] be grown from the 'head,'[4] yet
can be grown from the branch, as can all similar
trees and under-shrubs, for instance, as it appears,
rue gilliflower bergamot-mint tufted thyme cala-
mint. So the commonest ways of growth with all
plants are from a piece torn off or from seed; for all
plants that have seeds grow also from seed. And
they say that the bay too grows[5] from a piece
torn off, if one takes off the young shoots and plants
them; but it is necessary that the piece torn off
should have part of the root or stock[6] attached to it.
However the pomegranate and 'spring apple'[7] will
grow even without this, and a slip of almond[8] grows
if it is planted. The olive grows, one may say, in
more ways than any other plant; it grows from a
piece of the trunk or of the stock,[9] from the root,
from a twig, and from a stake, as has been said.[10] Of
other plants the myrtle also can be propagated in
several ways; for this too grows from pieces of wood

[4] πρώρας, cf. Col. 3. 10. 1. caput vitis vocat πρώραν. Sch.
restores the word, C.P. 3. 14. 7.
[5] cf. C.P. 1. 3. 2.      [6] i.e. a 'heel' (Lat. perna).
[7] cf. C.P. 2. 11. 6; Athen. 3. 23.     [8] cf. Geop. 10. 3. 9.
[9] καὶ ἀπὸ τοῦ ξύλου om. Julius Pontedeva on Varro 1. 39. 3;
a gloss on ἀπὸ τοῦ πρέμνου κατακ.     [10] 2. 1. 2.

φύεται. δεῖ δὲ καὶ τούτου καὶ τῆς ἐλάας τὰ ξύλα διαιρεῖν μὴ ἐλάττω σπιθαμιαίων καὶ τὸν φλοιὸν μὴ περιαιρεῖν.

Τὰ μὲν οὖν δένδρα βλαστάνει καὶ γίνεται κατὰ τοὺς εἰρημένους τρόπους· αἱ γὰρ ἐμφυτεῖαι καὶ οἱ ἐνοφθαλμισμοὶ καθάπερ μίξεις τινές εἰσιν ἢ κατ᾿ ἄλλον τρόπον γενέσεις, περὶ ὧν ὕστερον λεκτέον.

II. Τῶν δὲ φρυγανωδῶν καὶ ποιωδῶν τὰ μὲν πλεῖστα ἀπὸ σπέρματος ἢ ῥίζης τὰ δὲ καὶ ἀμφοτέρως· ἔνια δὲ καὶ ἀπὸ τῶν βλαστῶν, ὥσπερ εἴρηται. ῥοδωνία δὲ καὶ κρινωνία κατακοπέντων τῶν καυλῶν, ὥσπερ καὶ ἡ ἄγρωστις. φύεται δὲ ἡ κρινωνία καὶ ἡ ῥοδωνία καὶ ὅλου τοῦ καυλοῦ τεθέντος. ἰδιωτάτη δὲ ἡ ἀπὸ δακρύου· καὶ γὰρ οὕτω δοκεῖ τὸ κρίνον φύεσθαι, ὅταν ξηρανθῇ τὸ ἀπορρυέν. φασὶ δὲ καὶ ἐπὶ τοῦ ἱπποσελίνου· καὶ γὰρ τοῦτο ἀφίησι δάκρυον. φύεται δέ τις καὶ κάλαμος, ἐάν τις διατέμνων τὰς ἠλακάτας πλαγίας τιθῇ καὶ κατακρύψῃ κόπρῳ καὶ γῇ. ἰδίως δὲ ἀπὸ ῥίζης [τῷ] φύεσθαι καὶ τὰ κεφαλόρριζα.

2   Τοσαυταχῶς δὲ οὔσης τῆς δυνάμεως τὰ μὲν πολλὰ τῶν δένδρων, ὥσπερ ἐλέχθη πρότερον, ἐν πλείοσι τρόποις φύεται· ἔνια δὲ ἀπὸ σπέρματος

---

¹ ἐμφυτεῖαι conj. R. Const.; ἐμφυλέαι (with erasures) U; ἐμφυλείαι V; ἐμφυλείαι Ald.
² 2. 1. 3 ; cf. C.P. 1. 4. 4 and 6.
³ i.e. bulbil. cf. 6. 6. 8 ; 9. 1. 4 ; C.P. 1. 4. 6 ; Plin 21. 24.
⁴ ἐπὶ conj. W.; ἀπὸ P₂Ald.
⁵ δέ τις καὶ Ald.; τις om. W. after Sch.

and also from pieces of the stock. It is necessary however with this, as with the olive, to cut up the wood into pieces not less than a span long and not to strip off the bark.

Trees then grow and come into being in the above-mentioned ways; for as to methods of grafting [1] and inoculation, these are, as it were, combinations of different kinds of trees; or at all events these are methods of growth of a quite different class and must be treated of at a later stage.

II. Of under-shrubs and herbaceous plants the greater part grow from seed or a root, and some in both ways; some of them also grow from cuttings, as has been said,[2] while roses and lilies grow from pieces of the stems, as also does dog's-tooth grass. Lilies and roses also grow when the whole stem is set. Most peculiar is the method of growth from an exudation [3]; for it appears that the lily grows in this way too, when the exudation that has been produced has dried up. They say the same of [4] alexanders, for this too produces an exudation. There is a certain [5] reed also which grows if one cuts it in lengths from joint to joint and sets them [6] sideways, burying it in dung and soil. Again they say that plants which have a bulbous root are peculiar in their way of growing [7] from the root.

The capacity for growth being shewn in so many ways, most trees, as was said before,[8] originate in several ways; but some come [9] only from seed, as silver-

[6] cf. 1. 4. 4; Plin. 17. 145; Col. 4. 32. 2 ; τιθῇ conj. Sch.; ἢ Ald.; ⁚ θῇ.
[7] i.e. by offset bulbs. Text probably defective; cf. C.P. 1. 4. 1.   τῷ U; τὸ UMV.   [8] 2. 1. 1.
[9] φύεται I conj.: φησὶν ἐστιν or φασὶν ἐστιν MSS.; ὡς φασὶν ἐστιν Ald.; παραγίνεται conj. W.

φύεται μόνον, οἷον ἐλάτη πεύκη πίτυς ὅλως πᾶν
τὸ κωνοφόρον· ἔτι δὲ καὶ φοῖνιξ, πλὴν εἰ ἄρα ἐν
Βαβυλῶνι καὶ ἀπὸ τῶν ῥάβδων [ὥς] φασί τινες
μολεύειν.[1] κυπάριττος δὲ παρὰ μὲν τοῖς ἄλλοις
ἀπὸ σπέρματος, ἐν Κρήτῃ δὲ καὶ ἀπὸ τοῦ στελέχους, οἷον ἐπὶ[3] τῆς ὀρείας ἐν Τάρρᾳ· παρὰ τούτοις
γάρ ἐστιν ἡ κουριζομένη κυπάριττος· αὕτη δὲ ἀπὸ
τῆς τομῆς βλαστάνει πάντα τρόπον τεμνομένη
καὶ ἀπὸ γῆς καὶ ἀπὸ τοῦ μέσου καὶ ἀπὸ τοῦ ἀνω-
τέρω· βλαστάνει δὲ ἐνιαχοῦ καὶ ἀπὸ τῶν ῥιζῶν
σπανίως δέ.

3 Περὶ δὲ δρυὸς ἀμφισβητοῦσιν· οἱ μὲν γὰρ ἀπὸ
σπέρματός φασι μόνον, οἱ δὲ καὶ ἀπὸ ῥίζης
γλίσχρως· οἱ δὲ καὶ ἀπ' αὐτοῦ τοῦ στελέχους
κοπέντος. ἀπὸ παρασπάδος δὲ καὶ ῥίζης οὐδὲν
φύεται τῶν μὴ παραβλαστανόντων.

4 Ἁπάντων δὲ ὅσων πλείους αἱ γενέσεις, ἡ ἀπὸ
παρασπάδος καὶ ἔτι μᾶλλον ἡ ἀπὸ παραφυάδος
ταχίστη καὶ εὐαυξής, ἐὰν ἀπὸ ῥίζης ἡ παραφυὰς
ᾖ. καὶ τὰ μὲν οὕτως ἢ ὅλως ἀπὸ φυτευτηρίων
πεφυτευμένα πάντα δοκεῖ τοὺς καρποὺς ἐξομοιοῦν.
ὅσα δ' ἀπὸ τοῦ καρποῦ τῶν δυναμένων καὶ οὕτως
βλαστάνειν, ἅπανθ' ὡς εἰπεῖν χείρω, τὰ δὲ καὶ
ὅλως ἐξίσταται τοῦ γένους, οἷον ἄμπελος μηλέα
συκῆ ῥοιὰ ἄπιος· ἔκ τε γὰρ τῆς κεγχραμίδος οὐδὲν
γίνεται γένος ὅλως ἥμερον, ἀλλ' ἢ ἐρινεὸς ἢ
ἀγρία συκῆ, διαφέρουσα πολλάκις καὶ τῇ χροίᾳ·
καὶ γὰρ ἐκ μελαίνης λευκὴ καὶ ἐκ λευκῆς μέλαινα

---

[1] μολεύειν conj. Sch.; μωλύειν MSS.; μοσχεύειν conj. R.
Const. (cf. C.P. 1. 2 1). But cf. Hesych. s.v. μολεύειν.
[2] Plin. 16. 141.     [3] ἐπὶ conj. W.; τὸ UMVAld.

fir fir Aleppo pine, and in general all those that bear
cones : also the date-palm, except that in Babylon it
may be that, as some say, they take cuttings [1] from
it. The cypress in most regions grows from seed,
but in Crete [2] from the trunk also, for instance in [3]
the hill country about Tarra ; for there grows the
cypress which they clip, and when cut it shoots in
every possible way, from the part which has been cut,
from the ground, from the middle, and from the
upper parts ; and occasionally, but rarely, it shoots
from the roots also.

About the oak accounts differ ; some say it only
grows from seed, some from the root also, but not
vigorously, others again that it grows from the trunk
itself, when this is cut. But no tree grows from a
piece torn off or from a root except those which
make side-growths.

However in all the trees which have several
methods of originating the quickest method and that
which promotes the most vigorous growth is from a
piece torn off, or still better from a sucker, if this is
taken from the root. And, while all the trees which
are propagated thus or by some kind of slip [4] seem to
be alike in their fruits to the original tree, those raised
from the fruit, where this method of growing is also
possible, are nearly all inferior, while some quite lose
the character of their kind, as vine apple fig pomegranate pear. As for the fig,[5] no cultivated kind is
raised from its seed, but either the ordinary wild fig
or some wild kind is the result, and this often
differs in colour from the parent ; a black fig gives a

[4] φυτευτήριον : a general term including παραφυάς and
ταρασπάς.
[5] cf. C.P. 1. 9.

THEOPHRASTUS

γίνεται· ἔκ τε τῆς ἀμπέλου τῆς γενναίας ἀγεννής·
καὶ πολλάκις ἕτερον γένος· ὁτὲ δὲ ὅλως οὐδὲν
ἥμερον ἀλλ' ἄγριον ἐνίοτε καὶ τοιοῦτον ὥστε μὴ
ἐκπέττειν τὸν καρπόν· αἱ δ' ὥστε μηδὲ ἁδρύνειν
ἀλλὰ μέχρι τοῦ ἀνθῆσαι μόνον ἀφικνεῖσθαι.
5 Φύονται¹ δὲ καὶ ἐκ τῶν τῆς ἐλάας πυρήνων
ἀγριέλαιος, καὶ ἐκ τῶν τῆς ῥόας κόκκων τῶν
γλυκέων² ἀγεννεῖς, καὶ ἐκ τῶν ἀπυρήνων σκληραί,
πολλάκις δὲ καὶ ὀξεῖαι. τὸν αὐτὸν δὲ τρόπον
καὶ ἐκ τῶν ἀπίων καὶ ἐκ τῶν μηλέων· ἐκ μὲν γὰρ
τῶν ἀπίων μοχθηρὰ ἡ ἀχράς, ἐκ δὲ τῶν μηλέων
χείρων τε τῷ γένει καὶ ἐκ γλυκείας ὀξεῖα, καὶ ἐκ
στρουθίου Κυδώνιος. χείρων δὲ καὶ ἡ ἀμυγδαλῆ
καὶ τῷ χυλῷ καὶ τῷ σκληρὰ ἐκ μαλακῆς· δι' ὃ
καὶ αὐξηθεῖσαν ἐγκεντρίζειν κελεύουσιν, εἰ δὲ μὴ
τὸ μόσχευμα μεταφυτεύειν πολλάκις.
6 Χείρων δὲ καὶ ἡ δρῦς· ἀπὸ γοῦν τῆς ἐν Πύρρᾳ⁵
πολλοὶ φυτεύσαντες οὐκ ἐδύνανθ' ὁμοίαν ποιεῖν.
διάφνην δὲ καὶ μυρρίνην διαφέρειν ποτέ φασιν, ὡς
ἐπὶ τὸ πολὺ δ' ἐξίστασθαι καὶ οὐδὲ τὸ χρῶμα
διασώζειν, ἀλλ' ἐξ ἐρυθροῦ καρποῦ γίνεσθαι
μέλαιναν, ὥσπερ καὶ τὴν ἐν Ἀντάνδρῳ· πολλάκις
δὲ καὶ τὴν κυπάριττον ἐκ θηλείας ἄρρενα.
μάλιστα δὲ τούτων ὁ φοῖνιξ δοκεῖ διαμένειν
ὥσπερ εἰπεῖν τελείως τῶν ἀπὸ σπέρματος, καὶ
πεύκη ἡ κωνοφόρος καὶ πίτυς ἡ φθειροποιός.
ταῦτα μὲν οὖν ἐν τοῖς ἡμερωμένοις. ἐν δὲ τοῖς

¹ φύονται conj. W.; φυτεύονται Ald.H.; φύεται Vo.cod.Cas.
² γλυκέων conj. St.; γλαυκίων UMVAld.
³ cf. Athen. 3. 20 and 23.     ⁴ cf. C.P. 1. 9. 1.
⁵ In Lesbos ; cf. 3. 9. 5.     ⁶ cf. C.P. 1. 9. 2.

white, and conversely. Again the seed of an excellent vine produces a degenerate result, which is often of quite a different kind; and at times this is not a cultivated kind at all, but a wild one of such a character that it does not ripen its fruit; with others again the result is that the seedlings do not even mature fruit, but only get as far as flowering.

Again the stones of the olive give[1] a wild olive, and the seeds of a sweet pomegranate[2] give a degenerate kind, while the stoneless kind gives a hard sort and often an acid fruit. So also is it with seedlings of pears and apples; pears give a poor sort of wild pears, apples produce an inferior kind which is acid instead of sweet; quince produces wild quince.[3] Almond again raised from seed is inferior in taste and in being hard instead of soft; and this is why men[4] bid us graft on to the almond, even when it is fully grown, or, failing that, frequently plant the offsets.

The oak also deteriorates from seed: at least many persons having raised trees from acorns of the oak at Pyrrha[5] could not produce one like the parent tree. On the other hand they say that bay and myrtle sometimes improve by seeding, though usually they degenerate and do not even keep their colour, but red fruit gives black—as happened with the tree in Antandros; and frequently seed of a 'female' cypress produces a 'male' tree. The date-palm seems to be about the most constant of these trees, when raised from seed, and also the 'cone-bearing pine'[6] (stone-pine) and the 'lice-bearing pine.'[7] So much for degeneration in cultivated trees; among wild kinds it is plain that more in proportion

[7] Plin. 16. 49. The 'lice' are the seeds which were eaten. cf. Hdt. 4. 109, φθειροτραγέουσι; Theocr. 5. 49.

113

ἀγρίοις δῆλον ὅτι πλείω κατὰ λόγον ὡς ἰσχυρο-
τέροις· ἐπεὶ θάτερόν γε καὶ ἄτοπον, εἰ δὴ χείρω
καὶ ἐν ἐκείνοις καὶ ὅλως ἐν τοῖς ἀπὸ σπέρματος
μόνον· εἰ μή τι τῇ θεραπείᾳ δύνανται μεταβάλλειν.

7 Διαφέρουσι δὲ καὶ τόποι τόπων καὶ ἀὴρ ἀέρος·
ἐνιαχοῦ γὰρ ἐκφέρειν ἡ χώρα δοκεῖ τὰ ὅμοια,
καθάπερ καὶ ἐν Φιλίπποις· ἀνάπαλιν ὀλίγα καὶ
ὀλιγαχοῦ λαμβάνειν μεταβολήν, ὥστε ἐκ σπέρματος ἀγρίου ποιεῖν ἥμερον ἢ ἐκ χείρονος ἁπλῶς
βέλτιον· τοῦτο γὰρ ἐπὶ τῆς ῥόας μόνον ἀκηκόαμεν
ἐν Αἰγύπτῳ καὶ ἐν Κιλικίᾳ συμβαίνειν· ἐν
Αἰγύπτῳ μὲν γὰρ τὴν ὀξεῖαν καὶ σπαρεῖσαν καὶ
φυτευθεῖσαν γλυκεῖαν γίνεσθαί πως ἢ οἰνώδη·
περὶ δὲ Σόλους τῆς Κιλικίας περὶ ποταμὸν τὸν
Πίναρον, οὗ ἡ μάχη πρὸς Δαρεῖον ἐγένετο, πᾶσαι
γίνονται ἀπύρηνοι.

8 Εὔλογον δὲ καὶ εἴ τις τὸν παρ' ἡμῶν φοίνικα
φυτεύοι ἐν Βαβυλῶνι, κάρπιμόν τε γίνεσθαι καὶ
ἐξομοιοῦσθαι τοῖς ἐκεῖ. τὸν αὐτὸν δὲ τρόπον καὶ
εἴ τις ἑτέρα προσάλληλον ἔχει καρπὸν τόπῳ·
κρείττων γὰρ οὗτος τῆς ἐργασίας καὶ τῆς θεραπείας. σημεῖον δ' ὅτι μεταφερόμενα τἀκεῖθεν
ἄκαρπα τὰ δὲ καὶ ὅλως ἀβλαστῆ γίνεται.

9 Μεταβάλλει δὲ καὶ τῇ τροφῇ καὶ διὰ τὴν

[1] i.e. that they should improve from seed.
[2] Whereas wild trees are produced only from seed.
[3] i.e. improve a degenerate seedling.
[4] ἁπλῶς : ? om. Sch.   [5] cf. C.P. 1. 9. 2.

114

degenerate from seed, since the parent trees are stronger. For the contrary [1] would be very strange, seeing that degenerate forms are found even in cultivated trees,[2] and among these only in those which are raised from seed. (As a general rule these are degenerate, though men may in some cases effect a change [3] by cultivation).

*Effects of situation, climate, tendance.*

Again differences in situation and climate affect the result. In some places, as at Philippi, the soil seems to produce plants which resemble their parent; on the other hand a few kinds in some few places seem to undergo a change, so that wild seed gives a cultivated form, or a poor form one actually better.[4] We have heard that this occurs, but only with the pomegranate, in Egypt [5] and Cilicia; in Egypt a tree of the acid kind both from seeds and from cuttings produces one whose fruit has a sort of sweet taste,[6] while about Soli in Cilicia near the river Pinaros (where the battle with Darius was fought) all those pomegranates raised from seed are without stones.

If anyone were to plant our palm at Babylon, it is reasonable to expect that it would become fruitful and like the palms of that country. And so would it be with any other country which has fruits that are congenial to that particular locality; for the locality [7] is more important than cultivation and tendance. A proof of this is the fact that things transplanted thence become unfruitful, and in some cases refuse to grow altogether.

There are also modifications due to feeding [8] and

[6] Or 'wine-like.' Cited by Apollon. *Hist. Mir.* 43.
[7] οὗτοι conj. W.; αὐτὸς Ald.
[8] τῇ τροφῇ conj. W.; τῆς τροφῆς UMVAld.

THEOPHRASTUS

ἄλλην ἐπιμέλειαν, οἷς καὶ τὸ ἄγριον ἐξημεροῦται
καὶ αὐτῶν δὲ τῶν ἡμέρων ἔνια ἀπαγριοῦται, οἷον
ῥόα καὶ ἀμυγδαλῆ. ἤδη δέ τινες καὶ ἐκ κριθῶν
ἀναφῦναί φασι πυροὺς καὶ ἐκ πυρῶν κριθὰς καὶ
10 ἐπὶ τοῦ αὐτοῦ πυθμένος ἄμφω. ταῦτα μὲν οὖν
ὡς μυθωδέστερα δεῖ δέχεσθαι. μεταβάλλει δ᾽
οὖν τὰ μεταβάλλοντα τὸν τρόπον τοῦτον αὐτο-
μάτως· ἐξαλλαγῇ δὲ χώρας, ὥσπερ ἐν Αἰγύπτῳ
καὶ Κιλικίᾳ περὶ τῶν ῥοῶν εἴπομεν, οὐδὲ διὰ
μίαν θεραπείαν.

Ὡσαύτως δὲ καὶ ὅπου τὰ κάρπιμα ἄκαρπα
γίνεται, καθάπερ τὸ πέρσιον τὸ ἐξ Αἰγύπτου καὶ
ὁ φοῖνιξ ἐν τῇ Ἑλλάδι καὶ εἰ δή τις κομίσειε τὴν
ἐν Κρήτῃ λεγομένην αἴγειρον. ἔνιοι δέ φασι καὶ
τὴν ὄην ἐὰν εἰς ἀλεεινὸν ἔλθῃ σφόδρα τόπον
ἄκαρπον γίνεσθαι· φύσει γὰρ ψυχρόν. εὔλογον
δὲ ἀμφότερα συμβαίνειν κατὰ τὰς ἐναντιώσεις,
εἴπερ μηδ᾽ ὅλως ἔνια φύεσθαι θέλει μεταβάλλοντα τοὺς τόπους.    καὶ κατὰ μὲν τὰς χώρας
αἱ τοιαῦται μεταβολαί.

11  Κατὰ δὲ τὴν φυτείαν τὰ ἀπὸ τῶν σπερμάτων
φυτευόμενα, καθάπερ ἐλέχθη· παντοῖαι γὰρ αἱ
ἐξαλλαγαὶ καὶ τούτων. τῇ θεραπείᾳ δὲ μεταβάλλει ῥόα καὶ ἀμυγδαλῆ· ῥόα μὲν κόπρον ὑείαν
λαβοῦσα καὶ ὕδατος πλῆθος ῥυτοῦ· ἀμυγδαλῆ δὲ
ὅταν πάτταλόν τις ἐνθῇ, καὶ τὸ δάκρυον ἀφαιρῇ
τὸ ἐπιρρέον πλείω χρόνον καὶ τὴν ἄλλην ἀποδιδῷ

---

¹ ἔνια ἀπαγριοῦται οἷον conj. W.; ἔνια καὶ ἀπορῇ τε ῥόα UV;
ἐ. καὶ ἀπορῇ τὰ ῥόα M ; ἐ. καὶ ἀπορρεῖ τὰ ῥόα Ald.
² i.e. cultivation has nothing to do with it.
³ 2. 2. 7.    ⁴ cf. 3. 3. 4.    ⁵ Plin. 17. 242.
⁶ i.e. improve.  cf. 2. 2. 6 ad fin.

116

attention of other kinds, which cause the wild to
become cultivated, or again cause some cultivated
kinds to go wild,[1] such as pomegranate and almond.
Some say that wheat has been known to be produced
from barley, and barley from wheat, or again both
growing on the same stool ; but these accounts should
be taken as fabulous. Anyhow those things which do
change in this manner do so spontaneously,[2] and the
alteration is due to a change of position (as we said[3]
happens with pomegranates in Egypt and Cilicia),
and not to any particular method of cultivation.

So too is it when fruit-bearing trees become unfruitful, for instance the *persion* when moved from
Egypt, the date-palm when planted in Hellas, or the
tree which is called 'poplar' in Crete,[4] if anyone
should transplant it. [5] Some again say that the
sorb becomes unfruitful if it comes into a very warm
position, since it is by nature cold-loving. It is
reasonable to suppose that both results follow because
the natural circumstances are reversed, seeing that
some things entirely refuse to grow when their place
is changed. Such are the modifications due to
position.

As to those due to method of culture, the changes
which occur in things grown from seed are as was
said ; (for with things so grown also the changes are
of all kinds). Under cultivation the pomegranate
and the almond change character,[6] the pomegranate
if it receives pig-manure[7] and a great deal of river
water, the almond if one inserts a peg and[8] removes for
some time the gum which exudes and gives the other

[7] *cf. C.P.* 2. 14. 2 ; 3. 9. 3 ; Plin. 17. 259 ; Col. 5. 10. 15
and 16.
[8] *cf.* 2. 7. 6 ; *C.P.* 1. 17. 10 ; 2. 14. 1 ; Plin. 17. 252.

THEOPHRASTUS

12 θεραπείαν. ὡσαύτως δὲ δῆλον ὅτι καὶ ὅσα
ἐξημεροῦται τῶν ἀγρίων ἢ ἀπαγριοῦται τῶν
ἡμέρων· τὰ μὲν γὰρ θεραπείᾳ τὰ δ' ἀθεραπευσίᾳ
μεταβάλλει· πλὴν εἴ τις λέγοι μηδὲ μεταβολὴν
ἀλλ' ἐπίδοσιν εἰς τὸ βέλτιον εἶναι καὶ χεῖρον· οὐ
γὰρ οἷόν τε τὸν κότινον ποιεῖν ἐλάαν οὐδὲ τὴν
ἀχράδα ποιεῖν ἄπιον οὐδὲ τὸν ἐρινεὸν συκῆν. ὃ
γὰρ ἐπὶ τοῦ κοτίνου φασὶ συμβαίνειν, ὥστ' ἐὰν
περικοπεὶς¹ τὴν θαλίαν ὅλως μεταφυτευθῇ φέρειν
φαυλίας,² μετακίνησίς τις γίνεται οὐ μεγάλη.
ταῦτα μὲν οὖν ὁποτέρως δεῖ λαβεῖν οὐθὲν ἂν
διαφέροι.

III. Φασὶ δ' οὖν αὐτομάτην τινὰ γίνεσθαι τῶν
τοιούτων μεταβολήν, ὁτὲ μὲν τῶν καρπῶν ὁτὲ δὲ
καὶ ὅλως αὐτῶν τῶν δένδρων, ἃ καὶ σημεῖα νομί-
ζουσιν οἱ μάντεις· οἷον ῥόαν ὀξεῖαν γλυκεῖαν
ἐξενεγκεῖν καὶ γλυκεῖαν ὀξεῖαν· καὶ πάλιν ἁπλῶς
αὐτὰ τὰ δένδρα μεταβάλλειν, ὥστε ἐξ ὀξείας
γλυκεῖαν γίνεσθαι καὶ ἐκ γλυκείας ὀξεῖαν· χεῖρον
δὲ τὸ εἰς γλυκεῖαν μεταβάλλειν. καὶ ἐξ ἐρινεοῦ
συκῆν καὶ ἐκ συκῆς ἐρινεόν· χεῖρον δὲ τὸ ἐκ
συκῆς. καὶ ἐξ ἐλάας κότινον καὶ ἐκ κοτίνου
ἐλάαν· ἥκιστα δὲ τοῦτο. πάλιν δὲ συκῆν ἐκ

---

¹ περικοπεὶς conj. W.; περισκοπτεῖς U; περικόπτης Ald.
² φαυλίας conj. Salm.; φαύλους U; θάλος Ald. cf. Plin.
16. 244. These olives produced little oil, but were valued
for perfumery : see C.P. 6. 8. 3 and 5; de odor., 15.
³ οὐ add. Salm.; om. MSS. (?) Ald. H.

attention required. In like manner plainly some wild things become cultivated and some cultivated things become wild; for the one kind of change is due to cultivation, the other to neglect :—however it might be said that this is not a change but a natural development towards a better or an inferior form; (for that it is not possible to make a wild olive pear or fig into a cultivated olive pear or fig). As to that indeed which is said to occur in the case of the wild olive, that if the tree is transplanted with its top-growth entirely cut off,[1] it produces 'coarse olives,'[2] this is no[3] very great change. However it can make no difference which way[4] one takes this.

*Of spontaneous changes in the character of trees, and of certain marvels.*

III. [5]Apart from these changes it is said that in such plants there is a spontaneous kind of change, sometimes of the fruit, sometimes of the tree itself as a whole, and soothsayers call such changes portents. For instance, an acid pomegranate, it is said, may produce sweet fruit, and conversely; and again, in general, the tree itself sometimes undergoes a change, so that it becomes sweet[6] instead of acid, or the reverse happens. And the change to sweet is considered a worse portent. Again a wild fig may turn into a cultivated one, or the contrary change take place; and the latter is a worse portent. So again a culti-vated olive may turn into a wild one, or conversely, but the latter change is rare. So again a white fig

[4] *i.e.* whether nature or man is said to cause the admitted change.　[5] Plin. 17. 242.
[6] *i.e. all* the fruit are now acid instead of sweet, or the reverse. Sch. brackets ἐξ ὀξείας . . . ὀξεῖαν.

λευκῆς μέλαιναν καὶ ἐκ μελαίνης λευκήν. ὁμοίως
δὲ τοῦτο καὶ ἐπὶ ἀμπέλου.

2 Καὶ ταῦτα μὲν ὡς τέρατα καὶ παρὰ φύσιν ὑπο-
λαμβάνουσιν· ὅσα δὲ συνήθη τῶν τοιούτων οὐδὲ
θαυμάζουσιν ὅλως· οἷον τὸ τὴν κάπνειον ἄμπελον
καλουμένην καὶ ἐκ μέλανος βότρυος λευκὸν καὶ
ἐκ λευκοῦ μέλανα φέρειν· οὐδὲ γὰρ οἱ μάντεις τὰ
τοιαῦτα κρίνουσιν· ἐπεὶ οὐδὲ ἐκεῖνα, παρ᾽ οἷς
πέφυκεν ἡ χώρα μεταβάλλειν, ὥσπερ ἐλέχθη
περὶ τῆς ῥόας ἐν Αἰγύπτῳ· ἀλλὰ τὸ ἐνταῦθα
θαυμαστόν, διὰ τὸ μίαν μόνον ἢ δύο, καὶ ταύτας
ἐν τῷ παντὶ χρόνῳ σπανίας. οὐ μὴν ἀλλ᾽ εἴπερ
συμβαίνει, μᾶλλον ἐν τοῖς καρποῖς γίνεσθαι τὴν
παραλλαγὴν ἢ ἐν ὅλοις τοῖς δένδροις.

3 Ἐπεὶ καὶ τοιαύτη τις ἀταξία γίνεται περὶ τοὺς
καρπούς· οἷον ἤδη ποτὲ συκῆ τὰ σῦκα ἔφυσεν ἐκ
τοῦ ὄπισθεν τῶν θρίων· καὶ ῥόα δὲ καὶ ἄμπελος
ἐκ τῶν στελεχῶν, καὶ ἄμπελος ἄνευ φύλλων καρπὸν ἤνεγκεν. ἐλάα δὲ τὰ μὲν φύλλα ἀπέβαλε τὸν
δὲ καρπὸν ἐξήνεγκεν· ὃ καὶ Θετταλῷ τῷ Πεισι-
στράτου γενέσθαι λέγεται. συμβαίνει δὲ καὶ διὰ
χειμῶνας τοῦτο καὶ δι᾽ ἄλλας αἰτίας ἔνια τῶν
δοκούντων εἶναι παρὰ λόγον οὐκ ὄντων δέ· οἷον
ἐλάα ποτ᾽ ἀποκαυθεῖσα τελέως ἀνεβλάστησεν
ὅλη, καὶ αὐτὴ καὶ ἡ θαλία. ἐν δὲ τῇ Βοιωτίᾳ
καταβρωθέντων τῶν ἐρνῶν ὑπ᾽ ἀττελέβων πάλιν

---

[1] ἐπὶ conj. Sch.; ἐξ Ald. H.
[2] cf. C.P. 5. 3. 1 and 2; Arist. de gen. an. 4. 4; Hesych.
s.v. καπνίας; Schol. ad Ar. Vesp. 151.   [3] 2. 2. 7.
[4] εἰκὸς has perhaps dropped out. Sch.
[5] θρίων conj. R. Const., cf. C.P. 5. 1. 7 and 8; 5. 2. 2;
ἐρινεῶν P₂Ald. cf. also Athen. 3. 11.

may change into a black one, and conversely; and similar changes occur in[1] the vine.

Now these changes they interpret as miraculous and contrary to nature; but they do not even feel any surprise at the ordinary changes, for instance, when the 'smoky' vine,[2] as it is called, produces alike white grapes instead of black or black grapes instead of white. Of such changes the soothsayers take no account, any more than they do of those instances in which the soil produces a natural change, as was said[3] of the pomegranate in Egypt. But it is surprising when such a change occurs in our own country, because there are only one or two instances and these separated by wide intervals of time. However, if such changes occur, it is natural[4] that the variation should be rather in the fruit than in the tree as a whole. In fact the following irregularity also occurs in fruits; a fig-tree has been known to produce its figs from behind the leaves,[5] pomegranate and vines from the stem, while the vine has been known to bear fruit without leaves. The olive again has been known to lose its leaves and yet produce its fruit; this is said to have happened to Thettalos, son of Pisistratus. This may be due to inclement weather; and some changes, which seem to be abnormal, but are not really so, are due to other accidental causes; [6] for instance, there was an olive that, after being completely burnt down, sprang up again entire, the tree and all its branches. And in Boeotia an olive whose young shoots[7] had been eaten off by locusts grew again: in this case however[8] the

[6] cf. Hdt. 8. 55; Plin. 17. 241.
[7] ἐρνῶν conj. Sch.; ἐργων P₂Ald.; κλαδων mU.
[8] i.e. the portent was not so great as in the other case quoted, as the tree itself had not been destroyed.

121

ἀνεβλάστησε· τὰ δ' οἷον ἀπέπεσεν. ἥκιστα δ'
ἴσως τὰ τοιαῦτα ἄτοπα διὰ τὸ φανερὰς ἔχειν τὰς
αἰτίας, ἀλλὰ μᾶλλον τὸ μὴ ἐκ τῶν οἰκείων τόπων
φέρειν τοὺς καρποὺς ἢ μὴ οἰκείους· καὶ μάλιστα δ'
εἰ τῆς ὅλης φύσεως γίνεται μεταβολή, καθάπερ
ἐλέχθη. περὶ μὲν οὖν τὰ δένδρα τοιαῦταί
τινές εἰσι μεταβολαί.

IV. Τῶν δὲ ἄλλων τό τε σισύμβριον εἰς μίν-
θαν δοκεῖ μεταβάλλειν, ἐὰν μὴ κατέχηται τῇ
θεραπείᾳ, δι' ὃ καὶ μεταφυτεύουσι πολλάκις, καὶ
ὁ πυρὸς εἰς αἶραν. ταῦτα μὲν οὖν ἐν τοῖς δένδροις
αὐτομάτως, εἴπερ γίνεται. τὰ δ' ἐν τοῖς ἐπετείοις
διὰ παρασκευῆς· οἷον ἡ τίφη καὶ ἡ ζειὰ μετα-
βάλλουσιν εἰς πυρὸν ἐὰν πτισθεῖσαι σπείρωνται,
καὶ τοῦτ' οὐκ εὐθὺς ἀλλὰ τῷ τρίτῳ ἔτει. σχεδὸν
δὲ παραπλήσιον τοῦτό γε τῷ τὰ σπέρματα κατὰ
τὰς χώρας μεταβάλλειν· μεταβάλλει γὰρ καὶ
ταῦτα καθ' ἑκάστην χώραν καὶ σχεδὸν ἐν τῷ ἴσῳ
χρόνῳ καὶ ἡ τίφη. μεταβάλλουσι δὲ καὶ οἱ
ἄγριοι πυροὶ καὶ αἱ κριθαὶ θεραπευόμεναι καὶ
ἐξημερούμεναι κατὰ τὸν ἴσον χρόνον.

2    Καὶ ταῦτα μὲν ἔοικε χώρας τε μεταβολῇ καὶ
θεραπείᾳ γίνεσθαι· καὶ ἔνια ἀμφοτέροις, τὰ δὲ τῇ
θεραπείᾳ μόνον· οἷον πρὸς τὸ τὰ ὄσπρια μὴ γίνεσθαι ἀτεράμονα βρέξαντα κελεύουσιν ἐν νίτρῳ

---

¹ οἰκείους· καὶ I conj.; οἰκειοῦται UMV; οἰκείως Ald.H.; ἐοικότας
conj. W.        ² εἰ ins. Sch.        ³ 2. 3. 1.
⁴ cf. 6. 7. 2; Plin. 19. 176.
⁵ i.e. to prevent the change which cultivated soil induces.

shoots had, so to speak, only been shed. But after all such phenomena are perhaps far from strange, since the cause in each case is obvious; rather is it strange that trees should bear fruit not at the places where it naturally forms, or else fruit which does not belong to the character[1] of the tree. And most surprising of all is it when,[2] as has been said,[3] there is a change in the entire character of the tree. Such are the changes which occur in trees.

*Of spontaneous and other changes in other plants.*

IV. [4]Of other plants it appears that bergamot-mint turns into cultivated mint, unless it is fixed by special attention; and this is why men frequently transplant[5] it; [6]so too wheat turns into darnel. Now in trees such changes, if they occur, are spontaneous, but in annual plants they are deliberately brought about: for instance, one-seeded wheat and rice-wheat change[7] into wheat, if bruised before they are sown; and this does not happen at once, but in the third year. This change resembles that produced in the seeds by difference of soil[8]; for these grains vary according to the soil, and the change takes about the same time as that which occurs in one-seeded wheat. Again wild wheats and barleys also with tendance and cultivation change in a like period.

These changes appear to be due to change of soil and cultivation, and in some cases the change is due to both, in others to cultivation alone; for instance, in order that pulses may not become uncookable,[9]

[6] But see reff. under αἴρα in Index.
[7] cf. C.P. 5. 6. 12; Plin. 18. 93.
[8] χώραν conj. St.; ὥραν Ald.H.
[9] ἀτεράμονα conj. W.; ἀτέραμνα UAld. cf. 8. 8. 6 and 7: C.P. 4. 7. 2; 4. 12. 1 and 8; Geop. 2. 35. 2; 2. 41.

THEOPHRASTUS

νύκτα τῇ ὑστεραίᾳ σπείρειν ἐν ξηρᾷ· φακοὺς ὥστε
ἁδροὺς γίνεσθαι φυτεύουσιν ἐν βολίτῳ· τοὺς
ἐρεβίνθους δέ, ὥστε μεγάλους, αὐτοῖς τοῖς κελύφεσι βρέξαντα σπείρειν. μεταβάλλουσι δὲ καὶ
κατὰ τὰς ὥρας τοῦ σπόρου πρὸς κουφότητα καὶ
ἀλυπίαν· οἷον ἐάν τις τοὺς ὀρόβους ἐαρινοὺς
σπείρῃ τρισάλυποι γίνονται, καὶ οὐχ ὡς οἱ μετο-
πωρινοὶ βαρεῖς.
3  Γίνεται δὲ καὶ ἐν τοῖς λαχάνοις μεταβολὴ
διὰ τὴν θεραπείαν· οἷον τὸ σέλινον, ἐὰν σπαρὲν
καταπατηθῇ καὶ κυλινδρωθῇ, ἀναφύεσθαί φασιν
οὖλον. μεταβάλλει δὲ καὶ τὴν χώραν ἐξαλλάτ-
τοντα, καθάπερ καὶ τἆλλα. καὶ τὰ μὲν τοιαῦτα
κοινὰ πάντων ἐστίν. εἰ δὲ κατά τινα πήρωσιν ἢ
ἀφαίρεσιν μέρους δένδρον ἄγονον γίνεται, καθάπερ τὰ ζῷα, τοῦτο σκεπτέον· οὐδὲν γοῦν φανερὸν
κατά γε τὴν διαίρεσιν εἰς τὸ πλείω καὶ ἐλάττω
φέρειν ὥσπερ κακούμενον, ἀλλ' ἢ ἀπόλλυται τὸ
ὅλον ἢ διαμένον καρποφορεῖ. τὸ δὲ γῆρας κοινή
τις φθορὰ πᾶσιν.
4  Ἄτοπον δ' ἂν δόξειε μᾶλλον εἰ ἐν τοῖς ζώοις
αἱ τοιαῦται μεταβολαὶ φυσικαὶ καὶ πλείους· καὶ
γὰρ κατὰ τὰς ὥρας ἔνια δοκεῖ μεταβάλλειν, ὥσπερ ὁ ἱέραξ καὶ ἔποψ καὶ ἄλλα τῶν ὁμοίων
ὀρνέων. καὶ κατὰ τὰς τῶν τόπων ἀλλοιώσεις,
ὥσπερ ὁ ὕδρος εἰς ἔχιν ξηραινομένων τῶν λιβά-

¹ νύκτα l conj.; νυκτὶ MSS.
² ἐν βολίτῳ conj. Milus. on Geop. 3. 27 ; ἔμβολον UMV
Ald.  cf. C.P. 5. 6. 11 ; Col. 2. 10. 15 ; Plin. 18. 198.
³ cf. C.P. 5. 6. 11 ; Geop. 2. 3. 6.
⁴ ἀλυπίαν conj. Sch.; δι' ἀλυπίας M ; δι' ἀλυπίαν Ald.

124

men bid one moisten the seed in nitre for a night [1]
and sow it in dry ground the next day. To make
lentils vigorous they plant the seeds in dung [2]; to
make chick-peas large they bid one moisten the
seed while still in the pods,[3] before sowing. Also
the time of sowing makes differences which conduce
to digestibility and harmlessness [4] : thus, if one sows
vetches [5] in spring, they become quite harmless and
are not indigestible like those sown in autumn.

Again in pot-herbs change is produced by cultivation; for instance, they say that,[6] if celery seed
is trodden and rolled in after sowing, it comes up
curly; it also varies from change of soil, like other
things. Such variations are common to all; we must
now consider whether a tree, like animals, becomes
unproductive from mutilation or removal of a part.
At all events it does not appear that division [7] is an
injury, as it were, which affects the amount of fruit
produced; either the whole tree perishes, or else,
if it survives,[8] it bears fruit. Old age however is a
cause which in all plants puts an end to life. . . . .[9]

It would seem more surprising if [10] the following
changes occurred in animals naturally and frequently;
some animals do indeed seem to change according to
the seasons, for instance, the hawk the hoopoe and
other similar birds. So also changes in the nature
of the ground produce changes in animals, for instance,
the water-snake changes into a viper, if the marshes

[5] cf. Plin. 18. 139; Col. 2. 10. 34.
[6] cf. C.P. 5. 6. 7; Geop. 12. 23. 2.
[7] γε conj. Sch.; τε Ald.
[8] διάμενον conj. Sch; διαμένοντα Ald.
[9] Something seems to have been lost at the end of § 3.
[10] εἰ ins. Sch.; τοιαῦται may however mean 'the above-
mentioned,' and refer to something which has been lost.

125

THEOPHRASTUS

δων. φανερώτατα δὲ καὶ κατὰ τὰς γενέσεις ἔνια,
καὶ μεταβάλλει διὰ πλειόνων ζώων· οἷον ἐκ
κάμπης γίνεται χρυσαλλὶς εἶτ᾽ ἐκ ταύτης ψυχή·
καὶ ἐπ᾽ ἄλλων δ᾽ ἐστὶ τοῦτο πλειόνων, οὐδὲν ἴσως
ἄτοπον, οὐδ᾽ ὅμοιον τὸ ζητούμενον. ἀλλ᾽ ἐκεῖνο
συμβαίνει περὶ τὰ δένδρα καὶ ὅλως πᾶσαν τὴν
ὕλην, ὥσπερ ἐλέχθη καὶ πρότερον, ὥστε αὐτομάτην μεταβλαστάνειν μεταβολῆς τινος γινομένης
ἐκ τῶν οὐρανίων τοιαύτης.   τὰ μὲν οὖν περὶ
τὰς γενέσεις καὶ μεταβολὰς ἐκ τούτων θεωρητέον.

V. Ἐπεὶ δὲ καὶ αἱ ἐργασίαι καὶ αἱ θεραπεῖαι
μεγάλα συμβάλλονται, καὶ ἔτι πρότερον αἱ
φυτεῖαι καὶ ποιοῦσι μεγάλας διαφοράς, λεκτέον
καὶ περὶ τούτων.

Καὶ πρῶτον περὶ τῶν φυτειῶν. αἱ μὲν οὖν
ὧραι πρότερον εἴρηνται καθ᾽ ἃς δεῖ. τὰ δὲ φυτὰ
λαμβάνειν κελεύουσιν ὡς κάλλιστα καὶ ἐξ ὁμοίας
γῆς εἰς ἣν μέλλεις φυτεύειν, ἢ χείρονος· τοὺς δὲ
γυροὺς προορύττειν ὡς πλείστου χρόνου καὶ
βαθυτέρους αἰεὶ καὶ τοῖς ἐπιπολαιορριζοτέροις.

---

[1] i.e. in the instance given the development of an insect
exhibits, not one, but a series of changes from one creature
to another.
[2] Whereas the metamorphoses mentioned above are independent of climatic conditions.
[3] δὲ conj. W.; τε Ald.
[4] κάλλιστα conj. W., cf. C.P. 3. 24. 1; τάχιστα MVAld.;
τὰ χίστα U.

dry up. Most obvious are certain changes in regard
to the way in which animals are produced, and such
changes run through a series of creatures [1]; thus a
caterpillar changes into a chrysalis, and this in turn
into the perfect insect; and the like occurs in a
number of other cases. But there is hardly anything
abnormal in this, nor is the change in plants, which
is the subject of our enquiry, analogous to it. That
kind of change occurs in trees and in all woodland
plants generally, as was said before, and its effect is
that, when a change of the required character occurs
in the climatic conditions, a spontaneous change in
the way of growth ensues.[2]   These instances must
suffice for investigation of the ways in which plants
are produced or modified.

*Of methods of propagation, with notes on cultivation.*

V. Since however methods of cultivation and tendance largely contribute, and, before these, methods
of planting, and cause great differences, of these too
we must speak.

And first of methods of planting: as to the seasons,
we have already stated at what seasons one should
plant. Further [3] we are told that the plants chosen
should be the best possible,[4] and should be taken
from soil resembling that in which you are going to
plant them, or else inferior [5]; also the holes should
be dug [6] as long as possible beforehand, and should
always be deeper than the original holes, even for
those whose roots do not run very deep.

[5] *i.e.* the shift should be into better soil, if possible. *cf.
C.P.* 3. 5. 2.
[6] γυροὺς προορύττειν conj. R. Const.; πυροὺς προσορύττειν
UMVAld. *cf. C.P.* 3. 4. 1.

2 Λέγουσι δέ τινες ὡς οὐδεμία κατωτέρω διϊκνεῖται
τριῶν ἡμιποδίων· δι᾽ ὃ καὶ ἐπιτιμῶσι τοῖς ἐν
μείζονι βάθει φυτεύουσιν· οὐκ ἐοίκασι δὲ ὀρθῶς
λέγειν ἐπὶ πολλῶν· ἀλλ᾽ ἐὰν ἢ χώματος ἐπιλάβ-
ηται βαθέος ἢ καὶ χώρας τοιαύτης ἢ καὶ τόπου,
πολλῷ μακροτέραν ὠθεῖ τὸ τῇ φύσει βαθύρριζον.
πεύκην δέ τις ἔφη μεταφυτεύων μεμοχλευμένην
μείζω τὴν ῥίζαν ἔχειν ὀκτάπηχυν καίπερ οὐχ ὅλης
ἐξαιρεθείσης ἀλλ᾽ ἀπορραγείσης.

3 Τὰ δὲ φυτευτήρια ἐὰν μὲν ἐνδέχηται ὑπόρριζα,
εἰ δὲ μή, δεῖ μᾶλλον ἀπὸ τῶν κάτω ἢ τῶν ἄνω
λαμβάνειν, πλὴν ἀμπέλου· καὶ τὰ μὲν ἔχοντα
ῥίζας ὀρθὰ ἐμβάλλειν, τὰ δὲ μὴ ἔχοντα ὑποβάλλειν τοῦ φυτευτηρίου ὅσον σπιθαμὴν ἢ μικρῷ
πλεῖον. ἔνιοι δὲ κελεύουσι καὶ τῶν ὑπορρίζων
ὑποβάλλειν, τιθέναι δὲ καὶ τὴν θέσιν ὁμοίως ἥνπερ
εἶχεν ἐπὶ τῶν δένδρων τὰ πρόσβορρα καὶ τὰ πρὸς
ἕω καὶ τὰ πρὸς μεσημβρίαν. ὅσα δὲ ἐνδέχεται
τῶν φυτῶν καὶ προμοσχεύειν· τὰ μὲν ἐπ᾽ αὐτῶν
τῶν δένδρων, οἷον ἐλάας ἀπίου μηλέας συκῆς· τὰ
δ᾽ ἀφαιροῦντας, οἷον ἀμπέλου· ταύτην γὰρ οὐχ
οἷόν τε ἐπ᾽ αὐτῆς μοσχεύειν.

4 Ἐὰν δὲ μὴ ὑπόρριζα τὰ φυτὰ μηδὲ ὑπόπρεμνα

---

¹ ἀλλ᾽ ἐὰν . . . τοιούτου. ἐὰν ἢ μὲν σώματος M ; so V, but ἢ ;
ἢ om. PAld.; χώματος H ; κενώματος for σώματος and εὐδιόδου
for ἢ καὶ τόπου conj. W. χώρας refers to exposure, etc.,
τόπου (sc. τοιούτου) to quality of soil ; so G.
² Plin. 16. 129 ; Xen. Oec. 19. 3.    ³ cf. C.P. 3. 6.

Some say that no root goes down further than a foot and a half, and accordingly they blame those who plant deeper. However there are many instances in which it appears that what they say does not hold good; a plant which is naturally deep-rooting pushes much deeper if it finds either a deep mass of soil or a position which favours such growth or again the kind of ground which favours it.[1] In fact,[2] a man once said that when he was transplanting a fir which he had uprooted with levers, he found that it had a root more than eight cubits long, though the whole of it had not been removed, but it was broken off.

The slips for planting should be taken, if possible, with roots attached, or, failing that, from the lower[3] rather than from the higher parts of the tree, except in the case of the vine ; those that have roots should be set upright,[4] while in the case of those which have none about[5] a handsbreadth or rather more of the slip should be buried. Some say that part even of those which have roots should be buried, and that the position[6] should be the same as that of the tree from which the slip was taken, facing north or east or south, as the case may be. With those plants with which it is possible, shoots from the boughs should also, they say, be planted, some being set on the trees themselves,[7] as with olive pear apple and fig, but in other cases, as in that of the vine, they must be set separately, for that the vine cannot be grafted on itself.

If the slips cannot be taken with root or stock

[4] cf. C.P. 3. 6. 4 ; Xen. Oec. 19. 9.
[5] ὅσον conj. Sch.; οἷον P, Ald.
[6] cf. C.P. 3. 3. 2.    [7] i.e. grafted.

λαμβάνειν, καθάπερ τῆς ἐλάας, σχίσαντά τε τὸ
ξύλον κάτωθεν καὶ λίθον ἐμβαλόντα φυτεύειν·
ὁμοίως δὲ καὶ τῆς ἐλάας καὶ συκῆς καὶ τῶν ἄλλων. φυτεύεται δὲ ἡ συκῆ καὶ ἐάν τις κράδην
παχεῖαν ἀποξύνας σφύρᾳ παίῃ, ἄχρι οὗ ἂν
ἀπολίπῃ μικρὸν ὑπὲρ τῆς γῆς, εἶτ᾿ αὐτῆς ἄμμον
βαλὼν ἄνωθεν ἐπιχώσῃ· καὶ γίνεσθαι δή φασι
καὶ καλλίω ταῦτα τὰ φυτά, μέχρι οὗ ἂν ᾖ
νέα.

5    Παραπλησία καὶ τῶν ἀμπέλων, ὅταν ἀπὸ
τοῦ παττάλου· προοδοποιεῖ γὰρ ὁ πάτταλος
ἐκείνῳ τῷ κλήματι διὰ τὴν ἀσθένειαν· φυτεύουσιν οὕτω καὶ ῥόαν καὶ ἄλλα τῶν δένδρων.
ἡ συκῆ δέ, ἐὰν ἐν σκίλλῃ φυτευθῇ, θᾶττον παραγίνεται καὶ ἧττον ὑπὸ σκωλήκων κατεσθίεται.
ὅλως δὲ πᾶν ἐν σκίλλῃ φυτευόμενον εὐβλαστὲς
καὶ θᾶττον αὐξάνεται. ὅσα δὲ ἐκ τοῦ στελέχους
καὶ διακοπτόμενα φυτεύεται, κάτω τρέποντα τὴν
τομὴν δεῖ φυτεύειν, διακόπτειν δὲ μὴ ἐλάττω
σπιθαμιαίων, ὥσπερ ἐλέχθη, καὶ τὸν φλοιὸν
προσεῖναι· φύεται δ᾿ ἐκ τῶν τοιούτων ἔρνη· βλα-
στανόντων δ᾿ ἀεὶ προσχωννύειν, ἄχρι οὗ ἂν γένηται ἄρτιον· αὕτη μὲν οὖν τῆς ἐλάας ἰδία καὶ τοῦ
μυρρίνου, αἱ δ᾿ ἄλλαι κοινότεραι πᾶσιν.

6    Ἄριστον δὲ καὶ ῥιζώσασθαι καὶ φυτείας μάλιστα τῆς τυχούσης ἡ συκῆ. φυτεύειν δὲ ῥόας μὲν

---

¹ ἡ before τῆς om. W.    ² τε τὸ conj. W.; τό τε MVP.
³ καὶ τῆς ἐλαίας U ; ἐλάας MVP ; so W.
⁴ Plin. 17, 123.    ⁵ cf. C.P. 3. 12. 1.
⁶ cf. 7. 13. 4 ; C.P. 5. 6. 10 (where another bulb, σχῖνος, is
mentioned as being put to the same use) ; Athen. 3. 13 ;
Plin. 17. 87.

attached, as with the olive,[1] they say that one must [2] split the wood at the lower end and plant with a stone on top; and the fig and other trees must be treated in like manner with the olive.[3] The fig [4] is also propagated by sharpening a stout shoot and driving it in with a hammer, till only a small piece of it is left above ground, and then piling sand above so as to earth it up; and they say that the plants thus raised grow finer up to a certain age.

Similar is the method used with vines, when they are propagated by the 'peg'[5] method: for the peg makes a passage for that sort of shoot on account of its weakness; and in the same manner men plant the pomegranate and other trees. The fig progresses more quickly and is less eaten by grubs, if the cutting is set in a squill-bulb[6]; in fact anything so planted is vigorous and grows faster. All those trees which are propagated by pieces cut from the stem should be planted with the cut part downwards,[7] and the pieces cut off should not be less than a handsbreadth in length, as was said,[8] and the bark should be left on. From such pieces new shoots grow, and as they grow, one should keep on heaping up earth about them, till the tree becomes strong.[9] This kind of propagation is peculiar to the olive and myrtle, while the others are more or less common to all trees.

The fig is better than any other tree at striking roots, and will, more than any other tree, grow by any method of propagation. [10] We are told that,

[7] cf. Geop. 9. 11. 8.

[8] 2. 5. 3, where however the method of propagation is different.

[9] ἄρτιον Ald.; ἀρτιτελῆ conj. W. (quoad satis corroboratur G; donec robur planta capiat Plin. 17. 124); ἀρτιτεων U; ἀρτιτεων MV; ἀρτιτεων P₂. [10] cf. C.P. 3. 7.

καὶ μυρρίνους καὶ δάφνας πυκνὰς κελεύουσι, μὴ
πλέον διεστώσας ἢ ἐννέα πόδας, μηλέας δὲ μικρῷ
μακρότερον, ἀπίους δὲ καὶ ὄγχνας ἔτι μᾶλλον,
ἀμυγδαλᾶς δὲ καὶ συκᾶς πολλῷ πλέον, ὡσαύτως
δὲ καὶ τὴν ἐλάαν.¹ ποιεῖσθαι δὲ καὶ πρὸς τὸν
τόπον τὰς ἀποστάσεις· ἐν γὰρ τοῖς ὀρεινοῖς ἐλάττους ἢ ἐν τοῖς πεδεινοῖς.

7   Μέγιστον δὲ ὡς εἰπεῖν τὸ τὴν πρόσφορον
ἑκάστῳ χώραν ἀποδιδόναι· τότε γὰρ εὐθενεῖ
μάλιστα. ὡς δ' ἁπλῶς εἰπεῖν ἐλάᾳ μὲν καὶ συκῇ
καὶ ἀμπέλῳ τὴν πεδεινήν φασιν οἰκειοτάτην εἶναι,
τοῖς δὲ ἀκροδρύοις τὰς ὑπωρείας. χρὴ δὲ καὶ ἐν
αὐτοῖς τοῖς ὁμογενέσι μὴ ἀγνοεῖν τὰς οἰκείας. ἐν
πλείστῃ δὲ ὡς εἰπεῖν διαφορᾷ τὰ τῶν ἀμπέλων
ἐστίν·² ὅσα γάρ ἐστι γῆς εἴδη, τοσαῦτά τινές φασι
καὶ ἀμπέλων εἶναι. φυτευόμενα μὲν οὖν κατὰ
φύσιν ἀγαθὰ γίνεσθαι παρὰ φύσιν δὲ ἄκαρπα.
ταῦτα μὲν οὖν ὥσπερ κοινὰ πάντων.

VI. Τῶν δὲ φοινίκων ἴδιος ἡ φυτεία παρὰ
τἆλλα καὶ ἡ μετὰ ταῦτα θεραπεία. φυτεύουσι
γὰρ πλείους εἰς ταὐτὸ τιθέντες δύο κάτω καὶ δύο
ἄνωθεν ἐπιδοῦντες, πρανεῖς δὲ πάντας. τὴν γὰρ
ἔκφυσιν οὐκ ἐκ τῶν ὑπτίων καὶ κοίλων ποιεῖται,
καθάπερ τινές φασιν, ἀλλ' ἐκ τῶν ἄνω, δι' ὃ καὶ
ἐν τῇ ἐπιζεύξει τῶν ἐπιτιθεμένων οὐ δεῖ περικα-
λύπτειν τὰς ἀρχὰς ὅθεν ἡ ἔκφυσις· φανεραὶ δ'

¹ ἐλάαν conj. Bod. (cf. Plin. 17. 88) ; ῥοιὰν UAld.H.
² ἐλάττονι conj. Sch.; ἔλαττον Ald.
³ i.e. apples pears plums, etc.

132

in planting the pomegranate myrtle or bay, one should set two trees close together, not further than nine feet apart, apples a little further, pears and wild pears still further, almonds and figs further still, and in like manner the olive.[1] Again the distance apart must be regulated by the nature of the ground, being less [2] in hilly parts than in low ground.

Most important of all, one may say, is it to assign to each the suitable soil; for then is the tree most vigorous. Speaking generally, they say that low ground is most suitable for the olive fig and vine, and the lower slopes of hills for fruit trees.[3] Nor should one fail to note what soil suits each variety even of those closely related. There is the greatest difference, one may say, between the different kinds of vine: for they say that there are as many kinds of vine as there are of soil. If they are planted as their nature requires, they turn out well, if otherwise, they are unfruitful. And these remarks apply almost equally to all trees.

*Of the propagation of the date-palm; of palms in general.*

VI. [4] The method of propagating date-palms is peculiar and exceptional, as also is their subsequent cultivation. They plant several seeds together, putting two below and two above, which are fastened on; but all face downwards.[5] For germination starts not, as some say, from the 'reverse' or hollow side,[6] but from the part [7] which is uppermost; wherefore in joining on the seeds which are placed above one must not cover up the points from which the growth

[4] Plin. 13. 32.
[5] *i.e.* with the grooved side downwards.
[6] *i.e.* the grooved side.   [7] *i.e.* the round side.

εἰσὶ τοῖς ἐμπείροις. διὰ τοῦτο δ' εἰς τὸ αὐτὸ
πλείους τιθέασιν ὅτι ἀπὸ τοῦ ἑνὸς ἀσθενὴς ἡ
φυτεία. τούτων δὲ αἵ τε ῥίζαι πρὸς ἀλλήλας
συμπλέκονται καὶ εὐθὺς αἱ πρῶται βλαστήσεις,
ὥστε ἓν γίνεσθαι τὸ στέλεχος.

2 Ἡ μὲν οὖν ἀπὸ τῶν καρπῶν φυτεία τοιαύτη
τις· ἡ δ' ἀφ' αὑτοῦ, ὅταν ἀφέλωσι τὸ ἄνω ἐν
ᾧπερ ὁ ἐγκέφαλος· ἀφαιροῦσι δὲ ὅσον δίπηχυ·
σχίσαντες δὲ τοῦτο κάτω τιθέασι τὸ ὑγρόν· φιλεῖ
δὲ χώραν ἁλμώδη· δι' ὃ καὶ ὅπου μὴ τοιαύτη
τυγχάνει περιπάττουσιν ἅλας οἱ γεωργοί· τοῦτο
δὲ δεῖ ποιεῖν μὴ περὶ αὐτὰς τὰς ῥίζας ἀλλ' ἄποθεν
ἀποστήσαντα περιπάττειν ὅσον ἡμίεκτον· ὅτι δὲ
τοιαύτην ζητεῖ χώραν κἀκεῖνο ποιοῦνται σημεῖον·
πανταχοῦ γὰρ ὅπου πλῆθος φοινίκων ἁλμώδεις αἱ
χῶραι· καὶ γὰρ ἐν Βαβυλῶνί φασιν, ὅπου οἱ
φοίνικες πεφύκασι, καὶ ἐν Λιβύῃ δὲ καὶ ἐν Αἰγύπτῳ
καὶ Φοινίκῃ καὶ τῆς Συρίας δὲ τῆς κοίλης, ἐν ᾗ ᾗ γ'
οἱ πλεῖστοι τυγχάνουσιν, ἐν τρισὶ μόνοις τόποις
ἁλμώδεσιν εἶναι τοὺς δυναμένους θησαυρίζεσθαι·
τοὺς δ' ἐν τοῖς ἄλλοις οὐ διαμένειν ἀλλὰ σήπεσθαι,
χλωροὺς δ' ἡδεῖς εἶναι καὶ καταναλίσκειν οὕτω.

3 Φιλεῖ δὲ καὶ ὑδρείαν σφόδρα τὸ δένδρον· περὶ
δὲ κόπρου διαμφισβητοῦσιν· οἱ μὲν γὰρ οὔ φασι
χαίρειν ἀλλ' ἐναντιώτατον εἶναι, οἱ δὲ καὶ
χρῆσθαι καὶ ἐπίδοσιν πολλὴν ποιεῖν. δεῖν δ'
ὑδρεύειν εὖ μάλα κατὰ τῆς κόπρου, καθάπερ οἱ ἐν

---

[1] *i.e.* 'cabbage.'
[2] τοῦτο . . . ὑγρόν : I have inserted δὲ, otherwise retaining
the reading of Ald.; τούτου κάτω· τιθέασι δ' ἔνυγρον conj .W.
*cf.* Plin. 13. 36. τὸ ὑγρόν, viz. the cut end.
[3] ἁλμώδη conj. W.; ἀμμώδη P₂Ald.H.

134

is to come ; and these can be recognised by experts.
And the reason why they set several together is that
a plant that grows from one only is weak. The roots
which grow from these seeds become entangled
together and so do the first shoots from the very
start, so that they combine to make a single stem.

Such is the method of growing from the fruits.
But propagation is also possible from the tree itself,
by taking off the top, which contains the 'head.'[1]
They take off about two cubits' length, and, splitting
it, set the moist end.[2] It likes a soil which contains
salt[3] ; wherefore, where such soil is not available,
the growers sprinkle salt about it ; and this must not
be done about the actual roots : one must keep the
salt some way off and sprinkle about a gallon. To
shew that it seeks such a soil they offer the following
proof ; wherever date-palms grow abundantly, the
soil is salt,[4] both in Babylon, they say, where the tree
is indigenous, in Libya in Egypt and in Phoenicia ;
while in Coele-Syria, where are[5] most palms, only in
three districts, they say, where the soil is salt, are
dates produced which can be stored ; those that grow
in other districts do not keep, but rot, though when
fresh they are sweet and men use[6] them at that
stage.

[7]The tree is likewise very fond of irrigation ; as
to dung there is a difference of opinion : some say
that the date-palm does not like it, but that it is most
injurious, others that it gladly accepts[8] it and makes
good growth thereby, but plenty of water should be

[4] ἁλμώδεις conj. W.; ἁμμώδεις Ald.H.
[5] ἐν ᾗ ᾗ γ' οἱ conj. W.; ἷς 'Ινδοι U ; ἦν 'Ινδοι MVAld.
[6] καταναλίσκειν Ald.; καταναλίσκεσθαι conj. W.
[7] Plin. 13. 28.
[8] καὶ χρῆσθαι conj. Sch.; κεχρῆσθαι Ald.; ? κεχάρησθαι.

Ῥόδῳ. τοῦτο μὲν οὖν ἐπισκεπτέον· ἴσως γὰρ οἱ μὲν οὕτως οἱ δ' ἐκείνως θεραπεύουσιν, καὶ μετὰ μὲν τοῦ ὕδατος ὠφέλιμον ἡ κόπρος ἄνευ δὲ τούτου βλαβερά. ὅταν δὲ ἐνιαύσιος γένηται, μεταφυτεύουσι καὶ τῶν ἁλῶν συμπαραβάλλουσι, καὶ πάλιν ὅταν διετής· χαίρει γὰρ σφόδρα τῇ μεταφυτείᾳ.

4 Μεταφυτεύουσι δὲ οἱ μὲν ἄλλοι τοῦ ἦρος· οἱ δὲ ἐν Βαβυλῶνι περὶ τὸ ἄστρον, ὅτε καὶ ὅλως οἵ γε πολλοὶ φυτεύουσιν, ὡς καὶ παραγινομένου καὶ αὐξανομένου θᾶττον. νέου μὲν ὄντος οὐχ ἅπτονται, πλὴν ἀναδοῦσι τὴν κόμην, ὅπως ὀρθοφυῇ τ' ᾖ καὶ αἱ ῥάβδοι μὴ ἀπαρτῶνται. μετὰ δὲ ταῦτα περιτέμνουσιν, ὁπόταν ἁδρὸς ἤδη γένηται καὶ πάχος ἔχῃ. ἀπολείπουσι δὲ ὅσον σπιθαμὴν τῶν ῥάβδων. φέρει δὲ ἕως μὲν ἂν ᾖ νέος ἀπύρηνον τὸν καρπόν, μετὰ δὲ τοῦτο πυρηνώδη.

5 Ἄλλοι δέ τινες λέγουσιν ὡς οἵ γε κατὰ Συρίαν οὐδεμίαν προσάγουσιν ἐργασίαν ἀλλ' ἢ διακαθαίρουσι καὶ ἐπιβρέχουσιν, ἐπιζητεῖν δὲ μᾶλλον τὸ ναματιαῖον ὕδωρ ἢ τὸ ἐκ τοῦ Διός· εἶναι δὲ πολὺ τοιοῦτον ἐν τῷ αὐλῶνι ἐν ᾧ καὶ τὰ φοινικόφυτα τυγχάνει, τὸν αὐλῶνα δὲ τοῦτον λέγειν τοὺς Σύρους ὅτι διατείνει διὰ τῆς Ἀραβίας μέχρι τῆς ἐρυθρᾶς θαλάσσης καὶ πολλοὺς φάσκειν ἐληλυθέναι· τούτου δὲ ἐν τῷ κοιλοτάτῳ πεφυκέναι τοὺς φοίνικας. ταῦτα μὲν οὖν τάχ' ἀμφοτέρως ἂν εἴη· κατὰ γὰρ τὰς χώρας, ὥσπερ καὶ

---

¹ cf. 7. 5. 1.  ² Plin. 13. 37.
³ συμπαραβάλλουσι conj. Sch. from G ; συμπαραλαμβάνουσι UAld.  ⁴ cf. Plin. 13. 38.

given, after manuring, as the Rhodians use. This then is matter for enquiry; it may be that there are two distinct methods of cultivation, and that dung, if accompanied by watering,[1] is beneficial, though without it it is harmful. [2]When the tree is a year old, they transplant it and give plenty [3] of salt, and this treatment is repeated when it is two years old, for it delights greatly in being transplanted.

[4]Most transplant in the spring, but the people of Babylon about the rising of the dog-star, and this is the time when most people propagate it, since it then germinates and grows more quickly. As long as it is young, they do not touch it, except that they tie up the foliage, so that it may grow straight [5] and the slender branches may not hang down.[6] At a later stage they prune it, when it is more vigorous and has become a stout tree, leaving the slender branches only about a handsbreadth long. So long as it is young, it produces its fruit without a stone, but later on the fruit has a stone.

However some say that the people of Syria use no cultivation, except cutting out wood and watering, also that the date-palm requires spring water rather than water from the skies; and that such water is abundant in the valley in which are the palm-groves. And they add that the Syrians say that this valley [7] extends through Arabia to the Red Sea,[8] and that many profess to have visited it,[9] and that it is in the lowest part of it that the date-palms grow. Now both accounts may be true, for it is not strange that

[5] ὀρθυφυῆ τ᾿ ᾖ conj. W.; ὀρθοφύηται P₂Ald.
[6] ἀπαιωπῶνται conj. R. Const.; ἀποβθῶνται P₂MAld.
[7] cf. Diod. 3. 41.
[8] i.e. the Arabian Gulf.
[9] ἐληλυθέναι Ald.: διεληλυθέται conj. W.

αὐτὰ τὰ δένδρα, διαφέρειν καὶ τὰς ἐργασίας οὐκ
ἄτοπον.

6 Γένη δὲ τῶν φοινίκων ἐστὶ πλείω· πρῶτον μὲν
καὶ ὥσπερ ἐν μεγίστῃ διαφορᾷ τὸ μὲν κάρπιμον
τὸ δὲ ἄκαρπον, ἐξ ὧν οἱ περὶ Βαβυλῶνα τάς τε
κλίνας καὶ τἆλλα σκεύη ποιοῦνται. ἔπειτα τῶν
καρπίμων οἱ μὲν ἄρρενες αἱ δὲ θήλειαι· διαφέρουσι
δὲ ἀλλήλων, καθ' ἃ ὁ μὲν ἄρρην ἄνθος πρῶτον
φέρει ἐπὶ τῆς σπάθης, ἡ δὲ θήλεια καρπὸν εὐθὺ
μικρόν. αὐτῶν δὲ τῶν καρπῶν διαφοραὶ πλείους·
οἱ μὲν γὰρ ἀπύρηνοι οἱ δὲ μαλακοπύρηνοι· τὰς
χροιὰς οἱ μὲν λευκοὶ οἱ δὲ μέλανες οἱ δὲ ξανθοί·
τὸ δ' ὅλον οὐκ ἐλάττω χρώματά φασιν εἶναι τῶν
συκῶν οὐδ' ἁπλῶς τὰ γένη· διαφέρειν δὲ καὶ κατὰ
τὰ μεγέθη καὶ κατὰ τὰ σχήματα· καὶ γὰρ σφαι-
ροειδεῖς ἐνίους ὡσανεὶ μῆλα καὶ τὰ μεγέθη τηλι-
κούτους ὡς τέτταρας εἰς τὸν πῆχυν εἶναι, [ἕπτα
καὶ εὐπόδους]· ἄλλους δὲ μικροὺς ἡλίκους ἐρεβίνθους. καὶ τοῖς χυλοῖς δὲ πολὺ διαφέροντας.

7 Κράτιστον δὲ καὶ τῶν λευκῶν καὶ τῶν μελάνων
τὸ βασιλικὸν καλούμενον γένος ἐν ἑκατέρῳ καὶ
μεγέθει καὶ ἀρετῇ· σπάνια δ' εἶναι ταῦτα λέγουσι·
σχεδὸν γὰρ ἐν μόνῳ τῷ Βαγώου κήπῳ τοῦ
παλαιοῦ περὶ Βαβυλῶνα. ἐν Κύπρῳ δὲ ἴδιόν τι
γένος φοινίκων ἐστὶν ὃ οὐ πεπαίνει τὸν καρπόν,
ἀλλ' ὠμὸς ὢν ἡδὺς σφόδρα καὶ γλυκύς ἐστι· τὴν
δὲ γλυκύτητα ἰδίαν ἔχει. ἔνιοι δ' οὐ μόνον δια-

---

¹ Plin. 13. 39.
² πρῶτον conj. Sch.; πρῶτος UMVAld.
³ πῆχυν conj. R. Const. from Plin. 13. 45. and G, cf. Diod.
2. 53; στάχυν UMVAld.
⁴ ἕπτα καὶ εὐπόδους UMV: the words perhaps conceal a

in different soils the methods of cultivation should
differ, like the trees themselves.

[1] There are several kinds of palm. To begin with,
to take first the most important difference;—some
are fruitful and some not; and it is from this latter
kind that the people of Babylon make their beds
and other furniture. Again of the fruitful trees
some are 'male,' others 'female'; and these differ
from one another in that the 'male' first [2] bears a
flower on the spathe, while the 'female' at once
bears a small fruit. Again there are various differences
in the fruits themselves; some have no stones, others
soft stones; as to colour, some are white, some black,
some yellow; and in general they say that there is
not less variety of colour and even of kind than in
figs; also that they differ in size and shape, some being
round like apples and of such a size that four of them
make up a cubit [3] in length, . . . [4] while others are
small,[5] no bigger than chick-peas; and that there is
also much difference in flavour.

The best kind alike in size and in quality, whether
of the white or black variety, is that which in either
form is called 'the royal palm'; but this, they say,
is rare; it grows hardly anywhere except in the
park of the ancient Bagoas,[6] near Babylon. In
Cyprus [7] there is a peculiar kind of palm which does
not ripen its fruit, though, when it is unripe, it is
very sweet and luscious, and this lusciousness is of a
peculiar kind. Some palms again [8] differ not merely

gloss on πῆχυν, e.g. εἰς πῆχυς δύο πόδες (Salm.); om. G; ἐνίοτε
καὶ ἐπὶ πόδα conj. W.       [5] Plin. 13. 42.
  [6] Βαγώου: Βάττου MSS. corr. by R. Const. from Plin. 13.
41. τοῦ παλαίου apparently distinguishes this Bagoas from
some more recent wearer of the name.
  [7] Plin. 13. 33.       [8] Plin. 13. 28.

φέρουσι τοῖς καρποῖς ἀλλὰ καὶ αὐτῷ τῷ δένδρῳ
κατά τε τὸ μῆκος καὶ τὴν ἄλλην μορφήν· οὐ γὰρ
μεγάλοι καὶ μακροὶ ἀλλὰ βραχεῖς, ἔτι δὲ καρπι-
μώτεροι τῶν ἄλλων καὶ καρποφοροῦντες εὐθὺς
τριετεῖς· πολλοὶ δὲ καὶ οὗτοι περὶ Κύπρον. εἰσὶ
δὲ καὶ περὶ Συρίαν καὶ περὶ Αἴγυπτον φοίνικες
οἳ φέρουσι τετραετεῖς καὶ πενταετεῖς ἀνδρομήκεις
ὄντες.

8    Ἕτερον δ' ἔτι γένος ἐν Κύπρῳ, ὃ καὶ τὸ φύλλον
πλατύτερον ἔχει καὶ τὸν καρπὸν μείζω πολλῷ
καὶ ἰδιόμορφον· μεγέθει μὲν ἡλίκος ῥόα τῷ σχήματι δὲ προμήκης, οὐκ εὔχυλος δὲ ὥσπερ ἄλλοι
ἀλλ' ὅμοιος[1] ταῖς ῥόαις, ὥστε μὴ καταδέχεσθαι
ἀλλὰ διαμασησαμένους ἐκβάλλειν. γένη μὲν οὖν,
ὥσπερ εἴρηται, πολλά. θησαυρίζεσθαι δὲ μόνους
δύνασθαί φασι τῶν ἐν Συρίᾳ τοὺς ἐν τῷ αὐλῶνι,
τοὺς δ' ἐν Αἰγύπτῳ καὶ Κύπρῳ καὶ παρὰ τοῖς
ἄλλοις χλωροὺς ἀναλίσκεσθαι.

9    Ἔστι δὲ ὁ φοῖνιξ ὡς μὲν ἁπλῶς εἰπεῖν μονοστέλεχες καὶ μονοφυές· οὐ μὴν ἀλλὰ γίνονταί
τινες καὶ διφυεῖς, ὥσπερ ἐν Αἰγύπτῳ, καθάπερ
δικρόαν ἔχοντες· τὸ δ' ἀνάστημα τοῦ στελέχους
ἀφ' οὗ ἡ σχίσις καὶ πεντάπηχυ· πρὸς ἄλληλα δέ
πως ἰσάζοντα. φασὶ δὲ καὶ τοὺς ἐν Κρήτῃ
πλείους εἶναι τοὺς διφυεῖς, ἐνίους δὲ καὶ τριφυεῖς·[2]
ἐν δὲ τῇ Λαπαίᾳ τινὰ καὶ πεντακέφαλον· οὐκ
ἄλογον γοῦν ἐν ταῖς εὐτροφωτέραις χώραις πλείω
γίνεσθαι τὰ τοιαῦτα καὶ τὸ ὅλον δὲ τὰ εἴδη πλείω
καὶ τὰς διαφοράς.

---

[1] ὅμοιος conj. Bod.; ὁμοίως UMVAld.    [2] cf. §5.
[3] Plin. 13. 38 ; cf. 4. 2. 7, where the name (κουκιόφορον) of
this tree is given.

in their fruits but in the character of the tree itself
as to stature and general shape; for instead of being
large and tall they are low growing; but these are
more fruitful than the others, and they begin to bear
as soon as they are three years old; this kind too is
common in Cyprus.  Again in Syria and Egypt
there are palms which bear when they are four or
five years old, at which age they are the height of
a man.

There is yet another kind in Cyprus, which has
broader leaves and a much larger fruit of peculiar
shape; in size it is as large as a pomegranate, in
shape it is long; it is not however juicy like others,
but like[1] a pomegranate, so that men do not
swallow it, but chew it and then spit it out.  Thus,
as has been said, there are many kinds.  The only
dates that will keep, they say, are those which grow
in the Valley[2] of Syria, while those that grow in
Egypt Cyprus and elsewhere are used when fresh.

The palm, speaking generally, has a single and
simple stem; however there are some with two
stems, as in Egypt,[3] which make a fork, as it were;
the length of the stem up to the point where it
divides is as much as five cubits, and the two
branches of the fork are about equal in length.  They
say that the palms in Crete more often than not
have this double stem, and that some of them have
three stems; and that in Lapaia one with five heads
has been known.  It is after all not surprising[4]
that in more fertile soils such instances should be
commoner, and in general that more kinds and more
variation should be found under such conditions.

[4] οὐκ ἄλογον γοῦν conj. W. (οὐκ ἄλογον δ' Sch.); οὐ καλῶς
γοῦν Ald.MU (marked doubtful).

10 Ἄλλο δέ τι γένος ἐστὶν ὅ φασι γίνεσθαι πλεῖστον περὶ τὴν Αἰθιοπίαν, ὅ καλοῦσι κόϊκας· οὗτοι δὲ θαμνώδεις, οὐχὶ ἓν τὸ στέλεχος ἔχοντες ἀλλὰ πλείω καὶ ἐνίοτε συνηρτημένα μέχρι τινὸς εἰς ἕν, τὰς δὲ ῥάβδους οὐ μακρὰς μὲν ἀλλ᾽ ὅσον πηχυαίας, ἀλλὰ λείας, ἐπὶ δὲ τῶν ἄκρων τὴν κόμην. ἔχουσι δὲ καὶ τὸ φύλλον πλατὺ καὶ ὥσπερ ἐκ δυοῖν συγκείμενον ἐλαχίστοιν. καλοὶ δὲ καὶ τῇ ὄψει φαίνονται· τὸν δὲ καρπὸν καὶ τῷ σχήματι καὶ τῷ μεγέθει καὶ τῷ χυλῷ διάφορον ἔχουσι· στρογγυλώτερον γὰρ καὶ μείζω καὶ εὐστομώτερον ἧττον δὲ γλυκύν. πεπαίνουσι δὲ ἐν τρισὶν ἔτεσιν ὥστ᾽ ἀεὶ καρπὸν ἔχειν, ἐπικαταλαμβάνοντος τοῦ νέου τὸν ἔνον· ποιοῦσι δὲ καὶ ἄρτους ἐξ αὐτῶν· περὶ μὲν οὖν τούτων ἐπισκεπτέον.

11 Οἱ δὲ χαμαιρριφεῖς καλούμενοι τῶν φοινίκων ἕτερόν τι γένος ἐστὶν ὥσπερ ὁμώνυμον· καὶ γὰρ ἐξαιρεθέντος τοῦ ἐγκεφάλου ζῶσι καὶ κοπέντες ἀπὸ τῶν ῥιζῶν παραβλαστάνουσι. διαφέρουσι δὲ καὶ τῷ καρπῷ καὶ τοῖς φύλλοις· πλατὺ γὰρ καὶ μαλακὸν ἔχουσι τὸ φύλλον, δι᾽ ὃ καὶ πλέκουσιν ἐξ αὐτοῦ τάς τε σπυρίδας καὶ τοὺς φορμούς· πολλοὶ δὲ καὶ ἐν τῇ Κρήτῃ γίνονται καὶ ἔτι μᾶλλον ἐν Σικελίᾳ. ταῦτα μὲν οὖν ἐπὶ πλεῖον εἴρηται τῆς ὑποθέσεως.

---

[1] Plin. 13. 47.
[2] κόϊκας conj. Salm. cf. 1. 10. 5, and the probable reading in Plin. l.c.
[3] συνηρτημένα μέχρι τινὸς εἰς ἓν conj. W.; συνηρτημένας μὲν

142

[1] There is another kind which is said to be abundant in Ethiopia, called the doum-palm[2]; this is a shrubby tree, not having a single stem but several, which sometimes are joined together up to a certain point[3]; and the leaf-stalks are not long,[4] only the length of a cubit, but they are plain,[5] and the leafage is borne only at the tip. The leaf is broad and, as it were, made up of at least[6] two leaflets. This tree is fair to look upon, and its fruit in shape size and flavour differs from the date, being rounder larger and pleasanter to the taste, though not so luscious. It ripens in three years, so that there is always fruit on the tree, as the new fruit overtakes that of last year. And they make bread out of it. These reports then call for enquiry.

[7] The dwarf-palm, as it is called, is a distinct kind, having nothing but its name[8] in common with other palms. For if the head is removed, it survives, and, if it is cut down, it shoots again from the roots. It differs too in the fruit and leaves; for the leaf is broad and flexible, and so they weave their baskets and mats out of it. It is common in Crete and still more so in Sicily.[9] However in these matters we have said more than our purpose required.

οἷς ἕν U; συνηρτημένα μέχρι τινός εἰσι Ald.; συνηρτημένας μὲν μέχρι τινὸς εἶεν MV.

[4] μὲν ins. W. after Sch. (omitted above).

[5] i.e. without leaflets, except at the tip.

[6] ἐλαχίστοιν Bas.; ἐλαχίστων U. cf. Arist. Eth. N. 5. 3. 3, ἐν ἐλαχίστοις δυοῖν.

[7] Plin. 13. 39.     [8] For ὁμώνυμον cf. 9. 10. 1 n.

[9] A dwarf palm is now abundant at Selinunte: cf. Verg. Aen. 3. 705, palmosa Selinus.

THEOPHRASTUS

12 Ἐν δὲ ταῖς τῶν ἄλλων φυτείαις ἀνάπαλιν
τίθενται τὰ φυτευτήρια, καθάπερ τῶν κλημάτων.
οἱ μὲν οὖν οὐθὲν διαφέρειν φασὶν ἥκιστα δὲ ἐπὶ
τῶν ἀμπέλων· ἔνιοι δὲ ῥόαν δασύνεσθαι καὶ
σκιάζειν μᾶλλον τὸν καρπόν· ἔτι δὲ ἧττον ἀποβάλλειν τοὺς κυτίνους. συμβαίνειν δὲ τοῦτό φασι
καὶ ἐπὶ τῆς συκῆς· οὐ γὰρ ἀποβάλλειν ἀνάπαλιν
φυτευθεῖσαν, ἔτι δ᾽ εὐβατωτέραν γίνεσθαι· οὐκ
ἀποβάλλειν δὲ οὐδ᾽ ἐάν τις ἀποκλάσῃ φυομένης
εὐθὺς τὸ ἄκρον.
Αἱ μὲν οὖν φυτεῖαι καὶ γενέσεις ὃν τρόπον
ἔχουσι σχεδὸν ὡς τύπῳ περιλαβεῖν εἴρηνται.
VII. Περὶ δὲ τῆς ἐργασίας καὶ τῆς θεραπείας
τὰ μέν ἐστι κοινὰ τὰ δὲ ἴδια καθ᾽ ἕκαστον. κοινὰ
μὲν ἥ τε σκαπάνη καὶ ἡ ὑδρεία καὶ ἡ κόπρωσις,
ἔτι δὲ ἡ διακάθαρσις καὶ ἀφαίρεσις τῶν αὔων.
διαφέρουσι δὲ τῷ μᾶλλον καὶ ἧττον. τὰ μὲν
φίλυδρα καὶ φιλόκοπρα τὰ δ᾽ οὐχ ὁμοίως, οἷον ἡ
κυπάριττος, ἥπερ οὐ φιλόκοπρον οὐδὲ φίλυδρον,
ἀλλὰ καὶ ἀπόλλυσθαί φασιν ἐάν γε νέαν οὖσαν
ἐφυδρεύωσι πολλῷ. ῥόα δὲ καὶ ἄμπελος φίλυδρα.
συκῇ δὲ εὐβλαστοτέρα μὲν ὑδρευομένη τὸν δὲ
καρπὸν ἴσχει χείρω πλὴν τῆς Λακωνικῆς· αὕτη δὲ
φίλυδρος.

¹ ἀνάπαλιν conj. Sch.; τἀνάπαλιν Ald.   cf. C.P. 2. 9. 4;
Geop. 10. 45; Plin. 17. 84.   ² οὖν ins. H.
³ δασύνεσθαι: see LS. reff. s.v. δασύς.
⁴ cf. C.P. 2. 9. 3.
⁵ εὐβατωτέραν (i.e. 'more manageable'). The reference is
to a method of keeping the tree dwarf (Bod.). Plin. l.c. has

144

*Further notes on the propagation of trees.*

To return to the other trees :—in propagating them they set the cuttings upside down,[1] as with vine-shoots. Some however[2] say that that makes no difference, and least of all in propagating the vine ; while others contend that the pomegranate thus propagated has a bushier growth[3] and shades the fruit better, and also that it is then[4] less apt to shed the flower. This also occurs, they say, with the fig ; when it is set upside down, it does not shed its fruit, and it makes a more accessible[5] tree ; and it does not shed its fruit, even if one breaks off the top[6] as it begins to grow.

Thus we have given a general sketch of what we find about methods of propagation, and of the ways in which these trees are reproduced.

*Of the cultivation of trees.*

VII. [7] As to cultivation and tendance some require-ments apply equally to all trees, some are peculiar to one. Those which apply equally to all are spade-work watering and manuring, and moreover pruning and removal of dead wood. But different trees differ in the degree. Some love moisture and manure, some not so much, as the cypress,[8] which[9] is fond neither of manure nor of water, but actually dies, they say, if it is overwatered when young. But the pomegranate and vine are water-loving. The fig grows more vigorously if it is watered, but then its fruit is inferior, except in the case of the Laconian variety, which is water-loving.[10]

*scansilem* (so also G), which seems to be a rendering of εὔβατ. εὐβατοτέραν U.

[8] τὸ ἄκρον conj. R. Const. after G ; τὸν καρπὸν UMVP₂Ald.
[7] Plin. 17. 246.     [5] Plin. 17. 247.
[9] ᾗπερ conj. W. from G ; ὥσπερ Ald.     [10] *cf. C.P.* 3. 6. 6.

145

THEOPHRASTUS

2 Διακαθαίρεσθαι δὲ πάντα ζητεῖ· βελτίω γὰρ
τῶν αὔων ἀφαιρουμένων ὥσπερ ἀλλοτρίων, ἃ καὶ
τὰς αὐξήσεις καὶ τὰς τροφὰς ἐμποδίζει. δι᾽ ὃ
καὶ... ὅταν ᾖ γεράνδρυον ὅλως κόπτουσιν· ἡ γὰρ
βλάστησις νέα γίνεται τοῦ δένδρου. πλείστης δὲ
διακαθάρσεώς φησιν Ἀνδροτίων δεῖσθαι μύρρινον
καὶ ἐλάαν· ὅσῳ γὰρ ἂν ἐλάττω καταλίπῃς, ἄμεινον
βλαστήσει καὶ τὸν καρπὸν οἴσει πλείω· πλὴν
ἀμπέλου δῆλον ὅτι· ταύτῃ γὰρ ἀναγκαιότερον
καὶ πρὸς βλάστησιν καὶ πρὸς εὐκαρπίαν. ἁπλῶς
δὲ καὶ ταύτην καὶ τὴν ἄλλην θεραπείαν πρὸς τὴν
ἰδίαν φύσιν ἑκάστῳ ποιητέον.

3 Δεῖσθαι δέ φησιν Ἀνδροτίων καὶ κόπρου
δριμυτάτης καὶ πλείστης ὑδρείας, ὥσπερ καὶ τῆς
διακαθάρσεως, ἐλάαν καὶ μύρρινον καὶ ῥόαν· οὐ
γὰρ ἔχειν μήτραν οὐδὲ νόσημα κατὰ γῆς οὐδέν·
ἀλλ᾽ ἐπειδὰν παλαιὸν ᾖ τὸ δένδρον, ἀποτέμνειν
δεῖν τοὺς ἀκρεμόνας ἔπειτα τὸ στέλεχος θεραπεύειν ὥσπερὰν ἐξ ἀρχῆς φυτευθέν· οὕτω δὲ
φασι πολυχρονιώτερα καὶ ἰσχυρότατα μύρρινον
εἶναι καὶ ἐλάαν. ταῦτα μὲν οὖν ἐπισκέψαιτ᾽
ἄν τις, εἰ καὶ μὴ πάντα ἀλλὰ περί γε τῆς
μήτρας.

4 Ἡ δὲ κόπρος οὔτε πᾶσιν ὁμοίως οὔθ᾽ ἡ αὐτὴ
πᾶσιν ἁρμόττει· τὰ μὲν γὰρ δριμείας δεῖται τὰ
δ᾽ ἧττον τὰ δὲ παντελῶς κούφης. δριμυτάτη δὲ
ἡ τοῦ ἀνθρώπου· καθάπερ καὶ Χαρτόδρας
ἀρίστην μὲν ταύτην εἶναί φησι, δευτέραν δὲ τὴν
ὑείαν, τρίτην δὲ αἰγός, τετάρτην δὲ προβάτου,

---

[1] Plin. 17. 248.　　[2] Name of tree missing.　Sch.
[3] cf. C.P. 3. 10. 4.　　[4] ταύτῃ conj. W.; ταύτης Ald.

146

[1] All trees require pruning; for they are improved
by removal of the dead wood, which is, as it were, a
foreign body, and prevents growth and nourishment.
Wherefore when the (tree)[2] becomes old, they cut
off all its boughs: for then the tree breaks afresh.
Androtion[3] says that the myrtle and olive need more
pruning than any other trees; for the smaller you
leave them, the better they will grow, and they will
bear better fruit. But the vine of course needs
pruning even more; for it is in the case of this tree[4]
more necessary for promoting both growth and
fruitfulness. However, speaking generally, both
this and other kinds of tendance must be suited to
the particular natural character in each case.

Androtion further says that the olive the myrtle
and the pomegranate require the most pungent
manure and the heaviest watering, as well as the
most thorough pruning, for that then they do not
get 'softwood'[5] nor any disease underground; but
when the tree is old, he adds, one should cut off the
boughs, and then attend to the stem as though it
were a tree just planted. Thus[6] treated they say
that the myrtle and olive are longer lived and
very robust. These statements might be a subject
for further enquiry, or, if not all of them, at least what
is stated of the 'softwood.'

Manure does not suit all alike, nor is the same
manure equally good for all. Some need it pungent,
some less so, some need it quite light. The most
pungent is human dung: thus Chartodras[7] says
that this is the best, pig-manure being second to it,
goat-manure third, fourth that of sheep, fifth that of

[5] i.e. effete sap-wood.   [6] οὕτω conj. W.; οἱ Ald.
[7] Name perhaps corrupt.

πέμπτην δὲ βοός, ἕκτην δὲ τὴν λοφούρων. ἡ δὲ
συρματῖτις ἄλλη καὶ ἄλλως· ἡ μὲν γὰρ ἀσθενε-
στέρα ταύτης ἡ δὲ κρείττων.

5 Τὴν δὲ σκαπάνην πᾶσιν οἴονται συμφέρειν,
ὥσπερ καὶ τὴν ὅσκαλσιν τοῖς ἐλάττοσιν· εὐτρα-
φέστερα γὰρ γίνεσθαι. τρέφειν δὲ δοκεῖ καὶ ὁ κονι-
ορτὸς ἔνια καὶ θάλλειν ποιεῖν, οἷον τὸν βότρυν, δι'
ὃ καὶ ὑποκονίουσι πολλάκις· οἱ δὲ καὶ τὰς συκᾶς
ὑποσκάπτουσιν ἔνθα τούτου δεῖ. Μεγαροῖ δὲ
καὶ τοὺς σικύους καὶ τὰς κολοκύντας, ὅταν οἱ
ἐτησίαι πνεύσωσι, σκάλλοντες κονιορτοῦσι καὶ
οὕτω γλυκυτέρους καὶ ἀπαλωτέρους ποιοῦσιν
οὐχ ὑδρεύοντες. τοῦτο μὲν οὖν ὁμολογούμενον.
τὴν δ' ἄμπελον οὔ φασί τινες δεῖν [ἢ] ὑποκονίειν
οὐδ' ὅλως ἅπτεσθαι περκάζοντος τοῦ βότρυος,
ἀλλ' εἴπερ ὅταν ἀπομελανθῇ. οἱ δὲ τὸ ὅλον μηδὲ
τότε πλὴν ὅσον ὑποτῖλαι τὴν βοτάνην· ὑπὲρ μὲν
οὖν τούτων ἀμφισβητοῦσιν.

6 Ἐὰν δέ τι μὴ φέρῃ καρπὸν ἀλλ' εἰς βλάστησιν
τρέπηται, σχίζουσι τοῦ στελέχους τὸ κατὰ γῆν
καὶ λίθον ἐντιθέασιν ὅπως ἂν ῥαγῇ, καί φασι
φέρειν. ὁμοίως δὲ καὶ ἐάν τις τῶν ῥιζῶν τινας
περιτέμῃ, δι' ὃ καὶ τῶν ἀμπέλων ὅταν τραγῶσι
τοῦτο ποιοῦσι τὰς ἐπιπολῆς. τῶν δὲ συκῶν
πρὸς τῷ περιτέμνειν καὶ τέφραν περιπάττουσι
καὶ κατασχάζουσι τὰ στελέχη καί φασι φέρειν
μᾶλλον. ἀμυγδαλῇ δὲ καὶ πάτταλον ἐγκόψαντες

---

¹ Lit. ' bushy tails,' *i.e.* horses asses mules.
² *cf.* C.P. 3. 16. 3.   ³ δεῖ ins. H ; so apparently G read.
⁴ δεῖν ὑποκονίειν οὐδ' ὅλως conj. W. (so Sch., but keeping
[ἢ] after δεῖν); δεῖν ἢ ὑποκινιεῖν οὐδ' ὅλως UMV; δεῖν ἢ ὑποκο-
νιεῖν ἢ ὅλως Ald.   ⁵ Plin. 17. 253 and 254.

oxen, and sixth that of beasts of burden.[1] Litter
manure is of different kinds and is applied in various
ways : some kinds are weaker, some stronger.

Spade-work is held to be beneficial to all trees,
and also hoeing for the smaller ones, as they then
become more vigorous. Even dust[2] is thought to
fertilise some things and make them flourish, for
instance the grape ; wherefore they often put dust to
the roots of the vine. Some also dig in dust about
the figs in places where it is deficient.[3] In Megara,
when the etesian winds are past, they cover the
cucumber and gourd plants with dust by raking, and
so make the fruits sweeter and tenderer by not
watering. On this point there is general agreement.
But some say that dust should not be put to the vine,[4]
and that it should not be meddled with at all when
the grape is turning, or, if at all, only when it has
turned black. Some again say that even then nothing
should be done except to pluck up the weeds. So
on this point there is a difference of opinion.

[5] If a tree does not bear fruit but inclines to a
leafy growth, they split that part of the stem which
is underground and insert a stone corresponding[6] to
the crack thus made, and then, they say, it will bear.
The same result follows, if one cuts off some of the
roots, and accordingly they thus treat the surface
roots of the vine when it runs to leaf. In the case
of figs, in addition to root-pruning,[7] they also sprinkle
ashes about the tree, and make gashes in the stems,
and then, they say, it bears better. [8] Into the almond
tree they drive an iron peg, and, having thus made

[6] ὅπως ἂν ῥαγῇ Ald.: so G ; ? ὅπου ; ὅπως ἀνεθγῃ conj. W.
cf. Geop. 5. 35.    [7] Plin. l.c.
[8] cf. 2. 2. 11 ; C.P. 1. 17. 10 ; 2. 14. 1 ; Plin. 7. 253.

σιδηροῦν ὅταν τετράνωσιν ἄλλον ἀντεμβάλλουσι δρύϊνον καὶ τῇ γῇ κρύπτουσιν· ὃ καὶ καλοῦσί τινες κολάζειν ὡς ὑβρίζον τὸ δένδρον.

[1] Ταὐτὸν δὲ τοῦτο καὶ ἐπὶ τῆς ἀπίου καὶ ἐπ᾽ ἄλλων τινὲς ποιοῦσιν. ἐν Ἀρκαδίᾳ δὲ καὶ εὐθύνειν καλοῦσι τὴν ὕαν· πολὺ γὰρ τὸ δένδρον τοῦτο παρ᾽ αὐτοῖς ἐστι. καί φασιν, ὅταν πάθῃ τοῦτο, τὰς μὲν μὴ φερούσας φέρειν τὰς δὲ μὴ πεττούσας ἐκπέττειν καλῶς. ἀμυγδαλῆν δὲ καὶ ἐκ πικρᾶς γίγνεσθαι γλυκεῖαν, ἐάν τις περιορύξας τὸ στέλεχος καὶ τιτράνας ὅσον τε παλαιστιαῖον τὸ πανταχόθεν ἀπορρέον δάκρυον ἐπὶ ταὐτὸ ἐᾷ καταρρεῖν. τοῦτο μὲν οὖν ἂν εἴη πρός τε τὸ φέρειν ἅμα καὶ πρὸς τὸ εὐκαρπεῖν.

VIII. Ἀποβάλλει δὲ πρὸ τοῦ πέψαι τὸν καρπὸν ἀμυγδαλῆ μηλέα ῥόα ἄπιος καὶ μάλιστα δὴ πάντων συκῆ καὶ φοῖνιξ, πρὸς ἃ καὶ τὰς βοηθείας ζητοῦσι· ὅθεν καὶ ὁ ἐρινασμός· ἐκ γὰρ τῶν ἐκεῖ κρεμαννυμένων ἐρινῶν ψῆνες ἐκδυόμενοι κατεσθίουσι καὶ πιαίνουσι τὰς κορυφάς. διαφέρουσι δὲ καὶ αἱ χῶραι πρὸς τὰς ἀποβολάς· περὶ γὰρ Ἰταλίαν οὔ φασιν ἀποβάλλειν, δι᾽ ὃ οὐδ᾽ ἐρι-

---

[1] The operation being performed at the base of the tree. cf. § 7.    [2] ἐκπέττειν conj. R. Const.; εἰσπέττειν U.M.Ald.
[3] Plin. 17. 252.
[4] τὸ πανταχόθεν conj. W.; πανταχόθεν τὸ MSS.; so apparently G.   cf. C.P. 2. 14. 4.
[5] πέψαι conj. Sch.; πέμψαι Ald.
[6] ἐκεῖ κρεμαννυμένων ἐρινῶν I conj.; ἐκεῖ κρεμαννυμένων Ald.; ἐπικρεμαμένων ἐρινῶν conj. W.; but the present partic. is used C.P. 2. 9. 5.

a hole, insert in its place a peg of oak-wood and
bury it[1] in the earth, and some call this 'punishing'
the tree, since its luxuriance is thus chastened.

Some do the same with the pear and with other
trees. In Arcadia they have a similar process which is
called 'correcting' the sorb (for that tree is common in that country). And they say that under
this treatment those trees that would not bear do
so, and those that would not ripen their fruit now
ripen[2] them well. [3] It is also said that the almond
becomes sweet, instead of bitter, if one digs round
the stem and, having bored a hole about a palmsbreadth, allows the gum which exudes from all
sides[4] to flow down into it and collect. The object
of this would be alike to make the tree bear and to
improve the fruit.

*Of remedies for the shedding of the fruit: caprification.*

VIII. Trees which are apt to shed their fruit before
ripening[5] it are almond apple pomegranate pear
and, above all, fig and date-palm; and men try to
find the suitable remedies for this. This is the
reason for the process called 'caprification'; gall-
insects come out of the wild figs which are hanging
there,[6] eat the tops of the cultivated figs and so
make them swell.[7] The shedding of the fruit differs
according to the soil: in Italy[8] they say that it
does not occur, and so they do not use caprification,[9]

---

[7] πιαίνουσι MVAld.; διείρουσι conj. W. ? πεπαίνουσι, 'ripen,'
which is the word used in the parallel pass. *C.P.* 2. 9. 6, the
object of the process being to cause the figs to dry.
[8] Plin. 15. 81. 'Italy' means South Italy. *cf.* 4. 5. 5 and
6; 5. 8. 1.
[9] ἐρινάζουσιν conj. Bod.; ἐρινοῦσιν Ald. H.

νάζουσιν· οὐδ' ἐν τοῖς καταβορείοις καὶ λεπτογείοις, οἷον ἐπὶ Φαλύκῳ τῆς Μεγαρίδος· οὐδὲ τῆς
Κορινθίας ἔν τισι τόποις. ὡσαύτως δὲ καὶ ἡ
τῶν πνευμάτων κατάστασις· βορείοις γὰρ μᾶλλον
ἢ νοτίοις ἀποβάλλουσι, κἂν ψυχρότερα καὶ
πλείω γένηται μᾶλλον· ἔτι δ' αὐτῶν τῶν δένδρων
ἡ φύσις· τὰ πρώϊα γὰρ ἀποβάλλει, τὰ δ' ὄψια
οὐκ ἐκβάλλει, καθάπερ ἡ Λακωνικὴ καὶ αἱ ἄλλαι.
δι' ὃ καὶ οὐκ ἐρινάζουσι ταύτας. ταῦτα μὲν
οὖν ἔν τε τοῖς τόποις καὶ τοῖς γένεσι καὶ τῇ
καταστάσει τοῦ ἀέρος ἔχει τὰς διαφοράς.

2 Οἱ δὲ ψῆνες ἐκδύονται μὲν ἐκ τοῦ ἐρινεοῦ,
καθάπερ εἴρηται· γίνονται δ' ἐκ τῶν κεγχραμίδων.
σημεῖον δὲ λέγουσιν, ὅτι ἐπειδὰν ἐκδύωσιν οὐκ
ἔνεισι κεγχραμίδες. ἐκδύονται δὲ οἱ πολλοὶ
ἐγκαταλιπόντες ἢ πόδα ἢ πτερόν. γένος δέ τι
καὶ ἕτερόν ἐστι τῶν ψηνῶν, ὃ καλοῦσι κεντρίνας·
οὗτοι δ' ἀργοὶ καθάπερ κηφῆνες· καὶ τοὺς εἰσδυο-
μένους τῶν ἑτέρων κτείνουσιν αὐτοὶ δὲ ἐναπο-
θνήσκουσιν. ἐπαινοῦσι δὲ μάλιστα τῶν ἐρινῶν
τὰ μέλανα τὰ ἐκ τῶν πετρωδῶν χωρίων· πολλὰς
3 γὰρ ἔχει ταῦτα κεγχραμίδας. γιγνώσκεται δὲ
τὸ ἐρινασμένον τῷ ἐρυθρὸν εἶναι καὶ ποικίλον καὶ
ἰσχυρόν· τὸ δ' ἀνερίναστον λευκὸν καὶ ἀσθενές·
προστιθέασι δὲ τοῖς δεομένοις ὅταν ὕῃ. ὅπου
δὲ πλεῖστος κονιορτός, ἐνταῦθα πλεῖστα καὶ

---

¹ cf. 8. 2. 11.
² ψυχρότερα καὶ πλείω conj. Sch.; τεχνοτέρα καὶ πλείων MV
Ald. ; τεχρότερα καὶ πλείω U.
³ πρώϊα conj. Sch. from G ; πρῶτα Ald. H.
⁴ Plin. 17. 255 and 256.

nor is it practised in places which face north nor in those with light soils, as at Phalykos[1] in the Megarid, nor in certain parts of the district of Corinth. Also conditions as to wind make a difference; the fruit is shed more with northerly than with southerly winds, and this also happens more if the winds are cold and frequent.[2] Moreover the character of the tree itself makes a difference; for some kinds, such as the Laconian and other such kinds, shed their early[3] figs but not the later ones. Wherefore caprification is not practised with these. Such are the changes to which the fig is subject in respect of locality kind and climatic conditions.

[4] Now the gall-insects come, as has been said, out of the wild fig, and they are engendered from the seeds. The proof given of this is that, when they come out, there are no seeds left in the fruit; and most of them in coming out leave a leg or a wing behind. There is another kind of gall-insect which is called *kentrines*; these insects are sluggish, like drones, they kill those of the other kind who are entering the figs, and they themselves die in the fruit. The black kind of wild fig which grows in rocky places is most commended for caprification, as these figs contain numerous seeds.[5] A fig which has been subject to caprification is known by being red and parti-coloured and stout, while one which has not been so treated is pale and sickly. The treatment is applied to the trees which need it, after rain. The wild figs are most plentiful and most potent

[5] *i.e.* and so should produce more gall-insects: in *C.P.*
2. 9. 6 it is implied that the insect is produced by putrefac-
tion of the seeds of the wild fig.

ἰσχυρότατα τὰ ἐρινὰ γίνεται. φασὶ δὲ ἐρινάζειν καὶ τὸ πόλιον, ὁπόταν αὐτῷ καρπὸς ᾖ πολύς, καὶ τοὺς τῆς πτελέας κωρύκους· ἐγγίνεται γὰρ καὶ ἐν τούτοις θηρίδι᾿ ἄττα. κνῖπες ὅταν ἐν ταῖς συκαῖς γίνωνται κατεσθίουσι τοὺς ψῆνας. ἄκος δὲ τούτου φασὶν εἶναι τοὺς καρκίνους προσπερονᾶν· πρὸς γὰρ τούτους τρέπεσθαι τοὺς κνῖπας. ἀλλὰ γὰρ δὴ ταῖς μὲν συκαῖς αὗται βοήθειαι.

4 Τοῖς δὲ φοίνιξιν αἱ ἀπὸ τῶν ἀρρένων πρὸς τοὺς θήλεις· οὗτοι γάρ εἰσιν οἱ ἐπιμένειν ποιοῦντες καὶ ἐκπέττειν, ὃ καλοῦσί τινες ἐκ τῆς ὁμοιότητος ὀλυνθάζειν. γίνεται δὲ τόνδε τὸν τρόπον. ὅταν ἀνθῇ τὸ ἄρρεν, ἀποτέμνουσι τὴν σπάθην ἐφ᾿ ἧς τὸ ἄνθος εὐθὺς ὥσπερ ἔχει, τόν τε χνοῦν καὶ τὸ ἄνθος καὶ τὸν κονιορτὸν κατασείουσι κατὰ τοῦ καρποῦ τῆς θηλείας· κἂν τοῦτο πάθῃ, διατηρεῖ καὶ οὐκ ἀποβάλλει. φαίνεται δ᾿ ἀμφοῖν ἀπὸ τοῦ ἄρρενος τοῖς θήλεσι βοήθεια γίνεσθαι· θῆλυ γὰρ καλοῦσι τὸ καρποφόρον· ἀλλ᾿ ἡ μὲν οἷον μῖξις· ἡ δὲ κατ᾿ ἄλλον τρόπον.

---

[1] ὁπότ᾿ ἂν ... πολύς conj. W. from G, cum copiose fructificat; ὁπόταν αἰγίπυρος ᾖ πολύς MSS. U adds καὶ before ὁπόταν.

[2] κωρύκους I conj. In 3. 14. 1. the elm is said to bear κωρυκίδες which contain gnat-like creatures; these growths are called κωρυκώδη τινὰ κοῖλα 3. 15. 4; and in 3. 7. 3. the

where there is most dust. And they say that hulwort also, when it fruits freely,[1] and the 'gall-bags'[2] of the elm are used for caprification. For certain little creatures are engendered in these also. When the *knips* is found in figs, it eats the gall-insects. It is to prevent this, it is said, that they nail up the crabs ; for the *knips* then turns its attention to these. Such are the ways of assisting the fig-trees.

With dates it is helpful to bring the male to the female ; for it is the male which causes the fruit to persist and ripen, and this process some call, by analogy, 'the use of the wild fruit.'[3] The process is thus performed : when the male palm is in flower, they at once cut off the spathe on which the flower is, just as it is, and shake the bloom with the flower and the dust over the fruit of the female, and, if this is done to it, it retains the fruit and does not shed it. In the case both of the fig and of the date it appears that the 'male' renders aid to the 'female,' —for the fruit-bearing tree is called 'female'— but while in the latter case there is a union of the two sexes, in the former the result is brought about somewhat differently.

same thing is referred to as τὸ θυλακῶδες τοῦτο, where τοῦτο = 'the well-known'; *cf.* also 9. 1. 2, where Sch. restores ιαρύκους ; *cf.* Pall. 4. 10. 28. κυπαίρους (?) U ; κυπέρους MV; ιύπεριν Ald.; κυττάρους conj. W.

[3] ὑλυνθάζειν, from ὄλυνθος, a kind of wild fig, as ἐρινάζειν, from ἐρινός, the wild fig used for caprification. *cf.* C.P. 3. 18. 1.

BOOK III

Γ

I. Ἐπεὶ δὲ περὶ τῶν ἡμέρων δένδρων εἴρηται, λεκτέον ὁμοίως καὶ περὶ τῶν ἀγρίων, εἴ τέ τι ταὐτὸν καὶ ἕτερον ἔχουσι τοῖς ἡμέροις εἴ θ᾽ ὅλως ἴδιον τῆς φύσεως.

Αἱ μὲν οὖν γενέσεις ἁπλαῖ τινες αὐτῶν εἰσι· πάντα γὰρ ἢ ἀπὸ σπέρματος ἢ ἀπὸ ῥίζης φύεται. τοῦτο δ᾽ οὐχ ὡς οὐκ ἐνδεχόμενον καὶ ἄλλως, ἀλλ᾽ ἴσως διὰ τὸ μὴ πειρᾶσθαι μηδένα μηδὲ φυτεύειν· ἐκφύοιτο[1] δ᾽ ἂν εἰ λαμβάνοιεν τόπους ἐπιτηδείους καὶ θεραπείαν τὴν ἁρμόττουσαν· ὥσπερ καὶ νῦν τὰ ἀλσώδη καὶ φίλυδρα, λέγω δ᾽ οἷον πλάτανον ἰτέαν λεύκην αἴγειρον πτελέαν· ἅπαντα γὰρ ταῦτα καὶ τὰ τοιαῦτα φυτευόμενα βλαστάνει καὶ τάχιστα καὶ κάλλιστα ἀπὸ τῶν παρασπάδων, ὥστε καὶ μεγάλας οὔσας ἤδη καὶ ἰσοδένδρους ἄν τις μεταθῇ διαμένειν· φυτεύεται δὲ τὰ πολλὰ αὐτῶν καὶ καταπηγνύμενα, καθάπερ ἡ λεύκη καὶ ἡ αἴγειρος.

2 Τούτων μὲν οὖν πρὸς τῇ σπερματικῇ καὶ τῇ ἀπὸ τῶν ῥιζῶν καὶ αὕτη γένεσίς ἐστι· τῶν δὲ

---

[1] ἐκφύοιτο conj. W.; ἐπιφύοιτο UMVAld.

# BOOK III

*Of the ways in which wild trees originate.*

I. Now that we have spoken of cultivated trees, we must in like manner speak of wild ones, noting in what respects they agree with or differ from cultivated trees, and whether in any respects their character is altogether peculiar to themselves.

Now the ways in which they come into being are fairly simple ; they all grow either from seed or from a root. But the reason of this is not that they could not possibly grow in any other way, but merely perhaps that no one even tries to plant them otherwise ; whereas they might grow [1] from slips, if they were provided with a suitable position and received the fitting kind of tendance, as may be said even now of the trees of woodland and marsh, such as plane willow abele black poplar and elm ; all these and other similar trees grow very quickly and well when they are planted from pieces torn off, so that [2] they survive, even if at the time of shifting they are already tall and as big as trees. Most of these are simply planted by being set firmly, for instance, the abele and the black poplar.

Such is the way in which these originate as well as from seed or from roots ; the others grow only

[2] ὥστε καὶ μεγ. conj. Sch.; καὶ ὥστε καὶ μεγ. UM ; καὶ ὥστε μεγ. PAld.

ἄλλων ἐκεῖναι· πλὴν ὅσα μόνον ἀπὸ σπέρματος
φύεται, καθάπερ ἐλάτη πεύκη πίτυς. ὅσα δὲ ἔχει
σπέρμα καὶ καρπόν, κἂν ἀπὸ ῥίζης γίνηται, καὶ
ἀπὸ τούτων· ἐπεὶ καὶ τὰ δοκοῦντα ἄκαρπα εἶναι
γεννᾶν φασιν, οἷον πτελέαν ἰτέαν. σημεῖον δὲ
λέγουσιν οὐ μόνον ὅτι φύεται πολλὰ τῶν ῥιζῶν
ἀπηρτημένα καθ' οὓς ἂν ᾖ τόπους, ἀλλὰ καὶ τὰ
συμβαίνοντα θεωροῦντες, οἷον ἐν Φενεῷ τῆς
Ἀρκαδίας, ὡς ἐξερράγη τὸ συναθροισθὲν ὕδωρ ἐν
τῷ πεδίῳ φραχθέντων τῶν βερέθρων· ὅπου μὲν
ἐγγὺς ἦσαν ἰτέαι πεφυκυῖαι τοῦ καταποθέντος
τόπου, τῷ ὑστέρῳ ἔτει μετὰ τὴν ἀναξήρανσιν
ἐνταῦθα αὖθις ἀναφῦναί φασιν ἰτέαν· ὅπου δὲ
πτελέαι αὖθις πτελέας, καθάπερ καὶ ὅπου πεῦκαι
καὶ ἔλαται πεύκας καὶ ἐλάτας, ὥσπερ μιμουμένων
κἀκείνων.

3 Ἀλλὰ τὴν ἰτέαν ταχὺ προκαταβάλλειν πρὸ
τοῦ τελείως ἁδρῦναι καὶ πέψαι τὸν καρπόν·
δι' ὃ καὶ τὸν ποιητὴν οὐ κακῶς προσαγορεύειν
αὐτὴν ὠλεσίκαρπον.

Τῆς δὲ πτελέας κἀκεῖνο σημεῖον ὑπολαμβά-
νουσιν· ὅταν γὰρ ἀπὸ τῶν πνευμάτων εἰς τοὺς
ἐχομένους τόπους ὁ καρπὸς ἀπενεχθῇ, φύεσθαί
φασι. παραπλήσιον δὲ ἔοικεν εἶναι τὸ συμβαῖνον
ὃ καὶ ἐπὶ τῶν φρυγανικῶν καὶ ποιωδῶν τινών
ἐστιν· οὐκ ἐχόντων γὰρ σπέρμα φανερόν, ἀλλὰ

---

[1] cf. 5. 4. 6.
[2] 'Katavothra' (now called ' the devil's holes,' see Lawson,
cited below) ; cf. Paus. 8. 14 ; Catull. 68. 109 ; Plut. de sera
numinis vindicta, 557 c ; Plin. 31. 36 ; Frazer, Pausanias and
other Greek Sketches, pp. 315 foll. ; Lawson, Modern Greek
Folklore and Ancient Greek Religion, p. 85.

in these two ways—while some of them, such as
silver-fir fir and Aleppo pine grow *only* from seed.
All those that have seed and fruit, even if they grow
from a root, will grow from seed too; for they say
that even those which, like elm and willow, appear
to have no fruit reproduce themselves. For proof
they give the fact that many such trees come up at a
distance from the roots of the original tree, whatever the position may be; and further, they have
observed a thing which occasionally happens; for instance, when at Pheneos[1] in Arcadia the water which
had collected in the plain since the underground
channels[2] were blocked burst forth, where there
were willows growing near the inundated region, the
next year after it had dried up they say that willows
grew again; and where there had been elms, elms[3]
grew, even as, where there had been firs and silver-
firs, these trees reappeared—as if the former trees
followed the example[4] of the latter.

But the willow is said to shed its fruit early, before
it is completely matured and ripened; and so the
poet[5] not unfittingly calls it "the willow which loses
its fruit."

That the elm also reproduces itself the following
is taken to be a proof: when the fruit is carried by
the winds to neighbouring spots, they say that young
trees grow from it. Something similar to this
appears to be what happens in the case of certain
under-shrubs and herbaceous plants; though they
have no visible seed, but some of them only a sort of

---

[3] πτελέας αὖθις πτελέας conj. St.; πτελέας ἀντὶ πελέας U;
πτελέας ἀντὶ πτελέας MV; πτελέας αὖθις πτελέας P; πτελέα
αὖθις πτελέας Ald.

[4] *i.e.* by growing from seed, as conifers normally do.

[5] Homer, *Od.* 10. 510; *cf.* Plin. 16. 110.

τῶν μὲν οἷον χνοῦν τῶν δ' ἄνθος, ὥσπερ τὸ θύμον,
ὅμως ἀπὸ τούτων βλαστάνουσιν. ἐπεὶ ἥ γε
πλάτανος ἔχει φανερῶς καὶ ἀπὸ τούτων φύεται.
τοῦτο δ' ἐξ ἄλλων τε δῆλον κἀκεῖνο μέγιστον
σημεῖον· ὤφθη γὰρ ἤδη ποτὲ πεφυκυῖα πλάτανος
ἐν τρίποδι χαλκῷ.

4   Ταύτας τε δὴ τὰς γενέσεις ὑποληπτέον εἶναι
τῶν ἀγρίων καὶ ἔτι τὰς αὐτομάτους, ἃς καὶ οἱ
φυσιολόγοι λέγουσιν· Ἀναξαγόρας μὲν τὸν ἀέρα
πάντων φάσκων ἔχειν σπέρματα καὶ ταῦτα
συγκαταφερόμενα τῷ ὕδατι γεννᾶν τὰ φυτά·
Διογένης δὲ σηπομένου τοῦ ὕδατος καὶ μίξιν
τινὰ λαμβάνοντος πρὸς τὴν γῆν· Κλείδημος δὲ
συνεστάναι μὲν ἐκ τῶν αὐτῶν τοῖς ζῴοις, ὅσῳ
δὲ θολερωτέρων καὶ ψυχροτέρων τοσοῦτον ἀπέχειν
τοῦ ζῷα εἶναι. [λέγουσι δέ τινες καὶ ἄλλοι περὶ
τῆς γενέσεως.]

5   Ἀλλ' αὕτη μὲν ἀπηρτημένη πώς ἐστι τῆς
αἰσθήσεως. ἄλλαι δὲ ὁμολογούμεναι καὶ ἐμφα-
νεῖς, οἷον ὅταν ἔφοδος γένηται ποταμοῦ παρεκβάν-
τος τὸ ῥεῖθρον ἢ καὶ ὅλως ἑτέρωθι ποιησαμένου,
καθάπερ ὁ Νέσος ἐν τῇ Ἀβδηρίτιδι πολλάκις
μεταβαίνει, καὶ ἅμα τῇ μεταβάσει τοσαύτην
ὕλην συγγεννᾷ τοῖς τόποις, ὥστε τῷ τρίτῳ ἔτει
συνηρεφεῖν. καὶ πάλιν ὅταν ἐπομβρίαι κατά-
σχωσι πλείω χρόνον· καὶ γὰρ ἐν ταύταις βλαστήσεις γίνονται φυτῶν. ἔοικε δὲ ἡ μὲν τῶν ποταμῶν
ἔφοδος ἐπάγειν σπέρματα καὶ καρπούς, καὶ τοὺς
ὀχετούς φασι τὰ τῶν ποιωδῶν· ἡ δ' ἐπομβρία

1 cf. C.P. 1. 5. 2.
2 Sc. of Apollonia, the 'Ionian' philosopher.
3 cf. C.P. 1. 10. 3 ; 3. 23. 1 ; Arist. Meteor. 2. 9.

162

down, and others only a flower, such as thyme, young plants nevertheless grow from these. As for the plane, it obviously has seeds, and seedlings grow from them. This is evident in various ways, and here is a very strong proof—a plane-tree has before now been seen which came up in a brass pot.

Such we must suppose are the ways in which wild trees originate, apart from the spontaneous ways of which natural philosophers tell. [1] Anaxagoras says that the air contains the seeds of all things, and that these, carried down by the rain, produce the plants; while Diogenes [2] says that this happens when water decomposes and mixes in some sort with earth. [3] Kleidemos maintains that plants are made of the same elements as animals, but that they fall short of being animals in proportion as their composition is less pure and as they are colder. [4] And there are other philosophers also who speak of spontaneous generation.

But this kind of generation is somehow beyond the ken of our senses. There are other admitted and observable kinds, as when a river in flood gets over its banks or has altogether changed its course, even as the Nesos in the district of Abdera often alters its course, and in so doing causes such a growth of forest in that region that by the third year it casts a thick shade. The same result ensues when heavy rains prevail for a long time; during these too many plants shoot up. Now, as the flooding of a river, it would appear, conveys seeds of fruits of trees, and, as they say, irrigation channels convey the [5] seeds of herbaceous plants, so heavy

---

[4] λέγουσι . . . γενεσέως apparently a gloss (W.).
[5] τὰ conj. W.; τὴν MAld.

τοῦτο ποιεῖ ταὐτό· συγκαταφέρει γὰρ πολλὰ
τῶν σπερμάτων, καὶ ἅμα σῆψίν τινα τῆς γῆς καὶ
τοῦ ὕδατος· ἐπεὶ καὶ ἡ μίξις αὐτὴ τῆς Αἰγυπτίας
6 γῆς δοκεῖ τινα γεννᾶν ὕλην. ἐνιαχοῦ δέ, ἂν μόνον
ὑπεργάσωνται καὶ κινήσωσιν, εὐθὺς ἀναβλαστάνει
τὰ οἰκεῖα τῆς χώρας, ὥσπερ ἐν Κρήτῃ κυπάριττοι.
γίνεται δὲ παραπλήσιόν τι τούτῳ καὶ ἐν τοῖς
ἐλάττοσιν· ἅμα γὰρ κινουμένης ἀναβλαστάνει
πόα τις ἐν ἑκάστοις. ἐν δὲ τοῖς ἡμιβρόχοις ἐὰν
ὑπονεάσῃς φαίνεσθαί φασι τρίβολον. αὗται μὲν
οὖν ἐν τῇ μεταβολῇ τῆς χώρας εἰσίν, εἴτε καὶ
ἐνυπαρχόντων σπερμάτων εἴτε καὶ αὐτῆς πως
διατιθεμένης· ὅπερ ἴσως οὐκ ἄτοπον ἐγκατα-
κλειομένων ἅμα τῶν ὑγρῶν· ἐνιαχοῦ δὲ καὶ ὑδάτων
ἐπιγινομένων ἰδιώτερον ἀνατεῖλαι ὕλης πλῆθος,
ὥσπερ ἐν Κυρήνῃ πιττώδους τινὸς γενομένου καὶ
παχέος· οὕτως γὰρ ἀνεβλάστησεν ἡ πλησίον ὕλη
πρότερον οὐκ οὖσα. φασὶ δὲ καὶ τό γε σίλφιον
οὐκ ὂν πρότερον ἐκ τοιαύτης τινὸς αἰτίας φανῆναι. τρόποι μὲν οὖν τοιοῦτοι τῶν τοιούτων
γενέσεων.

II. Πάντα δὲ κάρπιμα ἢ ἄκαρπα, καὶ ἀείφυλλα
ἢ φυλλοβόλα, καὶ ἀνθοῦντα ἢ ἀνανθῆ· κοιναὶ

---

[1] ἢ δ' . . . ταὐτὸ conj. W.; ἢ δ' ἐπ. τοῦτ' αὖ ἐποίει ταὐτό
UMV (δ' αὖ marked doubtful in U); ἢ δ' ἐπ. τοῦτ' αὐτὸ ἐποίει
Ald.    [2] Plin. 16. 142.
[3] i.e. and is released by working the ground.
[4] cf. C.P. 1. 5. 1; Plin. 16. 143, who gives the date
A.U.C. 130; cf. 19. 41.

164

rain acts in the same way[1]; for it brings down
many of the seeds with it, and at the same time
causes a sort of decomposition of the earth and of
the water. In fact, the mere mixture of earth with
water in Egypt seems to produce a kind of vegetation. And in some places, if the ground is merely
lightly worked and stirred, the plants native to the
district immediately spring up; [2] for instance, the
cypress in Crete. And something similar to this
occurs even in smaller plants; as soon as the earth
is stirred, wherever it may be, a sort of vegetation
comes up. And in partly saturated soil, if you
break up the ground, they say that caltrop appears.
Now these ways of origination are due to the change
which takes place in the soil, whether there were
seeds in it already, or whether the soil itself somehow produces the result. And the latter explanation
is perhaps not strange, seeing that the moist element is also locked up in the soil.[3] Again, in some
places they say that after rain a more singular
abundance of vegetation has been known to spring
up; for instance, at Cyrene, after a heavy pitchy
shower had fallen: for it was under these circumstances that there sprang up the wood[4] which is
near the town, though till then it did not exist.
They say also that silphium[5] has been known to
appear from some such cause, where there was none
before. [6] Such are the ways in which these kinds
of generation come about.

*Of the differences between wild and cultivated trees.*

II. All trees are either fruit-bearing or without
fruit, either evergreen or deciduous, either flowering

[5] cf. 6. 3.　　[6] τοιοῦτοι MSS.; τοσοῦτοι conj. W.

THEOPHRASTUS

γάρ τινες διαιρέσεις ἐπὶ πάντων εἰσὶν ὁμοίως
ἡμέρων τε καὶ ἀγρίων. ἴδια δὲ πρὸς τὰ ἥμερα
τῶν ἀγρίων ὀψικαρπία τε καὶ ἰσχὺς καὶ πολυ-
καρπία τῷ προφαίνειν· πεπαίνει τε γὰρ ὀψιαίτερον καὶ τὸ ὅλον ἀνθεῖ καὶ βλαστάνει ὡς ἐπὶ τὸ
πᾶν· καὶ ἰσχυρότερα τῇ φύσει· καὶ προφαίνει
μὲν πλείω καρπὸν ἐκπέττει δ' ἧττον, εἰ μὴ καὶ
πάντα ἀλλά γε τὰ ὁμογενῆ, οἷον ἐλάας καὶ ἀπίου
κότινος καὶ ἀχράς. ἅπαντα γὰρ οὕτως, πλὴν
εἴ τι σπάνιον, ὥσπερ ἐπὶ τῶν κρανείων καὶ τῶν
οὔων· ταῦτα γὰρ δή φασι πεπαίτερα καὶ ἡδύτερα
τὰ ἄγρια τῶν ἡμέρων εἶναι· καὶ εἰ δή τι ἄλλο μὴ
προσδέχεται γεωργίαν ἢ δένδρον ἢ καί τι τῶν
ἐλαττόνων, οἷον τὸ σίλφιον καὶ ἡ κάππαρις καὶ
τῶν χεδροπῶν ὁ θέρμος, ἃ καὶ μάλιστ' ἂν τις
2 ἄγρια τὴν φύσιν εἴποι. τὸ γὰρ μὴ προσδεχόμενον
ἡμέρωσιν, ὥσπερ ἐν τοῖς ζώοις, τοῦτο ἄγριον τῇ
φύσει. καίτοι φησὶν Ἵππων ἅπαν καὶ ἥμερον
καὶ ἄγριον εἶναι, καὶ θεραπευόμενον μὲν ἥμερον
μὴ θεραπευόμενον δὲ ἄγριον, τῇ μὲν ὀρθῶς λέγων
τῇ δὲ οὐκ ὀρθῶς. ἐξαμελούμενον γὰρ ἅπαν
χεῖρον γίνεται καὶ ἀπαγριοῦται, θεραπευόμενον
δὲ οὐχ ἅπαν βέλτιον, ὥσπερ εἴρηται. ὁ δὴ
χωριστέον καὶ τὰ μὲν ἄγρια τὰ δ' ἥμερα λεκτέον,

---

¹ εἰ μὴ . . . ὁμογενῆ conj. W.: εἰ μὴ καὶ πάντα τὰ ἄλλα καὶ
τὰ ὁμοιογενῆ UMVAld.H.
² cf. C.P. 3. 1. 4.    ³ cf. 1. 3. 5 n.
⁴ i.e. the terms 'cultivated' and 'wild' do not denote
distinct 'kinds.'

166

or flowerless ; for certain distinctions apply to all trees alike, whether cultivated or wild.  To wild trees, as compared with cultivated ones, belong the special properties of fruiting late, of greater vigour, of abundance of fruit, produced if not matured ; for they ripen their fruit later, and in general their time of flowering and making growth is later ; also they are more vigorous in growth, and so, though they produce more fruit, they ripen it less ; if[1] this is not universally true, at least it holds good of the wild olive and pear as compared with the cultivated forms of these trees. This is generally true with few exceptions, as in the cornelian cherry and sorb ; for the wild forms of these, they say, ripen their fruit better, and it is sweeter than in the cultivated forms.  [2] And the rule also does not hold good of anything which does not admit of cultivation, whether it be a tree or one of the smaller plants, as silphium caper and, among leguminous plants, the lupin ; these one might say are specially wild in their character.  For, as with animals which do not submit to domestication, so a plant which does not submit to cultivation may be called wild in its essential character.  However Hippon[3] declares that of every plant there exists both a cultivated and a wild form, and that 'cultivated' simply means[4] that the plant has received attention, while ' wild ' means that it has not ; but though he is partly right, he is partly wrong.  It is true that any plant deteriorates by neglect and so becomes wild ; but it is not true that every plant may be improved by attention,[5] as has been said.  Wherefore[6] we must make our distinction and call some things wild, others culti-

[5] *i.e.* and so become ' cultivated.'
[6] δ δὴ MSS. ; δὰδ conj. Sch. from G.

ὥσπερ τῶν ζώων τὰ συνανθρωπευόμενα καὶ τὰ
δεχόμενα τιθασείαν.

3 Ἀλλὰ τοῦτο μὲν οὐδὲν ἴσως διαφέρει ποτέρως
ῥητέον. ἅπαν δὲ τὸ ἐξαγριούμενον τοῖς τε
καρποῖς χεῖρον γίνεται καὶ αὐτὸ βραχύτερον
καὶ φύλλοις καὶ κλωσὶ καὶ φλοιῷ καὶ τῇ ὅλῃ
μορφῇ· καὶ γὰρ πυκνότερα καὶ οὐλότερα καὶ
σκληρότερα καὶ ταῦτα καὶ ὅλη ἡ φύσις γίνεται,
ὡς ἐν τούτοις μάλιστα τῆς διαφορᾶς τῶν ἡμέρων
καὶ τῶν ἀγρίων γινομένης. δι' ὃ καὶ ὅσα τῶν
ἡμερουμένων τοιαῦτα τυγχάνει, ταῦτα ἄγριά
φασιν εἶναι, καθάπερ τὴν πεύκην καὶ τὴν κυπάριττον, ἢ ὅλως ἢ τὴν ἄρρενα, καὶ τὴν καρύαν δὲ
καὶ τὴν διοσβάλανον.

4 Ἔτι τε τῷ φιλόψυχρα καὶ ὀρεινὰ μᾶλλον εἶναι·
καὶ γὰρ τοῦτο λαμβάνεται πρὸς τὴν ἀγριότητα
τῶν δένδρων καὶ ὅλως τῶν φυτῶν, εἴτ' οὖν καθ'
αὑτὸ λαμβανόμενον εἴτε κατὰ συμβεβηκός.

Ὁ μὲν οὖν τῶν ἀγρίων ἀφορισμὸς εἴθ' οὕτως
ἢ καὶ ἄλλως ληπτέος, οὐδὲν ἂν ἴσως διενέγκοι
πρὸς τὰ νῦν· ἐκεῖνο δὲ ἀληθές, ὥς γε τῷ τύπῳ
καὶ ἁπλῶς εἰπεῖν, ὅτι μᾶλλον ὀρεινὰ τὰ ἄγρια καὶ
εὐθενεῖ τὰ πλείω καὶ μᾶλλον ἐν τούτοις τοῖς
τόποις, ἐὰν μή τις λαμβάνῃ τὰ φίλυδρα καὶ
παραποτάμια καὶ ἀλσώδη. ταῦτα γὰρ καὶ τὰ
5 τοιαῦτα τυγχάνει πεδεινὰ μᾶλλον. οὐ μὴν ἀλλ'
ἔν γε τοῖς μεγάλοις ὄρεσιν, οἷον Παρνησῷ τε
καὶ Κυλλήνῃ καὶ Ὀλύμπῳ τῷ Πιερικῷ τε καὶ
τῷ Μυσίῳ καὶ εἴ που τοιοῦτον ἕτερον, ἅπαντα

¹ τιθασείαν conj. W., cf. Plat. Pol. 264 c ; τιθάσιον UMAld.

168

vated—the latter class corresponding to those animals
which live with man and can be tamed.[1]

But perhaps it does not matter which way this
should be put. Any tree which runs wild deteriorates
in its fruits, and itself becomes dwarfed in leaves
branches bark and appearance generally; for under
cultivation these parts, as well as the whole
growth of the tree, become closer, more compact[2]
and harder; which indicates that the difference
between cultivated and wild is chiefly shown in these
respects. And so those trees which show these
characteristics under cultivation they say are really
wild, for instance fir cypress, or at least the 'male'
kind, hazel and chestnut.

Moreover these wild forms are distinguished by
having greater liking for cold and for hilly country:
for that too is regarded as a means of recognising
wild trees and wild plants generally, whether it is so
regarded in itself or as being only incidentally a
distinguishing mark.

So the definition of wild kinds, whether it should
be thus made or otherwise, perhaps makes no
difference for our present purpose. But it is certainly
true, speaking[3] broadly and generally, that the wild
trees are more to be found in hilly country, and that
the greater part of them flourish more in such regions,
with the exception of those which love water or grow
by river sides or in woods; these and such-like trees
are rather trees of the plain. However on great
mountains, such as Parnassus Cyllene the Pierian and
the Mysian Olympus, and such regions anywhere

[2] οὐλότερα conj. W. from G, *spissiora*; ὀρθότερα MSS.  cf.
C.P. 6. 11. 8.
[3] ἅς γε conj. Sch.; ὥστε UM; ὡς ἐν Ald.H.

φύεται διὰ τὴν πολυειδίαν τῶν τόπων· ἔχουσι
γὰρ καὶ λιμνώδεις καὶ ἐνύγρους καὶ ξηροὺς καὶ
γεώδεις καὶ πετρώδεις καὶ τοὺς ἀνὰ μέσον λει-
μῶνας καὶ σχεδὸν ὅσαι διαφοραὶ τῆς γῆς· ἔτι δὲ
τοὺς μὲν κοίλους καὶ εὐδιεινοὺς τοὺς δὲ μετεώρους
καὶ προσηνέμους· ὥστε δύνασθαι παντοῖα καὶ τὰ
ἐν τοῖς πεδίοις φέρειν.

6    Οὐδὲν δ' ἄτοπον οὐδ' εἰ ἔνια μὴ οὕτω πάμφορα
τῶν ὀρῶν, ἀλλ' ἰδιωτέρας τινὸς ὕλης ἢ πάσης ἢ τῆς
πλείστης, οἷον ἐν τῇ Κρήτῃ τὰ Ἰδαῖα·[1] κυπάριττος
γὰρ ἐκεῖ· καὶ τὰ περὶ Κιλικίαν καὶ Συρίαν, ἐν
οἷς κέδρος· ἐνιαχοῦ δὲ τῆς Συρίας τέρμινθος. αἱ
γὰρ διαφοραὶ τῆς χώρας τὴν ἰδιότητα ποιοῦσιν.
ἀλλ' εἴρηται τὸ ἴδιον ὡς ἐπὶ πᾶν.

III. Ἴδια δὲ τὰ τοιάδε τῶν ὀρεινῶν, ἃ ἐν τοῖς
πεδίοις οὐ φύεται, [περὶ τὴν Μακεδονίαν][3] ἐλάτη
πεύκη πίτυς ἀγρία φίλυρα ζυγία φηγὸς πύξος
ἀνδράχλη μίλος ἄρκευθος τέρμινθος ἐρινεὸς
φιλύκη ἀφάρκη καρύα διοσβάλανος πρῖνος. τὰ
δὲ καὶ ἐν τοῖς πεδίοις μυρίκη πτελέα λεύκη ἰτέα
αἴγειρος κρανεία θηλυκρανεία κλήθρα δρῦς λακάρη ἀχρὰς μηλέα ὀστρύα κήλαστρον μελία παλίουρος ὀξυάκανθος <σφένδαμνος,> ἣν ἐν μὲν τῷ

---

[1] ἐν . . . Ἰδαῖα conj. W. (after Sch., who conj. τὰ ἐν); τὰ
ἐν κρήτῃ τῇ Ἰδαίᾳ UAld.
[2] i.e. it is not meant that a tree which is 'special' to
Mount Ida (e.g.) occurs only there.
[3] περὶ τὴν Μακ.? a gloss; περὶ τε τὴν Μακ. MP₂Ald.; τε om. P.

else, all kinds grow, because of the diversity of
positions afforded them. For such mountains offer
positions which are marshy, wet, dry, deep-soiled or
rocky; they have also their meadow land here and
there, and in fact almost every variety of soil; again
they present positions which lie low and are sheltered, as well as others which are lofty and exposed
to wind; so that they can bear all sorts, even those
which belong to the plains.

Yet it is not strange that there should be some
mountains which do not thus bear all things, but
have a more special kind of vegetation to a great
extent if not entirely; for instance the range of Ida
in Crete[1]; for there the cypress grows; or the hills
of Cilicia and Syria, on which the Syrian cedar
grows, or certain parts of Syria, where the terebinth
grows. For it is the differences of soil which give
a special character to the vegetation. [2] (However
the word 'special' is used here in a somewhat
extended sense.)

*Of mountain trees: of the differences found in wild trees.*

III. The following trees are peculiar to mountain
country and do not grow in the plains; [3] let us
take Macedonia as an example. Silver-fir fir 'wild
pine' lime *zygia* Valonia oak box andrachne yew
Phoenician cedar terebinth wild fig alaternus hybrid
arbutus hazel chestnut kermes-oak. The following
grow also in the plain: tamarisk elm abele willow
black poplar cornelian cherry cornel alder oak *lakare*
(bird-cherry) wild pear apple hop-hornbeam holly
manna-ash Christ's thorn cotoneaster maple,[4] which

[4] σφενδαμνος add. Palm. in view of what follows; ὀξυάκαρτα
ἀκανθος UPAld.Bas.; ἀκανθος P₂.

ὄρει πεφυκυῖαν ζυγίαν καλοῦσιν, ἐν δὲ τῷ πεδίῳ
γλεῖνον. οἱ δ' ἄλλως διαιροῦσι καὶ ἕτερον ποιοῦσιν εἶδος σφενδάμνου καὶ ζυγίας.

2 Ἅπαντα δὲ ὅσα κοινὰ τῶν ὀρῶν καὶ τῶν
πεδίων, μείζω μὲν καὶ καλλίω τῇ ὄψει τὰ ἐν τοῖς
πεδίοις γίνεται, κρείττω δὲ τῇ χρείᾳ τῇ τε τῶν
ξύλων καὶ τῇ τῶν καρπῶν τὰ ὀρεινά· πλὴν
ἀχράδος καὶ ἀπίου καὶ μηλέας· αὗται δ' ἐν τοῖς
πεδίοις κρείττους οὐ μόνον τοῖς καρποῖς ἀλλὰ καὶ
τοῖς ξύλοις· ἐν γὰρ τοῖς ὄρεσι μικραὶ καὶ ὀζώδεις
καὶ ἀκανθώδεις γίνονται· πάντα δὲ καὶ ἐν τοῖς
ὄρεσιν, ὅταν ἐπιλάβωνται τῶν οἰκείων τόπων, καὶ
καλλίω φύεται καὶ εὐθενεῖ μᾶλλον· ὡς δὲ ἁπλῶς
εἰπεῖν τὰ ἐν τοῖς ὁμαλέσι τῶν ὀρῶν καὶ μάλιστα,
τῶν δὲ ἄλλων τὰ ἐν τοῖς κάτω καὶ κοίλοις· τὰ δ'
ἐπὶ τῶν ἄκρων χείριστα, πλὴν εἴ τι τῇ φύσει
3 φιλόψυχρον· ἔχει δὲ καὶ ταῦτ' αὖ τινα διαφορὰν
ἐν τοῖς ἀνομοίοις τῶν τόπων, ὑπὲρ ὧν ὕστερον
λεκτέον· νῦν δὲ διαιρετέον ἕκαστον κατὰ τὰς διαφορὰς τὰς εἰρημένας.

Λείφυλλα μὲν οὖν ἐστι τῶν ἀγρίων ἃ καὶ
πρότερον ἐλέχθη, ἐλάτη πεύκη πίτυς ἀγρία πύξος
ἀνδράχλη μίλος ἄρκευθος τέρμινθος φιλύκη
ἀφάρκη δάφνη φελλόδρυς κήλαστρον ὀξυάκανθος
πρῖνος μυρίκη· τὰ δὲ ἄλλα πάντα φυλλοβολεῖ·
πλὴν εἴ τι περιττὸν ἐνιαχοῦ, καθάπερ ἐλέχθη περὶ
τῆς ἐν τῇ Κρήτῃ πλατάνου καὶ δρυὸς καὶ εἴ που
τόπος τις ὅλως εὔτροφος.

---

[1] δ' ἄλλως conj. Sch. from G; δ' αὖ Ald.    [2] Plin. 16, 77.
[3] i.e. are not always of the poorest quality.    ταῦτ' αὖ τινα
conj. W.; ταῦτα αὐτῶν Ald.H    [4] 1. 9. 3.

when it grows in the mountains, is called *zygia*,
when in the plain, *gleinos*: others however,[1] classify
differently and make maple and *zygia* distinct trees.

[2] All those trees which are common to both hill
and plain are taller and finer in appearance when
they grow in the plain; but the mountain forms are
better as to producing serviceable timber and fruits,
with the exception of wild pear pear and apple;
these are in the plain better in fruit and also in
timber; for in the hills they grow small with many
knots and much spinous wood. But even on the
mountains all trees grow fairer and are more vigorous
when they have secured a suitable position; and, to
speak generally, those which grow on the level parts
of the mountains are specially fair and vigorous;
next to these come those which grow on the lower
parts and in the hollows; while those that grow on
the heights are of the poorest quality, except any
that are naturally cold-loving. But even these shew
some variation[3] in different positions, of which we
must speak later; for the present we must in our
distinctions in each case take account only of the
differences already mentioned.

Now among wild trees those are evergreen which
were mentioned before,[4] silver-fir fir ' wild pine ' box
andrachne yew Phoenician cedar terebinth alaternus
hybrid arbutus bay *phellodrys*[5] (holm-oak) holly
cotoneaster kermes-oak tamarisk; but all the others
shed their leaves, unless it be that in certain places
they keep them exceptionally, as was said[6] of the
plane and oak in Crete and in any other place which
is altogether favourable to luxuriant growth.

[5] φελλόδρυς conj. Bod., *cf*. 1. 9. 3 ; φελλὸς δρῦς UMV(?)Ald.
[6] 1. 9. 5.

THEOPHRASTUS

4  Κάρπιμα δὲ τὰ μὲν ἄλλα πάντα· περὶ δὲ ἰτέας
καὶ αἰγείρου καὶ πτελέας, ὥσπερ ἐλέχθη, διαμφισβητοῦσιν. ἔνιοι δὲ τὴν αἴγειρον μόνην ἀκαρπεῖν
φασιν, ὥσπερ καὶ οἱ ἐν Ἀρκαδίᾳ, τὰ δὲ ἄλλα
πάντα τὰ ἐν τοῖς ὄρεσι καρποφορεῖν. ἐν Κρήτῃ
δὲ καὶ αἴγειροι κάρπιμοι πλείους εἰσί· μία μὲν ἐν
τῷ στομίῳ τοῦ ἄντρου τοῦ ἐν τῇ Ἴδῃ, ἐν ᾧ τὰ
ἀναθήματα ἀνάκειται, ἄλλη δὲ μικρὰ πλησίον·
ἀπωτέρω δὲ μάλιστα δώδεκα σταδίους περί τινα
κρήνην Σαύρου καλουμένην πολλαί. εἰσὶ δὲ καὶ
ἐν τῷ πλησίον ὄρει τῆς Ἴδης ἐν τῷ Κινδρίῳ
καλουμένῳ καὶ περὶ Πραισίαν δὲ ἐν τοῖς ὄρεσιν.
οἱ δὲ μόνον τῶν τοιούτων τὴν πτελέαν κάρπιμον
εἶναί φασι, καθάπερ οἱ περὶ Μακεδονίαν.

5  Μεγάλη δὲ διαφορὰ πρὸς καρπὸν καὶ ἀκαρπίαν
καὶ ἡ τῶν τόπων φύσις, ὥσπερ ἐπί τε τῆς περσέας
ἔχει καὶ τῶν φοινίκων· ἡ μὲν ἐν Αἰγύπτῳ καρποφορεῖ καὶ εἴ που τῶν πλησίον τόπων, ἐν Ῥόδῳ δὲ
μέχρι τοῦ ἀνθεῖν μόνον ἀφικνεῖται. ὁ δὲ φοῖνιξ
περὶ μὲν Βαβυλῶνα θαυμαστός, ἐν τῇ Ἑλλάδι δὲ
οὐδὲ πεπαίνει, παρ' ἐνίοις δὲ ὅλως οὐδὲ προφαίνει
καρπόν.

6  Ὁμοίως δὲ καὶ ἕτερα πλείω τοιαῦτ' ἐστίν· ἐπεὶ
καὶ τῶν ἐλαττόνων ποαρίων καὶ ὑλημάτων ἐν τῇ

¹ 2. 2. 10.
² cf. 2. 2. 10. It appears that the buds of the poplar were
mistaken for fruit (Sch.); cf. Diosc. 1. 81. Later writers
perpetuated the error by calling them κόκκοι.
³ τοῦ ἐν τῇ Ἴδῃ conj. Sch.; τοῦ ἐν τῷ Ἴδῃ U; τοῦ ἐν τῷ Ἴδης
MV; ἐν τῇ Ἴδῃ Ald.H.

174

Most trees are fruit-bearing, but about willow
black poplar and elm men hold different opinions,
as was said [1]; and some, as the Arcadians, say that only
the black poplar is without fruit, but that all the
other mountain trees bear fruit. However in Crete
there are a number of black poplars which bear fruit [2];
there is one at the mouth of the cave on mount Ida,[3]
in which the dedicatory offerings are hung, and
there is another small one not far off, and there are
quite a number about a spring called the Lizard's
Spring about twelve furlongs off. There are also
some in the hill-country of Ida in the same neighbourhood, in the district called Kindria and in the
mountains about Praisia.[4] Others again, as the
Macedonians, say that the elm is the only tree of this
class which bears fruit.

Again the character of the position makes a great
difference as to fruit-bearing, as in the case of the
*persea* [5] and the date-palm. The *persea* of Egypt
bears fruit, and so it does wherever it grows in the
neighbouring districts, but in Rhodes [6] it only gets
as far as flowering. The date-palm in the neighbourhood of Babylon is marvellously fruitful; in Hellas it
does not even ripen its fruit, and in some places it
does not even produce any.

The same may be said of various other trees: in
fact even [7] of smaller herbaceous plants and bushes
some are fruitful, others not, although the latter are

---

[3] Πραισίαν conj. Meurs. *Creta*; τιρασίαν UMVAld.
[5] cf. 4. 2. 5. περσέαι conj. R. Const.; περσείας U; περσίας Ald.
[6] 'Ρόδῳ conj. R. Const. from G, so too Plin. 16. 111; ῥόα Ald. cf. 1. 13. 5. for a similar corruption.
[7] ἐπεὶ καὶ conj. Sch. from G; ἐπεὶ δὲ καὶ Ald.

αὐτῇ χώρᾳ καὶ συνόρῳ χώρᾳ τὰ μὲν κάρπιμα τὰ
δ᾽ ἄκαρπα γίνεται· καθάπερ καὶ τὸ κενταύριον ἐν
τῇ Ἠλείᾳ, τὸ μὲν ἐν τῇ ὀρεινῇ κάρπιμον, τὸ δ᾽ ἐν
τῷ πεδίῳ ἄκαρπον ἀλλὰ μόνον ἀνθεῖ, τὸ δ᾽ ἐν τοῖς
κοίλοις τύποις οὐδ᾽ ἀνθεῖ πλὴν κακῶς. δοκεῖ δ᾽
οὖν καὶ τῶν ἄλλων τῶν ὁμογενῶν καὶ ἐν μιᾷ
προσηγορίᾳ τὸ μὲν ἄκαρπον εἶναι τὸ δὲ κάρπιμον,
οἷον πρῖνος ὁ μὲν κάρπιμος ὁ δ᾽ ἄκαρπος· καὶ
7 κλήθρα δὲ ὡσαύτως· ἀνθεῖ δ᾽ ἄμφω. σχεδὸν δὲ
ὅσα καλοῦσιν ἄρρενα τῶν ὁμογενῶν ἄκαρπα· καὶ
τούτων τὰ μὲν πολλὰ ἀνθεῖν φασι τὰ δ᾽ ὀλίγον
τὰ δ᾽ ὅλως οὐδ᾽ ἀνθεῖν· τὰ δὲ ἀνάπαλιν, τὰ μὲν
ἄρρενα μόνα καρποφορεῖν, οὐ μὴν ἀλλ᾽ ἀπό γε
τῶν ἀνθῶν φύεσθαι τὰ δένδρα, καθάπερ καὶ ἀπὸ
τῶν καρπῶν ὅσα κάρπιμα· καὶ ἐν ἀμφοῖν οὕτως
ἐνίοτε πυκνὴν εἶναι τὴν ἔκφυσιν ὥστε τοὺς
ὀρεοτύπους οὐ δύνασθαι διϊέναι μὴ ὁδοποιη-
σαμένους.

8 Ἀμφισβητεῖται δὲ καὶ περὶ τῶν ἀνθῶν ἐνίων,
ὥσπερ εἴπομεν. οἱ μὲν γὰρ καὶ δρῦν ἀνθεῖν
οἴονται καὶ τὴν Ἡρακλεῶτιν καρύαν καὶ διοσβάλανον, ἔτι δὲ πεύκην καὶ πίτυν· οἱ δ᾽ οὐδὲν
τούτων, ἀλλὰ τὸν ἴουλον τὸν ἐν ταῖς καρύαις καὶ
τὸ βρύον τὸ δρύϊνον καὶ τὸν κύτταρον τὸν πιτύ-

---

¹ χώρᾳ καὶ Ald. ; ἢ καὶ conj. St.
² i.e. the 'males' are sterile whether they flower or not.
καὶ τούτων τὰ μὲν πολλὰ I conj.; τούτων τὰ πολλὰ τὰ μὲν Ald.
³ ? i.e. the flowers of the 'female' tree.
⁴ i.e. (a) in those trees whose 'male' form is sterile,
whether it bears flowers or not ; (b) in those whose 'male'

growing in the same place as the former, or [1] quite
near it. Take for instance the centaury in Elea; where
it grows in hill-country, it is fruitful; where it grows
in the plain, it bears no fruit, but only flowers; and
where it grows in deep valleys, it does not even
flower, unless it be scantily. Any way it appears
that, even of other plants which are of the same
kind and all go by the same name, one will be
without fruit, while another bears fruit; for instance,
one kermes-oak will be fruitful, another not; and the
same is true of the alder, though both produce
flowers. And, generally speaking, all those of any
given kind which are called 'male' trees are without
fruit, and that though [2] some of these, they say,
produce many flowers, some few, some none at all.
On the other hand they say that in some cases it is
only the 'males' that bear fruit. but that, in spite
of this, the trees grow from the flowers,[3] (just as in
the case of fruit-bearing trees they grow from the
fruit). And they add that in both cases,[4] the crop
of seedlings [5] which comes up is sometimes so thick
that the woodmen cannot get through except by
clearing a way.

There is also a doubt about the flower of some
trees, as we said. Some think that the oak bears
flowers, and also the filbert the chestnut and even
the fir and Aleppo pine : some however think that
none of these has a flower, but that,—resembling [6]
and corresponding to the wild figs which drop off
prematurely, we have in the nuts the catkin,[7] in the

form alone bears fruit, but the fruit is infertile. The passage
is obscure : W. gives up the text.

[5] ἐκφυσιν. *cf.* 7. 4. 3.
[6] δυοιον conj. W.; δυοίαν UAld. *cf.* 3. 7. 3.
[7] *cf.* 3. 5. 5.

ἰνον ὅμοιον καὶ ἀνάλογον εἶναι τοῖς προαπο-
πτώτοις ἐρινοῖς. οἱ δὲ περὶ Μακεδονίαν οὐδὲ
ταῦτά φασιν ἀνθεῖν ἄρκευθον ὀξύην ἀρίαν σφένδαμνον. ἔνιοι δὲ τὰς ἀρκεύθους δύο εἶναι, καὶ τὴν
μὲν ἑτέραν ἀνθεῖν μὲν ἄκαρπον δ᾽ εἶναι, τὴν δὲ
ἑτέραν οὐκ ἀνθεῖν μὲν καρπὸν δὲ φέρειν εὐθὺς
προφαινόμενον, ὥσπερ καὶ τὰς συκᾶς τὰ ἐρινά.
συμβαίνει δ᾽ οὖν ὥστε ἐπὶ δύο ἔτη τὸν καρπὸν
ἔχειν μόνον τοῦτο τῶν δένδρων. ταῦτα μὲν οὖν
ἐπισκεπτέον.

IV. Ἡ δὲ βλάστησις τῶν μὲν ἅμα γίνεται καὶ
τῶν ἡμέρων, τῶν δὲ μικρὸν ἐπιλειπομένη, τῶν δ᾽
ἤδη πλέον, ἁπάντων δὲ κατὰ τὴν ἠρινὴν ὥραν.
ἀλλὰ τῶν καρπῶν ἡ παραλλαγὴ πλείων· ὥσπερ
δὲ καὶ πρότερον εἴπομεν, οὐ κατὰ τὰς βλαστήσεις
αἱ πεπάνσεις ἀλλὰ πολὺ διαφέρουσιν· ἐπεὶ καὶ
τῶν ὀψικαρποτέρων, ἃ δή τινές φασιν ἐνιαυτο-
φορεῖν, οἷον ἄρκευθον καὶ πρῖνον, ὅμως αἱ βλαστήσεις τοῦ ἦρος. αὐτὰ δ᾽ αὐτῶν τὰ ὁμογενῆ τῷ
πρότερον καὶ ὕστερον διαφέρει κατὰ τοὺς τόπους·
πρῶτα μὲν γὰρ βλαστάνει τὰ ἐν τοῖς ἕλεσιν, ὡς
οἱ περὶ Μακεδονίαν λέγουσι, δεύτερα δὲ τὰ ἐν τοῖς
πεδίοις, ἔσχατα δὲ τὰ ἐν τοῖς ὄρεσιν.

2    Αὐτῶν δὲ τῶν καθ᾽ ἕκαστα δένδρων τὰ μὲν

---

[1] i.e. the male flower, cf. Schol. on Ar. Vesp. 1111.
Θεόφραστος κυρίως λέγει κύτταρον τὴν προάνθησιν τῆς πίτυος :
but no explanation of such a use of the word suggests itself.
cf. 3. 3. 8 ; 4. 8. 7.
[2] ἀρίαν conj. Sch., cf. 3. 4. 2; 3. 16. 3; 3. 17. 1 ; ὀξύνην ἀγρίαν
Ald.

oak the oak-moss, in the pine the 'flowering tuft.'[1] The people of Macedonia say that these trees also produce no flowers—Phoenician cedar beech *aria*[2] (holm-oak) maple. Others distinguish two kinds of Phoenician cedar, of which one bears flowers but bears no fruit, while the other, though it has no flower, bears a fruit which shows itself at once[3]—just as wild figs produce their abortive fruit. However that may be,[4] it is a fact that this is the only tree which keeps its fruit for two years. These matters then need enquiry.

*Of the times of budding and fruiting of wild, as compared with cultivated, trees.*

IV. Now the budding of wild trees occurs in some cases at the same time as that of the cultivated forms, but in some cases somewhat, and in some a good deal later; but in all cases it is during the spring season. But there is greater diversity in the time of fruiting; as we said before, the times of ripening do not correspond to those of budding, but there are wide differences. For even in the case of those trees which are somewhat late in fruiting,—which some say take a year to ripen their fruit—such as Phoenician cedar and kermes-oak, the budding nevertheless takes place in the spring. Again there are differences of time between individual trees of the same kind, according to the locality; those in the marshes bud earliest, as the Macedonians say, second to them those in the plains, and latest those in the mountains.

Again of particular trees some wild ones bud

---

[3] *i.e.* without antecedent flower.
[4] δ' οὖν conj. W.; σχεδόν UMVAld.

THEOPHRASTUS

συναναβλαστάνει τοῖς ἡμέροις, οἷον ἀνδράχλη
ἀφάρκη· ἀχράς δὲ μικρῷ ὕστερον τῆς ἀπίου. τὰ
δὲ καὶ πρὸ ζεφύρου καὶ μετὰ πνοὰς εὐθὺ ζεφύρου.
καὶ πρὸ ζεφύρου μὲν κρανεία καὶ θηλυκρανεία,
μετὰ ζέφυρον δὲ δάφνη κλήθρα, πρὸ ἰσημερίας δὲ
μικρὸν φίλυρα ζυγία φηγὸς συκῆ· πρωΐβλαστα
δὲ καὶ καρύα καὶ δρῦς καὶ ἀκτέος· ἔτι δὲ μᾶλλον
τὰ ἄκαρπα δοκοῦντα καὶ ἀλσώδη, λεύκη πτελέα
ἰτέα αἴγειρος· πλάτανος δὲ μικρῷ ὀψιαίτερον
τούτων. τὰ δὲ ἄλλα ὥσπερ ἐνισταμένου τοῦ
ἦρος, οἷον ἐρινεὸς φιλύκη ὀξυάκανθος παλίουρος
τέρμινθος καρύα διοσβάλανος· μηλέα δ᾽ ὀψί-
βλαστος· ὀψιβλαστότατον δὲ σχεδὸν ἴψος ἀρία
τετραγωνία θύεια μίλος. αἱ μὲν οὖν βλαστήσεις
οὕτως ἔχουσιν.

3 Αἱ δὲ ἀνθήσεις ἀκολουθοῦσι μὲν ὡς εἰπεῖν κατὰ
λόγον, οὐ μὴν ἀλλὰ παραλλάττουσι, μᾶλλον δὲ
καὶ ἐπὶ πλέον ἡ τῶν καρπῶν τελείωσις. κρανεία
μὲν γὰρ ἀποδίδωσι περὶ τροπὰς θερινὰς ἡ πρώϊος
σχεδὸν ὥσπερ πρῶτον· ἡ δ᾽ ὄψιος, ἣν δή τινες
καλοῦσι θηλυκρανείαν, μετ᾽ αὐτὸ τὸ μετόπωρον·
ἔστι δὲ ὁ ταύτης καρπὸς ἄβρωτος καὶ τὸ ξύλον
ἀσθενὲς καὶ χαῦνον· τοσαύτη δὴ διαφορὰ περὶ
4 ἄμφω. τέρμινθος δὲ περὶ πυροῦ ἀμητὸν ἡ μικρῷ

¹ See below, n. 4.
² τὰ ἀκ. δοκ. καὶ ἀλσ. conj. W.; τὰ ἀκ. καὶ δοκ. καὶ ἀλσ. U
MP; τὰ ἀκ. τὰ δοκ. ἀλσ. Ald.
³ ὥσπερ apologises for the unusual sense given to ἐνιστ.

180

along with the cultivated forms, as andrachne and
hybrid arbutus ; and the wild pear is a little later
than the cultivated. Some again bud both before
zephyr begins to blow, and immediately after it has
been blowing. Before it come cornelian cherry and
cornel, after it bay and alder ; a little before the
spring equinox come lime *zygia* Valonia oak fig.
Hazel[1] oak and elder are also early in budding, and
still more those trees which seem to have no fruit
and to grow in groves,[2] abele elm willow black
poplar ; and the plane is a little later than these.
The others which bud when the spring is, as it were,
becoming established,[3] are such as wild fig alaternus
cotoneaster Christ's thorn terebinth hazel[4] chestnut.
The apple is late in budding, latest of all generally
are *ipsos*[5] (cork-oak) *aria* (holm-oak) *tetragonia*
odorous cedar yew. Such are the times of budding.

The flowering times in general follow in proportion ;
but they present some irregularity, and so in still
more cases and to a greater extent do the times at
which the fruit is matured. The cornelian cherry produces its fruit about the summer solstice ; the early
kind, that is to say, and this tree is about the earliest
of all.[6] The late form, which some call 'female
cornelian cherry' (cornel), fruits quite at the end of
autumn. The fruit of this kind is inedible and its
wood is weak and spongy ; that is what the difference
between the two kinds amounts to. The terebinth
produces its fruit about the time of wheat-harvest or

(usually ' beginning '). τὰ δ' ἄλλα ὥσπερ ἐνιστ. conj. W.; τὰ
δ' ἄλλως περ' U ; τὰ δὲ ἄλλως περιενιστάμενον M Ald. H.
  [4] καρύα can hardly be right both here and above.
  [5] See Index.
  [6] σχεδὸν ὥσπερ πρῶτον not in G, nor in Plin. (16. 105) ; text
perhaps defective.

ὀψιαίτερον ἀποδίδωσι καὶ μελία καὶ σφένδαμνος
τοῦ θέρους τὸν καρπόν· κλήθρα δὲ καὶ καρύα καὶ
ἀχράδων τι γένος μετοπώρου· δρῦς δὲ καὶ διοσβάλανος ὀψιαίτερον ἔτι περὶ Πλειάδος δύσιν,
ὡσαύτως δὲ καὶ φιλύκη καὶ πρῖνος καὶ παλίουρος
καὶ ὀξυάκανθος μετὰ Πλείαδος δύσιν· ἡ δ᾽ ἀρία
χειμῶνος ἀρχομένου· καὶ ἡ μηλέα μὲν τοῖς πρώτοις
ψύχεσιν, ἀχρὰς δὲ ὀψία χειμῶνος· ἀνδράχλη δὲ
καὶ ἀφάρκη τὸ μὲν πρῶτον πεπαίνουσιν ἅμα τῷ
βότρυϊ περκάζοντι, τὸ δὲ ὕστερον, δοκεῖ γὰρ ταῦτα
δίκαρπα, ἀρχομένου τοῦ χειμῶνος, ἐλάτη δὲ καὶ
5 μίλος ἀνθοῦσι μικρὸν πρὸ ἡλίου τροπῶν· [καὶ τῆς
γε ἐλάτης τὸ ἄνθος κρόκινον καὶ ἄλλως καλόν]
τὸν δὲ καρπὸν ἀφιᾶσι μετὰ δύσιν Πλειάδος.
πεύκη δὲ καὶ πίτυς προτεροῦσι τῇ βλαστήσει
μικρόν, ὅσον πεντεκαίδεκα ἡμέραις, τοὺς δὲ καρποὺς ἀποδιδόασι μετὰ Πλειάδα κατὰ λόγον.

Ταῦτα μὲν οὖν μετριωτέραν μὲν ἔχει παραλλα-
γήν· πάντων δὲ πλείστην ἡ ἄρκευθος καὶ ἡ κήλαστρος καὶ ἡ πρῖνος· ἡ μὲν γὰρ ἄρκευθος ἐνιαύσιον
ἔχειν δοκεῖ· περικαταλαμβάνει γὰρ ὁ νέος τὸν περυ-
σινόν. ὡς δέ τινές φασιν, οὐδὲ πεπαίνει, δι᾽ ὃ καὶ
προαφαιροῦσι καὶ χρόνον τινὰ τηροῦσιν· ἐὰν δὲ ἐᾷ
6 ἐπὶ τοῦ δένδρου τις, ἀποξηραίνεται. φασὶ δὲ καὶ τὴν
πρῖνον οἱ περὶ Ἀρκαδίαν ἐνιαυτῷ τελειοῦν· ἅμα
γὰρ τὸν ἔνον πεπαίνει καὶ τὸν νέον ὑποφαίνει·
ὥστε τοῖς τοιούτοις συμβαίνει συνεχῶς τὸν καρπὸν
ἔχειν. φασὶ δέ γε καὶ τὴν κήλαστρον ὑπὸ τοῦ

---

[1] ἀποδ. καὶ μελία U ; ἀποδίδωσι· μελία Ald.  Some confusion
in text, but sense clear.
[2] ὀψία : ? ἡ ὀψία W.

a little later, manna-ash[1] and maple in summer; alder hazel and a certain kind of wild pear in autumn; oak and chestnut later still, about the setting of the Pleiad; and in like manner alaternus kermes-oak Christ's-thorn cotoneaster after the setting of the Pleiad; *aria* (holm-oak) when winter is beginning, apple with the first cold weather, wild pear late[2] in winter. Andrachne and hybrid arbutus first ripen their fruit when the grape is turning, and again[3] when winter is beginning; for these trees appear to bear twice. As for[4] silver-fir and yew, they flower a little before the solstice; [5](the flower of the silver-fir is yellow and otherwise pretty); they bear their fruit after the setting of the Pleiad. Fir and Aleppo pine are a little earlier in budding, about fifteen days, but produce their fruit after the setting of the Pleiad, though proportionately earlier than silver-fir and yew.

In these trees then the difference of time is not considerable; the greatest difference is shewn in Phoenician cedar holly and kermes-oak; for Phoenician cedar appears to keep its fruit for a year, the new fruit overtaking that of last year; and, according to some, it does not ripen it at all; wherefore men gather it unripe and keep it, whereas if it is left on the tree, it shrivels up. The Arcadians say that the kermes-oak also takes a year to perfect its fruit; for it ripens last year's fruit at the same time that the new fruit appears on it; the result of which is that such trees always have fruit on them. They say also

[3] After ὕστερον Ald. adds ἀνθοῦντι (so also H and G); Plin. 13. 121. omits it; om. W. after Sch.
[4] γὰρ Ald.; δὲ conj. W.
[5] Probably an early gloss, W. *cf.* Plin. 16. 106.

THEOPHRASTUS

χειμῶνος ἀποβάλλειν. ὀψίκαρπα δὲ σφόδρα καὶ
φίλυρα καὶ πύξος. [τὸν δὲ καρπὸν ἄβρωτον
ἔχει παντὶ ζώῳ φίλυρα θηλυκρανεία πύξος.
ὀψίκαρπα δὲ καὶ κιττὸς καὶ ἄρκευθος καὶ
πεύκη καὶ ἀνδράχλη.] ὡς δὲ οἱ περὶ Ἀρκαδίαν
φασίν, ἔτι τούτων ὀψικαρπότερα σχεδὸν
δὲ πάντων ὀψιαίτερα τετραγωνία θύεια μίλος. αἱ μὲν οὖν τῶν καρπῶν ἀποβολαὶ καὶ
πεπάνσεις τῶν ἀγρίων τοιαύτας ἔχουσι διαφορὰς
οὐ μόνον πρὸς τὰ ἥμερα ἀλλὰ καὶ πρὸς ἑαυτά.

V. Συμβαίνει δ' ὅταν ἄρξωνται βλαστάνειν
τὰ μὲν ἄλλα συνεχῆ τήν τε βλάστησιν καὶ τὴν
αὔξησιν ποιεῖσθαι, πεύκην δὲ καὶ ἐλάτην καὶ
δρῦν διαλείπειν, καὶ τρεῖς ὁρμὰς εἶναι καὶ τρεῖς
ἀφιέναι βλαστούς, δι' ὃ καὶ τρίσλοποι· πᾶν γὰρ
δὴ δένδρον ὅταν βλαστάνῃ λοπᾷ· πρῶτον μὲν
ἄκρου ἔαρος εὐθὺς ἱσταμένου τοῦ Θαργηλιῶνος,
ἐν δὲ τῇ Ἴδῃ περὶ πεντεκαίδεκα μάλιστα ἡμέρας·
μετὰ δὲ ταῦτα διαλιπόντα περὶ τριάκοντα ἢ
μικρῷ πλείους ἐπιβάλλεται πάλιν ἄλλους βλαστοὺς ἀπ' ἄκρας τῆς κορυνήσεως τῆς ἐπὶ τῷ προ-
τέρῳ βλαστῷ· καὶ τὰ μὲν ἄνω τὰ δ' εἰς τὰ
πλάγια κύκλῳ ποιεῖται τὴν βλάστησιν, οἷον γόνυ

---

¹ φίλυρα Ald.; φιλυρέα conj. Sch.
² τὸν δὲ . . . . ἀνδράχλη. Apparently a gloss, W.
³ τετραγωνία conj. Sch. (τετρα- omitted after -τερα) : cf. § 2;
γωνία MV ; γωνίεια U.
⁴ τῶν ἀγρίων after πεπάνσεις conj. Sch.; after ἥμερα Ald.
⁵ Plin. 16. 100.

184

that holly loses its fruit owing to the winter. Lime [1] and box are very late in fruiting, (lime has a fruit which no animal can eat, and so have cornel and box. Ivy Phoenician cedar fir and andrachne are late fruiting [2]) though, according to the Arcadians, still later than these and almost latest of all are *tetragonia* [3] odorous cedar and yew. Such then are the differences as to the time of shedding and ripening their fruit between wild [4] as compared with cultivated trees, and likewise as compared with one another.

*Of the seasons of budding.*

V. [5] Now most trees, when they have once begun to bud, make their budding and their growth continuously, but with fir silver-fir and oak there are intervals. They make three fresh starts in growth and produce three separate sets of buds; wherefore also they lose their bark thrice [6] a year. For every tree loses its bark when it is budding. This first happens in mid-spring [7] at the very beginning of the month Thargelion, [8] on Mount Ida within about fifteen days of that time; later, after an interval of about thirty days or rather more, the tree [9] puts on fresh buds which start from the head of the knobby growth [10] which formed at the first budding-time; and it makes its budding partly on the top of this, [11] partly all round it laterally, [12] using the knob formed at the

---

[6] τρίσλοποι conj. Sch.; τρίσλοιποι UM₂V; τρίσλεποι M₁Ald. *cf.* 4. 15. 3 ; 5. 1. 1.

[7] ἔαρος conj. R. Const.; ἀέρος VAld.   *cf.* Plin. *l.c.*

[8] About May.

[9] What follows evidently applies only to the oak.

[10] κορυνήσεως conj. Sch.: κορύτης ἕως UMV; κορυφῆς ἕως Ald.

[11] *cf.* 3. 6. 2.   [12] τὰ add. Sch.

ποιησάμενα τὴν τοῦ πρώτου βλαστοῦ κορύνην,
ὥσπερ καὶ ἡ πρώτη βλάστησις ἔχει. γίνεται δὲ
τοῦτο περὶ τὸν Σκιρροφοριῶνα λήγοντα.

2  Κατὰ δὲ ταύτην τὴν βλάστησιν καὶ ἡ κηκὶς
φύεται πᾶσα, καὶ ἡ λευκὴ καὶ ἡ μέλαινα· φύεται
δὲ ὡς ἐπὶ τὸ πολὺ νυκτὸς ἀθρόος· ἐφ᾽ ἡμέραν δὲ
μίαν αὐξηθεῖσα, πλὴν τῆς πιττοειδοῦς, ἐὰν ὑπὸ
τοῦ καύματος ληφθῇ ξηραίνεται, καὶ ἀναυξὴς ἐπὶ
τὸ μεῖζον, ἐγίνετο γὰρ ἂν μείζων τῷ μεγέθει.
διόπερ τινὲς αὐτῶν οὐ μεῖζον ἔχουσι κυάμου τὸ
μέγεθος. ἡ δὲ μέλαινα καὶ ἐπὶ πλείους ἡμέρας
ἔγχλωρός ἐστι, καὶ αὐξάνονται καὶ λαμβάνουσιν
ἔνιαι μέγεθος μήλου.

Διαλείποντα δὲ μετὰ τοῦτο περὶ πεντεκαίδεκα
ἡμέρας πάλιν τὸ τρίτον ἐπιβάλλεται βλαστοὺς
Ἑκατομβαιῶνος, ἐλαχίστας ἡμέρας τῶν πρότε-
ρον· ἴσως γὰρ ἐξ ἢ ἑπτὰ τὸ πλεῖστον· ἡ δὲ
βλάστησις ὁμοία καὶ τὸν αὐτὸν τρόπον. παρελ-
θουσῶν δὲ τούτων οὐκέτι εἰς μῆκος ἀλλ᾽ εἰς
πάχος ἡ αὔξησις τρέπεται.

3  Πᾶσι μὲν οὖν τοῖς δένδροις αἱ βλαστήσεις
φανεραί, μάλιστα δὲ τῇ ἐλάτῃ καὶ τῇ πεύκῃ διὰ
τὸ στοιχεῖν τὰ γόνατα καὶ ἐξ ἴσου τοὺς ὄζους
ἔχειν. ὥρα δὲ καὶ πρὸς τὸ τέμνεσθαι τὰ ξύλα
τότε διὰ τὸ λοπᾶν· ἐν γὰρ τοῖς ἄλλοις καιροῖς
οὐκ εὐπεριαίρετος ὁ φλοιός, ἀλλὰ καὶ περιαιρεθέντος μέλαν τὸ ξύλον γίνεται καὶ τῇ ὄψει χεῖρον·
ἐπεὶ καὶ πρός γε τὴν χρείαν οὐδέν, ἀλλὰ καὶ

---

[1] About June.
[2] cf. 3. 7. 4 ; 3. 8. 6 ; Plin. 16. 27.
[3] ἔγχλωρος conj. Coraës ; εὔχλωρος Ald.
[4] διαλείποντα conj. St. ; διαλείπουσαι Ald. H.

first budding as a sort of joint, just as in the case of the first budding. This happens about the end of the month Skirrophorion.[1]

[2](It is only at the time of this second budding that the galls also are produced, both the white and the black; the liquid forming them is mostly produced in quantity at night, and, after swelling for one day —except the part which is of resinous character—it hardens if it is caught by the heat, and so cannot grow any more; otherwise it would have grown greater in bulk; wherefore in some trees the formation is not larger than a bean. The black gall is for several days of a pale green[3] colour: then it swells and sometimes attains the size of an apple.)

Then, after an interval[4] of about fifteen days, the tree for the third time puts on buds in the month Hekatombaion[5]; but this growth continues for fewer days than on either of the previous occasions, perhaps for six or seven at most. However the formation of the buds is as before and takes place in the same manner. After this period there is no increase in length, but the only increase is in thickness.

The periods of budding can be seen in all trees, but especially in fir and silver-fir, because the joints of these are in a regular series and have the knots at even distances. It is then the season also for cutting the timber, because the bark is being shed[6]; for at other times the bark is not easy to strip off, and moreover, if it is stripped off, the wood turns black[7] and is inferior in appearance; for as to its utility[8] this makes no difference, though the wood

[5] About July.
[6] λοπᾶν conj. Sch.; λυιπᾶν UMV; λιπᾶν Ald.
[7] cf. Plin. 16. 74.
[8] γε conj. Sch.; τε Ald.

THEOPHRASTUS

ἰσχυρότερον, ἐὰν μετὰ τὴν πέπανσιν τῶν καρπῶν τμηθῇ.

4 Ταῦτα μὲν οὖν ἴδια τῶν προειρημένων δένδρων. αἱ δὲ βλαστήσεις αἱ ἐπὶ Κυνὶ καὶ Ἀρκτούρῳ γινόμεναι μετὰ τὴν ἐαρινὴν σχεδὸν κοιναὶ πάντων· ἔνδηλοι δὲ μᾶλλον ἐν τοῖς ἡμέροις καὶ τούτων μάλιστα συκῇ καὶ ἀμπέλῳ καὶ ῥοιᾷ καὶ ὅλως ὅσα εὐτραφῆ καὶ ὅπου χώρα τοιαύτη· δι' ὃ καὶ τὴν ἐπ' Ἀρκτούρῳ πλείστην φασὶ γίνεσθαι περὶ Θετταλίαν καὶ Μακεδονίαν· ἅμα γὰρ συμβαίνει καὶ τὸ μετόπωρον καλὸν γίνεσθαι καὶ μακρόν, ὥστε καὶ τὴν μαλακότητα συμβάλλεσθαι τοῦ ἀέρος. ἐπεὶ καὶ ἐν Αἰγύπτῳ διὰ τοῦθ' ὡς εἰπεῖν αἰεὶ βλαστάνει τὰ δένδρα, ἢ καὶ μικρόν τινα διαλείπει χρόνον.

5 Ἀλλὰ τὰ μὲν περὶ τὰς ἐπιβλαστήσεις, ὥσπερ εἴρηται, κοινά, τὰ δὲ περὶ τὰς διαλείψεις ἀπὸ τῆς πρώτης ἴδια τῶν λεχθέντων. ἴδιον δ' ἐνίοις ὑπάρχει καὶ τὸ τῆς καλουμένης κάχρυος, οἷον τοῖς [τε] προειρημένοις· ἔχει γὰρ καὶ ἐλάτη καὶ πεύκη καὶ δρῦς, καὶ ἔτι φίλυρα καὶ καρύα καὶ διοσβάλανος καὶ πίτυς. αὗται δὲ γίνονται δρυὶ μὲν πρὸ τῆς βλαστήσεως ὑποφαινούσης τῆς ἠρινῆς ὥρας. ἔστι δ' ὡσπερεὶ κύησις φυλλικὴ μεταξὺ πίπτουσα τῆς ἐξ ἀρχῆς ἐποιδήσεως καὶ τῆς φυλλικῆς βλαστήσεως· τῇ δ' ὄῃ ἐστὶ τοῦ

---

¹ δένδρων conj. R. Const.; καρπῶν Ald. H.
² cf. C.P. 1. 10. 6; 1. 12. 4; 1. 13. 3; 1. 13. 5; 1. 13. 10; Plin. 16. 98.   ³ cf. C.P. 1. 14. 11.   ⁴ cf. 5. 1. 4; Plin. 16. 30.

188

is stronger if it is cut after the ripening of the fruit.

Now what has been said is peculiar to the above-mentioned trees.[1] [2] But the buddings which take place at the rising of the dog-star and at that of Arcturus after the spring budding are common to nearly all, though they may be most clearly seen in cultivated trees, and, among these, especially in fig vine pomegranate, and in general in all those that are luxuriant in growth or are growing in rich soil. Accordingly they say that the budding at the rising of Arcturus is most considerable in Thessaly and Macedonia[3]; for it also happens that the autumn in these countries is a fair and a long season; so that the mildness of the climate also contributes. Indeed it is for this reason, one may say, that in Egypt too the trees are always budding, or at least that the process is only suspended for quite a short time.

Now the facts as to the later buddings apply, as has been said, to all trees alike; but those which belong to the intervals after the first period of budding are peculiar to those mentioned above. Peculiar to some also is the growth of what are called 'winter buds,'[4] for instance in the above-mentioned trees; silver-fir fir and oak have them, and also lime hazel chestnut and Aleppo pine. These are found in the oak before the leaf-buds grow, when the spring season is just beginning. This growth consists of a sort of leaf-like formation,[5] which occurs between the first swelling of the leaf-buds and the time when they burst into leaf. In the sorb[6] it

[5] ἐστι ... φυλλικὴ: ἐστι conj. R. Const.; ὡσπερεὶ conj. Sch.; ἔτι δὲ ὥσπερ ἡ κύησις φυλακὴ U Ald. H.; φυλλικὴ m Bas. etc.
[6] τῇ δ' ὕῃ ἐστὶ conj. W. (cf. the description of ὕη, 3. 12. 8); τῇ δ' ἰδιότητι Ald.

μετοπώρου μετὰ τὴν φυλλοβολίαν εὐθὺς λιπαρά
τις καὶ ὥσπερ ἐπωδηκυῖα, καθαπερανεὶ μέλλουσα
βλαστάνειν, καὶ διαμένει τὸν χειμῶνα μέχρι τοῦ
ἦρος. ἡ δὲ Ἡρακλεωτικὴ μετὰ τὴν ἀποβολὴν τοῦ
καρποῦ φύει[2] τὸ βοτρυῶδες ἡλίκον σκώληξ εὐμε-
γέθης, ἐξ ἑνὸς μίσχου πλείω δή[4], ἃ καλοῦσί τινες
6 ἰούλους[3]. τούτων ἕκαστον ἐκ μικρῶν σύγκειται
μορίων φολιδωτῶν τῇ τάξει, καθάπερ οἱ στρόβιλοι
τῆς πεύκης, ὥστε μὴ ἀνομοίαν εἶναι τὴν ὄψιν
στροβίλῳ νέῳ καὶ χλωρῷ πλὴν προμηκέστερον
καὶ σχεδὸν ἰσόπαχες διόλου. τοῦτο δὲ αὔξεται
τὸν χειμῶνα· (καὶ ἅμα τῷ ἦρι χάσκει τὰ φολι-
δωτὰ καὶ ξανθὰ γίνεται), καὶ τὸ μῆκος λαμβάνει
καὶ τριδάκτυλον· ὅταν δὲ τοῦ ἦρος τὸ φύλλον
βλαστάνῃ, ταῦτ' ἀποπίπτει καὶ τὰ τοῦ καρύου
καλυκώδη περικάρπια γίνεται συμμεμυκότα[6] κατὰ
τοῦ μίσχου, τοσαῦτα ὅσα καὶ ἦν τὰ ἄνθη· τούτων
δ' ἐν ἑκάστῳ κάρυον ἕν. περὶ δὲ τῆς φιλύρας
ἐπισκεπτέον, καὶ εἴ τι ἄλλο καχρυοφόρον.

VI. Ἔστι δὲ καὶ τὰ μὲν εὐαυξῆ τὰ δὲ δυσαυξῆ.
εὐαυξῆ μὲν τά τε πάρυδρα, οἷον πτελέα πλάτανος
λεύκη αἴγειρος ἰτέα· καί τοι περὶ ταύτης ἀμφισ-
βητοῦσί τινες ὡς δυσαυξοῦς· καὶ τῶν καρποφόρων
δὲ ἐλάτη πεύκη δρῦς. εὐαυξέστατον δὲ . . . μίλος

---

¹ εὐθὺς λιπαρὰ conj. Sch.: τις add. W.; εὐθὺς αἱ παρὰ τῆς U.
² φύει conj. W.; φύεται Ald.   ³ i.e. catkins. cf. 3. 3. 8.
⁴ πλείω δὴ conj. Sch.; πιώδη U M V Ald.; πλείονα U ?.
⁵ cf. 3. 10. 4.
⁶ συμμεμυκότα κατὰ τοῦ μ.:  G evidently had a different
text ; ? συμπεφυκότα W.

occurs in the autumn after the shedding of the leaves, and has from the first a glistening look,[1] as though swelling had taken place, just as if it were about to burst into leaves: and it persists through the winter till the spring. The filbert after casting its fruit produces[2] its clustering growth,[3] which is as large as a good-sized grub: several[4] of these grow from one stalk, and some call them catkins. Each of these is made up of small processes arranged like scales, and resembles the cone of the fir, so that its appearance is not unlike that of a young green fir-cone, except that it is longer and almost of the same thickness throughout. This grows through the winter (when spring comes, the scale-like processes open and turn yellow); it grows to the length of three fingers, but, when in spring the leaves are shooting, it falls off, and the cup-like[5] fruit-cases of the nut are formed, closed all down[6] the stalk and corresponding[7] in number to the flowers: and in each of these is a single nut. The case of the lime and of any other tree that produces winter-buds needs further consideration.

*Of the comparative rate of growth in trees, and of the length of their roots.*

VI. Some trees are quick-growing, some slow. Quick-growing are those which grow by the waterside, as elm plane abele black poplar willow; (however some dispute about the last-named, and consider it a slow grower:) and of fruit-bearing trees, silver-fir fir oak. Quickest growing of all are . . .[5] yew *lakara*

---

[7] ὅσα καὶ ἦν τὰ ἄνθη conj. W.; ὅσα καὶ κατὰ ἄνθη Ald.

[5] Lacuna in text (Sch. W.). The following list of trees also appears to be in confusion, and includes some of both classes.

καὶ λάκαρα φηγὸς ἄρκευθος σφένδαμνος ὀστρύα
ζυγία μελία κλήθρα πίτυς ἀνδράχλη κρανεία
πύξος ἀχράς. καρποφορεῖ δ' εὐθὺς ἐλάτη πεύκη
πίτυς, κἂν ὀπηλικονοῦν μέγεθος λάβωσιν.

2 Ἡ δὲ αὔξησις καὶ ἡ βλάστησις τῶν μὲν ἄλλων
ἄτακτος κατὰ τοὺς τόπους τῶν βλαστῶν,¹ τῆς δ'
ἐλάτης ὡρισμένη καὶ συνεχὴς καὶ ὕστερον. ὅταν
γὰρ ἐκ τοῦ στελέχους τὰ πρῶτα σχισθῇ, πάλιν ἐξ
ἐκείνου ἡ ἑτέρα σχίσις² γίνεται κατὰ τὸν αὐτὸν
τρόπον, καὶ τοῦτ' ἀεὶ ποιεῖ κατὰ πάσας τὰς ἐπιβλαστήσεις. ἐν δὲ τοῖς ἄλλοις οὐδ' οἱ ὄζοι κατ'
ἀλλήλους πλὴν ἐπί τινων ὀλίγων, οἷον κοτίνου
καὶ ἄλλων· ἔχει δὲ καὶ τῇδε διαφορὰν ἡ αὔξησις
κοινῇ πάντων ὁμοίως ἡμέρων τε καὶ ἀγρίων· τὰ
μὲν γὰρ καὶ ἐκ τοῦ ἄκρου τῶν βλαστῶν καὶ ἐκ
τῶν πλαγίων φύεται, καθάπερ ἄπιος ῥόα συκῆ
μύρρινος σχεδὸν τὰ πλεῖστα· τὰ δ' ἐκ τοῦ ἄκρου
μὲν οὐκ ἀνίησιν ἐκ δὲ τῶν πλαγίων, καὶ αὐτὸ
προωθεῖται τὸ ὑπάρχον, ὥσπερ καὶ τὸ ὅλον στέλεχος καὶ οἱ ἀκρεμόνες. συμβαίνει δὲ τοῦτο ἐπὶ
τῆς Περσικῆς καρύας καὶ τῆς Ἡρακλεωτικῆς καὶ
3 ἄλλων.³ ἁπάντων δὲ τῶν τοιούτων εἰς ἓν φύλλον
ἀποτελευτῶσιν οἱ βλαστοί, δι' ὃ καὶ εὐλόγως οὐκ
ἐπιβλαστάνει καὶ αὐξάνεται μὴ ἔχοντα ἀρχήν.
(ὁμοία δὲ τρόπον τινὰ ἡ αὔξησις καὶ τοῦ σίτου·

---

¹ κατὰ . . . βλαστῶν conj. W.; κατὰ τοὺς τρόπους (corrected
to τόπους) καὶ βλαστούς U ; MVP insert τοὺς before βλαστούς.
² ἐκείνου . . . κατὰ conj. W.; ἐκείνου ἡ ἑτέρα σχίζεται τὰ ἴσα
καὶ UAld.
³ ἄλλων : ? ἐλάας W.; I suggest ἄλλων ἐλαῶν.

(bird-cherry) Valonia oak Phoenician cedar maple hop-hornbeam *zygia* manna-ash alder Aleppo pine andrachne cornelian cherry box wild pear. But silver-fir fir and Aleppo pine bear fruit from the very first, whatever size they have attained.

While the growth and budding of most trees are irregular as regards the position in which the buds appear,[1] the growth and budding of the silver-fir follow a regular rule, and its development afterwards is also in a regular sequence. For, when the trunk first divides, then again from the divided trunk the second division[2] takes place in like manner, and so the tree goes on with each fresh formation of buds. In other trees not even the knots are opposite to one another, except in some few cases, as wild olive and others.[3] Here too we find a difference in the manner of growth which belongs to all trees alike, both cultivated and wild: in some cases the growth is from the top of the shoots and also from the side-buds,[4] as in pear pomegranate fig myrtle and the majority of trees, one may say: in some cases the growth is not from the top, but only from the side-buds, and the already existing part is pushed out[5] further, as is the whole trunk with the upper branches. This occurs in the walnut and in the filbert as well as in other trees. In all such trees the buds end in a single leaf[6]; wherefore it is reasonable that they should not make fresh buds and growth from this point, as they have no point of departure. (To a certain extent the growth of corn is similar; for it

[4] ἐκ τοῦ . . . πλαγίων : ? ἐκ τοῦ ἄκρου καὶ ἐκ τῶν πλαγίων βλαστῶν. *cf.* 3. 5. 1.
[5] i.e. grows without dividing. *cf.* Plin. 16. 100. (of different trees).
[6] φύλλον perhaps conceals some other word.

193

THEOPHRASTUS

καὶ γὰρ οὗτος ἀεὶ τῇ προώσει τοῦ ὑπάρχοντος¹
αὐξάνεται, κἂν κολοβωθῇ τὰ φύλλα, καθάπερ ἐν
τοῖς ἐπιβοσκομένοις· πλὴν οὗτός γε οὐκ ἐκ τοῦ
πλαγίου παραφύει, καθάπερ ἔνια τῶν χεδροπῶν.)
αὕτη μὲν οὖν διαφορά τις ἂν εἴη βλαστήσεως
ἅμα καὶ αὐξήσεως.

4   Βαθύρριζα δὲ οὔ² φασί τινες εἶναι τὰ ἄγρια διὰ
τὸ φύεσθαι πάντα ἀπὸ σπέρματος, οὐκ ἄγαν
ὀρθῶς λέγοντες. ἐνδέχεται γὰρ ὅταν ἐμβιώσῃ⁴
πόρρω καθιέναι τὰς ῥίζας· ἐπεὶ καὶ τῶν λαχάνων
τὰ πολλὰ τοῦτο ποιεῖ, καίπερ ἀσθενέστερα ὄντα
καὶ ἐναργῶς φυόμενα <ἐν> τῇ γῇ. βαθυρριζότατον
δ' οὖν δοκεῖ τῶν ἀγρίων εἶναι ἡ πρῖνος· ἐλάτη δὲ
καὶ πεύκη μετρίως, ἐπιπολαιότατον δὲ θραύπαλος καὶ κοκκυμηλέα καὶ σποδιάς· αὕτη δ' ἐστὶν
ὥσπερ ἀγρία κοκκυμηλέα. ταῦτα μὲν οὖν καὶ
ὀλιγόρριζα· ὁ δὲ θραύπαλος πολύρριζον. συμβαίνει δὲ τοῖς ἄλλοις τοῖς μὴ κατὰ βάθους ἔχουσι,
καὶ οὐχ ἥκιστα ἐλάτῃ καὶ πεύκῃ, προρρίζοις ὑπὸ
τῶν πνευμάτων ἐκπίπτειν.

5   Οἱ μὲν οὖν περὶ Ἀρκαδίαν οὕτω λέγουσιν. οἱ
δ' ἐκ τῆς Ἴδης βαθυρριζότερον ἐλάτην δρυὸς ἀλλ'
ἐλάττους ἔχειν καὶ εὐθυρριζοτέραν εἶναι· βαθυρριζότατον δὲ καὶ τὴν κοκκυμηλέαν καὶ τὴν Ἡρακλεωτικήν, τὰς δὲ ῥίζας λεπτὰς καὶ ἰσχυρὰς τὴν
Ἡρακλεωτικήν, τὴν δὲ κοκκυμηλέαν πολύρριζον,
ἄμφω δ' ἐμβιῶναι δεῖν· δυσώλεθρον δὲ τὴν
κοκκυμηλέαν. ἐπιπολῆς δὲ σφένδαμνον καὶ

¹ τοῦ ὑπάρχοντος conj. Sch. from G ; τῇ ὑπαρχούσῃ Ald.
² οὐδ' : ἢ οὐκ W.    ³ Plin. 16. 127.
⁴ ἐμβιώσῃ : cf. 3. 6. 5 ; C.P. 1. 2. 1.

194

also regularly increases by pushing forward of the already existing part,[1] even if the leaves are mutilated, as in corn which is bitten down by animals. Corn however does not[2] make side-growths, as some leguminous plants do.) Here then we may find a difference which occurs both in the making of buds and in the making of fresh growth.

[3] Some say that wild trees are not deep rooting, because they all grow from seed; but this is not a very accurate statement. For it is possible that, when they are well established,[4] they may send their roots down far; in fact even most pot-herbs do this, though these are not so strong as trees, and are undoubtedly grown from seed planted in the ground.[5] The kermes-oak however seems to be the deepest rooting of wild trees; silver-fir and fir are only moderately so, and shallowest are joint-fir plum bullace (which is a sort of wild plum). The last two also have few roots, while joint-fir has many. Trees which do not root deep,[6] and especially silver-fir and fir, are liable to be rooted up by winds.

So the Arcadians say. But the people who live near Mount Ida say that the silver fir is deeper rooting[7] than the oak,[8] and has straighter roots, though they are fewer. Also that those which have the deepest roots are plum and filbert, the latter having strong slender roots, the former having many : but they add that both trees must be well established to acquire these characters; also that plum is very tenacious of life. Maple, they say,

---

[5] ἐναργῶς . . . γῇ : so G ; ἐν add. W.
[6] βάθους conj. Sch.; βάθος Ald.
[7] βαθυρριζότερον conj. W.; βαθυρριζότατον UMVAld.
[8] Proverbial for its hold on the ground ; cf. Verg. *Aen.* 4. 441 foll.

# THEOPHRASTUS

ὀλίγας· τὴν δὲ μελίαν πλείους καὶ εἶναι πυκνόρριζον καὶ βαθύρριζον. ἐπιπολῆς δὲ καὶ ἄρκευθον
καὶ κέδρον· καὶ κλήθρας λεπτὰς καὶ ὁμαλεῖς·
ἔτι δ' ὀξύην· καὶ γὰρ τοῦτ' ἐπιπολαιόρριζον καὶ
ὀλιγόρριζον. τὴν δὲ οὖαν ἐπιπολαίους μὲν ἰσχυρὰς δὲ καὶ παχείας καὶ δυσωλέθρους πλήθει δὲ
μετρίας. βαθύρριζα μὲν οὖν καὶ οὐ βαθύρριζα
τὰ τοιαῦτ' ἐστίν.

VII. Ἀποκοπέντος δὲ τοῦ στελέχους τὰ μὲν
ἄλλα πάνθ' ὡς εἰπεῖν παραβλαστάνει, πλὴν ἐὰν
αἱ ῥίζαι πρότερον τύχωσι πεπονηκυῖαι· πεύκη
δὲ καὶ ἐλάτη τελέως ἐκ ῥιζῶν αὐτοετεῖς αὐαίνονται
καὶ ἐὰν τὸ ἄκρον ἐπικοπῇ. συμβαίνει δὲ ἴδιόν
τι περὶ τὴν ἐλάτην· ὅταν γὰρ κοπῇ ἢ κολουσθῇ
ὑπὸ πνεύματος ἢ καὶ ἄλλου τινὸς περὶ τὸ λεῖον
τοῦ στελέχους—ἔχει γὰρ μέχρι τινὸς λεῖον καὶ
ἄοζον καὶ ὁμαλὸν ἱκανὸν ἴστω πλοίου—περι-
φύεται μικρόν, ὑποδεέστερον εἰς ὕψος, καὶ καλοῦσιν οἱ μὲν ἄμφαυξιν οἱ δὲ ἀμφίφυαν, τῷ μὲν
χρώματι μέλαν τῇ δὲ σκληρότητι ὑπερβάλλον,
ἐξ οὗ τοὺς κρατῆρας ποιοῦσιν οἱ περὶ Ἀρκαδίαν·
2 τὸ δὲ πάχος οἷον ἂν τύχῃ τὸ δένδρον, ὅσῳπερ
ἂν ἰσχυρότερον καὶ ἐγχυλότερον ἢ παχύτερον.
συμβαίνει δὲ κἀκεῖνο ἴδιον ἐν ταὐτῷ τούτῳ περὶ

---

[1] σφ. καὶ ὀλίγας conj. W.; σφ. κατ' ὀλίγον UMVAld.
[2] i.e. not very fibrous.
[3] cf. Hdt. 6. 37, and the proverb πίτυος τρόπον ἐκτρίβεσθαι.
[4] ὁμαλὸν conj. Scal.; ὅμοιον Ald.
[5] ἱκανὸν ἴστῳ πλοίου conj. W.; ἢ καὶ ἡλίκον πλεῖον Ald.; so
UH, but with πλοῖον.

has shallow roots and few of them [1]; but manna-ash has more and they are thickly matted and run deep ; Phoenician cedar and prickly cedar, they say, have shallow roots, those of alder are slender and 'plain,' [2] as also are those of beech ; for this too has few roots, and they are near the surface. Sorb, they say, has its roots near the surface, but they are strong and thick and hard to kill, though not very numerous. Such are the trees which are or are not deep-rooting.

*Of the effects of cutting down the whole or part of a tree.*

VII. Almost all trees shoot from the side if the trunk is cut down, unless the roots have previously been injured ; but fir and silver-fir wither away [3] completely from the roots within the year, if merely the top has been cut off. And there is a peculiar thing about the silver-fir ; when it is topped or broken off short by wind or some other cause affecting the smooth part of the trunk—for up to a certain height the trunk is smooth knotless and plain [4] (and so suitable for making a ship's mast [5]),— a certain amount of new growth forms round it, which does not however grow much vertically ; and this is called by some *amphauxis* [6] and by others *amphiphya* [6] ; it is black in colour and exceedingly hard, and the Arcadians make their mixing-bowls out of it ; the thickness is in proportion [7] to the tree, according as that is more or less vigorous and sappy, or again according to its thickness. There [8] is this peculiarity too in the silver-fir in the same connexion ;

[6] Two words meaning 'growth about.' *i.e. callus.*
[7] οἷον ἂν conj. W.: οἷον ἐἀν Ald.; ὅσει ἂν conj. Seal.
[8] Plin. 16. 123.

THEOPHRASTUS

τὴν ἐλάτην· ὅταν μὲν γάρ τις τοὺς ὄζους ἅπαντας
ἀφελὼν ἀποκόψῃ τὸ ἄκρον, ἀποθνήσκει ταχέως·
ὅταν δὲ τὰ κατωτέρω τὰ κατὰ τὸ λεῖον ἀφέλῃ,
ζῇ τὸ κατάλοιπον, περὶ ὃ δὴ καὶ ἡ ἄμφαυξις
φύεται. ζῇ δὲ δῆλον ὅτι τῷ ἔγχυλον εἶναι καὶ
χλωρόν, εἴπερ ἀπαράβλαστον. ἀλλὰ γὰρ τοῦτο
μὲν ἴδιον τῆς ἐλάτης.

3   Φέρει δὲ τὰ μὲν ἄλλα τόν τε καρπὸν τὸν
ἑαυτῶν καὶ τὰ κατ᾽ ἐνιαυτὸν ἐπιγινόμενα ταῦτα,
φύλλον ἄνθος βλαστόν· τὰ δὲ καὶ βρύον ἢ ἕλικα·
τὰ δὲ πλείω, καθάπερ ἥ τε πτελέα τόν τε βότρυν
καὶ τὸ θυλακῶδες τοῦτο, καὶ συκῆ καὶ τὰ ἐρινὰ
τὰ προαποπίπτοντα καὶ εἴ τινες ἄρα τῶν συκῶν
ὀλυνθοφοροῦσιν· ἴσως δὲ τρόπον τινὰ καρπὸς
οὗτος. ἀλλ᾽ ἡ Ἡρακλεωτικὴ καρύα τὸν ἴουλον
καὶ ἡ πρῖνος τὸν φοινικοῦν κόκκον ἡ δὲ δάφνη
τὸ βότρυον. φέρει μὲν καὶ ἡ καρποφόρος, εἰ μὴ
καὶ πᾶσα ἀλλά τοι γένος τι αὐτῆς, οὐ μὴν ἀλλὰ
πλέον ἡ ἄκαρπος, ἣν δὴ καὶ ἄρρενά τινες καλοῦσιν. ἀλλ᾽ ἡ πεύκη τὸν προαποπίπτοντα κύτταρον.

4   Πλεῖστα δὲ πάντων ἡ δρῦς παρὰ τὸν καρπόν,
οἷον τήν τε κηκίδα τὴν μικρὰν καὶ τὴν ἑτέραν

---

[1] *i.e.* and so does not, like other trees under like treatment, put its strength into these.   *cf. C.P.* 5. 17. 4.
[2] ἑαυτῶν conj. Sch. from G ; αὐτὴν Ald.
[3] The leaf-gall, *cf.* 2. 8. 3; 3. 14. 1.  For τοῦτο *cf.* 3. 18. 11 ;
4. 7. 1.   [4] Lat. *grossi. cf. C.P.* 5. 1. 8.
[5] τινὰ καρπὸς conj. Sch.; τινὰ ἄκαρπος UAld.

198

when, after taking off all the branches, one cuts off
the top, it soon dies ; yet, when one takes off the
lower parts, those about the smooth portion of the
trunk, what is left survives, and it is on this part
that the *amphauxis* forms. And plainly the reason
why the tree survives is that it is sappy and green
because it has no side-growths.[1]  Now this is peculiar
to the silver-fir.

*Of other things borne by trees besides their leaves flowers and*
*fruit.*

Now, while other trees bear merely their own [2]
fruit and the obvious parts which form annually, to
wit, leaf flower and bud, some bear also catkins or
tendrils, and some produce other things as well, for
instance the elm its ' cluster ' and the familiar bag-
like thing,[3] the fig both the immature figs which drop
off and (in some kinds) the untimely figs [4]—though
perhaps in a sense [5] these should be reckoned as
fruit.  Again filbert produces its catkin,[6] kermes-oak
its scarlet ' berry,'[7] and bay its ' cluster.'[8]  The
fruit-bearing sort of bay also produces this, or at all
events [9] one kind certainly does so ; however the
sterile kind, which some call the ' male,' produces
it in greater quantity. The fir again bears its 'tuft,'[10]
which drops off.

[11] The oak however bears more things besides [12] its
fruit than any other tree ; as the small gall [13] and its

[6] *cf.* 3. 3. 8 ; 3. 5. 5.
[7] *cf.* 3. 16. 1.  *i.e.* the kermes gall (whence Eng. 'crimson').
[8] βότρυον UMVAld., supported by G. and Plin. 16. 120 ;
but some editors read βρύον on the strength of 3. 11. 4. and
*C.P.* 2. 11. 4.      [9] ἀλλά τοι conj. W. ; ἀλλὰ καὶ Ald.
[10] *cf.* 3. 3. 8 n.   [11]  Plin. 16. 28.
[12] παρὰ conj. W., *cf.* § 6 ; φέρει Ald.      [13] *cf.* 3. 5. 2.

·τὴν πιττώδη μέλαιναν. ἔτι δὲ συκαμινῶδες ἄλλο
τῇ μορφῇ πλὴν σκληρὸν καὶ δυσκάτακτον,
σπάνιον δὲ τοῦτο· καὶ ἕτερον αἰδοιώδη σχέσιν
ἔχον, τελειούμενον δ' ἔτι σκληρὸν κατὰ τὴν
ἐπανάστασιν καὶ τετρυπημένον· προσεμφερὲς
τρόπον τινὰ τοῦτ' ἐστὶ καὶ ταύρου κεφαλῇ, περι-
καταγνύμενον δὲ ἔνδοθεν ἔχει πυρῆνος ἐλάας
ἰσοφυές. φύει δὲ καὶ τὸν ὑπ' ἐνίων καλούμενον
πῖλον· τοῦτο δ' ἐστὶ σφαιρίον ἐριῶδες μαλακὸν
περὶ πυρήνιον σκληρότερον πεφυκύς, ᾧ χρῶνται
πρὸς τοὺς λύχνους· καίεται γὰρ καλῶς, ὥσπερ
καὶ ἡ μέλαινα κηκίς. φύει δὲ καὶ ἕτερον σφαιρίον
κόμην ἔχον, τὰ μὲν ἄλλα ἀχρεῖον, κατὰ δὲ τὴν
ἐαρινὴν ὥραν ἐπίβαπτον χυλῷ μελιτηρῷ καὶ κατὰ
τὴν ἀφὴν καὶ κατὰ τὴν γεῦσιν.

5    Παραφύει δ' ἐνδοτέρω τῆς τῶν ῥαβδῶν μασχαλίδος ἕτερον σφαιρίον ἄμισχον ἢ καὶ κοιλόμισχον
ἴδιον καὶ ποικίλον· τοὺς μὲν γὰρ ἐπανεστηκότας
ὀμφαλοὺς ἐπιλεύκους ἢ ἐπεστιγμένους ἔχει μέλα-
νας τὸ δ' ἀνὰ μέσον κοκκοβαφὲς καὶ λαμπρόν·
ἀνοιγόμενον δ' ἐστὶ μέλαν καὶ ἐπίσαπρον. σπάνιον
δὲ παραφύει καὶ λιθάριον κισσηροειδὲς ἐπὶ
πλεῖον. ἔτι δ' ἄλλο τούτου σπανιαίτερον φυλλι-
κὸν συμπεπιλημένον πρόμηκες σφαιρίον. ἐπὶ δὲ
τοῦ φύλλου φύει κατὰ τὴν ῥάχιν σφαιρίον λευκὸν
διαυγὲς ὑδατῶδες, ὅταν ἁπαλὸν ᾖ· τοῦτο δὲ καὶ

¹ πυρῆνος ἐλάας ἰσοφυὲς conj. W.; πυρῆνος ἐλαίᾳ εἰρουφυην
UMV ; πυρῆνα ἐλαία εἰρουφύην Ald.
² περὶ πυρήνιον σκληρότερον I conj. ; περὶ πυρηνίου σκληρότητα
U ; περὶ πυρηνίου σκληρότερον M ; περιπυρηνίου σκληρότερον
VAld.  W. prints the reading of U.  For πῖλος see Index.

other black resinous gall. Again it has another growth, like a mulberry in shape, but hard and difficult to break; this however is not common. It has also another growth like the *penis* in shape, which, when it is further developed, makes a hard prominence and has a hole through it. This to a certain extent resembles also a bull's head, but, when split open, it contains inside a thing shaped like the stone of an olive.[1] The oak also produces what some call the 'ball'; this is a soft woolly spherical object enclosing a small stone which is harder,[2] and men use it for their lamps; for it burns well, as does the black gall. The oak also produces another hairy ball, which is generally useless, but in the spring season it is covered with a juice which is like honey both to touch and taste.

[3] Further the oak produces right inside the axil [4] of the branches another ball with no stalk or else [5] a hollow one; this is peculiar and of various colours: for the knobs which arise on it are whitish or black and spotted,[6] while the part between these is brilliant scarlet; but, when it is opened, it is black and rotten.[7] It also occasionally produces a small stone which more or less resembles pumice-stone; also, less commonly, there is a leaf-like ball, which is oblong and of close texture. Further the oak produces on the rib of the leaf a white transparent ball, which is watery, when it is young; and this sometimes con-

---

[3] Plin. 16. 29.
[4] ἐνδοτέρω . . . μασχαλίδος conj. R. Const.; ἐντεριώνης τῶν βοτῶν μασχαλίδας U.Ald. Plin., *l.c.*, *gignunt et aliae ramorum eius pilulas.* [5] ἢ ins. St.
[6] Plin., *l.c.*, *nigra varietate dispersa.*
[7] ἐπίσαπρον; Plin., *l.c.*, has *apertis amara inanitas est*, whence ἐπίπικρον conj. Sch.

μύας ἐνίοτε ἐνδὸν ἴσχει. τελειούμενον δὲ σκλη-
ρύνεται κηκίδος μικρᾶς λείας τρόπον.

6 Ἡ μὲν οὖν δρῦς τοσαῦτα φέρει παρὰ τὸν
καρπόν. οἱ γὰρ μύκητες ἀπὸ τῶν ῥιζῶν καὶ
παρὰ τὰς ῥίζας φυόμενοι κοινοὶ καὶ ἑτέρων εἰσίν.
ὡσαύτως δὲ καὶ ἡ ἰξία· καὶ γὰρ αὕτη φύεται
καὶ ἐν ἄλλοις· ἀλλ᾽ οὐδὲν ἧττον, ὥσπερ ἐλέχθη,
πλειστοφόρον ἐστίν· εἰ δέ γε δὴ καθ᾽ Ἡσίοδον
φέρει μέλι καὶ μελίττας, ἔτι μᾶλλον· φαίνεται δ᾽
οὖν καὶ ὁ μελιτώδης οὗτος χυλὸς ἐκ τοῦ ἀέρος
ἐπὶ ταύτῃ μάλιστα προσίζειν. φασὶ δὲ καὶ ὅταν
κατακαυθῇ γίνεσθαι λίτρον ἐξ αὐτῆς. ταῦτα
μὲν οὖν ἴδια τῆς δρυός.

VIII. Πάντων δέ, ὥσπερ ἐλέχθη, τῶν δένδρων
ὡς καθ᾽ ἕκαστον γένος λαβεῖν διαφοραὶ πλείους
εἰσίν· ἡ μὲν κοινὴ πᾶσιν, ᾗ διαιροῦσι τὸ θῆλυ καὶ
τὸ ἄρρεν, ὧν τὸ μὲν καρποφόρον τὸ δὲ ἄκαρπον
ἐπί τινων. ἐν οἷς δὲ ἄμφω καρποφόρα τὸ θῆλυ
καλλικαρπότερον καὶ πολυκαρπότερον· πλὴν
ὅσοι ταῦτα καλοῦσιν ἄρρενα, καλοῦσι γάρ τινες.
παραπλησία δ᾽ ἡ τοιαύτη διαφορὰ καὶ ὡς τὸ
ἥμερον διῄρηται πρὸς τὸ ἄγριον. ἑτέρα δὲ κατ᾽
εἶδος αὐτῶν τῶν ὁμογενῶν· ὑπὲρ ὧν λεκτέον ἅμα
συνεμφαίνοντας καὶ τὰς ἰδίας μορφὰς τῶν μὴ
φανερῶν καὶ γνωρίμων.

1 Plin. 16. 31.   2 Hes. Op. 233.
3 Plin. 16. 16.   4 λεκτέον add. Sch.

tains flies : but as it develops, it becomes hard, like a small smooth gall.

Such are the growths which the oak produces as well as its fruit. For as for the fungi [1] which grow from the roots or beside them, these occur also in other trees. So too with the oak-mistletoe ; for this grows on other trees also. However, apart from that, the oak, as was said, produces more things than any other tree ; and all the more so if, as Hesiod [2] says, it produces honey and even bees ; however, the truth appears to be that this honey-like juice comes from the air and settles on this more than on other trees. They say also that, when the oak is burnt, nitre is produced from it. Such are the things peculiar to the oak.

*Of 'male' and 'female' in trees: the oak as an example of this and other differences.*

VIII. [3] Taking, as was said, all trees according to their kinds, we find a number of differences. Common to them all is that by which men distinguish the 'male' and the 'female,' the latter being fruit-bearing, the former barren in some kinds. In those kinds in which both forms are fruit-bearing the 'female' has fairer and more abundant fruit ; however some call these the 'male' trees—for there are those who actually thus invert the names. This difference is of the same character as that which distinguishes the cultivated from the wild tree, while other differences distinguish different forms of the same kind : and these we must discuss,[4] at the same time indicating the peculiar forms, where these are not [5] obvious and easy to recognise.

[5] μὴ conj. St.; μήτε Ald.H.

THEOPHRASTUS

2 Δρυὸς δὴ γένη—ταύτην γὰρ μάλιστα διαιροῦσι·
καὶ ἔνιοί γε εὐθὺς τὴν μὲν ἥμερον καλοῦσι τὴν δ᾽
ἀγρίαν οὐ τῇ γλυκύτητι τοῦ καρποῦ διαιροῦντες·
ἐπεὶ γλυκύτατός γε ὁ τῆς φηγοῦ, ταύτην δ᾽
ἀγρίαν ποιοῦσιν· ἀλλὰ τῷ μᾶλλον ἐν τοῖς ἐργασίμοις φύεσθαι καὶ τὸ ξύλον ἔχειν λειότερον,
τὴν δὲ φηγὸν τραχὺ καὶ ἐν τοῖς ὀρεινοῖς—γένη
μὲν οὖν οἱ μὲν τέτταρα ποιοῦσιν οἱ δὲ πέντε.
διαλλάττουσι δ᾽ ἔνια τοῖς ὀνόμασιν, οἷον τὴν τὰς
γλυκείας φέρουσαν οἱ μὲν ἡμερίδα καλοῦντες οἱ
δ᾽ ἐτυμόδρυν. ὁμοίως δὲ καὶ ἐπ᾽ ἄλλων. ὡς δ᾽
οὖν οἱ περὶ τὴν Ἴδην διαιροῦσι, τάδ᾽ ἐστὶ τὰ εἴδη·
ἡμερὶς αἰγίλωψ πλατύφυλλος φηγὸς ἁλίφλοιος·
οἱ δὲ εὐθύφλοιον καλοῦσιν. κάρπιμα μὲν πάντα·
γλυκύτατα δὲ τὰ τῆς φηγοῦ, καθάπερ εἴρηται,
καὶ δεύτερον τὰ τῆς ἡμερίδος, ἔπειτα τῆς πλατυφύλλου, καὶ τέταρτον ἡ ἁλίφλοιος, ἔσχατον δὲ
3 καὶ πικρότατον ἡ αἰγίλωψ. οὐχ ἅπασαι δὲ
γλυκεῖαι ἐν τοῖς γένεσιν ἀλλ᾽ ἐνίοτε καὶ πικραί,
καθάπερ ἡ φηγός. διαφέρουσι δὲ καὶ τοῖς
μεγέθεσι καὶ τοῖς σχήμασι καὶ τοῖς χρώμασι
τῶν βαλάνων. ἴδιον δὲ ἔχουσιν ἥ τε φηγὸς καὶ
ἡ ἁλίφλοιος· ἀμφότεραι γὰρ παραλιθάζουσιν ἐν
τοῖς ἄρρεσι καλουμένοις ἐξ ἄκρων τῶν βαλάνων
ἑκατέρωθεν, αἱ μὲν πρὸς τῷ κελύφει αἱ δὲ πρὸς

1 Plin. 16. 16 and 17.
2 See Index, δρῦς and ἡμερίς. ἡμερίς, lit. 'cultivated oak.'
3 Plin. 16. 29.

204

[1] Take then the various kinds of oak; for in this tree men recognise more differences than in any other. Some simply speak of a cultivated and a wild kind, not recognising any distinction made by the sweetness of the fruit; (for sweetest is that of the kind called Valonia oak, and this they make the wild kind), but distinguishing the cultivated kind by its growing more commonly on tilled land and having smoother timber, while the Valonia oak has rough wood and grows in mountain districts. Thus some make four kinds, others five. They also in some cases vary as to the names assigned; thus the kind which bears sweet fruit is called by some *hemeris*, by others 'true oak.' So too with other kinds. However, to take the classification given by the people of Mount Ida, these [2] are the kinds: *hemeris* (gall-oak), *aigilops* (Turkey-oak), 'broad-leaved' oak (scrub oak), Valonia oak, sea-bark oak, which some call 'straight-barked' oak. [3] All these bear fruit; but the fruits of Valonia oak are the sweetest, as has been said; second to these those of *hemeris* (gall-oak), third those of the 'broad-leaved' oak (scrub oak), fourth sea-bark oak, and last *aigilops* (Turkey-oak), whose fruits are very bitter. [4] However the fruit is not always sweet in the kinds specified as such [5]; sometimes it is bitter, that of the Valonia oak for instance. There are also differences in the size shape and colour of the acorns. Those of Valonia oak and sea-bark oak are peculiar; in both of these kinds on what are called the 'male' trees the acorns become stony at one end or the other; in one kind this hardening takes place in the end which is

[4] Plin. 16. 19 21.
[5] οὐχ . . . ἐνίοτε conj. W.: text defective in Ald.H.

αὐτῇ τῇ σαρκί. δι' ὃ καὶ ἀφαιρεθέντων ὅμοια
γίνεται κοιλώματα τοῖς ἐπὶ τῶν ζώων.

4 Διαφέρουσι δὲ καὶ τοῖς φύλλοις καὶ τοῖς στελέχεσι καὶ τοῖς ξύλοις καὶ τῇ ὅλῃ μορφῇ. ἡ μὲν
γὰρ ἡμερὶς οὐκ ὀρθοφυὴς οὐδὲ λεία οὐδὲ μακρά·
περίκομος γὰρ ἡ φυτεία καὶ ἐπεστραμμένη καὶ
πολυμάσχαλος, ὥστε ὀζώδη καὶ βραχεῖαν γίνε-
σθαι· τὸ δὲ ξύλον ἰσχυρὸν μὲν ἀσθενέστερον δὲ
τῆς φηγοῦ· τοῦτο γὰρ ἰσχυρότατον καὶ ἀσαπέστατον. οὐκ ὀρθοφυὴς δὲ οὐδ' αὕτη ἀλλ' ἧττον
ἔτι τῆς ἡμερίδος, τὸ δὲ στέλεχος παχύτατον, ὥστε
καὶ τὴν ὅλην μορφὴν βραχεῖαν εἶναι· καὶ γὰρ
ἡ φυτεία περίκομος καὶ ταύτῃ καὶ οὐκ εἰς ὀρθόν.
ἡ δὲ αἰγίλωψ ὀρθοφυέστατον καὶ ὑψηλότατον
καὶ λειότατον καὶ τὸ ξύλον εἰς μῆκος ἰσχυρότατον.
οὐ φύεται δὲ ἐν τοῖς ἐργασίμοις ἢ σπανίως.

5 Ἡ δὲ πλατύφυλλος δεύτερον ὀρθοφυΐᾳ καὶ
μήκει, πρὸς δὲ τὴν χρείαν τὴν οἰκοδομικὴν χείριστον μετὰ τὴν ἁλίφλοιον, φαῦλον δὲ καὶ εἰς τὸ
καίειν καὶ ἀνθρακεύειν, ὥσπερ καὶ τὸ τῆς ἁλιφλοίου, καὶ θριπηδέστατον μετ' ἐκείνην· ἡ γὰρ
ἁλίφλοιος παχὺ μὲν ἔχει τὸ στέλεχος χαῦνον δὲ
καὶ κοῖλον ἐὰν ἔχῃ πάχος ὡς ἐπὶ τὸ πολύ, δι'
ὃ καὶ ἀχρεῖον εἰς τὰς οἰκοδομάς· ἔτι δὲ σήπεται
τάχιστα· καὶ γὰρ ἔνυγρόν ἐστι τὸ δένδρον· δι' ὃ
καὶ κοίλη γίνεται. φασὶ δέ τινες οὐδ' ἐγκάρδιον
εἶναι μόνῃ. λέγουσιν ὡς καὶ κεραυνόβλητες
αὗται μόναι γίνονται καίπερ ὕψος οὐκ ἔχουσαι

---

[1] i.e. at the ' top ' end ; πρὸς : ? ἐν, πρὸς being repeated by
mistake.
[2] ζώων MSS.; ᾠῶν conj. Palm.      [3] Plin. 16. 22.

attached to the cup, in the other in the flesh itself.[1]
Wherefore, when the cups are taken off, we find a
cavity like the visceral cavities in animals.[2]

[3] There are also differences in leaves trunk timber
and general appearance. *Hemeris* (gall-oak) is not
straight-growing nor smooth nor tall, for its growth
is very leafy [4] and twisted, with many side-branches,
so that it makes a low much-branched tree : its timber
is strong, but not so strong as that of the Valonia
oak, for that is the strongest and the least liable to
rot. This [5] kind too is not straight-growing, even less
so than the *hemeris* (gall-oak), but the trunk is very
thick, so that the whole appearance is stunted ; for
in growth this kind too is very leafy [4] and not erect.
The *aigilops* (Turkey oak) is the straightest growing
and also the tallest and smoothest, and its wood, cut
lengthways, is the strongest. It does not grow on
tilled land, or very rarely.

The 'broad-leaved' oak (scrub oak) [6] comes second
as to straightness of growth and length of timber to
be got from it, but for use in building it is the worst
next after the sea-bark oak, and it is even poor wood
for burning and making charcoal, as is also that of
the sea-bark oak, and next after this kind it is the
most worm-eaten. For the sea-bark oak has a thick
trunk, but it is generally spongy and hollow when
it is thick ; wherefore it is useless for building.
Moreover it rots very quickly, for the tree contains
much moisture ; and that is why it also becomes
hollow ; and some say that it is the only [7] oak which
has no heart. And some of the Aeolians say that
these are the only oaks which are struck by light-

[4] *i.e.* of bushy habit.     [6] αὕτη conj. Sch.: αὐτή UAld.
[5] Plin. 16. 23 and 24.    [7] μόνη conj. St.; μόνην Ald. H.

THEOPHRASTUS

τῶν Αἰολέων τινές, οὐδὲ πρὸς τὰ ἱερὰ χρῶνται
τοῖς ξύλοις.  κατὰ μὲν οὖν τὰ ξύλα καὶ τὰς
ὅλας μορφὰς ἐν τούτοις αἱ διαφοραί.

6   Κηκίδας δὲ πάντα φέρει τὰ γένη, μόνη δὲ εἰς
τὰ δέρματα χρησίμην ἡ ἡμερίς. ἡ δὲ τῆς αἰγί-
λωπος καὶ τῆς πλατυφύλλου τῇ μὲν ὄψει παρομοία τῇ τῆς ἡμερίδος, πλὴν λειοτέρα, ἀχρεῖος δέ.
φέρει καὶ τὴν ἑτέραν τὴν μέλαιναν ᾗ τὰ ἔρια
βάπτουσιν. ὃ δὲ καλοῦσί τινες φάσκον ὅμοιον
τοῖς ῥακίοις ἡ αἰγίλωψ μόνη φέρει πολιὸν καὶ
τραχύ· καὶ γὰρ πηχυαῖον κατακρεμάννυται,
καθάπερ τρύχος ὀθονίου μακρόν. φύεται δὲ
τοῦτο ἐκ τοῦ φλοιοῦ καὶ οὐκ ἐκ τῆς κορύνης
ὅθεν ἡ βάλανος, οὐδ' ἐξ ὀφθαλμοῦ ἀλλ' ἐκ τοῦ
πλαγίου τῶν ἄνωθεν ὄζων. ἡ δ' ἁλίφλοιος ἐπίμελαν τοῦτο φύει καὶ βραχύ.

7   Οἱ μὲν οὖν ἐκ τῆς Ἴδης οὕτως διαιροῦσιν. οἱ
δὲ περὶ Μακεδονίαν τέτταρα γένη ποιοῦσιν,
ἐτυμόδρυν ἢ τὰς γλυκείας, πλατύφυλλον ἢ τὰς
πικράς, φηγὸν ἢ τὰς στρογγύλας, ἄσπριν· ταύτην
δὲ οἱ μὲν ἄκαρπον ὅλως οἱ δὲ φαῦλον τὸν καρπόν,
ὥστε μηδὲν ἐσθίειν ζῷον πλὴν ὑός, καὶ ταύτην
ὅταν ἑτέραν μὴ ἔχῃ· καὶ τὰ πολλὰ λαμβάνεσθαι
περικεφαλαίᾳ. μοχθηρὰ δὲ καὶ τὰ ξύλα· πελε-

---

¹ Plin. 16. 26.
² φάσκον . . . ῥακίοις conj. Sch. (ῥακίοις Salm.) : φάσκος ὅμοιος
τοῖς βραχείοις UP₂; φάσκον ὁμοίως τοῖς βραγχίοις Ald.H. Plin.
16. 33, cf. 12. 108; Diosc. 1. 20; Hesych. s.v. φάσκος.
³ τραχὺ conj. W.; βραχὺ UP.    ⁴ κορύνης. cf. 3. 5. 1.

208

ning, although they are not lofty; nor do they use the wood for their sacrifices. Such then are the differences as to timber and general appearance.

[1] All the kinds produce galls, but only *hemeris* (gall-oak) produces one which is of use for tanning hides. That of *aigilops* (Turkey-oak) and that of the 'broad-leaved' oak (scrub oak) are in appearance like that of *hemeris* (gall-oak), but smoother and useless. This also produces the other gall, the black kind, with which they dye wool. The substance which some call tree-moss and which resembles rags[2] is borne only by the *aigilops* (Turkey-oak); it is grey and rough [3] and hangs down for a cubit's length, like a long shred of linen. This grows from the bark and not from the knob[4] whence the acorn starts; nor does it grow from an eye, but from the side of the upper boughs. The sea-bark oak also produces this, but it is blackish[5] and short.

Thus the people of Mount Ida distinguish. But the people of Macedonia make four kinds, 'true-oak,' or the oak which bears the sweet acorns, 'broad-leaved' oak (scrub oak), or that which bears the bitter ones, Valonia oak, or that which bears the round ones, and *aspris*[6] (Turkey-oak); [7] the last-named some say is altogether without fruit, some say it bears poor fruit, so that no animal eats it except the pig, and only he when he can get no others, and that after eating it the pig mostly gets an affection of the head.[8] The wood is also wretched; when hewn with the axe it is altogether

---

[5] ἐπίμελαν τοῦτο φύει conj. Scal.; ἐπιμ. τοῦτο φύσει U; ἐπὶ μελίαν τοῦτο φύει MVAld.

[6] See Index.     [7] Plin. 16. 24.

[8] περικεφαλαία : apparently the name of a disease.

THEOPHRASTUS

κηθέντα μὲν ὅλως ἀχρεῖα· καταρήγνυται γὰρ καὶ
διαπίπτει· ἀπελέκητα δὲ βελτίω, δι' ὃ καὶ οὕτω
χρῶνται. μοχθηρὰ δὲ καὶ εἰς καῦσιν καὶ εἰς
ἀνθρακείαν· ἀχρεῖος γὰρ ὅλως ὁ ἄνθραξ διὰ τὸ
πηδᾶν καὶ σπινθηρίζειν πλὴν τοῖς χαλκεῦσι.
τούτοις δὲ χρησιμώτερος τῶν ἄλλων· διὰ γὰρ τὸ
ἀποσβέννυσθαι, ὅταν παύσηται φυσώμενος, ὀλίγος
ἀναλίσκεται. [τὸ δὲ τῆς ἁλιφλοίου χρήσιμον εἰς
τοὺς ἄξονας μόνον καὶ τὰ τοιαῦτα.]   δρυὸς μὲν
οὖν ταύτας ποιοῦσι τὰς ἰδέας.

IX. Τῶν δὲ ἄλλων ἐλάττους· καὶ σχεδὸν τά
γε πλεῖστα διαιροῦσι ἄρρενι καὶ θήλει, καθάπερ
εἴρηται, πλὴν ὀλίγων ὧν ἐστι καὶ ἡ πεύκη·
πεύκης γὰρ τὸ μὲν ἥμερον ποιοῦσι τὸ δ' ἄγριον,
τῆς δ' ἀγρίας δύο γένη· καλοῦσι δὲ τὴν μὲν Ἰδαίαν
τὴν δὲ παραλίαν· τούτων δὲ ὀρθοτέρα καὶ μακροτέρα καὶ τὸ φύλλον ἔχουσα παχύτερον ἡ Ἰδαία,
τὸ δὲ φύλλον λεπτότερον καὶ ἀμενηνότερον ἡ
παραλία καὶ λειότερον τὸν φλοιὸν καὶ εἰς τὰ
δέρματα χρήσιμον· ἡ δὲ ἑτέρα οὔ. καὶ τῶν
στροβίλων ὁ μὲν τῆς παραλίας στρογγύλος τε
καὶ διαχάσκων ταχέως, ὁ δὲ τῆς Ἰδαίας μακρό-
τερος καὶ χλωρὸς καὶ ἧττον χάσκων ὡς ἂν
ἀγριώτερος· τὸ δὲ ξύλον ἰσχυρότερον τὸ τῆς
παραλίας· δεῖ γὰρ καὶ τὰς τοιαύτας διαφορὰς

[1] Plin. 16. 23.
[2] τὸ δὲ . . . τοιαῦτα : this sentence seems out of place, as
ἀλίφλοιος was not one of the ' Macedonian ' oaks mentioned
above (Sch.).

useless, for it breaks in pieces and falls asunder;
if it is not hewn with the axe it is better, wherefore they so use it. [1] It is even wretched for
burning and for making charcoal; for the charcoal
is entirely useless except to the smith, because it
springs about and emits sparks. But for use in the
smithy it is more serviceable than the other kinds,
since, as it goes out when it ceases to be blown, little
of it is consumed. [2] The wood of the sea-bark oak
is only useful for wheel-axles and the like purposes.
Such are the varieties of the oak [3] which men
make out.

*Of the differences in firs.*

IX. [4] The differences between other trees are fewer;
for the most part men distinguish them merely
according as they are 'male' or 'female,' as has been
said, except in a few cases including the fir; for in this
tree they distinguish the wild and the cultivated [5]
kinds, and make two wild kinds, calling one the 'fir
of Ida' (Corsican pine [6]) the other the 'fir of the
sea-shore' (Aleppo pine); of these the former is
straighter and taller and has thicker leaves,[7] while
in the latter the leaves are slenderer and weaker,
and the bark is smoother and useful for tanning
hides, which the other is not. Moreover the cone of
the seaside kind is round and soon splits open, while
that of the Idaean kind is longer and green and
does not open so much, as being of wilder character.
The timber of the seaside kind is stronger,—for one
must note such differences also between trees of the

---

[3] T. describes πρῖνος σμῖλαξ, and φελλόδρυς in 3. 16,
φελλός in 3. 17. 1.

[4] Plin. 16. 43.    [5] Stone pine. See Index.
[6] Plin. 16. 48.    [7] φύλλον W. conj.; ξύλον UMVP.

THEOPHRASTUS

λαμβάνειν τῶν συγγενῶν· γνώριμοι γὰρ διὰ τὴν
χρείαν.

2  Ὀρθότερον δὲ καὶ παχύτερον, ὥσπερ εἴπομεν,
ἡ Ἰδαία, καὶ πρὸς τούτοις πιττωδέστερον ὅλως τὸ
δένδρον, μελαντέρᾳ δὲ πίττῃ καὶ γλυκυτέρᾳ καὶ
λεπτοτέρᾳ καὶ εὐωδεστέρᾳ, ὅταν ᾖ ὠμή· ἑψη-
θεῖσα δὲ χείρων ἐκβαίνει διὰ τὸ πολὺν ἔχειν τὸν
ὀρρόν. ἐοίκασι δ' ἅπερ οὗτοι διαιροῦσιν ὀνόμασιν
ἰδίοις οἱ ἄλλοι διαιρεῖν τῷ ἄρρενι καὶ θήλει·
φασὶ δ' οἱ περὶ Μακεδονίαν καὶ ἄκαρπόν τι γένος
ὅλως εἶναι πεύκης, καὶ τὸ μὲν ἄρρεν βραχύτερόν
τε καὶ σκληροφυλλότερον, τὸ δὲ θῆλυ εὐμηκέστερον, καὶ τὰ φύλλα λιπαρὰ καὶ ἁπαλὰ καὶ
κεκλιμένα μᾶλλον ἔχειν· ἔτι δὲ τὰ ξύλα τῆς μὲν
ἄρρενος περίμητρα καὶ σκληρὰ καὶ ἐν ταῖς
ἐργασίαις στρεφόμενα, τῆς δὲ θηλείας εὐεργὰ καὶ
ἀστραβῆ καὶ μαλακώτερα.

3  Σχεδὸν δὲ κοινή τις ἡ διαφορὰ πάντων τῶν
ἀρρένων καὶ θηλειῶν, ὡς οἱ ὑλοτόμοι φασίν. ἅπαν
γὰρ τὸ ἄρρεν τῇ πελεκήσει καὶ βραχύτερον καὶ
ἐπεστραμμένον μᾶλλον καὶ δυσεργότερον καὶ τῷ
χρώματι μελάντερον, τὸ δὲ θῆλυ εὐμηκέστερον·
ἐπεὶ καὶ τὴν αἰγίδα τὴν καλουμένην ἡ θήλεια τῆς
πεύκης ἔχει· τοῦτο δ' ἐστὶ τὸ ἐγκάρδιον αὐτῆς·

---

¹ συγγενῶν conj. R. Const.; ἀγγείων UAld.; ἐγγείων MV mBas.
² γνώριμοι conj. R. Const.; γνώριμος UAld.H.; γνώριμα conj. W.
³ ὀρθότερον conj. R. Const.; ὀξύτερον UMVAld.
⁴ μελαντέρᾳ ... εὐωδεστέρᾳ conj. W.; μελάντεραι δὲ πίττῃ καὶ γλυκύτεραι καὶ λεπτότεραι καὶ εὐωδέστεραι UMV; μελαντέρα

212

same kind,[1] since it is by their use that the different characters are recognised.[2]

The Idaean kind is, as we have said, of straighter[3] and stouter growth, and moreover the tree is altogether more full of pitch, and its pitch is blacker sweeter thinner and more fragrant[4] when it is fresh; though, when it is boiled, it turns out inferior,[5] because it contains so much watery matter. However it appears that the kinds which these people distinguish by special names are distinguished by others merely as 'male' and 'female.' The people of Macedonia say that there is also a kind of fir which bears no fruit whatever, in which the 'male'[6] (Aleppo pine) is shorter and has harder leaves, while the 'female' (Corsican pine) is taller and has glistening delicate leaves which are more pendent. Moreover the timber of the 'male' kind has much heart-wood,[7] is tough, and warps in joinery work, while that of the 'female' is easy to work, does not warp,[8] and is softer.

This distinction between 'male' and 'female' may, according to the woodmen, be said to be common to all trees. Any wood of a 'male' tree, when one comes to cut it with the axe, gives shorter lengths, is more twisted, harder to work, and darker in colour; while the 'female' gives better lengths. For it is the 'female' fir which contains what is called the *aigis*[9]; this is the heart of the tree; the

δὲ καὶ γλυκυτέρα καὶ λεπτοτέρα καὶ εὐωδεστέρα Ald. λεπτοτέρᾳ, [2] less viscous.

[5] cf. 9. 2. 5; Plin. 16. 60. [6] Plin. 16. 47.
[7] περίμητρα conj. R. Const.: so Mold. explains; περιμήτρια UMV. cf. 3. 9. 6.
[8] ἀστραβῆ conj. R. Const.; εὐστραβῆ Ald.
[9] αἰγίδα: cf. 5. 1. 9; Plin. 16. 187.

αἴτιον δὲ ὅτι ἀπευκοτέρα καὶ ἧττον ἔνδαδος καὶ
λειοτέρα καὶ εὐκτεανωτέρα.¹ γίνεται δὲ ἐν τοῖς
μέγεθος ἔχουσι τῶν δένδρων, ὅταν ἐκπεσόντα περι-
σαπῇ τὰ λευκὰ τὰ κύκλῳ.² τούτων γὰρ περι-
αιρεθέντων καὶ καταλειφθείσης τῆς μήτρας ἐκ
ταύτης πελεκᾶται· ἔστι δὲ εὔχρουν σφόδρα καὶ
λεπτόϊνον. ὃ δὲ οἱ περὶ τὴν Ἴδην δαδουργοὶ
καλοῦσι συκῆν, τὸ ἐπιγιγνόμενον ἐν ταῖς πεύκαις,
ἐρυθρότερον τὴν χροιὰν τῆς δαδός, ἐν τοῖς ἄρρεσίν
ἐστι μᾶλλον· δυσῶδες δὲ τοῦτο καὶ οὐκ ὄζει δαδὸς
οὐδὲ καίεται ἀλλ᾽ ἀποπηδᾷ ἀπὸ τοῦ πυρός.

4 Πεύκης μὲν οὖν ταῦτα γένη ποιοῦσιν, ἥμερόν
τε καὶ ἄγριον, καὶ τῆς ἀγρίας ἄρρενά τε καὶ
θήλειαν καὶ τρίτην τὴν ἄκαρπον. οἱ δὲ περὶ τὴν
Ἀρκαδίαν οὔτε τὴν ἄκαρπον λέγουσιν οὔτε τὴν
ἥμερον πεύκην, ἀλλὰ πίτυν εἶναί φασι· καὶ γὰρ τὸ
στέλεχος ἐμφερέστατον εἶναι τῇ πίτυϊ καὶ ἔχειν
τήν τε λεπτότητα καὶ τὸ μέγεθος καὶ ἐν ταῖς
ἐργασίαις ταὐτὸ τὸ ξύλον· τὸ γὰρ τῆς πεύκης καὶ
παχύτερον καὶ λειότερον καὶ ὑψηλότερον εἶναι·
καὶ τὰ φύλλα τὴν μὲν πεύκην ἔχειν πολλὰ καὶ
λιπαρὰ καὶ βαθέα καὶ κεκλιμένα, τὴν δὲ πίτυν
καὶ τὴν κωνοφόρον ταύτην ὀλίγα τε καὶ αὐχμωδέ-
στερα καὶ πεφρικότα μᾶλλον <ἄμφω δὲ τριχόφυλλα.> ἔτι δὲ τὴν πίτταν ἐμφερεστέραν τῆς

---

¹ εὐκτεανωτέρα: εὐκτηδονωτέρα conj. R. Const.  cf. 5. 1. 9 ;
but text is supported by Hesych. s.v. ἰθυκτέανον.
² I omit καὶ before τὰ κύκλῳ.
³ Plin. 16. 44.

214

reason being that it is less resinous, less soaked with pitch, smoother, and of straighter grain.[1] This *aigis* is found in the larger trees, when, as they have fallen down, the white outside part[2] has decayed; when this has been stripped off and the core left, it is cut out of this with the axe; and it is of a good colour with fine fibre. However the substance which the torch-cutters of Mount Ida call the 'fig,'[3] which forms in the fir and is redder in colour than the resin, is found more in the 'male' trees; it has an evil smell, not like the smell of resin, nor will it burn, but it leaps away from the fire.

[4] Such are the kinds of fir which they make out, the cultivated and the wild, the latter including the 'male' and the 'female' and also the kind which bears no fruit. However the Arcadians say that neither the sterile kind nor the cultivated is a fir, but a pine; for, they say, the trunk closely resembles the pine and has its slenderness, its stature, and the same kind[5] of wood for purposes of joinery, the trunk of the fir being thicker smoother and taller; moreover that the fir has many leaves, which are glossy massed together[6] and pendent, while in the pine and in the above-mentioned cone-bearing tree[7] the leaves are few and drier and stiffer; though in both the leaves are hair-like.[8] Also, they say, the pitch of this tree is more like that of the pine; for

[4] ταῦτα γένη conj. R. Const. from G; ταυτά γε UMVAld.; Plin. 16. 45–49.

[5] ταὐτὸ conj. W.; αὐτὸ Ald.

[6] βαθέα: δασέα conj. R. Const. *cf.* 3. 16. 2.

[7] *i.e.* the cultivated πεύκη (so called). T. uses this periphrasis to avoid begging the question of the name.

[8] ἄμφω δὲ τριχ. ins. here by Sch.; in MSS. and Ald. the words occur in § 5 after πιττωδέστερον.

πίτυος· καὶ γὰρ τὴν πίτυν ἔχειν ὀλίγην τε καὶ
πικράν, ὥσπερ καὶ τὴν κωνοφόρον, τὴν δὲ πεύκην
εὐώδη καὶ πολλήν. φύεται δ' ἐν μὲν τῇ Ἀρκαδίᾳ
ἡ πίτυς ὀλίγη περὶ δὲ τὴν Ἠλείαν πολλή. οὗτοι
μὲν οὖν ὅλῳ τῷ γένει διαμφισβητοῦσιν.

5 Ἡ δὲ πίτυς δοκεῖ τῆς πεύκης καὶ διαφέρειν τῷ
λιπαρωτέρα τε εἶναι καὶ λεπτοφυλλοτέρα καὶ τὸ
μέγεθος ἐλάττων καὶ ἧττον ὀρθοφυής· ἔτι δὲ τὸν
κῶνον ἐλάττω φέρειν καὶ πεφρικότα μᾶλλον καὶ
τὸ κάρυον πιττωδέστερον· καὶ τὰ ξύλα λευκότερα
καὶ ὁμοιότερα τῇ ἐλάτῃ καὶ τὸ ὅλον ἄπευκα.
διαφορὰν δ' ἔχει καὶ ταύτην² μεγάλην πρὸς τὴν
πεύκην· πεύκην μὲν γὰρ ἐπικαυθεισῶν τῶν ῥιζῶν
οὐκ ἀναβλαστάνειν, τὴν πίτυν δέ φασί τινες ἀναβλαστάνειν, ὥσπερ καὶ ἐν Λέσβῳ ἐμπρησθέντος
τοῦ Πυρραίων ὄρους τοῦ πιτυώδους. νόσημα δὲ
ταῖς πεύκαις τοιοῦτόν τι λέγουσι συμβαίνειν οἱ
περὶ τὴν Ἴδην ὥστ', ὅταν μὴ μόνον τὸ ἐγκάρδιον
ἀλλὰ καὶ τὸ ἔξω τοῦ στελέχους ἔνδαδον γένηται,
τηνικαῦτα ὥσπερ ἀποπνίγεσθαι. τοῦτο δὲ αὐτόματον συμβαίνει δι' εὐτροφίαν τοῦ δένδρου, ὡς ἄν
τις εἰκάσειεν· ὅλον γὰρ γίνεται δάς· περὶ μὲν οὖν
τὴν πεύκην ἴδιον τοῦτο πάθος.

6 Ἐλάτη δ' ἐστὶν ἡ μὲν ἄρρην ἡ δὲ θήλεια, διαφορὰς δ' ἔχουσα τοῖς φύλλοις· ὀξύτερα γὰρ καὶ
κεντητικώτερα τὰ τοῦ ἄρρενος καὶ ἐπεστραμμένα
μᾶλλον, δι' ὃ καὶ οὐλότερον τῇ ὄψει φαίνεται τὸ
δένδρον ὅλον. καὶ τῷ ξύλῳ· λευκότερον γὰρ καὶ
μαλακώτερον καὶ εὐεργέστερον τὸ τῆς θηλείας καὶ

---

¹ πικρὸν conj. R. Const. from G ; μικρὰν VAld.
² καὶ ταύτην μεγάλην πρὸς conj. Sch.; καὶ τὴν μεγ. πρὸς
UMV; μεγάλην πρὸς Ald.

in the pine too it is scanty and bitter,[1] as in this
other cone-bearing tree, but in the fir it is fragrant
and abundant. Now the pine is rare in Arcadia,
but common in Elis. The Arcadians then dispute
altogether the nomenclature.

The pine appears to differ also from the fir in
being glossier and having finer leaves, while it is
smaller in stature and does not grow so straight ;
also in bearing a smaller cone, which is stiffer and
has a more pitchy kernel, while its wood is whiter,
more like that of the silver-fir, and wholly free from
pitch. And there is another great difference[2]
between it and the fir ; the fir, if it is burnt down
to the roots, does not shoot up again, while the
pine, according to some, will do so; for instance
this happened in Lesbos,[3] when the pine-forest of
Pyrrha[4] was burnt. The people of Ida say that the
fir is liable to a kind of disease ;—when not only the
heart but the outer part of the trunk becomes glutted[5]
with pitch, the tree then is as it were choked. This
happens of its own accord through the excessive
luxuriance of the tree, as one may conjecture ; for
it all turns into pitch-glutted wood. This then is an
affection peculiar to the fir.

[6] The silver-fir is either 'male' or 'female,' and
has differences in its leaves[7] ; those of the 'male'
are sharper more needle-like and more bent ; wherefore the whole tree has a more compact appearance.
There are also differences in the wood, that of the
'female' being whiter softer and easier to work,

[3] ἐν Λέσβῳ conj. W. from G, and Plin. 16. 46 ; εἰς Λέσβον
MSS.
[4] On the W. of Lesbos, modern Caloni. cf. 2. 2. 6 ; Plin. l.c.
[5] cf. 1. 6. 1 ; Plin. 16. 44.
[6] Plin. 16. 48.     [7] cf. 1. 8. 2,

217

τὸ ὅλον στέλεχος εὐμηκέστερον· τὸ δὲ τοῦ ἄρρενος ποικιλώτερον καὶ παχύτερον καὶ σκληρότερον
καὶ περίμητρον μᾶλλον ὅλως δὲ φαυλότερον τὴν
ὄψιν. ἐν δὲ τῷ κώνῳ τῷ μὲν τοῦ ἄρρενός ἐστι
κάρυα ὀλίγα ἐπὶ τοῦ ἄκρου, τῷ δὲ τῆς θηλείας
ὅλως οὐδέν, ὡς οἱ ἐκ Μακεδονίας ἔλεγον. ἔχει δὲ
πτέρυγας τὸ φύλλον καὶ ἐπ᾽ ἔλαττον, ὥστε τὴν
ὅλην μορφὴν εἶναι θολοειδῆ καὶ παρόμοιον μάλιστα ταῖς Βοιωτίαις κυνέαις· πυκνὸν δὲ οὕτως
ὥστε μήτε χιόνα διϊέναι μήθ᾽ ὑετόν. ὅλως δὲ καὶ
τῇ ὄψει τὸ δένδρον καλόν· καὶ γὰρ ἡ βλάστησις
ἰδία τις, ὥσπερ εἴρηται, παρὰ τὰς ἄλλας καὶ μόνη
τάξιν ἔχουσα· τῷ δὲ μεγέθει μέγα καὶ πολὺ τῆς
πεύκης εὐμηκέστερον.

7 Διαφέρει δὲ καὶ κατὰ τὸ ξύλον οὐ μικρόν· τὸ
μὲν γὰρ τῆς ἐλάτης ἰνῶδες καὶ μαλακὸν καὶ κοῦφον, τὸ δὲ τῆς πεύκης δαδῶδες καὶ βαρὺ καὶ
σαρκωδέστερον. ὄζους δὲ ἔχει πλείους μὲν ἡ
πεύκη σκληροτέρους δ᾽ ἡ ἐλάτη, σχεδὸν δὲ πάντων ὡς εἰπεῖν σκληροτέρους, τὸ δὲ ξύλον μαλακώτερον. ὅλως δὲ οἱ ὄζοι πυκνότατοι καὶ στερεώτατοι μόνον οὐ διαφανεῖς ἐλάτης καὶ πεύκης καὶ
τῷ χρώματι δαδώδεις καὶ μάλιστα διάφοροι τοῦ
ξύλου, μᾶλλον δὲ τῆς ἐλάτης. ἔχει δέ, ὥσπερ ἡ
πεύκη τὴν αἰγίδα, καὶ ἡ ἐλάτη τὸ λευκὸν λοῦσσον

---

[1] παχύτερον conj. W.; πλατύτερον Ald.
[2] Plin. 16. 48 and 49.  [3] For the tense see Intr. p. xx.
[4] φύλλον, i.e. the leafy shoot. Sch. considers φύλλον to
be corrupt, and refers the following description to the cone;
W. marks a lacuna after φύλλον. Pliny, l.c., seems to have
read φύλλον, but does not render καὶ ἐπ᾽ ἔλαττον . . . κυνέαις.
The words καὶ ἐπ᾽ ἔλαττον can hardly be sound as they stand.
For the description of the foliage cf. 1. 10. 5.

218

while the whole trunk is longer; that of the 'male'
is less of a uniform colour thicker[1] and harder, has
more heart-wood, and is altogether inferior in appearance. In the cone[2] of the 'male' are a few seeds at
the apex, while that of the 'female,' according to
what the Macedonians said,[3] contains none at all.
The foliage[4] is feathered and the height dispropor-
tionate so that the general appearance of the tree
is dome-like,[5] and closely resembles the Boeotian
peasant's hat[6]; and it is so dense that neither snow
nor rain penetrates it. And in general the tree has
a handsome appearance; for its growth is somewhat
peculiar, as has been said, compared with the others,
it being the only one which is regular, and in stature
it is large, much taller than the fir.

[7] There is also not a little difference in the wood:
that of the silver-fir is fibrous[8] soft and light, that of
the fir is resinous heavy and more fleshy. The fir
has more knots,[9] but the silver-fir harder ones;
indeed they may be said to be harder than those of
any tree, though the wood otherwise is softer. And
in general the knots of silver-fir and fir are of the
closest and most solid[10] texture and almost[11] transparent: in colour they are like resin-glutted wood,
and quite different from the rest of the wood; and
this is especially so[12] in the silver-fir. And just as
the fir has its *aigis*,[13] so the silver-fir has what is

[5] θολοειδῆ conj. Scal.; θηλοειδῆ U (erased); θηλοειδὲς MV;
*ut concameratum imitetur* G; ? θολωειδῆ; in Theocr. 15. 39.
θολία seems to be a sun-hat.
[6] κυνέαις: cf. Hesych. s.v. κυνῆ Βοιωτία, apparently a hat
worn in the fields.
[7] cf. 5. 1. 7.　　[8] cf. 5. 1. 5.　　[9] cf. 5. 1. 6.
[10] cf. 5. 1. 6, κερατώδεις.　　[11] οὐ ins. Sch.
[12] μᾶλλον δὲ conj. W.; μᾶλλον ἢ Ald.　　[13] cf. 3. 9. 3

THEOPHRASTUS

καλούμενον, οἷον ἀντίστροφον τῇ αἰγίδι, πλὴν τὸ
μὲν λευκὸν ἡ δ᾽ αἰγὶς εὔχρως διὰ τὸ ἔνδαδον.
πυκνὸν δὲ καὶ λευκὸν γίνεται καὶ καλὸν ἐκ τῶν
πρεσβυτέρων ἤδη δένδρων· ἀλλὰ σπάνιον τὸ
χρηστόν, τὸ δὲ τυχὸν δαψιλές, ἐξ οὗ τά τε τῶν
ζωγράφων πινάκια ποιοῦσι καὶ τὰ γραμματεῖα τὰ
πολλά· τὰ δ᾽ ἐσπουδασμένα ἐκ τοῦ βελτίονος.
8 Οἱ δὲ περὶ Ἀρκαδίαν ἀμφότερα καλοῦσιν
αἰγίδα καὶ τὴν τῆς πεύκης καὶ τὴν τῆς ἐλάτης,
καὶ εἶναι πλείω τὴν τῆς ἐλάτης ἀλλὰ καλλίω τὴν
τῆς πεύκης· εἶναι γὰρ τῆς μὲν ἐλάτης πολλήν τε
καὶ λείαν καὶ πυκνήν, τῆς δὲ πεύκης ὀλίγην, τὴν
μέντοι οὖσαν οὐλοτέραν καὶ ἰσχυροτέραν καὶ τὸ
ὅλον καλλίω. οὗτοι μὲν οὖν ἐοίκασι τοῖς ὀνόμασι
διαφωνεῖν. ἡ δὲ ἐλάτη ταύτας ἔχει τὰς διαφορὰς πρὸς τὴν πεύκην καὶ ἔτι τὴν περὶ τὴν ἄμφαυξιν, ἣν πρότερον εἴπομεν.
X. Ὀξύη δ᾽ οὐκ ἔχει διαφορὰς ἀλλ᾽ ἐστὶ μονο-
γενές· ὀρθοφυὲς δὲ καὶ λεῖον καὶ ἄνοζον καὶ πάχος
καὶ ὕψος ἔχον σχεδὸν ἴσον τῇ ἐλάτῃ· καὶ τἄλλα
δὲ παρόμοιον [τε] τὸ δένδρον· ξύλον δὲ εὔχρουν
ἰσχυρὸν εὔινον καὶ φλοιὸν λεῖον καὶ παχύν, φύλλον δ᾽ ἀσχιδὲς προμηκέστερον ἀπίου καὶ ἐπα-
κάνθιζον ἐξ ἄκρου, ῥίζας οὔτε πολλὰς οὔτε κατὰ
βάθους· ὁ δὲ καρπὸς λεῖος βαλανώδης ἐν ἐχίνῳ

¹ cf. Eur. I.A. 99 ; Hipp. 1254.
² τὰ δ᾽ conj. Scal.; καὶ Ald.
³ πεύκης conj. Scal. from G ; ἐλάτης Ald.
⁴ ἐλάτης conj. Scal. from G ; πεύκης Ald.

220

called its white ' centre,' which answers, as it were, to
the *aigis* of the fir, except that it is white, while
the other is bright-coloured because it is glutted with
pitch. It becomes close white and good in trees
which are of some age, but it is seldom found in good
condition, while the ordinary form of it is abundant
and is used to make painters' boards and ordinary
writing tablets,[1] superior ones being[2] made of the
better form.

However the Arcadians call both substances *aigis*,
alike that of the fir[3] and the corresponding part of
the silver-fir,[4] and say that, though the silver-fir
produces more, that of the fir is better; for that,
though that of the silver-fir is abundant[5] smooth and
close, that of the fir, though scanty, is compacter
stronger and fairer in general. The Arcadians then
appear to differ as to the names which they give.
Such are the differences in the silver-fir as compared with the fir, and there is also that of having
the *amphauxis*,[6] which we mentioned before.

*Of beech, yew, hop-hornbeam, lime.*

X. The beech presents no differences, there being
but one kind. It is a straight-growing smooth and
unbranched tree, and in thickness and height is
about equal to the silver-fir, which it also resembles
in other respects ; the wood is of a fair colour strong
and of good grain, the bark smooth and thick, the
leaf undivided, longer than a pear-leaf, spinous at the
tip,[7] the roots neither numerous nor running deep ;
the fruit is smooth like an acorn, enclosed in a shell,

[5] πολλὴν conj. Gesner ; οὔλην UmBas.; ὅλην MVAld.
[6] *cf.* 3. 7. 1.
[7] *i.e.* mucronate. *cf.* 3. 11. 3.

πλὴν [οὐκ] ἀνακάνθῳ καὶ λείῳ, καὶ οὐχ ὡς ἡ
διοσβάλανος ἀκανθώδει, προσεμφερὴς δὲ καὶ
κατὰ γλυκύτητα καὶ κατὰ τὸν χυλὸν ἐκείνῳ.
γίνεται δὲ καὶ ἐν τῷ ὄρει λευκή, ἣ καὶ χρήσιμον
ἔχει τὸ ξύλον πρὸς πολλά· καὶ γὰρ πρὸς ἁμαξ-
ουργίαν καὶ πρὸς κλινοπηγίαν καὶ εἰς διφρουρ-
γίαν καὶ εἰς τραπεζίαν καὶ εἰς ναυπηγίαν· ἡ δ' ἐν
τοῖς πεδίοις μέλαινα καὶ ἄχρηστος πρὸς ταῦτα·
τὸν δὲ καρπὸν ἔχουσι παραπλήσιον.

2 Μονογενὴς δὲ καὶ ἡ μίλος, ὀρθοφυὴς δὲ καὶ
εὐαυξὴς καὶ ὁμοία τῇ ἐλάτῃ, πλὴν οὐχ ὑψηλὸν
οὕτω, πολυμάσχαλον δὲ μᾶλλον. ὅμοιον δὲ καὶ
τὸ φύλλον ἔχει τῇ ἐλάτῃ, λιπαρώτερον δὲ καὶ
μαλακώτερον. τὸ δὲ ξύλον ἡ μὲν ἐξ Ἀρκαδίας
μέλαν καὶ φοινικοῦν, ἡ δ' ἐκ τῆς Ἴδης ξανθὸν
σφόδρα καὶ ὅμοιον τῇ κέδρῳ, δι' ὃ καὶ τοὺς πω-
λοῦντάς φασιν ἐξαπατᾶν ὡς κέδρον πωλοῦντας·
πᾶν γὰρ εἶναι καρδίαν, ὅταν ὁ φλοιὸς περιαιρεθῇ·
ὅμοιον δὲ καὶ τὸν φλοιὸν ἔχειν καὶ τῇ τραχύτητι
καὶ τῷ χρώματι τῇ κέδρῳ, ῥίζας δὲ μικρὰς καὶ
λεπτὰς καὶ ἐπιπολαίους. σπάνιον δὲ τὸ δένδρον
περὶ τὴν Ἴδην, περὶ δὲ Μακεδονίαν καὶ Ἀρκαδίαν
πολύ· καὶ καρπὸν φέρει στρογγύλον μικρῷ μείζω
κυάμου, τῷ χρώματι δ' ἐρυθρὸν καὶ μαλακόν·
φασὶ δὲ τὰ μὲν λόφουρα ἐὰν φάγῃ τῶν φύλλων
ἀποθνήσκειν, τὰ δὲ μηρυκάζοντα οὐδὲν πάσχειν.
τὸν δὲ καρπὸν ἐσθίουσι καὶ τῶν ἀνθρώπων τινὲς
καὶ ἔστιν ἡδὺς καὶ ἀσινής.

---

[1] ἐχῖνος being otherwise used of a prickly case, such as
that of the chestnut. πλὴν ἄναν. καὶ λείῳ conj. W.; πλὴν
οὐκ ἀνακάνθωι καὶ λείωι U ; πλὴν οὐκ ἐν ἀκάνθῳ MVAld.

which is however without prickles[1] and smooth, not spinous,[2] like the chestnut, though in sweetness and flavour it resembles it. In mountain country it also grows white and has[3] timber which is useful for many purposes, for making carts beds chairs and tables, and for shipbuilding[4]; while the tree of the plains is black and useless for these purposes; but the fruit is much the same in both.

[5] The yew has also but one kind, is straight-growing, grows readily, and is like the silver-fir, except that it is not so tall and is more branched. Its leaf is also like that of the silver-fir, but glossier and less stiff. As to the wood, in the Arcadian yew it is black or red, in that of Ida bright yellow and like prickly cedar; wherefore they say that dealers practise deceit, selling it for that wood: for that it is all heart, when the bark is stripped off; its bark also resembles that of prickly cedar in roughness and colour, its roots are few slender and shallow. The tree is rare about Ida, but common in Macedonia and Arcadia; it bears a round fruit a little larger than a bean, which is red in colour and soft; and they say that, if beasts of burden[6] eat of the leaves they die, while ruminants take no hurt. Even men sometimes eat the fruit, which is sweet and harmless.

[2] ἀκανθώδει conj. R. Const.; ἀκανθώδη Ald.H.
[3] λευκὴ ἢ καὶ conj. W.; λευκή τε καὶ Ald.H.
[4] cf. 5. 6. 4; 5. 7. 2 and 6.
[5] Plin. 16. 62. (description taken from this passage, but applied to fraxinus, apparently from confusion between μίλος and μελία).
[6] cf. 2. 7. 4 n.

3 Ἔστι δὲ καὶ ἡ ὄστρυς μονοειδής, ἣν καλοῦσί
τινες ὀστρύαν, ὁμοφυὲς τῇ ὀξύᾳ τῇ τε φυτείᾳ καὶ
τῷ φλοιῷ· φύλλα δὲ ἀπιοειδῆ τῷ σχήματι, πλὴν
προμηκέστερα πολλῷ καὶ εἰς ὀξὺ συνηγμένα καὶ
μείζω, πολύϊνα δέ, ἀπὸ τῆς μέσης εὐθείας καὶ
μεγάλης τῶν ἄλλων πλευροειδῶς κατατεινουσῶν
καὶ πάχος ἐχουσῶν· ἔτι δὲ ἐρρυτιδωμένα κατὰ
τὰς ἶνας καὶ χαραγμὸν ἔχοντα κύκλῳ λεπτόν· τὸ
δὲ ξύλον σκληρὸν καὶ ἄχρουν, ἔκλευκον· καρπὸν
δὲ μικρὸν πρόμακρον ὅμοιον κριθῇ ξανθόν· ῥίζας
δὲ ἔχει μετεώρους· ἔνυδρον δὲ καὶ φαραγγῶδες.
λέγεται δὲ ὡς οὐκ ἐπιτήδειον εἰς οἰκίαν εἰσφέ-
ρειν· δυσθανατεῖν γάρ φασι καὶ δυστοκεῖν οὗ
ἂν ᾖ.

4 Τῆς δὲ φιλύρας ἡ μὲν ἄρρην ἐστὶ ἡ δὲ θήλεια·
διαφέρουσι δὲ τῇ μορφῇ τῇ ὅλῃ καὶ τῇ τοῦ ξύλου καὶ
τῷ τὸ μὲν εἶναι κάρπιμον τὸ δ' ἄκαρπον. τὸ μὲν
γὰρ τῆς ἄρρενος ξύλον σκληρὸν καὶ ξανθὸν καὶ
ὀζωδέστερον καὶ πυκνότερόν ἐστι, ἔτι δ' εὐωδέστερον, τὸ δὲ τῆς θηλείας λευκότερον. καὶ ὁ
φλοιὸς τῆς μὲν ἄρρενος παχύτερος καὶ περιαιρεθεὶς
ἀκαμπὴς διὰ τὴν σκληρότητα, τῆς δὲ θηλείας λεπτότερος καὶ εὐκαμπής, ἐξ οὗ τὰς κίστας ποιοῦσιν·
καὶ ἡ μὲν ἄκαρπος καὶ ἀνανθής, ἡ δὲ θήλεια
καὶ ἄνθος ἔχει καὶ καρπόν· τὸ μὲν ἄνθος καλυκῶδες παρὰ τὸν τοῦ φύλλου μίσχον καὶ παρὰ

---

[1] cf. 1. 8. 2 (ὀστρυΐς), 3. 3. 1 ; C.P. 5. 12. 9 (ὀστρύη) ; Plin.
13. 117.
[2] μέσης . . . κατατεινουσῶν conj. Sch.; μέσης πλευροειδῶς
τῶν ἄλλων εὐθειῶν καὶ μεγάλην κατατεινουσῶν Ald. cf. 1. 10. 2 ;
3. 17. 3.

224

The *ostrys* (hop-hornbeam),[1] which some call *ostrya*, has also but one kind : it is like the beech in growth and bark : its leaves are in shape like a pear's, except that they are much longer, come to a sharp point, are larger, and have many fibres, which branch out like ribs from a large straight one[2] in the middle, and are thick ; also the leaves are wrinkled along the fibres and have a finely serrated edge : the wood is hard colourless and whitish ; the fruit is small oblong and yellow like barley ; it has shallow roots ; it loves water and is found in ravines. It is said to be unlucky to bring it into the house, since, wherever it is, it is supposed to cause a painful death[3] or painful labour in giving birth.

[4]The lime has both 'male' and 'female' forms, which differ in their general appearance, in that of the wood, and in being respectively fruit-bearing and sterile. The wood of the 'male' tree is hard yellow more branched closer, and also more fragrant[5] ; that of the 'female' is whiter. The bark of the 'male' is thicker, and, when stripped off, is unbending because of its hardness ; that of the 'female' is thinner[6] and flexible ; men make their writing-cases[7] out of it. The 'male' has neither fruit nor flower, but the 'female' has both flower and fruit ; the flower is cup-shaped, and appears alongside of the stalk of the leaf, or alongside of next year's

[3] δυσθανατεῖν I conj. ; δυσθάνατον P.Ald.; δυσθανατᾶν conj. Sch., but δυσθανατᾶν has a desiderative sense.
[4] Plin. 16. 65.
[5] ἔτι δ' εὐωδ. inserted here by Sch.; cf. Plin., l.c. In Ald. the words, with the addition τὸ τῆς θηλείας, occur after ποιοῦσιν.
[6] λεπτότερος conj. Sch ; λευκότερος Ald.
[7] cf. 3. 13. 1 ; Ar. Vesp. 529.

225

THEOPHRASTUS

τὴν εἰς νέωτα κάχρυν ἐφ' ἑτέρου μίσχου, χλοερὸν
δὲ ὅταν ᾖ καλυκῶδες, ἐκκαλυπτόμενον δὲ ἐπίξαν-
5 θον· ἡ δὲ ἄνθησις ἅμα τοῖς ἡμέροις. ὁ δὲ καρπὸς
στρογγύλος πρόμακρος ἡλίκος κύαμος ὅμοιος τῷ
τοῦ κιττοῦ, γωνίας ἔχων ὁ ἁδρὸς πέντε οἷον ἰνῶν
ἐξεχουσῶν καὶ εἰς ὀξὺ συναγομένων· ὁ δὲ μὴ
ἁδρὸς ἀδιαρθρότερος· διακνιζόμενος δὲ ὁ ἁδρὸς
ἔχει μίκρ' ἄττα καὶ λεπτὰ σπερμάτια ἡλίκα καὶ
ὁ τῆς ἀδραφάξυος. τὸ δὲ φύλλον καὶ ὁ φλοιὸς
ἡδέα καὶ γλυκέα· τὴν δὲ μορφὴν κιττῶδες τὸ
φύλλον, πλὴν ἐκ προσαγωγῆς μᾶλλον ἡ περι-
φέρεια, κατὰ τὸ πρὸς τῷ μίσχῳ κυρτότατον,
ἀλλὰ κατὰ μέσον εἰς ὀξύτερον τὴν συναγωγὴν
ἔχον καὶ μακρότερον, ἔπουλον δὲ κύκλῳ καὶ κεχαραγμένον. μήτραν δ' ἔχει τὸ ξύλον μικρὰν καὶ οὐ
πολὺ μαλακωτέραν τοῦ ἄλλου· μαλακὸν γὰρ καὶ
τὸ ἄλλο ξύλον.

XI. Τῆς δὲ σφενδάμνου, καθάπερ εἴπομεν, δύο
γένη ποιοῦσιν, οἱ δὲ τρία· ἓν μὲν δὴ τῷ κοινῷ
προσαγορεύουσι σφένδαμνον, ἕτερον δὲ ζυγίαν,
τρίτον δὲ κλινότροχον, ὡς οἱ περὶ Στάγειρα. διαφορὰ δ' ἐστὶ τῆς ζυγίας καὶ τῆς σφενδάμνου ὅτι
ἡ μὲν σφένδαμνος λευκὸν ἔχει τὸ ξύλον καὶ
εὐινότερον, ἡ δὲ ζυγία ξανθὸν καὶ οὐλον· τὸ δὲ
φύλλον εὐμέγεθες ἄμφω, τῇ σχίσει ὅμοιον τῷ

---

[1] cf. 3. 5. 5. and 6.
[2] διακνιζόμενος : διασχιζόμενος, 'when split open,' conj. W.
[3] cf. 1. 12. 4 ; C.P. 6. 12. 7.　　[4] 3. 3. 1.
[5] προσαγορεύουσι conj. W. from G ; προσαγορεύεται Ald.

226

winter-bud [1] on a separate stalk; it is green, when
in the cup-like stage, but brownish as it opens; it
appears at the same time as in the cultivated trees.
The fruit is rounded oblong as large as a bean,
resembling the fruit of the ivy; when mature, it
has five angular projections, as it were, made by
projecting fibres which meet in a point; the immature fruit is less articulated. When the mature
fruit is pulled to pieces,[2] it shows some small fine
seeds of the same size as those of orach. The leaf and
the bark [3] are well flavoured and sweet; the leaf is
like that of the ivy in shape, except that it rounds
more gradually, being most curved at the part next
the stalk, but in the middle contracting to a sharper
and longer apex, and its edge is somewhat puckered
and jagged. The timber contains little core, which
is not much softer than the other part; for the rest
of the wood is also soft.

*Of maple and ash.*

XI. Of the maple, as we have said,[4] some make [5]
two kinds, some three; one they call by the general
name 'maple,' another *zygia*, the third *klinotrokhos* [6];
this name, for instance, is used by the people of
Stagira. The difference between *zygia* and maple
proper is that the latter has white wood of finer
fibre, while that of *zygia* is yellow and of compact
texture. The leaf [7] in both trees is large, resembling that of the plane in the way in which it is

[6] κλινότροχον Ald.; κλινόστροχον U; ἰσότροχον conj. Salm.
from Plin. 16. 66 and 67, *cursicenium* or *crassivenium*. Sch.
thinks that the word conceals γλῖνος; cf. 3. 3. 1; 3. 11. 2.
[7] φύλλον conj. R. Const.; ξύλον UMVAld.H.G.

# THEOPHRASTUS

τῆς πλατάνου τετανὸν λεπτότερον δὲ καὶ ἀσαρκό-
τερον καὶ μαλακώτερον καὶ προμηκέστερον· τὰ δὲ
σχίσμαθ'[2] ὅλα[3] τ' εἰς ὀξὺ συνήκοντα καὶ οὐχ οὕτω
μεσοσχιδῆ ἀλλ' ἀκροσχιδέστερα· οὐ πολύϊνα[5] δὲ
ὡς κατὰ μέγεθος. ἔχει δὲ καὶ φλοιὸν μικρῷ
τραχύτερον τοῦ τῆς φιλύρας, ὑποπέλιον παχὺν καὶ
πυκνότερον ἢ ὁ τῆς πίτυος καὶ ἀκαμπῆ· ῥίζαι δ'
ὀλίγαι καὶ μετέωροι καὶ οὖλαι σχεδὸν αἱ πλεῖσται
2 καὶ αἱ τῆς ξανθῆς καὶ αἱ τῆς λευκῆς. γίνεται δὲ
μάλιστα ἐν τοῖς ἐφύδροις, ὡς οἱ περὶ τὴν Ἴδην λέγουσι, καὶ ἔστι σπάνιον. περὶ ἄνθους δὲ οὐκ ᾔδεσαν·
τὸν δὲ καρπὸν οὐ λίαν μὲν προμήκη, παρόμοιον δὲ
τῷ παλιούρῳ πλὴν προμηκέστερον. οἱ δ' ἐν τῷ
Ὀλύμπῳ τὴν μὲν ζυγίαν ὄρειον μᾶλλον, τὴν δὲ
σφένδαμνον καὶ ἐν τοῖς πεδίοις φύεσθαι· εἶναι δὲ
τὴν μὲν ἐν τῷ ὄρει φυομένην ξανθὴν καὶ εὔχρουν
καὶ οὖλην καὶ στερεάν, ᾖ καὶ πρὸς τὰ πολυτελῆ
τῶν ἔργων χρῶνται, τὴν δὲ πεδεινὴν λευκήν τε
καὶ μανοτέραν καὶ ἧττον οὖλην· καλοῦσι δ' αὐτὴν
ἔνιοι γλεῖνον, οὐ σφένδαμνον. . . . καὶ τῆς ἄρρενος
οὐλότερα τὰ ξύλα συνεστραμμένα, καὶ ἐν τῷ
πεδίῳ ταύτην φύεσθαι μᾶλλον καὶ βλαστάνειν
πρωΐτερον.
3 Ἔστι δὲ καὶ μελίας γένη δύο. τούτων δ' ἡ
μὲν ὑψηλὴ καὶ εὐμήκης ἐστὶ τὸ ξύλον ἔχουσα
λευκὸν καὶ εὔινον καὶ μαλακώτερον καὶ ἀνοζό-

---

¹ τετανὸν : cf. 3, 12. 5 ; 3. 15. 6.
² σχίσμαθ' conj. R. Const. from G; σχίμαθ' Ald.Cam.;
σχῆμαθ' Bas., which W. reads.
³ ὅλα : ? ὅλως.
⁴ i.e. do not run back so far.
⁵ πολύϊνα conj. R. Const.; πολύ· ἴνα δὲ Ald.; πολύ· ἴνα δὲ M.

divided; it is smooth,[1] but more delicate, less fleshy, softer, longer in proportion to its breadth, and the divisions[2] all[3] tend to meet in a point, while they do not occur so much in the middle of the leaf,[4] but rather at the tip; and for their size the leaves have not many fibres.[5] The bark too is somewhat rougher than that of the lime, of blackish colour thick closer[6] than that of the Aleppo pine and stiff; the roots are few shallow and compact for the most part, both those of the yellow and those of the white-wooded tree. This tree occurs chiefly in wet ground,[7] as the people of Mount Ida say, and is rare. About its flower they did[8] not know, but the fruit, they said, is not very oblong, but like that of Christ's thorn,[9] except that it is more oblong than that. But the people of Mount Olympus say that, while *zygia* is rather a mountain tree, the maple proper grows also in the plains; and that the form which grows in the mountains has yellow wood of a bright colour, which is of compact texture and hard, and is used even for expensive work, while that of the plains has white wood of looser make and less compact texture. And some call it *gleinos*[10] instead of maple. . . . .[11] The wood of the 'male' tree is of compacter texture and twisted: this tree, it is said, grows rather in the plain and puts forth its leaves earlier.

[12] There are also two kinds of ash. Of these one is lofty and of strong growth with white wood of good fibre, softer, with less knots, and of more compact

[6] πυκνότερον conj. Scal. from G ; πυρώτερον UAld.
[7] ἐφύδροις : ὑφύδροις conj. Sch.   cf. ὕφαμμος, ὑπόπετρος.
[8] cf. 3. 9. 6 n.; Intr. p. xx.   [9] cf. 3. 18. 3.
[10] cf. 3. 3. 1 ; Plin. 16. 67.
[11] W. marks a lacuna : the description of the 'female' tree seems to be missing.   [12] Plin. 16. 62-64.

τερον καὶ οὐλότερον· ἡ δὲ ταπεινοτέρα καὶ ἧττον
εὐαυξὴς καὶ τραχυτέρα καὶ σκληροτέρα καὶ ξαν-
θοτέρα. τὰ δὲ φύλλα τῷ μὲν σχήματι δαφνοειδῆ,
πλατυφύλλου δάφνης, εἰς ὀξύτερον δὲ συνηγμένα,
χαραγμὸν δέ τιν᾿ ἔχοντα κύκλῳ καὶ ἐπακανθί-
ζοντα· τὸ δὲ ὅλον, ὅπερ εἴποι τις ἂν φύλλον τῷ
ἅμα φυλλορροεῖν, ἀφ᾿ ἑνὸς μίσχου· καὶ περὶ
μίαν οἷον ἵνα κατὰ γόνυ καὶ συζυγίαν τὰ φύλλα
καθ᾿ ἕκαστον πέφυκε, συχνῶν διεχουσῶν τῶν
συζυγιῶν, ὁμοίως καὶ ἐπὶ τῆς οἴης. ἔστι δὲ τῶν
μὲν βραχέα τὰ γόνατα καὶ αἱ συζυγίαι τὸ πλῆθος
ἐλάττους, τῶν δὲ τῆς λευκῆς καὶ μακρὰ καὶ
πλείους· καὶ τὰ καθ᾿ ἕκαστον φύλλα μακρότερα
καὶ στενότερα, τὴν δὲ χρόαν πρασώδη. φλοιὸν
δὲ λεῖον ἔχει, καπυρὸν δὲ καὶ λεπτὸν καὶ τῇ
4 χρόᾳ πυρρόν. πυκνόρριζον δὲ καὶ παχύρριζον
καὶ μετέωρον. καρπὸν δὲ οἱ μὲν περὶ τὴν Ἴδην
οὐχ ὑπελάμβανον ἔχειν οὐδ᾿ ἄνθος· ἔχει δ᾿ ἐν
λοβῷ λεπτῷ καρπὸν καρυηρὸν ὡς τῶν ἀμυγδαλῶν ὑπόπικρον τῇ γεύσει. φέρει δὲ καὶ ἕτερ᾿
ἄττα οἷον βρύα, καθάπερ ἡ δάφνη, πλὴν στιφρό-
τερα· καὶ ἕκαστον καθ᾿ αὑτὸ σφαιροειδές, ὥσπερ
τὰ τῶν πλατάνων· τούτων δὲ τὰ μὲν περὶ τὸν
καρπόν, τὰ δ᾿ ἀπηρτημένα πολύ, καὶ τὰ πλεῖστα
οὕτω. φύεται δὲ ἡ μὲν λεία περὶ τὰ βαθυάγκη
μάλιστα καὶ ἔφυδρα, ἡ δὲ τραχεῖα καὶ περὶ τὰ ξηρὰ
καὶ πετρώδη. ἔνιοι δὲ καλοῦσι τὴν μὲν μελίαν

---

¹ οὐλότερον : ἀνουλότερον W. from Sch.'s conj.; ἄνουλος
does not occur elsewhere, and T. uses μανός as the opposite
of οὖλος.
² i.e. instead of considering the leaflet as the unit. For
the description cf. 3. 12. 5 ; 3. 15. 4.

texture[1]; the other is shorter, less vigorous in growth,
rougher harder and yellower. The leaves in shape
are like those of the bay, that is, the broad-leaved
bay, but they contract to a sharper point, and they
have a sort of jagged outline with sharp points.
The whole leaf (if one may consider this as[2] a 'leaf'
because it is all shed at once) grows on a single
stalk; on either side of a single fibre, as it were,
the leaflets grow at a joint in pairs, which are
numerous and distinct, just as in the sorb. In some
leaves the joints are short[3] and the pairs fewer in
number, but in those of the white kind the joint is
long and the pairs more numerous, while the leaflets
are longer narrower and leek-green in colour. Also
this tree has a smooth bark, which is dry thin and
red in colour. The roots are matted stout and
shallow.[4] As to the fruit, the people of Ida supposed
it to have none, and no flower either; however it
has a nut-like fruit in a thin pod, like the fruit of
the almond, and it is somewhat bitter in taste. And
it also bears certain other things like winter-buds,
as does the bay, but they are more solid,[5] and each
separate one is globular, like those of the plane;
some of these occur around the fruit, some, in fact
the greater number,[6] are at a distance from it. The
smooth kind[7] grows mostly in deep ravines and damp
places, the rough kind occurs also in dry and rocky
parts. Some, for instance the Macedonians, call the

[3] βραχέα conj. Scal. from G; τραχέα UAld.H.
[4] Bod. inserts οὐ before μετέωρον: cf. 3. 6. 5. (Idaean account.)
[5] στιφρότερα conj. Dalec.: στρυφνότερα MSS.
[6] πλεῖστα conj. R. Const.; πλεκτά UMVAld.
[7] cf. Plin., l.c.

231

τὴν δὲ βουμέλιον, ὥσπερ οἱ περὶ Μακεδονίαν.
5 μεῖζον δὲ καὶ μανότερον ἡ βουμέλιος, δι' ὃ καὶ
ἧττον οὖλον. φύσει δὲ τὸ μὲν πεδεινὸν καὶ τραχύ,
τὸ δ' ὀρεινὸν καὶ λεῖον· ἔστι δὲ ἡ μὲν ἐν τοῖς
ὄρεσι φυομένη εὔχρους καὶ λεία καὶ στερεὰ καὶ
γλίσχρα, ἡ δ' ἐν τῷ πεδίῳ ἄχρους καὶ μανὴ καὶ
τραχεῖα. (τὸ δ' ὅλον ὡς εἰπεῖν τὰ δένδρα ὅσα
καὶ ἐν τῷ πεδίῳ καὶ ἐν τῷ ὄρει φύεται, τὰ μὲν
ὀρεινὰ εὔχροά τε καὶ στερεὰ καὶ λεῖα γίνεται,
καθάπερ ὀξύη πτελέα τὰ ἄλλα· τὰ δὲ πεδεινὰ
μανότερα καὶ ἀχρούστερα καὶ χείρω, πλὴν ἀπίου
καὶ μηλέας καὶ ἀχράδος, ὡς οἱ περὶ τὸν Ὄλυμπόν
φασι· ταῦτα δ' ἐν τῷ πεδίῳ κρείττω καὶ τῷ
καρπῷ καὶ τοῖς ξύλοις· ἐν μὲν γὰρ τῷ ὄρει
τραχεῖς καὶ ἀκανθώδεις καὶ ὀζώδεις εἰσίν, ἐν δὲ τῷ
πεδίῳ λειότεροι καὶ μείζους καὶ τὸν καρπὸν ἔχουσι
γλυκύτερον καὶ σαρκωδέστερον· μεγέθει δὲ αἰεὶ
μείζω τὰ πεδεινά.)

XII. Κρανείας δὲ τὸ μὲν ἄρρεν τὸ δὲ θῆλυ,
ἣν δὴ καὶ θηλυκρανείαν καλοῦσιν. ἔχουσι δὲ
φύλλον μὲν ἀμυγδαλῇ ὅμοιον, πλὴν λιπωδέστερον
καὶ παχύτερον, φλοιὸν δ' ἰνώδη λεπτόν· τὸ δὲ
στέλεχος οὐ παχὺ λίαν, ἀλλὰ παραφύει ῥάβδους
ὥσπερ ἄγνος· ἐλάττους δὲ ἡ θηλυκρανεία καὶ
θαμνωδέστερόν ἐστιν. τοὺς δὲ ὄζους ὁμοίως
ἔχουσιν ἄμφω τῇ ἄγνῳ καὶ κατὰ δύο καὶ κατ'

---

[1] cf. Plin., l.c., and Index.
[2] μεῖζον δὲ καὶ μανότερον conj. W. from G ; μ. δὲ καὶ μανότερα
MVU (? μανότερον) ; μείζων δὲ καὶ μακροτέρα Ald.H.

one 'ash' (manna-ash), the other 'horse-ash[1]' (ash). The 'horse-ash' is a larger and more spreading[2] tree, wherefore it is of less compact appearance. It is naturally a tree of the plains and rough, while the other belongs to the mountains and is smooth[3]; the one which grows on the mountains is fair-coloured smooth hard and stunted, while that of the plains is colourless spreading and rough. (In general one may say of trees that grow in the plain and on the mountain respectively, that the latter are of fair colour hard and smooth,[4] as beech elm and the rest; while those of the plain are more spreading, of less good colour and inferior, except the pear apple[5] and wild pear, according to the people of Mount Olympus. These when they grow in the plain are better both in fruit and in wood; for on the mountain they are rough spinous and much branched, in the plain smoother larger and with sweeter and fleshier fruit. However the trees of the plain are always of larger size.)

*Of cornelian cherry, cornel, 'cedars,' medlar, thorns, sorb.*

XII. Of the cornelian cherry there is a 'male' and a 'female' kind (cornel), and the latter bears a corresponding name. Both have a leaf like that of the almond, but oilier and thicker; the bark is fibrous and thin, the stem is not very thick, but it puts out side-branches like the chaste-tree, those of the 'female' tree, which is more shrubby, being fewer. Both kinds have branches like those of the chaste-tree,

[3] καὶ τραχὺ . . . λεῖον conj. Sch.; καὶ λεῖον . . . τραχὺ Ald.
[4] λεῖα conj. Mold.; λευκὰ Ald.G.
[5] μηλέας conj. Scal., cf. 3. 3. 2; μελίας UMAld.H.

ἀλλήλους· τὸ δὲ ξύλον τὸ μὲν τῆς κρανείας
ἀκάρδιον καὶ στερεὸν ὅλον, ὅμοιον κέρατι τὴν
πυκνότητα καὶ τὴν ἰσχύν, τὸ δὲ τῆς θηλυκρανείας
ἐντεριώνην ἔχον καὶ μαλακώτερον καὶ κοιλαινό-
2 μενον· δι' ὃ καὶ ἀχρεῖον εἰς τὰ ἀκόντια. τὸ δ'
ὕψος τοῦ ἄρρενος δώδεκα μάλιστα πηχέων, ἡλίκη
τῶν σαρισσῶν ἡ μεγίστη· τὸ γὰρ ὅλον στέλεχος
ὕψος οὐκ ἴσχει. φασὶ δ' οἱ μὲν ἐν τῇ Ἴδῃ τῇ Τρωάδι
τὸ μὲν ἄρρεν ἄκαρπον εἶναι τὸ δὲ θῆλυ κάρπιμον.
πυρῆνα δ' ὁ καρπὸς ἔχει παραπλήσιον ἐλάᾳ, καὶ
ἐσθιόμενος γλυκὺς καὶ εὐώδης· ἄνθος δὲ ὅμοιον
τῷ τῆς ἐλάας, καὶ ἀπανθεῖ δὲ καὶ καρποφορεῖ
τὸν αὐτὸν τρόπον τῷ ἐξ ἑνὸς μίσχου πλείους
ἔχειν, σχεδὸν δὲ καὶ τοῖς χρόνοις παραπλησίως.
οἱ δ' ἐν Μακεδονίᾳ καρποφορεῖν μὲν ἄμφω φασὶν
τὸν δὲ τῆς θηλείας ἄβρωτον εἶναι· τὰς ῥίζας δ'
ὁμοίας ἔχει ταῖς ἄγνοις ἰσχυρὰς καὶ ἀνωλέθρους.
γίνεται δὲ καὶ περὶ τὰ ἔφυδρα καὶ οὐκ ἐν τοῖς
ξηροῖς μόνον· φύεται δὲ καὶ ἀπὸ σπέρματος καὶ
ἀπὸ παρασπάδος.
3 Κέδρον δὲ οἱ μέν φασιν εἶναι διττήν, τὴν μὲν
Λυκίαν τὴν δὲ Φοινικήν, οἱ δὲ μονοειδῆ, καθάπερ
οἱ ἐν τῇ Ἴδῃ. παρόμοιον δὲ τῇ ἀρκεύθῳ, διαφέρει
δὲ μάλιστα τῷ φύλλῳ· τὸ μὲν γὰρ τῆς κέδρου
σκληρὸν καὶ ὀξὺ καὶ ἀκανθῶδες, τὸ δὲ τῆς ἀρκεύθου
μαλακώτερον· δοκεῖ δὲ καὶ ὑψηλοφυέστερον εἶναι
ἡ ἄρκευθος· οὐ μὴν ἀλλ' ἔνιοί γε οὐ διαιροῦσι

---

[1] The Idaeans are evidently responsible for this statement.
T. himself (3. 4. 3) says the fruit is inedible.

[2] But (1. 11. 4) only certain varieties of the olive are said
to have this character; the next statement seems also inconsistent with 3. 4. 3. Perhaps T. is still reproducing his
Idaean authority.

arranged in pairs opposite one another. The wood
of the 'male' tree has no heart, but is hard throughout, like horn in closeness and strength; whereas
that of the 'female' tree has heart-wood and is softer
and goes into holes; wherefore it is useless for
javelins. The height of the 'male' tree is at most
twelve cubits, the length of the longest Macedonian
spear, the stem up to the point where it divides
not being very tall. The people of Mount Ida
in the Troad say that the 'male' tree is barren,
but that the 'female' bears fruit. The fruit has a
stone like an olive and is sweet to the taste and
fragrant[1]; the flower is like that of the olive, and the
tree produces its flowers and fruit in the same manner,
inasmuch as it has several growing from one stalk,[2]
and they are produced at almost the same time
in both forms. However the people of Macedonia
say that both trees bear fruit, though that of the
'female' is uneatable, and the roots are like those of
the chaste-tree, strong and indestructible. This tree
grows in wet ground and not only[3] in dry places;
and it comes from seed, and also can be propagated
from a piece torn off.

[4]The 'cedar,' some say, has two forms, the Lycian
and the Phoenician[5]; but some, as the people of
Mount Ida, say that there is only one form. It
resembles the *arkeuthos* (Phoenician cedar), differing
chiefly in the leaf, that of 'cedar' being hard sharp
and spinous, while that of *arkeuthos* is softer: the
latter tree also seems to be of taller growth. However some do not give them distinct names, but call

[3] μόνον ins. R. Const. from G.
[4] Plin. 13. 52.  See Index κέδρος and ἄρκευθος.
[5] Φοινίκην: Φοινικικὴν conj. W.  cf. 9. 2. 3 : Plin. l.c.

τοῖς ὀνόμασιν ἀλλ᾿ ἄμφω καλοῦσι κέδρους, πλὴν
παρασήμως τὴν κέδρον ὀξύκεδρον. ὀζώδη δ᾿
ἄμφω καὶ πολυμάσχαλα καὶ ἐπεστραμμένα ἔχοντα τὰ ξύλα· μήτραν δ᾿ ἡ μὲν ἄρκευθος ἔχει
μικρὰν καὶ πυκνὴν καὶ ὅταν κοπῇ ταχὺ σηπο-
μένην· ἡ δὲ κέδρος τὸ πλεῖστον ἐγκάρδιον καὶ
ἀσαπές, ἐρυθροκάρδια δ᾿ ἄμφω· καὶ ἡ μὲν τῆς
4 κέδρου εὐώδης ἡ δὲ τῆς ἑτέρας οὔ. καρπὸς δ᾿
ὁ μὲν τῆς κέδρου ξανθὸς μύρτου μέγεθος ἔχων
εὐώδης ἡδὺς ἐσθίεσθαι. ὁ δὲ τῆς ἀρκεύθου τὰ
μὲν ἄλλα ὅμοιος, μέλας δὲ καὶ στρυφνὸς καὶ
ὥσπερ ἄβρωτος· διαμένει δ᾿ εἰς ἐνιαυτόν, εἶθ᾿
ὅταν ἄλλος ἐπιφυῇ ὁ περυσινὸς ἀποπίπτει. ὡς
δὲ οἱ ἐν Ἀρκαδίᾳ λέγουσι, τρεῖς ἅμα καρποὺς
ἴσχει, τόν τε περυσινὸν οὔπω πέπονα καὶ
τὸν προπερύσινον ἤδη πέπονα καὶ ἐδώδιμον
καὶ τρίτον τὸν νέον ὑποφαίνει. ἔφη δὲ Σάτυρος
καὶ κομίσαι τοὺς ὀρεοτύπους αὐτῷ ἀνανθεῖς ἄμφω.
τὸν δὲ φλοιὸν ὅμοιον ἔχει κυπαρίττῳ τραχύτερον
δέ· ῥίζας δὲ μανὰς ἀμφότεραι καὶ ἐπιπολαίους.
φύονται περὶ τὰ πετρώδη καὶ χειμέρια καὶ τούτους
τοὺς τόπους ζητοῦσι.
5 Μεσπίλης δ᾿ ἐστὶ τρία γένη, ἀνθηδὼν σατάνειος ἀνθηδονοειδής, ὡς οἱ περὶ τὴν Ἴδην διαιροῦσι. φέρει δὲ ἡ μὲν σατάνειος τὸν καρπὸν
μείζω καὶ λευκότερον καὶ χαυνότερον καὶ τοὺς
πυρῆνας ἔχοντα μαλακωτέρους· αἱ δ᾿ ἕτεραι

---

¹ παρασήμως τὴν κέδρον U ; π. τὸν κέδρον M ; Ald. omits the
article ; παρασημασία κέδρου conj. W.
² μήτραν conj. Sch.; μᾶλλον UMVAld. Plin., 16. 198, sup-
ports μήτραν : he apparently read μήτραν δ᾿ ἡ μὲν ἀ. ἔχει μᾶλλον

them both 'cedar,' distinguishing them however as
'the cedar'[1] and 'prickly cedar.' Both are branching
trees with many joints and twisted wood.  On the
other hand *arkeuthos* has only a small amount of
close core,[2] which, when the tree is cut, soon rots,
while the trunk of 'cedar' consists mainly of heart
and does not rot.  The colour of the heart in each
case is red : that of the 'cedar' is fragrant, but not
that of the other.  The fruit of 'cedar' is yellow,
as large as the myrtle-berry, fragrant, and sweet
to the taste.  That of *arkeuthos* is like it in
other respects, but black, of astringent taste and
practically uneatable ; it remains on the tree for a
year, and then, when another grows, last year's fruit
falls off.  According to the Arcadians it has three
fruits on the tree at once, last year's, which is not
yet ripe, that of the year before last which is now
ripe and eatable, and it also shews the new fruit.
Satyrus[3] said that the wood-cutters gathered him
specimens of both kinds which were flowerless.  The
bark is[4] like that of the cypress but rougher.  Both[5]
kinds have spreading shallow roots.  These trees
grow in rocky cold parts and seek out such districts.
 [6] There are three kinds of *mespile*, *anthedon*
(oriental thorn), *sataneios* (medlar) and *anthedonoeides*
(hawthorn), as the people of mount Ida distinguish
them.  [7] The fruit of the medlar is larger paler
more spongy and contains softer stones ; in the other

τυκνήν ; but the words καὶ ὅταν . . . σηπομένην (which P. does
not render) seem inconsistent.  ? ins. οὐ before ταχὺ Sch.
[3] ? An enquirer sent out by the Lyceum : see Intr. p. xxi.
[4] ἔχει conj. W.; ἐδόκει Ald.
[5] ἀμφότεραι conj. W.; ἀμφοτέρας U ; ἀμφοτέρους Ald. H.
[6] Plin. 15. 84.
[7] *cf. C.P.* 2. 8. 2 ; 6. 14. 4 ; 6. 16. 1.

ἐλάττω τέ τι καὶ εὐωδέστερον καὶ στρυφνότερον,
ὥστε δύνασθαι πλείω χρόνον θησαυρίζεσθαι.
πυκνότερον δὲ καὶ τὸ ξύλον τούτων καὶ ξανθότερον,
τὰ δ᾽ ἄλλα ὅμοιον. τὸ δ᾽ ἄνθος πασῶν ὅμοιον
ἀμυγδαλῇ, πλὴν οὐκ ἐρυθρὸν ὥσπερ ἐκεῖνο ἀλλ᾽
ἐγχλωρότερον. . . . . . . μεγέθει μέγα τὸ δένδρον
καὶ περίκομον. φύλλον δὲ τὸ μὲν ἐπὶ . . . . . .
πολυσχιδὲς δὲ καὶ ἐν ἄκρῳ σελινοειδές, τὸ δ᾽
ἐπὶ τῶν παλαιοτέρων πολυσχιδὲς σφόδρα καὶ
ἐγγωνοειδὲς μείζοσι σχίσμασι, τετανὸν ἰνῶδες
λεπτότερον σελίνου καὶ προμηκέστερον καὶ τὸ
ὅλον καὶ τὰ σχίσματα, περικεχαραγμένον δὲ
ὅλον· μίσχον δ᾽ ἔχει λεπτὸν μακρόν· πρὸ τοῦ
φυλλορροεῖν δ᾽ ἐρυθραίνεται σφόδρα. πολύρριζον
δὲ τὸ δένδρον καὶ βαθύρριζον· δι᾽ ὃ καὶ χρόνιον
καὶ δυσώλεθρον. καὶ τὸ ξύλον ἔχει πυκνὸν καὶ
6 στερεὸν καὶ ἀσαπές. φύεται δὲ καὶ ἀπὸ σπέρματος καὶ ἀπὸ παρασπάδος. νόσημα δὲ αὐτῶν
ἐστιν ὥστε γηράσκοντα σκωληκόβρωτα γίνεσθαι·
καὶ οἱ σκώληκες μεγάλοι καὶ ἴδιοι ἢ οἱ ἐκ τῶν
δένδρων τῶν ἄλλων.

Τῶν δ᾽ οἰῶν δύο γένη ποιοῦσι, τὸ μὲν δὴ
καρποφόρον θῆλυ τὸ δὲ ἄρρεν ἄκαρπον· οὐ μὴν
ἀλλὰ διαφέρουσι τοῖς καρποῖς, τῷ τὰς μὲν
στρογγύλον τὰς δὲ προμήκη τὰς δ᾽ ὠοειδῆ φέρειν.
διαφέρουσι δὲ καὶ τοῖς χυλοῖς· ὡς γὰρ ἐπὶ τὸ

---

1 ἐλάττω τέ τι conj. W.; ἐλάττω εἰσὶ UAld.
2 W. suggests that some words are missing here, as it does
not appear to which kind of μεσπίλη the following description belongs; hence various difficulties. See Sch.
3 Probably a lacuna in the text. W. thus supplies the
sense; he suggests σικνοειδές for σελινοειδές.

238

kinds it is somewhat smaller,[1] more fragrant and of more astringent taste, so that it can be stored for a longer time. The wood also of these kinds is closer and yellower, though in other respects it does not differ. The flower in all the kinds is like the almond flower, except that it is not pink, as that is, but greenish . . . . .[2] In stature the tree is large and it has thick foliage. The leaf in the young tree is round[3] but much divided and like celery at the tip: but the leaf of older trees is very much divided and forms angles with larger divisions: it is smooth[4] fibrous thinner and more oblong than the celery leaf, both as a whole and in its divisions, and it has a jagged edge all round.[5] It has a long thin stalk, and the leaves turn bright red before they are shed. The tree has many roots, which run deep; wherefore it lives a long time and is hard to kill. The wood is close and hard and does not rot. The tree grows from seed and also from a piece torn off. It is subject to a disease which causes it to become worm-eaten[6] in its old age, and the worms are large and different[7] to those engendered by other trees.

[8] Of the sorb they make two kinds, the 'female' which bears fruit and the 'male' which is barren. There are moreover differences in the fruit of the 'female' kind ; in some forms it is round, in others oblong and egg-shaped. There are also differences

[4] τεταυὸν : cf. 3. 11. 1 ; 3. 15. 6.

[5] περικεχαραγμένον conj. Scal.; περικεθαρμένον U; περικεκαρμένον MVAld. cf. allusions to the leaf of μεσπίλη, 3. 13. 1 ; 3. 15. 6.

[6] cf. 4. 14. 10 ; Plin. 17. 221 ; Pall. 4. 10.

[7] ἴδιοι Ald. (for construction cf. Plat. Gorg. 481 c); ἰδίους UMV (the first ι corrected in U). W. adopts Sch.'s conj., ἡδίους, in allusion to the edible cossus : cf. Plin. l.c.

[8] Plin. 15. 85.

πᾶν εὐωδέστερα καὶ γλυκύτερα τὰ στρογγύλα,
τὰ δ' ὠοειδῆ πολλάκις ἐστὶν ὀξέα καὶ ἧττον
7 εὐώδη. φύλλα δ' ἀμφοῖν κατὰ μίσχον μακρὸν
ἰνοειδῆ πεφύκασι στοιχηδὸν ἐκ τῶν πλαγίων
πτερυγοειδῶς, ὡς ἑνὸς ὄντος τοῦ ὅλου λοβοὺς δὲ
ἔχοντος ἐσχισμένους ἕως τῆς ἰνός· πλὴν διεστᾶσιν
ἀφ' ἑαυτῶν ὑπόσυχνον τὰ κατὰ μέρος· φυλλοβολεῖ δὲ οὐ κατὰ μέρος ἀλλὰ ὅλον ἅμα τὸ
πτερυγῶδες. εἰσὶ δὲ περὶ μὲν τὰ παλαιότερα
καὶ μακρότερα πλείους αἱ συζυγίαι, περὶ δὲ τὰ
νεώτερα καὶ βραχύτερα ἐλάττους, πάντων δὲ ἐπ'
ἄκρου τοῦ μίσχου φύλλον περιττόν, ὥστε καὶ
πάντ' εἶναι περιττά. τῷ δὲ σχήματι δαφνοειδῆ
τῆς λεπτοφύλλου, πλὴν χαραγμὸν ἔχοντα καὶ
βραχύτερα καὶ οὐκ εἰς ὀξὺ τὸ ἄκρον συνῆκον
ἀλλ' εἰς περιφερέστερον. ἄνθος δὲ ἔχει βοτρυῶδες ἀπὸ μιᾶς κορύνης ἐκ πολλῶν μικρῶν καὶ
8 λευκῶν συγκείμενον. καὶ ὁ καρπὸς ὅταν εὐκαρπῇ
βοτρυῶδης· πολλὰ γὰρ ἀπὸ τῆς αὐτῆς κορύνης,
ὥστ' εἶναι καθάπερ κηρίον. σκωληκόβορος ἐπὶ
τοῦ δένδρου ὁ καρπὸς ἄπεπτος ὢν ἔτι γίνεται
μᾶλλον τῶν μεσπίλων καὶ ἀπίων καὶ ἀχράδων·
καίτοι πολὺ στρυφνότατος. γίνεται δὲ καὶ αὐτὸ
τὸ δένδρον σκωληκύβρωτον καὶ οὕτως αὐαίνεται
γηράσκον· καὶ ὁ σκώληξ ἴδιος ἐρυθρὸς δασύς.
καρποφορεῖ δ' ἐπιεικῶς νέα· τριετὴς γὰρ εὐθὺς
φύει. τοῦ μετοπώρου δ' ὅταν ἀποβάλῃ τὸ φύλλον,
εὐθὺς ἴσχει τὴν καχρυώδη κορύνην λιπαρὰν καὶ

---

¹ φύλλα ... στοιχηδὸν conj. W.; φύλλον δ' ἀμφοῖν τὸ μὲν
μίσχον μακρὸν ἰνοειδῆ· πεφ. [δὲ] στοιχηδὸν UMVAld.
² ἀφ' ἑαυτῶν (=ἀπ' ἀλλήλων) conj. Scal.; ἀπ' αὐτῶν U: so
W., who however renders inter se.

in taste; the round fruits are generally more fragrant and sweeter, the oval ones are often sour and less fragrant. The leaves in both grow attached to a long fibrous stalk, and project on each side in a row [1] like the feathers of a bird's wing, the whole forming a single leaf but being divided into lobes with divisions which extend to the rib; but each pair are some distance apart,[2] and, when the leaves fall,[3] these divisions do not drop separately, but the whole wing-like structure drops at once. When the leaves are older and longer, the pairs are more numerous; in the younger and shorter leaves they are fewer; but in all at the end of the leaf-stalk there is an extra leaflet, so that the total number of leaflets is an odd number. In form the leaflets resemble [4] the leaves of the 'fine-leaved' bay, except that they are jagged and shorter and do not narrow to a sharp point but to a more rounded end. The flower [5] is clustering and made up of a number of small white blossoms from a single knob. The fruit too is clustering, when the tree fruits well; for a number of fruits are formed from the same knob, giving an appearance like a honeycomb. The fruit gets eaten by worms on the tree before it is ripe to a greater extent than that of medlar pear or wild pear, and yet it is much more astringent than any of these. The tree itself also gets worm-eaten, and so withers away as it ages; and the worm [6] which infests it is a peculiar one, red and hairy. This tree bears fruit when it is quite young, that is as soon as it is three years old. In autumn, when it has shed its leaves, it immediately produces its winter-bud-like knob.[7]

[3] Plin. 16. 92.  [4] For construction *cf.* 3. 11. 3.
[5] *i.e.* inflorescence.  [6] Plin. 17. 221.  [7] *cf.* 3. 5. 5.

ἐπωδηκυῖαν ὡσὰν ἤδη βλαστικόν, καὶ διαμένει
9 τὸν χειμῶνα. ἀνάκανθον δέ ἐστι καὶ ἡ οἴη καὶ
ἡ μεσπίλη· φλοιὸν δ' ἔχει λεῖον ὑπολίπαρον,
ὅσπερ μὴ γεράνδρυα, τὴν δὲ χρόαν ξανθὸν
ἐπιλευκαίνοντα· τὰ δὲ γεράνδρυα τραχὺν καὶ
μέλανα. τὸ δὲ δένδρον εὐμέγεθες ὀρθοφυὲς
εὔρυθμον τῇ κόμῃ· σχεδὸν γὰρ ὡς ἐπὶ τὸ πολὺ
στροβιλοειδὲς σχῆμα λαμβάνει κατὰ τὴν κόμην,
ἐὰν μή τι ἐμποδίσῃ. τὸ δὲ ξύλον στερεὸν πυκνὸν
ἰσχυρὸν εὔχρουν, ῥίζας δὲ οὐ πολλὰς μὲν οὐδὲ
κατὰ βάθους, ἰσχυρὰς δὲ καὶ παχείας καὶ ἀνωλέθρους ἔχει. φύεται δὲ καὶ ἀπὸ ῥίζης καὶ ἀπὸ
παρασπάδος καὶ ἀπὸ σπέρματος· τόπον δὲ ζητεῖ
ψυχρὸν ἔνικμον, φιλόζωον δ' ἐν τούτῳ καὶ
δυσώλεθρον· οὐ μὴν ἀλλὰ καὶ φύεται ἐν τοῖς
ὄρεσιν.

XIII. Ἴδιον δὲ τῇ φύσει δένδρον ὁ κέρασός
ἐστι· μεγέθει μὲν μέγα· καὶ γὰρ εἰς τέτταρας
καὶ εἴκοσι πήχεις· ἔστι δ' ὀρθοφυὲς σφόδρα·
πάχος δὲ ὥστε καὶ δίπηχυν τὴν περίμετρον ἀπὸ
τῆς ῥίζης ἔχειν. φύλλον δ' ὅμοιον τῷ τῆς
μεσπίλης σκληρὸν δὲ σφόδρα καὶ παχύτερον,
ὥστε τῇ χροιᾷ πόρρωθεν φανερὸν εἶναι τὸ δένδρον.
φλοιὸν δὲ τὴν λειότητα καὶ τὴν χρόαν καὶ τὸ
πάχος ὅμοιον φιλύρᾳ, δι' ὃ καὶ τὰς κίστας ἐξ
αὐτοῦ ποιοῦσιν ὥσπερ καὶ ἐκ τοῦ τῆς φιλύρας.
περιπέφυκε δὲ αὐτὸς οὔτε ὀρθοφυὴς οὔτε κύκλῳ
κατ' ἴσον, ἀλλ' ἑλικηδὸν περιείληφε κάτωθεν ἄνω

---

1 ὅσπερ μὴ conj. Bod.; ὥσπερ τὰ Ald; ὥστε τὰ M.
2 κόμην Ald.H.; κορυφὴν conj. Sch.; vertice G.
3 Plin. 16. 125; cf. 16. 74; 17. 234.
4 παχύτερον: so quoted by Athen. 2. 34; πλατύτερον MSS.

which is glistening and swollen as though the tree
were just about to burst into leaf, and this persists
through the winter. The sorb, like the medlar, is
thornless; it has smooth rather shiny bark, (except
when [1] the tree is old), which in colour is a whitish
yellow; but in old trees it is rough and black. The
tree is of a good size, of erect growth and with well
balanced foliage; for in general it assumes a cone-
like shape as to its foliage,[2] unless something inter-
feres. The wood is hard close strong and of a good
colour; the roots are not numerous and do not run
deep, but they are strong and thick and indestructible. The tree grows from a root, from a piece
torn off, or from seed, and seeks a cold moist position;
in such a position it is tenacious of life and hard to
kill: however it also grows on mountains.

*Of bird-cherry, elder, willow.*

XIII. [3] The *kerasos* (bird-cherry) is peculiar in
character; it is of great stature, growing as much as
twenty-four cubits high; and it is of very erect
growth; as to thickness, it is as much as two cubits
in circumference at the base. The leaves are like
those of the medlar, but very tough and thicker,[4] so
that the tree is conspicuous by its colour from a
distance. The bark [5] in smoothness colour and thickness is like that of the lime; wherefore men make
their writing-cases [6] from it, as from the bark of that
tree. [7] This bark does not grow straight nor evenly
all round the tree, but runs round it [8] in a spiral

[3] *cf.* 4. 15. 1; Hesych. *s.v.* κέρασος.
[6] *cf.* 3. 10. 4; Ar. *Vesp.* 529.
[7] περιπέφυκε . . . περιπεφυκός ; text as restored by Sch. and
others, following U as closely as possible.
[8] περιείληφε conj. R. Const.

# THEOPHRASTUS

προσάγων, ὥσπερ ἡ διαγραφὴ τῶν φύλλων· καὶ
λοπιζόμενος οὗτος ἐκδέρεται, ἐκεῖνος δ' ἐπίτομος
2 γίνεται καὶ οὐ δύναται· μέρος δ' αὐτοῦ τι τὸν
αὐτὸν τρόπον ἀφαιρεῖται κατὰ πάχος σχιζόμενον
λεπτὸν ὡς ἂν φύλλον, τὸ δὲ λοιπὸν προσμένειν
τε δύναται καὶ σώζει τὸ δένδρον ὡσαύτως περιπεφυκός. περιαιρουμένου δὲ ὅταν λοπᾷ τοῦ
φλοιοῦ συνεκραίνει καὶ τότε τὴν ὑγρότητα· καὶ
ὅταν ὁ ἔξω χιτὼν περιαιρεθῇ, μόνον ὁ ὑπολιπὴς
ἐπιμελαίνεται ὥσπερ μυξώδει ὑγρασίᾳ, καὶ πάλιν
ὑποφύεται τῷ δευτέρῳ ἔτει χιτὼν ἄλλος ἀντ'
ἐκείνου πλὴν λεπτότερος. πέφυκε καὶ τὸ ξύλον
ὅμοιον ταῖς ἰσὶ τῷ φλοιῷ στρεπτῶς ἑλιττόμενον·
καὶ οἱ ῥάβδοι φύονται τὸν αὐτὸν τρόπον εὐθύς·
τοὺς ὄζους δ' αὐξανομένου συμβαίνει τοὺς μὲν
3 κάτω ἀεὶ ἀπόλλυσθαι τοὺς δ' ἄνω αὔξειν. τὸ δ'
ὅλον οὐ πολύοζον τὸ δένδρον ἀλλ' ἀνοζότερον
πολὺ τῆς αἰγείρου. πολύρριζον δὲ καὶ ἐπιπολαιόρριζον οὐκ ἄγαν δὲ παχύρριζον· ἡ δ'
ἐπιστροφὴ καὶ τῆς ῥίζης καὶ τοῦ φλοιοῦ τοῦ περὶ
αὐτὴν ἡ αὐτή. ἄνθος δὲ λευκὸν ἀπίῳ καὶ μεσπίλῃ
ὅμοιον, ἐκ μικρῶν ἀνθῶν συγκείμενον κηριῶδες.
ὁ δὲ καρπὸς ἐρυθρὸς ὅμοιος διοσπύρῳ τὸ σχῆμα,
τὸ δὲ μέγεθος ἡλίκον κύαμος, πλὴν τοῦ διοσπύρου
μὲν ὁ πυρὴν σκληρὸς τοῦ δὲ κεράσου μαλακός.
φύεται δ' ὅπου καὶ ἡ φίλυρα, τὸ δὲ ὅλον ὅπου
ποταμοὶ καὶ ἔφυδρα.
4 Φύεται δὲ καὶ ἡ ἀκτὴ μάλιστα παρ' ὕδωρ καὶ

---

[1] Which is an ellipse, the segment of a cylinder : so Sch.
explains.
[2] ἐκεῖνος: i.e. lower down the trunk, where the spiral is
less open.    [3] ἐπίτομος: cf. 5. 1. 12.

(which becomes closer as it gets higher up the tree)
like the outline of the leaves.[1] And this part of
it can be stripped off by peeling, whereas with the
other part[2] this is not possible and it has to be cut
in short lengths.[3] In the same manner part is
removed by being split off in flakes as thin as a leaf,
while the rest can be left and protects the tree, growing about it as described. If the bark is stripped off
when the tree is peeling, there is also at the time a
discharge of the sap; further, when only the outside
coat is stripped off, what remains turns black with a
kind[4] of mucus-like moisture; and in the second
year another coat grows to replace what is lost, but
this is thinner. The wood in its fibres is like the
bark, twisting spirally,[5] and the branches grow in
the same manner from the first; and, as the tree
grows, it comes to pass that the lower branches keep
on perishing, while the upper ones increase. However the whole tree is not much branched, but has
far fewer branches than the black poplar. Its roots
are numerous and shallow and not very thick; and
there is a similar twisting of the root and of the bark
which surrounds it. [6] The flower is white, like that
of the pear and medlar, composed of a number of
small blossoms arranged like a honeycomb. The
fruit is red, like that of *diospyros* in shape, and in size
it is as large as a bean. However the stone of the
*diospyros* fruit is hard, while that of the bird-cherry
is soft. The tree grows where the lime grows, and
in general where there are rivers and damp places.
[7] The elder also grows chiefly by water and in shady

---

[4] ὥσπερ conj. Sch.; περ MV; πως Ald.H.
[5] στρεπτῶς ἑλιττόμενον conj. Sch.; στρεπτῷ ἑλιττομέναι U;
στρεπτῷ ἑλιττομένῳ Ald. [6] cf. 3. 12. 7. [7] Plin. 17. 151.

ἐν τοῖς σκιεροῖς, οὐ μὴν ἀλλὰ καὶ ἐν τοῖς μὴ
τοιούτοις· θαμνῶδες δὲ ῥάβδοις ἐπετείοις αὐξα-
νομέναις μέχρι τῆς φυλλορροίας εἰς μῆκος, εἶτα
μετὰ ταῦτα εἰς πάχος· τὸ δὲ ὕψος τῶν ῥάβδων
οὐ μέγα λίαν ἀλλὰ καὶ μάλιστα ὡς ἑξάπηχυ·
τῶν δὲ στελεχῶν πάχος τῶν γερανδρύων ὅσον
περικεφαλαίας,¹ φλοιὸς δὲ λεῖος λεπτὸς καπυρός·²
τὸ δὲ ξύλον χαῦνον καὶ κοῦφον ξηρανθέν, ἐντεριώνην δὲ ἔχον μαλακήν, ὥστε δι' ὅλου καὶ
κοιλαίνεσθαι τὰς ῥάβδους, ἐξ ὧν καὶ τὰς βακτηρίας ποιοῦσι τὰς κούφας. ξηρανθὲν δὲ ἰσχυρὸν
καὶ ἀγήρων ἐὰν βρέχηται, κἂν ᾖ λελοπισμένον·
λοπίζεται δὲ αὐτόματον ξηραινόμενον. ῥίζας δὲ
ἔχει μετεώρους οὐ πολλὰς δὲ οὐδὲ μεγάλας.
5 φύλλον δὲ τὸ μὲν καθ' ἕκαστον μαλακόν, πρόμηκες ὡς τὸ τῆς πλατυφύλλου δάφνης, μεῖζον
δὲ καὶ πλατύτερον καὶ περιφερέστερον ἐκ μέσου
καὶ κάτωθεν, τὸ δ' ἄκρον εἰς ὀξὺ μᾶλλον συνῆκον
κύκλῳ δ' ἔχον χαραγμόν· τὸ δὲ ὅλον, περὶ ἕνα
μίσχον παχὺν καὶ ἰνώδη ὡσὰν κλωνίον τὰ μὲν
ἔνθεν τὰ δὲ ἔνθεν κατὰ γόνυ καὶ συζυγίαν πεφύκασι τῶν φύλλων διέχοντα ἀπ' ἀλλήλων, ἐν δὲ
ἐξ ἄκρου τοῦ μίσχου. ὑπέρυθρα δὲ τὰ φύλλα
ἐπιεικῶς καὶ χαῦνα καὶ σαρκώδη· φυλλορροεῖ
δὲ τοῦτο ὅλον, διόπερ φύλλον ἄν τις εἴποι τὸ ὅλον.
ἔχουσι δὲ καὶ οἱ κλῶνες οἱ νέοι γωνοειδῆ τινα.
6 τὸ δ' ἄνθος λευκὸν ἐκ μικρῶν λευκῶν πολλῶν
ἐπὶ τῇ τοῦ μίσχου σχίσει κηριῶδες· εὐωδίαν

---

¹ περικεφαλαίας, some part of a ship's prow : so Pollux.
² καπυρός conj. Sch.; καὶ πυρσός U (?) ; καὶ πυρρός V; καὶ
πουρός M.    ³ Sc. pith.

places, but likewise in places which are not of this
character. It is shrubby, with annual branches which
go on growing in length till the fall of the leaf, after
which they increase in thickness. The branches do
not grow to a very great height, about six cubits at
most. The thickness of the stem of old trees is
about that of the 'helmet'[1] of a ship; the bark is
smooth thin and brittle[2]; the wood is porous and
light when dried, and has a soft heart-wood,[3] so that
the boughs are hollow right through, and men make
of them their light walking-sticks. When dried it is
strong and durable if it is soaked, even if it is stripped
of the bark; and it strips itself of its own accord as it
dries. The roots are shallow and neither numerous
nor large. The single leaflet is soft and oblong, like
the leaf of the 'broad-leaved' bay, but larger broader
and rounder at the middle and base, though the tip
narrows more to a point and is jagged[4] all round.
The whole leaf is composed of leaflets growing about
a single thick fibrous stalk, as it were, to which they
are attached at either side in pairs at each joint;
and they are separate from one another, while one
is attached to the tip of the stalk. The leaves are
somewhat reddish porous and fleshy: the whole is
shed in one piece ; wherefore one may consider the
whole structure as a 'leaf.'[5] The young twigs too
have certain crooks[6] in them. The flower[7] is white,
made up of a number of small white blossoms
attached to the point where the stalk divides,
in form like a honeycomb, and it has the heavy

[4] χαραγμόν conj. R. Const. from G; παραγμόν UMV;
σπαραγμον Ald.     [5] cf. 3. 11. 3 n.
[6] γωνοειδῆ U; ? γωνιοειδῆ; G seems to have read γονατοειδῆ;
Sch. considers the text defective or mutilated.
[7] cf. 3. 12. 7 n.

247

δὲ ἔχει λειριώδη ἐπιβαρεῖαν. ἔχει δὲ καὶ τὸν
καρπὸν ὁμοίως πρὸς ἑνὶ μίσχῳ παχεῖ βοτρυώδη
δέ· γίνεται δὲ καταπεπαινόμενος[1] μέλας, ὠμὸς δὲ
ὢν ὀμφακώδης· μεγέθει δὲ μικρῷ μείζων ὀρόβου·
τὴν ὑγρασίαν δὲ οἰνώδη τῇ ὄψει· καὶ τὰς χεῖρας
τελειούμενοι βάπτονται καὶ τὰς κεφαλάς·[2] ἔχει δὲ
καὶ τὰ ἐντὸς σησαμοειδῆ τὴν ὄψιν.

7     Πάρυδρον δὲ καὶ ἡ ἰτέα καὶ πολυειδές· ἡ μὲν
μέλαινα καλουμένη τῷ τὸν φλοιὸν ἔχειν μέλανα
καὶ φοινικοῦν, ἡ δὲ λευκὴ τῷ λευκόν. καλλίους
δὲ ἔχει τὰς ῥάβδους καὶ χρησιμωτέρας εἰς τὸ
πλέκειν ἡ μέλαινα, ἡ δὲ λευκὴ καπυρωτέρας. ἔστι
δὲ καὶ τῆς μελαίνης καὶ τῆς λευκῆς ἔνιον γένος
μικρὸν καὶ οὐκ ἔχον αὔξησιν εἰς ὕψος, ὥσπερ καὶ
ἐπ᾽ ἄλλων τοῦτο δένδρων, οἷον κέδρου φοίνικος.
καλοῦσι δ᾽ οἱ περὶ Ἀρκαδίαν οὐκ ἰτέαν ἀλλὰ
ἑλίκην τὸ δένδρον· οἴονται δέ, ὥσπερ ἐλέχθη, καὶ
καρπὸν ἔχειν αὐτὴν γόνιμον.

XIV.     Ἔστι δὲ τῆς πτελέας δύο γένη, καὶ τὸ μὲν
ὀρειπτελέα καλεῖται τὸ δὲ πτελέα· διαφέρει δὲ τῷ
θαμνωδέστερον εἶναι τὴν πτελέαν εὐαυξέστερον δὲ
τὴν ὀρειπτελέαν. φύλλον δὲ ἀσχιδὲς περικεχαραγμένον ἡσυχῇ, προμηκέστερον δὲ τοῦ τῆς ἀπίου,

---

[1] καταπεπαινόμενος conj. W. ; καὶ πεπ. VAld.
[2] καὶ . . . βάπτονται I conj., following Scal., W., etc., but
keeping closer to U : certain restoration perhaps impossible ;
καὶ τὰς χεῖρας τελείους ἀναβλάστει δὲ καὶ τὰς κεφαλάς U ; χεῖρας
δὲ τελείους· ἀναβλασεῖ MV ; om. G.
[3] Plin. 16. 174 and 175.

fragrance of lilies. The fruit is in like manner attached to a single thick stalk, but in a cluster: as it becomes quite ripe,[1] it turns black, but when unripe it is like unripe grapes; in size the berry is a little larger than the seed of a vetch; the juice is like wine in appearance, and in it men bathe [2] their hands and heads when they are being initiated into the mysteries. The seeds inside the berry are like sesame.

[3] The willow also grows by the water, and there are many kinds. There is that which is called the black willow [4] because its bark is black and red, and that which is called the white [4] from the colour of its bark. The black kind has boughs which are fairer and more serviceable for basket-work, while those of the white are more brittle.[5] There is a form both of the black and of the white which is small and does not grow to a height,—just as there are dwarf forms of other trees, such as prickly cedar and palm. The people of Arcadia call the tree [6] not 'willow' but *helike*: they believe, as was said,[7] that it bears fruitful seed.

*Of elm, poplars, alder, [semyda, bladder-senna].*

XIV. [8] Of the elm there are two kinds, of which one is called the 'mountain elm,' the other simply the 'elm': the difference is that the latter is shrubbier, while the mountain elm grows more vigorously. The leaf is undivided and slightly jagged, longer than that of the pear, but rough

[4] See Index.
[5] καπυρωτέρας conj. Sch.: καὶ πυρωτέρας U ; καὶ πυροτέρας MVAld. *cf.* 3. 13. 4.
[6] Sc. *ἰτέα* generally.    [7] 3. 1. 2.    [8] Plin. 16. 72.

τραχὺ δὲ καὶ οὐ λεῖον. μέγα δὲ τὸ δένδρον καὶ
τῷ ὕψει καὶ τῷ μεγέθει. πολὺ δ᾽ οὐκ ἔστι περὶ
τὴν Ἴδην ἀλλὰ σπάνιον· τόπον δὲ ἔφυδρον φιλεῖ.
τὸ δὲ ξύλον ξανθὸν καὶ ἰσχυρὸν καὶ εὔινον καὶ
γλίσχρον·[1] ἅπαν γὰρ καρδία· χρῶνται δ᾽ αὐτῷ
καὶ πρὸς θυρώματα πολυτελῆ, καὶ χλωρὸν μὲν
εὔτομον ξηρὸν δὲ δύστομον. ἄκαρπον δὲ νομί-
ζουσιν, ἀλλ᾽ ἐν ταῖς κωρυκίσι τὸ κόμμι καὶ θηρί᾽
ἄττα κωνωποειδῆ φέρει. τὰς δὲ κάχρυς ἰδίας
ἴσχει τοῦ μετοπώρου πολλὰς καὶ μικρὰς καὶ
μελαίνας, ἐν δὲ ταῖς ἄλλαις ὥραις οὐκ ἐπέ-
σκεπται.

2 Ἡ δὲ λεύκη καὶ ἡ αἴγειρος μονοειδής, ὀρθοφυῆ
δὲ ἄμφω, πλὴν μακρότερον πολὺ καὶ μανότερον
καὶ λειότερον ἡ αἴγειρος, τὸ δὲ σχῆμα τῶν φύλλων
παρόμοιον. ὅμοιον δὲ καὶ τὸ ξύλον τεμνόμενον
τῇ λευκότητι. καρπὸν δ᾽ οὐδέτερον τούτων οὐδὲ
ἄνθος ἔχειν δοκεῖ.

Ἡ κερκὶς δὲ παρόμοιον τῇ λεύκῃ καὶ τῷ μεγέθει
καὶ τῷ τοὺς κλάδους ἐπιλεύκους ἔχειν· τὸ δὲ
φύλλον κιττῶδες μὲν ἀγώνιον δὲ ἐκ τοῦ ἄλλου,
τὴν δὲ μίαν προμήκη καὶ εἰς ὀξὺ συνήκουσαν· τῷ
δὲ χρώματι σχεδὸν ὅμοιον τὸ ὕπτιον καὶ τὸ
πρανές· μίσχῳ δὲ προσηρτημένον μακρῷ καὶ
λεπτῷ, δι᾽ ὃ καὶ οὐκ ὀρθὸν ἀλλ᾽ ἐγκεκλιμένον.
φλοιὸν δὲ τραχύτερον τῆς λεύκης καὶ μᾶλλον
ὑπόλεπρον, ὥσπερ ὁ τῆς ἀχράδος. ἄκαρπον δέ.

3 Μονογενὲς δὲ καὶ ἡ κλήθρα· φύσει δὲ καὶ

---

¹ γλίσχρον conj. St.; αἰσχρόν Ald. H.  cf. 5. 3. 4.
² cf. 5. 5. 2.
³ cf. τὸ θυλακῶδες τοῦτο, 3. 7. 3 ; 2. 8. 3 n.; 9. 1. 2.

rather than smooth. The tree is large, being both tall and wide-spreading. It is not common about Ida, but rare, and likes wet ground. The wood is yellow strong fibrous and tough[1]; for it is all heart. Men use it for expensive doors[2]: it is easy to cut when it is green, but difficult when it is dry. The tree is thought to bear no fruit, but in the 'wallets'[3] it produces its gum and certain creatures like gnats; and it has in autumn its peculiar 'winter-buds'[4] which are numerous small and black, but these have not been observed at other seasons.

The abele and the black poplar have each but a single kind: both are of erect growth, but the black poplar is much taller and of more open growth, and is smoother, while the shape of its leaves is similar to those of the other. The wood also of both, when cut, is much the same in whiteness. Neither of these trees appears to have fruit or flower.[5]

The aspen is a tree resembling the abele both in size and in having whitish branches, but the leaf is ivy-like: while however it is otherwise without angles, its one angular[6] projection is long and narrows to a sharp point: in colour the upper and under sides are much alike. The leaf is attached to a long thin stalk: wherefore the leaf is not set straight, but has a droop.[7] The bark of the abele is rougher and more scaly, like that of the wild pear, and it bears no fruit.

The alder also has but one form: in growth it is

[4] κάχρυς, here probably a gall, mistaken for winter-bud.
[5] cf., however, 3. 3. 4; 4. 10. 2, where T. seems to follow a different authority.
[6] Supply γωνίαν from ἀγώνιον.
[7] ἐγκεκλιμένον: sc. is not in line with the stalk.

ὀρθοφυές, ξύλον δ᾽ ἔχον μαλακὸν καὶ ἐντεριώνην
μαλακήν, ὥστε δι᾽ ὅλου κοιλαίνεσθαι τὰς λεπτὰς
ῥάβδους. φύλλον δ᾽ ὅμοιον ἀπίῳ, πλὴν μεῖζον
καὶ ἰνωδέστερον. τραχύφλοιον δὲ καὶ ὁ φλοιὸς
ἔσωθεν ἐρυθρός, δι᾽ ὃ καὶ βάπτει τὰ δέρματα.
ῥίζας δὲ ἐπιπολαίους . . . ἡλίκον δάφνης. φύεται
δὲ ἐν τοῖς ἐφύδροις ἀλλόθι δ᾽ οὐδαμοῦ.

4 [Σημύδα δὲ τὸ μὲν φύλλον ἔχει ὅμοιον τῇ
Περσικῇ καλουμένῃ καρύᾳ πλὴν μικρῷ στενότερον, τὸν φλοιὸν δὲ ποικίλον, ξύλον δὲ ἐλαφρόν·
χρήσιμον δὲ εἰς βακτηρίας μόνον εἰς ἄλλο δὲ
οὐδέν.

Ἡ δὲ κολυτέα ἔχει τὸ μὲν φύλλον ἐγγὺς τοῦ
τῆς ἰτέας, πολύοζον δὲ καὶ πολύφυλλον καὶ τὸ
δένδρον ὅλως μέγα· τὸν δὲ καρπὸν ἔλλοβον,
καθάπερ τὰ χεδροπά· λοβοῖς γὰρ πλατέσι καὶ
οὐ στενοῖς τὸ σπερμάτιον τὸ ἐνὸν μικρὸν καὶ οὐ
μέγα· σκληρὸν δὲ μετρίως οὐκ ἄγαν· οὐδὲ πολύκαρπον ὡς κατὰ μέγεθος. σπάνιον δὲ τὸ ἐν
λοβοῖς ἔχειν τὸν καρπόν· ὀλίγα γὰρ τοιαῦτα τῶν
δένδρων.]

XV. Ἡ δὲ Ἡρακλεωτικὴ καρύα—φύσει γὰρ
καὶ τοῦτ᾽ ἄγριον τῷ τε μηδὲν ἢ μὴ πολὺ
χείρω γίνεσθαι <ἢ> τῶν ἡμέρων τὸν καρπόν, καὶ
τῷ δύνασθαι χειμῶνας ὑποφέρειν καὶ τῷ πολὺ
φύεσθαι κατὰ τὰ ὄρη καὶ πολύκαρπον ἐν τοῖς
ὀρείοις· ἔτι δὲ τῷ μηδὲ στελεχῶδες ἀλλὰ θαμ-

---

[1] Part of the description of the flower, and perhaps of the
fruit, seems to be missing. Sch.
[2] cf. 4. 8. 1 ; but in 1. 4. 3 the alder is classed with 'amphibious' trees, and in 3. 3. 1 with 'trees of the plain.'
[3] Betulam, G from Plin. 16. 74.

also erect, and it has soft wood and a soft heart-wood, so that the slender boughs are hollow throughout. The leaf is like that of the pear, but larger and more fibrous. It has rough bark, which on the inner side is red: wherefore it is used for dyeing hides. It has shallow roots . . . [1] the flower is as large as that of the bay. It grows in wet places [2] and nowhere else.

The *semyda* [3] has a leaf like that of the tree called the 'Persian nut'(walnut), but it is rather narrower: the bark is variegated and the wood light: it is only of use for making walking-sticks and for no other purpose.

The bladder-senna [4] has a leaf near that of the willow, but is many-branched and has much foliage; and the tree altogether is a large one. The fruit is in a pod, as in leguminous plants: the pods in fact are broad rather than narrow, and the seed in them is comparatively small, and is moderately hard, but not so very hard. For its size the tree does not bear much fruit. It is uncommon to have the fruit in a pod; in fact there are few such trees.

*Of filbert, terebinth, box,* krataigos.

XV. The filbert is also naturally a wild tree, in that its fruit is little, if at all, inferior to that of the tree in cultivation, that it can stand winter, that it grows commonly on the mountains, and that it bears abundance of fruit in mountain regions [5]: also because it does not make a trunk, but is shrubby with

[4] Sch. remarks that the description of κολυτέα is out of place: cf. 3. 17. 2. W. thinks the whole section spurious. The antitheses in the latter part suggest a different context, in which κολυτέα was described by comparison with some other tree. [5] ὀρείοις conj. W.; φοραῖς Ald.

νῶδες εἶναι ῥάβδοις ἄνευ μασχαλῶν καὶ ἀνόζοις
μακραῖς δὲ καὶ παχείαις ἐνίαις·—οὐ μὴν ἀλλὰ
καὶ ἐξημεροῦται. διαφορὰν δὲ ἔχει τῷ τὸν
καρπὸν ἀποδιδόναι βελτίω καὶ μεῖζον τὸ φύλλον·
κεχαραγμένον δ' ἀμφοῖν· ὁμοιότατον τὸ τῆς
κλήθρας, πλὴν πλατύτερον καὶ αὐτὸ τὸ δένδρον
μεῖζον. καρπιμώτερον δ' αἰεὶ γίνεται κατα-
2 κοπτόμενον τὰς ῥάβδους. γένη δὲ δύο ἀμφοῖν·
αἱ μὲν γὰρ στρογγύλον αἱ δὲ πρόμακρον φέρουσι
τὸ κάρυον· ἐκλευκότερον δὲ τὸ τῶν ἡμέρων. καὶ
καλλικαρπεῖ μάλιστά γ' ἐν τοῖς ἐφύδροις. ἐξημεροῦται δὲ τὰ ἄγρια μεταφυτευόμενα. φλοιὸν
δ' ἔχει λεῖον ἐπιπόλαιον λεπτὸν λιπαρὸν ἰδίως
στιγμὰς λευκὰς ἔχοντα ἐν αὐτῷ· τὸ δὲ ξύλον
σφόδρα γλίσχρον, ὥστε καὶ τὰ λεπτὰ πάνυ ῥαβ-
δία περιλοπίσαντες κανέα ποιοῦσι, καὶ τὰ παχέα
δὲ καταξύσαντες. ἔχει δὲ καὶ ἐντεριώνην λεπτὴν
ξανθήν, ἢ κοιλαίνεται. ἴδιον δ' αὐτῶν τὸ περὶ
τὸν ἴουλον, ὥσπερ εἴπομεν.
3 Τῆς δὲ τερμίνθου τὸ μὲν ἄρρεν τὸ δὲ θῆλυ. τὸ
μὲν οὖν ἄρρεν ἄκαρπον, δι' ὃ καὶ καλοῦσιν ἄρρεν·
τῶν δὲ θηλειῶν ἡ μὲν ἐρυθρὸν εὐθὺς φέρει τὸν
καρπὸν ἡλίκον φακὸν ἄπεπτον, ἡ δὲ χλοερὸν
ἐνέγκασα μετὰ ταῦτα ἐρυθραίνει, καὶ ἅμα τῇ
ἀμπέλῳ πεπαίνουσα τὸ ἔσχατον ποιεῖ μέλανα,
μέγεθος ἡλίκον κύαμον, ῥητινώδη δὲ καὶ θυω-
δέστερον. ἔστι δὲ τὸ δένδρον περὶ μὲν τὴν Ἴδην
καὶ Μακεδονίαν βραχὺ θαμνῶδες ἐστραμμένον,
περὶ δὲ Δαμασκὸν τῆς Συρίας μέγα καὶ πολὺ
καὶ καλόν· ὄρος γάρ τί φασιν εἶναι πάμμεστον

---

[1] cf. C.P. 2. 12. 6.　　[2] cf. Geop. 10. 68.
[3] λεῖον conj. W.; πλέον UMVAld.

unbranched stems without knots ; though some of
these are long and stout. Nevertheless it also submits
to cultivation. The cultivated form differs in producing better fruit and larger leaves ; in both forms the
leaf has a jagged edge : the leaf of the alder most
closely resembles it, but is broader, and the tree itself
is bigger.  [1] The filbert is always more fruitful if it
has its slender boughs cut off.  [2] There are two kinds
of each sort; some have a round, others an oblong
nut ; that of the cultivated tree is paler, and it fruits
best in damp places. The wild tree becomes
cultivated by being transplanted. Its bark is smooth,[3]
consisting of one layer, thin glossy and with peculiar
white blotches on it. The wood is extremely tough,
so that men make baskets even of the quite thin
twigs, having stripped them of their bark, and of
the stout ones when they have whittled them. Also
it has a small amount of yellow heart-wood, which
makes [4] the branches hollow. Peculiar to these trees
is the matter of the catkin, as we mentioned.[5]

[6] The terebinth has a ' male ' and a ' female ' form.
The ' male ' is barren, which is why it is called
male ' ; the fruit of one of the ' female ' forms is
red from the first and as large as an unripe [7] lentil ;
the other produces a green fruit which subsequently
turns red, and, ripening at the same time as the
grapes, becomes eventually black and is as large as a
bean, but resinous and somewhat aromatic. About
Ida and in Macedonia the tree is low shrubby and
twisted, but in the Syrian Damascus, where it
abounds, it is tall and handsome ; indeed they say

[4] $\frac{a}{b}$ Ald.H.; $\dot{\eta}$ W. with U.  cf. 3. 13. 4.
[5] 3. 7. 3.        [6] Plin. 13. 54.
[7] καὶ before ἄπεπτον om. St.

4 τερμίνθων, ἄλλο δ᾽ οὐδὲν πεφυκέναι. ξύλον δὲ ἔχει γλίσχρον καὶ ῥίζας ἰσχυρὰς κατὰ βάθους, καὶ τὸ ὅλον ἀνώλεθρον· ἄνθος δὲ ὅμοιον τῷ τῆς ἐλάας, τῷ χρώματι δὲ ἐρυθρόν. φύλλον, περὶ ἕνα μίσχον πλείω δαφνοειδῆ κατὰ συζυγίαν, ὥσπερ καὶ τὸ τῆς οἴης· καὶ τὸ ἐξ ἄκρου περιττόν· πλὴν ἐγγωνιώτερον τῆς οἴης καὶ δαφνοειδέστερον δὲ κύκλῳ καὶ λιπαρὸν ἅπαν ἅμα τῷ καρπῷ. φέρει δὲ καὶ κωρυκώδη τινὰ κοῖλα, καθάπερ ἡ πτελέα, ἐν οἷς θηρίδια ἐγγίγνεται κωνωποειδῆ· ἐγγίγνεται δέ τι καὶ ῥητινῶδες ἐν τούτοις καὶ γλίσχρον· οὐ μὴν ἐνθεῦτέν γε ἡ ῥητίνη συλλέγεται ἀλλ᾽ ἀπὸ τοῦ ξύλου. ὁ δὲ καρπὸς οὐκ ἀφίησι ῥητίνης πλῆθος, ἀλλὰ προσέχεται μὲν ταῖς χερσί, κἂν μὴ πλυθῇ μετὰ τὴν συλλογὴν συνέχεται· πλυνόμενος δὲ ὁ μὲν λευκὸς καὶ ἄπεπτος ἐπιπλεῖ, ὁ δὲ μέλας ὑφίσταται.

5 Ἡ δὲ πύξος μεγέθει μὲν οὐ μεγάλη, τὸ δὲ φύλλον ὅμοιον ἔχει μυρρίνῳ. φύεται δ᾽ ἐν τοῖς ψυχροῖς τόποις καὶ τραχέσι· καὶ γὰρ τὰ Κύτωρα τοιοῦτον, οὗ ἡ πλείστη γίνεται· ψυχρὸς δὲ καὶ ὁ Ὄλυμπος ὁ Μακεδονικός· καὶ γὰρ ἐνταῦθα γίνεται πλὴν οὐ μεγάλη· μεγίστη δὲ καὶ καλλίστη ἐν Κύρνῳ· καὶ γὰρ εὐμήκεις καὶ πάχος ἔχουσαι πολὺ παρὰ τὰς ἄλλας. δι᾽ ὃ καὶ τὸ μέλι οὐχ ἡδὺ ὄζον τῆς πύξου.

---

[1] πλείω : sc. φύλλα, in loose apposition to φύλλον. Apparently the leaf is said to resemble that of οἴη in its composite structure, but that of the bay in shape : cf. 3. 12. 7.

[2] ἅπαν ἅμα conj. W.; ἅμα ἅπαν UAld.

[3] cf. 2. 8. 3 ; 3. 7. 3 ; 3. 14. 1. κωρυκώδη conj. R. Const.; κορυώδη Ald.; κωρυώδη H.; καρυώδη in Bas.

256

that there is a certain hill which is covered with
terebinths, though nothing else grows on it. It has
tough wood and strong roots which run deep, and the
tree as a whole is impossible to destroy. The flower
is like that of the olive, but red in colour. The leaf
is made up of a number of leaflets,[1] like bay leaves,
attached in pairs to a single leaf-stalk. So far it
resembles the leaf of the sorb; there is also the
extra leaflet at the tip : but the leaf is more angular
than that of the sorb, and the edge resembles
more the leaf of the bay ; the leaf is glossy all
over,[2] as is the fruit. It bears also some hollow
bag-like[3] growths, like the elm, in which are found
little creatures like gnats ; and resinous sticky
matter is found also in these bags ; but the resin is
gathered from the wood and not from these. The
fruit does not discharge much resin, but it clings to
the hands, and, if it is not washed after gathering, it
all sticks together ; if it is washed, the part which is
white and unripe floats,[4] but the black part sinks.

The box is not a large tree, and it has a leaf like
that of the myrtle. It grows in cold rough places ;
for of this character is Cytora,[5] where it is most
abundant. The Macedonian Olympus is also a cold
region ; [6] for there too it grows, though not to a
great size. It is largest and fairest in Corsica,[7]
where the tree grows taller and stouter than anywhere
else ; wherefore the honey there is not sweet, as it
smells of the box.

[4] ἐπιπλεῖ conj. R. Const. from G ; ἐπὶ πλεῖον Ald.; ἐπὶ πλεῖ
(erased) U.
[5] cf. Cytore buxifer, Catull. 4. 13 ; Plin. 16. 70.
[6] cf. 5. 7. 7.
[7] Κύρνῳ conj. R. Const. from Plin. l.c.; Κυρήνωι U ; Κυρήνῃ
Ald.

6 Πλήθει δὲ πολὺ κράταιγός ἐστιν, οἱ δὲ κρα-
ταιγόνα καλοῦσιν· ἔχει δὲ τὸ μὲν φύλλον ὅμοιον
μεσπίλῃ τετανόν, πλὴν μεῖζον ἐκείνου καὶ πλατύτερον ἢ προμηκέστερον, τὸν δὲ χαραγμὸν οὐκ
ἔχον ὥσπερ ἐκεῖνο. γίνεται δὲ τὸ δένδρον οὔτε
μέγα λίαν οὔτε παχύ· τὸ δὲ ξύλον ποικίλον
ἰσχυρὸν ξανθόν· ἔχει δὲ φλοιὸν λεῖον ὅμοιον
μεσπίλῃ· μονόρριζον δ᾽ εἰς βάθος ὡς ἐπὶ τὸ πολύ.
καρπὸν δ᾽ ἔχει στρογγύλον ἡλίκον ὁ κότινος·
πεπαινόμενος δὲ ξανθύνεται καὶ ἐπιμελαίνεται·
κατὰ δὲ τὴν γεῦσιν καὶ τὸν χυλὸν μεσπιλῶδες·
διόπερ οἷον ἀγρία μεσπίλη δόξειεν ἂν εἶναι.
μονοειδὲς δὲ καὶ οὐκ ἔχον διαφοράς.
XVI. Ὁ δὲ πρῖνος φύλλον μὲν ἔχει δρυῶδες,
ἔλαττον δὲ καὶ ἐπακανθίζον, τὸν δὲ φλοιὸν λειότερον δρυός. αὐτὸ δὲ τὸ δένδρον μέγα, καθάπερ
ἡ δρῦς, ἐὰν ἔχῃ τόπον καὶ ἔδαφος· ξύλον δὲ
πυκνὸν καὶ ἰσχυρόν· βαθύρριζον δὲ ἐπιεικῶς καὶ
πολύρριζον. καρπὸν δὲ ἔχει βαλανώδη· μικρὰ
δὲ ἡ βάλανος· περικαταλαμβάνει δὲ ὁ νέος τὸν
ἔνον· ὀψὲ γὰρ πεπαίνει, δι᾽ ὃ καὶ διφορεῖν τινές
φασι. φέρει δὲ παρὰ τὴν βάλανον καὶ κόκκον
τινὰ φοινικοῦν· ἴσχει δὲ καὶ ἰξίαν καὶ ὑφέαρ·
ὥστε ἐνίοτε συμβαίνει τέτταρας ἅμα καρποὺς
ἔχειν αὐτόν, δύο μὲν τοὺς ἑαυτοῦ δύο δ᾽ ἄλλους
τόν τε τῆς ἰξίας καὶ τὸν τοῦ ὑφέαρος. καὶ τὴν

---

[1] Quoted by Athen. 2. 34; cf. Plin. 16. 120; 26. 99;
27, 62 and 63.
[2] τετανόν: cf. 3. 11. 1; 3. 12. 5. Athen., l.c., has τετα-
μένον.
[3] ἐκεῖνο Athen. l.c.; κἀκεῖνο Ald.
[4] ξανθὸν before ἰσχυρόν Athen. l.c.

[1] The *krataigos* is a very common tree; some call it *kra'aigon*. It has a smooth[2] leaf like that of the medlar, but longer, and its breadth is greater than its length, while the edge is not jagged like that[3] of the medlar. The tree does not grow very tall or thick; its wood is mottled strong and brown[4]; it has a smooth bark like that of the medlar; it has generally a single root, which runs deep. The fruit is round and as large as that of the wild olive[5]; as it ripens it turns brown and black; in taste and flavour it is like that of the medlar; wherefore this might seem to be a sort of wild form of that tree.[6] There is only one form of it and it shews no variation.

*Of certain other oaks, arbutus, andrachne, wig-tree.*

XVI. The kermes-oak[7] has a leaf like that of the oak, but smaller and spinous,[8] while its bark is smoother than that of the oak. The tree itself is large, like the oak, if it has space and root-room; the wood is close and strong; it roots fairly deep and it has many roots. The fruit is like an acorn, but the kermes-oak's acorn is small; the new one overtakes that of last year, for it ripens late.[9] Wherefore some say that it bears twice. Besides the acorn it bears a kind of scarlet berry[10]; it also has oak-mistletoe[11] and mistletoe; so that sometimes it happens that it has four fruits on it at once, two which are its own and two others, namely those of the oak-mistletoe[11] and

[5] κότινος Athen. *l.c.*; κόϲιμος UMVAld.
[6] μεσπίλη added from Athen. *l.c.*
[7] *cf.* 3. 7. 3.    [8] *cf.* 3. 16. 2.    [9] *cf.* 3. 4. 1, 4 and 6.
[10] Plin. 16. 32; Simon. *ap.* Plut. *Theseus* 17.
[11] *cf. C.P.* 2. 17. 1.

THEOPHRASTUS

μὲν ἰξίαν φέρει ἐκ τῶν πρὸς βορρᾶν, τὸ δὲ ὑφέαρ
ἐκ τῶν πρὸς μεσημβρίαν.

2 Οἱ δὲ περὶ Ἀρκαδίαν δένδρον τι σμίλακα
καλοῦσιν, ὅ ἐστιν ὅμοιον τῷ πρίνῳ, τὰ δὲ φύλλα
οὐκ ἀκανθώδη ἔχει ἀλλ᾽ ἁπαλώτερα καὶ βαθύτερα
καὶ διαφορὰς ἔχοντα πλείους· οὐδὲ τὸ ξύλον
ὥσπερ ἐκεῖνο στερεὸν καὶ πυκνόν, ἀλλὰ καὶ
μαλακὸν ἐν ταῖς ἐργασίαις.

3 Ὁ δὲ καλοῦσιν οἱ Ἀρκάδες φελλόδρυν τοιάνδε
ἔχει τὴν φύσιν· ὡς μὲν ἁπλῶς εἰπεῖν ἀνὰ μέσον
πρίνου καὶ δρυός ἐστιν· καὶ ἔνιοί γε ὑπολαμβάνουσιν εἶναι θῆλυν πρῖνον· δι᾽ ὃ καὶ ὅπου μὴ
φύεται πρῖνος τούτῳ χρῶνται πρὸς τὰς ἁμάξας
καὶ τὰ τοιαῦτα, καθάπερ οἱ περὶ Λακεδαίμονα καὶ
Ἠλείαν. καλοῦσι δὲ οἵ γε Δωριεῖς καὶ ἀρίαν τὸ
δένδρον· ἔστι δὲ μαλακώτερον μὲν καὶ μανότερον
τοῦ πρίνου, σκληρότερον δὲ καὶ πυκνότερον τῆς
δρυός· καὶ τὸ χρῶμα φλοῖσθέντος τοῦ ξύλου
λευκότερον μὲν τοῦ πρίνου, οἰνωπότερον δὲ τῆς
δρυός· τὰ δὲ φύλλα προσέοικε μὲν ἀμφοῖν, ἔχει
δὲ μείζω μὲν ἢ ὡς πρῖνος ἐλάττω δὲ ἢ ὡς δρῦς·
καὶ τὸν καρπὸν τοῦ μὲν πρίνου κατὰ μέγεθος
ἐλάττω ταῖς ἐλαχίσταις δὲ βαλάνοις ἴσον, καὶ
γλυκύτερον μὲν τοῦ πρίνου πικρότερον δὲ τῆς
δρυός. καλοῦσι δέ τινες τὸν μὲν τοῦ πρίνου καὶ
τὸν ταύτης καρπὸν ἄκυλον, τὸν δὲ τῆς δρυὸς
βάλανον. μήτραν δὲ ἔχει φανερωτέραν ἢ ὁ
πρῖνος· καὶ ἡ μὲν φελλόδρυς τοιαύτην τινὰ ἔχει
φύσιν.

---

[1] Plin. 16. 19. See Index.
[2] βαθύτερα MSS.; εὐθύτερα conj. Dalec.
[3] Plin. l.c. See Index.

260

of the mistletoe. It produces the oak-mistletoe on the north side and the mistletoe on the south.

The Arcadians have a tree which they call *smilax* [1] (holm-oak), which resembles the kermes-oak, but has not spinous leaves, its leaves being softer and longer [2] and differing in several other ways. Nor is the wood hard and close like that of the kermes-oak, but quite soft to work.

The tree which the Arcadians call 'cork-oak' [3] (holm-oak) has this character:—to put it generally, it is between the kermes-oak and the oak ; and some suppose it to be the 'female' kermes-oak ; wherefore, where the kermes-oak does not grow, they use this tree for their carts and such-like purposes; for instance it is so used by the peoples of Lacedaemon and Elis. The Dorians also call the tree *aria*.[4] Its wood is softer and less compact than that of the kermes-oak, but harder and closer than that of the oak. When it is barked,[5] the colour of the wood is paler than that of the kermes-oak, but redder than that of the oak. The leaves resemble those of both trees, but they are somewhat large, if we consider the tree as a kermes-oak, and somewhat small if we regard it as an oak. The fruit is smaller in size than that of the kermes-oak, and equal to the smallest acorns ; it is sweeter than that of the kermes-oak, bitterer than that of the oak. Some call the fruit of the kermes-oak and of the *aria* 'mast,' [6] keeping the name 'acorn' for the fruit of the oak. It has a core which is more obvious than in kermes-oak. Such is the character of the 'cork-oak.'

[4] Already described ; *cf.* 3. 4. 2 ; 3. 17. 1.
[5] *cf.* Paus. *Arcadia*, 8. 12.
[6] ἄκυλον : *cf.* Hom. *Od.* 10. 242.

THEOPHRASTUS

4 Ἡ δὲ κόμαρος, ἡ τὸ μεμαίκυλον φέρουσα τὸ
ἐδώδιμον, ἐστὶ μὲν οὐκ ἄγαν μέγα, τὸν δὲ φλοιὸν
ἔχει λεπτὸν μὲν παρόμοιον μυρίκῃ, τὸ δὲ φύλλον
μεταξὺ πρίνου καὶ δάφνης. ἀνθεῖ δὲ τοῦ Πυανε-
ψιῶνος· τὰ δὲ ἄνθη πέφυκεν ἀπὸ μιᾶς κρεμάστρας
ἐπ᾽ ἄκρων βοτρυδόν· τὴν δὲ μορφὴν ἕκαστόν
ἐστιν ὅμοιον μύρτῳ προμήκει καὶ τῷ μεγέθει δὲ
σχεδὸν τηλικοῦτον· ἄφυλλον δὲ καὶ κοῖλον ὥσπερ
ᾠὸν ἐκκεκολαμμένον τὸ στόμα δὲ ἀνεῳγμένον·
ὅταν δ᾽ ἀπανθήσῃ, καὶ ἡ πρόσφυσις τετρύπηται,
τὸ δ᾽ ἀπανθῆσαν λεπτὸν καὶ ὥσπερ σφόνδυλος
περὶ ἄτρακτον ἢ κάρνειος Δωρικός· ὁ δὲ καρπὸς
ἐνιαυτῷ πεπαίνεται, ὥσθ᾽ ἅμα συμβαίνει τοῦτόν
τ᾽ ἔχειν καὶ τὸν ἕτερον ἀνθεῖν.

5 Παρόμοιον δὲ τὸ φύλλον καὶ ἡ ἀνδράχλη ἔχει
τῷ κομάρῳ, μέγεθος οὐκ ἄγαν μέγα· τὸν δὲ φλοιὸν
λεῖον ἔχει καὶ περιρρηγνύμενον· καρπὸν δ᾽ ἔχει
ὅμοιον τῇ κομάρῳ.

6 Ὅμοιον δ᾽ ἐστὶ τούτοις τὸ φύλλον καὶ τὸ τῆς
κοκκυγέας· τὸ δὲ δένδρον μικρόν. ἴδιον δὲ ἔχει
τὸ ἐκπαππποῦσθαι τὸν καρπόν· τοῦτο γὰρ οὐδ᾽
ἐφ᾽ ἑνὸς ἀκηκόαμεν ἄλλου δένδρου. ταῦτα μὲν
οὖν κοινότερα πλείοσι χώραις καὶ τόποις.

---

¹ Plin. 15. 98 and 99 ; Diosc. 1. 122.    ² October.
³ ἐκκεκολαμμένον MV, cf. Arist. H.A. 6. 3 ; ἐγκεκολαμμένον
UAld.    ⁴ cf. 1. 13. 3.
⁵ κάρνειος, an unknown word, probably corrupt ; κίονος
Δωρικοῦ conj. Sch., 'drum of a Doric column.' cf. Athen.
5. 39.

262

[1] The arbutus, which produces the edible fruit called *memaikylon*, is not a very large tree; its bark is thin and like that of the tamarisk, the leaf is between that of the kermes-oak and that of the bay. It blooms in the month Pyanepsion [2]; the flowers grow in clusters at the end of the boughs from a single attachment; in shape each of them is like an oblong myrtle flower and it is of about the same size; it has no petals, but forms a cup like an empty eggshell,[3] and the mouth is open: when the flower drops off, there is a hole [4] also through the part by which it is attached, and the fallen flower is delicate and like a whorl on a spindle or a Doric *karneios*.[5] The fruit takes a year to ripen, so that it comes to pass that this and the new flower are on the tree together.

[6] The andrachne has a leaf like that of the arbutus and is not a very large tree; the bark is smooth [7] and cracked,[8] the fruit is like that of the arbutus.

The leaf of the wig-tree [9] is also like that of the last named tree, but it is a small tree. Peculiar to it is the fact that the fruit passes into down [10]: we have not heard of such a thing in any other tree. These trees are found in a good many positions and regions.

[6] Plin. 13. 120.
[7] Λεῖον conj. Sch.; λευκὸν UAld. In Pletho's excerpt the passage has Λεῖον, and Plin., *l.c.*, evidently read Λεῖον.
[8] περιρρηγνύμενον. Plin., *l.c.*, seems to have read περιπηγνύμενον. *cf.* 1. 5. 2; 9. 4. 3.
[9] Plin. 13. 121. κοκκυγέας conj. Sch. after Plin. *l.c.*, *cf.* Hesych. *s.v.* κεκκοκυγωμένην: κοκκομηλέας U; κοκκυμηλέας P.Ald.
[10] ἐκπαπποῦσθαι: *fructum amittere lanugine* Plin. *l.c.* *cf.* 6. 8. 4.

THEOPHRASTUS

XVII. Ἔνια δὲ ἰδιώτερα, καθάπερ καὶ ὁ φελλός·
γίνεται μὲν ἐν Τυρρηνίᾳ, τὸ δὲ δένδρον ἐστὶ στελεχῶδες μὲν καὶ ὀλιγόκλαδον, εὔμηκες δ᾿ ἐπιεικῶς
καὶ εὐαυξές· ξύλον ἰσχυρόν· τὸν δὲ φλοιὸν παχὺν
σφόδρα καὶ καταρρηγνύμενον, ὥσπερ ὁ τῆς πίτυος,
πλὴν κατὰ μείζω. τὸ δὲ φύλλον ὅμοιον ταῖς
μελίαις παχὺ προμηκέστερον· οὐκ ἀείφυλλον
ἀλλὰ φυλλοβολοῦν. καρπὸν δὲ [ἀεὶ] φέρει
βαλανηρὸν ὅμοιον τῇ ἀρίᾳ. περιαιροῦσι δὲ τὸν
φλοιὸν καί φασι δεῖν πάντα ἀφαιρεῖν, εἰ δὲ μὴ
χεῖρον γίνεται τὸ δένδρον· ἐξαναπληροῦται δὲ
πάλιν σχεδὸν ἐν τρισὶν ἔτεσιν.

2   Ἴδιον δὲ καὶ ἡ κολουτέα περὶ Λιπάραν· δένδρον
μὲν εὐμέγεθες, τὸν δὲ καρπὸν φέρει ἐν λοβοῖς
ἡλίκον φακόν, ὃς πιαίνει τὰ πρόβατα θαυμαστῶς.
φύεται δὲ ἀπὸ σπέρματος καὶ ἐκ τῆς τῶν προβάτων κόπρου κάλλιστα. ὥρα δὲ τῆς φυτείας ἅμα
Ἀρκτούρῳ δυομένῳ· δεῖ δὲ φυτεύειν προβρέχοντας
ὅταν ἤδη διαφύηται ἐν τῷ ὕδατι. φύλλον δ᾿ ἔχει
παρόμοιον τήλει. βλαστάνει δὲ τὸ πρῶτον
μονοφυὲς ἐπὶ ἔτη μάλιστα τρία ἐν οἷς καὶ τὰς
βακτηρίας τέμνουσι· δοκοῦσι γὰρ εἶναι καλαί·
καὶ ἐάν τις κολούσῃ ἀποθνήσκει· καὶ γὰρ ἀπα-
ράβλαστόν ἐστιν· εἶτα σχίζεται καὶ ἀποδενδροῦται τῷ τετάρτῳ ἔτει.

¹ Plin. 16. 34.
² Τυρρηνίᾳ conj. R. Const.; πυρρηνίαι UMV; πυρρηνίᾳ Ald.
³ ἀεὶ must be corrupt : probably repeated from ἀείφυλλον.
⁴ βαλανηρὸν conj. Sch.; βαλανήφορον UMVAld.
⁵ ἀρίᾳ conj. R. Const. from G ; ἀγρίᾳ P₂MVAld.; ἀγρίαι U.

XVII. [1] Some however are more local, such as the cork-oak : this occurs in Tyrrhenia[2] ; it is a tree with a distinct trunk and few branches, and is fairly tall and of vigorous growth. The wood is strong, the bark very thick and cracked, like that of the Aleppo pine, save that the cracks are larger. The leaf is like that of the manna-ash, thick and somewhat oblong. The tree is not evergreen but deciduous. It has always[3] an acorn-like[4] fruit like that of the *aria*[5] (holm-oak). They strip off the bark,[6] and they say that it should all be removed,[7] otherwise the tree deteriorates : it is renewed again in about three years.

The *kolutea*[8] too is a local tree, occurring in the Lipari islands. It is a tree of good size, and bears its fruit, which is as large as a lentil. in pods ; this fattens sheep wonderfully. It grows from seed, and also grows very well from sheep-droppings. The time for sowing it is the setting of Arcturus ; and one should first soak the seed and sow it when it is already sprouting in the water. It has a leaf like *'clis*[9] (fenugreek). At first it grows for about three years with a single stem, and in this period men cut their walking-sticks from it ; for it seems that it makes excellent ones. And, if the top is cut off during this period, it dies, for it makes no side-shoots. After this period it divides, and in the fourth year develops into a tree.

[6] *cf.* 1. 5. 2 ; 4. 15. 1 ; Plin. 17. 234.
[7] ἀφαιρεῖν conj. Coraes ; διαιρεῖν P₂Ald.
[8] *cf.* 1. 11. 2 ; 3. 17. 3.
[9] τήλει conj. R. Const. from G, *faeno graeco* ; τίλει UMV : ʹύλῃ Ald.

## THEOPHRASTUS

3 Ἡ δὲ περὶ τὴν Ἴδην, ἣν καλοῦσι κολοιτίαν,¹
ἕτερον εἶδός ἐστιν, θαμνοειδὲς δὲ καὶ ὀζῶδες καὶ
πολυμάσχαλον, σπάνιον δέ, οὐ πολύ· ἔχει δὲ
φύλλον δαφνοειδὲς πλατυφύλλου δάφνης, πλὴν
στρογγυλώτερον καὶ μεῖζον ὥσθ' ὅμοιον φαίνεσθαι
τῷ τῆς πτελέας, προμηκέστερον δέ, τὴν χρόαν
ἐπὶ θάτερα χλοερὸν ὄπισθεν δὲ ἐπιλευκαῖνον, καὶ
πολύϊνον ἐκ τῶν ὄπισθεν ταῖς λεπταῖς ἰσὶ ἔκ τε
τῆς ῥάχεως καὶ μεταξὺ τῶν πλευροειδῶν ἀπὸ
τῆς μέσης κατατεινουσῶν· φλοιὸν δ' οὐ λεῖον
ἀλλ' οἷον τὸν τῆς ἀμπέλου· τὸ δὲ ξύλον σκληρὸν
καὶ πυκνόν· ῥίζας δὲ ἐπιπολαίους καὶ λεπτὰς
καὶ μανὰς οὐλὰς δ' ἐνίοτε, καὶ ξανθὰς σφόδρα.
καρπὸν δὲ οὐκ ἔχειν φασὶν οὐδὲ ἄνθος· τὴν δὲ
κορυνώδη κάχρυν καὶ τοὺς ὀφθαλμοὺς τοὺς παρὰ
τὰ φύλλα λείους σφόδρα καὶ λιπαροὺς καὶ
λευκοὺς τῷ σχήματι δὲ καχρυώδεις· ἀποκοπὲν δὲ
καὶ ἐπικανθὲν παραφύεται καὶ ἀναβλαστάνει.
4 Ἴδια δὲ καὶ τάδε τὰ περὶ τὴν Ἴδην ἐστίν, οἷον
ἥ τε Ἀλεξάνδρεια καλουμένη δάφνη καὶ συκῆ τις
καὶ ἄμπελος. τῆς μὲν οὖν δάφνης ἐν τούτῳ τὸ
ἴδιον, ὅτι ἐπιφυλλόκαρπόν ἐστιν, ὥσπερ καὶ ἡ
κεντρομυρρίνη· ἀμφότεραι γὰρ τὸν καρπὸν ἔχουσιν ἐκ τῆς ῥάχεως τοῦ φύλλου.
5 Ἡ δὲ συκῆ θαμνῶδες μὲν καὶ οὐχ ὑψηλόν,
πάχος δ' ἔχον ὥστε καὶ πηχυαῖον εἶναι τὴν περί-
μετρον· τὸ δὲ ξύλον ἐπεστραμμένον γλίσχρον·
κάτωθεν μὲν λεῖον καὶ ἄνοζον ἄνωθεν δὲ περί-

¹ κολοιτίαν (? κολοιτέαν) U. cf. 1. 11. 2; 3. 17. 2. Whichever spelling is correct should probably be adopted in all
three places. ² cf. 3. 11. 3.

266

The tree found about Mount Ida, called $kol_{ia}$,[1] is a distinct kind and is shrubby and branching with many boughs; but it is rather rare. It has a leaf like that of the 'broad-leaved' bay,[2] but round and larger, so that it looks like that of the elm but it is more oblong: the colour on both sides is green, but the base is whitish; in this part it is very fibrous, because of its fine fibres which spring partly from the midrib,[3] partly between the ribs[4] (so to call them) which run out from the midrib. The bark is not smooth but like that of the vine; the wood is hard and close, the roots are shallow slender and spreading, (though sometimes they are compact), and they are very yellow. They say that this shrub has no fruit nor flower, but has its knobby winter-bud and its 'eyes'; these grow alongside of the leaves, and are very smooth glossy and white, and in shape are like a winter-bud. When the tree is cut or burnt down, it grows from the side and springs up again.

There are also three trees peculiar to Mount Ida, the tree called Alexandrian laurel, a sort of fig, and a 'vine' (currant grape). The peculiarity of the laurel is that it bears fruit on its leaves, like the 'prickly myrtle' (butcher's broom): both have their fruit on the midrib of the leaf.

The 'fig'[5] is shrubby and not tall, but so thick that the stem is a cubit in circumference. The wood is twisted and tough; below it is smooth and unbranched, above it has thick foliage: the colour both

---

[3] ἐκ τε τῆς ῥαχέως καὶ conj. W.; καὶ ταῖς ῥίζαις καὶ Ald.   cf. 3. 10. 3, and ἐκ τῆς ῥαχέως below, 3. 17. 4.

[4] πλευροειδῶν: πλευροειδῶν conj. St.

[5] See Index.  Plin. 15. 68; cf. Athen. 3. 11.

THEOPHRASTUS

κ..ον· χρῶμα δὲ καὶ φύλλου καὶ φλοιοῦ πελιόν,
δὲ σχῆμα τῶν φύλλων ὅμοιον τῷ τῆς φιλύρας
αἱ μαλακὸν καὶ πλατὺ καὶ τὸ μέγεθος παρα-
πλήσιον· ἄνθος μεσπιλῶδες καὶ ἀνθεῖ ἅμα τῇ
μεσπίλῃ. ὁ δὲ καρπός, ὃν καλοῦσι σῦκον, ἐρυθρὸς
ἡλίκος ἐλάας πλὴν στρογγυλώτερος, ἐσθιόμενος
δὲ μεσπιλώδης· ῥίζας δὲ ἔχει παχείας ὡσὰν
συκῆς ἡμέρου καὶ γλίσχρας. ἀσαπὲς δέ ἐστι τὸ
δένδρον καὶ καρδίαν ἔχει στερεὰν οὐκ ἐντεριώνην.

6 Ἡ δὲ ἄμπελος φύεται μὲν τῆς Ἴδης περὶ τὰς
Φαλάκρας καλουμένας· ἔστι δὲ θαμνῶδες ῥαβ-
δίοις μικροῖς· τείνονται δὲ οἱ κλῶνες ὡς πυγω-
νιαῖοι, πρὸς οἷς ῥᾶγές εἰσιν ἐκ πλαγίου μέλαιναι
τὸ μέγεθος ἡλίκος κύαμος γλυκεῖαι· ἔχουσι δὲ
ἐντὸς γιγαρτῶδές τι μαλακόν· φύλλον στρογγύλον
ἀσχιδὲς μικρόν.

XVIII. Ἔχει δὲ καὶ τἆλλα σχεδὸν ὄρη φύσεις
τινὰς ἰδίας τὰ μὲν δένδρων τὰ δὲ θάμνων τὰ δ'
ἄλλων ὑλημάτων. ἀλλὰ γὰρ περὶ μὲν τῆς ἰδιό-
τητος εἴρηται πλεονάκις ὅτι γίνεται καθ' ἑκάστους
τόπους. ἡ δὲ ἐν αὐτοῖς τοῖς ὁμογενέσιν διαφορά,
καθάπερ ἡ τῶν δένδρων καὶ τῶν θάμνων, ὁμοίως
ἐστὶ καὶ τῶν ἄλλων, ὥσπερ εἴρηται, τῶν πλείστων,
ὥσπερ καὶ ῥάμνου καὶ παλιούρου καὶ οἴσου [καὶ
οἴτου] καὶ ῥοῦ καὶ κιττοῦ καὶ βάτου καὶ ἑτέρων
πολλῶν.

---

¹ Lit. grape-stone.
² I omit ἡ before διαφορά with Sch.

268

of leaf and bark is a dull green, the shape of the leaf is like that of the lime; it is soft and broad, and in size it also corresponds; the flower is like that of the medlar, and the tree blooms at the same time as that tree. The fruit, which they call a 'fig,' is red, and as large as an olive, but it is rounder and is like the medlar in taste; the roots are thick like those of the cultivated fig, and tough. The tree does not rot, and it has a solid heart, instead of ordinary heart-wood.

The 'vine' (currant grape) grows about the place called Phalakrai in the district of Ida; it is shrubby with small twigs; the branches are about a cubit long, and attached to them at the side are black berries, which are the size of a bean and sweet; inside they have a sort of soft stone[1]; the leaf is round undivided and small.

*Of the differences in various shrubs—buckthorn, withy, Christ's thorn, bramble, sumach, ivy, smilax, [spindle-tree].*

XVIII. Most other mountains too have certain peculiar products, whether trees shrubs or other woody plants. However we have several times remarked as to such peculiarities that they occur in all regions. Moreover the variation[2] between things of the same kind which we find in trees obtains also among shrubs and most other things, as has been said: for instance, we find it in buckthorn Christ's thorn withy[3] sumach ivy bramble and many others.

---

[3] [καὶ οἴτου] bracketed by W.; καὶ ἴσου Ald.; καὶ ἴσου καὶ οἴτου MVP; καὶ οἴσου καὶ οἴτου U. Only οἶσος is mentioned in the following descriptions.

2 Ῥάμνος τε γάρ ἐστιν ἡ μὲν μέλαινα ἡ δὲ λευκή, καὶ ὁ καρπὸς διάφορος, ἀκανθοφόροι δὲ ἄμφω.

Τοῦ τε οἴσου τὸ μὲν λευκὸν τὸ δὲ μέλαν· καὶ τὸ ἄνθος ἑκατέρου καὶ ὁ καρπὸς κατὰ λόγον ὁ μὲν λευκὸς ὁ δὲ μέλας· ἔνιοι δὲ καὶ ὥσπερ ἀνὰ μέσον, ὧν καὶ τὸ ἄνθος ἐπιπορφυρίζει καὶ οὔτε οἰνωπὸν οὔτε ἔκλευκόν ἐστιν ὥσπερ τῶν ἑτέρων. ἔχει δὲ καὶ τὰ φύλλα λεπτότερα καὶ λειότερα καὶ τὰς ῥάβδους τὸ λευκόν.

3 Ὅ τε παλίουρος ἔχει διαφορὰς . . . ἅπαντα δὲ ταῦτα καρποφόρα. καὶ ὅ γε παλίουρος ἐν λοβῷ τινι τὸν καρπὸν ἔχει καθαπερεὶ φύλλῳ, ἐν ᾧ τρία ἢ τέτταρα γίνεται. χρῶνται δ' αὐτῷ πρὸς τὰς βῆχας οἱ ἰατροὶ κόπτοντες· ἔχει γάρ τινα γλισχρότητα καὶ λίπος, ὥσπερ τὸ τοῦ λίνου σπέρμα. φύεται δὲ καὶ ἐπὶ τοῖς ἐφύδροις καὶ ἐν τοῖς ξηροῖς, ὥσπερ ὁ βάτος. [οὐχ ἧττον δέ ἐστι τὸ δένδρον πάρυδρον.] φυλλοβόλον δὲ καὶ οὐχ ὥσπερ ἡ ῥάμνος ἀείφυλλον.

4 Ἔτι δὲ καὶ τοῦ βάτου πλείω γένη, μεγίστην δὲ ἔχοντες διαφορὰν ὅτι ὁ μὲν ὀρθοφυὴς καὶ ὕψος ἔχων, ὁ δ' ἐπὶ τῆς γῆς καὶ εὐθὺς κάτω νεύων καὶ ὅταν συνάπτῃ τῇ γῇ ῥιζούμενος πάλιν, ὃν δὴ καλοῦσί τινες χαμαίβατον. τὸ δὲ κυνόσβατον τὸν καρπὸν ὑπέρυθρον ἔχει καὶ παραπλήσιον τῷ τῆς ῥόας· ἔστι δὲ θάμνου καὶ δένδρου μεταξὺ καὶ παρόμοιον ταῖς ῥόαις, τὸ δὲ φύλλον ἀκανθῶδες.

---

[1] cf. 1. 9. 4 ; 3. 18. 12 ; C.P. 1. 10. 7.

[2] Some words are missing, which described various forms of παλίουρος, alluded to in πάντα ταῦτα (Sch.). cf. 4. 3. 3, where an African παλίουρος is described.

[3] καθαπερεὶ φύλλῳ conj. W., cf. 3. 11. 2 ; καθάπερ τὸ φύλλον UMV.

[1] Thus of buckthorn there is the black and the white form, and there is difference in the fruit, though both bear thorns.

Of the withy there is a black and a white form; the flower and fruit of each respectively correspond in colour to the name; but some specimens are, as it were, intermediate, the flower being purplish, and neither wine-coloured nor whitish as in the others. The leaves in the white kind are also slenderer and smoother, as also are the branches.

There is variation also in the Christ's thorn . . .[2] all these forms are fruit-bearing. Christ's thorn has its fruit in a sort of pod, resembling a leaf,[3] which contains three or four seeds. Doctors bruise[4] them and use them against coughs; for they have a certain viscous and oily character, like linseed. The shrub grows in wet and dry places alike, like the bramble.[5] But it is deciduous, and not evergreen like buckthorn.

Of the bramble again there are several kinds, shewing very great variation; one is erect and tall, another runs along the ground and from the first bends downwards, and, when it touches the earth, it roots again; this some call the 'ground bramble.' The 'dog's bramble' (wild rose) has a reddish fruit, like that of the pomegranate[6]; and, like the pomegranate, it is intermediate between a shrub and a tree; but the leaf is spinous.[7]

[4] κόπτοντες: for the tense cf. 3. 17. 2, προβρέχοντας.

[5] οὐχ . . . πάρυδρον probably a gloss, W.

[6] ῥόαις UMV (?) Ald.; ῥυδαῖς conj. Sch. from Plin. 16. 180. Athen. (2. 82) cites the passage with ῥοραπ. τῇ ῥοιᾳ. The Schol. on Theocr. 5. 92 seems to have traces of both readings.

[7] ἀκανθῶδες conj. Sch. from Schol. on Theocr. (see last note), which quotes the passage with ἀκανθῶδες; ἀγνῶδες UAld.; so also Athen. l.c. Plin. (24. 121) seems to have read ἰχνῶδες (vestigio hominis simile).

5 Τῆς δὲ ῥοῦ τὸ μὲν ἄρρεν τὸ δὲ θῆλυ καλοῦσι
τῷ τὸ μὲν ἄκαρπον εἶναι τὸ δὲ κάρπιμον. οὐκ
ἔχει δὲ οὐδὲ τὰς ῥάβδους ὑψηλὰς οὐδὲ παχείας,
φύλλον δ' ὅμοιον πτελέᾳ πλὴν μικρὸν προμηκέστερον καὶ ἐπίδασυ. τῶν δὲ κλωνίων τῶν νέων
ἐξ ἴσου τὰ φύλλα εἰς δύο, κατ' ἄλληλα δὲ ἐκ τῶν
πλαγίων ὥστε στοιχεῖν.² βάπτουσι δὲ τούτῳ καὶ
οἱ σκυτοδέψαι τὰ δέρματα τὰ λευκά. ἄνθος
λευκὸν βοτρυῶδες,³ τῷ σχήματι δὲ τὸ ὁλοσχερὲς
ὄστλιγγας ἔχον ὥσπερ καὶ ὁ βότρυς· ἀπανθή-
σαντος δὲ ὁ καρπὸς ἅμα τῇ σταφύλῃ ἐρυθραίνεται,
καὶ γίνονται οἷον φακοὶ λεπτοὶ συγκείμενοι·
βοτρυῶδες δὲ τὸ σχῆμα καὶ τούτων. ἔχει δὲ τὸ
φαρμακῶδες τοῦτο ὃ καλεῖται ῥοῦς ἐν αὑτῷ
ὀστῶδες, ὃ καὶ τῆς ῥοῦ διῃττημένης ἔχει πολλάκις·
ῥίζα δ' ἐπιπόλαιος καὶ μονοφυὴς ὥστε ἀνα-
κάμπτεσθαι ῥᾳδίως ὁλόρριζα· τὸ δὲ ξύλον ἐντεριώνην ἔχει, εὔφθαρτον δὲ καὶ κοπτόμενον. ἐν
πᾶσι δὲ γίγνεται τοῖς τόποις, εὐθενεῖ δὲ μάλιστα
ἐν τοῖς ἀργιλώδεσι.

6 Πολυειδὴς δὲ ὁ κιττός· καὶ γὰρ ἐπίγειος, ὁ δὲ
εἰς ὕψος αἰρόμενος· καὶ τῶν ἐν ὕψει πλείω γένη.
τρία δ' οὖν φαίνεται τὰ μέγιστα ὅ τε λευκὸς καὶ
ὁ μέλας καὶ τρίτον ἡ ἕλιξ. εἴδη δὲ καὶ ἑκάστου
τούτων πλείω. λευκὸς γὰρ ὁ μὲν τῷ καρπῷ
μόνον, ὁ δὲ καὶ τοῖς φύλλοις ἐστί. πάλιν δὲ τῶν
λευκοκάρπων μόνον ὁ μὲν ἁδρὸν καὶ πυκνὸν καὶ
συνεστηκότα τὸν καρπὸν ἔχει καθαπερεὶ σφαῖραν,

---

¹ Plin. 13. 55; 24. 91.
² στοιχεῖν: cf. 3. 5. 3; Plin. 13. 55.
³ βοτρυῶδες conj. W.; βοτρυηδόν U; βοτρυδόν Ald.
⁴ ὁ ῥοῦς masc. cf. Diosc. 1. 108.

[1] Of the sumach they recognise a 'male' and a 'female' form, the former being barren, the latter fruit-bearing. The branches are not lofty nor stout, the leaf is like that of the elm, but small more oblong and hairy. On the young shoots the leaves grow in pairs at equal distances apart, corresponding to each other on the two sides, so that they are in regular rows.[2] Tanners use this tree for dyeing white leather. The flower is white and grows in clusters; the general form of it, with branchlets, is like that of the grape-bunch; when the flowering is over, the fruit reddens like the grape, and the appearance of it is like small lentils set close together; the form of these too is clustering.[3] The fruit contains the drug called by the same name,[4] which is a bony substance; it is often still found even when the fruit has been put through a sieve. The root is shallow and single, so that these trees are easily bent right over,[5] root and all. The wood has heart-wood, and it readily perishes and gets worm-eaten.[6] The tree occurs in all regions, but flourishes most in clayey soils.

[7] The ivy also has many forms; one kind grows on the ground, another grows tall, and of the tall-growing ivies there are several kinds. However the three most important seem to be the white the black and the *helix*. And of each of these there are several forms. Of the 'white' one is white only in its fruit, another in its leaves also. Again to take only white-fruited sorts, one of these has its fruit well formed close and compact like a ball; and this

[5] *i.e.* nearly uprooted by wind.
[6] κοπτόμενον : *cf.* 8. 11. 2, 3 and 5.
[7] Plin. 16. 144-147.

ὃν δὴ καλοῦσί τινες κορυμβίαν, οἱ δ᾽ Ἀθήνησιν
Ἀχαρνικόν. ὁ δὲ ἐλάττων διακεχυμένος ὥσπερ
καὶ ὁ μέλας· ἔχει δὲ καὶ ὁ μέλας διαφορὰς ἀλλ᾽
οὐχ ὁμοίως φανεράς.

7 Ἡ δὲ ἕλιξ ἐν μεγίσταις διαφοραῖς· καὶ γὰρ
τοῖς φύλλοις πλεῖστον διαφέρει τῇ τε μικρότητι
καὶ τῷ γωνοειδῆ καὶ εὐρυθμότερα εἶναι· τὰ δὲ τοῦ
κιττοῦ περιφερέστερα καὶ ἁπλᾶ· καὶ τῷ μήκει
τῶν κλημάτων καὶ ἔτι τῷ ἄκαρπος εἶναι. διατείνονται γάρ τινες τῷ μὴ ἀποκιττοῦσθαι τῇ
φύσει τὴν ἕλικα ἀλλὰ τὴν ἐκ τοῦ κιττοῦ τελειου-
μένην. (εἰ δὲ πᾶσα ἀποκιττοῦται, καθάπερ τινές
φασιν, ἡλικίας ἂν εἴη καὶ διαθέσεως οὐκ εἴδους
διαφορά, καθάπερ καὶ τῆς ἀπίου πρὸς τὴν
ἀχράδα.) πλὴν τό γε φύλλον καὶ ταύτης πολὺ
διαφέρει πρὸς τὸν κιττόν. σπάνιον δὲ τοῦτο καὶ
ἐν ὀλίγοις ἐστὶν ὥστε παλαιούμενον μεταβάλλειν,
8 ὥσπερ ἐπὶ τῆς λεύκης καὶ τοῦ κρότωνος. εἴδη
δ᾽ ἐστὶ πλείω τῆς ἕλικος, ὡς μὲν τὰ προφανέ-
στατα καὶ μέγιστα λαβεῖν τρία, ἥ τε χλοερὰ καὶ
ποιώδης ἥπερ καὶ πλείστη, καὶ ἑτέρα ἡ λευκή, καὶ
τρίτη ἡ ποικίλη, ἣν δὴ καλοῦσί τινες Θρᾳκίαν.

---

¹ cf. Theocr. 11. 46.     ² Plin. 16. 145 foll.
³ i.e. is the most ' distinct ' of the ivies.
⁴ cf. 1. 10. 1 ; Diosc. 2. 179.
⁵ i.e. as an explanation of the barrenness of *helix*.
⁶ i.e. and so becomes fertile.
⁷ διατείνονται: cf. *C.P.* 4. 6. 1.  διατ. τῷ . . . apparently
= "insist on the view that," . . . but the dative is strange.
The sentence, which is highly elliptical, is freely emended by
most editors.

kind some call *korymbias*, but the Athenians call it the
'Acharnian' ivy. Another kind is smaller and loose
in growth like the black ivy.[1] There are also variations in the black kind, but they are not so well
marked.

[2] The *helix* presents the greatest differences[3]; the
principal difference is in the leaves,[4] which are small
angular and of more graceful proportions, while
those of the ivy proper are rounder and simple;
there is also difference in the length of the twigs,
and further in the fact that this tree is barren. For,[5]
as to the view that the *helix* by natural development
turns into the ivy,[6] some insist[7] that this is not so,
the only true ivy according to these being that which
was ivy from the first[8]; (whereas if, as some say, the
*helix* invariably[9] turns into ivy, the difference would
be merely one of age and condition, and not of kind,
like the difference between the cultivated and the
wild pear). However the leaf even of the full-
grown *helix* is very different from that of the ivy,
and it happens but rarely and in a few specimens
that in this plant a change in the leaf occurs as it
grows older, as it does in the abele and the castor-oil
plant.[10] [11] There are several forms of the *helix*, of
which the three most conspicuous and important are
the green 'herbaceous' kind (which is the commonest), the white, and the variegated, which some call
the 'Thracian' *helix*. Each of these appears to

[8] *i.e.* and *helix* being a distinct plant which is always
barren.
[9] πᾶσα conj. Sch.; πᾶς Ald.
[10] Sc. as well as in *ivy*; *cf.* 1. 10. 1, where this change is
said to be characteristic of these three trees. (The rendering
attempted of this obscure section is mainly from W.'s note.)
[11] Plin. 16. 148 foll.

THEOPHRASTUS

ἑκάστη δὲ τούτων δοκεῖ διαφέρειν· καὶ γὰρ τῆς
χλοώδους ἡ μὲν λεπτοτέρα καὶ ταξιφυλλοτέρα
καὶ ἔτι πυκνοφυλλοτέρα, ἡ δ' ἧττον πάντα ταῦτ'
ἔχουσα. καὶ τῆς ποικίλης ἡ μὲν μεῖζον ἡ δ'
ἔλαττον τὸ φύλλον, καὶ τὴν ποικιλίαν διαφέρουσα. ὡσαύτως δὲ καὶ τὰ τῆς λευκῆς τῷ
μεγέθει καὶ τῇ χροιᾷ διαφέρουσιν. εὐαυξεστάτη
δὲ ἡ ποιώδης καὶ ἐπὶ πλεῖστον προϊοῦσα. φανερὰν
δ' εἶναί φασιν τὴν ἀποκιττουμένην οὐ μόνον τοῖς
φύλλοις ὅτι μείζω καὶ πλατύτερα ἔχει ἀλλὰ
καὶ τοῖς βλαστοῖς· εὐθὺς γὰρ ὀρθοὺς ἔχει, καὶ
οὐχ ὥσπερ ἡ ἑτέρα κατακεκαμμένη, καὶ διὰ τὴν
λεπτότητα καὶ διὰ τὸ μῆκος· τῆς δὲ κιττώδους
καὶ βραχύτεροι καὶ παχύτεροι. καὶ ὁ κιττὸς
ὅταν ἄρχηται σπερμοῦσθαι μετέωρον ἔχει καὶ
ὀρθὸν τὸν βλαστόν.

9 Πολύρριζος μὲν οὖν ἅπας κιττὸς καὶ πυκνόρρι-
ζος συνεστραμμένος ταῖς ῥίζαις καὶ ξυλώδεσι καὶ
παχείαις καὶ οὐκ ἄγαν βαθύρριζος, μάλιστα δ' ὁ
μέλας, καὶ τοῦ λευκοῦ ὁ τραχύτατος καὶ ἀγριώ-
τατος· δι' ὃ καὶ χαλεπὸς παραφύεσθαι πᾶσι τοῖς
δένδροις· ἀπόλλυσι γὰρ πάντα καὶ ἀφαναίνει
παραιρούμενος τὴν τροφήν. λαμβάνει δὲ μάλιστα
πάχος οὗτος καὶ ἀποδενδροῦται καὶ γίνεται αὐτὸ
καθ' αὑτὸ κιττοῦ δένδρον. ὡς δ' ἐπὶ τὸ πλεῖον
εἶναι πρὸς ἑτέρῳ φιλεῖ καὶ ζητεῖ καὶ ὥσπερ
10 ἐπαλλόκαυλόν ἐστιν. ἔχει δ' εὐθὺς καὶ τῆς

1 ταξιφυλλοτέρα conj. W. from Plin. 16. 149, folia in ordinem digesta ; μακροφυλλοτέρα MSS. cf. 1. 10. 8.
2 κατακεκαμμένη conj. W.; κατακεκαυμένη UAld.; κατακεκαμμένους conj. Sch.
3 κιττώδους MSS.; ποιώδους conj. St. 4 cf. C.P. 1. 16. 4.

276

present variations; of the green one form is slenderer
and has more regular[1] and also closer leaves, the
other has all these characteristics in a less degree.
Of the variegated kind again one sort has a larger,
one a smaller leaf, and the variegation is variable.
In like manner the various forms of the white *helix*
differ in size and colour. The 'herbaceous' kind is
the most vigorous and covers most space. They say
that the form which is supposed to turn into ivy is
clearly marked not only by its leaves, because they
are larger and broader, but also by its shoots; for
these are straight from the first, and this form does
not bend over[2] like the other; also because the
shoots are slenderer and larger, while those of the
ivy-like[3] form are shorter and stouter. [4] The ivy
too, when it begins to seed, has its shoots upward-
growing and erect.

All ivies have numerous close roots, which are
tangled together woody and stout, and do not run
very deep; but this is specially true of the black
kind and of the roughest and wildest forms of the
white. Wherefore it is mischievous to plant this
against any tree; for it destroys and starves any
tree by withdrawing the moisture. This form also
more than the others grows stout and becomes tree-
like, and in fact becomes itself an independent ivy
tree, though in general it likes and seeks to be[5]
against another tree, and is, as it were, parasitic.[6]
[7] Moreover from the first it has also this natural

[1] εἶναι conj. W.; αἰεὶ UM; ἀεὶ Ald.
[6] *i.e.* depends on another tree; not, of course, in the
strict botanical sense. *cf.* 3. 18. 11. ἐπαλλόκαυλον conj.
Scal.; ἐπαυλόκαλον MVAld.U (with υ corrected). *cf.* περι-
αλλόκαυλος. 7. 8. 1: *C.P.* 2. 18. 2.
[7] Plin. 16. 152.

φύσεώς τι τοιοῦτον· ἐκ γὰρ τῶν βλαστῶν ἀφίησιν ἀεὶ ῥίζας ἀνὰ μέσον τῶν φύλλων, αἴσπερ ἐνδύεται τοῖς δένδροις καὶ τοῖς τειχίοις οἷον ἐξεπίτηδες πεποιημέναις ὑπὸ τῆς φύσεως· δι᾽ ὃ καὶ ἐξαιρούμενος τὴν ὑγρότητα καὶ ἕλκων ἀφαναίνει, καὶ ἐὰν ἀποκοπῇ κάτωθεν δύναται διαμένειν καὶ ζῆν. ἔχει δὲ καὶ ἑτέραν διαφορὰν κατὰ τὸν καρπὸν οὐ μικράν· ὁ μὲν γὰρ ἐπίγλυκύς ἐστιν ὁ δὲ σφόδρα πικρὸς καὶ τοῦ λευκοῦ καὶ τοῦ μέλανος· σημεῖον δ᾽ ὅτι τὸν μὲν ἐσθίουσιν οἱ ὄρνιθες τὸν δ᾽ οὔ. τὰ μὲν οὖν περὶ τὸν κιττὸν οὕτως ἔχει.

11   Ἡ δὲ σμῖλαξ¹ ἐστι μὲν ἐπαλλόκαυλον,² ὁ δὲ καυλὸς³ ἀκανθώδης καὶ ὥσπερ ὀρθάκανθος, τὸ δὲ φύλλον κιττῶδες μικρὸν ἀγώνιον, κατὰ τὴν μίσχου πρόσφυσιν τυληρόν.⁴ ἴδιον δ᾽ ὅτι τήν τε διὰ μέσου ταύτην⁵ ὥσπερ ῥάχιν λεπτὴν ἔχει καὶ τὰς στημονίους διαλήψεις οὐκ ἀπὸ ταύτης, ὥσπερ τὰ τῶν ἄλλων, ἀλλὰ περὶ αὐτὴν περιφερεῖς ἠγμένας ἀπὸ τῆς προσφύσεως τοῦ μίσχου τῷ φύλλῳ. παρὰ δὲ τοῦ καυλοῦ τὰ γόνατα καὶ παρὰ τὰς διαλείψεις τὰς φυλλικὰς ἐκ τῶν αὐτῶν μίσχων τοῖς φύλλοις παραπέφυκεν ἴουλος λεπτὸς καὶ ἑλικτός· ἄνθος δὲ λευκὸν καὶ εὐῶδες λείρινον·

---

¹ σμῖλαξ : ? μῖλαξ W.  cf. 1. 10. 5; Plin. 16. 153-155.
² ἐπαλλόκαυλον conj. Sch.; ἐπαυλόκαυλον V.  cf. 3. 18. 10.
³ καυλὸς conj. R. Const.; καρπὸς UMVAld.
⁴ τυληρόν conj. W.; νοτηρόν Ald.U (corrected).
⁵ ταύτην: cf. τὸ θυλακῶδες τοῦτο, 3. 7. 3.  Is the pronoun

characteristic, that it regularly puts forth roots from the shoots between the leaves, by means of which it gets a hold of trees and walls, as if these roots were made by nature on purpose. Wherefore also by withdrawing and drinking up the moisture it starves its host, while, if it is cut off below, it is able to survive and live. There are also other not inconsiderable differences in the fruit; both in the white and in the black kind it is in some cases rather sweet, in others extremely bitter; in proof whereof birds eat one but not the other. Such are the facts about ivy.

The smilax[1] is parasitic,[2] but its stem[3] is thorny and has, as it were, straight thorns; the leaf is ivy-like small and without angles, and makes a callus[4] at the junction with the stalk. A peculiarity of it is its conspicuous[5] slender midrib, so to call it, which divides it in two; also the fact that the thread-like branchings[6] do not start from this, as in other leaves, but are carried in circles round it, starting from the junction of the leaflet with the leaf. And at the joints of the stem[7] and the spaces between the leaves there grows from the same stalk as the leaves a fine spiral tendril.[8] The flower is white and fragrant like a lily.[9] The fruit

deictic, referring to an actual specimen shewn in lecture? cf. also 4. 7. 1.

[6] διαλήψεις Ald.; διαλείψεις UMV. A mistake probably due to διαλείψεις below, where it is right. διάληψις is the Aristotelian word for a 'division.'

[7] τοῦ καυλοῦ τὰ γόνατα conj. Sch.; τὸν καυλὸν τὸν ἄτονον Ald.

[8] This must be the meaning of ἴουλος here, qualified by ἑλικτός; but elsewhere it = catkin. cf. 3. 5. 5.

[9] λείρινον conj. R. Const. from Plin. l.c. olente lilium; ἡρινόν UAld.

THEOPHRASTUS

τὸν δὲ καρπὸν ἔχει προσεμφερῆ τῷ στρύχνῳ καὶ
τῷ μηλώθρῳ καὶ μάλιστα τῇ καλουμένῃ σταφυλῇ
12 ἀγρίᾳ· κατακρέμαστοι δ' οἱ βότρυες κιττοῦ τρό-
πον· παρεγγίζει δ' ὁ παραθριγκισμὸς πρὸς τὴν
σταφυλήν· ἀπὸ γὰρ ἑνὸς σημείου οἱ μίσχοι οἱ
ῥαγικοί. ὁ δὲ καρπὸς ἐρυθρός, ἔχων πυρῆνας τὸ
μὲν ἐπὶ πᾶν δύο, ἐν τοῖς μείζοσι τρεῖς ἐν δὲ τοῖς
μικροῖς ἕνα· σκληρὸς δ' ὁ πυρὴν εὖ μάλα καὶ τῷ
χρώματι μέλας ἔξωθεν. ἴδιον δὲ τὸ τῶν βοτρύων,
ὅτι ἐκ πλαγίων τε τὸν καυλὸν παραθριγκίζουσιν,
καὶ κατ' ἄκρον ὁ μέγιστος βότρυς τοῦ καυλοῦ,
ὥσπερ ἐπὶ τῆς ῥάμνου καὶ τοῦ βάτου. τοῦτο δὲ
δῆλον ὡς καὶ ἀκρόκαρπον καὶ πλαγιόκαρπον.
13 [Τὸ δ' εὐώνυμος καλούμενον δένδρον φύεται μὲν
ἄλλοθί τε καὶ τῆς Λέσβου ἐν τῷ ὄρει τῷ Ὀρδύν-
νῳ καλουμένῳ· ἔστι δὲ ἡλίκον ῥόα καὶ τὸ φύλλον
ἔχει ῥοῶδες, μεῖζον δὲ ἡ χαμαιδάφνης, καὶ μαλακὸν δὲ ὥσπερ ἡ ῥόα. ἡ δὲ βλάστησις ἄρχεται
μὲν αὐτῷ περὶ τὸν Ποσειδεῶνα· ἀνθεῖ δὲ τοῦ
ἦρος· τὸ δὲ ἄνθος ὅμοιον τὴν χρόαν τῷ λευκῷ
ἴῳ· ὄζει δὲ δεινὸν ὥσπερ φόνου. ὁ δὲ καρπὸς
ἐμφερὴς τὴν μορφὴν μετὰ τοῦ κελύφους τῷ τοῦ
σησάμου λοβῷ· ἔνδοθεν δὲ στερεὸν πλὴν διῃρη-
μένον κατὰ τὴν τετραστοιχίαν. τοῦτο ἐσθιό-

¹ Presumably σ. ὁ ἐδώδιμος. See Index.
² παρεγγίζει δ' ὁ παραθριγκισμὸς I conj., cf. παραθριγκίζουσι
below ; παρωγγίζει δὲ παραθριvακίζει δὲ ὡς U; παραγγίζει δὲ
παραθρηνακίζει δὲ ὡς MV; παραθριγκίζει δὲ ὡς conj. W.
280

is like the *strykhnos*[1] and the *melothron* (bryony),
and most of all like the berry which is called the
' wild grape' (bryony). The clusters hang down as
in the ivy, but the regular setting[2] of the berries
resembles the grape-cluster more closely; for the
stalks which bear the berries start from a single
point. The fruit is red, having generally two stones,
the larger ones three and the smaller one; the
stone is very hard and in colour black outside. A
peculiarity of the clusters is that they make a row[3]
along the sides of the stalk, and the longest cluster
is at the end of the stalk, as in the buckthorn and
the bramble. It is clear that the fruit is produced
both at the end and at the sides.

[4] The tree called the spindle-tree[5] grows, among
other places, in Lesbos, on the mountain called
Ordynnos.[6] It is as large as the pomegranate and
has a leaf like that of that tree, but larger than that
of the periwinkle,[7] and soft, like the pomegranate
leaf. It begins to shoot about the month Poseideon,[8]
and flowers in the spring; the flower in colour is
like the gilliflower, but it has a horrible smell, like
shed blood.[9] The fruit, with its case, is like the
pod of sesame[10]; inside it is hard, but it splits easily
according to its four divisions. This tree, if eaten

---

[3] παραθριγκίζουσιν conj. Sch.; παραθρυγκίζουσαν U (corrected); παραθρυγγίζουσι M.
[4] This section down to the word ἀνόχῳ is clearly out of place: εὐώνυμος was not one of the plants proposed for discussion 3. 18. 1. It should come somewhere among the descriptions of trees characteristic of special localities.
[5] Plin. 13. 118.    [6] cf. Plin. 5. 140.
[7] This irrelevant comparison probably indicates confusion in the text, as is shewn also by Pletho's excerpt of part of this section: see Sch.
[8] January.    [9] φόνον: cf. 6. 4. 6.    [10] cf. 8. 5. 2.

μενον ὑπὸ τῶν προβάτων ἀποκτιννύει, καὶ τὸ
φύλλον καὶ ὁ καρπός, καὶ μάλιστα τὰς αἶγας
ἐὰν μὴ καθάρσεως τύχῃ. καθαίρεται δὲ ἀνόχῳ.] περὶ μὲν οὖν δένδρων καὶ θάμνων
εἴρηται· ἐν δὲ τοῖς ἑξῆς περὶ τῶν λειπομένων
λεκτέον.

by sheep, is fatal[1] to them, both the leaf and the fruit, and it is especially fatal to goats unless they are purged by it; and the purging is effected by diarrhoea.[2]     So we have spoken of trees and shrubs ; in what follows we must speak of the plants which remain.

[1] In Pletho's excerpt (see above) this is said of periwinkle.
[2] *i.e.* and not by vomiting.

BOOK IV

Δ

I. Αἱ μὲν οὖν διαφοραὶ τῶν ὁμογενῶν τεθεώρηνται πρότερον. ἅπαντα δ' ἐν τοῖς οἰκείοις τόποις καλλίω γίνεται καὶ μᾶλλον εὐσθενεῖ· καὶ γὰρ τοῖς ἀγρίοις εἰσὶν ἑκάστοις οἰκεῖοι, καθάπερ τοῖς ἡμέροις· τὰ μὲν γὰρ φιλεῖ τοὺς ἐφύδρους καὶ ἑλώδεις, οἷον αἴγειρος λεύκη ἰτέα καὶ ὅλως τὰ παρὰ τοὺς ποταμοὺς φυόμενα, τὰ δὲ τοὺς εὐσκεπεῖς καὶ εὐηλίους, τὰ δὲ μᾶλλον τοὺς παλισκίους. πεύκη μὲν γὰρ ἐν τοῖς προσείλοις καλλίστη καὶ μεγίστη, ἐν δὲ τοῖς παλισκίοις ὅλως οὐ φύεται· ἐλάτη δὲ ἀνάπαλιν ἐν τοῖς παλισκίοις καλλίστη τοῖς δ' εὐείλοις οὐχ ὁμοίως.

2    Ἐν Ἀρκαδίᾳ γοῦν περὶ τὴν Κράνην καλουμένην τόπος ἐστί τις κοῖλος καὶ ἄπνους, εἰς ὃν οὐδέποθ' ὅλως ἥλιον ἐμβάλλειν φασίν· ἐν τούτῳ δὲ πολὺ διαφέρουσιν αἱ ἐλάται καὶ τῷ μήκει καὶ τῷ πάχει, οὐ μὴν ὁμοίως γε πυκναὶ οὐδ' ὡραῖαι ἀλλ' ἥκιστα, καθάπερ καὶ αἱ πεῦκαι αἱ ἐν τοῖς παλισκίοις· δι' ὃ καὶ πρὸς τὰ πολυτελῆ τῶν ἔργων, οἷον θυρώματα καὶ εἴ τι ἄλλο σπουδαῖον, οὐ χρῶνται τούτοις ἀλλὰ πρὸς τὰς ναυπηγίας μᾶλλον καὶ τὰς οἰκοδομάς· καὶ γὰρ δοκοὶ κάλλι-

286

# BOOK IV

*Of the importance of position and climate.*

1. The differences between trees of the same kind
have already been considered. Now all grow fairer
and are more vigorous in their proper positions ; for
wild, no less than cultivated trees, have each their
own positions : some love wet and marshy ground, as
black poplar abele willow, and in general those that
grow by rivers ; some love exposed[1] and sunny
positions ; some prefer a shady place. The fir is
fairest and tallest in a sunny position, and does not
grow at all in a shady one ; the silver-fir on the
contrary is fairest in a shady place, and not so
vigorous in a sunny one.

Thus there is in Arcadia near the place called
Krane a low-lying district sheltered from wind, into
which they say that the sun never strikes ; and in
this district the silver-firs excel greatly in height and
stoutness, though they have not such close grain
nor such comely wood, but quite the reverse,—like
the fir when it grows in a shady place. Wherefore men do not use these for expensive work, such
as doors or other choice articles, but rather for
ship-building and house-building. For excellent

[1] εὐσκεπεῖς should mean 'sheltered,' but cannot in this
context, nor in *C.P.* 1. 13. 11 and 12 : the word seems to
have been confused with εὔσκοπος.

287

σται καὶ τανεῖαι καὶ κέραιαι αἱ ἐκ τούτων, ἔτι δ᾽
ἱστοὶ τῷ μήκει διαφέροντες ἀλλ᾽ οὐχ ὁμοίως
ἰσχυροί· καὶ ἐκ τῶν προσείλων ἅμα τῇ βραχύτητι
πυκνότεροί τε ἐκείνων καὶ ἰσχυρότεροι γίνονται.
3 Χαίρει δὲ σφόδρα καὶ ἡ μῖλος τοῖς παλισκίοις
καὶ ἡ πάδος καὶ ἡ θραύπαλος. περὶ δὲ τὰς
κορυφὰς τῶν ὀρέων καὶ τοὺς ψυχροὺς τόπους θυία
μὲν φύεται καὶ εἰς ὕψος, ἐλάτη δὲ καὶ ἄρκευθος
φύεται μὲν οὐκ εἰς ὕψος δέ, καθάπερ καὶ περὶ τὴν
ἄκραν Κυλλήνην· φύεται δὲ καὶ ἡ κήλαστρος
ἐπὶ τῶν ἄκρων καὶ χειμεριωτάτων. ταῦτα μὲν
οὖν ἄν τις θείη φιλόψυχρα· τὰ δ᾽ ἄλλα πάντα
ὡς εἰπεῖν [οὐ] μᾶλλον χαίρει τοῖς προσείλοις.
οὐ μὴν ἀλλὰ καὶ τοῦτο συμβαίνει κατὰ τὴν
χώραν τὴν οἰκείαν ἑκάστῳ τῶν δένδρων. ἐν
Κρήτῃ γοῦν φασιν ἐν τοῖς Ἰδαίοις ὄρεσι καὶ ἐν τοῖς
Λευκοῖς καλουμένοις ἐπὶ τῶν ἄκρων ὅθεν οὐδέποτ᾽
ἐπιλείπει χιὼν κυπάριττον εἶναι· πλείστη γὰρ
αὕτη τῆς ὕλης καὶ ὅλως ἐν τῇ νήσῳ καὶ ἐν τοῖς
ὄρεσιν.
4 Ἔστι δέ, ὥσπερ καὶ πρότερον εἴρηται, καὶ τῶν
ἀγρίων καὶ τῶν ἡμέρων τὰ μὲν ὀρεινὰ τὰ δὲ
πεδεινὰ μᾶλλον. ἀναλογία δὲ καὶ ἐν αὐτοῖς τοῖς
ὄρεσι τὰ μὲν ἐν τοῖς ὑποκάτω τὰ δὲ περὶ τὰς
κορυφάς, ὥστε καὶ καλλίω γίνεται καὶ εὐσθενῆ.
πανταχοῦ δὲ καὶ πάσης τῆς ὕλης πρὸς βορρᾶν
τὰ ξύλα πυκνότερα καὶ οὐλότερα καὶ ἁπλῶς
καλλίω· καὶ ὅλως δὲ πλείω ἐν τοῖς προσβορείοις
φύεται. αὐξάνεται δὲ καὶ ἐπιδίδωσι τὰ πυκνὰ

---

[1] I omit αἱ before κέραιαι with P.
[2] ἅμα I conj. ; ἀλλὰ Ald.; om. W. after Sch.; ἀλλ᾽ ἅμα
conj. St.

rafters beams and yard-arms[1] are made from these, and also masts of great length which are not however equally strong ; while masts made of trees grown in a sunny place are necessarily[2] short but of closer grain and stronger than the others.

Yew *pados* and joint-fir rejoice exceedingly in shade. On mountain tops and in cold positions odorous cedar grows even to a height, while silver-fir and Phoenician cedar grow, but not to a height,—for instance on the top of Mount Cyllene ; and holly also grows in high and very wintry positions. These trees then we may reckon as cold-loving : all others, one may say in general, prefer a sunny position. However this too depends partly on the soil appropriate to each tree ; thus they say that in Crete on the mountains of Ida and on those called the White Mountains the cypress is found on the peaks whence the snow never disappears ; for this is the principal tree both in the island generally and in the mountains.

Again, as has been said[3] already, both of wild and of cultivated trees some belong more to the mountains, some to the plains. And on the mountains themselves in proportion to the height some grow fairer[4] and more vigorous in the lower regions, some about the peaks. However it is true of all trees anywhere that with a north aspect the wood is closer and more compact[5] and better generally ; and, generally speaking, more trees grow in positions facing the north. Again trees which are close

[2] 3. 2 4.
[4] Something seems to have dropped out before ὥστε.
[5] οὐλότερα conj. W. from mutilated word in U ; καλλιώτερα MV ; καλλίω Ald.

## THEOPHRASTUS

μὲν ὄντα μᾶλλον εἰς μῆκος, δι' ὃ καὶ ἄνοζα καὶ
εὐθέα καὶ ὀρθοφυῆ γίνεται, καὶ κωπεῶνες ἐκ
τούτων κάλλιστοι· <τὰ δὲ μανὰ> μᾶλλον εἰς
βάθος καὶ πάχος, δι' ὃ καὶ σκολιώτερα καὶ
ὀζωδέστερα καὶ τὸ ὅλον στερεώτερα καὶ πυκνότερα
φύεται.

5 Σχεδὸν δὲ τὰς αὐτὰς ἔχει διαφορὰς τούτοις
καὶ ἐν τοῖς παλισκίοις καὶ ἐν τοῖς εὐείλοις καὶ ἐν
τοῖς ἀπνόοις καὶ εὐπνόοις· ὀζωδέστερα γὰρ καὶ
βραχύτερα καὶ ἧττον εὐθέα τὰ ἐν τοῖς εὐείλοις
ἢ τοῖς προσηνέμοις. ὅτι δὲ ἕκαστον ζητεῖ καὶ
χώραν οἰκείαν καὶ κρᾶσιν ἀέρος φανερὸν τῷ τὰ
μὲν φέρειν ἐνίους τόπους τὰ δὲ μὴ φέρειν μήτε
αὐτὰ γιγνόμενα μήτε φυτευόμενα ῥᾳδίως, ἐὰν δὲ
καὶ ἀντιλάβηται μὴ καρποφορεῖν, ὥσπερ ἐπὶ τοῦ
φοίνικος ἐλέχθη καὶ τῆς Αἰγυπτίας συκαμίνου
καὶ ἄλλων· εἰσὶ γὰρ πλείω καὶ ἐν πλείοσι χώραις
τὰ μὲν ὅλως οὐ φυόμενα τὰ δὲ φυόμενα μὲν
ἀναυξῆ δὲ καὶ ἄκαρπα καὶ τὸ ὅλον φαῦλα. περὶ
ὧν ἴσως λεκτέον ἐφ' ὅσον ἔχομεν ἱστορίας.

II. Ἐν Αἰγύπτῳ γάρ ἐστιν ἴδια δένδρα πλείω,
ἥ τε συκάμινος καὶ ἡ περσέα καλουμένη καὶ ἡ
βάλανος καὶ ἡ ἄκανθα καὶ ἕτερ' ἄττα.

Ἔστι δὲ ἡ μὲν συκάμινος παραπλησία πως τῇ
ἐνταῦθα συκαμίνῳ· καὶ γὰρ τὸ φύλλον παρόμοιον

---

¹ κωπεῶνες : cf. 5. 1. 7.  ² τὰ δὲ μανὰ add. W.
³ cf. 5. 1. 8.  ⁴ 2. 2. 10.
⁵ ὅλως . . . μὲν conj. W.; ὅλως οὐ φυτευόμενα U ; ὅλως φυτευόμενα MVPAld.

together grow and increase more in height, and so become unbranched straight and erect, and the best oar-spars[1] are made from these, while those that grow far apart[2] are of greater bulk and denser habit[3]; wherefore they grow less straight and with more branches, and in general have harder wood and a closer grain.

Such trees exhibit nearly the same differences, whether the position be shady or sunny, windless or windy; for trees growing in a sunny or windy position are more branched shorter and less straight. Further that each tree seeks an appropriate position and climate is plain from the fact that some districts bear some trees but not others; (the latter do not grow there of their own accord. nor can they easily be made to grow), and that, even if they obtain a hold, they do not bear fruit—as was said[4] of the date-palm the sycamore and others; for there are many trees which in many places either do not grow at all, or,[5] if they do, do not thrive nor bear fruit, but are in general of inferior quality. And perhaps we should discuss this matter, so far as our enquiries go.

*Of the trees special to Egypt, and of the carob.*

II. [6] Thus in Egypt there are a number of trees which are peculiar[7] to that country, the sycamore the tree called *persea* the *balanos* the acacia and some others.

Now the sycamore to a certain extent resembles the tree which bears that name[8] in our country; its

[6] Plin. 13. 56 and 57.
[7] Bια conj. R. Const.; Eα Ald.
[8] i.e. mulberry. See Index.

THEOPHRASTUS

ἔχει καὶ τὸ μέγεθος καὶ τὴν ὅλην πρόσοψιν, τὸν
δὲ καρπὸν ἰδίως φέρει παρὰ τὰ ἄλλα, καθάπερ
ἐλέχθη καὶ ἐν τοῖς ἐξ ἀρχῆς· οὐ γὰρ ἀπὸ τῶν
βλαστῶν οὐδ᾽ ἀπὸ τῶν ἀκρεμόνων ἀλλ᾽ ἐκ τοῦ
στελέχους, μέγεθος μὲν ἡλίκον σῦκον καὶ τῇ ὄψει
δὲ παραπλήσιον, τῷ χυλῷ δὲ καὶ τῇ γλυκύτητι
τοῖς ὀλύνθοις, πλὴν γλυκύτερον πολὺ καὶ κεγχραμίδας ὅλως οὐκ ἔχοντα, πλήθει δὲ πολύν.
καὶ πέττειν οὐ δύναται μὴ ἐπικνισθέντα· ἀλλ᾽
ἔχοντες ὄνυχας σιδηροῦς ἐπικνίζουσιν· ἃ δ᾽ ἂν
ἐπικνισθῇ τεταρταῖα πέττεται· τούτων δ᾽ ἀφαιρεθέντων πάλιν ἄλλα φύεται καὶ ἄλλα καὶ ἐκ
τοῦ αὐτοῦ τόπου μηδὲν παραλλάττοντα· καὶ
τοῦθ᾽ οἱ μὲν τρὶς οἱ δὲ πλεονάκις φασὶ γίνεσθαι.
2 πολύοπον δὲ τὸ δένδρον σφόδρα ἐστὶ καὶ τὸ ξύλον
αὐτοῦ εἰς πολλὰ χρήσιμον. ἴδιον δὲ ἔχειν δοκεῖ
παρὰ τἆλλα· τμηθὲν γὰρ εὐθὺς χλωρόν ἐστι·
αἰαίνεται δὲ ἐμβύθιον· εἰς βόθρον δὲ ἐμβάλλουσι
καὶ εἰς τὰς λίμνας εὐθὺς καὶ ταριχεύουσι
βρεχόμενον δ᾽ ἐν τῷ βυθῷ ξηραίνεται· καὶ ὅταν
τελέως ξηρὸν γένηται, τότε ἀναφέρεται καὶ ἐπινεῖ
καὶ δοκεῖ τότε καλῶς τεταριχεῦσθαι· γίνεται γὰρ
κοῦφον καὶ μανόν. ἡ μὲν οὖν συκάμινος ἔχει
ταύτας τὰς ἰδιότητας.
3 Ἔοικε δέ τις παραπλησία ἡ φύσις εἶναι καὶ
τῆς ἐν Κρήτῃ καλουμένης Κυπρίας συκῆς· καὶ
γὰρ ἐκείνη φέρει τὸν καρπὸν ἐκ τοῦ στελέχους
καὶ ἐκ τῶν παχυτάτων ἀκρεμόνων, πλὴν ὅτι
βλαστόν τινα ἀφίησι μικρὸν ἄφυλλον ὥσπερ
ῥιζίον, πρὸς ᾧ γε ὁ καρπός. τὸ δὲ στέλεχος μέγα

[1] 1. 1. 7; cf. 1. 14 2.
[2] cf. C.P. 1. 17. 9; Diosc. 1. 127; Athen. 2. 36. This

292

leaf is similar, its size, and its general appearance;
but it bears its fruit in a quite peculiar manner, as
was said at the very outset[1]; it is borne not on the
shoots or branches, but on the stem; in size it is as
large as a fig, which it resembles also in appearance,
but in flavour and sweetness it is like the 'immature
figs,' except that it is much sweeter and contains
absolutely no seeds, and it is produced in large
numbers. It cannot ripen unless it is scraped; but
they scrape it with iron 'claws'[2]; the fruits thus
scraped ripen in four days. If these are removed,
others and others again grow from exactly the same
point, and this some say occurs three times over,
others say it can happen more times than that.
Again the tree is very full of sap, and its wood is
useful for many purposes. There is another peculiar
property which it appears to possess; when it is
cut, it is at first green, but it dries in deep water[3];
they put it at once in a hole or in pools and so season
it; and it becomes dry by being soaked in the deep
water, and when it is completely dry, it is fetched up
and floats and is then thought to be duly seasoned;
for it is now light and porous. Such are the
peculiarities of the sycamore.

Somewhat similar appears to be the character of
the tree which in Crete is called the 'Cyprian fig'[4]
(sycamore). For this also bears its fruit on the stem
and on the thickest branches; but in this case there
is a small leafless shoot, like a root, to which the
fruit is attached. The stem is large and like the

scraping was the prophet Amos' occupation: cf. Amos 7. 14.
comm.
[3] ἐμβύθιον conj. W.; εἰς βύθον UMVPAld. ? ἐν βύθῳ ὄν.
[4] See Index. cf. Athen. 3. 11; Plin. 13. 58; Diosc. 1. 127. 3.

καὶ παρόμοιον τῇ λεύκῃ, φύλλον δὲ τῇ πτελέᾳ.
πεπαίνει δὲ τέτταρας καρπούς, ὅσαιπερ αὐτοῦ καὶ
αἱ βλαστήσεις· οὐδένα δὲ πεπαίνει μὴ ἐπιτμη-
θέντος τοῦ ἐρινοῦ καὶ ἐκρυέντος τοῦ ὀποῦ. ἡ δὲ
γλυκύτης προσεμφερὴς τῷ σύκῳ καὶ τὰ ἔσωθεν
τοῖς ἐρινοῖς· μέγεθος ἡλίκον κοκκύμηλον.

4 (Ταύτῃ δὲ παραπλησία καὶ ἦν οἱ Ἴωνες κερωνίαν καλοῦσιν· ἐκ τοῦ στελέχους γὰρ καὶ αὕτη
φέρει τὸν πλεῖστον καρπόν, ἀπὸ δὲ τῶν ἀκρεμόνων,
ὥσπερ εἴπομεν, ὀλίγον. ὁ δὲ καρπὸς ἔλλοβος, ὃν
καλοῦσί τινες Αἰγύπτιον σῦκον διημαρτηκότες·
οὐ γίνεται γὰρ ὅλως περὶ Αἴγυπτον ἀλλ᾿ ἐν Συρίᾳ
καὶ ἐν Ἰωνίᾳ δὲ καὶ περὶ Κνίδον καὶ Ῥόδον.
ἀείφυλλον δὲ καὶ ἄνθος ἔκλευκον ἔχον καί τι
βαρύτητος, μὴ μετεωρίζον δὲ σφόδρα καὶ ὅλως
ἐκ τῶν κάτω παραβλαστητικὸν ἄνωθεν δὲ
ὑποξηραινόμενον. ἔχει δὲ ἅμα καὶ τὸν ἔνον καὶ
τὸν νέον καρπόν· ἀφαιρουμένου γὰρ θατέρου μετὰ
Κύνα καὶ ὁ ἕτερος εὐθὺς φανερὸς κυούμενος·
κύεται γὰρ ὥσπερ βότρυς ὁμοσχήμων· εἶτ᾿ αὐξη-
θεὶς ἀνθεῖ περὶ Ἀρκτοῦρον καὶ ἰσημερίαν· ἀπὸ
τούτου δὴ διαμένει τὸν χειμῶνα μέχρι Κυνός. ἡ
μὲν οὖν ὁμοιότης ὅτι στελεχόκαρπα καὶ ταῦτα·
διαφοραὶ δὲ αἱ εἰρημέναι πρὸς τὴν συκάμινον.)

5 Ἐν Αἰγύπτῳ δ᾿ ἐστὶν ἕτερον ἡ περσέα καλούμενον, τῇ μὲν προσόψει μέγα καὶ καλόν, παραπλήσιον δὲ μάλιστα τῇ ἀπίῳ καὶ φύλλοις καὶ
ἄνθεσι καὶ ἀκρεμόσι καὶ τῷ ὅλῳ σχήματι· πλὴν

---

¹ ὅσαιπερ conj. R. Const., etc., cf. Athen. l.c.; ὅσα ὑπὲρ
αὐτοῦ U (corrected); ὅσα ὑπὲρ αὐτὸν M; ὅσα ὑπὲρ αὐτοῦ Ald.
² Plin. 13. 59.   ³ 1. 14. 2.

abele, but the leaf is like that of the elm. It ripens
its fruit four times a year, having also [1] four periods
of growth; but it ripens no fruit unless the 'fig' is
split and the juice let out. The sweet taste resembles
that of the fig, and the inside of the fruit is like
that of wild figs: it is as large as a plum.

[2] (Like this too is the tree which the Ionians call
carob: for this too bears most of its fruit on the
stem, though it bears a little also on the branches, as
we said.[3] The fruit is in a pod; some call it the
'Egyptian fig'—erroneously; for it does not occur at
all in Egypt, but in Syria and Ionia and also in
Cnidos and Rhodes. It is evergreen and has a
whitish flower and is somewhat acrid; it does not
attain to a great height, and it sends out side-shoots
entirely from its lower parts, while it withers above.
It has on it at the same time both last year's fruit
and the new fruit; for if the one is removed after the
rising of the dog-star, immediately the other is seen
swelling up; for there swells [4] up as it were another
similar cluster. This then increases and flowers
about the rising of Arcturus and the equinox; and
thenceforward it [5] persists through the winter to the
rising of the dog-star. The likeness then consists in
the fact that these trees too bear fruit on their stems,
and the differences between them and the sycamore
are as has been said.)

[6] In Egypt there is another tree called the *persea*,
which in appearance is large and fair, and it most
resembles the pear in leaves flowers branches and
general form, but it is evergreen, while the other is

[4] κύεται conj. W. from G; κύει MSS.
[5] i.e. the cluster, now in the fruit stage.
[6] Plin. 13. 60 and 61.

τὸ μὲν ἀείφυλλον τὸ δὲ φυλλοβόλον. καρπὸν δὲ
φέρει πολὺν καὶ πᾶσαν ὥραν· περικαταλαμβάνει
γὰρ ὁ νέος ἀεὶ τὸν ἔνον· πέττει δὲ ὑπὸ τοὺς
ἐτησίας· τὸν δ' ἄλλον ὠμότερον ἀφαιροῦσι καὶ
ἀποτιθέασιν.[1] ἔστι δὲ τὸ μέγεθος ἡλίκον ἄπιος,
τῷ σχήματι δὲ πρόμακρος ἀμυγδαλώδης, χρῶμα
δὲ αὐτοῦ ποιῶδες. ἔχει δὲ ἐντὸς κάρυον, ὥσπερ
τὸ κοκκύμηλον, πλὴν ἔλαττον πολὺ καὶ μαλακώ-
τερον· τὴν δὲ σάρκα γλυκεῖαν σφόδρα καὶ ἡδεῖαν
καὶ εὔπεπτον· οὐδὲν γὰρ ἐνοχλεῖ πολὺ προσ-
ενεγκαμένων. εὔριζον δὲ τὸ δένδρον καὶ μήκει
καὶ πάχει καὶ πλήθει πολύ· ἔχει δὲ καὶ ξύλον
ἰσχυρὸν καὶ καλὸν τῇ ὄψει μέλαν, ὥσπερ ὁ λωτός,
ἐξ οὗ καὶ τὰ ἀγάλματα καὶ τὰ κλινία καὶ
τραπέζια καὶ τἆλλα τὰ τοιαῦτα ποιοῦσιν.

6  Ἡ δὲ βάλανος ἔχει μὲν τὴν προσηγορίαν ἀπὸ
τοῦ καρποῦ· φύλλον δ' αὐτῇ παραπλήσιον τῷ
τῆς μυρρίνης πλὴν προμηκέστερον. ἔστι δὲ τὸ
δένδρον εὐπαχὲς μὲν καὶ εὐμέγεθες, οὐκ εὐφυὲς
δὲ ἀλλὰ παρεστραμμένον. τοῦ καρποῦ δὲ τοῖς
κελύφεσι χρῶνται οἱ μυρεψοὶ κόπτοντες· εὐῶδες
γὰρ ἔχει τὸν δὲ καρπὸν αὐτὸν ἀχρεῖον. ἔστι δὲ
καὶ τῷ μεγέθει καὶ τῇ ὄψει παραπλήσιος τῷ τῆς
καππάριος· ξύλον δὲ ἰσχυρὸν καὶ εἰς ἄλλα τε
χρήσιμον καὶ εἰς τὰς ναυπηγίας.

7  Τὸ δὲ καλούμενον κουκιόφορόν ἐστιν ὅμοιον τῷ
φοίνικι· τὴν δὲ ὁμοιότητα κατὰ τὸ στέλεχος
ἔχει καὶ τὰ φύλλα· διαφέρει δὲ ὅτι ὁ μὲν φοῖνιξ
μονοφυὲς καὶ ἁπλοῦν ἐστι, τοῦτο δὲ προσαυξηθὲν
σχίζεται καὶ γίνεται δίκρουν, εἶτα πάλιν ἑκάτερον

---

[1] ἀποτιθέασιν conj. R. Const. from G (recondunt); τιθέασι
UMVAld.

296

deciduous. It bears abundant fruit and at every season, for the new fruit always overtakes that of last year. It ripens its fruit at the season of the etesian winds: the other fruit they gather somewhat unripe and store[1] it. In size it is as large as a pear, but in shape it is oblong, almond-shaped, and its colour is grass-green. It has inside a stone like the plum, but much smaller and softer; the flesh is sweet and luscious and easily digested; for it does no hurt if one eats it in quantity. The tree has good roots as to length thickness and number. Moreover its wood is strong and fair in appearance, black like the nettle-tree: out of it men make their images beds tables and other such things.

[2] The *balanos* gets its name from its fruit[3]; its leaf is like that of the myrtle[4] but it is longer. The tree is of a good stoutness[5] and stature, but not of a good shape, being crooked. The perfumers use the husks of the fruit, which they bruise; for this is fragrant, though the fruit itself is useless. In size and appearance it is like the fruit of the caper; the wood is strong and useful for shipbuilding and other purposes.

[6] The tree called the doum-palm is like the date-palm; the resemblance is in the stem and the leaves, but it differs in that the date-palm is a tree with a single undivided stem, while the other, as it increases, splits and becomes forked,[7] and then each of the two

---

[2] Plin. 13. 61.

[3] *i.e.* it is like an acorn (βάλανος).

[4] μυρρίνης MVPAld.; μυρίκης U.

[5] εὐπαχὲς conj. Sch.; εὐπαθὲς U; ἀπαθὲς Ald. H.

[6] Plin. 13. 62.

[7] *cf.* 2. 6. 9, where the same tree is evidently indicated. δίκρουν conj. Salm., Scal., etc.; ἄκρον U Ald. H.

THEOPHRASTUS

τούτων ὁμοίως· ἔτι δὲ τὰς ῥάβδους βραχείας ἔχει
σφόδρα καὶ οὐ πολλάς. χρῶνται δὲ τῷ φύλλῳ,
καθάπερ τῷ φοίνικι, πρὸς τὰ πλέγματα. καρπὸν
δὲ ἴδιον ἔχει πολὺ διαφέροντα καὶ μεγέθει καὶ
σχήματι καὶ χυλῷ· μέγεθος μὲν γὰρ ἔχει σχεδὸν
χειροπληθές· στρογγύλον δὲ καὶ οὐ προμήκη·
χρῶμα ἐπίξανθον· χυλὸν δὲ γλυκὺν καὶ εὔστομον·
οὐκ ἀθρόον δέ, ὥσπερ ὁ φοῖνιξ, ἀλλὰ κεχωρισμένον
καθ᾽ ἕνα· πυρῆνα δὲ μέγαν καὶ σφόδρα σκληρόν,
ἐξ οὗ τοὺς κρίκους τορνεύουσι τοὺς εἰς τοὺς
στρωματεῖς τοὺς διαποικίλους· διαφέρει δὲ πολὺ
τὸ ξύλον τοῦ φοίνικος· τὸ μὲν γὰρ μανὸν καὶ
ἰνῶδες καὶ χαῦνον, τὸ δὲ πυκνὸν καὶ βαρὺ καὶ
σαρκῶδες καὶ διατμηθὲν οὖλον σφόδρα καὶ
σκληρόν ἐστιν. καὶ οἵ γε δὴ Πέρσαι πάνυ
ἐτίμων αὐτὸ καὶ ἐκ τούτου τῶν κλινῶν ἐποιοῦντο
τοὺς πόδας.

8   Ἡ δὲ ἄκανθα καλεῖται μὲν διὰ τὸ ἀκανθῶδες
ὅλον τὸ δένδρον εἶναι πλὴν τοῦ στελέχους· καὶ
γὰρ ἐπὶ τῶν ἀκρεμόνων καὶ ἐπὶ τῶν βλαστῶν
καὶ ἐπὶ τῶν φύλλων ἔχει. μεγέθει δὲ μέγα, καὶ
γὰρ δωδεκάπηχυς ἐξ αὐτῆς ἐρέψιμος ὕλη τέμνεται.
διττὸν δὲ τὸ γένος αὐτῆς, ἡ μὲν γάρ ἐστι λευκὴ
ἡ δὲ μέλαινα· καὶ ἡ μὲν λευκὴ ἀσθενής τε καὶ
εὔσηπτος· ἡ δὲ μέλαινα ἰσχυροτέρα τε καὶ
ἄσηπτος, δι᾽ ὃ καὶ ἐν ταῖς ναυπηγίαις χρῶνται
πρὸς τὰ ἐγκοίλια αὐτῇ. τὸ δένδρον δὲ οὐκ ἄγαν
ὀρθοφυές. ὁ δὲ καρπὸς ἔλλοβος, καθάπερ τῶν
χεδροπῶν, ᾧ χρῶνται οἱ ἐγχώριοι πρὸς τὰ δέρματα
ἀντὶ κηκίδος. τὸ δ᾽ ἄνθος καὶ τῇ ὄψει καλόν,
ὥστε καὶ στεφάνους ποιεῖν ἐξ αὐτοῦ, καὶ φαρμα-

branches forks again: moreover the twigs are very short and not numerous. They use the leaf, like the palm-leaf, for plaiting. It has a peculiar fruit, very different from that of the date-palm in size form and taste; for in size it is nearly big enough to fill the hand, but it is round rather than long; the colour is yellowish, the flavour sweet and palatable. It does not grow bunched together, like the fruit of the date-palm, but each fruit grows separately; it has a large and very hard stone, out of which they turn the rings for embroidered bed-hangings.[1] The wood is very different to that of the date-palm; whereas the latter is of loose texture fibrous and porous,[2] that of the doum-palm is close heavy and fleshy, and when split is exceedingly compact and hard. The Persians[3] used to esteem it highly and made the feet of their couches out of it.

[4] The *akantha* (acacia) is so called because the whole tree is spinous (*akanthodes*) except the stem; for it has spines on the branches shoots and leaves. It is of large stature, since lengths of timber for roofing of twelve cubits are cut from it. There are two kinds, the white and the black; the white is weak and easily decays, the black is stronger and less liable to decay; wherefore they use it in shipbuilding for the ribs.[5] The tree is not very erect in growth. The fruit is in a pod, like that of leguminous plants, and the natives use it for tanning hides instead of gall. [6] The flower is very beautiful in appearance, so that they make garlands of it, and it has medicinal

---

[1] Plin. *l.c.*, *velares annulos*; *cf.* Athen. 12. 71, *ad fin.*
[2] χαῦνον conj. Sch.; χλωρὸν Ald.
[3] *i.e.* during their occupation of Egypt.
[4] Plin. 13. 63; Athen. 15. 25.
[5] *cf.* Hdt. 2. 96.    [6] *cf.* Athen. *l.c.*

κῶδες, δι' ὃ καὶ συλλέγουσιν οἱ ἰατροί. γίνεται
δὲ ἐκ ταύτης καὶ τὸ κόμμι· καὶ ῥέει καὶ πλη-
γείσης καὶ αὐτόματον ἄνευ σχάσεως. ὅταν δὲ
κοπῇ, μετὰ τρίτον ἔτος εὐθὺς ἀναβεβλάστηκε·
πολὺ δὲ τὸ δένδρον ἐστί, καὶ δρυμὸς μέγας περὶ
τὸν Θηβαϊκὸν νόμον, οὗπερ καὶ ἡ δρῦς καὶ ἡ
περσέα πλείστη καὶ ἡ ἐλάα.
9  Καὶ γὰρ ἡ ἐλάα περὶ τοῦτον τὸν τόπον ἐστί,
τῷ ποταμῷ μὲν οὐκ ἀρδευομένη, πλείω γὰρ ἢ
τριακόσια στάδια ἀπέχει, ναματιαίοις δ' ὕδασιν·
εἰσὶ γὰρ κρῆναι πολλαί. τὸ δ' ἔλαιον οὐδὲν
χεῖρον τοῦ ἐνθάδε, πλὴν κακωδέστερον διὰ τὸ
σπανίοις τοῖς ἁλσὶ χρῆσθαι· φύσει δὲ τὸ ξύλον
τοῦ δένδρου καὶ σκληρὸν καὶ παραπλήσιον
τεμνόμενον τὴν χρόαν τῷ λωτίνῳ.
10  Ἄλλο δέ τι δένδρον ἡ κοκκυμηλέα, μέγα μὲν
τῷ μεγέθει καὶ τὴν φύσιν τοῦ καρποῦ ὅμοιον τοῖς
μεσπίλοις, καὶ τὸ μέγεθος παραπλήσιον πλὴν
ἔχοντα πυρῆνα στρογγύλον· ἄρχεται δὲ ἀνθεῖν
μηνὸς Πυανεψιῶνος, τὸν δὲ καρπὸν πεπαίνει περὶ
ἡλίου τροπὰς χειμερινάς· ἀείφυλλον δ' ἐστίν.
οἱ δὲ περὶ τὴν Θηβαΐδα κατοικοῦντες διὰ τὴν
ἀφθονίαν τοῦ δένδρου ξηραίνουσι τὸν καρπὸν καὶ
τὸν πυρῆνα ἐξαιροῦντες κόπτουσι καὶ ποιοῦσι
παλάθας.
11  Ἄλημα δὲ ἴδιόν τι φύεται περὶ Μέμφιν, οὐ
κατὰ φύλλα καὶ βλαστοὺς καὶ τὴν ὅλην μορφὴν

---

1 cf. Hdt. l.c.
2 σχάσεως conj. R. Const.; σχίσεως Ald.
3 πλείστη conj. R. Const.; πλεκτὴ UMVAld.
4 cf. C.P. 6. 8. 7, where this olive is said to produce no oil.
5 cf. Strabo, 17. 1. 35.

properties, wherefore physicians gather it. [1] Gum is also produced from it, which flows both when the tree is wounded and also of its own accord without any incision [2] being made. When the tree is cut down, after the third year it immediately shoots up again ; it is a common tree, and there is a great wood of it in the Thebaid, where grow the oak, the *persea* in great abundance,[3] and the olive.

[4] For the olive also grows in that district, though it is not watered by the river, being more than 300 furlongs distant from it, but by brooks ; for there are many springs. The oil produced is not inferior to that of our country, except that it has a less pleasing smell,[5] because it has not a sufficient natural supply of salt.[6] The wood of the tree is hard in character, and, when split, is like in colour [7] to that of the nettle-tree.

[8] There is another tree, the (Egyptian) plum (sebesten), which is of great stature, and the character of its fruit [9] is like the medlar (which it resembles in size), except that it has a round stone. It begins to flower in the month Pyanepsion,[10] and ripens its fruit about the winter solstice, and it is evergreen.[11] The inhabitants of the Thebaid, because of the abundance of the tree, dry the fruit : they take out the stones, bruise it, and make cakes of it.

There is a peculiar bush [12] which grows about Memphis, whose peculiarity does not lie in its leaves

---

[3] σπανίοις . . . φύσει conj. W.; σπανίας τοῖς ἁλσὶ χρ. τῇ φύσει Ald.; so U, but omitting τῇ.

[7] *i.e.* black. *cf.* 4. 3. 1.      [8] Plin. 13. 64 and 65.

[9] τοῦ καρποῦ add. Scal. from G and Plin. *l.c.*    [10] October.

[11] ἀείφυλλον conj. Scal. from G and Plin. *l.c.*; φύλλον UMV Ald.

[12] *Mimosa asperata* ; see Index, App. (2). ὕλημα conj. Scal. from G (*materia*) ; οἴδημα M Ald. U (corrected).

THEOPHRASTUS

ἔχον τὸ ἴδιον ἀλλ' εἰς τὸ συμβαῖνον περὶ αὐτὸ
πάθος· ἡ μὲν γὰρ πρόσοψις ἀκανθώδης ἐστὶν
αὐτοῦ, καὶ τὸ φύλλον παρόμοιον ταῖς πτερ-
ίσιν· ὅταν δέ τις ἅψηται τῶν κλωνίων, ὥσπερ
ἀφαυαινόμενα τὰ φύλλα συμπίπτειν φασὶν εἶτα
μετά τινα χρόνον ἀναβιώσκεσθαι πάλιν καὶ
θάλλειν. καὶ τὰ μὲν ἴδια τῆς χώρας, ὅσα γ'
ἂν δένδρα τις ἢ θάμνους εἴποι, τά γ' ἐπιφανέ-
στατα ταῦτ' ἐστί. περὶ γὰρ τῶν ἐν τῷ ποταμῷ
καὶ τοῖς ἕλεσιν ὕστερον ἐροῦμεν, ὅταν καὶ περὶ
τῶν ἄλλων ἐνύδρων.

12 [Ἄπαντα δὲ ἐν τῇ χώρᾳ τὰ δένδρα τὰ τοιαῦτα
μεγάλα καὶ τοῖς μήκεσι καὶ τοῖς πάχεσιν· ἐν
γοῦν Μέμφιδι τηλικοῦτο δένδρον εἶναι λέγεται
τὸ πάχος, ὃ τρεῖς ἄνδρες οὐ δύνανται περιλαμβά-
νειν. ἔστι δὲ καὶ τμηθὲν τὸ ξύλον καλόν· πυκνόν
τε γὰρ σφόδρα καὶ τῷ χρώματι λωτοειδές.]

III. Ἐν Λιβύῃ δὲ ὁ λωτὸς πλεῖστος καὶ κάλλιστος καὶ ὁ παλίουρος καὶ ἔν τισι μέρεσι τῇ τε
Νασαμωνικῇ καὶ παρ' Ἄμμωνι καὶ ἄλλοις ὁ
φοῖνιξ· ἐν δὲ τῇ Κυρηναίᾳ κυπάρισσος καὶ ἐλάαι
τε κάλλισται καὶ ἔλαιον πλεῖστον. ἰδιώτατον
δὲ πάντων τὸ σίλφιον· ἔτι κρόκον πολὺν ἡ χώρα
φέρει καὶ εὔοσμον. ἔστι δὲ τοῦ λωτοῦ τὸ μὲν
ὅλον δένδρον ἴδιον εὐμέγεθες ἡλίκον ἄπιος ἢ
μικρὸν ἔλαττον· φύλλον δὲ ἐντομὰς ἔχον καὶ
πρινῶδες· τὸ μὲν ξύλον μέλαν· γένη δὲ αὐτοῦ
πλείω διαφορὰς ἔχοντα τοῖς καρποῖς· ὁ δὲ καρπὸς

---

¹ πάθος : cf. l. 1. 1 n.
² cf. Schol. ad Nic. Ther. 683 of a sensitive plant called
σκορπίουρος or ἰσχύουσα. ἀφαυαινόμενα conj. Scal.; ἀφαυλινό-
μενα UMVP₂Ald.

shoots and general form, but in the strange property [1] which belongs to it. Its appearance is spinous and the leaf is like ferns, but, when one touches the twigs, they say that the leaves as it were wither up [2] and collapse and then after a time come to life again and flourish. Such are the most conspicuous things peculiar to the country, to speak only of trees or shrubs. For we will speak later of the things which grow in the river and the marshes, when we come to speak of the other water plants.

[3] All the trees of this kind in that country are large, both in height and stoutness: thus at Memphis there is said to be a tree of such girth that three men cannot embrace it. The wood too, when split, is good, being of extremely close grain and in colour like the nettle-tree.

*Of the trees and shrubs special to Libya.*

III. [4] In Libya the *lotos* is most abundant and fairest; so also is the Christ's thorn, and in some parts, such as the Nasamonian district and near the temple of Zeus Ammon, the date-palm. In the Cyrenaica the cypress grows and the olives are fairest and the oil most abundant. Most special of all to this district is the silphium, and the land also bears abundant fragrant saffron-crocus. As to the *lotos*— the whole tree is peculiar, of good stature, as tall as a pear-tree, or nearly so; the leaf is divided and like that of the kermes-oak, and the wood is black. There are several sorts, which differ in their fruits; the fruit

[3] This section is evidently out of place: its probable place is at the end of § 10, so that the description will belong to the 'Egyptian plum.'

[4] See Index. Plin. 13. 104–106.

THEOPHRASTUS

ἡλίκος κύαμος, πεπαίνεται δέ, ὥσπερ οἱ βότρυες,
μεταβάλλων τὰς χροιάς· φύεται δέ, καθάπερ τὰ
μύρτα, παρ' ἄλληλα πυκνὸς ἐπὶ τῶν βλαστῶν·
ἐσθιόμενος δ' ὁ ἐν τοῖς Λωτοφάγοις καλουμένοις
γλυκὺς καὶ ἡδὺς καὶ ἀσινὴς καὶ ἔτι πρὸς τὴν
κοιλίαν ἀγαθός· ἡδίων δ' ὁ ἀπύρηνος, ἔστι γὰρ
καὶ τοιοῦτόν τι γένος· ποιοῦσι δὲ καὶ οἶνον ἐξ
αὐτοῦ.

2 Πολὺ δὲ τὸ δένδρον καὶ πολύκαρπον· τό γ'
οὖν Ὀφέλλου στρατόπεδον, ἡνίκα ἐβάδιζεν εἰς
Καρχηδόνα, καὶ τούτῳ φασὶ τραφῆναι πλείους
ἡμέρας ἐπιλιπόντων τῶν ἐπιτηδείων. ἔστι μὲν
οὖν καὶ ἐν τῇ νήσῳ τῇ Λωτοφαγίτιδι καλουμένῃ
πολύς· αὕτη δ' ἐπίκειται καὶ ἀπέχει μικρόν· οὐ
μὴν οὐθέν γε μέρος ἀλλὰ πολλῷ πλεῖον ἐν τῇ
ἠπείρῳ· πλεῖστον γὰρ ὅλως ἐν τῇ Λιβύῃ, καθάπερ
εἴρηται, τοῦτο καὶ ὁ παλίουρός ἐστιν· ἐν γὰρ
Εὐεσπερίσι τούτοις καυσίμοις χρῶνται. διαφέρει
δὲ οὗτος ὁ λωτὸς τοῦ παρὰ τοῖς Λωτοφάγοις.

3 Ὁ δὲ παλίουρος θαμνωδέστερος τοῦ λωτοῦ·
φύλλον δὲ παρόμοιον ἔχει τῷ ἐνταῦθα, τὸν δὲ
καρπὸν διάφορον· οὐ γὰρ πλατὺν ἀλλὰ στρογγύλον καὶ ἐρυθρόν, μέγεθος δὲ ἡλίκον τῆς κέδρου ἢ
μικρῷ μεῖζον· πυρῆνα δὲ ἔχει οὐ συνεσθιόμενον
καθάπερ ταῖς ῥοαῖς· ἡδὺν δὲ τὸν καρπόν· καὶ ἐάν
τις οἶνον ἐπιχέῃ καὶ αὐτὸν ἡδίω γίνεσθαί φασι
καὶ τὸν οἶνον ἡδίω ποιεῖν.

---

[1] cf. Hdt. 4. 177; Athen. 14. 651; Scyl. Peripl. Lotophagi.
[2] A ruler of Cyrene, who invaded Carthaginian territory in
conjunction with Agathocles, B.C. 308.
[3] τῇ λωτοφαγιτίδι conj. W.; τῇ Λωτοφαγίᾳ Φάριδι UMAld.
[4] μέρος : μείων conj. Sch. (non minor G).

is as large as a bean, and in ripening like grapes it
changes its colour: it grows, like myrtle-berries,
close together on the shoots; to eat, that which grows
among the people called the Lotus-eaters [1] is sweet
pleasant and harmless, and even good for the stomach;
but that which has no stone is pleasanter (for
there is also such a sort), and they also make wine
from it.

The tree is abundant and produces much fruit;
thus the army of Ophellas,[2] when it was marching
on Carthage, was fed, they say, on this alone for
several days, when the provisions ran short. It is
abundant also in the island called the island of
the Lotus-eaters; [3] this lies off the mainland at
no great distance: it grows however in no less
quantity,[4] but even more abundantly [5] on the mainland; for, as has been said,[6] this tree is common in
Libya generally as well as the Christ's thorn; for in
the islands called Euesperides [7] they use these trees
as fuel. However this *lotos* [8] differs from that found
in the land of the Lotus-eaters.

[9] The (Egyptian) 'Christ's thorn' is more shrubby
than the *lotos*; it has a leaf like the tree of the same
name of our country, but the fruit is different; for
it is not flat, but round and red, and in size as large
as the fruit of the prickly cedar or a little larger;
it has a stone which is not eaten with the fruit, as in
the case of the pomegranate, but the fruit is sweet,
and, if one pours wine over it, they say that it
becomes sweeter and that it makes the wine sweeter.

[5] πλεῖον U; ? πλεῖον with MV.
[6] 4. 3. 1.    [7] cf. Hdt. 4. 191.
[8] cf. Hdt. 2. 96.
[9] See Index.  Plin. 13. 111.

THEOPHRASTUS

4 "Ενιοι δὲ τὸ τοῦ λωτοῦ δένδρον θαμνῶδες εἶναι
καὶ πολύκλαδον, τῷ στελέχει δὲ εὐπαχές· τὸν δὲ
καρπὸν μέγα τὸ κάρυον ἔχειν· τὸ δ᾽ ἐκτὸς οὐ
σαρκῶδες ἀλλὰ δερματωδέστερον· ἐσθιόμενον δὲ
οὐχ οὕτω γλυκὺν ὡς εὔστομον· καὶ τὸν οἶνον ὃν
ἐξ αὐτοῦ ποιοῦσιν οὐ διαμένειν ἀλλ᾽ ἢ δύο ἢ
τρεῖς ἡμέρας εἶτ᾽ ὀξύνειν. ἡδίω μὲν οὖν τὸν
καρπὸν τὸν ἐν τοῖς Λωτοφάγοις, ξύλον δὲ
κάλλιον τὸ ἐν Κυρηναίᾳ· θερμοτέραν δὲ εἶναι
τὴν χώραν τὴν τῶν Λωτοφάγων· τοῦ ξύλου δὲ
τὴν ῥίζαν εἶναι μελαντέραν μὲν πολὺ πυκνὴν δὲ
ἧττον καὶ εἰς ἐλάττω χρησίμην· εἰς γὰρ τὰ
ἐγχειρίδια καὶ τὰ ἐπικολλήματα χρῆσθαι, τῷ
ξύλῳ δὲ εἴς τε τοὺς αὐλοὺς καὶ εἰς ἄλλα πλείω.

5 Ἐν δὲ τῇ μὴ νομένῃ τῆς Λιβύης ἄλλα τε πλείω
φύεσθαι καὶ φοίνικας μεγάλους καὶ καλούς· οὐ
μὴν ἀλλ᾽ ὅπου μὲν φοῖνιξ ἁλμυρίδα τε εἶναι καὶ
ἔφυδρον τὸν τόπον, οὐκ ἐν πολλῷ δὲ βάθει ἀλλὰ
μάλιστα ἐπ᾽ ὀργυίαις τρισίν. τὸ δ᾽ ὕδωρ ἔνθα
μὲν γλυκὺ σφόδρα ἔνθα δὲ ἁλυκὸν πλησίον ὄντων
ἀλλήλοις· ὅπου δὲ τὰ ἄλλα φύεται ξηρὸν καὶ
ἄνυδρον· ἐνιαχοῦ δὲ καὶ τὰ φρέατα εἶναι ἑκατὸν
ὀργυιῶν, ὥστε ὑποζυγίοις ἀπὸ τροχηλιᾶς ἀνιμᾶν·
δι᾽ ὃ καὶ θαυμαστὸν πῶς ποτε ὠρύχθη τηλικαῦτα
βάθη· τὸ δ᾽ οὖν τῶν ὑδάτων τῶν ὑπὸ τοὺς
φοίνικας καὶ ἐν Ἄμμωνος εἶναι διαφορὰν ἔχον
τὴν εἰρημένην. φύεσθαι δὲ ἐν τῇ μὴ νομένῃ τὸ
θύμον πολὺ καὶ ἄλλα ἴδιά τε καὶ πλείω γίνεσθαι

---

[1] Sch. after Scal. places this section before § 3, making the account of this tree consecutive.　[2] Plin. 13. 17. 104–106.
[3] εὔπαχες conj. R. Const.; εὐσταχές U; εὐσταχες MP₂Ald.
[4] cf. Hdt. 2. 96.

306

[1] Some say that the *lotos* [2] is shrubby and much branched, though it has a stout [3] stem ; and that the stone in the fruit is large, while the outside is not fleshy but somewhat leathery ; and that to eat it is not so much sweet as palatable : and that the wine which they make out of it does not keep more than two or three days, after which it gets sour ; and so that the fruit [4] found in the Lotus-eaters' country is sweeter, while the wood in the Cyrenaica is better ; and that the country of the Lotus-eaters is hotter ; and that the root is much blacker than the wood, but of less close grain, and of use for fewer purposes ; for they use it only for dagger-handles and tessellated work,[5] while the wood is used for pipes and many other things.

In the part of Libya where no rain falls they say that, besides many other trees, there grow tall and fine date-palms ; however they add that, where the date-palm is found, the soil [6] is salt and contains water, and that at no great depth, not more than three fathoms. They say also that the water is in some places quite sweet, but in others quite close by it is brackish ; that where however other things grow, the soil is dry and waterless ; and that in places even the wells are a hundred fathoms deep, so that they draw water by means of a windlass worked by beasts. Wherefore it is wonderful how at any time digging to such depths was carried out. Such, they say, is the special character of the water supply which feeds the date-palms in the district also of the temple of Zeus Ammon. Further it is said that in the land where no rain falls thyme [7] is

[5] ἐπικολλήματα : lit. ' pieces glued on ' ; *cf.* Plin. *l.c.*
[6] *cf.* Hdt. 3. 183.
[7] θύμον mBas.H. ; θάμνον UMVAld. *cf.* 6. 2. 3.

307

x 2

ἐνταῦθα, καὶ πτῶκα καὶ δορκάδα καὶ στρουθὸν
6 καὶ ἕτερα τῶν θηρίων. ἀλλὰ ταῦτα μὲν ἄδηλον
εἰ ἐκτοπίζει που πιόμενα· (διὰ γὰρ τὸ τάχος
δύναται μακράν τε καὶ ταχὺ παραγενέσθαι),
ἄλλως τε κεὶ δι᾽ ἡμερῶν τινων πίνουσι, καθάπερ
καὶ τὰ ἥμερα παρὰ τρίτην ἢ τετάρτην ποτίζεται
ταῦτα· τὸ δὲ τῶν ἄλλων ζώων, οἷον ὄφεων
σαυρῶν καὶ τῶν τοιούτων, φανερὸν ὅτι ἄποτα.
τοὺς δὲ Λίβυας λέγειν ὅτι τὸν ὄνον ἐσθίει ταῦτα
ὃς καὶ παρ᾽ ἡμῖν γίνεται, πολύπουν τε καὶ μέλαν
συσπειρώμενον εἰς ἑαυτό· τοῦτον δὲ πολύν τε
γίνεσθαι σφόδρα καὶ ὑγρὸν τὴν φύσιν εἶναι.
7 Δρόσον δὲ ἀεὶ πίπτειν ἐν τῇ μὴ ὑομένῃ πολλήν,
ὥστε δῆλον ὅτι τὸν μὲν φοίνικα καὶ εἴ τι ἄλλο
φύεται ἐν ἀνύδροις τό τε ἐκ τῆς γῆς ἀνιὸν ἐκτρέφει
καὶ πρὸς τούτῳ ἡ δρόσος. ἱκανὴ γὰρ ὡς κατὰ
μεγέθη καὶ τὴν φύσιν αὐτῶν ξηρὰν οὖσαν καὶ ἐκ
τοιούτων συνεστηκυῖαν. καὶ δένδρα μὲν ταῦτα
πλεῖστα καὶ ἰδιώτατα. περὶ δὲ τοῦ σιλφίου
λεκτέον ὕστερον ποῖόν τι τὴν φύσιν.

IV. Ἐν δὲ τῇ Ἀσίᾳ παρ᾽ ἑκάστοις ἴδι᾽ ἄττα
τυγχάνει· τὰ μὲν γὰρ φέρουσιν αἱ χῶραι τὰ δ᾽

---

¹ Lepus Aegyptiacus. cf. Arist. H.A. 8. 28.
² ὡς κατὰ conj. Scal. from G ; ὥστε τὰ Ald.H.

abundant, and that there are various other peculiar plants there, and that there are found the hare [1] gazelle ostrich and other animals. However it is uncertain whether these do not migrate in order to find drink somewhere, (for by reason of their fleetness they are able to appear at a distant place in a short space of time), especially if they can go for several days without drinking, even as these animals, when domesticated, are only given drink every third or fourth day. While as to other animals, such as snakes lizards and the like, it is plain that they go without drink. And we are told that according to the Libyans, these animals eat the wood-louse, which is of the same kind that is found also in our country, being black, with many feet, and rolling itself into a ball ; this, they say, is extremely common and is juicy by nature.

They say also that dew always falls abundantly in the land in which no rain falls, so that it is plain that the date-palm, as well as anything else which grows in waterless places, is kept alive by the moisture which rises from the ground, and also by the dew. For the latter is sufficient, considering [2] the size of such trees and their natural character, which is dry and formed of dry components. And trees of that character are most abundant in, and most specially belong to such country. The character of the silphium we must discuss later.

*Of the trees and herbs special to Asia.*

IV. In different parts of Asia also there are special trees, for the soil of the various regions produces some but not others. [3] Thus they say that

[3] Plin. 16. 144.

THEOPHRASTUS

οὐ φύουσιν· οἷον κιττὸν καὶ ἐλάαν οὔ φασιν εἶναι
τῆς Ἀσίας ἐν τοῖς ἄνω τῆς Συρίας ἀπὸ θαλάττης
πένθ᾽ ἡμερῶν· ἀλλ᾽ ἐν Ἰνδοῖς φανῆναι κιττὸν
ἐν τῷ ὄρει τῷ Μηρῷ καλουμένῳ, ὅθεν δὴ καὶ τὸν
Διόνυσον εἶναι μυθολογοῦσι. δι᾽ ὃ καὶ Ἀλέξανδρος ἀπ᾽ ἐξοδίας λέγεται ἀπιὼν ἐστεφανωμένος
κιττῷ εἶναι καὶ αὐτὸς καὶ ἡ στρατιά· τῶν δὲ
ἄλλων ἐν Μηδίᾳ μόνον· περικλείειν γὰρ αὕτη
δοκεῖ καὶ συνάπτειν πως τῷ Πόντῳ. καίτοι γε
διεφιλοτιμήθη Ἅρπαλος ἐν τοῖς παραδείσοις τοῖς
περὶ Βαβυλῶνα φυτεύων πολλάκις καὶ πραγ-
ματευόμενος, ἀλλ᾽ οὐδὲν ἐποίει πλέον· οὐ γὰρ
ἐδύνατο ζῆν ὥσπερ τἆλλα τὰ ἐκ τῆς Ἑλλάδος.
τοῦτο μὲν οὖν οὐ δέχεται ἡ χώρα διὰ τὴν τοῦ
ἀέρος κρᾶσιν· ἀναγκαίως δὲ δέχεται καὶ πύξον
καὶ φίλυραν· καὶ γὰρ περὶ ταῦτα πονοῦσιν οἱ ἐν
τοῖς παραδείσοις. ἕτερα δὲ ἴδια φέρει καὶ δένδρα
2 καὶ ὑλήματα· καὶ ἔοικεν ὅλως ὁ τόπος ὁ πρὸς
ἀνατολὰς καὶ μεσημβρίαν ὥσπερ καὶ ζῷα καὶ
φυτὰ φέρειν ἴδια παρὰ τοὺς ἄλλους· οἷον ἥ τε
Μηδία χώρα καὶ Περσὶς ἄλλα τε ἔχει πλείω καὶ
τὸ μῆλον τὸ Μηδικὸν ἢ τὸ Περσικὸν καλούμενον.
ἔχει δὲ τὸ δένδρον τοῦτο φύλλον μὲν ὅμοιον καὶ
σχεδὸν ἴσον τῷ τῆς ἀνδράχλης, ἀκάνθας δὲ οἵας
ἄπιος ἢ ὀξυάκανθος, λείας δὲ καὶ ὀξείας σφόδρα
καὶ ἰσχυράς· τὸ δὲ μῆλον οὐκ ἐσθίεται μέν,

---

¹ ἐλάαν conj. Spr.; ἐλάτην MSS. cf. Hdt. 1. 193; Xen.
Anab. 4. 4. 13; Arr. Ind. 40.
² κιττὸν conj. W., cf. Arr. Anab. 5. 1. 6; καὶ τὴν UMV;
καὶ τῷ Ald.H. ³ λέγεται add. W.
⁴ ἐξοδίας UMVP; Ἰνδίας W. with Ald.
⁵ κιττῷ εἶναι conj. W.; εἶτα μεῖναι U; εἶτα μὴ εἶναι MVPAld.

310

ivy and olive[1] do not grow in Asia in the parts of
Syria which are five days' journey from the sea ; but
that in India ivy[2] appears on the mountain called
Meros, whence, according to the tale, Dionysus
came. Wherefore it is said[3] that Alexander, when
he came back from an expedition,[4] was crowned
with ivy,[5] himself and his army. But elsewhere in
Asia it is said to grow only in Media, for that country
seems in a way to surround and join on to the Euxine
Sea.[6] However,[7] when Harpalus took great pains
over and over again to plant it in the gardens of
Babylon, and made a special point of it, he failed :
since it could not live like the other things introduced from Hellas. The country then does not[8]
admit this plant on account of the climate, and it
grudgingly admits the box and the lime ; for even
these give much trouble to those engaged in the
gardens. It also produces some peculiar trees and
shrubs. And in general the lands of the East and
South appear to have peculiar plants, as they have
peculiar animals ; for instance, Media and Persia have,
among many others, that which is called the
' Median ' or ' Persian apple ' (citron).[9] This tree[10]
has a leaf like to and almost identical with that of
the andrachne, but it has thorns like those of the
pear[11] or white-thorn, which however are smooth
and very sharp and strong. The ' apple ' is not

---

[6] *i.e.* and so Greek plants may be expected to grow there.
But the text is probably defective ; *cf.* the citation of this
passage, Plut. *Quaest. Conv.* 3. 2. 1.
[7] καίτοι γε. This sentence does not connect properly with
the preceding. [8] οὐ add. Sch.
[9] Plin. 12. 15 and 16 ; cited also Athen. 3. 26.
[10] *cf.* Verg. *G.* 2. 131–135.
[11] ἄπιος : ? here=ἀχράς R. Const. *cf. C.P.* 1. 15. 2.

εὔοσμον δὲ πάνυ καὶ τὸ φύλλον τοῦ δένδρου· κἂν εἰς ἱμάτια τεθῇ τὸ μῆλον ἄκοπα διατηρεῖ. χρήσιμον δ᾽ ἐπειδὰν τύχῃ <τις> πεπωκὼς φάρμακον <θανάσιμον· δοθὲν γὰρ ἐν οἴνῳ διακόπτει τὴν κοιλίαν καὶ ἐξάγει τὸ φάρμακον·> καὶ πρὸς στόματος εὐωδίαν· ἐὰν γάρ τις ἐψήσῃ ἐν ζωμῷ, ἢ ἐν ἄλλῳ τινὶ τὸ ἔσωθεν τοῦ μήλου ἐκπιέσῃ εἰς τὸ στόμα καὶ καταροφήσῃ, ποιεῖ τὴν ὀσμὴν ἡδεῖαν.

3 σπείρεται δὲ τοῦ ἦρος εἰς πρασιὰς ἐξαιρεθὲν τὸ σπέρμα διειργασμένας ἐπιμελῶς, εἶτα ἀρδεύεται διὰ τετάρτης ἢ πέμπτης ἡμέρας· ὅταν δὲ ἁδρὸν ᾖ, διαφυτεύεται πάλιν τοῦ ἔαρος εἰς χωρίον μαλακὸν καὶ ἔφυδρον καὶ οὐ λίαν λεπτόν· φιλεῖ γὰρ τὰ τοιαῦτα. φέρει δὲ τὰ μῆλα πᾶσαν ὥραν· τὰ μὲν γὰρ ἀφήρηται τὰ δὲ ἀνθεῖ τὰ δὲ ἐκπέττει. τῶν δὲ ἀνθῶν ὅσα, ὥσπερ εἴπομεν, ἔχει καθάπερ ἠλακάτην ἐκ μέσου τιν᾽ ἐξέχουσαν, ταῦτά ἐστι γόνιμα, ὅσα δὲ μὴ ἄγονα. σπείρεται δὲ καὶ εἰς ὄστρακα διατετρημένα, καθάπερ καὶ οἱ φοίνικες. τοῦτο μὲν οὖν, ὥσπερ εἴρηται, περὶ τὴν Περσίδα καὶ τὴν Μηδίαν ἐστίν.

4 Ἡ δὲ Ἰνδικὴ χώρα τήν τε καλουμένην ἔχει συκῆν, ἣ καθίησιν ἐκ τῶν κλάδων τὰς ῥίζας ἀν᾽ ἕκαστον ἔτος, ὥσπερ εἴρηται πρότερον· ἀφίησι δὲ οὐκ ἐκ τῶν νέων ἀλλ᾽ ἐκ τῶν ἔνων καὶ ἔτι παλαιοτέρων· αὗται δὲ συνάπτουσαι τῇ γῇ ποιοῦσιν ὥσπερ δρύφακτον κύκλῳ περὶ τὸ δένδρον, ὥστε γίνεσθαι καθάπερ σκηνήν, οὗ δὴ καὶ

---

[1] τις add. W. from Athen. l.c.; θανάσιμον . . . φάρμακον add. Sch. from Athen. l.c.    [2] Plin. 11. 278; 12. 16.
[3] ἁδρὸν ᾖ W. from Athen. l.c., whence διαφυτεύεται W. etc. for διαφυτεύηται Ald.H. ἁδρόν τι UMVAld.

eaten, but it is very fragrant, as also is the leaf of the tree. And if the 'apple' is placed among clothes, it keeps them from being moth-eaten. It is also useful when one[1] has drunk deadly poison; for being given in wine it upsets the stomach and brings up the poison; also for producing sweetness of breath;[2] for, if one boils the inner part of the 'apple' in a sauce, or squeezes it into the mouth in some other medium, and then inhales it, it makes the breath sweet. The seed is taken from the fruit and sown in spring in carefully tilled beds, and is then watered every fourth or fifth day. And, when it is growing vigorously,[3] it is transplanted, also in spring, to a soft well-watered place, where the soil is not too fine; for such places it loves. And it bears its 'apples' at all seasons; for when some have been gathered, the flower of others is on the tree and it is ripening others. Of the flowers, as we have said,[4] those which have, as it were, a distaff[5] projecting in the middle are fertile, while those that have it not are infertile. It is also sown, like date-palms, in pots[6] with a hole in them. This tree, as has been said, grows in Persia and Media.

[7] The Indian land has its so-called 'fig-tree' (banyan), which drops its roots from its branches every year, as has been said above[8]; and it drops them, not from the new branches, but from those of last year or even from older ones; these take hold of the earth and make, as it were, a fence about the tree, so that it becomes like a tent, in

[4] 1. 13. 4.     [5] *i.e.* the pistil.
[6] Plin. 12. 16, *fictilibus in vasis, dato per cavernas radicibus spiramento*: the object, as Plin. explains, was to export it for medical use.
[7] Plin. 12. 22 and 23.     [8] 1. 7. 3.

THEOPHRASTUS

εἰώθασι διατρίβειν. εἰσὶ δὲ αἱ ῥίζαι φυόμεναι διάδηλοι πρὸς τοὺς βλαστούς· λευκότεραι γὰρ καὶ δασεῖαι καὶ σκολιαὶ καὶ ἄφυλλοι.[1][2] ἔχει δὲ καὶ τὴν ἄνω κόμην πολλήν, καὶ τὸ ὅλον δένδρον εὔκυκλον καὶ τῷ μεγέθει μέγα σφόδρα· καὶ γὰρ ἐπὶ δύο στάδια ποιεῖν φασι τὴν σκιάν· καὶ τὸ πάχος τοῦ στελέχους ἔνια πλειόνων ἢ ἑξήκοντα βημάτων, τὰ δὲ πολλὰ τετταράκοντα.[3] τὸ δέ γε φύλλον οὐκ ἔλαττον ἔχει πέλτης, καρπὸν δὲ σφόδρα μικρὸν ἡλίκον ἐρέβινθον ὅμοιον δὲ σύκῳ· δι᾽ ὃ καὶ ἐκάλουν αὐτὸ οἱ Ἕλληνες συκῆν· ὀλίγον δὲ θαυμαστῶς τὸν καρπὸν οὐχ ὅτι κατὰ τὸ τοῦ δένδρου μέγεθος ἀλλὰ καὶ τὸ ὅλον. φύεται δὲ καὶ τὸ δένδρον περὶ τὸν Ἀκεσίνην ποταμόν.

5 Ἔστι δὲ καὶ ἕτερον δένδρον καὶ τῷ μεγέθει μέγα καὶ ἡδύκαρπον θαυμαστῶς καὶ μεγαλόκαρπον· καὶ χρῶνται τροφῇ τῶν Ἰνδῶν οἱ σοφοὶ καὶ μὴ ἀμπεχόμενοι.

Ἕτερον δὲ οὗ τὸ φύλλον τὴν μὲν μορφὴν πρόμηκες τοῖς τῶν στρουθῶν πτεροῖς ὅμοιον, ἃ παρατίθενται παρὰ τὰ κράνη, μῆκος δὲ ὡς διπηχυαῖον.

Ἄλλο τέ ἐστιν οὗ ὁ καρπὸς μακρὸς καὶ οὐκ εὐθὺς ἀλλὰ σκολιὸς ἐσθιόμενος δὲ γλυκύς. οὗτος ἐν τῇ κοιλίᾳ δηγμὸν ἐμποιεῖ καὶ δυσεντερίαν, δι᾽ ὃ Ἀλέξανδρος ἀπεκήρυξε μὴ ἐσθίειν. ἔστι δὲ καὶ ἕτερον οὗ ὁ καρπὸς ὅμοιος τοῖς κρανέοις.

---

[1] οὗ conj. W.; αἷς UMVAld.
[2] ἄφυλλοι conj. Dalec.; δίφυλλοι UVAld.; so also MH., omitting καί.
[3] ἑξήκοντα . . . τετταράκοντα MSS.; ἓξ . . . τεττάρων conj. Salm. cf. Plin. l.c.; Strabo 15. 1, 21,

which [1] men sometimes even live. The roots as they
grow are easily distinguished from the branches,
being whiter hairy crooked and leafless.[2] The
foliage above is also abundant, and the whole tree is
round and exceedingly large. They say that it
extends its shade for as much as two furlongs ; and
the thickness of the stem is in some instances more
than sixty [3] paces, while many specimens are as
much as forty [3] paces through. The leaf is quite as
large as a shield,[4] but the fruit is very small,[5] only as
large as a chick-pea, and it resembles a fig. And
this is why the Greeks [6] named this tree a 'fig-tree.'
The fruit is curiously scanty, not only relatively to
the size of the tree, but absolutely. The tree also
grows near the river Akesines.[7]

There is also another tree [8] which is very large
and has wonderfully sweet and large fruit ; it is
used for food by the sages of India who wear no
clothes.

There is another tree [9] whose leaf is oblong in
shape, like the feathers of the ostrich ; this they
fasten on to their helmets, and it is about two cubits
long.

There is also another [10] whose fruit is long and not
straight, but crooked, and it is sweet to the taste.
This causes griping in the stomach and dysentery ;
wherefore Alexander ordered that it should not be
eaten. There is also another [11] whose fruit is like the
fruit of the cornelian cherry.

[4] πέλτη : a small round shield.  [5] cf. C.P. 2. 10. 2.
[6] i.e. in Alexander's expedition.  [7] Chenab.
[8] Jack-fruit. See Index App. (3).  Plin. 12. 24.
[9] Banana. See Index App. (4).
[10] Mango. See Index App. (5).  Plin. 12. 24.
[11] Jujube. See Index App. (6).

Καὶ ἔτερα δὲ πλείω καὶ διαφέροντα τῶν ἐν τοῖς Ἕλλησιν ἀλλ' ἀνώνυμα. θαυμαστὸν δ' οὐδὲν τῆς ἰδιότητος· σχεδὸν γάρ, ὥς γε δή τινές φασιν, οὐθὲν ὅλως τῶν δένδρων οὐδὲ τῶν ὑλημάτων οὐδὲ τῶν ποιωδῶν ὅμοιόν ἐστι τοῖς ἐν τῇ Ἑλλάδι πλὴν ὀλίγων.

6 Ἴδιον δὲ καὶ ἡ ἐβένη τῆς χώρας ταύτης· ταύτης δὲ δύο γένη, τὸ μὲν εὔξυλον καὶ καλὸν τὸ δὲ φαῦλον. σπάνιον δὲ τὸ καλὸν θάτερον δὲ πολύ. τὴν δὲ χρόαν οὐ θησαυριζομένη λαμβάνει τὴν εὔχρουν ἀλλ' εὐθὺς τῇ φύσει. ἔστι δὲ τὸ δένδρον θαμνῶδες, ὥσπερ ὁ κύτισος.

7 Φασὶ δ' εἶναι καὶ τέρμινθον, οἱ δ' ὅμοιον τερμίνθῳ, ὃ τὸ μὲν φύλλον καὶ τοὺς κλῶνας καὶ τἆλλα πάντα ὅμοια ἔχει τῇ τερμίνθῳ τὸν δὲ καρπὸν διάφορον· ὅμοιον γὰρ ταῖς ἀμυγδαλαῖς. εἶναι γὰρ καὶ ἐν Βάκτροις τὴν τέρμινθον ταύτην καὶ κάρυα φέρειν ἡλίκα ἀμύγδαλα διὰ τὸ μὴ μεγάλα· καὶ τῇ ὄψει δὲ παρόμοια, πλὴν τὸ κέλυφος οὐ τραχύ, τῇ δ' εὐστομίᾳ καὶ ἡδονῇ κρείττω τῶν ἀμυγδάλων. δι' ὃ καὶ χρῆσθαι τοὺς ἐκεῖ μᾶλλον.

8 Ἐξ ὧν δὲ τὰ ἱμάτια ποιοῦσι τὸ μὲν φύλλον ὅμοιον ἔχει τῇ συκαμίνῳ, τὸ δὲ ὅλον φυτὸν τοῖς κυνορόδοις ὅμοιον. φυτεύουσι δὲ ἐν τοῖς πεδίοις αὐτὸ κατ' ὄρχους, δι' ὃ καὶ πόρρωθεν ἀφορῶσι ἄμπελοι φαίνονται. ἔχει δὲ καὶ φοίνικας ἔνια

1 Plin. 12. 25.
2 See Index. Plin. 12. 17-19.
3 Pistachio-nut. See Index App. (7). Plin. 12. 25. Nic. Ther. 894.

There are also many more [1] which are different to
those found among the Hellenes, but they have no
names. There is nothing surprising in the fact that
these trees have so special a character; indeed, as
some say, there is hardly a single tree or shrub or
herbaceous plant, except quite a few, like those in
Hellas.

The ebony [2] is also peculiar to this country; of
this there are two kinds, one with good handsome
wood, the other inferior. The better sort is rare, but
the inferior one is common. It does not acquire its
good colour by being kept, but it is natural to it from
the first. The tree is bushy, like laburnum.

Some say that a 'terebinth' [3] grows there also,
others that it is a tree like the terebinth; this in
leaf twigs and all other respects resembles that
tree, but the fruit is different, being like almonds.
In fact they say that this sort of terebinth grows also
in Bactria and bears nuts only as big as almonds,
inasmuch as they are not large for the size of the
tree [4]; and they closely resemble almonds in appearance, except that the shell is not rough; and in
palatableness and sweetness they are superior to
almonds; wherefore the people of the country use
them in preference to almonds.

[5] The trees from which they make their clothes
have a leaf like the mulberry, but the whole tree
resembles the wild rose. They plant them in the
plains in rows, wherefore, when seen from a distance,
they look like vines. Some parts also have many

[4] διά . . . μέγαλα: Sch. omits these words, and W. considers them corrupt; but G seems to have had them in his
text. The translation is tentative.
[5] Cotton-plant. cf. 4. 7. 7 and 8. Plin. 12. 25.

THEOPHRASTUS

μέρη πολλούς. καὶ ταῦτα μὲν ἐν δένδρου
φύσει.

9 Φέρει δὲ καὶ σπέρματα ἴδια, τὰ μὲν τοῖς
χεδροποῖς ὅμοια τὰ δὲ τοῖς πυροῖς καὶ ταῖς
κριθαῖς. ἐρέβινθος μὲν γὰρ καὶ φακὸς καὶ τἆλλα
τὰ παρ' ἡμῖν οὐκ ἔστιν· ἕτερα δ' ἐστὶν ὥστε
παραπλήσια ποιεῖν τὰ ἐψήματα καὶ μὴ δια-
γιγνώσκειν, ὥς φασιν, ἂν μή τις ἀκούσῃ. κριθαὶ
δὲ καὶ πυροὶ καὶ ἄλλο τι γένος ἀγρίων κριθῶν,
ἐξ ὧν καὶ ἄρτοι ἡδεῖς καὶ χόνδρος καλός. ταύτας
οἱ ἵπποι ἐσθίοντες τὸ πρῶτον διεφθείροντο, κατὰ
μικρὸν δὲ οὖν ἐθισθέντες ἐν ἀχύροις οὐδὲν
ἔπασχον.

10 Μάλιστα δὲ σπείρουσι τὸ καλούμενον ὄρυζον,
ἐξ οὗ τὸ ἔψημα. τοῦτο δὲ ὅμοιον τῇ ζειᾷ καὶ
περιπτισθὲν οἷον χόνδρος εὔπεπτον δέ, τὴν ὄψιν
πεφυκὸς ὅμοιον ταῖς αἴραις καὶ τὸν πολὺν χρόνον
ἐν ὕδατι, ἀποχεῖται δὲ οὐκ εἰς στάχυν ἀλλ' οἷον
φόβην, ὥσπερ ὁ κέγχρος καὶ ὁ ἔλυμος. ἄλλο δὲ
ὃ ἐκάλουν οἱ Ἕλληνες φακόν· τοῦτο δὲ ὅμοιον
μὲν τῇ ὄψει καὶ τὸ βούκερας, θερίζεται δὲ περὶ
Πλειάδος δύσιν.

11 Διαφέρει δὲ καὶ αὕτη ἡ χώρα τῷ τὴν μὲν
φέρειν ἔνια τὴν δὲ μὴ φέρειν· ἡ γὰρ ὀρεινὴ καὶ
ἄμπελον ἔχει καὶ ἐλάαν καὶ τὰ ἄλλα ἀκρόδρυα·
πλὴν ἄκαρπον τὴν ἐλάαν, καὶ σχεδὸν καὶ τὴν
φύσιν ὥσπερ μεταξὺ κοτίνου καὶ ἐλάας ἐστὶ καὶ

---

[1] cf. 8. 4. 2. whence it appears that the original text here
contained a fuller account. Plin. 18. 71.
[2] Sorghum halepense. [3] Sc. of Alexander.
[4] The verb seems to have dropped out (W.).

318

date-palms.   So much for what come under the
heading of 'trees.'

These lands bear also peculiar grains, some like
those of leguminous plants, some like wheat and
barley.   For the chick-pea lentil and other such
plants found in our country do not occur; but there
are others, so that they make similar mashes, and
one cannot, they say, tell the difference, unless one
has been told.   They have however barley wheat [1]
and another kind of wild barley, [2] which makes sweet
bread and good porridge. [3]   When the horses [3] ate
this, at first it proved fatal to them, but by degrees
they became accustomed to it mixed with bran and
took no hurt.

But above all they sow the cereal called rice, of
which they make their mash.   This is like rice-wheat,
and when bruised makes a sort of porridge, which is
easily digested; in its appearance as it grows it is
like darnel, and for most of its time of growth it is [4]
in water; however it shoots [5] up not into an ear, but
as it were into a plume, [6] like the millet and Italian
millet.   There was another plant [7] which the Hellenes [8] called lentil; this is like in appearance to
'ox-horn' (fenugreek), but it is reaped about the
setting of the Pleiad.

Moreover this country shews differences in that
part of it bears certain things which another part
does not; thus the mountain country has the vine
and olive and the other fruit-trees; but the olive is
barren, [9] and in its character it is as it were almost
between a wild and a cultivated olive, and so it

[5] ἀποχεῖται: cf. 8. 8. 1.     [6] cf. 8. 3. 4.
[7] *Phaseolus Mungo*; see Index App. (8).
[8] i.e. of Alexander's expedition.      [9] Plin. 12. 14.

THEOPHRASTUS

τῇ ὅλῃ μορφῇ· καὶ τὸ φύλλον τοῦ μὲν πλατύτερον τοῦ δὲ στενότερον. ταῦτα μὲν οὖν κατὰ
τὴν Ἰνδικήν.

12 Ἐν δὲ τῇ Ἀρίᾳ χώρᾳ καλουμένῃ ἄκανθά ἐστιν,
ἐφ' ἧς γίνεται δάκρυον ὅμοιον τῇ σμύρνῃ καὶ τῇ
ὄψει καὶ τῇ ὀσμῇ· τοῦτο δὲ ὅταν ἐπιλάμψῃ ὁ
ἥλιος καταρρεῖ. πολλὰ δὲ καὶ ἄλλα παρὰ τὰ
ἐνταῦθα καὶ ἐν τῇ χώρᾳ καὶ ἐν τοῖς ποταμοῖς
γίνεται. ἐν ἑτέροις δὲ τόποις ἐστὶν ἄκανθα λευκὴ
τρίοζος, ἐξ ἧς καὶ σκυτάλια καὶ βακτηρίας ποι-
οῦσιν· ὀπώδης δὲ καὶ μανή· ταύτην δὲ καλοῦσιν
Ἡρακλέους.

Ἄλλο δὲ ὕλημα μέγεθος μὲν ἡλίκον ῥάφανος,
τὸ δὲ φύλλον ὅμοιον δάφνῃ καὶ τῷ μεγέθει καὶ
τῇ μορφῇ. τοῦτο δ' εἴ τι φάγοι ἐναποθνήσκει.
δι' ὃ καὶ ὅπου ἵπποι τούτους ἐφύλαττον διὰ
χειρῶν.

13 Ἐν δὲ τῇ Γεδρωσίᾳ χώρᾳ πεφυκέναι φασὶν ἓν
μὲν ὅμοιον τῇ δάφνῃ φύλλον ἔχον, οὗ τὰ ὑποζύγια
καὶ ὁτιοῦν εἰ φάγοι μικρὸν ἐπισχόντα διεφθείροντο παραπλησίως διατιθέμενα καὶ σπώμενα
ὁμοίως τοῖς ἐπιλήπτοις.

Ἕτερον δὲ ἄκανθάν τινα εἶναι· ταύτην δὲ
φύλλον μὲν οὐδὲν ἔχειν πεφυκέναι δ' ἐκ μιᾶς
ῥίζης· ἐφ' ἑκάστῳ δὲ τῶν ὄζων ἄκανθαν ἔχειν
ὀξεῖαν σφόδρα, καὶ τούτων δὲ καταγνυμένων ἢ
προστριβομένων ὀπὸν ἐκρεῖν πολύν, ὃς ἀποτυφλοῖ

---

¹ καὶ σχεδὸν ... μορφῇ conj. W.; σχεδὸν δὲ καὶ τὴν φύσιν
ἅπερ μετ. κοτ. καὶ ἐλ. ἐστι δὲ τῇ ὅλῃ μορφῇ καὶ τὸ φ. Ald.; so
also U, omitting the first καί.
² *Balsamodendron Mukul*; see Index App. (9). Plin. 12.
33.

320

is also in its general appearance,[1] and the leaf is broader than that of the one and narrower than that of the other. So much for the Indian land.

In the country called Aria there is a 'thorn'[2] on which is found a gum resembling myrrh[3] in appearance and smell, and this drops when the sun shines on it. There are also many other plants besides those of our land, both in the country and in its rivers. In other parts there is a white 'thorn'[4] which branches in three, of which they make batons and sticks; its wood is sappy and of loose texture, and they call it the thorn 'of Herakles.'

There is another shrub[5] as large as a cabbage, whose leaf is like that of the bay in size and shape. And if any animal should eat this, it is certain to die of it. Wherefore, wherever there were horses,[6] they kept them under control.

In Gedrosia they say that there grows one tree[7] with a leaf like that of the bay, of which if the beasts or anything else ate, they very shortly died with the same convulsive symptoms as in epilepsy.

And they say that another tree[8] there is a sort of 'thorn' (spurge), and that this has no leaf and grows from a single root; and on each of its branches it has a very sharp spine, and if these are broken or bruised a quantity of juice flows out, which blinds animals or

---

[3] σμύρνη conj. Sch. from 9. 1. 2; Plin. *l.c.*; τῇ Ἰλλυρίᾳ Ald. H.
[4] See Index.
[5] *Asafoetida*; see Index App. (10). Plin. 12. 33.
[6] *i.e.* in Alexander's expedition. Probably a verb, such as ὠσφραίνοντο, has dropped out after ἵπποι (Sch.). *Odore equos invitans* Plin. *l.c.*
[7] *Nerium odorum*; see Index App. (11). *cf.* 4. 4. 13; Strabo 15. 2. 7; Plin. *l.c.*
[8] Plin. *l.c.*; Arrian, *Anab.* 6. 22. 7.

τἆλλα ζῷα πάντα καὶ πρὸς τοὺς ἀνθρώπους εἴ
τις προσραίνειεν αὐτοῖς. ἐν δὲ τόποις τισὶ πεφυκέναι τινὰ βοτάνην, ὑφ᾽ ἧ συνεσπειρωμένους ὄφεις
εἶναι μικροὺς σφόδρα· τούτοις δ᾽ εἴ τις ἐμβὰς
πληγείη θνήσκειν. ἀποπνίγεσθαι δὲ καὶ ἀπὸ
τῶν φοινίκων τῶν ὠμῶν εἴ τις φάγοι, καὶ τοῦτο
ὕστερον κατανοηθῆναι. τοιαῦται μὲν οὖν δυνάμεις καὶ ζώων καὶ φυτῶν ἴσως καὶ παρ᾽ ἄλλοις
εἰσί.

14 Περιττότερα δὲ τῶν φυομένων καὶ πλεῖστον
ἐξηλλαγμένα πρὸς τὰ ἄλλα τὰ εὔοσμα τὰ περὶ
Ἀραβίαν καὶ Συρίαν καὶ Ἰνδούς, οἷον ὅ τε
λιβανωτὸς καὶ ἡ σμύρνα καὶ ἡ κασία καὶ τὸ
ὀποβάλσαμον καὶ τὸ κινάμωμον καὶ ὅσα ἄλλα
τοιαῦτα· περὶ ὧν ἐν ἄλλοις εἴρηται διὰ πλειόνων.
ἐν μὲν οὖν τοῖς πρὸς ἔω τε καὶ μεσημβρίαν καὶ
ταῦτ᾽ ἴδια καὶ ἕτερα δὲ τούτων πλείω ἐστίν.

V. Ἐν δὲ τοῖς πρὸς ἄρκτον οὐχ ὁμοίως· οὐθὲν
γὰρ ὅτι ἄξιον λόγου λέγεται παρὰ τὰ κοινὰ τῶν
δένδρων ἃ καὶ φιλόψυχρά τε τυγχάνει καὶ ἔστι
καὶ παρ᾽ ἡμῖν, οἷον πεύκη δρῦς ἐλάτη πύξος
διοσβάλανος φίλυρα καὶ τὰ ἄλλα δὲ τὰ τοιαῦτα·
σχεδὸν γὰρ οὐδὲν ἕτερον παρὰ ταῦτά ἐστιν, ἀλλὰ
τῶν ἄλλων ὑλημάτων ἔνια ἃ τοὺς ψυχροὺς
μᾶλλον ζητεῖ τόπους, καθάπερ κενταύριον
ἀψίνθιον, ἔτι δὲ τὰ φαρμακώδη ταῖς ῥίζαις καὶ
τοῖς ὀποῖς, οἷον ἐλλέβορος ἐλατήριον σκαμμωνία,
σχεδὸν πάντα τὰ ῥιζοτομούμενα.

2 Τὰ μὲν γὰρ ἐν τῷ Πόντῳ καὶ τῇ Θρᾴκῃ γίνεται,

---

¹ τὰ ἀλλὰ δὲ : ? om. τὰ ; δὲ om. Sch.

even a man, if any drops of it should fall on him. Also they say that in some parts grows a herb under which very small snakes lie coiled up, and that, if anyone treads on these and is bitten, he dies. They also say that, if anyone should eat of unripe dates, he chokes to death, and that this fact was not discovered at first. Now it may be that animals and plants have such properties elsewhere also.

Among the plants that grow in Arabia Syria and India the aromatic plants are somewhat exceptional and distinct from the plants of other lands; for instance, frankincense myrrh cassia balsam of Mecca cinnamon and all other such plants, about which we have spoken at greater length elsewhere. So in the parts towards the east and south there are these special plants and many others besides.

*Of the plants special to northern regions.*

V. In the northern regions it is not so, for nothing worthy of record is mentioned except the ordinary trees which love the cold and are found also in our country, as fir oak silver-fir box chestnut lime, as well as other similar trees. There is hardly any other [1] besides these; but of shrubs there are some which for choice [2] seek cold regions, as centaury and wormwood, and further those that have medicinal properties in their roots and juices, such as hellebore squirting cucumber scammony, and nearly all those whose roots are gathered.[3]

Some of these grow in Pontus and Thrace, some

---

[2] I have moved μᾶλλον, which in the MSS. comes before τῶν ἄλλων.

[3] *i.e.* which have medicinal uses.

## THEOPHRASTUS

τὰ δὲ περὶ τὴν Οἴτην καὶ τὸν Παρνασὸν καὶ τὸ
Πήλιον καὶ τὴν Ὄσσαν καὶ τὸ Τελέθριον· καὶ ἐν
τούτοις δέ τινές φασι πλεῖστον· πολλὰ δὲ καὶ
ἐν τῇ Ἀρκαδίᾳ καὶ ἐν τῇ Λακωνικῇ· φαρμακώδεις
γὰρ καὶ αὗται. τῶν δὲ εὐωδῶν οὐδὲν ἐν ταύταις,
πλὴν ἴρις ἐν τῇ Ἰλλυρίδι καὶ περὶ τὸν Ἀδρίαν·
ταύτῃ γὰρ χρηστὴ καὶ πολὺ διαφέρουσα τῶν
ἄλλων· ἀλλ᾽ ἐν τοῖς ἀλεεινοῖς καὶ τοῖς πρὸς
μεσημβρίαν ὥσπερ ἀντικείμενα τὰ εὐώδη. ἔχουσι
δὲ καὶ κυπάριττον οἱ ἀλεεινοὶ μᾶλλον, ὥσπερ
Κρήτη Λυκία Ῥόδος, κέδρον δὲ καὶ τὰ Θρᾴκια
ὄρη καὶ τὰ Φρύγια.

3    Τῶν δὲ ἡμερουμένων ἥκιστά φασιν ἐν τοῖς
ψυχροῖς ὑπομένειν δάφνην καὶ μυρρίνην, καὶ
τούτων δὲ ἧττον ἔτι τὴν μυρρίνην· σημεῖον δὲ
λέγουσιν ὅτι ἐν τῷ Ὀλύμπῳ δάφνη μὲν πολλή,
μύρρινος δὲ ὅλως οὐκ ἔστιν. ἐν δὲ τῷ Πόντῳ
περὶ Παντικάπαιον οὐδ᾽ ἕτερον καίπερ σπουδα-
ζόντων καὶ πάντα μηχανωμένων πρὸς τὰς ἱερο-
σύνας· συκαῖ δὲ πολλαὶ καὶ εὐμεγέθεις καὶ
ῥοιαὶ δὲ περισκεπαζόμεναι· ἄπιοι δὲ καὶ μηλέαι
πλεῖσται καὶ παντοδαπώταται καὶ χρησταί·
αὗται δ᾽ ἐαριναὶ πλὴν εἰ ἄρα ὄψιαι· τῆς δὲ
ἀγρίας ὕλης ἐστὶ δρῦς πτελέα μελία καὶ ὅσα
τοιαῦτα· πεύκη δὲ καὶ ἐλάτη καὶ πίτυς οὐκ ἔστιν
οὐδὲ ὅλως οὐδὲν ἔνδαδον· ὑγρὰ δὲ αὕτη καὶ
χείρων πολὺ τῆς Σινωπικῆς, ὥστ᾽ οὐδὲ πολὺ
χρῶνται αὐτῇ πλὴν πρὸς τὰ ὑπαίθρια.    ταῦτα

---

[1] Τελέθριον conj. Sch. (in Euboea), cf. 9. 15. 4; Πελέθριον
UMVP; Παρθένιον Ald.G.

[2] Whose rhizome was used for perfumes; cf. 1. 7. 2; de
odor. 22. 23. 28. 32; Dykes, The Genus Iris, p. 237, gives an
interesting account of the modern uses of 'orris-root.'

324

about Oeta Parnassus Pelion Ossa and Telethrion,[1] and in these parts some say that there is great abundance; so also is there in Arcadia and Laconia, for these districts too produce medicinal plants. But of the aromatic plants none grows in these lands, except the iris[2] in Illyria on the shores of the Adriatic; for here it is excellent and far superior to that which grows elsewhere; but in hot places and those which face the south the fragrant plants grow, as if by contrast to the medicinal plants. And the warm places have also the cypress in greater abundance; for instance, Crete Lycia Rhodes, while the prickly cedar grows in the Thracian and the Phrygian mountains.

Of cultivated plants they say that those least able to thrive in cold regions are the bay and myrtle, especially the myrtle, and they give for proof [3] that on Mount Olympus the bay is abundant, but the myrtle does not occur at all. In Pontus about Panticapaeum neither grows, though they are anxious to grow them and take special pains [4] to do so for religious purposes. But there are many well grown fig-trees and pomegranates, which are given shelter; pears and apples are abundant in a great variety of forms and are excellent. These are spring-fruiting trees, except that they may fruit later here than elsewhere. Of wild trees there are oak elm manna-ash and the like (while there is no fir silver-fir nor Aleppo pine, nor indeed any resinous tree). But the wood of such trees [5] in this country is damp and much inferior to that of Sinope, so that they do not much use it except for outdoor purposes. These

[3] Plin. 16. 137.
[4] Plin., l.c., says that Mithridates made this attempt.
[5] i.e. oak, etc.

μὲν οὖν περὶ τὸν Πόντον ἢ ἔν τισί γε τόποις αὐτοῦ.

4 Ἐν δὲ τῇ Προποντίδι γίνεται καὶ μύρρινος καὶ δάφνη πολλαχοῦ ἐν τοῖς ὄρεσιν. ἴσως δ' ἔνια καὶ τῶν τόπων ἴδια θετέον· ἕκαστοι γὰρ ἔχουσι τὰ διαφέροντα, ὥσπερ εἴρηται, κατὰ τὰς ὕλας οὐ μόνον τῷ βελτίω καὶ χείρω τὴν αὐτὴν ἔχειν ἀλλὰ καὶ τῷ φέρειν ἢ μὴ φέρειν· οἷον ὁ μὲν Τμῶλος ἔχει καὶ ὁ Μύσιος Ὄλυμπος πολὺ τὸ κάρυον καὶ τὴν διοσβάλανον, ἔτι δὲ ἄμπελον καὶ μηλέαν καὶ ῥόαν· ἡ δὲ Ἴδη τὰ μὲν οὐκ ἔχει τούτων τὰ δὲ σπάνια· περὶ δὲ Μακεδονίαν καὶ τὸν Πιερικὸν Ὄλυμπον τὰ μὲν ἔστι τὰ δ' οὐκ ἔστι τούτων· ἐν δὲ τῇ Εὐβοίᾳ καὶ περὶ τὴν Μαγνησίαν τὰ μὲν Εὐβοϊκὰ πολλὰ τῶν δὲ ἄλλων οὐθέν· οὐδὲ δὴ περὶ τὸ Πέλιον οὐδὲ τὰ ἄλλα τὰ ἐνταῦθα ὄρη.

5 Βραχὺς δ' ἐστὶ τόπος ὃς ἔχει καὶ ὅλως τὴν ναυπηγήσιμον ὕλην· τῆς μὲν γὰρ Εὐρώπης δοκεῖ τὰ περὶ τὴν Μακεδονίαν καὶ ὅσα τῆς Θρᾴκης καὶ περὶ Ἰταλίαν· τῆς δὲ Ἀσίας τά τε ἐν Κιλικίᾳ καὶ τὰ ἐν Σινώπῃ καὶ Ἀμίσῳ, ἔτι δὲ ὁ Μύσιος Ὄλυμπος καὶ ἡ Ἴδη πλὴν οὐ πολλήν· ἡ γὰρ Συρία κέδρον ἔχει καὶ ταύτῃ χρῶνται πρὸς τὰς τριήρεις.

6 Ἀλλὰ καὶ τὰ φίλυδρα καὶ τὰ παραποτάμια ταῦθ' ὁμοίως· ἐν μὲν γὰρ τῷ Ἀδρίᾳ πλάτανον οὔ φασιν εἶναι πλὴν περὶ τὸ Διομήδους ἱερόν· σπανίαν δὲ καὶ ἐν Ἰταλίᾳ πάσῃ· καίτοι πολλοὶ καὶ μεγάλοι ποταμοὶ παρ' ἀμφοῖν· ἀλλ' οὐκ

---

[1] See Index.
[2] καὶ ὅσα : text probably defective, but sense clear. ? καὶ ὅσα τῆς Θ. ἔχει καὶ τὰ περὶ Ἰ.

are the trees of Pontus, or at least of certain districts of that country.

In the land of Propontis myrtle and bay are found in many places on the mountains. Perhaps however some trees should be put down as special to particular places. For each district, as has been said, has different trees, differing not only in that the same trees occur but of variable quality, but also as to producing or not producing some particular tree. For instance, Tmolus and the Mysian Olympus have the hazel and chestnut [1] in abundance, and also the vine apple and pomegranate; while Mount Ida has some of these not at all and others only in small quantity; and in Macedonia and on the Pierian Olympus some of these occur, but not others; and in Euboea and Magnesia the sweet chestnut [1] is common, but none of the others is found; nor yet on Pelion or the other mountains of that region.

Again it is only a narrow extent of country which produces wood fit for shipbuilding at all, namely in Europe the Macedonian region, and certain parts [2] of Thrace and Italy; in Asia Cilicia Sinope and Amisus, and also the Mysian Olympus, and Mount Ida; but in these parts it is not abundant. For Syria has Syrian cedar, and they use this for their galleys.

The like is true of trees which love water and the riverside; in the Adriatic region they say that the plane is not found, except near the Shrine of Diomedes,[3] and that it is scarce throughout Italy[4]; yet there are many large rivers in both countries, in spite of which the localities do not seem to

[3] On one of the islands of Diomedes, off the coast of Apulia; now called Isole di Tremiti. cf. Plin. 12. 6.
[4] cf. 2. 8. 1 n.

327

ἔοικε φέρειν ὁ τόπος· ἐν Ῥηγίῳ γοῦν ἃς Διονύσιος
πρεσβύτερος ὁ τύραννος ἐφύτευσεν ἐν τῷ παρα-
δείσῳ, αἵ εἰσι νῦν ἐν τῷ γυμνασίῳ, φιλοτιμηθεῖσαι[1]
οὐ δεδύνηνται λαβεῖν μέγεθος.

7 Ἔνιοι δὲ πλείστην ἔχουσι πλάτανον, οἱ δὲ
πτελέαν καὶ ἰτέαν, οἱ δὲ μυρίκην, ὥσπερ ὁ Αἷμος.
ὥστε τὰ μὲν τοιαῦτα, καθάπερ ἐλέχθη, τῶν τόπων
ἴδια θετέον ὁμοίως ἔν τε τοῖς ἀγρίοις καὶ τοῖς
ἡμέροις. οὐ μὴν ἀλλὰ τάχ᾽ ἂν εἴη καὶ τούτων
ἐπί τινων ὥστε διακοσμηθέντων δύνασθαι τὴν
χώραν φέρειν, ὃ καὶ νῦν ξυμβαῖνον ὁρῶμεν καὶ
ἐπὶ ζώων ἐνίων καὶ φυτῶν.

VI. Μεγίστην δὲ διαφορὰν αὐτῆς τῆς φύσεως
τῶν δένδρων καὶ ἁπλῶς τῶν ὑλημάτων ὑποληπτέον ἣν καὶ πρότερον εἴπομεν, ὅτι τὰ μὲν ἔγγαια
τὰ δ᾽ ἔνυδρα τυγχάνει, καθάπερ τῶν ζώων, καὶ τῶν
φυτῶν· οὐ μόνον ἐν τοῖς ἔλεσι καὶ ταῖς λίμναις
καὶ τοῖς ποταμοῖς γὰρ ἀλλὰ καὶ ἐν τῇ θαλάττῃ
φύεται καὶ ὑλήματα ἔνια ἔν τε τῇ ἔξω καὶ δένδρα·
ἐν μὲν γὰρ τῇ περὶ ἡμᾶς μικρὰ πάντα τὰ φυόμενα,
καὶ οὐδὲν ὑπερέχον ὡς εἰπεῖν τῆς θαλάττης·[2] ἐν
ἐκείνῃ δὲ καὶ τὰ τοιαῦτα καὶ ὑπερέχοντα, καὶ
ἕτερα δὲ μείζω δένδρα.

2 Τὰ μὲν οὖν περὶ ἡμᾶς ἐστι τάδε· φανερώτατα
μὲν καὶ κοινότατα πᾶσιν τό τε φῦκος καὶ τὸ
βρύον καὶ ὅσα ἄλλα τοιαῦτα· φανερώτατα δὲ καὶ

---

[1] φιλοτιμηθεῖσαι conj. St.; φιλοτιμηθεὶς MSS ; Plin. 12. 7.
[2] θαλάττης conj. Scal. from G ; ἐλάτης Ald. H.

produce this tree. At any rate those which King Dionysius the Elder planted at Rhegium in the park, and which are now in the grounds of the wrestling school and are thought much of,[1] have not been able to attain any size.

Some of these regions however have the plane in abundance, and others the elm and willow, others the tamarisk, such as the district of Mount Haemus. Wherefore such trees we must, as was said, take to be peculiar to their districts, whether they are wild or cultivated. However it might well be that the country should be able to produce some of these trees, if they were carefully cultivated: this we do in fact find to be the case with some plants, as with some animals.

*Of the aquatic plants of the Mediterranean.*

VI. However the greatest difference in the natural character itself of trees and of tree-like plants generally we must take to be that mentioned already, namely, that of plants, as of animals, some belong to the earth, some to water. Not only in swamps, lakes and rivers, but even in the sea there are some tree-like growths, and in the ocean there are even trees. In our own sea all the things that grow are small, and hardly any of them rise above the surface[2]; but in the ocean we find the same kinds rising above the surface, and also other larger trees.

Those found in our own waters are as follows: most conspicuous of those which are of general occurrence are seaweed[3] oyster-green and the like; most obvious of those peculiar to certain parts are the

[3] Plin. 13. 135.

ἰδιώτατα κατὰ τοὺς τόπους ἐλάτη συκῆ δρῦς
ἄμπελος φοῖνιξ. τούτων δὲ τὰ μὲν πρόσγεια
τὰ δὲ πόντια τὰ δ' ἀμφοτέρων τῶν τόπων κοινά.
καὶ τὰ μὲν πολυειδῆ, καθάπερ τὸ φῦκος, τὰ δὲ
μίαν ἰδέαν ἔχοντα. τοῦ γὰρ φύκους τὸ μέν ἐστι
πλατύφυλλον ταινιοειδὲς χρῶμα ποῶδες ἔχον,
ὃ δὴ καὶ πράσον καλοῦσί τινες, οἱ δὲ ζωστῆρα·
ῥίζαν δὲ ἔχει δασεῖαν ἔξωθεν ἔνδοθεν δὲ λεπυριώδη,
μακρὰν δὲ ἐπιεικῶς καὶ εὐπαχῆ παρομοίαν τοῖς
κρομυογητείοις.

3 Τὸ δὲ τριχόφυλλον, ὥσπερ τὸ μάραθον, οὐ
ποῶδες ἀλλ' ἔξωχρον οὐδὲ ἔχον καυλὸν ἀλλ'
ὀρθόν πως ἐν αὑτῷ· φύεται δὲ τοῦτο ἐπὶ τῶν
ὀστράκων καὶ τῶν λίθων, οὐχ ὥσπερ θάτερον
πρὸς τῇ γῇ· πρόσγεια δ' ἄμφω, καὶ τὸ μὲν
τριχόφυλλον πρὸς αὐτῇ τῇ γῇ, πολλάκις δὲ ὥσπερ
ἐπικλύζεται μόνον ὑπὸ τῆς θαλάττης, θάτερον δὲ
ἀνωτέρω.

4 Γίνεται δὲ ἐν μὲν τῇ ἔξω τῇ περὶ Ἡρακλέους
στήλας θαυμαστόν τι τὸ μέγεθος, ὥς φασι, καὶ τὸ
πλάτος μεῖζον ὡς παλαιστιαῖον. φέρεται δὲ
τοῦτο εἰς τὴν ἔσω θάλατταν ἅμα τῷ ῥῷ τῷ
ἔξωθεν καὶ καλοῦσιν αὐτὸ πράσον· ἐν ταύτῃ δ'
ἔν τισι τόποις ὥστ' ἐπάνω τοῦ ὀμφαλοῦ. λέγεται
δὲ ἐπέτειον εἶναι καὶ φύεσθαι μὲν τοῦ ἦρος
λήγοντος, ἀκμάζειν δὲ τοῦ θέρους, τοῦ μετοπώρου
δὲ φθίνειν, κατὰ δὲ τὸν χειμῶνα ἀπόλλυσθαι καὶ
ἐκπίπτειν. ἅπαντα δὲ καὶ τἆλλα τὰ φυόμενα
χείρω καὶ ἀμαυρότερα γίνεσθαι τοῦ χειμῶνος.

---

[1] See Index : συκῆ, δρῦς, etc.
[2] ταινιοειδὲς conj. Dalec. : τεταινοειδὲς UP₂Ald.H.; τὰ τενο-
ειδὲς MV.    [3] cf. Diosc. 4. 99 ; Plin. 13. 136.

sea-plants called 'fir' 'fig' 'oak' 'vine' 'palm.'[1]
Of these some are found close to land, others
in the deep sea, others equally in both positions.
And some have many forms, as seaweed, some but
one. Thus of seaweed there is the broad-leaved
kind, riband-like[2] and green in colour, which some
call 'green-weed' and others 'girdle-weed.' This
has a root which on the outside is shaggy, but the
inner part is made of several coats, and it is fairly
long and stout, like *kromyogeteion* (a kind of onion).

[3] Another kind has hair-like leaves like fennel,
and is not green but pale yellow; nor has it a stalk,
but it is, as it were, erect in itself; this grows on
oyster-shells and stones, not, like the other, attached
to the bottom: but both are plants of the shore,
and the hair-leaved kind grows close to land, and
sometimes is merely washed over by the sea[4]; while
the other is found further out.

Again in the ocean about the pillars of Heracles
there is a kind[5] of marvellous size, they say, which
is larger, about a palmsbreadth.[6] This is carried into
the inner sea along with the current from the outer
sea, and they call it 'sea-leek' (riband-weed);
and in this sea in some parts it grows higher than
a man's waist. It is said to be annual, and to come
up at the end of spring, and to be at its best in
summer, and to wither in autumn, while in winter it
perishes and is thrown up on shore. Also, they say,
all the other plants of the sea become weaker and
feebler in winter. These then are, one may say, the

[4] *i.e.* grows above low water mark.
[5] See Index: φῦκος (2).
[6] *i.e.* the 'leaf': the comparison is doubtless with τὸ
πλατύ, §2; ὡς UMVAld.; ἢ W. after Sch.'s conj.

THEOPHRASTUS

ταῦτα μὲν οὖν οἷον πρόσγεια περί γε τὴν
θάλατταν. τὸ δὲ πόντιον φῦκος ὃ οἱ σπογγιεῖς
ἀνακολυμβῶσι πελάγιον.

5 Καὶ ἐν Κρήτῃ δὲ φύεται πρὸς τῇ γῇ ἐπὶ τῶν
πετρῶν πλεῖστον καὶ κάλλιστον ᾧ βάπτουσιν οὐ
μόνον τὰς ταινίας ἀλλὰ καὶ ἔρια καὶ ἱμάτια· καὶ
ἕως ἂν ᾖ πρόσφατος ἡ βαφή, πολὺ καλλίων ἡ
χρόα τῆς πορφύρας· γίνεται δ᾿ ἐν τῇ προσβόρρῳ
καὶ πλεῖον καὶ κάλλιον, ὥσπερ αἱ σπογγιαὶ καὶ
ἄλλα τοιαῦτα.

6 Ἄλλο δ᾿ ἐστὶν ὅμοιον τῇ ἀγρώστει· καὶ γὰρ τὸ
φύλλον παραπλήσιον ἔχει καὶ τὴν ῥίζαν γονα-
τώδη καὶ μακρὰν καὶ πεφυκυῖαν πλαγίαν, ὥσπερ
ἡ τῆς ἀγρώστιδος· ἔχει δὲ καὶ καυλὸν καλαμώδη,
καθάπερ ἡ ἄγρωστις· μεγέθει δὲ ἔλαττον πολὺ
τοῦ φύκους.

Ἄλλο δὲ τὸ βρύον, ὃ φύλλον μὲν ἔχει ποῶδες
τῇ χρόᾳ, πλατὺ δὲ καὶ οὐκ ἀνόμοιον ταῖς θριδα-
κίναις, πλὴν ῥυτιδωδέστερον καὶ ὥσπερ συν-
εσπασμένον. καυλὸν δὲ οὐκ ἔχει, ἀλλ᾿ ἀπὸ μιᾶς
ἀρχῆς πλείω τὰ τοιαῦτα καὶ πάλιν ἀπ᾿ ἄλλης·
φύεται δὲ ἐπὶ τῶν λίθων τὰ τοιαῦτα πρὸς τῇ γῇ
καὶ τῶν ὀστράκων. καὶ τὰ μὲν ἐλάττω σχεδὸν
ταῦτ᾿ ἐστίν.

7 Ἡ δὲ δρῦς καὶ ἡ ἐλάτη παράγειοι μὲν ἄμφω·
φύονται δ᾿ ἐπὶ λίθοις καὶ ὀστράκοις ῥίζας μὲν οὐκ
ἔχουσαι, προσπεφυκυῖαι δὲ ὥσπερ αἱ λεπάδες.
ἀμφότεραι μὲν οἷον σαρκόφυλλα· προμηκέστερον
δὲ τὸ φύλλον πολὺ καὶ παχύτερον τῆς ἐλάτης

---
[1] Plin. 13. 136, cf. 32. 22; Diosc. 4. 99.
[2] litmus; see Index, φῦκος (5).
[3] Plin. l.c.; grass-wrack, see Index, φῦκος (6).

332

sea-plants which are found near the shore. But the
'seaweed of ocean,' which is dived for by the
sponge-fishers, belongs to the open sea.

[1] In Crete there is an abundant and luxuriant
growth [2] on the rocks close to land, with which they
dye not only their ribbons, but also wool and
clothes. And, as long as the dye is fresh, the
colour is far more beautiful than the purple dye;
it occurs on the north coast in greater abundance
and fairer, as do the sponges and other such things.

[3] There is another kind like dog's-tooth grass;
the leaf is very like, the root is jointed and long,
and grows out sideways, like that of that plant; it
has also a reedy stalk like the same plant, and in
size it is much smaller than ordinary seaweed.

[4] Another kind is the oyster-green, which has a
leaf green in colour, but broad and not unlike
lettuce leaves; but it is more wrinkled [5] and as it
were crumpled. It has no stalk, but from a single
starting-point grow many of the kind, and again
from another starting-point. These things grow on
stones close to land and on oyster-shells. These
are about all the smaller kinds.

[6] The 'sea-oak' and 'sea-fir' both belong to the
shore; they grow on stones and oyster-shells, having
no roots, but being attached to them like limpets.[7]
Both have more or less fleshy leaves; but the leaf
of the 'fir' grows much longer and stouter, and is [5]

---

[4] Plin. 13. 137; 27. 56; βρύον conj. Scal. from G and Plin.
*l.c.*; βότρυον U Ald. H.

[5] ῥυτιδωδέστερον conj. Scal. from G and Plin. *l.c.*; χρυσιωδέ-
cτερον Ald.; ῥυσιωδέστερον mBas.

[6] Plin. *l.c.*     [7] λεπάδες Ald.; λοπάδες W. with UMV.

[5] προμηκέστερον . . . πέφυκε καὶ conj. W.; προμ. δὲ τὸ φύλλον
ταχὺ καὶ παχύτερον τῆς ἐλάτης· πολὺ δὲ καὶ Ald.

πέφυκε καὶ οὐκ ἀνόμοιον τοῖς τῶν ὀσπρίων λοβοῖς,
κοῖλον δ' ἔνδοθεν καὶ οὐδὲν ἔχον ἐν αὑτοῖς· τὸ δὲ
τῆς δρυὸς λεπτὸν καὶ μυρικωδέστερον· χρῶμα δ'
ἐπιπόρφυρον ἀμφοῖν. ἡ δὲ ὅλη μορφὴ τῆς μὲν
ἐλάτης ὀρθὴ καὶ αὑτῆς καὶ τῶν ἀκρεμόνων, τῆς δὲ
δρυὸς σκολιωτέρα καὶ μᾶλλον ἔχουσα πλάτος·
8 γίνεται δὲ ἄμφω καὶ πολύκαυλα καὶ <μονόκαυλα,>
μονοκαυλότερον δὲ ἡ ἐλάτη· τὰς δὲ ἀκρεμονικὰς
ἀποφύσεις ἡ μὲν ἐλάτη μακρὰς ἔχει καὶ εὐθείας
καὶ μανάς, ἡ δὲ δρῦς βραχυτέρας καὶ σκολιωτέρας
καὶ πυκνοτέρας. τὸ δ' ὅλον μέγεθος ἀμφοτέρων
ὡς πυγωνιαῖον ἢ μικρὸν ὑπεραῖρον, μεῖζον δὲ ὡς
ἁπλῶς εἰπεῖν τὸ τῆς ἐλάτης. χρήσιμον δὲ ἡ δρῦς
εἰς βαφὴν ἐρίων ταῖς γυναιξίν. ἐπὶ μὲν τῶν
ἀκρεμόνων προσηρτημένα τῶν ὀστρακοδέρμων
ζώων ἔνια· καὶ κάτω δὲ πρὸς αὐτῷ τῷ καυλῷ
περιπεφυκότων τινῶν γ' ὅλῳ, ἐν τούτοις δεδυκότες
ὀνίννοι τε καὶ ἄλλ' ἄττα καὶ τὸ ὅμοιον πολύποδι.

9 Ταῦτα μὲν οὖν πρόσγεια καὶ ῥᾴδια θεωρηθῆναι·
φασὶ δέ τινες καὶ ἄλλην δρῦν εἶναι ποντίαν ἣ καὶ
καρπὸν φέρει, καὶ ἡ βάλανος αὐτῆς χρησίμη·
τοὺς δὲ σκινθοὺς καὶ κολυμβητὰς λέγειν ὅτι καὶ
ἕτεραι μεγάλαι τινὲς τοῖς μεγέθεσιν εἴησαν.
Ἡ δὲ ἄμπελος ἀμφοτέρωσε γίνεται· καὶ γὰρ
πρὸς τῇ γῇ καὶ ποντία· μείζω δ' ἔχει καὶ τὰ
φύλλα καὶ τὰ κλήματα καὶ τὸν καρπὸν ἡ
ποντία.
Ἡ δὲ συκῆ ἄφυλλος μὲν τῷ δὲ μεγέθει οὐ
μεγάλη, χρῶμα δὲ τοῦ φλοιοῦ φοινικοῦν.

---

¹ αὑτοῖς Ald.H.; αὑτῷ conj. W.
² I have inserted μονόκαυλα.

not unlike the pods of pulses, but is hollow inside and contains nothing in the 'pods.'[1] That of the 'oak' is slender and more like the tamarisk; the colour of both is purplish. The whole shape of the 'fir' is erect, both as to the stem and the branches, but that of the 'oak' is less straight and the plant is broader. Both are found both with many stems and with one,[2] but the 'fir' is more apt to have a single stem. The branchlike outgrowths in the 'fir' are long straight and spreading, while in the 'oak' they are shorter less straight and closer. The whole size of either is about a cubit or rather more, but in general that of the 'fir' is the longer. The 'oak' is useful to women for dyeing wool. To the branches are attached certain creatures with shells, and below they are also found attached to the stem itself, which in some cases they completely cover;[3] and among these are found millepedes and other such creatures, including the one which resembles a cuttlefish.

These plants occur close to land and are easy to observe; but some report[4] that there is another 'sea oak' which even bears fruit and has a useful 'acorn.' and that the sponge fishers[5] and divers told them that there were other large kinds.

[6] The 'sea-vine' grows under both conditions, both close to land and in the deep sea; but the deep sea form has larger leaves branches and fruit.

[7] The 'sea-fig' is leafless and not of large size, and the colour of the bark is red.

[3] τινῶν γ' ὅλῳ conj. W; τινῶν ὅλων Ald.; τινῶν γε ὅλων U; text uncertain: the next clause has no connecting particle.
[4] Plin. 13. 137.
[5] σκίνθους, a vox nihili: perhaps conceals a proper name, e.g. Σικελικούς; σπογγεῖς conj. St.
[6] Plin. 13. 138.    [7] Plin. l.c.

335

10   Ὁ δὲ φοῖνιξ ἐστι μὲν πόντιον βραχυστέλεχες
δὲ σφόδρα, καὶ σχεδὸν εὐθεῖαι αἱ ἐκφύσεις τῶν
ῥάβδων· καὶ κάτωθεν οὐ κύκλῳ αὗται, καθάπερ
τῶν ῥάβδων αἱ ἀκρεμόνες, ἀλλ᾽ ὡσὰν ἐν πλάτει
κατὰ μίαν συνεχεῖς, ὀλιγαχοῦ δὲ καὶ ἀπαλλάττουσαι. τῶν δὲ ῥάβδων ἢ τῶν ἀποφύσεων
τούτων ὁμοία τρόπον τινὰ ἡ φύσις τοῖς τῶν
ἀκανθῶν φύλλοις τῶν ἀκανικῶν, οἷον σόγκοις
καὶ τοῖς τοιούτοις, πλὴν ὀρθαὶ καὶ οὐχ, ὥσπερ
ἐκεῖνα, περικεκλασμέναι καὶ τὸ φύλλον ἔχουσαι
διαβεβρωμένον ὑπὸ τῆς ἄλμης· ἐπεὶ τό γε δι᾽
ὅλου ἥκειν τὸν μέσον γε καυλὸν καὶ ἡ ἄλλη ὄψις
παραπλησία. τὸ δὲ χρῶμα καὶ τούτων καὶ τῶν
καυλῶν καὶ ὅλου τοῦ φυτοῦ ἐξέρυθρόν τε σφόδρα
καὶ φοινικοῦν.
Καὶ τὰ μὲν ἐν τῇδε τῇ θαλάττῃ τοσαῦτά ἐστιν.
ἡ γὰρ σπογγιὰ καὶ αἱ ἀπλυσίαι καλούμεναι καὶ
εἴ τι τοιοῦτον ἑτέραν ἔχει φύσιν.
VII. Ἐν δὲ τῇ ἔξω τῇ περὶ Ἡρακλέους στήλας
τό τε πράσον, ὥσπερ εἴρηται, φύεται καὶ τὰ
ἀπολιθούμενα ταῦτα, οἷον θῦμα καὶ τὰ δαφνοειδῆ
καὶ τὰ ἄλλα. τῆς δὲ ἐρυθρᾶς καλουμένης ἐν τῇ
Ἀραβίᾳ μικρὸν ἐπάνω Κόπτου ἐν μὲν τῇ γῇ

---

[1] κάτωθεν . . , ἀπαλλάττουσαι probably beyond certain restoration : I have added καὶ before κάτωθεν (from G), altered
κυκλωθὲν to κύκλῳ, put a stop before καὶ κάτωθεν, and restored
ἀπαλλάττουσαι (Ald.H.).   [2] cf. 6. 4. 8; 7. 8. 3.
[3] περικεκλασμένα, i.e. towards the ground. cf. Diosc. 3.
68 and 69, where Plin. (27. 13) renders (φύλλα) ὑποπερικλᾶται
ad terram infracta.

The 'sea-palm' is a deep-sea plant, but with a
very short stem, and the branches which spring from
it are almost straight; and these under water are
not set all round the stem, like the twigs which grow
from the branches, but extend, as it were, quite
flat in one direction, and are uniform; though
occasionally they are irregular.[1] The character of
these branches or outgrowths to some extent resembles the leaves of thistle-like spinous plants,
such as the sow-thistles[2] and the like, except that
they are straight and not bent over[3] like these,
and have their leaves eaten away by the brine; in
the fact that the central stalk[4] at least runs through
the whole, they resemble these, and so does the
general appearance. The colour both of the branches
and of the stalks and of the plant as a whole is a
deep red or scarlet.

Such are the plants found in this sea. For sponges
and what are called *aplysiai*[5] and such-like growths
are of a different character.

*Of the aquatic plants of the 'outer sea' (i.e. Atlantic, Persian
Gulf, etc.).*

VII. In the outer sea near the pillars of Heracles
grows the 'sea-leek,' as has been said[6]; also the
well known[7] plants which turn to stone, as *thyma*,
the plants like the bay and others. And in the
sea called the Red Sea[8] a little above Coptos[9]

---

[4] *i.e.* midrib.
[5] Some kind of sponge. ἀπλυσίαι conj. R. Const; πλύσιαι
UAld.; πλυσίαι M; πλούσιαι V.   [6] 4. 6. 4.
[7] ταῦτα: *cf.* 3. 7. 3; 3. 18. 11.
[8] Plin. 13. 139.
[9] Κόπτου conj. Scal.; κόπου MV; κόλπου UAld.; *Capto* G
and Plin. *l.c.*

δένδρον οὐδὲν φύεται πλὴν τῆς ἀκάνθης τῆς
διψάδος καλουμένης· σπανία δὲ καὶ αὕτη διὰ τὰ
καύματα καὶ τὴν ἀνυδρίαν· οὐχ ὕει γὰρ ἀλλ᾽ ἢ
δι᾽ ἐτῶν τεττάρων ἢ πέντε καὶ τότε λάβρως καὶ
ἐπ᾽ ὀλίγον χρόνον.

2 Ἐν δὲ τῇ θαλάττῃ φύεται, καλοῦσι δ᾽ αὐτὰ
δάφνην καὶ ἐλάαν. ἔστι δὲ ἡ μὲν δάφνη ὁμοία
τῇ ἀρίᾳ ἡ δὲ ἐλάα <τῇ ἐλάᾳ> τῷ φύλλῳ· καρπὸν
δὲ ἔχει ἡ ἐλάα παραπλήσιον ταῖς ἐλάαις· ἀφίησι
δὲ καὶ δάκρυον, ἐξ οὗ οἱ ἰατροὶ φάρμακον ἔναιμον
συντιθέασιν ὃ γίνεται σφόδρα ἀγαθόν. ὅταν δὲ
ὕδατα πλείω γένηται, μύκητες φύονται πρὸς τῇ
θαλάττῃ κατά τινα τόπον, οὗτοι δὲ ἀπολιθοῦνται
ὑπὸ τοῦ ἡλίου. ἡ δὲ θάλαττα θηριώδης· πλείστους δὲ ἔχει τοὺς καρχαρίας, ὥστε μὴ εἶναι
κολυμβῆσαι.

Ἐν δὲ τῷ κόλπῳ τῷ καλουμένῳ Ἡρώων, ἐφ᾽ ὃν
καταβαίνουσιν οἱ ἐξ Αἰγύπτου, φύεται μὲν δάφνη
τε καὶ ἐλάα καὶ θύμον, οὐ μὴν χλωρά γε ἀλλὰ
λιθοειδῆ τὰ ὑπερέχοντα τῆς θαλάττης, ὅμοια δὲ
καὶ τοῖς φύλλοις καὶ τοῖς βλαστοῖς τοῖς χλωροῖς.
ἐν δὲ τῷ θύμῳ καὶ τὸ τοῦ ἄνθους χρῶμα διάδηλον
ὡσὰν μήπω τελέως ἐξηνθηκός. μήκη δὲ τῶν
δενδρυφίων ὅσον εἰς τρεῖς πήχεις.

3 Οἱ δέ, ὅτε ἀνάπλους ἦν τῶν ἐξ Ἰνδῶν ἀποστα-
λέντων ὑπὸ Ἀλεξάνδρου, τὰ ἐν τῇ θαλάττῃ
φυόμενα, μέχρι οὗ μὲν ἂν ᾖ ἐν τῷ ὑγρῷ, χρῶμά
φασιν ἔχειν ὅμοιον τοῖς φυκίοις, ὁπόταν δ᾽ ἐξ-

---

[1] cf. Strabo 16. 1. 147.　　[2] See Index.
[3] The name of a tree seems to have dropped out : I have
inserted τῇ ἐλάᾳ: cf. ταῖς ἐλάαις below. Bretzl suggests ἰδέᾳ
for ἀρίᾳ.

in Arabia there grows on the land no tree except that called the 'thirsty' acacia, and even this is scarce by reason of the heat and the lack of water; for it never rains except at intervals of four or five years, and then the rain comes down heavily and is soon over.

[1] But there are plants in the sea, which they call 'bay' and 'olive' (white mangrove[2]). In foliage the 'bay' is like the *aria* (holm-oak), the 'olive' like the real olive.[3] The latter has a fruit like olives, and it also discharges a gum,[4] from which the physicians[4] compound a drug[5] for stanching blood, which is extremely effective. And when there is more rain than usual, mushrooms grow in a certain place close to the sea, which are turned to stone by the sun. The sea is full of beasts, and produces sharks[6] in great numbers, so that diving is impossible.

In the gulf called 'the Gulf of the Heroes,'[7] to which the Egyptians go down, there grow a 'bay,' an 'olive,' and a 'thyme'; these however are not green, but like stones so far as they project above the sea, but in leaves and shoots they are like their green namesakes. In the 'thyme' the colour of the flower is also conspicuous, looking as though the flower had not yet completely developed. These treelike growths are about three cubits in height.

[8] Now some, referring to the occasion when there was an expedition of those returning from India sent out by Alexander, report that the plants which grow in the sea, so long as they are kept damp, have a colour

[4] *cf*. Diosc. 1. 105 and 106.
[5] *cf*. Athen. 4. 83 ; Plin. 12. 77.
[6] Plin. 13. 139.     [7] *cf*. 9. 4. 4.     [8] Plin. 13. 140.

339
z 2

THEOPHRASTUS

ἐνεχθέντα τεθῇ πρὸς τὸν ἥλιον, ἐν ὀλίγῳ χρόνῳ
ἐξομοιοῦσθαι τῷ ἁλί. φύεσθαι δὲ καὶ σχοίνους
λιθίνους παρ' αὐτὴν τὴν θάλατταν, οὓς οὐδεὶς ἂν
διαγνοίη τῇ ὄψει πρὸς τοὺς ἀληθινούς. θαυμασιώτερον δέ τι τούτου λέγουσι· φύεσθαι γὰρ
δενδρύφι' ἄττα τὸ μὲν χρῶμα ἔχοντα ὅμοιον
κέρατι βοὸς τοῖς δὲ ὄζοις τραχέα καὶ ἀπ' ἄκρου
πυρρά· ταῦτα δὲ θραύεσθαι μὲν εἰ συγκλῴη τις·
ἐκ δὲ τούτων πυρὶ ἐμβαλλόμενα, καθάπερ τὸν
σίδηρον, διάπυρα γινόμενα πάλιν ὅταν ἀποψύ-
χοιτο καθίστασθαι καὶ τὴν αὐτὴν χρόαν λαμβάνειν.

4 Ἐν δὲ ταῖς νήσοις ταῖς ὑπὸ τῆς πλημμυρίδος
καταλαμβανομέναις δένδρα μεγάλα πεφυκέναι
ἡλίκαι πλάτανοι καὶ αἴγειροι αἱ μέγισται· συμβαίνειν δέ, ὅθ' ἡ πλημμυρὶς ἐπέλθοι, τὰ μὲν ἄλλα
κατακρύπτεσθαι ὅλα, τῶν δὲ μεγίστων ὑπερέχειν
τοὺς κλάδους, ἐξ ὧν τὰ πρυμνήσια ἀνάπτειν, εἶθ'
ὅτε πάλιν ἄμπωτις γίνοιτο ἐκ τῶν ῥιζῶν. ἔχειν
δὲ τὸ δένδρον φύλλον μὲν ὅμοιον τῇ δάφνῃ, ἄνθος
δὲ τοῖς ἴοις καὶ τῷ χρώματι καὶ τῇ ὀσμῇ, καρπὸν
δὲ ἡλίκον ἐλία καὶ τοῦτον εὐώδη σφόδρα· καὶ τὰ
μὲν φύλλα οὐκ ἀποβάλλειν, τὸ δὲ ἄνθος καὶ τὸν
καρπὸν ἅμα τῷ φθινοπώρῳ γίνεσθαι, τοῦ δὲ ἔαρος
ἀπορρεῖν.

5 Ἄλλα δ' ἐν αὐτῇ τῇ θαλάττῃ πεφυκέναι, ἀείφυλλα μὲν τὸν δὲ καρπὸν ὅμοιον ἔχειν τοῖς
θέρμοις.

Περὶ δὲ τὴν Περσίδα τὴν κατὰ τὴν Καρμανίαν,
καθ' ὃ ἡ πλημμυρὶς γίνεται, δένδρα ἐστὶν εὐμεγέθη
ὅμοια τῇ ἀνδράχλῃ καὶ τῇ μορφῇ καὶ τοῖς φύλλοις·
καρπὸν δὲ ἔχει πολὺν ὅμοιον τῷ χρώματι ταῖς

340

like sea-weeds, but that when they are taken out and put in the sun, they shortly become like salt. They also say that rushes of stone grow close to the sea, which none could distinguish at sight from real rushes. They also report a more marvellous thing than this ; they say that there are certain tree-like growths which in colour resemble an ox-horn, but whose branches are rough, and red at the tip ; these break if they are doubled up, and some of them, if they are cast on a fire, become red-hot like iron, but recover when they cool and assume their original colour.

[1] On the islands which get covered by the tide they say that great trees [2] grow, as big as planes or the tallest poplars, and that it came to pass that, when the tide [3] came up, while the other things were entirely buried, the branches of the biggest trees projected and they fastened the stern cables to them, and then, when the tide ebbed again, fastened them to the roots. And that the tree has a leaf like that of the bay, and a flower like gilliflowers in colour and smell, and a fruit the size of that of the olive, which is also very fragrant. And that it does not shed its leaves, and that the flower and the fruit form together in autumn and are shed in spring.

[4] Also they say there are plants which actually grow in the sea, which are evergreen and have a fruit like lupins.

[5] In Persia in the Carmanian district, where the tide is felt, there are trees [6] of fair size like the andrachne in shape and in leaves ; and they bear much fruit like

[1] Plin. 13. 141.
[2] Mangroves. See Index App. (12).
[3] cf. Arr. Anab. 6. 22. 6.
[4] Plin. l.c. Index App. (13).   [5] Plin. 12. 37.
[6] White mangroves. Index App. (14).

ἀμυγδάλαις ἔξωθεν, τὸ δ' ἐντὸς συνελίττεται
καθάπερ συνηρτημένον πᾶσιν. ὑποβέβρωται δὲ
ταῦτα τὰ δένδρα πάντα κατὰ μέσον ὑπὸ τῆς
θαλάττης καὶ ἕστηκεν ὑπὸ τῶν ῥιζῶν, ὥσπερ
πολύπους. ὅταν γὰρ ἡ ἄμπωτις γένηται θεωρεῖν
6 ἐστιν. ὕδωρ δὲ ὅλως οὐκ ἔστιν ἐν τῷ τόπῳ· κατα-
λείπονται δέ τινες διώρυχες δι' ὧν διαπλέουσιν·
αὗται δ' εἰσὶ θαλάττης· ᾧ καὶ δῆλον οἴονταί τινες
ὅτι τρέφονται ταύτῃ καὶ οὐ τῷ ὕδατι, πλὴν εἴ τι
ταῖς ῥίζαις ἐκ τῆς γῆς ἕλκουσιν. εὔλογον δὲ καὶ
τοῦθ' ἁλμυρὸν εἶναι· καὶ γὰρ οὐδὲ κατὰ βάθους
αἱ ῥίζαι. τὸ δὲ ὅλον ἓν τὸ γένος εἶναι τῶν τ' ἐν
τῇ θαλάττῃ φυομένων καὶ τῶν ἐν τῇ γῇ ὑπὸ τῆς
πλημμυρίδος καταλαμβανομένων· καὶ τὰ μὲν ἐν
τῇ θαλάττῃ μικρὰ καὶ φυκώδη φαινόμενα, τὰ δ'
ἐν τῇ γῇ μεγάλα καὶ χλωρὰ καὶ ἄνθος εὔοδμον
ἔχοντα, καρπὸν δὲ οἷον θέρμος.
7 Ἐν Τύλῳ δὲ τῇ νήσῳ, κεῖται δ' αὕτη ἐν τῷ
Ἀραβίῳ κόλπῳ, τὰ μὲν πρὸς ἔω τοσοῦτο πλῆθος
εἶναί φασι δένδρων ὅτ' ἐκβαίνει ἡ πλημμυρὶς
ὥστ' ἀποχυρῶσθαι. πάντα δὲ ταῦτα μεγέθη μὲν
ἔχειν ἡλίκα συκῆ, τὸ δὲ ἄνθος ὑπερβάλλον τῇ
εὐωδίᾳ, καρπὸν δὲ ἄβρωτον ὅμοιον τῇ ὄψει τῷ
θέρμῳ. φέρειν δὲ τὴν νῆσον καὶ τὰ δένδρα τὰ
ἐριοφόρα πολλά. ταῦτα δὲ φύλλον μὲν ἔχειν
παρόμοιον τῇ ἀμπέλῳ πλὴν μικρόν, καρπὸν δὲ
οὐδένα φέρειν· ἐν ᾧ δὲ τὸ ἔριον ἡλίκον μῆλον
ἐαρινὸν συμμεμυκός· ὅταν δὲ ὡραῖον ᾖ, ἐκπετάν-

---

[1] Plin. *l.c.* *Sicco litore radicibus nudis polyporum modo complexae steriles arenas aspectantur*: he appears to have had a fuller text.

in colour to almonds on the outside, but the inside
is coiled up as though the kernels were all united.
[1] These trees are all eaten away up to the middle by
the sea and are held up by their roots, so that they
look like a cuttle-fish. For one may see this at
ebb-tide. And there is no rain at all in the district,
but certain channels are left, along which they sail,
and which are part of the sea. Which, some think,
makes it plain that the trees derive nourishment from
the sea and not from fresh water, except what they
draw up with their roots from the land. And it is
reasonable to suppose that this too is brackish; for
the roots do not run to any depth. In general they
say that the trees which grow in the sea and those
which grow on the land and are overtaken by the
tide are of the same kind, and that those which grow
in the sea are small and look like seaweed, while
those that grow [2] on land are large and green and
have a fragrant flower and a fruit like a lupin.

In the island of Tylos,[3] which is situated in the
Arabian gulf,[4] they say that on the east side there is
such a number of trees when the tide goes out that
they make a regular fence. All these are in size
as large as a fig-tree, the flower is exceedingly
fragrant, and the fruit, which is not edible, is like in
appearance to the lupin. They say that the island
also produces the 'wool-bearing' tree (cotton-plant)
in abundance. This has a leaf like that of the vine,
but small, and bears no fruit; but the vessel in which
the 'wool' is contained is as large as a spring apple,

[2] φυκώδη φαινόμενα τὰ δ' ἐν conj. W.; φυκ. φυ. δ' ἐν MVAld.;
U has φερόμενα (?).
[3] cf. 5. 4. 6; Plin. 12. 38 and 39; modern name Bahrein.
[4] i.e. Persian Gulf.

νυσθαι καὶ ἐξείρειν¹ τὸ ἔριον, ἐξ οὗ τὰς σινδόνας
ὑφαίνουσι, τὰς μὲν εὐτελεῖς τὰς δὲ πολυτελε-
στάτας.
8 Γίνεται δὲ τοῦτο καὶ ἐν Ἰνδοῖς, ὥσπερ ἐλέχθη²,
καὶ ἐν Ἀραβίᾳ. εἶναι δὲ ἄλλα δένδρα τὸ ἄνθος
ἔχοντα ὅμοιον τῷ λευκοΐῳ, πλὴν ἄοδμον³ καὶ τῷ
μεγέθει τετραπλάσιον τῶν ἴων⁴. καὶ ἕτερον δέ τι
δένδρον πολύφυλλον ὥσπερ τὸ ῥόδον· τοῦτο δὲ
τὴν μὲν νύκτα συμμύειν ἅμα δὲ τῷ ἡλίῳ ἀνιόντι
διοίγνυσθαι, μεσημβρίας δὲ τελέως διεπτύχθαι,
πάλιν δὲ τῆς δείλης συνάγεσθαι κατὰ μικρὸν καὶ
τὴν νύκτα συμμύειν· λέγειν δὲ καὶ τοὺς ἐγχωρίους ὅτι καθεύδει. γίνεσθαι δὲ καὶ φοίνικας ἐν
τῇ νήσῳ καὶ ἀμπέλους καὶ τἆλλα ἀκρόδρυα καὶ
συκᾶς οὐ φυλλορροούσας. ὕδωρ δὲ οὐράνιον γίνεσθαι μέν, οὐ μὴν χρῆσθαί γε πρὸς τοὺς καρπούς·
ἀλλ᾽ εἶναι κρήνας ἐν τῇ νήσῳ πολλάς, ἀφ᾽ ὧν
πάντα βρέχειν, ὃ καὶ συμφέρειν μᾶλλον τῷ σίτῳ
καὶ τοῖς δένδρεσιν. δι᾽ ὃ καὶ ὅταν ὕσῃ τοῦτο ἐπ-
αφιέναι καθαπερεὶ καταπλύνοντας ἐκεῖνο. καὶ
τὰ μὲν ἐν τῇ ἔξω θαλάττῃ δένδρα τά γε νῦν
τεθεωρημένα σχεδὸν τοσαῦτά ἐστιν.
VIII. Ὑπὲρ δὲ τῶν ἐν τοῖς ποταμοῖς καὶ τοῖς
ἕλεσι καὶ ταῖς λίμναις μετὰ ταῦτα λεκτέον. τρία
δέ ἐστιν εἴδη τῶν ἐν τούτοις, τὰ μὲν δένδρα τὰ δ᾽

---

¹ ἐξείρειν conj. W.; ἐξειαίρειν P₂; ἐξαίρειν Ald.   ² 4. 5. 8.
³ Tamarind. See Index App. (15). Plin. 12. 40.
⁴ πλὴν ἄοδμον conj. H. Steph.; πλείονα ὄδμον UMAld.
⁵ τῷ μεγέθει καὶ I conj.; καὶ τῷ μεγέθει UMVP; καὶ om. Ald.
⁶ Tamarind also. See Index App. (16).   ⁷ i.e. leaflets.
⁸ Ficus laccifera. See Index App. (17).   οὐ φυλλορροούσας
conj. W., cf. G and Plin. l.c.; αἳ φυλλορροοῦσιν Ald.H.

and closed, but when it is ripe, it unfolds and puts forth [1] the 'wool,' of which they weave their fabrics, some of which are cheap and some very expensive.

This tree is also found, as was said,[2] in India as well as in Arabia. They say that there are other trees[3] with a flower like the gilliflower, but scentless[4] and in size[5] four times as large as that flower. And that there is another tree[6] with many leaves[7] like the rose, and that this closes at night, but opens at sunrise, and by noon is completely unfolded : and at evening again it closes by degrees and remains shut at night, and the natives say that it goes to sleep. Also that there are date-palms on the island and vines and other fruit-trees, including evergreen[8] figs. Also that there is water from heaven, but that they do not use it for the fruits, but that there are many springs on the island, from which they water everything, and that this is more beneficial[9] to the corn and the trees. Wherefore, even when it rains, they let this water over the fields,[10] as though they were washing away the rain water. Such are the trees as so far observed which grow in the outer sea.

*Of the plants of rivers, marshes, and lakes, especially in Egypt.*

VIII. Next we must speak of plants which live in rivers marshes and lakes. Of these there are three classes, trees. plants of 'herbaceous'[11] character, and

[9] ἢ καὶ συμφέρειν conj. Sch.: & καὶ συμφέρει Ald.; U has συμφέρειν.

[10] *cf. C.P.* 2. 5. 5, where Androsthenes, one of Alexander's admirals, is given as the authority for this statement.

[11] The term τὰ ποιώδη seems to be given here a narrower connotation than usual, in order that τὰ λοχμώδη may be distinguished.

345

ὥσπερ ποιώδη τὰ δὲ λοχμώδη. λέγω δὲ ποιώδη
μὲν οἷον τὸ σέλινον τὸ ἕλειον καὶ ὅσα ἄλλα τοι-
αῦτα· λοχμώδη δὲ κάλαμον κύπειρον φλεὼ σχοῖ-
νον βούτομον, ἅπερ σχεδὸν κοινὰ πάντων τῶν
ποταμῶν καὶ τῶν τοιούτων τόπων.
Ἐνιαχοῦ δὲ καὶ βάτοι καὶ παλίουροι καὶ τὰ
ἄλλα δένδρα, καθάπερ ἰτέα λεύκη πλάτανος. τὰ
μὲν οὖν μέχρι τοῦ κατακρύπτεσθαι, τὰ δὲ ὥστε
μικρὸν ὑπερέχειν, τῶν δὲ αἱ μὲν ῥίζαι καὶ μικρὸν
τοῦ στελέχους ἐν τῷ ὑγρῷ, τὸ δὲ ἄλλο σῶμα πᾶν
ἔξω. τοῦτο γὰρ καὶ ἰτέᾳ καὶ κλήθρᾳ καὶ πλατάνῳ
καὶ φιλύρᾳ καὶ πᾶσι τοῖς φιλύδροις συμβαίνει.
2  Σχεδὸν δὲ καὶ ταῦτα κοινὰ πάντων τῶν ποταμῶν ἐστιν· ἐπεὶ καὶ ἐν τῷ Νείλῳ πέφυκεν· οὐ
μὴν πολλή γε ἡ πλάτανος, ἀλλὰ σπανιωτέρα ἔτι
ταύτης ἡ λεύκη, πλείστη δὲ μελία καὶ βουμέλιος.
τῶν γοῦν ἐν Αἰγύπτῳ φυομένων τὸ μὲν ὅλον
πολὺ πλῆθός ἐστιν πρὸς τὸ ἀριθμήσασθαι καθ'
ἕκαστον· οὐ μὴν ἀλλ' ὥς γε ἁπλῶς εἰπεῖν ἅπαντα
ἐδώδιμα καὶ χυλοὺς ἔχοντα γλυκεῖς. διαφέρειν
δὲ δοκεῖ τῇ γλυκύτητι καὶ τῷ τρόφιμα μάλιστα
εἶναι τρία ταῦτα, ὅ τε πάπυρος καὶ τὸ καλούμενον σάρι καὶ τρίτον ὃ μνάσιον καλοῦσι.
3  Φύεται δὲ ὁ πάπυρος οὐκ ἐν βάθει τοῦ ὕδατος
ἀλλ' ὅσον ἐν δύο πήχεσιν, ἐνιαχοῦ δὲ καὶ ἐν
ἐλάττονι. πάχος μὲν οὖν τῆς ῥίζης ἡλίκον καρπὸς χειρὸς ἀνδρὸς εὐρώστου, μῆκος δὲ ὑπὲρ τε-
τράπηχυ· φύεται δὲ ὑπὲρ τῆς γῆς αὐτῆς, πλαγίας
ῥίζας εἰς τὸν πηλὸν καθιεῖσα λεπτὰς καὶ πυκνάς,
ἄνω δὲ τοὺς παπύρους καλουμένους τριγώνους,

---

¹ τῶν γοῦν κ.τ.λ.: text probably defective ; what follows
appears to relate to τὰ ποιώδη.

346

plants growing in clumps. By 'herbaceous' I mean
here such plants as the marsh celery and the like;
by 'plants growing in clumps' I mean reeds galingale *phleo* rush sedge—which are common to almost
all rivers and such situations.

And in some such places are found brambles
Christ's thorn and other trees, such as willow abele
plane. Some of these are water plants to the extent
of being submerged, while some project a little from
the water; of some again the roots and a small part
of the stem are under water, but the rest of the
body is altogether above it. This is the case with
willow alder plane lime, and all water-loving trees.

These too are common to almost all rivers, for
they grow even in the Nile. However the plane is
not abundant by rivers, while the abele is even more
scarce, and the manna-ash and ash are commonest.
At any rate of those [1] that grow in Egypt the list is
too long to enumerate separately; however, to speak
generally, they are all edible and have sweet flavours.
But they differ in sweetness, and we may distinguish
also three as the most useful for food, namely the
papyrus, the plant called *sari,* and the plant which
they call *mnasion.*

[2] The papyrus does not grow in deep water, but
only in a depth of about two cubits, and sometimes
shallower. The thickness of the root is that of the
wrist of a stalwart man, and the length above four
cubits [3]; it grows above the ground itself, throwing
down slender matted roots into the mud, and
producing above the stalks which give it its name
'papyrus'; these are three-cornered and about ten

[2] Plin. 13. 71-73.
[3] τετράπηχυ: δέκα πήχεις MSS. See next note.

THEOPHRASTUS

μέγεθος ὡς δέκα πήχεις, κόμην ἔχοντας ἀχρεῖον
ἀσθενῆ καρπὸν δὲ ὅλως οὐδένα· τούτους δ' ἀναδί-
4 δωσι κατὰ πολλὰ μέρη. χρῶνται δὲ ταῖς μὲν
ῥίζαις ἀντὶ ξύλων οὐ μόνον τῷ κάειν ἀλλὰ καὶ τῷ
σκεύη ἄλλα ποιεῖν ἐξ αὐτῶν παντοδαπά· πολὺ
γὰρ ἔχει τὸ ξύλον καὶ καλόν. αὐτὸς δὲ ὁ πάπυρος πρὸς πλεῖστα χρήσιμος· καὶ γὰρ πλοῖα
ποιοῦσιν ἐξ αὐτοῦ, καὶ ἐκ τῆς βίβλου ἱστία τε
πλέκουσι καὶ ψιάθους καὶ ἐσθῆτά τινα καὶ
στρωμνὰς καὶ σχοινία τε καὶ ἕτερα πλείω. καὶ
ἐμφανέστατα δὴ τοῖς ἔξω τὰ βιβλία· μάλιστα δὲ
καὶ πλείστη βοήθεια πρὸς τὴν τροφὴν ἀπ' αὐτοῦ
γίνεται. μασῶνται γὰρ ἅπαντες οἱ ἐν τῇ χώρᾳ
τὸν πάπυρον καὶ ὠμὸν καὶ ἐφθὸν καὶ ὀπτόν· καὶ
τὸν μὲν χυλὸν καταπίνουσι, τὸ δὲ μάσημα ἐκβάλ-
λουσιν. ὁ μὲν οὖν πάπυρος τοιοῦτός τε καὶ ταύτας παρέχεται τὰς χρείας. γίνεται δὲ καὶ ἐν
Συρίᾳ περὶ τὴν λίμνην ἐν ᾗ καὶ ὁ κάλαμος ὁ
εὐώδης· ὅθεν καὶ Ἀντίγονος εἰς τὰς ναῦς ἐποιεῖτο
τὰ σχοινία.
5   Τὸ δὲ σάρι φύεται μὲν ἐν τῷ ὕδατι περὶ τὰ ἕλη
καὶ τὰ πεδία, ἐπειδὰν ὁ ποταμὸς ἀπέλθῃ, ῥίζαν δὲ
ἔχει σκληρὰν καὶ συνεστραμμένην, καὶ ἐξ αὐτῆς
φύεται τὰ σάρια καλούμενα· ταῦτα δὲ μῆκος μὲν
ὡς δύο πήχεις, πάχος δὲ ἡλίκον ὁ δάκτυλος ὁ
μέγας τῆς χειρός· τρίγωνον δὲ καὶ τοῦτο, καθάπερ
ὁ πάπυρος, καὶ κόμην ἔχον παραπλήσιον. μα-
σώμενοι δὲ ἐκβάλλουσι καὶ τοῦτο τὸ μάσημα, τῇ
ῥίζῃ δὲ οἱ σιδηρουργοὶ χρῶνται· τὸν γὰρ ἄνθρακα
ποιεῖ χρηστὸν διὰ τὸ σκληρὸν εἶναι τὸ ξύλον.
6   Τὸ δὲ μνάσιον ποιῶδές ἐστιν, ὥστ' οὐδεμίαν
παρέχεται χρείαν πλὴν τὴν εἰς τροφήν.

348

cubits [1] long, having a plume which is useless and
weak, and no fruit whatever; and these stalks the
plant sends up at many points. They use the roots
instead of wood, not only for burning, but also for
making a great variety of articles: for the wood is
abundant and good. The 'papyrus' itself [2] is useful
for many purposes; for they make boats from it,
and from the rind they weave sails mats a kind of
raiment coverlets ropes and many other things.
Most familiar to foreigners are the papyrus-rolls
made of it; but above all the plant also is of very
great use in the way of food. [3] For all the natives
chew the papyrus both raw boiled and roasted; they
swallow the juice and spit out the quid. Such is
the papyrus and such its uses. It grows also in
Syria about the lake in which grows also sweet-
flag; and Antigonus made of it the cables for his
ships.

[4] The *sari* grows in the water in marshes and
plains, when the river has left them; it has a hard
twisted root, and from it grow what they call the
*saria* [5]; these are about two cubits long and as
thick as a man's thumb: this stalk too is three-
cornered, like the papyrus, and has similar foliage.
This also they chew, spitting out the quid; and
smiths use the root, for it makes excellent charcoal,
because the wood is hard.

*Mnasion* is herbaceous, so that it has no use except
for food.

[1] δέκα πήχεις: τετραπήχεις MSS. The two numbers seem
to have changed places (Bartels ap. Sch.). *cf.* Plin. *l.c.*
[2] *i.e.* the stalk.
[3] *cf.* Diod. 1. 80.    [4] Plin. 13. 128.
[5] *i.e.* stalks, like those of the papyrus.

349

## THEOPHRASTUS

Καὶ τὰ μὲν γλυκύτητι διαφέροντα ταῦτά ἐστι.
φύεται δὲ καὶ ἕτερον ἐν τοῖς ἕλεσι καὶ ταῖς λίμναις ὃ οὐ συνάπτει τῇ γῇ, τὴν μὲν φύσιν ὅμοιον
τοῖς κρίνοις, πολυφυλλότερον δὲ καὶ παρ᾽ ἄλληλα
τὰ φύλλα καθάπερ ἐν διστοιχίᾳ· χρῶμα δὲ χλωρὸν ἔχει σφόδρα. χρῶνται δὲ οἱ ἰατροὶ πρός τε
τὰ γυναικεῖα αὐτῷ καὶ πρὸς τὰ κατάγματα.
7 [Ταῦτα δὲ γίνεται ἐν τῷ ποταμῷ εἰ μὴ ὁ ῥοῦς
ἐξέφερεν· συμβαίνει δὲ ὥστε καὶ ἀποφέρεσθαι·
ἕτερα δ᾽ ἀπ᾽ αὐτῶν πλείω.]
Ὁ δὲ κύαμος φύεται μὲν ἐν τοῖς ἕλεσι καὶ λίμναις, καυλὸς δὲ αὐτοῦ μῆκος μὲν ὁ μακρότατος
εἰς τέτταρας πήχεις, πάχος δὲ δακτυλιαῖος,
ὅμοιος δὲ καλάμῳ μαλακῷ ἀγονάτῳ. διαφύσεις
δὲ ἔνδοθεν ἔχει δι᾽ ὅλου διειλημμένας ὁμοίας τοῖς
κηρίοις· ἐπὶ τούτῳ δὲ ἡ κωδύα, παρομοία σφηκίῳ
περιφερεῖ, καὶ ἐν ἑκάστῳ τῶν κυττάρων κύαμος
μικρὸν ὑπεραίρων αὐτῆς, πλῆθος δὲ οἱ πλεῖστοι
τριάκοντα. τὸ δὲ ἄνθος διπλάσιον ἢ μήκωνος,
χρῶμα δὲ ὅμοιον ῥόδῳ κατακορές· ἐπάνω δὲ τοῦ
ὕδατος ἡ κωδύα. παραφύεται δὲ φύλλα μεγάλα
παρ᾽ ἕκαστον τῶν κυάμων, ὧν ἴσα τὰ μεγέθη
πετάσῳ Θετταλικῇ τὸν αὐτὸν ἔχοντα καυλὸν τῷ
τῶν κυάμων. συντρίψαντι δ᾽ ἕκαστον τῶν κυάμων φανερόν ἐστι τὸ πικρὸν συνεστραμμένον, ἐξ

¹ *Ottelia alismoeides.* See Index App. (18).
² ταῦτα ... πλείω conj. W. after Sch.; I have also transposed the two sentences, after Sch. The whole passage in [ ]
(which is omitted by G) is apparently either an interpolation
or defective. σημαίνει δὲ ὥσπερ καὶ ἀποφέρεσθαι· ἕτερα δὲ ἀπ᾽
αὐτῶν τὰ πλεῖα· ταῦτα δὲ γίνεται ἐν τῷ ποταμῷ· εἰ μὴ ὁ ῥοῦς
ἐξέφερεν Ald.; so also U, but αὐτῶν πλείω.

350

Such are the plants which excel in sweetness of taste. There is also another plant [1] which grows in the marshes and lakes, but which does not take hold of the ground; in character it is like a lily, but it is more leafy, and has its leaves opposite to one another, as it were in a double row; the colour is a deep green. Physicians use it for the complaints of women and for fractures.

Now these plants grow in the river, unless the stream has thrown them up on land; it sometimes happens that they are borne down the stream, and that then other plants grow from them.[2]

[3] But the 'Egyptian bean' grows in the marshes and lakes; the length of its stalk at longest is four cubits, it is as thick as a man's finger, and resembles a pliant [4] reed without joints. Inside it has tubes which run distinct from one another right through, like a honey-comb: on this is set the 'head,' which is like a round wasps' nest, and in each of the cells is a 'bean,' which slightly projects from it; at most there are thirty of these. The flower is twice as large as a poppy's, and the colour is like a rose, of a deep shade; the 'head' is above the water. Large leaves grow at the side of each plant, equal [5] in size to a Thessalian hat [6]; these have a stalk exactly like that [7] of the plant. If one of the 'beans' is crushed, you find the bitter substance coiled up, of which the

[2] Plin. 18. 121 and 122.
[4] μαλακῷ Ald.H.G Plin. *l.c.* Athen. 3. 2 cites the passage with μακρῷ.
[5] ἴσα conj. W.; καὶ Ald.
[6] πετάσῳ conj. Sch. from Diosc. 2. 106; πίλῳ Ald.H.; οἱ πέτασοι are mentioned below (§ 9) without explanation. The comparison is omitted by G and Plin. *l.c.*
[7] *i.e.* that which carries the κωδύα.

8 οὐ γίνεται ὁ πῖλος. τὰ μὲν οὖν περὶ τὸν καρπὸν τοιαῦτα. ἡ δὲ ῥίζα παχυτέρα τοῦ καλάμου τοῦ παχυτάτου καὶ διαφύσεις ὁμοίως ἔχουσα τῷ καυλῷ. ἐσθίουσι δ᾽ αὐτὴν καὶ ὠμὴν καὶ ἐφθὴν καὶ ὀπτήν, καὶ οἱ περὶ τὰ ἕλη τούτῳ σίτῳ χρῶνται. φύεται μὲν οὖν ὁ πολὺς αὐτόματος· οὐ μὴν ἀλλὰ καὶ καταβάλλουσιν ἐν πηλῷ ἀχυρώσαντες εὖ μάλα πρὸς τὸ κατειεχθῆναί τε καὶ μεῖναι καὶ μὴ διαφθαρῆναι· καὶ οὕτω κατασκευάζουσι τοὺς κυαμῶνας· ἂν δ᾽ ἅπαξ ἀντιλάβηται, μένει διὰ τέλους. ἰσχυρὰ γὰρ ἡ ῥίζα καὶ οὐ πόρρω τῆς τῶν καλάμων πλὴν ἐπακανθίζουσα· δι᾽ ὃ καὶ ὁ κροκόδειλος φεύγει μὴ προσκόψῃ τῷ ὀφθαλμῷ τῷ μὴ ὀξὺ καθορᾶν· γίνεται δὲ οὗτος καὶ ἐν Συρίᾳ καὶ κατὰ Κιλικίαν, ἀλλ᾽ οὐκ ἐκπέττουσιν αἱ χῶραι· καὶ περὶ Τορώνην τῆς Χαλκιδικῆς ἐν λίμνῃ τινὶ μετρίᾳ τῷ μεγέθει· καὶ αὐτοῦ πέττεται τελέως καὶ τελεοκαρπεῖ.

9 Ὁ δὲ λωτὸς καλούμενος φύεται μὲν ὁ πλεῖστος ἐν τοῖς πεδίοις, ὅταν ἡ χώρα κατακλυσθῇ. τούτου δὲ ἡ μὲν τοῦ καυλοῦ φύσις ὁμοία τῇ τοῦ κυάμου, καὶ οἱ πέτασοι δὲ ὡσαύτως, πλὴν ἐλάττους καὶ λεπτότεροι. ἐπιφύεται δὲ ὁμοίως ὁ καρπὸς τῷ τοῦ κυάμου. τὸ ἄνθος αὐτοῦ λευκὸν ἐμφερὲς τῇ στενότητι τῶν φύλλων τοῖς τοῦ κρίνου, πολλὰ δὲ καὶ πυκνὰ ἐπ᾽ ἀλλήλοις φύεται. ταῦτα δὲ ὅταν μὲν ὁ ἥλιος δύῃ συμμύει καὶ συγκαλύπτει τὴν κωδύαν, ἅμα δὲ τῇ ἀνατολῇ διοί-

---

[1] ὁ πῖλος UMV; ἡ πῖλος Ald.H.; ?=germen Sch.
[2] cf. Diosc. 2. 107.
[3] καὶ καταβ. conj. W.; καταβ. Ald.; καταβ. δ᾽ UMV.
[4] Plin. 13. 107 and 108.

*pilos* [1] is made. So much for the fruit. The root is thicker than the thickest reed, and is made up of distinct tubes, like the stalk. [2] They eat it both raw boiled and roasted, and the people of the marshes make this their food. It mostly grows of its own accord; however they also sow [3] it in the mud, having first well mixed the seed with chaff, so that it may be carried down and remain in the ground without being rotted; and so they prepare the 'bean' fields, and if the plant once takes hold it is permanent. For the root is strong and not unlike that of reeds, except that it is prickly on the surface. Wherefore the crocodile avoids it, lest he may strike his eye on it, since he has not sharp sight. This plant also grows in Syria and in parts of Cilicia, but these countries cannot ripen it; also about Torone in Chalcidice in a certain lake of small size; and this lake ripens it perfectly and matures its fruit.

[4] The plant called the *lotos* (Nile water-lily) grows chiefly in the plains when the land is inundated. The character of the stalk of this plant is like that of the 'Egyptian bean,' and so are the 'hat-like' leaves, [5] except that they are smaller and slenderer. And the fruit [6] grows on the stalk in the same way as that of the 'bean.' The flower is white, resembling in the narrowness of its petals those of the lily, [7] but there are many petals growing close one upon another. When the sun sets, these close [8] and cover up the 'head,' but with sunrise they open and

[5] *cf.* 4. 8. 7.
[6] καρπὸς conj. W.; λωτὸς MSS. Possibly the fruit was specially called λωτός.
[7] *cf.* Hdt. 2. 92; Diosc. 4. 113.
[8] δύη, συμμύει conj. St.; συμμύει MV; συμμύη U; συμμύη (omitting καί) Ald. H.

γεται καὶ ὑπὲρ τοῦ ὕδατος γίνεται. τοῦτο δὲ
ποιεῖ μέχρι ἂν ἡ κωδύα ἐκτελεωθῇ καὶ τὰ ἄνθη
10 περιρρυῇ. τῆς δὲ κωδύας τὸ μέγεθος ἡλίκον
μήκωνος τῆς μεγίστης, καὶ διέζωσται ταῖς κατα-
τομαῖς τὸν αὐτὸν τρόπον τῇ μήκωνι· πλὴν πυκνό-
τερος ἐν ταύταις ὁ καρπός. ἔστι δὲ παρόμοιος
τῷ κέγχρῳ. ἐν δὲ τῷ Εὐφράτῃ τὴν κωδύαν φασὶ
καὶ τὰ ἄνθη δύνειν καὶ ὑποκαταβαίνειν τῆς ὀψίας
μέχρι μεσῶν νυκτῶν καὶ τῷ βάθει πόρρω· οὐδὲ
γὰρ καθιέντα τὴν χεῖρα λαβεῖν εἶναι. μετὰ δὲ
ταῦτα ὅταν ὄρθρος ᾖ πάλιν ἐπανιέναι καὶ πρὸς
ἡμέραν ἔτι μᾶλλον, ἅμα τῷ ἡλίῳ φανερὸν <ὂν>
ὑπὲρ τοῦ ὕδατος καὶ ἀνοίγειν τὸ ἄνθος, ἀνοιχθέν-
τος δὲ ἔτι ἀναβαίνειν· συχνὸν δὲ τὸ ὑπεραῖρον
11 εἶναι τὸ ὕδωρ. τὰς δὲ κωδύας ταύτας οἱ Αἰγύ-
πτιοι συνθέντες εἰς τὸ αὐτὸ σήπουσιν· ἐπὰν δὲ
σαπῇ τὸ κέλυφος, ἐν τῷ ποταμῷ κλύζοντες ἐξαι-
ροῦσι τὸν καρπόν, ξηράναντες δὲ καὶ πτίσαντες
ἄρτους ποιοῦσι καὶ τούτῳ χρῶνται σιτίῳ. ἡ δὲ
ῥίζα τοῦ λωτοῦ καλεῖται μὲν κόρσιον, ἐστὶ δὲ
στρογγύλη, τὸ μέγεθος ἡλίκον μῆλον Κυδώνιον·
φλοιὸς δὲ περίκειται περὶ αὐτὴν μέλας ἐμφερὴς
τῷ κασταναϊκῷ καρύῳ· τὸ δὲ ἐντὸς λευκόν, ἑψό-
μενον δὲ καὶ ὀπτώμενον γίνεται λεκιθῶδες, ἡδὺ δὲ
ἐν τῇ προσφορᾷ· ἐσθίεται δὲ καὶ ὠμή, ἀρίστη
δὲ ἐν [τῷ] ὕδατι ἐφθὴ καὶ ὀπτή. καὶ τὰ μὲν
ἐν τοῖς ὕδασιν σχεδὸν ταῦτά ἐστιν.
12 Ἐν δὲ τοῖς ἀμμώδεσι χωρίοις, ἅ ἐστιν οὐ πόρρω

¹ cf. Diosc. l.c.  ² cf. C.P. 2. 19. 1; Plin. 13. 109.
³ ὀψίας conj. W. from Plin. l.c.; ? ὀψίας ὥρας.
⁴ <ὂν> add. W.
⁵ κέλυφος i.e. fruit: καρπόν i.e. seeds.

appear above the water. This the plant does until the 'head' is matured and the flowers have fallen off. [1] The size of the 'head' is that of the largest poppy, and it has grooves all round it in the same way as the poppy, but the fruit is set closer in these. This is like millet. [2] In the Euphrates they say that the 'head' and the flowers sink and go under water in the evening [3] till midnight, and sink to a considerable depth; for one can not even reach them by plunging one's hand in; and that after this, when dawn comes round, they rise and go on rising towards day-break, being [4] visible above the water when the sun appears: and that then the plant opens its flower, and, after it is open, it still rises; and that it is a considerable part which projects above the water. These 'heads' the Egyptians heap together and leave to decay, and when the 'pod' [5] has decayed, they wash the 'head' in the river and take out the 'fruit,' [5] and, having dried and pounded [6] it, they make loaves of it, which they use for food. The root of the *lotos* is called *korsion*, [7] and it is round and about the size of a quince; it is enclosed in a black 'bark,' like the shell of a chestnut. The inside is white; but when it is boiled or roasted, it becomes of the colour of the yolk of an egg and is sweet to taste. The root is also eaten raw, though it is best when boiled in water or roasted. [8] Such are the plants found in water.

In sandy places which are not [9] far from the river

[6] πτίσαντες: cf. Hdt. 2. 92.    [7] cf. Strabo 17. 2. 4.
[8] ἐσθίεται ... ὀπτή conj. Sch. from Plin. *l.c.* and G ; ἐσθ. δὲ καὶ ὠμόν· ἀρίστη δὲ ἐν τοῖς ὕδασιν αὐτὴ ὠμή Ald.; ἀρίστη δὲ καὶ τοῖς ὕδασιν αὐτὴν UMV, then ομή U, ὠμῇ V, ὠμή M ; ἀρίστη δὲ ἐν τῷ ὕδατι ἑφθὴ ἢ καὶ ὀπτή H.
[9] οὐ was apparently not in Pliny's text ; (21. 88.)

THEOPHRASTUS

τοῦ ποταμοῦ, φύεται κατὰ γῆς ὃ καλεῖται μαλιν-
αθάλλη, στρογγύλον τῷ σχήματι μέγεθος δὲ
ἡλίκον μέσπιλον ἀπύρηνον δὲ ἄφλοιον· φύλλα
δὲ ἀφίησιν ἀπ᾽ αὐτοῦ ὅμοια κυπείρῳ· ταῦτα
συνάγοντες οἱ κατὰ τὴν χώραν ἕψουσιν ἐν βρυτῷ
τῷ ἀπὸ τῶν κριθῶν καὶ γίνεται γλυκέα σφόδρα·
χρῶνται δὲ πάντες ὥσπερ τραγήμασι.

13 Τοῖς δὲ βουσὶ καὶ τοῖς προβάτοις ἅπαντα μὲν
τὰ φυόμενα ἐδώδιμά ἐστιν, ἒν δέ τι γένος ἐν ταῖς
λίμναις καὶ τοῖς ἕλεσι φύεται διαφέρον, ὃ καὶ
χλωρὸν νέμονται καὶ ξηραίνοντες παρέχουσι κατὰ
χειμῶνα τοῖς βουσὶν ὅταν ἐργάσωνται· καὶ τὰ
σώματα ἔχουσιν εὖ σίτου ἄλλο λαμβάνοντες
οὐθέν.

14 Ἔστι δὲ καὶ ἄλλο παραφυόμενον αὐτόματον
ἐν τῷ σίτῳ· τοῦτο δέ, ὅταν ὁ σῖτος ᾖ καθαρός,
ὑποπτίσαντες καταβάλλουσι τοῦ χειμῶνος ὑγ-
ρὰν εἰς γῆν· βλαστήσαντος δὲ τεμόντες καὶ
ξηράναντες παρέχουσι καὶ τοῦτο βουσὶ καὶ
ἵπποις καὶ τοῖς ὑποζυγίοις σὺν τῷ καρπῷ τῷ ἐπι-
γινομένῳ· ὁ δὲ καρπὸς μέγεθος μὲν ἡλίκον σήσαμον, στρογγύλος δὲ καὶ τῷ χρώματι χλωρός,
ἀγαθὸς δὲ διαφερόντως. ἐν Αἰγύπτῳ μὲν οὖν
τὰ περιττὰ σχεδὸν ταῦτα ἄν τις λάβοι.

IX. Ἕκαστοι δὲ τῶν ποταμῶν ἐοίκασιν ἴδιόν
τι φέρειν, ὥσπερ καὶ τῶν χερσαίων. ἐπεὶ οὐδὲ
ὁ τρίβολος ἐν ἅπασιν οὐδὲ πανταχοῦ φύεται,
ἀλλ᾽ ἐν τοῖς ἑλώδεσι τῶν ποταμῶν· ἐν μεγίστῳ
δὲ βάθει πενταπήχει ἢ μικρῷ μείζονι, καθάπερ

---

[1] Plin. l.c. anthalium, whence Salm. conj. ἀνθάλλιον.
[2] Saccharum biflorum. See Index App. (19).
[3] εὖ σίτου ἄλλο conj. W.; εὐσιτοῦντα Ald.

356

there grows under ground the thing called *malina-thalle*[1]; this is round in shape and as large as a medlar, but has no stone and no bark. It sends out leaves like those of galingale. These the people of the country collect and boil in beer made from barley, and they become extremely sweet, and all men use them as sweetmeats.

All the things that grow in such places may be eaten by oxen and sheep, but there is one kind of plant[2] which grows in the lakes and marshes which is specially good for food : they graze their cattle on it when it is green, and also dry it and give it in the winter to the oxen after their work ; and these keep in good condition when they have no other[3] kind of food.

There is also another plant[4] which comes up of its own accord among the corn ; this, when the harvest is cleared, they crush slightly[5] and lay during the winter on[6] moist ground ; when it shoots, they cut and dry it and give this also to the cattle and horses and beasts of burden with the fruit which forms on it. The fruit in size is as large as sesame, but round and green in colour, and exceedingly good. Such one might take to be specially remarkable plants of Egypt.

IX. Every river seems to bear some peculiar plant, just as does each part of the dry land. [7] For not even the water-chestnut grows in all rivers nor everywhere, but only in marshy rivers, and only in those whose depth is not more or not much more than five cubits,

[4] *Corchorus trilocularis.* See Index App. (20).
[5] G seems to have read ὑποπτίσαντες (*leviter pinsentes*) : ὑποπτήσαντες W. with Ald.H.
[6] εἰς conj. W.; τὴν Ald.
[7] Plin. 21. 98 ; Diosc. 4. 15.

THEOPHRASTUS

περὶ τὸν Στρυμόνα· σχεδὸν δὲ ἐν τοσούτῳ καὶ
ὁ κάλαμος καὶ τὰ ἄλλα. ὑπερέχει δὲ οὐθὲν
αὐτοῦ πλὴν αὐτὰ τὰ φύλλα ὥσπερ ἐπινέοντα
καὶ κρύπτοντα τὸν τρίβολον, ὁ δὲ τρίβολος αὐτὸς
ἐν τῷ ὕδατι νεύων εἰς βυθόν. τὸ δὲ φύλλον ἐστὶ
πλατὺ προσεμφερὲς τῷ τῆς πτελέας, μίσχον δὲ
2 ἔχει σφόδρα μακρόν· ὁ δὲ καυλὸς ἐξ ἄκρου
παχύτατος, ὅθεν τὰ φύλλα καὶ ὁ καρπός, τὰ
δὲ κάτω λεπτότερος ἀεὶ μέχρι τῆς ῥίζης· ἔχει
δὲ ἀποπεφυκότα ἀπ᾽ αὐτοῦ τριχώδη τὰ μὲν
πλεῖστα παράλληλα τὰ δὲ καὶ παραλλάττοντα,
κάτωθεν ἀπὸ τῆς ῥίζης μεγάλα τὰ δὲ ἄνω ἀεὶ ἐλάττω προϊοῦσιν, ὥστε τὰ τελευταῖα μικρὰ πάμπαν
εἶναι καὶ τὴν διαφορὰν μεγάλην τὴν ἀπὸ τῆς
ῥίζης πρὸς τὸν καρπόν. ἔχει δὲ ἐκ τοῦ ἑνὸς
καυλοῦ καὶ παραβλαστήματα πλείω· καὶ γὰρ
τρία καὶ τέτταρα, μέγιστον δ᾽ αἰεὶ τὸ πλησιαί-
τερον τῆς ῥίζης, εἶτα τὸ μετὰ τοῦτο καὶ τὰ
ἄλλα κατὰ λόγον. τὸ δὲ παραβλάστημά ἐστιν
ὥσπερ καυλὸς ἄλλος λεπτότερος μὲν τοῦ πρώτου,
τὰ δὲ φύλλα καὶ τὸν καρπὸν ἔχων ὁμοίως. ὁ
δὲ καρπὸς μέλας καὶ σκληρὸς σφόδρα. ῥίζαν
δὲ ἡλίκην καὶ ποίαν ἔχει σκεπτέον. ἡ μὲν οὖν
φύσις τοιαύτη. φύεται μὲν ἀπὸ τοῦ καρποῦ
τοῦ πίπτοντος καὶ ἀφίησι βλαστὸν τοῦ ἦρος·
3 φασὶ δὲ οἱ μὲν εἶναι ἐπέτειον οἱ δὲ διαμένειν
τὴν μὲν ῥίζαν εἰς χρόνον, ἐξ ἧς καὶ τὴν βλάστησιν εἶναι τοῦ καυλοῦ. τοῦτο μὲν οὖν σκεπτέον. ἴδιον δὲ παρὰ τἄλλα τὸ τῶν παραφυομένων
ἐκ τοῦ καυλοῦ τριχωδῶν· οὔτε γὰρ φύλλα ταῦτα
οὔτε καυλός· ἐπεὶ τό γε τῆς παραβλαστήσεως
κοινὸν καλάμου καὶ ἄλλων.

358

as the Strymon. (In rivers of such a depth grow
also reeds and other plants.) No part of it projects
from the water except just the leaves; these float as
it were and conceal the 'chestnut,' which is itself
under water and bends down towards the bottom.
The leaf is broad, like that of the elm, and has a
very long stalk. The stem is thickest at the top,
whence spring the leaves and the fruit; below it gets
thinner down to the root. It has springing from it
hair-like growths, most of which are parallel to each
other, but some are irregular; below, starting from
the root, they are large, but, as one gets higher up
the plant, they become smaller, so that those at the
top are quite small and there is a great contrast
between the root and the top where the fruit grows.
The plant also has on the same stalk several side-
growths; of these there are three or four, and the
largest is always that which is nearer to the root,
the next largest is the one next above it, and so on
in proportion: this sidegrowth is like another stalk,
but slenderer than the original one, though like that
it has leaves and fruit. The fruit is black and
extremely hard. The size and character of the root
are matter for further enquiry. Such is the character
of this plant. It grows from the fruit which falls,
and begins to grow in spring. Some say that it is
annual, others that the root persists for a time, and
that from it grows the new stalk. This then is
matter for enquiry. However quite peculiar to this
plant is the hair-like character of the growths which
spring from the stalk; for these are neither leaves
nor stalk; though reeds and other things have also
sidegrowths.

X. Τὰ μὲν οὖν ἴδια θεωρητέον ἰδίως δῆλον ὅτι,
τὰ δὲ κοινὰ κοινῶς.¹ διαιρεῖν δὲ χρὴ καὶ ταῦτα
κατὰ τοὺς τόπους, οἷον εἰ τὰ μὲν ἕλεια τὰ δὲ
λιμναῖα τὰ δὲ ποτάμια μᾶλλον ἢ καὶ κοινὰ πάντων τῶν τόπων· διαιρεῖν δὲ καὶ ποῖα ταὐτὰ² ἐν τῷ
ὑγρῷ καὶ τῷ ξηρῷ φύεται, καὶ ποῖα ἐν τῷ ὑγρῷ
μόνον, ὡς ἁπλῶς εἰπεῖν πρὸς τὰ κοινότατα εἰρη-
μένα πρότερον.³

Ἐν δ' οὖν τῇ λίμνῃ τῇ περὶ Ὀρχομενὸν τάδ'
ἐστὶ τὰ φυόμενα δένδρα καὶ ὑλήματα, ἰτέα
ἐλαίαγνος σίδη κάλαμος ὅ τε αὐλητικὸς καὶ ὁ
ἕτερος κύπειρον φλεὼς τύφη, ἔτι γε μήνανθος
ἴκμη καὶ τὸ καλούμενον ἵππον. ὃ γὰρ προσαγορεύουσι λέμνα τούτου τὰ πλείω καθ' ὕδατός ἐστι.

2   Τούτων δὲ τὰ μὲν ἄλλα γνώριμα· ὁ δ' ἐλαίαγνος
καὶ ἡ σίδη καὶ ἡ μήνανθος καὶ ἡ ἴκμη καὶ τὸ
ἵππον ἴσως μὲν φύεται καὶ ἑτέρωθι, προσαγορεύεται δὲ ἄλλοις ὀνόμασι· λεκτέον δὲ περὶ αὐτῶν.
ἔστι δὲ ὁ μὲν ἐλαίαγνος φύσει μὲν θαμνῶδες καὶ
παρόμοιον τοῖς ἄγνοις, φύλλον δὲ ἔχει τῷ μὲν
σχήματι παραπλήσιον μαλακὸν δέ, ὥσπερ αἱ
μηλέαι καὶ χνοῶδες. ἄνθος δὲ τῷ τῆς λεύκης
ὅμοιον ἔλαττον· καρπὸν δὲ οὐδένα φέρει. φύεται
δὲ ὁ πλεῖστος μὲν ἐπὶ τῶν πλοάδων νήσων· εἰσὶ
γάρ τινες καὶ ἐνταῦθα πλοάδες, ὥσπερ ἐν Αἰγύπτῳ

¹ τὰ δὲ κοινὰ κοινῶς conj. Sch. from G ; τὰ δὲ κοινῶς Ald.H.
² ταὐτὰ conj. Sch.; ταῦτα Ald.
³ πρὸς τὰ κοιν. εἰρ. πρ. conj. W. supported by G ; κοινότατα
προσειρημένα πρότερον Ald.H.

360

*Of the plants peculiar to the lake of Orchomenos (Lake Copais),
especially its reeds; and of reeds in general.*

X. Plants peculiar to particular places must be
considered separately, while a general account may
be given of those which are generally distributed.[1]
But even the latter must be classified according to
locality; thus some belong to marshes, others to
lakes, others to rivers, or again others may be common
to all kinds of locality: we must also distinguish which
occur alike[2] in wet and in dry ground, and which
only in wet ground, marking these off in a general
way from those mentioned above as being most
impartial.[3]

Now in the lake near Orchomenos grow the
following trees and woody plants: willow goat-willow
water-lily reeds (both that used for making pipes and
the other kind) galingale *phleos* bulrush; and also
'moon-flower' duckweed and the plant called
marestail: as for the plant called water-chickweed
the greater part of it grows under water.[4]

Now of these most are familiar: the goat-willow
water-lily 'moon-flower' duckweed and marestail
probably grow also elsewhere, but are called by
different names. Of these we must speak. The
goat-willow is of shrubby habit and like the chaste-
tree: its leaf resembles that leaf in shape, but it is
soft like that of the apple,[5] and downy. The bloom[6]
is like that of the abele, but smaller, and it bears no
fruit. It grows chiefly on the floating islands; (for
here too there are floating islands, as in the marshes

[4] τούτου τὰ πλείω καθ' ὕδ. conj. Sch.; τοῦτο πλείω τὸ καθ' ὕδ.
U M; τοῦτο πλεῖον τὸ καθ' ὕδ. Ald.
[5] μηλέαι perhaps here = quince (μηλέα Κυδωνία).
[6] ἄνθος here = catkin.

THEOPHRASTUS

περὶ τὰ ἕλη καὶ ἐν Θεσπρωτίδι καὶ ἐν ἄλλαις λίμ-
ναις· ἐλάττων δὲ καθ᾽ ὕδατος· ὁ μὲν οὖν ἐλαίαγνος
τοιοῦτον.

3 Ἡ δὲ σίδη τὴν μὲν μορφήν ἐστιν ὁμοία τῇ
μήκωνι· καὶ γὰρ τὸ ἄνω κυτινῶδες τοιοῦτον ἔχει,
πλὴν μεῖζον ὡς κατὰ λόγον· μεγέθει δὲ ὅλος ὁ
ὄγκος ἡλίκον μῆλον· ἔστι δὲ οὐ γυμνόν, ἀλλὰ ὑμένες
περὶ αὐτὴν λευκοί, καὶ ἐπὶ τούτοις ἔξωθεν φύλλα
ποώδη παραπλήσια τοῖς τῶν ῥόδων ὅταν ἐν
κάλυξιν ὦσι, τέτταρα τὸν ἀριθμόν· ἀνοιχθεῖσα
δὲ τοὺς κόκκους ἐρυθροὺς μὲν ἔχει τῷ σχήματι
δὲ οὐχ ὁμοίους ταῖς ῥόαις ἀλλὰ περιφερεῖς μικροὺς
δὲ καὶ οὐ πολλῷ μείζους κέγχρου· τὸν δὲ χυλὸν
ὑδατώδη τινά, καθάπερ ὁ τῶν πυρῶν. ἀδρύνεται
δὲ τοῦ θέρους, μίσχον δὲ ἔχει μακρόν. τὸ δὲ
ἄνθος ὅμοιον ῥόδου κάλυκι, μεῖζον δὲ καὶ σχεδὸν
διπλάσιον τῷ μεγέθει. τοῦτο μὲν οὖν καὶ τὸ
φύλλον ἐπὶ τοῦ ὕδατος· μετὰ δὲ ταῦτα, ὅταν
ἀπανθήσῃ καὶ συστῇ τὸ περικάρπιον, κατακλίνε-
σθαί φασιν εἰς τὸ ὕδωρ μᾶλλον, τέλος δὲ συνάπτειν
τῇ γῇ καὶ τὸν καρπὸν ἐκχεῖν.

4 Καρποφορεῖν δὲ τῶν ἐν τῇ λίμνῃ τοῦτο καὶ τὸ
βούτομον καὶ τὸν φλεών. εἶναι δὲ τοῦ βουτόμου
μέλανα, τῷ δὲ μεγέθει παραπλήσιον τῷ τῆς
σίδης. τοῦ δὲ φλεὼ τὴν καλουμένην ἀνθήλην,

---

[1] ἐλάττων . . . ὕδατος : sense doubtful.  G. seems to render
a different reading.
[2] i.e. the flower-head, which, as well as the plant, was
called σίδη.
[3] μήκωνι can hardly be right : suspected by H.
[4] cf. Athen. 14. 64.
[5] i.e. petals.

362

of Egypt, in Thesprotia, and in other lakes). When it grows under water, it is smaller.[1] Such is the goat-willow.

The water-lily[2] is in shape like the poppy.[3] For the top of it has this character, being shaped like the pomegranate flower,[4] but it is longer in proportion to the size of the plant. Its size in fact as a whole is that of an apple ; but it is not bare, having round it white membranes,[5] and attached to these on the outside are grass-green 'leaves,'[6] like those of roses when they are still in bud, and of these there are four ; when it is opened it shews its seeds, which are red ; in shape however they are not like pomegranate[7] seeds, but round small and not much longer than millet seeds ; the taste is insipid, like that of wheat-grains. It ripens in summer and has a long stalk. The flower is like a rose-bud, but larger, almost twice as large. Now this and the leaf float on the water : but later, when the bloom is over and the fruit-case[8] has formed, they say that it sinks deeper into the water, and finally reaches the bottom and sheds its fruit.

Of the plants of the lake they say that water-lily sedge and *phleos* bear fruit, and that that of the sedge is black, and in size like that of the water-lily. The fruit of *phleos* is what is called the 'plume,'[9]

---

[6] i.e. sepals.

[7] ῥόαις conj. Bod. from Nic. *Ther.* 887 and Schol.; ῥίζαις UMVAld H.

[8] περικάρπιον conj. W.; κατακάρπιον MSS. κατα- probably lue to κατακλίνεσθαι.

[9] cf. Diosc. 3. 118. ἀνθήλην, sc. καρπὸν εἶναι. But Sch. suggests that further description of the fruit has dropped out, and that the clause ᾧ . . . κονίας does not refer to the fruit.

THEOPHRASTUS

ᾧ χρῶνται πρὸς τὰς κονίας.¹ τοῦτο δ' ἐστὶν οἷον
πλακουντῶδές τι μαλακὸν ἐπίπυρρον. ἔτι δὲ
καὶ τοῦ φλεὼ καὶ τοῦ βουτόμου τὸ μὲν θῆλυ
ἄκαρπον, χρήσιμον δὲ πρὸς τὰ πλόκανα, τὸ δὲ
ἄρρεν ἀχρεῖον.
Περὶ δὲ τῆς ἴκμης καὶ μηνάνθους καὶ τοῦ ἵπνου
σκεπτέον.
5 Ἰδιώτατον δὲ τούτων ἐστὶν ἡ τύφη καὶ τῷ
ἄφυλλον εἶναι καὶ τῷ μὴ πολύρριζον τοῖς ἄλλοις
ὁμοίως· ἐπεὶ τἆλλα οὐχ ἧττον εἰς τὰ κάτω τὴν
ὁρμὴν ἔχει καὶ τὴν δύναμιν· μάλιστα δὲ τὸ
κύπειρον, ὥσπερ καὶ ἡ ἄγρωστις, δι' ὃ καὶ δυσώ-
λεθρα καὶ ταῦτα καὶ ὅλως ἅπαν τὸ γένος τὸ τοιοῦτον. ἡ δὲ ῥίζα τοῦ κυπείρου πολύ τι τῶν ἄλλων
παραλλάττει τῇ ἀνωμαλίᾳ, τῷ τὸ μὲν εἶναι παχύ
τι καὶ σαρκῶδες αὐτῆς τὸ δὲ λεπτὸν καὶ ξυλῶδες·
καὶ τῇ βλαστήσει καὶ τῇ γενέσει· φύεται γὰρ
ἀπὸ τοῦ πρεμνώδους ἑτέρα λεπτὴ κατὰ πλάγιον,
εἶτ' ἐν ταύτῃ συνίσταται πάλιν τὸ σαρκῶδες, ἐν ᾧ
καὶ ὁ βλαστὸς ἀφ' οὗ ὁ καυλός· ἀφίησι δὲ καὶ
εἰς βάθος τὸν αὐτὸν τρόπον ῥίζας, δι' ὃ καὶ πάντων
μάλιστα δυσώλεθρον καὶ ἔργον ἐξελεῖν.
6 (Σχεδὸν δὲ παραπλησίως φύεται ἡ ἄγρωστις ἐκ
τῶν γονάτων· αἱ γὰρ ῥίζαι γονατώδεις, ἐξ ἑκάστου δ' ἀφίησιν ἄνω βλαστὸν καὶ κάτωθεν
ῥίζαν. ὡσαύτως δὲ καὶ ἡ ἄκανθα ἡ ἀκανώδης,
ἀλλ' οὐ καλαμώδης οὐδὲ γονατώδης ἡ ῥίζα ταύ-

¹ κονίας : ? κονιάσεις (plastering), a conjecture mentioned
by Sch.

and it is used as a soap-powder.[1] It is something
like a cake, soft and reddish. Moreover the 'female'
plant both of *phleos* and sedge is barren, but useful
for basket-work,[2] while the 'male' is useless.

Duckweed 'moon-flower' and marestail require
further investigation.

Most peculiar of these plants is the bulrush, both
in being leafless and in not having so many roots as
the others; for the others tend downwards quite as
much as upwards, and shew their strength in that
direction; and especially is this true of galingale, and
also of dog's-tooth grass; wherefore these plants
too and all others like them are hard to destroy.
The root of galingale exceeds all the others in the
diversity of characters which it shews, in that part
of it is stout and fleshy, part slender and woody.
So also is this plant peculiar in its way of shooting
and originating; for from the trunk-like stock[3]
grows another slender root[4] sideways, and on this
again forms the fleshy part which contains the shoot
from which the stalk springs.[5] In like manner it
also sends out roots downwards; wherefore of all
plants it is hardest to kill, and troublesome to get
rid of.

(Dog's-tooth grass grows in almost the same way
from the joints; for the roots are jointed, and from
each joint it sends a shoot upwards and a root downwards. The growth of the spinous plant called
corn-thistle[6] is similar, but it is not reedy and its

[2] *cf.* Hdt. 3. 98.    [3] *i.e.* rhizome.
[4] *i.e.* stolon; *cf.* 1. 6. 8.
[5] ἀφ' οὗ ὁ καυλός transposed by W.; in Ald. these words
come before ἐν ᾧ.
[6] ἡ ἀκανώδης I conj.; κεάνωτος UMV; κεάνωθος Ald.; ἡ
κεάνωθος most edd.; G omits the word.

τῆς. ταῦτα μὲν οὖν ἐπὶ πλεῖον διὰ τὴν ὁμοιότητα εἴρηται.)

Φύεται δ' ἐν ἀμφοῖν καὶ ἐν τῇ γῇ καὶ ἐν τῷ ὕδατι ἰτέα κάλαμος, πλὴν τοῦ αὐλητικοῦ, κύπειρον τύφη φλεὼς βούτομος· ἐν δὲ τῷ ὕδατι μόνον σίδη. περὶ γὰρ τῆς τύφης ἀμφισβητοῦσι. καλλίω δὲ καὶ μείζω τῶν ἐν ἀμφοῖν φυομένων αἰεὶ τὰ ἐν τῷ ὕδατι γίνεσθαί φασι. φύεσθαι δ' ἔνια τούτων καὶ ἐπὶ τῶν πλοάδων, οἷον τὸ κύπειρον καὶ τὸ βούτομον καὶ τὸν φλεών, ὥστε πάντα τὰ μέρη ταῦτα κατέχειν.

7 Ἐδώδιμα δ' ἐστὶ τῶν ἐν τῇ λίμνῃ τάδε· ἡ μὲν σίδη καὶ αὐτὴ καὶ τὰ φύλλα τοῖς προβάτοις, ὁ δὲ βλαστὸς τοῖς ὑσίν, ὁ δὲ καρπὸς τοῖς ἀνθρώποις. τοῦ δὲ φλεὼ καὶ τῆς τύφης καὶ τοῦ βουτόμου τὸ πρὸς ταῖς ῥίζαις ἁπαλόν, ὃ μάλιστα ἐσθίει τὰ παιδία. ῥίζα δ' ἐδώδιμος ἡ τοῦ φλεὼ μόνη τοῖς βοσκήμασιν. ὅταν δ' αὐχμὸς ᾖ καὶ μὴ γένηται τὸ κατὰ κεφαλὴν ὕδωρ, ἅπαντα αὐχμεῖ τὰ ἐν τῇ λίμνῃ, μάλιστα δὲ ὁ κάλαμος, ὑπὲρ οὗ καὶ λοιπὸν εἰπεῖν· ὑπὲρ γὰρ τῶν ἄλλων σχεδὸν εἴρηται.

XI. Τοῦ δὴ καλάμου δύο φασὶν εἶναι γένη, τόν τε αὐλητικὸν καὶ τὸν ἕτερον· ἐν γὰρ εἶναι τὸ γένος τοῦ ἑτέρου, διαφέρειν δὲ ἀλλήλων ἰσχύι <καὶ παχύτητι> καὶ λεπτότητι καὶ ἀσθενείᾳ· καλοῦσι δὲ τὸν μὲν ἰσχυρὸν καὶ παχὺν χαρακίαν τὸν δ' ἕτερον πλόκιμον· καὶ φύεσθαι τὸν μὲν

---

[1] i.e. we have gone beyond the list of typical plants of Orchomenus given 4. 10. 1, because we have found others of which much the same may be said.

[2] cf. 4. 10. 2.

[3] αὐτή : cf. 4. 10. 3 n.

root is not jointed. We have enlarged on these matters [1] because of the resemblance.)

The willow and the reed (not however the reed used for pipes) galingale bulrush *phleos* sedge grow both on land and in the water, water-lily only in the water. (As to bulrush indeed there is a difference of opinion.) However they say that those plants which grow in the water are always finer and larger than those that grow in both positions; also that some of these plants grow also on the floating islands,[2] for instance galingale sedge and *phleos*; thus all parts of the lake contain these plants.

Of the plants of the lake the parts good for food are as follows: of the water-lily both the flower[3] and the leaves are good for sheep, the young shoots for pigs, and the fruit for men. Of *phleos* galingale and sedge the part next the roots is tender, and is mostly eaten by children. The root of *phleos* is the only part which is edible by cattle. When there is a drought and there is no water from overhead,[4] all the plants of the lake are dried up, but especially the reed; of this it remains to speak, since we have said almost enough about the rest.

XI. [5] Of the reed there are said to be two kinds, the one used for making pipes and the other kind. For that of the latter there is only one kind, though individual plants differ in being strong and stout,[6] or on the other hand slender and weak. The strong stout one they call the 'stake-reed,' the other the 'weaving reed.' The latter they say grows on the

[4] κεφαλὴν UMVAld.; for the case *cf.* Xen. *Hell.* 7. 2. 8 and 11; κεφαλῆς conj. W.
[5] Plin. 16. 168 and 169.
[6] καὶ παχύτητι add. Dalec. from G.

# THEOPHRASTUS

πλόκιμον ἐπὶ τῶν πλοάδων τὸν δὲ χαρακίαν ἐπὶ
τοῖς κώμυσι· κώμυθας δὲ καλοῦσι οὗ ἂν ᾖ συν-
ηθροισμένος κάλαμος καὶ συμπεπλεγμένος ταῖς
ῥίζαις· τοῦτο δὲ γίνεται καθ' οὓς ἂν τόπους
τῆς λίμνης εὔγειον ᾖ χωρίον· γίνεσθαι δέ ποτε
τὸν χαρακίαν καὶ οὗ ὁ αὐλητικός, μακρότερον
μὲν τοῦ ἄλλου χαρακίου σκωληκόβρωτον δέ.
τούτου μὲν οὖν ταύτας λέγουσι τὰς διαφοράς.

2 Περὶ δὲ τοῦ αὐλητικοῦ τὸ μὲν φύεσθαι δι' ἐννεατηρίδος, ὥσπερ τινές φασι, καὶ ταύτην εἶναι
τὴν τάξιν οὐκ ἀληθές, ἀλλὰ τὸ μὲν ὅλον αὐξη-
θείσης γίνεται τῆς λίμνης· ὅτι δὲ τοῦτ' ἐδόκει
συμβαίνειν ἐν τοῖς πρότερον χρόνοις μάλιστα δι'
ἐννεατηρίδος, καὶ τὴν γένεσιν τοῦ καλάμου ταύτην ἐποίουν τὸ συμβεβηκὸς ὡς τάξιν λαμβάνοντες.

3 γίνεται δὲ ὅταν ἐπομβρίας γενομένης ἐμμένῃ
τὸ ὕδωρ δύ' ἔτη τοὐλάχιστον, ἂν δὲ πλείω καὶ
καλλίων· τούτου δὲ μάλιστα μνημονεύουσι γεγονό-
τος τῶν ὕστερον χρόνων ὅτε συνέβη τὰ περὶ
Χαιρώνειαν· πρὸ τούτων γὰρ ἔφασαν ἔτη πλείω
βαθυνθῆναι τὴν λίμνην· μετὰ δὲ ταῦτα ὕστερον,
ὡς ὁ λοιμὸς ἐγένετο σφοδρός, πλησθῆναι μὲν
αὐτήν, οὐ μείναντος δὲ τοῦ ὕδατος ἀλλ' ἐκλιπόν-
τος χειμῶνος οὐ γενέσθαι τὸν κάλαμον· φασὶ γὰρ
καὶ δοκεῖ βαθυνομένης τῆς λίμνης αὐξάνεσθαι
τὸν κάλαμον εἰς μῆκος, μείναντα δὲ τὸν ἐπιόντα
ἐνιαυτὸν ἁδρύνεσθαι· καὶ γίνεσθαι τὸν μὲν ἁδρυ-
θέντα ζευγίτην, ᾧ δ' ἂν μὴ συμπαραμείνῃ τὸ

---

¹ κώμυσι : lit 'bundles.'
² δύ' ἔτη conj. W.; διετῆ UMVAld.
³ B.C. 338.

floating islands, the stout form in the ' reed-beds ' [1] :
this name they give to the places where there is a
thick mass of reed with its roots entangled together.
This occurs in any part of the lake where there is
rich soil. It is said that the ' stake-reed ' is also
sometimes found in the same places as the reed used
for pipes, in which places it is longer than the ' stake-
reed ' found elsewhere, but gets worm-eaten. These
then are the differences in reeds of which they tell.

As to the reed used for pipes, it is not true, as some
say, that it only grows once in nine years and that
this is its regular rule of growth ; it grows in general
whenever the lake is full : but, because in former
days this was supposed to happen generally once in
nine years, they made the growth of the reed to
correspond, taking what was really an accident to be
a regular principle. As a matter of fact it grows
whenever after a rainy season the water remains in
the lake for at least two years,[2] and it is finer if the
water remains longer ; this is specially remembered
to have happened in recent times at the time of the
battle of Chaeronea.[3] For before that period they
told me that the lake was for several years deep [4] ;
and, at a time later than that, when there was a
severe visitation of the plague, it filled up ; but, as
the water did not remain but failed in winter, the
reed did not grow : for they say, apparently with
good reason, that, when the lake is deep, the reed
increases in height, and, persisting for the next year,
matures its growth ; and that the reed which thus
matures is suitable for making a reed mouthpiece,[5]
while that for which the water has not remained is

[4] ἔτη πλείω conj. Scal. from G ; ἔτι πλείω UMV ; ἔτι πλείον
Ald.
[5] See n. on τὸ στόμα τῶν γλωττῶν, § 4.

ὕδωρ βομβυκίαν.¹ τὴν μὲν οὖν γένεσιν εἶναι τοιαύτην.

4 Διαφέρειν δὲ τῶν ἄλλων καλάμων ὡς καθ᾽ ὅλου λαβεῖν εὐτροφίᾳ τινὶ τῆς φύσεως· εὐπληθέστερον γὰρ εἶναι καὶ εὐσαρκότερον καὶ ὅλως δὲ θῆλυν τῇ προσόψει. καὶ γὰρ τὸ φύλλον πλατύτερον ἔχειν καὶ λευκότερον τὴν δὲ ἀνθήλην ἐλάττω τῶν ἄλλων, τινὰς δὲ ὅλως οὐκ ἔχειν, οὓς καὶ προσ- αγορεύουσιν εὐνουχίας· ἐξ ὧν ἄριστα μέν φασί τινες γίνεσθαι τὰ ζεύγη, κατορθοῦν δὲ ὀλίγα παρὰ τὴν ἐργασίαν.

Τὴν δὲ τομὴν ὡραίαν εἶναι πρὸ ᾽Αντιγενίδου μέν, ἡνίκ᾽ ηὔλουν ἀπλάστως, ὑπ᾽ ᾽Αρκτοῦρον Βοη- δρομιῶνος μηνός· τὸν γὰρ οὕτω τμηθέντα συχνοῖς μὲν ἔτεσιν ὕστερον γίνεσθαι χρήσιμον καὶ προ- καταυλήσεως δεῖσθαι πολλῆς, συμμύειν δὲ τὸ στόμα τῶν γλωττῶν, ὃ πρὸς τὴν διακτηρίαν εἶναι 5 χρήσιμον. ἐπεὶ δὲ εἰς τὴν πλάσιν μετέβησαν, καὶ ἡ τομὴ μετεκινήθη· τέμνουσι γὰρ δὴ νῦν τοῦ Σκιρροφοριῶνος καὶ ῾Εκατομβαιῶνος ὥσπερ πρὸ τροπῶν μικρὸν ἢ ὑπὸ τροπάς. γίνεσθαι δέ φασι τρίενόν τε χρήσιμον καὶ καταυλήσεως βραχείας

---

¹ βομβυκίαν. In one kind of pipe the performer blew, not directly on to the 'reed,' but into a cap in which it was enclosed ; this cap, from the resemblance in shape to a cocoon, was called βόμβυξ.
² εἶναι add. W.
³ Plin. 16. 169-172.    ⁴ September.
⁵ i.e. between the free end of the vibrating 'tongue' and

suitable for making a 'cap.'[1] Such then, it is said,
is [2] the reed's way of growth.

[3] Also it is said to differ from other reeds, to speak
generally, in a certain luxuriance of growth, being of
a fuller and more fleshy character, and, one may say,
'female' in appearance. For it is said that even the
leaf is broader and whiter, though the plume is
smaller than that of other reeds, and some have no
plume at all; these they call 'eunuch-reeds.' From
these they say that the best mouthpieces are made,
though many are spoiled in the making.

Till the time of Antigenidas, before which men
played the pipe in the simple style, they say that
the proper season for cutting the reeds was the
month Boëdromion [4] about the rising of Arcturus;
for, although the reed so cut did not become fit for
use for many years after and needed a great deal of
preliminary playing upon, yet the opening [5] of the
reed-tongues is well closed, which is a good thing for
the purpose of accompaniment.[6] But when a change
was made to the more elaborate style of playing, the
time of cutting the reeds was also altered; for in
our own time they cut them in the mouths Skirrophorion [7] or Hekatombaion [8] about the solstice or a
little earlier.[9] And they say that the reed becomes
fit for use in three years and needs but little
preliminary playing upon, and that the reed-tongues

the body or 'lay' of the reed mouthpiece: the instrument
implied throughout is apparently one with a single vibrating
'tongue' (reed) like the modern clarinet.

[6] διακτηρίαν UMV; διακτορίαν Ald. ? πρὸς τὸ ἀκροατήριον,
'for the concert-room'; *quod erat illis theatrorum moribus
utilius* Plin. *l.c.*

[7] June. [8] July.

[9] ὥσπερ conj. W.; ὥσπερεὶ UH.; ὡς περὶ MVAld.

B B 2

## THEOPHRASTUS

δεῖσθαι καὶ κατασπάσματα τὰς γλώττας ἴσχειν·
τοῦτο δὲ ἀναγκαῖον τοῖς μετὰ πλάσματος αὐ-
λοῦσι. τοῦ μὲν οὖν ζευγίτου ταύτας εἶναι τὰς
ὥρας τῆς τομῆς.

6 Ἡ δ' ἐργασία γίνεται τοῦτον τὸν τρόπον· ὅταν
συλλέξωσι τιθέασιν ὑπαίθριον τοῦ χειμῶνος ἐν
τῷ λέμματι· τοῦ δ' ἦρος περικαθάραντες καὶ
ἐκτρίψαντες εἰς τὸν ἥλιον ἔθεσαν. τοῦ θέρους δὲ
μετὰ ταῦτα συντεμόντες εἰς τὰ μεσογονάτια πάλιν
ὑπαίθριον τιθέασι χρόνον τινά. προσλείπουσι
δὲ τῷ μεσογονατίῳ τὸ πρὸς τοὺς βλαστοὺς γόνυ·
τὰ δὲ μήκη τὰ τούτων οὐ γίνεται διπαλαίστων
ἐλάττω. βέλτιστα μὲν οὖν εἶναι τῶν μεσογονα-
τίων πρὸς τὴν ζευγοποιΐαν ὅλου τοῦ καλάμου τὰ
μέσα· μαλακώτατα δὲ ἴσχειν ζεύγη τὰ πρὸς τοὺς
7 βλαστούς, σκληρότατα δὲ τὰ πρὸς τῇ ῥίζῃ· συμ-
φωνεῖν δὲ τὰς γλώττας τὰς ἐκ τοῦ αὐτοῦ μεσογο-
νατίου, τὰς δὲ ἄλλας οὐ συμφωνεῖν· καὶ τὴν μὲν
πρὸς τῇ ῥίζῃ ἀριστερὰν εἶναι, τὴν δὲ πρὸς τοὺς
βλαστοὺς δεξιάν. τμηθέντος δὲ δίχα τοῦ μεσο-
γονατίου τὸ στόμα τῆς γλώττης ἑκατέρας γίνεσθαι κατὰ τὴν τοῦ καλάμου τομήν· ἐὰν δὲ ἄλλον
τρόπον ἐργασθῶσιν αἱ γλῶτται, ταύτας οὐ πάνυ
συμφωνεῖν· ἡ μὲν οὖν ἐργασία τοιαύτη.

---

[1] κατασπάσματα : lit. 'convulsions'; i.e. the strong vibra-
tions of a 'tongue,' the free end of which is kept away from
the body or 'lay' of the mouthpiece. Such a 'reed' would
have the effect of giving to the pipes a fuller and louder tone.
[2] i.e. so as to make a closed end.

have ample vibration,[1] which is essential for those
who play in the elaborate style. Such, they tell us,
are the proper seasons for cutting the reed used for
the reed mouthpiece.

The manufacture is carried out in the following
manner. Having collected the reed-stems they lay
them in the open air during the winter, leaving on
the rind; in the spring they strip this off, and,
having rubbed the reeds thoroughly, put them in
the sun. Later on, in the summer, they cut the
sections from knot to knot into lengths and again
put them for some time in the open air. They
leave the upper knot on this internodal section [2];
and the lengths thus obtained are not less than two
palmsbreadths long. Now they say that for making
mouthpieces the best lengths are those of the middle
of the reed, whereas the lengths towards the upper
growths make very soft mouthpieces and those next
to the root very hard ones. They say too that the
reed-tongues made out of the same length are of the
same quality, while those made from different lengths
are not; also that the one from the length next to
the root forms a left-hand [3] reed-tongue, and that
from the length towards the upper growths a right-
hand [3] reed-tongue. Moreover, when the length is
slit, the opening of the reed-tongues in either case
is made towards the point at which the reed was
cut [4]; and, if the reed-tongues are made in any other
manner, they are not quite of the same quality. Such
then is the method of manufacture.

[3] i.e. the vibrating 'tongues' (reeds) for the left-hand
and the right-hand pipe of the Double Pipe respectively.
[4] i.e. not at the closed end, but at the end which was
'lower' when the cane was growing: cf. §6, προσλείπουσι δὲ
κ.τ.λ.

8 Φύεται δὲ πλεῖστος μὲν μεταξὺ τοῦ Κηφισοῦ
καὶ τοῦ Μέλανος· οὗτος δὲ ὁ τόπος προσαγορεύεται μὲν Πελεκανία· τούτου δ' ἔστιν ἄττα
Χύτροι καλούμενοι βαθύσματα τῆς λίμνης, ἐν οἷς
κάλλιστόν φασι γίνεσθαι· <γίνεσθαι> δὲ καὶ καθ'
ὃ ἡ Προβατία καλουμένη καταφέρεται· τοῦτο δ'
ἐστὶ ποταμὸς ῥέων ἐκ Λεβαδείας. κάλλιστος δὲ
δοκεῖ πάντων γίνεσθαι περὶ τὴν Ὀξεῖαν καλουμένην Καμπήν· ὁ δὲ τόπος οὗτός ἐστιν ἐμβολὴ
τοῦ Κηφισοῦ. γειτνιᾷ δ' αὐτῷ πεδίον εὔγειον, ὃ
9 προσαγορεύουσι Ἱππίαν. πρόσβορρος δὲ τόπος
ἄλλος τῆς Ὀξείας Καμπῆς ἐστιν, ὃν καλοῦσι
Βοηδρίαν· φύεσθαι δέ φασι καὶ κατὰ ταύτην
εὐγενῆ τὸν κάλαμον. τὸ δὲ ὅλον, οὗ ἂν ᾖ βαθύ-
γειον καὶ εὔγειον χωρίον καὶ ἰλυῶδες καὶ ὁ
Κηφισὸς ἀναμίσγεται καὶ πρὸς τούτοις βάθυσμα
τῆς λίμνης, κάλλιστον γίνεσθαι κάλαμον. περὶ
γὰρ τὴν Ὀξεῖαν Καμπὴν καὶ τὴν Βοηδρίαν πάντα
ταῦτα ὑπάρχειν. ὅτι δὲ ὁ Κηφισὸς μεγάλην ἔχει
ῥοπὴν εἰς τὸ ποιεῖν καλὸν τὸν κάλαμον σημεῖον
ἔχουσι· καθ' ὃν γὰρ τόπον ὁ Μέλας καλούμενος
ἐμβάλλει βαθείας οὔσης τῆς λίμνης καὶ τοῦ
ἐδάφους εὐγείου καὶ ἰλυώδους, ἢ ὅλως μὴ γίνεσθαι
ἢ φαῦλον.    ἡ μὲν οὖν γένεσις καὶ φύσις τοῦ
αὐλητικοῦ καὶ ἡ κατεργασία καὶ τίνας ἔχει διαφορὰς πρὸς τοὺς ἄλλους ἱκανῶς εἰρήσθω.
10 Γένη δὲ οὐ ταῦτα μόνον ἀλλὰ πλείω τοῦ καλάμου τυγχάνει φανερὰς ἔχοντα τῇ αἰσθήσει δια-
φοράς· ὁ μὲν γὰρ πυκνὸς καὶ τῇ σαρκὶ καὶ τοῖς

---

[1] cf. Plut. Sulla, 20.
[2] i.e. the so-called 'Lake' Copaïs.
[3] καὶ add. W.

This reed grows in greatest abundance between
the Kephisos and the Black River[1]; this district is
called Pelekania, and in it are certain 'pots,' as they
are called, which are deep holes in the marsh,[2] and
in these holes they say that it grows fairest; it is also[3]
said to be found[4] where the river called the 'Sheep
River' comes down, which is a stream that flows from
Lebadeia. But it appears to grow fairest of all near
'the Sharp Bend'; this place is the mouth of the
Kephisos; near it is a rich plain called Hippias.
There is another region north of the Sharp Bend
called Boedrias; and here too they say that the reed
grows fine, and in general that it is fairest wherever
there is a piece of land with deep rich alluvial soil,
where also Kephisos mingles[5] his waters with the
soil, and where there is further a deep hole in the
marsh; for that about the Sharp Bend and Boedrias
all these conditions are found. As proof that the
Kephisos has a great effect in producing the reed of
good quality they have the fact that, where the river
called the 'Black River' flows into the marsh, though
the marsh is there deep and the bottom of good
alluvial soil, it either does not grow at all or at best
but of poor quality. Let this suffice for an account
of the growth and character of the reed used for
pipes, of the manufacture, and of its distinctive
features as compared with other reeds.

But these are not the only kinds of reed: there are
several others[6] with distinctive characters which are
easily recognised; there is one that is of compact
growth in flesh and has its joints close together:

[1] γίνεσθαι add. Sch.; φασι γίνεσθαι δὲ καθ' [3] UMVP: so
Ald., but καθ' ὅν.
[5] ἀναυίσγεται: ? ἀναυίσγηται; cf. Plut. Sull. l.c.
[6] Plin. 16. 164-167; Diosc. 1. 85.

γόνασιν, ὁ δὲ μανὸς καὶ ὀλιγογόνατος· καὶ ὁ μὲν
κοῖλος, ὃν καλοῦσί τινες συριγγίαν, οὐδὲν γὰρ ὡς
εἰπεῖν ἔχει ξύλου καὶ σαρκός· ὁ δὲ στερεὸς καὶ
συμπλήρης μικροῦ. καὶ ὁ μὲν βραχύς, ὁ δὲ
εὐαυξὴς καὶ ὑψηλὸς καὶ παχύς. ὁ δὲ λεπτὸς καὶ
πολύφυλλος, ὁ δὲ ὀλιγόφυλλος καὶ μονόφυλλος.
ὅλως δὲ πολλαί τινές εἰσι διαφοραὶ κατὰ τὰς
χρείας· ἕκαστος γὰρ πρὸς ἕκαστα χρήσιμος.

11  Ὀνόμασι δὲ ἄλλοι ἄλλοις προσαγορεύουσι·
κοινότατον δέ πως ὁ δόναξ, ὃν καὶ λοχμωδέστατόν
γέ φασιν εἶναι καὶ μάλιστα φύεσθαι παρὰ τοὺς
ποταμοὺς καὶ τὰς λίμνας. διαφέρειν δ' ὅμως
παντὸς καλάμου πολὺ τόν τε ἐν τῷ ξηρῷ καὶ τὸν
ἐν τοῖς ὕδασι φυόμενον. ἴδιος δὲ καὶ ὁ τοξικός, ὃν
δὴ Κρητικόν τινες καλοῦσιν· ὀλιγογόνατος μὲν
σαρκωδέστερος δὲ πάντων καὶ μάλιστα κάμψιν
δεχόμενος, καὶ ὅλως ἄγεσθαι δυνάμενος ὡς ἂν
θέλῃ τις θερμαινόμενος.

12  Ἔχουσι δέ, ὥσπερ ἐλέχθη, καὶ κατὰ τὰ φύλλα
μεγάλας διαφορὰς οὐ πλήθει καὶ μεγέθει μόνον
ἀλλὰ καὶ χροιᾷ. ποικίλος γὰρ ὁ Λακωνικὸς
καλούμενος. ἔτι δὲ τῇ θέσει καὶ προσφύσει·
κάτωθεν γὰρ ἔνιοι πλεῖστα φέρουσι τῶν φύλλων,
αὐτὸς δὲ ὥσπερ ἐκ θάμνου πέφυκε. σχεδὸν δέ
τινές φασι καὶ τῶν λιμναίων ταύτην εἶναι τὴν
διαφοράν, τὸ πολύφυλλον καὶ παρόμοιον ἔχειν
τρόπον τινὰ τὸ φύλλον τῷ τοῦ κυπείρου καὶ

another that is of open growth, with few joints; there is the hollow reed called by some the 'tube-reed,'[1] inasmuch as it has hardly any wood or flesh; there is another which is solid and almost entirely filled with substance; there is another which is short, and another which is of strong growth tall and stout; there is one which is slender and has many leaves, another which has few leaves or only one. And in general there are many differences in natural character and in usefulness, each kind being useful for some particular purpose.

Some distinguish the various kinds by different names; commonest perhaps is the pole-reed, which is said to be of very bushy habit, and to grow chiefly by rivers and lakes. And it is said that there is a wide difference in reeds in general between those that grow on dry land and those that grow in the water. Quite distinct again is the 'archer's' reed, which some call the 'Cretan': this has few joints and is fleshier than any of the others; it can also be most freely bent, and in general, when warmed, may be turned about as one pleases.

The various kinds have also, as was said, great differences in the leaves, not only in number and size, but also in colour. That called the 'Laconian' reed is parti-coloured. They also differ in the position and attachment of the leaves; some have most of their leaves low down, and the reed itself grows out of a sort of a bush. Indeed some say that this may be taken as the distinctive character of those which grow in lakes, namely, that these have many leaves, and that their foliage in a manner

συριγγίαν conj. Sch. from Plin. *l.c.*, *syringiam*; *cf.* Diosc. *l.c.*, *Geop.* 2. 6. 23. συριγί U; σύριγγι MV; σύριγγα Ald.H.

φλεὼ καὶ θρύου καὶ βουτόμου· σκέψασθαι δὲ δεῖ τοῦτο.

13 Γένος δέ τι καλάμου φύεται καὶ ἐπίγειον, ὃ οὐκ εἰς ὀρθὸν ἀλλ' ἐπὶ γῆς ἀφίησι τὸν καυλόν, ὥσπερ ἡ ἄγρωστις, καὶ οὕτως ποιεῖται τὴν αὔξησιν. ἔστι δὲ ὁ μὲν ἄρρην στερεός, καλεῖται δὲ ὑπό τινων εἰλετίας. . . .

Ὁ δὲ Ἰνδικὸς ἐν μεγίστῃ διαφορᾷ καὶ ὥσπερ ἕτερον ὅλως τὸ γένος· ἔστι δὲ ὁ μὲν ἄρρην στερεός, ὁ δὲ θῆλυς κοῖλος· διαιροῦσι γὰρ καὶ τοῦτον τῷ ἄρρενι καὶ θήλει. φύονται δ' ἐξ ἑνὸς πυθμένος πολλοὶ καὶ οὐ λοχμώδεις· τὸ δὲ φύλλον οὐ μακρὸν ἀλλ' ὅμοιον τῇ ἰτέᾳ· τῷ δὲ μεγέθει μεγάλοι καὶ εὐπαγεῖς, ὥστε ἀκοντίοις χρῆσθαι. φύονται δὲ οὗτοι περὶ τὸν Ἀκεσίνην ποταμόν. ἅπας δὲ κάλαμος εὔζωος καὶ τεμνόμενος καὶ ἐπικαιόμενος καλλίων βλαστάνει· ἔτι δὲ παχύρριζος καὶ πολύρριζος, δι' ὃ καὶ δυσώλεθρος. ἡ δὲ ῥίζα γονατώδης, ὥσπερ ἡ τῆς ἀγρωστίδος, πλὴν οὐ παντὸς ὁμοίως. ἀλλὰ περὶ μὲν καλάμων ἱκανῶς εἰρήσθω.

XII. Κατάλοιπον δὲ εἰπεῖν ὡσὰν ἐκ τοῦ γένους τούτου περὶ σχοίνου· καὶ γὰρ καὶ τοῦτο τῶν ἐνύδρων θετέον. ἔστι δὲ αὐτοῦ τρία εἴδη, καθάπερ τινὲς διαιροῦσιν, ὅ τε ὀξὺς καὶ ἄκαρπος, ὃν δὴ καλοῦσιν ἄρρενα, καὶ ὁ κάρπιμος, ὃν μελαγκρανὶν

---

[1] θρύον, a kind of grass (see Index ; cf. Hom. Il. 21. 351), conj. Sch. ; βρύον MSS. ; however Plut. Nat. Quaest. 2 gives βρύον along with τύφη and φλεώς in a list of marsh plants.

[2] δὲ δεῖ τοῦτο conj. W. ; δὲ τοῦτο UMVAld.

378

resembles that of galingale *phleos thryon* [1] and sedge ;
but this needs [2] further enquiry.

There is also a kind of reed (bush-grass) which
grows on land, and which is not erect, but sends out
its stem over the ground, like the dog's-tooth grass,
and so makes its growth. The 'male' reed is solid :
some call it *eiletias*. . . . . [3]

The Indian reed (bamboo) is very distinct, and
as it were a totally different kind ; the 'male' is
solid and the 'female' hollow (for in this kind too
they distinguish a 'male' and a 'female' form) ; a
number of reeds of this kind grow from one base and
they do not form a bush ; the leaf is not long, but
resembles the willow leaf ; these reeds are of great
size and of good substance, so that they are used for
javelins. They grow by the river Akesines.[4] All
reeds are tenacious of life, and, if cut or burnt down,
grow up again more vigorously ; also their roots are
stout and numerous, so that the plant is hard to
destroy. The root is jointed, like that of the dog's-
tooth grass, but this is not equally so in all kinds.
However let this suffice for an account of reeds.

*Of rushes.*

XII. It remains to speak of the rush,[5] as though
t belonged to this class of plants, inasmuch as we
must reckon this also among water plants. Of this
there are three kinds [6] as some distinguish, the
'sharp' rush, which is barren and is called the
'male'; the 'fruiting' kind which we call the 'black-

---

[3] Sch. marks a lacuna ; there is nothing to correspond to
ὁ μὲν ἄρρην.    [4] Chenab.
[5] cf. 1. 5. 3 ; 1. 8. 1 ; Plin. 21. 112–115 ; Diosc. 4. 52.
[6] See Index.

καλοῦμεν διὰ τὸ μέλανα τὸν καρπὸν ἔχειν, παχύτερος δὲ οὗτος καὶ σαρκωδέστερος· καὶ τρίτος τῷ
μεγέθει καὶ τῇ παχύτητι καὶ εὐσαρκίᾳ διαφέρων
ὁ καλούμενος ὀλόσχοινος.

2 Ἡ μὲν οὖν μελαγκρανὶς αὐτός τις καθ᾽ αὑτόν· ὁ
δ᾽ ὀξὺς καὶ ὀλόσχοινος ἐκ τοῦ αὐτοῦ φύονται· ὃ
καὶ ἄτοπον φαίνεται, καὶ θαυμαστόν γ᾽ ἦν ἰδεῖν
ὅλης κομισθείσης τῆς σχοινιᾶς· οἱ πολλοὶ γὰρ
ἦσαν ἄκαρποι πεφυκότες ἐκ τοῦ αὐτοῦ, κάρπιμοι
δὲ ὀλίγοι. τοῦτο μὲν οὖν ἐπίσκεπτέον. ἐλάττους δὲ ὅλως οἱ κάρπιμοι· πρὸς γὰρ τὰ πλέγματα
χρησιμώτερος ὁ ὀλόσχοινος διὰ τὸ σαρκῶδες καὶ
μαλακόν. κορυνᾷ δ᾽ ὅλως ὁ κάρπιμος ἐξ αὐτοῦ
τοῦ γραμμώδους ἐξοιδήσας, κἄπειτα ἐκτίκτει
καθάπερ ὠά. πρὸς μιᾷ γὰρ ἀρχῇ γραμμώδει
ἔχει τοὺς περισταχυώδεις μίσχους, ἐφ᾽ ὧν ἄκρωι
παραπλαγίους τὰς τῶν ἀγγείων ἔχει στρογγυλό-
τητας ὑποχασκούσας· ἐν τούτοις δὲ τὸ σπερμάτιον ἀκιδῶδές ἐστι μέλαν ἑκάστῳ προσεμφερὲς
3 τῷ τοῦ ἀστερίσκου πλὴν ἀμενηνότερον. ῥίζαν δὲ
ἔχει μακρὰν καὶ παχυτέραν πολὺ τοῦ σχοίνου·
αὕτη δ᾽ αὐαίνεται καθ᾽ ἕκαστον ἐνιαυτόν, εἶθ᾽
ἑτέρα πάλιν ἀπὸ τῆς κεφαλῆς τοῦ σχοίνου καθίε-
ται· τοῦτο δὲ καὶ ἐν τῇ ὄψει φανερὸν ἰδεῖν τὰς
μὲν αὔας τὰς δὲ χλωρὰς καθιεμένας· ἡ δὲ κεφαλὴ
ὁμοία τῇ τῶν κρομύων καὶ τῇ τῶν γητείων, συμ-

---

¹ θ. γ᾽ ἦν ἰδεῖν conj. W. from G ; θ. ἐν γ᾽ εἰδεῖν U ; θ. ἔν γε
ἰδεῖν MVP ; θ. ἐνιδεῖν Ald.
² οἱ κάρπιμοι conj. R. Const.; οἱ καρποί Ald.H.
³ γὰρ seems meaningless ; G has autem.
⁴ κορυνᾷ ; cf. 3. 5. 1.
⁵ γραμμώδει conj. R. Const.; γραμμώδεις Ald.H.

head' because it has black fruit; this is stouter and
fleshier: and third the 'entire rush,' as it is called,
which is distinguished by its size stoutness and
fleshiness.

Now the 'black-head' grows by itself, but the
'sharp' rush and the 'entire' rush grow from the
same stock, which seems extraordinary, and indeed
it was strange to see it¹ when the whole clump of
rushes was brought before me; for from the same
stock there were growing 'barren' rushes, which
were the most numerous, and also a few 'fruiting'
ones. This then is a matter for further enquiry.
The 'fruiting'² ones are in general scarcer, for³ the
'entire rush' is more useful for wicker-work because
of its fleshiness and pliancy. The 'fruiting' rush in
general produces a club-like⁴ head which swells
straight from the wiry stem, and then bears egg-like
bodies; for attached to a single wiry⁵ base it has its
very spike-like⁶ branches all round it, and on the
ends of these it has its round vessels borne laterally
and gaping⁷; in each of these is the small seed,
which is pointed and black, and like that of the
Michaelmas daisy, except that it is less solid. It
has a long root, which is stouter than that of the
ordinary rush: this withers every year, and then
another strikes down again from the 'head'⁸ of the
plant. And it is easy to observe that some of the
roots as they are let down are withered, some green.
The 'head' is like that of an onion or long onion,

⁶ περισταχυώθεις seems an impossible word; ? περὶ αὐτὸν
τοὺς σταχυώδεις.
⁷ ὑποχασκούσας conj. Sch.; ἐπισχαζούσας Ald. H.
⁸ i.e. the part above ground; cf. Plin. l.c.   Sch. has dis-
posed of the idea that κεφαλή is here a 'bulbous' root.

πεφυκυῖά πως ἐκ πλειόνων εἰς ταὐτὸ καὶ πλατεῖα κάτωθεν ἔχουσα κελύφη ὑπέρυθρα. συμβαίνει δ᾿ οὖν ἴδιον ἐπὶ τῶν ῥιζῶν εἰ ἀναίνονται κατ᾿ ἐνιαυτὸν καὶ ἐκ τοῦ ἄνωθεν πάλιν ἡ γένεσις. τῶν μὲν οὖν σχοίνων τοιαύτη τις φύσις.

4 Εἰ δὲ καὶ ὁ βάτος καὶ ὁ παλίουρος ἔνυδρά πώς ἐστιν ἢ πάρυδρα, καθάπερ ἐνιαχοῦ, φανεραὶ σχεδὸν καὶ αἱ τούτων διαφοραί· περὶ ἀμφοῖν γὰρ εἴρηται πρότερον.

[Τῶν δὲ νήσων τῶν πλοάδων τῶν ἐν Ὀρχομενῷ τὰ μὲν μεγέθη παντοδαπὰ τυγχάνει, τὰ δὲ μέγιστα αὐτῶν ἐστιν ὅσον τριῶν σταδίων τὴν περίμετρον. ἐν Αἰγύπτῳ δὲ μάλιστα μεγάλα σφόδρα συνίσταται, ὥστε καὶ ὗς ἐν αὐταῖς ἐγγίνεσθαι πολλούς, οὓς καὶ κυνηγετοῦσι διαβαίνοντες.] καὶ περὶ μὲν ἐνύδρων ταῦτ᾿ εἰρήσθω.

XIII. Περὶ δὲ βραχυβιότητος φυτῶν καὶ δένδρων τῶν ἐνύδρων ἐπὶ τοσοῦτον ἔχομεν ὡς ἂν καθ᾿ ὅλου λέγοντες, ὅτι βραχυβιώτερα τῶν χερσαίων ἐστί, καθάπερ καὶ τὰ ζῷα. τοὺς δὲ καθ᾿ ἕκαστον βίους ἱστορῆσαι δεῖ τῶν χερσαίων. τὰ μὲν οὖν ἄγριά φασιν οὐδεμίαν ἔχειν ὡς εἰπεῖν οἱ ὀρεοτύποι διαφοράν, ἀλλὰ πάντα εἶναι μακρόβια καὶ οὐθὲν βραχύβιον· αὐτὸ μὲν τοῦτο ἴσως ἀληθὲς λέγοντες· ἅπαντα γὰρ ὑπερτείνει πολὺ τὴν τῶν ἄλλων ζωήν. οὐ μὴν ἀλλ᾿ ὅμως ἐστὶ τὰ μὲν μᾶλλον τὰ δ᾿ ἧττον μακρόβια, καθάπερ ἐν τοῖς ἡμέροις· ποῖα

---

being, as it were, made up of several united together; it is broad, and underneath it has reddish scales. Now it is a peculiar fact about the roots of this plant that they wither every year and that the fresh growth of roots comes from the part of the plant which is above ground. Such is the character of rushes.

Bramble and Christ's thorn may be considered to some extent plants of the water or the waterside, as they are in some districts; but the distinctive characters of these plants are fairly clear, for we have spoken of both already.[1]

The floating islands of Orchomenos[2] are of various sizes, the largest being about three furlongs in circumference. But in Egypt very large ones form, so that even a number of boars are found in them, and men go across to the islands to hunt them. Let this account of water-plants suffice.

*Of the length or shortness of the life of plants, and the causes.*

XIII. As to the comparative shortness of life of plants and trees of the water we may say thus much as a general account, that, like the water-animals, they are shorter-lived than those of the dry land. But we must enquire into the lives of those of the dry land severally. Now the woodmen say that the wild kinds are almost[3] without exception long-lived, and none of them is short-lived: so far they may be speaking the truth; all such plants do live far longer than others. However, just as in the case of cultivated plants, some are longer-lived than others,

[2] *cf.* 4. 10. 2, to which § this note perhaps belongs.
[3] ὡς εἰπεῖν conj. Sch.: ὡς εἰπεῖ U: ὡς εἰποι MV: ὡς ἂν εἴποιεν Ald. H.

δὲ ταῦτα σκεπτέον. τὰ δὲ ἥμερα φανερῶς διαφέρει τῷ τὰ μὲν εἶναι μακρόβια τὰ δὲ βραχύβια·
ὡς δ' ἁπλῶς εἰπεῖν τὰ ἄγρια τῶν ἡμέρων μακρο-
βιώτερα καὶ ὅλως τῷ γένει καὶ τὰ ἀντιδιῃρημένα
καθ' ἕκαστον, οἷον κότινος ἐλάας καὶ ἀχρὰς ἀπίου
ἐρινεὸς συκῆς· ἰσχυρότερα γὰρ καὶ πυκνότερα
καὶ ἀγονώτερα τοῖς περικαρπίοις.

2  Τὴν δὲ μακροβιότητα μαρτυροῦσιν ἐπί γέ τινων
καὶ ἡμέρων καὶ ἀγρίων καὶ αἱ παραδεδομέναι
φῆμαι παρὰ τῶν μυθολόγων· ἐλάαν μὲν γὰρ
λέγουσι τὴν Ἀθήνῃσι, φοίνικα δὲ τὸν ἐν Δήλῳ,
κότινον δὲ τὸν ἐν Ὀλυμπίᾳ, ἀφ' οὗ ὁ στέφανος·
φηγοὺς δὲ τὰς ἐν Ἰλίῳ τὰς ἐπὶ τοῦ Ἴλου μνήμα-
τος· τινὲς δέ φασι καὶ τὴν ἐν Δελφοῖς πλάτανον
Ἀγαμέμνονα φυτεῦσαι καὶ τὴν ἐν Καφύαις τῆς
Ἀρκαδίας. ταῦτα μὲν οὖν ὅπως ἔχει τάχ' ἂν
ἕτερος εἴη λόγος· ὅτι δέ ἐστι μεγάλη διαφορὰ
τῶν δένδρων φανερόν· μακρόβια μὲν γὰρ τά τε
προειρημένα καὶ ἕτερα πλείω· βραχύβια δὲ καὶ
τὰ τοιαῦτα ὁμολογουμένως, οἷον ῥοιὰ συκῆ μηλέα,
καὶ τούτων ἡ ἠρινὴ μᾶλλον καὶ ἡ γλυκεῖα τῆς
ὀξείας, ὥσπερ τῶν ῥοῶν ἡ ἀπύρηνος. βραχύβια
δὲ καὶ ἀμπέλων ἔνια γένη καὶ μάλιστα τὰ πολύ-
καρπα· δοκεῖ δὲ καὶ τὰ πάρυδρα βραχυβιώτερα

[1] καὶ τὰ ἀντ. conj. W.; κατὰ ἀντ. UMV; τὰ ἀντ. Ald.H.
[2] περικαρπίοις : cf. C.P. 1. 17. 5.
[3] On the Acropolis : cf. Hdt. 8. 55 ; Soph. O.C. 694 foll.

and we must consider which these are. Cultivated
plants plainly differ as to the length of their lives,
but, to speak generally, wild plants are longer-lived
than cultivated ones, both taken as classes, and also
when one compares [1] the wild and cultivated forms
of particular plants: thus the wild olive pear and fig
are longer-lived than the corresponding cultivated
trees; for the wild forms of these are stronger and of
closer growth, and they do not produce such well-
developed fruit-pulp.[2]

To the long-lived character of some plants, both
cultivated and wild, witness is borne also by the tales
handed down in mythology, as of the olive at Athens,[3]
the palm in Delos,[4] and the wild olive at Olympia,
from which the wreaths for the games are made;
or again of the Valonia oaks at Ilium, planted on the
tomb of Ilos. Again some say that Agamemnon
planted the plane at Delphi, and the one at Kaphyai [5]
in Arcadia. Now how this is may perhaps be
another story, but anyhow it is plain that there is a
great difference between trees in this respect: the
kinds that have been mentioned, and many others
besides, are long-lived, while the following are ad-
mittedly short-lived—pomegranate fig apple: and
among apples the 'spring' sort and the 'sweet'
apple are shorter-lived than the 'sour' apple, even
as the 'stoneless' pomegranate is shorter-lived than
the other kinds. Also some kinds of vine are short-
lived, especially those which bear much fruit; and it
appears that trees which grow by water are shorter-

[4] Under which Leto gave birth to Artemis and Apollo: cf.
Paus. 8. 48. 3; Cic. de Leg. 1. 1.; Plin. 16. 238.
[5] Its planting is ascribed to Menelaus by Paus. 8. 23. 3.

τῶν ἐν τοῖς ξηροῖς εἶναι, οἷον ἰτέα λεύκη ἀκτὴ
αἴγειρος.

3    Ἔνια δὲ γηράσκει μὲν καὶ σήπεται ταχέως,
παραβλαστάνει δὲ πάλιν ἐκ τῶν αὐτῶν, ὥσπερ αἱ
δάφναι καὶ αἱ μηλέαι τε καὶ αἱ ῥόαι καὶ τῶν
φιλύδρων τὰ πολλά· περὶ ὧν καὶ σκέψαιτ᾿ ἄν
τις πότερα ταὐτὰ δεῖ λέγειν ἢ ἕτερα· καθάπερ εἴ
τις τὸ στέλεχος ἀποκόψας, ὥσπερ ποιοῦσιν οἱ
γεωργοί, πάλιν ἀναθεραπεύοι τοὺς βλαστούς,¹ ἢ εἰ
καὶ ὅλως ἐκκόψειεν ἄχρι τῶν ῥιζῶν καὶ ἐπικαύ-
σειεν· καὶ γὰρ ταῦτα ποιοῦσιν, ὁτὲ δὲ καὶ ἀπὸ
τοῦ αὐτομάτου συμβαίνει· πότερα δὴ τοῦτο ταὐτὸ
δεῖ λέγειν ἢ ἕτερον; ἢ μὲν γὰρ ἀεὶ τὰ μέρη τὰς
αὐξήσεις καὶ φθίσεις φαίνεται παραλλάττοντα
καὶ ἔτι τὰς διακαθάρσεις τὰς ὑπ᾿ αὐτῶν, ταύτῃ
μὲν ἂν δόξειε ταὐτὸν εἶναι· τί γὰρ ἂν ἐπὶ τούτων
4    ἢ ἐκείνων διαφέροι; ἢ δ᾿ ὥσπερ οὐσία καὶ φύσις
τοῦ δένδρου μάλιστ᾿ ἂν φαίνοιτο τὸ στέλεχος, ὅταν
μεταλλάττῃ τοῦτο, κἂν τὸ ὅλον ἕτερον ὑπολάβοι
τις, εἰ μὴ ἄρα διὰ τὸ ἀπὸ τῶν αὐτῶν ἀρχῶν εἶναι
ταὐτὸ θείη· καίτοι πολλάκις συμβαίνει καὶ τὰς
ῥίζας ἑτέρας εἶναι καὶ μεταβάλλειν τῶν μὲν σηπο-
μένων τῶν δ᾿ ἐξ ἀρχῆς βλαστανουσῶν. ἐπεί, ἐὰν
ἀληθὲς ᾖ, ὥς γέ τινές φασι, τὰς ἀμπέλους μακρο-

---

¹ cf. C.P. 2. 11. 5.
² ἀναθεραπεύοι conj. W.; ἀναθεραπεύει Ald.
³ ἢ εἰ καὶ ὅλως conj. W.; ἃ εἰ καὶ καλῶς U; ἀεὶ καὶ καλῶς
MV; καὶ εἰ καλῶς Ald. H.
⁴ Sc. and then encourage new growth.

lived than those which live in dry places : this is true
of willow abele elder and black poplar.

Some trees, though they grow old and decay
quickly, shoot up again from the same stock,[1] as
bay apple pomegranate and most of the water-
loving trees. About these one might enquire
whether one should call the new growth the same
tree or a new one ; to take a similar case, if, after
cutting down the trunk, one should, as the husband-
men do, encourage[2] the new shoots to grow again,
or if[3] one should cut the tree right down to the
roots and burn the stump,[4] (for these things are
commonly done, and they also sometimes occur
naturally); are we then here too, to call the new
growth the same tree, or another one ? In so far as
it is always the parts of the tree which appear to
alternate their periods of growth and decay and also
the prunings which they themselves thus make, so
far the new and the old growth might seem to be the
same tree ; for what difference can there be in the
one as compared with the other ?[5] On the other
hand, in so far as the trunk would seem to be above
all the essential part of the tree, which gives it its
special character, when this changes, one might
suppose that the whole tree becomes something
different—unless indeed one should lay down that to
have the same starting-point constitutes identity ;
whereas it often[6] happens that the roots too are
different and undergo a change, since some decay
and others grow afresh.[7] For if it be true, as some
assert, that the reason why the vine is the longest

[5] *i.e.* how can the substitution of one set of 'parts' for
another destroy the identity of the tree as a whole?
[6] πολλάκις conj. Sch. from G : πολλὰ καὶ Ald.H.
[7] And so the 'starting-point' too is not constant.

βιωτάτας εἶναι τῷ μὴ φύειν ἑτέρας ἀλλ᾽ ἐξ αὐτῶν
ἀεὶ συναναπληροῦσθαι, γελοῖον ἂν ἴσως δοκοίη τοιαύτη σύγκρισις ἐὰν <μὴ> μένῃ τὸ στέλεχος· αὕτη
γὰρ οἷον ὑπόθεσις καὶ φύσις δένδρων. τοῦτο μὲν
οὖν ὁποτέρως ποτὲ λεκτέον οὐθὲν ἂν διενέγκαι
5 πρὸς τὰ νῦν. τάχα δ᾽ ἂν εἴη μακροβιώτατον τὸ
πάντως δυνάμενον ἀνταρκεῖν, ὥσπερ ἡ ἐλάα καὶ
τῷ στελέχει καὶ τῇ παραβλαστήσει καὶ τῷ
δυσωλέθρους ἔχειν τὰς ῥίζας. δοκεῖ δὲ ὁ βίος
τῆς γε μιᾶς εἶναι, καθ᾽ ὃν τὸ στέλεχος δεῖ τὴν
ἀρχὴν τιθέντα μέτρον ἀναμετρεῖν τὸν χρόνον,
μάλιστα περὶ ἔτη διακόσια. εἰ δ᾽ ὅπερ ἐπὶ τῶν
ἀμπέλων λέγουσί τινες, ὡς παραιρουμένων τῶν
ῥιζῶν κατὰ μέρος δύναται διαμένειν τὸ στέλεχος,
καὶ ἡ ὅλη φύσις ὁμοία καὶ ὁμοιοφόρος ὁποσονοῦν
χρόνον, μακροβιώτατον ἂν εἴη πάντων. φασὶ δὲ
δεῖν οὕτω ποιεῖν ὅταν ἤδη δοκῇ καταφέρεσθαι·
κλήματά τε ἐπιβάλλειν καὶ καρποῦσθαι τὸν
ἐνιαυτόν· μετὰ δὲ ταῦτα κατασκάψαντα ἐπὶ
θάτερα τῆς ἀμπέλου περικαθᾶραι πάσας τὰς
ῥίζας, εἶτ᾽ ἐμπλῆσαι φρυγάνων καὶ ἐπαμήσασθαι
6 τὴν γῆν· τούτῳ μὲν οὖν τῷ ἔτει κακῶς φέρειν
σφόδρα, τῷ δ᾽ ὑστέρῳ βέλτιον, τῷ δὲ τρίτῳ καὶ

---

[1] ἐξ αὐτῶν Ald., sc. τῶν ῥιζῶν; ἐκ τῶν αὐτῶν conj. W.
[2] i.e. such an argument practically assumes the permanence
of the trunk, which in the case of the vine can hardly be
considered apart from the root. δοκοίη τοιαύτη σύγκρισις I
conj. from G; δικαιοτάτη σύγκρισις MVAld.; δικαιοτάτηι
συγκρίσεις U; δοκοίη εἶναι ἡ σύγκρισις conj. Sch.; so W. in
his earlier edition: in his later editions he emends wildly.

388

lived of trees, is that, instead of producing new
roots, it always renews itself from the existing ones,[1]
such an illustration must surely lead to an absurd conclusion,[2] unless [3] we assume that the stock persists,
as it must do, since it is, as it were, the fundamental
and essential part of a tree. However it cannot
matter much for our present purpose which account
is the right one. Perhaps we may say that the
longest-lived tree is that which in all ways is able to
persist,[4] as does the olive by its trunk, by its power
of developing sidegrowth, and by the fact that its
roots are so hard to destroy. It appears that the
life of the individual olive (in regard to which one
should make the trunk the essential part and standard[5]
in estimating the time), lasts for about two hundred
years.[6] But if it is true of the vine, as some say, that,
if the roots are partly removed, the trunk is able to
survive, and the whole character of the tree remains
the same and produces like fruits for any period,
however long, then the vine will be the longest-lived
of all trees. They say that, when the vine seems to
be deteriorating, this is what one should do :—one
should encourage the growth of branches and gather
the fruit that year ; and after that one should dig on
one side of the vine and prune away all the roots on
that side, and then fill the hole with brushwood and
heap up the soil. In that year, they say, the vine
bears very badly, but better in the next, while in the

---

[3] I have inserted μὴ, which G seems to have read.
[4] ἀνταρκεῖν U, cf. Ar. Eq. 540 ; αἰταρκεῖν Ald.
[5] καθ' ὃν τὸ στέλεχος δεῖ τὴν ἀρχὴν τιθέντα I conj. ; so G ;
καθ' ὃν στέλεχος ἤδη τὴν ἀρχὴν τιθέντα μέτρον Ald.H.; εἰ
δεῖ for ἤδη U ; καθ' ὃ τοῦ στελέχους δεῖ τὸν ὄγκον τιθέντα μέτρον
conj. W. ; καθ' ὃν τὸ στ. ἤδη ἀρχὴν καὶ μέτρον χρὴ conj. Sch.
cf. end of § 4. [6] Plin. 16. 241.

τετάρτῳ καθίστασθαι καὶ φέρειν πολλοὺς καὶ καλούς, ὥστε μηδὲν διαφέρειν ἢ ὅτε ἤκμαζεν· ἐπειδὰν δὲ πάλιν ἀποπληγῇ,¹ θάτερον μέρος παρασκάπτειν καὶ θεραπεύειν ὁμοίως, καὶ οὕτως αἰεὶ διαμένειν· ποιεῖν δὲ τοῦτο μάλιστα δι᾽ ἐτῶν δέκα· δι᾽ ὃ καὶ κόπτειν οὐδέποτε τοὺς τοῦτο ποιοῦντας, ἀλλ᾽ ἐπὶ γενεὰς πολλὰς ταὐτὰ τὰ στελέχη διαμένειν, ὥστε μηδὲ μεμνῆσθαι τοὺς φυτεύσαντας· τοῦτο μὲν οὖν ἴσως τῶν πεπειραμένων ἀκούοντα δεῖ πιστεύειν. τὰ δὲ μακρόβια καὶ βραχύβια διὰ τῶν εἰρημένων θεωρητέον.

XIV. Νοσήματα δὲ τοῖς μὲν ἀγρίοις οὔ φασι ξυμβαίνειν ὑφ᾽ ὧν ἀναιροῦνται, φαύλως δὲ διατίθεσθαι καὶ μάλιστα ἐπιδήλως ὅταν χαλαζοκοπηθῇ ἢ βλαστάνειν μέλλοντα ἢ ἀρχόμενα ἢ ἀνθοῦντα, καὶ ὅταν ἢ πνεῦμα ψυχρὸν ἢ θερμὸν ἐπιγένηται κατὰ τούτους τοὺς καιρούς. ὑπὸ δὲ τῶν ὡραίων χειμώνων οὐδὲ ἂν ὑπερβάλλοντες ὦσιν οὐδὲν πάσχειν, ἀλλὰ καὶ ξυμφέρειν πᾶσι χειμασθῆναι· μὴ χειμασθέντα γὰρ κακοβλαστότερα γίνεσθαι. τοῖς δὲ ἡμέροις ἐστὶ πλείω νοσήματα, καὶ τὰ μὲν ὥσπερ κοινὰ πᾶσιν ἢ τοῖς πλείστοις τὰ δ᾽ ἴδια κατὰ γένη.⁴ κοινὰ δὴ τό τε σκωληκοῦσθαι καὶ ἀστροβολεῖσθαι καὶ ὁ σφακελισμός. ἅπαντα γὰρ ὡς εἰπεῖν καὶ σκώληκας

---

¹ ἀποπληγῇ : ἀπολήγῃ conj. Sch.
² Plin. 17. 216.   ³ cf. C.P. 5. 8. 3.
⁴ κατὰ γένη conj. W.; καὶ τὰ γένη UMV; καὶ κατὰ γένη Ald.

third and fourth it becomes normal again and bears
many fair clusters, so that it is quite as good as when
it was in its prime. And when it goes off again,[1]
they say one should dig on the other side and apply
the same treatment; and that so treated the tree
lasts for ever: and this should be done at intervals of
about ten years. And this is why those who adopt
this treatment never cut down the vine, but the same
stems remain for many generations, so that even
those who planted the trees cannot remember doing
so. However perhaps one should enquire of those
who have had experience before accepting this statement. These examples may serve for considering
which trees are long-lived and which short-lived.

*Of diseases and injuries done by weather conditions.*

XIV. [2] As to diseases—they say that wild trees
are not liable to diseases which destroy them, but
that they get into poor condition, and that most
obviously when they are smitten with hail when
either they are about to bud or are just budding
or are in bloom; also when either a cold or a hot
wind comes at such seasons: but that from season-
able storms, even if they be violent, they take no
hurt,[3] but rather that it is good for them all to be
exposed to weather: for, unless they are, they do
not grow so well. Cultivated kinds however, they
say, are subject to various diseases, some of which
are, one may say, common to all or to most, while
others are special to particular kinds.[4] General
diseases are those[5] of being worm-eaten, of being
sun-scorched, and rot.[6] All trees, it may be said,

[5] κοινὰ δὴ τό τε conj. W.; κοινὰ καὶ τότε UMV; κοινά· οἷον
τότε Ald.H.    [6] *cf.* 8. 10. 1.

ἴσχει πλὴν τὰ μὲν ἐλάττους τὰ δὲ πλείους, καθάπερ συκῆ μηλέα καὶ ἄπιος. ὡς δὲ ἁπλῶς εἰπεῖν ἥκιστα σκωληκοῦνται τὰ δριμέα καὶ ὀπώδη, καὶ ἀστροβολεῖται ὡσαύτως· μᾶλλον δὲ τοῖς νέοις ἢ τοῖς ἐν ἀκμῇ τοῦτο συμβαίνει, πάντων δὲ μάλιστα τῇ τε συκῇ καὶ τῇ ἀμπέλῳ.

3 Ἡ δ' ἐλάα πρὸς τῷ τοὺς σκώληκας ἴσχειν, οἳ δὴ καὶ τὴν συκῆν διαφθείρουσιν ἐντίκτοντες, φύει καὶ ἧλον· οἱ δὲ μύκητα καλοῦσιν, ἔνιοι δὲ λοπάδα· τοῦτο δ' ἐστὶν οἷον ἡλίου καῦσις. διαφθείρονται δ' ἐνίοτε καὶ αἱ νέαι ἐλάαι διὰ τὴν ὑπερβολὴν τῆς πολυκαρπίας. ἡ δὲ ψώρα καὶ οἱ προσφυόμενοι κοχλίαι συκῆς εἰσιν· οὐ πανταχοῦ δὲ τοῦτο συμβαίνει ταῖς συκαῖς, ἀλλ' ἔοικε καὶ τὰ νοσήματα γίνεσθαι κατὰ τοὺς τόπους, ὥσπερ τοῖς ζώοις· ἐπεὶ παρ' ἐνίοις οὐ ψωριῶσι, καθάπερ οὐδὲ περὶ τὴν Αἰνείαν.

4 Ἁλίσκεται δὲ συκῆ μάλιστα καὶ σφακελισμῷ καὶ κράδῳ. καλεῖται δὲ σφακελισμὸς μὲν ὅταν αἱ ῥίζαι μελανθῶσι, κράδος δ' ὅταν οἱ κλάδοι· καὶ γὰρ καλοῦσί τινες κράδους, ὅθεν καὶ τοὔνομα τῇ νόσῳ· ὁ δ' ἐρινεὸς οὔτε κραδᾷ οὔτε σφακελίζει οὔτε ψωριᾷ οὔτε σκωληκοῦται ταῖς ῥίζαις ὁμοίως· οὐδὲ δὴ τὰ ἐρινά τινες ἀποβάλλουσιν οὐδ' ἐὰν ἐμφυτευθῶσιν εἰς συκῆν.

---

¹ ὀπώδη UMVAld.; εὐώδη H., evidently from Plin. 17. 221. cf. C.P. 5. 9. 4 and 5.

² λοπάδα; Plin. 17. 223, *patella*. The ἧλος is an abortive bud, called in Italian *porc̓o*.

³ ἡλίου καῦσις conj. Scal. from Plin. *l.c. veluti solis exustio*: so also G; ἡλοιαυτον U; ἧλοι αὐτὸν V; ἧλοι αὐτῶν M; ἧλοι αὐτῶν Ald. which W. prints provisionally.

have worms, but some less, as fig and apple, some more, as pear. Speaking generally, those least liable to be worm-eaten are those which have a bitter acrid [1] juice, and these are also less liable to sun-scorch. Moreover this occurs more commonly in young trees than in those which have come to their strength, and most of all it occurs in the fig and the vine.

The olive, in addition to having worms (which destroy the fig too by breeding in it), produces also a 'knot' (which some call a fungus, others a bark-blister [2]), and it resembles the effect of sun-scorch.[3] Also sometimes young olives are destroyed by excessive fruitfulness. The fig is also liable to scab, and to snails which cling to it. However this does not happen to figs everywhere, but it appears that, as with animals, diseases are dependent on local conditions; for in some parts, as about Aineia,[4] the figs do not get scab.

The fig is also often a victim to rot and to *krados*. It is called rot when the roots turn black, it is called *krados* when the branches do so; for some call the branches *kradoi* [5] (instead of *kladoi*), whence the name is transferred to the disease. The wild fig does not suffer from *krados* rot or scab, nor does it get so worm-eaten in its roots [6] as the cultivated tree; indeed some wild figs do not even shed their early fruit—not even if they are grafted [7] into a cultivated tree.

---

[4] *cf.* 5. 2. 1.    [5] Evidently a dialectic form.
[6] ῥίζαις PAld.; συκαῖς W. after conj. of Sch.
[7] ἐμφυτευθῶσιν conj. Sch.; ἔτι φυτ. UMV; ἔνια φυτ. Ald. Apparently the object of such grafting was the 'caprification' of the cultivated tree (*cf.* 2. 8. 3); but grafting for this purpose does not seem to be mentioned elsewhere.

5 Ἡ δὲ ψώρα μάλιστα γίνεται ὅταν ὕδωρ ἐπὶ
Πλειάδι γένηται μὴ πολύ· ἐὰν δὲ πολύ, ἀπο-
κλύζεται· συμβαίνει δὲ τότε καὶ τὰ ἐρινὰ ἀπορρεῖν καὶ τοὺς ὀλύνθους. τῶν δὲ σκωλήκων τῶν
ἐν ταῖς συκαῖς οἱ μὲν ἐξ αὐτῆς γίνονται οἱ δὲ
ἐντίκτονται ὑπὸ τοῦ καλουμένου κεράστου· πάντες
δὲ εἰς κεράστην ἀποκαθίστανται· φθέγγονται δὲ
οἷον τριγμόν. νοσεῖ δὲ συκῆ καὶ ἐὰν ἐπομβρία
γένηται· τά τε γὰρ πρὸς τὴν ῥίζαν καὶ αὐτὴ ἡ
ῥίζα ὥσπερ μαδᾷ· τοῦτο δὲ καλοῦσι λοπᾶν.
6 ἡ δ᾽ ἄμπελος τραγᾷ· τοῦτο δὲ μάλιστα αὐτῆς
ἐστι πρὸς τῷ ἀστροβολεῖσθαι, ἢ ὅταν ὑπὸ
πνευμάτων βλαστοκοπηθῇ ἢ ὅταν τῇ ἐργασίᾳ
συμπάθῃ ἢ τρίτον ὑπτία τμηθῇ.

Ῥυὰς δὲ γίνεται, ὃ καλοῦσί τινες ψίνεσθαι,
ὅταν ἐπινιφθῇ κατὰ τὴν ἀπάνθησιν ἢ ὅταν
κρειττωθῇ· τὸ δὲ πάθος ἐστὶν ὥστε ἀπορρεῖν τὰς
ῥᾶγας καὶ τὰς ἐπιμενούσας εἶναι μικράς. ἔνια δὲ
καὶ ῥιγώσαντα νοσεῖ, καθάπερ ἡ ἄμπελος· ἀμ-
βλοῦνται γὰρ οἱ ὀφθαλμοὶ τῆς πρωτοτόμου· καὶ
πάλιν ὑπερθερμανθέντα· ζητεῖ γὰρ καὶ τούτων τὴν
συμμετρίαν ὥσπερ καὶ τῆς τροφῆς. ὅλως δὲ πᾶν
τὸ παρὰ φύσιν ἐπικίνδυνον.

---

1 cf. C.P. 5. 9. 10 ; Col. 5. 9. 15.
2 cf. 5. 4. 5 ; C.P. 5. 10. 5 ; Plin. 17. 221.
3 αὐτὴ ἡ ῥίζα I conj.: αὐτὴν τὴν ῥίζαν U ; om. Ald.
4 cf. C.P. 5. 9. 12 ; Plin. 17. 225.
5 i.e. shedding of the 'bark' of the roots. λοπᾶν conj.
Sch., cf. C.P. 5. 9. 9 ; λοπάδα Ald.H., cf. 4. 14. 3 ; but the
word here points to a different disease.
6 ὑπτία τομή seems to be a technical term for pruning in
such a way that the growth of the new wood is encouraged

Scab[1] chiefly occurs when there is not much rain after the rising of the Pleiad; if rain is abundant, the scab is washed off, and at such times it comes to pass that both the spring and the winter figs drop off. Of the worms found in fig-trees some have their origin in the tree, some are produced in it by the creature called the 'horned worm'; but they all turn into the 'horned worm';[2] and they make a shrill noise. The fig also becomes diseased if there is heavy rain; for then the parts towards the root and the root itself[3] become, as it were, sodden,[4] and this they call 'bark-shedding.'[5] The vine suffers from over-luxuriance; this, as well as sun-scorch, specially happens to it either when the young shoots are cut by winds, or when it has suffered from bad cultivation, or, thirdly, when it has been pruned upwards.[6]

The vine becomes a 'shedder,'[7] a condition which some call 'casting of the fruit,' if the tree is snowed upon at the time when the blossom falls, or else when it becomes over lusty;[8] what happens is that the unripe grapes drop off, and those that remain on the tree are small. Some trees also contract disease from frost, for instance the vine; for then the eyes of the vine that was pruned early become abortive; and this also happens from excessive heat, for the vine seeks regularity in these conditions too, as in its nourishment. And in general anything is dangerous which is contrary to the normal course of things.

and so there is less fruit: exact sense obscure; ? 'from below' (i.e. with the blade of the knife pointing upwards). cf. C.P. l.c.; Col. 4. 24. 15; Plin. l.c., in supinum excisis.

[7] cf. C.P. 5. 9. 13.

[8] κρειττωθῇ: i.e. the growth is over-luxuriant. The word occurs elsewhere only in the parallel passage C.P. l.c., where occurs also the subst. κρείττωσις, evidently a technical term.

…

7 Μεγάλα δὲ ξυμβάλλεται καὶ τὰ τραύματα καὶ
αἱ πληγαὶ τῶν περισκαπτόντων εἰς τὸ μὴ φέρειν
τὰς μεταβολὰς ἢ καυμάτων ἢ χειμώνων· ἀσθενὲς
γὰρ ὂν διὰ τὴν ἕλκωσιν καὶ τὸν πόνον εὐχειρω-
τότατόν ἐστι ταῖς ὑπερβολαῖς. σχεδὸν δέ, ὥς τινες
οἴονται, τὰ πλεῖστα τῶν νοσημάτων ἀπὸ πληγῆς
γίνεται· καὶ γὰρ τὰ ἀστρόβλητα καλούμενα καὶ
τὰ σφακελίζοντα διὰ τὸ ἀπὸ ταύτης εἶναι τῶν
ῥιζῶν τὸν πόνον. οἴονται δὲ καὶ δύο ταύτας εἶναι
μόνας νόσους· οὐ μὴν ἀλλὰ τοῦτό γ᾽ οὐκ ἄγαν
ὁμολογούμενόν ἐστι.
[Πάντων δ᾽ ἀσθενέστατον ἡ μηλέα ἡ ἠρινὴ καὶ
τούτων ἡ γλυκεῖα.]

8 Ἔνιαι δὲ πηρώσεις οὐκ εἰς φθορὰν γίνονται
ὅλων ἀλλ᾽ εἰς ἀκαρπίαν· οἷον ἐάν τις τῆς πίτυος
ἀφέλῃ τὸ ἄκρον ἢ τοῦ φοίνικος, ἄκαρπα γίνεσθαι
ἄμφω δοκεῖ καὶ οὐχ ὅλως ἀναιρεῖσθαι.

Γίνονται δὲ νόσοι καὶ τῶν καρπῶν αὐτῶν, ἐὰν
μὴ κατὰ καιρὸν τὰ πνεύματα καὶ τὰ οὐράνια
γένηται· συμβαίνει γὰρ ὁτὲ μὲν ἀποβάλλειν
γενομένων ἢ μὴ γενομένων ὑδάτων, οἷον τὰς συκᾶς,
ὁτὲ δὲ χείρους γίνεσθαι σηπομένους καὶ καταπνιγο-
μένους ἢ πάλιν ἀναξηραινομένους παρὰ τὸ δέον.
χείριστον δὲ ἐὰν ἀπανθοῦσί τισιν ἐφύσῃ, καθάπερ
ἐλάᾳ καὶ ἀμπέλῳ· συναπορρεῖ γὰρ ὁ καρπὸς δι᾽
ἀσθένειαν.

---

¹ Plin. 17. 227.
² εὐχειρωτότατον conj. W. after Lobeck ; εὐχειρότατον Ald.
³ πόνον conj. H. from G ; τόπον MV Ald.
⁴ This sentence is clearly out of place : the plural τούτων
has nothing to refer to. cf. 4. 13. 2. It is represented however by Plin. l.c.

[1] Moreover the wounds and blows inflicted by men who dig about the vines render them less able to bear the alternations of heat and cold; for then the tree is weak owing to the wounding and to the strain put upon it, and falls an easy prey [2] to excess of heat and cold. Indeed, as some think, most diseases may be said to be due to a blow; for that even the diseases known as 'sun-scorch' and 'rot' occur because the roots have suffered in this way.[3] In fact they think that there are only these two diseases; but there is not general agreement on this point.

The 'spring apple' and especially the sweet form of it, has the weakest constitution.[4]

[5] Some mutilations however do not cause destruction of the whole [6] tree, but only produce barrenness; for instance, if one takes away the top of the Aleppo pine or the date-palm, the tree in both cases appears to become barren, but not to be altogether destroyed.

There are also diseases of the fruits themselves, which occur if the winds and rains do not come in due season. For it comes to pass [7] that sometimes trees, figs, for example, shed their fruit when rain does or does not come, and [8] sometimes the fruit is spoilt by being rotted and so choked off,[9] or again by being unduly dried up. It is worst of all for some trees, as olive and vine, if rain falls on them as they are dropping their blossom; [10] for then the fruit, having no strength, drops also.

[5] Plin. 17. 228 and 229.
[6] ὕλων conj. W.; τινων P₂Ald.H. cf. C.P. 5. 17. 3 and 6.
[7] cf. C.P. 5. 10. 5.
[8] δὲ add. Sch. [9] cf. C.P. l.c.
[10] ἀπανθοῦσι conj. Sch. from G and Plin. l.c.; ἐπανθοῦσι Ald.H.

9  Ἐν Μιλήτῳ δὲ τὰς ἐλάας, ὅταν ὦσι περὶ τὸ
ἀνθεῖν, κάμπαι κατεσθίουσιν, αἱ μὲν τὰ φύλλα αἱ
δὲ τὰ ἄνθη, ἕτεραι τῷ γένει, καὶ ψιλοῦσι τὰ
δένδρα· γίνονται δὲ ἐὰν ᾖ νότια καὶ εὐδιεινά· ἐὰν
δὲ ἐπιλάβῃ καύματα ῥήγνυνται.
    Περὶ δὲ Τάραντα προφαίνουσι μὲν ἀεὶ πολὺν
καρπόν, ὑπὸ δὲ τὴν ἀπάνθησιν τὰ πολλ᾽ ἀπόλλυται.    τὰ μὲν οὖν τοιαῦτα τῶν τόπων ἴδια.
10  Γίνεται δὲ καὶ ἄλλο νόσημα περὶ τὰς ἐλάας
ἀράχνιον καλούμενον· φύεται γὰρ τοῦτο καὶ διαφθείρει τὸν καρπόν. ἐπικάει δὲ καὶ καύματά
τινα καὶ ἐλάαν καὶ βότρυν καὶ ἄλλους καρπούς.
οἱ δὲ καρποὶ σκωληκοῦνταί τινων, οἷον ἐλάας
ἀπίου μηλέας μεσπίλης ῥόας. καὶ ὅ γε τῆς ἐλάας
σκώληξ ἐὰν μὲν ὑπὸ τὸ δέρμα γένηται διαφθείρει
τὸν καρπόν, ἐὰν δὲ τὸν πυρῆνα διαφάγῃ ὠφελεῖ·
κωλύεται δὲ ὑπὸ τῷ δέρματι εἶναι ὕδατος ἐπ᾽
Ἀρκτούρῳ γενομένου. γίνονται δὲ καὶ ἐν ταῖς
δρυπεπέσι σκώληκες, αἵπερ καὶ χείρους εἰς τὴν
ῥύσιν· ὅλως δὲ καὶ δοκοῦσιν εἶναι σαπραί· δι᾽ ὃ
καὶ γίνονται τοῖς νοτίοις καὶ μᾶλλον ἐν τοῖς
ἐφύδροις. ἐγγίνονται δὲ καὶ κνῖπες ἔν τισι τῶν
δένδρων, ὥσπερ ἐν τῇ δρυῒ καὶ τῇ συκῇ· καὶ
δοκοῦσιν ἐκ τῆς ὑγρότητος συνίστασθαι τῆς ὑπὸ
τὸν φλοιὸν συνισταμένης· αὕτη δέ ἐστι γλυκεῖα
γενομένοις. γίνονται δὲ καὶ ἐν λαχάνοις τισίν

---

¹ cf. C.P. 5. 10. 3.
² Tarentum : cf. C.P. l.c.
³ ἀπάνθησιν conj. W.; ἄνθησιν Ald.
⁴ Plin. 17. 229–231.
⁵ ἀράχνιον conj. Sch. after Meurs.; ἀρίχνιον UP₂; ἀρχίχνιον
MVP; ἀρχίνιον Ald. cf. C.P. 5. 10. 2.
398

[1] In Miletus the vines at the time of flowering are eaten by caterpillars, some of which devour the flowers, others, a different kind, the leaves; and they strip the tree; these appear if there is a south wind and sunny weather; if the heat overtakes them, the trees split.

About Taras [2] the olives always shew much fruit, but most of it perishes at the time when the blossom falls.[3] Such are the drawbacks special to particular regions.

[4] There is also another disease incident to the olive, which is called cobweb; [5] for this forms [6] on the tree and destroys the fruit. Certain hot [7] winds also scorch both olive vine-cluster and other fruits. And the fruits of some get worm-eaten,[8] as olive pear apple medlar pomegranate. Now the worm which infests the olive, if it appears below the skin, destroys the fruit; but if it devours the stone it is beneficial. And it is prevented from appearing under the skin if there is rain after [9] the rising of Arcturus. Worms also occur in the fruit which ripens on the tree, and these are more harmful as affecting the yield of oil. Indeed these worms seem to be altogether rotten; wherefore they appear when there is a south wind and particularly in damp places. The *knips* [10] also occurs in certain trees, as the oak and fig, and it appears that it forms from the moisture which collects under the bark, which is sweet to the taste. Worms also occur [11] in some

---

[6] φύεται Ald.; ἐμφύεται conj. Sch. from *C.P. l.c.*, but the text is perhaps defective.

[7] *cf. C.P.* 5. 10. 5.  [8] *cf. C.P.* 5. 10. 1.

[9] ἐπ' conj. Sch., *cf. C.P.* 5. 10. 1; ὑπ' U; ἀπ' Ald.H.

[10] *cf.* 2. 8. 3.

[11] The subject of γίνονται is probably σκώληκες, not κνῖπες.

## THEOPHRASTUS

ἔνθα δὲ κάμπαι διαφερούσης δῆλον ὅτι τῆς ἀρχῆς.

11   Καὶ τὰ μὲν νοσήματα σχεδὸν ταῦτα καὶ ἐν τούτοις ἐστίν.[1] ἔνια δὲ πάθη τῶν κατὰ τὰς ὥρας καὶ τῶν κατὰ τοὺς τόπους[2] γινομένων ἀναιρεῖν πέφυκεν, ἃ οὐκ ἄν τις εἴποι νόσους, οἷον λέγω τὴν ἔκπηξιν[3] καὶ ὃ καλοῦσί τινες καυθμόν. ἄλλα δὲ παρ' ἑκάστοις πέφυκε πνεύματα ἀπολλύναι καὶ ἀποκάειν· οἷον ἐν Χαλκίδι τῆς Εὐβοίας Ὀλυμπίας ὅταν πνεύσῃ μικρὸν πρὸ τροπῶν ἢ μετὰ τροπὰς χειμερινὰς ψυχρός· ἀποκάει γὰρ τὰ δένδρα καὶ οὕτως αὖα ποιεῖ καὶ ξηρὰ ὡς οὐδ' ἂν ὑφ' ἡλίου καὶ χρόνου πολλοῦ γένοιτ' ἄν, δι' ὃ καὶ καλοῦσι καυθμόν· ἐγένετο δὲ πρότερον πολλάκις ἤδη καὶ ἐπ' Ἀρχίππου δι' ἐτῶν τεσσαράκοντα σφοδρός.

12   Πονοῦσι δὲ μάλιστα τῶν τόπων οἱ κοῖλοι καὶ οἱ αὐλῶνες καὶ ὅσοι περὶ τοὺς ποταμοὺς καὶ ἁπλῶς οἱ ἀπνευστότατοι· τῶν δένδρων δὲ μάλιστα συκῆ, δεύτερον δὲ ἐλάα. ἐλάας δὲ μᾶλλον ὁ κότινος ἐπόνησεν ἰσχυρότερος ὤν, ὃ καὶ θαυμαστὸν ἦν· αἱ δὲ ἀμυγδαλαῖ τὸ πάμπαν ἀπαθεῖς· ἀπαθεῖς δὲ καὶ αἱ μηλέαι καὶ αἱ ἄπιοι καὶ αἱ ῥόαι ἐγένοντο· δι' ὃ καὶ τοῦτο ἦν θαυμαστόν. ἀποκάεται δὲ εὐθὺς ἐκ τοῦ στελέχους, καὶ ὅλως δὲ μᾶλλον καὶ πρότερον ὡς εἰπεῖν ἅπτεται <τὰ ἄνω> τῶν κάτω. φανερὰ δὲ γίνεται τὰ μὲν ἅμα περὶ τὴν βλάστησιν,

---

[1] Plin. 17. 232.

[2] τῶν κατὰ τοὺς τόπους conj. Sch. from Plin. *l.c.*; τῶν καθ' αὑτὰ Ald.

[3] ἔκπηξιν conj. Sch.; ἔκπληξιν UMP₂Ald. *cf. C.P.* 5. 12. 2, πῆξις.

[4] *cf. C.P.* 5. 12. 4.

400

pot-herbs, as also do caterpillars, though the origin of these is of course different.

Such are in general the diseases, and the plants in which they occur. Moreover[1] there are certain affections due to season or situation[2] which are likely to destroy the plant, but which one would not call diseases: I mean such affections as freezing[3] and what some call 'scorching.' Also[4] there are winds which blow in particular districts that are likely to destroy or scorch; for instance the 'Olympian' wind of Chalcis in Euboea, when it blows cold a little before or after the winter solstice; for this wind scorches up the trees and makes them more dry and withered than they would become from the sun's heat even in a long period; wherefore its effect is called 'scorching.' In old times it occurred very frequently, and it recurred with great violence in the time of Archippus, after an interval of forty years.

[5] The places which suffer most in this way are hollow places, valleys, the ground near rivers, and, in general, places which are least open to wind; the tree which suffers most is the fig, and next to that the olive. The wild olive, being stronger, suffered more than the cultivated tree, which was surprising. But the almonds were altogether unscathed, as also were the apples pears and pomegranates; wherefore this too was a surprising fact. The tree gets scorched by this wind right down to the trunk, and in general the upper are caught more and earlier than the lower parts.[6] The effects are seen partly at the actual

---

[5] cf. C.P. 5. 12. 7; Plin. 17. 232 and 233.
[6] κάτω UMVP; ἄνω W. after Sch.'s conj.: text probably defective; I have added τὰ ἄνω. cf. C.P. 5. 12. 5.

ἡ δὲ ἐλάα διὰ τὸ ἀείφυλλον ὕστερον· ὅσαι μὲν οὖν
ἂν φυλλοβολήσωσιν ἀναβιώσκονται πάλιν, ὅσαι
δ᾽ ἂν μὴ τελέως ἀπόλλυνται. παρ᾽ ἐνίοις δέ τινες
ἀποκαυθεῖσαι καὶ τῶν φύλλων αὐανθέντων ἀνε-
βλάστησαν πάλιν ἄνευ τοῦ ἀποβαλεῖν καὶ τὰ
φύλλα ἀνεβίωσεν. ἐνιαχοῦ δὲ καὶ πολλάκις
τοῦτο συμβαίνει, καθάπερ καὶ ἐν Φιλίπποις.

13 Τὰ δ᾽ ἐκπαγέντα, ὅταν μὴ τελέως ἀπόληται,
τάχιστα ἀναβλαστάνει, ὥστε εὐθὺς τὴν ἄμπελον
καρποφορεῖν, ὥσπερ ἐν Θετταλίᾳ. ἐν δὲ τῷ
Πόντῳ περὶ Παντικάπαιον αἱ μὲν ἐκπήξεις
γίνονται διχῶς, ὁτὲ μὲν ὑπὸ ψύχους ἐὰν χειμέριον
ᾖ τὸ ἔτος, ὁτὲ δὲ ὑπὸ πάγων ἐάν γε πολὺν χρόνον
διαμένωσι. ἀμφότερα δὲ μάλιστα γίγνονται
μετὰ τροπὰς περὶ τὰς τετταράκοντα. γίνονται
δὲ οἱ μὲν πάγοι ταῖς αἰθρίαις, τὰ δὲ ψύχη μάλιστα
ὑφ᾽ ὧν ἡ ἔκπηξις ὅταν αἰθρίας οὔσης αἱ λεπίδες
καταφέρωνται. ταῦτα δ᾽ ἐστὶν ὥσπερ τὰ ξύσματα
πλὴν πλατύτερα, καὶ φερόμενα φανερὰ πεσόντα
δὲ οὐ διαμένει· περὶ δὲ τὴν Θρᾴκην ἐκπήγνυνται.

14 Ἀλλὰ γὰρ αἱ μὲν νόσοι πόσαι τε καὶ ποῖαι καὶ
τίνες γίνονται καὶ πάλιν αἱ δι᾽ ὑπερβολὴν
χειμῶνος ἢ καυμάτων φθοραὶ καὶ αἱ διὰ πνευμάτων ψυχρότητα ἢ θερμότητα διὰ τούτων
θεωρείσθωσαν· ὧν ἐνίας οὐθὲν ἂν κωλύοι καὶ τοῖς
ἀγρίοις εἶναι κοινὰς καὶ κατὰ τὴν ὅλην τῶν
δένδρων φθορὰν καὶ ἔτι μᾶλλον κατὰ τὴν τῶν
καρπῶν· ὃ καὶ συμβαῖνον ὁρῶμεν· οὐκ εὐκαρπεῖ

---

[1] Plin. 17. 233.
[2] ἐκπαγέντα conj. Sch.: ἐκπλαγέντα U; ἐκπληγέντα Ald.
[3] ἐάν γε conj. Sch.; ἐὰν δὲ U; ἐὰν π. χ. δ. γε Ald.

time of budding, but in the olive, because it is evergreen, they do not appear till later; those trees therefore which have shed their leaves come to life again, but those that have not done so are completely destroyed. In some places trees have been known, after being thus scorched and after their leaves have withered, to shoot again without shedding their leaves, and the leaves have come to life again. Indeed in some places, as at Philippi, this happens several times.

[1] Trees which have been frost-bitten,[2] when they are not completely destroyed, soon shoot again, so that the vine immediately bears fruit, for instance in Thessaly. In Pontus near Panticapaeum the frost-bite occurs in two ways, either just from cold, if the season is wintry, or from long[3] spells of frost; in either case this generally occurs in the[4] forty days after the winter solstice. The frosts occur in fine weather, but the cold spells, which cause the frost-bite, chiefly when in fine weather the 'flakes'[5] fall: these are like filings, but broader, and can be seen as they fall, but when they have fallen, they disappear—though in Thrace they freeze solid.

Let this suffice for consideration of the diseases, their number and nature, including the fatal effects of excessive cold and heat or of cold or hot winds. And it may well be that certain of these also affect wild trees, producing entire destruction of the tree and still more that of the fruit. Indeed we see this actually happen; for wild trees also often fail to

[4] περί conj. Sch., cf. C.P. 5. 12. 4; μετὰ UMVAld.
[5] λεπίδες conj. Scal. from G (squammulae); ῥεπίδες Ald. cf. Idt. 4. 31.

γὰρ οὐδ᾽ ἐκεῖνα πολλάκις, ἀλλ᾽ οὐχ ὁμοίως οἶμαι
παρατετήρηται.

XV. Λοιπὸν δ᾽ εἰπεῖν ὅσα παραιρουμένων
τινῶν μορίων ἀπόλλυται. κοινὴ μὲν δὴ πᾶσι
φθορὰ τοῦ φλοιοῦ περιαιρεθέντος κύκλῳ· πᾶν
γὰρ ὡς εἰπεῖν οὕτως ἀπόλλυσθαι δοκεῖ πλὴν
ἀνδράχλη· καὶ αὕτη δὲ ἐάν τις τὴν σάρκα σφόδρα
πιέσῃ καὶ τὸν μέλλοντα βλαστὸν διακόψῃ· πλὴν
εἰ ἄρα φελλοῦ· τοῦτον γάρ φασι καὶ εὐσθενεῖν
μᾶλλον περιαιρουμένου δῆλον ὅτι τοῦ ἔξω καὶ
τοῦ κάτω πρὸς τῇ σαρκί, καθάπερ καὶ τῆς ἀνδράχλης. ἐπεὶ καὶ τοῦ κεράσου περιαιρεῖται καὶ
τῆς ἀμπέλου καὶ τῆς φιλύρας, ἐξ οὗ τὰ σχοινία,
καὶ μαλάχης τῶν ἐλαττόνων, ἀλλ᾽ οὐχ ὁ κύριος
οὐδ᾽ ὁ πρῶτος, ἀλλ᾽ ὁ ἐπιπολῆς, ὃς καὶ αὐτόματος
ἐνίοτε ἀποπίπτει διὰ τὴν ὑπόφυσιν θατέρου.

2   Καὶ γὰρ φλοιορραγῆ ἔνια τῶν δένδρων ἐστίν,
ὥσπερ καὶ ἡ ἀνδράχλη καὶ ἡ πλάτανος. ὡς δέ
τινες οἴονται, πάλιν ὑποφύεται νέος, ὁ δὲ ἔξωθεν
ἀποξηραίνεται καὶ ῥήγνυται καὶ αὐτόματος
ἀποπίπτει πολλῶν, ἀλλ᾽ οὐχ ὁμοίως ἐπίδηλος.
φθείρονται μὲν οὖν, ὡς οἴονται, πάντα περιαιρουμένου, διαφέρει δὲ τῷ θᾶττον καὶ βραδύτερον καὶ

[1] Plin. 17. 234 ; cf. C.P. 5. 15. 1.
[2] cf. 1. 5. 2.
[3] βλαστὸν conj. Sch. from G ; καρπὸν UAld.H.
[4] Plin. 17. 234-236.

produce a good crop of fruit ; but, I imagine, they have not been so well observed.

*Of the effects on trees of removing bark, head, heart-wood, roots, etc.; of various causes of death.*

XV. [1] Next we must mention what trees perish when certain parts are removed. All perish alike, if the bark is stripped off all round ; one may say that every tree, except the andrachne,[2] perishes under these circumstances ; and this tree does so also, if one does violence to the flesh, and so breaks off the new growth [3] which is forming. However one should perhaps except the cork-oak ; for this, they say, is all the stronger if its bark is stripped off, that is, the outer bark and also that which lies below it next the flesh—as with the andrachne. For the bark is also stripped from the bird-cherry the vine and the lime (and from this the ropes are made), and, among smaller plants, from the mallow ; but in these cases it is not the real nor the first bark which is taken, but that which grows above that, which even of its own accord sometimes falls off because fresh bark is forming underneath.

[4] In fact some trees, as andrachne and plane, have a bark which cracks.[5] As some think, in many cases a new bark forms [6] underneath, while the outer bark withers and cracks and in many cases falls off of its own accord ; but the process is not so obvious as it is in the above mentioned cases. Wherefore, as they think, all trees are destroyed by stripping the bark, though the destruction is not in all cases equally

[5] *cf. C.P.* 3. 18. 3. φλοιορραγῇ ἔνια conj. Mold.; φλοιορραγία μία UMV; φυλλορογία μία Ald.
[6] ὑποφύεται conj. W.; ὑποφύει Ald.H.

μᾶλλον καὶ ἧττον. ἔνια γὰρ πλείω χρόνον διαμένει, καθάπερ συκῆ καὶ φίλυρα καὶ δρῦς· οἱ δὲ
καὶ ζῆν φασι ταῦτα, ζῆν δὲ καὶ πτελέαν καὶ
φοίνικα· τῆς δὲ φιλύρας καὶ συμφύεσθαι τὸν
φλοιὸν πλὴν μικροῦ· τῶν δὲ ἄλλων οἷον πωροῦ-
σθαι καὶ ἰδίαν τινὰ φύσιν ἔχειν. βοηθεῖν δὲ
πειρῶνται διαπλάττοντες πηλῷ καὶ περιδοῦντες
φλοιοῖς καὶ καλάμοις καὶ τοῖς τοιούτοις, ὅπως μὴ
ψύχηται μηδ᾽ ἀποξηραίνηται. καὶ ἤδη φασί που
ἀναφῦναι, καθάπερ καὶ ἐν Ἡρακλείᾳ τῇ Τραχινίᾳ,
3 τὰς συκᾶς. δεῖ δὲ ἅμα τῇ τῆς χώρας ἀρετῇ καὶ
τῇ τοῦ ἀέρος κράσει καὶ τὰ ἐπιγιγνόμενα τοιαῦτα
εἶναι· χειμώνων γὰρ ἢ καυμάτων ἐπιγινομένων
σφοδρῶν εὐθὺς ἀπόλλυνται· διαφέρουσι δὲ καὶ
αἱ ὧραι· περὶ γὰρ τὴν βλάστησιν ἐλάτης ἢ
πεύκης, ὅτε καὶ λοπῶσι, τοῦ Θαργηλιῶνος ἢ
Σκιρροφοριῶνος ἄν τις περιέλῃ, παραχρῆμα ἀπόλλυται. τοῦ δὲ χειμῶνος πλείω χρόνον ἀντ-
έχει καὶ ἔτι μᾶλλον τὰ ἰσχυρότατα, καθάπερ πρῖνος καὶ δρῦς· χρονιωτέρα γὰρ ἡ τούτων φθορά.
4 δεῖ δὲ καὶ τὴν περιαίρεσιν ἔχειν τι πλάτος,
πάντων μὲν μάλιστα δὲ τῶν ἰσχυροτάτων· ἐπεὶ
ἄν τις μικρὰν παντελῶς ποιήσῃ, οὐδὲν ἄτοπον τὸ
μὴ ἀπόλλυσθαι· καίτοι φασί γέ τινες, ἐὰν ὁποσονοῦν, συμφθείρεσθαι πάντως· ἀλλ᾽ ἐπὶ τῶν
ἀσθενεστέρων τοῦτ᾽ εἰκός. ἔνια γὰρ κἂν μὴ
κύκλῳ περιαιρεθῇ φθείρεσθαί φασιν, ἃ καὶ

---

¹ καὶ add. W. (text defective in MSS. except U).

rapid or complete. Some in fact, as fig lime and oak,
survive for some time ; indeed some say that these
recover, and also the elm and date-palm, and
that the bark even of the lime almost entirely
closes up again, while in other trees it forms as it
were a callus and[1] acquires a peculiar new character.
Men try to help the tree by plastering it with mud
and tying pieces of bark reeds or something of the
kind about it, so that it may not take cold nor
become dried up. And they say that the bark has
been known to grow again :[2] for instance that that
of the fig-trees at the Trachinian Heraclea did so.
However this does not only depend on the quality of
the soil and on the climate ; the other circumstances
which ensue must also be favourable ; for, if great
cold or heat ensues, the tree perishes at once. The
season also makes a difference. For if one strips the
bark of a silver-fir or fir at the time when the buds
are shooting during Thargelion or Skirrophorion,[3] at
which season it is separable, the tree dies at once.
If it is done however in winter, the tree holds out
longer ; and this is especially true of the strongest
trees, such as kermes-oak and oak : these it takes
longer to kill. However the piece stripped off must
be of a certain breadth to cause the death of the
tree, especially in the case of the strongest trees : for,
if one does it only a little, it is not surprising that
the tree should not be killed ; though some indeed
say that, if it is done at all,[4] the tree certainly dies ;
this however is probably true only of the weaker
kinds. For some, they say, if they are in bad barren

[2] ἀναφῦναι conj. Sch. from G ; φῦναι Ald.H.
[3] May June.
[4] ὁποσοιοῦν conj. Sch. from G ; ὁπωσοῦν Ald.

λυπρὰν ἔχει χώραν καὶ ἄτροφον. αὕτη μὲν δή, καθάπερ εἴρηται, κοινὴ φθορὰ πάντων. XVI. Ἣν δὲ καλοῦσιν ἐπικοπὴν τῶν δένδρων, μόνον πεύκης ἐλάτης πίτυος φοίνικος, οἱ δὲ καὶ κέδρου καὶ κυπαρίττου φασί. ταῦτα γάρ, ἐὰν περιαιρεθῇ τὴν κόμην ἄνωθεν καὶ ἐπικοπῇ τὸ ἄκρον, φθείρεται πάντα καὶ οὐ βλαστάνει, καθάπερ οὐδ᾽ ἐπικαυθέντα ἢ πάντα ἢ ἔνια. τὰ δ᾽ ἄλλα πάντα καὶ περικοπέντα βλαστάνει, καὶ ἔνιά γε καλλίω γίνεται, καθάπερ ἡ ἐλάα. διαφθείρεται δὲ τὰ πολλὰ κἂν σχισθῇ τὸ στέλεχος· οὐδὲν γὰρ ὑπομένειν δοκεῖ πλὴν ἀμπέλου καὶ συκῆς καὶ ῥόας καὶ μηλέας· ἔνια δὲ κἂν ἑλκωθῇ καὶ μεῖζον καὶ βαθύτερον ἀπόλλυται. τὰ δ᾽ οὐδὲν πάσχει, καθάπερ ἡ πεύκη δαδουργουμένη, καὶ ἐξ ὧν δὴ τὰς ῥητίνας συλλέγουσιν, οἷον ἐλάτης τερμίνθου· καὶ γὰρ δὴ τούτων εἰς βάθος ἡ τρῶσις καὶ ἕλκωσις. καὶ γὰρ ἐξ ἀφόρων φοράδες γίνονται καὶ ἐξ ὀλιγοφόρων πολυφόροι.

2 Τὰ δὲ καὶ πελέκησιν ὑπομένει καὶ ὀρθὰ καὶ πεσόντα ὑπὸ πνεύματος, ὥστε πάλιν ἀνίστασθαι καὶ ζῆν καὶ βλαστάνειν, οἷον ἰτέα καὶ πλάτανος. ὅπερ συνέβη καὶ ἐν Ἀντάνδρῳ καὶ ἐν Φιλίπποις· ἐκπεσούσης γὰρ ὡς ἀπέκοψαν τοὺς ἀκρεμόνας καὶ ἐπελέκησαν, ἀνεφύη νύκτωρ ἡ πλάτανος κουφισθεῖσα τοῦ βάρους καὶ ἀνεβίω καὶ ὁ φλοιὸς περιέφυ πάλιν. παραπεπελεκημένη δ᾽ ἐτύγχανεν ἐκ τῶν δύο μερῶν· ἦν δὲ τὸ δένδρον μέγα μῆκος

1 Plin. 17. 236 ; cf. 3. 7. 2 ; C.P. 5. 17. 3.
2 cf. 3. 9. 5.
3 ἄνωθεν καὶ conj. W.: καὶ ἄνωθεν Ald.
4 cf. 1. 3. 3 ; 1. 14. 2.

soil, die even if the bark is not stripped all round. This then, as has been said, is a universal cause of death.

XVI. [1] The process which is called topping of trees is fatal only to fir silver-fir Aleppo pine[2] and date-palm, though some add prickly cedar and cypress. These, if they are stripped of their foliage at the top[3] and the crown is cut off, perish wholly and do not shoot again, as is the case with some, if not with all, if they are burnt. But all other trees shoot again after being lopped, and some, such as the olive,[4] become all the fairer. However most trees perish if the stem is split;[5] for no tree seems able to stand this, except vine fig pomegranate and apple; and some perish even if they are wounded severely and deeply. Some however take no harm[6] from this, as the fir when it is cut for tar, and those trees from which the resins are collected, as silver-fir and terebinth; though these trees are in fact then deeply wounded and mangled. Indeed they actually become fruitful[7] instead of barren, or are made to bear plentifully instead of scantily.

Some trees again submit to being hewn both when they are standing and when they have been blown down, so that they rise up again and live and shoot, for instance the willow and the plane. [8] This was known to happen in Antandros and at Philippi; a plane in Antandros having fallen and had its boughs lopped off and the axe applied to its trunk, grew again in the night when thus relieved of the weight, and the bark grew about it again. It happened that it had been hewn two thirds of the way round; it

---

[5] cf. C.P. 5. 16. 4; Plin. 17. 238.   [6] cf. C.P. 5. 16. 2.
[7] φοράδες conj. Sch.; φορίδες Ald.   [8] Plin. 16. 133.

THEOPHRASTUS

μὲν μεῖζον ἢ δεκάπηχυ, πάχος δ' ὥστε μὴ ῥαδίως
3 ἂν περιλαβεῖν τέτταρας ἄνδρας. ἡ δὲ ἐν Φιλίπποις ἰτέα περιεκόπη μὲν τοὺς ἀκρεμόνας, οὐ μὴν
παρεπελεκήθη. μάντις δέ τις ἔπεισεν αὐτοὺς
θυσίαν τε ποιεῖσθαι καὶ τηρεῖν τὸ δένδρον ὡς
σημεῖον ἀγαθὸν γεγονός. ἀνέστη δὲ καὶ ἐν
Σταγείροις ἐν τῷ μουσείῳ λεύκη τις ἐκπεσοῦσα.
4 Τῆς δὲ μήτρας ἐξαιρουμένης οὐθὲν ὡς εἰπεῖν
φθείρεται δένδρον. σημεῖον δὲ ὅτι πολλὰ κοῖλα
τῶν μέγεθος ἐχόντων δένδρων ἐστίν. οἱ δὲ περὶ
Ἀρκαδίαν φασὶ μέχρι τινὸς μὲν ζῆν τὸ δένδρον,
τελέως δὲ ἐξ ἅπαντος ἐξαιρεθείσης καὶ πεύκην
φθείρεσθαι καὶ ἐλάτην καὶ ἄλλο πᾶν.
5 Κοινὴ δὲ φθορὰ πάντων κἂν αἱ ῥίζαι περι-
κοπῶσιν ἢ πᾶσαι ἢ αἱ πλεῖσται καὶ μέγισται
καὶ κυριώταται τοῦ ζῆν. αὗται μὲν οὖν ἐξ
ἀφαιρέσεως.

Ἡ δ' ὑπὸ τοῦ ἐλαίου προσθέσει τινὶ μᾶλλον ἢ
ἀφαιρέσει· πολέμιον γὰρ δὴ καὶ τοῦτο πᾶσι· καὶ
ἔλαιον ἐπιχέουσι τοῖς ὑπολείμμασι τῶν ῥιζῶν.
ἰσχύει δὲ μᾶλλον τὸ ἔλαιον ἐν τοῖς νέοις καὶ ἄρτι
φυομένοις· ἀσθενέστερα γάρ, δι' ὃ καὶ ἅπτεσθαι
κωλύουσι.

Φθοραὶ δὲ καὶ ὑπ' ἀλλήλων εἰσὶ τῷ παραι-
ρεῖσθαι τὰς τροφὰς καὶ ἐν τοῖς ἄλλοις ἐμποδίζειν.
χαλεπὸς δὲ καὶ ὁ κιττὸς παραφυόμενος, χαλεπὸς
δὲ καὶ ὁ κύτισος· ἀπόλλυσι γὰρ πάνθ' ὡς εἰπεῖν·

---

[1] τινὸς μὲν ζῆν τὸ δ. conj. W.; τινος ἐὰν (corrected) τοῦ δένδρου
U; τινος ἐξηρέθη τοῦ δ. MVAld.
[2] cf. Plin. 17. 234; C.P. 5. 15. 6.
[3] πᾶσι καὶ ἔλαιον ἐπιχέουσι conj. Sch.; πᾶσιν ἔλαιον ἐπιχεύ-
ουσιν UMP₂Ald.

410

was a large tree, more than ten cubits high, and of such girth that four men could not easily have encircled it. The willow at Philippi which grew again had had its branches lopped off, but the trunk had not been hewn. A certain seer persuaded the people to offer sacrifice and take care of the tree, since what had occurred was a good omen. Also at Stageira an abele in the school gardens which had fallen got up again.

Hardly any tree is destroyed by taking out the core; a proof of which is the fact that many large trees are hollow. The people of Arcadia say that the tree under these circumstances lives for a time,[1] but that, if the tree is entirely deprived of its core, fir or silver-fir or any other tree perishes.

All trees alike are destroyed when the roots are cut off, whether all or most of them, if those removed are the largest and the most essential to life. Such then are the causes of death which come from the removal of a part of the tree.

On the other hand the destruction which oil [2] causes is due rather to a kind of addition than to removal; for oil is hostile to all trees, and[3] so men pour it [4] over what remains of the roots. However oil is more potent with young trees which are just growing; for then they are weaker: wherefore men do not allow them to be touched at that time.

[5] Again trees may destroy one another, by robbing them of nourishment and hindering them in other ways. Again an overgrowth of ivy [6] is dangerous,[7] and so is tree-medick, for this destroys almost any-

[4] i.e. to complete the destruction of a tree. cf. Plut. Quaest. Conv. 2. 6. 2.
[5] Plin. 17. 239 and 240.   [6] cf. C.P. 5. 15. 4.
[7] χαλεπὸς δὲ καὶ Ald.; χαλεπὸς δ' ἐστὶν conj. W.

ἰσχυρότερον δὲ τούτου τὸ ἅλιμον· ἀπόλλυσι γὰρ
τὸν κύτισον.

6 Ἔνια δὲ οὐ φθείρει μὲν χείρω δὲ ποιεῖ ταῖς
δυνάμεσι τῶν χυλῶν καὶ τῶν ὀσμῶν, οἷον ἡ
ῥάφανος καὶ ἡ δάφνη τὴν ἄμπελον. ὀσφραίνεσθαι
γάρ φασι καὶ ἕλκειν. δι᾽ ὃ καὶ ὅταν ὁ βλαστὸς
πλησίον γένηται πάλιν ἀναστρέφειν καὶ ἀφορᾶν
ὡς πολεμίας οὔσης τῆς ὀσμῆς. Ἀνδροκύδης δὲ
καὶ παραδείγματι τούτῳ κατεχρήσατο πρὸς τὴν
βοήθειαν τὴν ἀπὸ τῆς ῥαφάνου γινομένην πρὸς
τὸν οἶνον, ὡς ἐξελαύνουσαν τὴν μέθην· φεύγειν
γὰρ δὴ καὶ ζῶσαν τὴν ἄμπελον τὴν ὀσμήν. αἱ
μὲν οὖν φθοραὶ πῶς τε γίνονται καὶ πόσαι καὶ
ποσαχῶς φανερὸν ἐκ τῶν προειρημένων.

---

[1] ἕλκει: lit. 'draws it in'; cf. ἕλκειν ἀέρα, μέθυ, etc.
[2] cf. C.P. 2. 18. 4. ὁ βλαστὸς πλησίον conj. Dalec. from G ;
ὁ πλησίον βλαστός Ald.H.

thing. But *halimon* is more potent even than this, for it destroys tree-medick.

Again some things, though they do not cause death, enfeeble the tree as to the production of flavours and scents; thus cabbage and sweet bay have this effect on the vine. For they say that the vine scents the cabbage and is infected[1] by it. Wherefore the vine-shoot,[2] whenever it comes near this plant, turns back and looks away,[3] as though the smell were hostile to it. Indeed Androkydes[4] used this fact as an example to demonstrate the use of cabbage against wine, to expel the fumes of drunkenness; for,[5] said he, even when it is alive, the vine avoids the smell. It is now clear from what has been said how the death of a tree may be caused, how many are the causes of death, and in what several ways they operate.

[3] ἀφορᾶν conj. Sch.; εὐφορεῖν U; ἀφορεῖν Ald.; *averti* G; *recedere* Plin. *l.c.*; ἐκχωρεῖν conj. W.
[4] A medical man who preached temperance to Alexander; *cf.* Plin. 14. 58; 17. 240.
[5] γὰρ δὴ καὶ conj. Dalec. from G; γὰρ δεῖ καὶ Ald.

BOOK V

E

I. Περὶ δὲ τῆς ὕλης, ποία τέ ἐστιν ἑκάστη, καὶ πόθ᾽ ὡραία τέμνεσθαι, καὶ πρὸς ποῖα τῶν ἔργων χρησίμη, καὶ ποία δύσεργος ἢ εὔεργος, καὶ εἴ τι ἄλλο τῆς τοιαύτης ἱστορίας ἔχεται, πειρατέον ὁμοίως εἰπεῖν.

Ὡραῖα δὴ τέμνεσθαι τῶν ξύλων τὰ μὲν οὖν στρογγύλα καὶ ὅσα πρὸς φλοϊσμὸν ὅταν βλαστάνῃ· τότε γὰρ εὐπεριαίρετος ὁ φλοιός, ὃ δὴ καλοῦσι λοπᾶν, διὰ τὴν ὑγρότητα τὴν ὑπογινομένην αὐτῷ. μετὰ δὲ ταῦτα δυσπεριαίρετος³ καὶ τὸ ξύλον μέλαν γίνεται καὶ δυσειδές. τὰ δὲ τετράγωνα μετὰ τὸν λοπητόν· ἀφαιρεῖται γὰρ ἡ πελέκησις τὴν δυσείδειαν. ὅλως πᾶν πρὸς ἰσχὺν ὡραιότατον οὐ μόνον πεπαυμένον τῆς βλαστήσεως ἀλλ᾽ ἔτι μᾶλλον ἐκπεπᾶναν τὸν καρπόν. ἀλλὰ διὰ τὸν φλοϊσμὸν ἀώροις οὖσιν ὡραίοις συμβαίνει γίνεσθαι τοῖς στρογγύλοις, ὥστε ἐναντίαι αἱ ὧραι κατὰ συμβεβηκός. εὐ-

---

¹ Plin. 16. 188.  ² cf. 3. 5. 1.
³ δυσπεριαιρετός conj. Sch.; δυσπερικάθαρτος Ald.

# BOOK V

OF THE TIMBER OF VARIOUS TREES AND ITS USES.

I. In like manner we must endeavour to speak of timber, saying of what nature is that of each tree, what is the right season for cutting it, which kinds are hard or easy to work, and anything else that belongs to such an enquiry.

### Of the seasons of cutting.

[1] Now these are the right seasons for cutting timber :—for 'round' timber and that whose bark is to be stripped the time is when the tree is coming into leaf. For then the bark is easily stripped (which process they call ' peeling '[2]) because of the moisture which forms beneath it. At a later time it is hard to strip,[3] and the timber obtained is black and uncomely. However square logs can be cut after the time of peeling, since trimming with the axe removes the uncomeliness. In general any wood is at the best season as to strength when it has not merely ceased coming into leaf, but has even ripened its fruit ; however on account of the bark-stripping it comes to pass that ' round ' timber is in season [4] when it is cut before it is ripe, so that, as it happens, the seasons are here reversed. Moreover the wood

---

[4] *i.e.* in practice the timber is cut before the ideally proper time.

VOL. I.                                    E E

χρούστερα δὲ τὰ ἐλάτινα γίνεται κατὰ τὸν πρῶτον λοπητόν.

2 Ἐπεὶ δὲ μάλιστ᾽ ἢ μόνον περιαιροῦσι τὸν φλοιὸν ἐλάτης πεύκης πίτυος, ταῦτα μὲν τέμνεται τοῦ ἦρος· τότε γὰρ ἡ βλάστησις· τὰ δὲ ἄλλα ὁτὲ μὲν μετὰ πυροτομίαν, ὁτὲ δὲ μετὰ τρυγητὸν καὶ Ἀρκτοῦρον, οἷον ἀρία πτελέα σφένδαμνος μελία ζυγία ὀξύα φίλυρα φηγός τε καὶ ὅλως ὅσα κατορύττεται· δρῦς δὲ ὀψιαίτατα κατὰ χειμῶνα μετὰ τὸ μετόπωρον· ἐὰν δὲ ὑπὸ τὸν λοπητὸν τμηθῇ, σήπεται τάχιστα ὡς εἰπεῖν, ἐάν τε ἔμ-φλοιος ἐάν τε ἄφλοιος· καὶ μάλιστα μὲν τὰ ἐν τῷ πρώτῳ λοπητῷ, δεύτερα δὲ τὰ ἐν τῷ δευτέρῳ, τρίτα δὲ καὶ ἥκιστα τὰ ἐν τῷ τρίτῳ· τὰ δὲ μετὰ τὴν πέπανσιν τῶν καρπῶν ἄβρωτα διαμένει, κἂν ἀλόπιστα ᾖ· πλὴν ὑπὸ τὸν φλοιὸν ὑποδυό-μενοι σκώληκες ἐπιπολῆς ἐγγράφουσι τὸ στέλεχος, οἷς καὶ σφραγῖσι χρῶνταί τινες· ὡραῖον δὲ τμη-θὲν τὸ δρύϊνον ἀσαπές τε καὶ ἀθριπηδέστατον γίνεται καὶ σκληρὸν καὶ πυκνὸν ὥσπερ κέρας· πᾶν γὰρ ὅμοιόν ἐστιν ἐγκαρδίῳ· πλὴν τό γε τῆς ἁλιφλοίου καὶ τότε φαῦλον.

3 Συμβαίνει δὲ καὶ τοῦτο ὑπεναντίον, ὅταν τε κατὰ τὴν βλάστησιν τέμνωνται καὶ ὅταν μετὰ τοὺς καρπούς. τότε μὲν γὰρ ἀναξηραίνεται τὰ στελέχη καὶ οὐ βλαστάνει τὰ δένδρα· μετὰ δὲ τοὺς καρποὺς παραβλαστάνει. δυστομώτερα δὲ

---

¹ cf. 3. 5. 1.   ² ἢ add. Sch.
³ φηγός τε conj. Scal.; πηγός τε U; φηγόσιν τε V; πηγόσιν τε MAld.
⁴ κατορύττεται conj. Sch. from G; ὀρύττεται Ald. cf. 5. 4. 3; 5. 7. 5.   ⁵ Plin. 16. 189.

of the silver-fir is of a better colour at the time [1] of the first peeling.

But since they strip the bark of [2] hardly any trees except silver-fir fir and pine, these trees are cut in the spring; for then is the time of coming into leaf. Other trees are cut sometimes after wheat-harvest, sometimes after the vintage and the rising of Arcturus, as *aria* (holm-oak) elm maple manna-ash *zygia* beech lime Valonia oak,[3] and in general all those whose timber is for underground use.[4] The oak is cut latest of all, in early winter at the end of autumn. [5] If it is cut at the time of peeling, it rots almost more quickly than at any other time, whether it has the bark on or not. This is especially so if it is cut during the first peeling, less so during the second, and least during the third. What is cut after the ripening of the fruit remains untouched by worms, even if it has not peeled : however worms get in under the bark and mark the surface of the stem, and such marked pieces of wood some use as seals.[6] Oak-wood if cut in the right season does not rot and is remarkably free from worms, and its texture is hard and close like horn ; for it is like the heart of a tree throughout, except that that of the kind called sea-bark oak is even at that time of poor quality.[7]

Again, if the trees are cut at the time of coming into leaf, the result is the opposite of that which follows when they are cut after fruiting : for in the former case the trunks dry up and the trees do not sprout into leaf,[8] whereas after the time of fruiting they sprout at the sides. At this season however

[6] *cf.* Ar. *Thesm.* 427 : θριπήδεστα σφραγίδια.
[7] *cf.* 3. 8. 5.
[8] Βλαστάνει M ; παραβλαστάνει W. with Ald.

419

E E 2

διὰ τὴν σκληρότητα κατὰ ταύτην τὴν ὥραν. κελεύουσι δὲ καὶ δεδυκυίας τῆς σελήνης τέμνειν ὡς σκληροτέρων καὶ ἀσαπεστέρων γινομένων. ἐπεὶ δὲ αἱ πέψεις τῶν καρπῶν **παραλλάττουσι,** δῆλον ὅτι καὶ αἱ ἀκμαὶ πρὸς τὴν τομὴν παραλλάττουσιν· ἀεὶ γὰρ ὀψιαίτεραι αἱ τῶν ὀψικαρ-
4 ποτέρων. δι᾽ ὃ καὶ πειρῶνταί τινες ὁρίζειν καθ᾽ ἑκάστην· οἷον πεύκην μὲν καὶ ἐλάτην ὅταν ὑπολοπῶσιν· ἔτι δὲ ὀξύαν καὶ φίλυραν καὶ σφένδαμνον καὶ ζυγίαν τῆς ὀπώρας· δρῦν δέ, ὥσπερ εἴρηται, μετὰ τὸ φθινόπωρον. φασὶ δέ τινες πεύκην ὡραίαν εἶναι τοῦ ἦρος, ὅταν γε ἔχῃ τὴν καλουμένην κάχρυν, καὶ τὴν πίτυν ὅταν ὁ βότρυς αὐτῆς ἀνθῇ. ποῖα μὲν οὖν ὡραῖα καθ᾽ ἕκαστον χρόνον οὕτω διαιροῦνται. πάντων δὲ δῆλον ὅτι βελτίω τὰ τῶν ἀκμαζόντων δένδρων ἢ τῶν νέων κομιδῇ καὶ γεγηρακότων· τὰ μὲν γὰρ ὑδατώδη, τὰ δὲ γεώδη.
5 Πλείστας δὲ χρείας καὶ μεγίστας ἡ ἐλάτη καὶ ἡ πεύκη παρέχονται, καὶ ταῦτα κάλλιστα καὶ μέγιστα τῶν ξύλων ἐστί. διαφέρουσι δὲ ἀλλήλων ἐν πολλοῖς· ἡ μὲν γὰρ πεύκη σαρκωδεστέρα τε καὶ ὀλιγόϊνος· ἡ δ᾽ ἐλάτη καὶ πολύϊνος καὶ ἄσαρκος, ὥστε ἐναντίως ἑκάτερον ἔχειν τῶν μερῶν, τὰς μὲν ἶνας ἰσχυρὰς τὴν δὲ σάρκα

---

[1] αἱ add. Sch.

[2] ὑπολοπῶσιν conj. Sch.; εἰ πέλειν εἰσι U; ὑπελειψεισιν MV; ὑπελινῶσιν Ald.

[3] ταύτην conj. St.; καὶ τὴν Ald. H.

they are harder to cut because the wood is tougher.
It is also recommended to do the cutting when the
moon has set, since then the wood is harder and
less likely to rot. But, since the times when the
fruit ripens are different for different trees, it is
clear that the right moment for cutting also differs,
being later for those[1] trees which fruit later.
Wherefore some try to define the time for the
cutting of each tree; for instance for fir and silver-
fir the time is, they say, when they begin to peel[2]:
for beech lime maple and *zygia* in autumn; for oak,[3]
as has been said, when autumn is past. Some however say that the fir is ripe for cutting in spring,
when it has on it the thing called 'catkin,'[4] and the
pine when its 'cluster'[5] is in bloom. Thus they
distinguish which trees are ripe for cutting at various
times; however it is clear that in all cases the wood
is better when the tree is in its prime than when it
is quite young or has grown old. the wood of quite
young trees being too succulent, and that of old ones
too full of mineral matter.

*Of the wood of silver-fir and fir.*

Silver-fir and fir are the most useful trees and in
the greatest variety of ways, and their[6] timber is
the fairest and largest. Yet they differ from one
another in many respects; the fir is fleshier and has
few fibres, while the silver-fir has many fibres and is
not fleshy, so that in respect of each component it is
the reverse of the other, having stout fibres[7] but soft

[4] *cf.* 1. 1. 2 n.; 3. 5. 5.
[5] *i.e.* the male inflorescence.
[6] ταῦτα conj. Sch. from G; αὐτὰ Ald.H.
[7] *cf.* 3. 9. 7; Plin. 16. 184.

μαλακὴν καὶ μανήν· δι' ὃ τὸ μὲν βάρυ τὸ δὲ
κοῦφον· τὸ μὲν γὰρ ἔνδαδον τὸ δὲ ἄδαδον, ᾗ καὶ
6 λευκότερον. ἔχει δὲ καὶ ὄζους πλείους μὲν ἡ
πεύκη, σκληροτέρους δὲ ἡ ἐλάτη πολλῷ, μᾶλλον·
δὲ καὶ σκληροτάτους πάντων· ἄμφω δὲ πυκνοὺς
καὶ κερατώδεις καὶ τῷ χρώματι ξανθοὺς καὶ
δαδώδεις. ὅταν δὲ τμηθῶσι, ῥεῖ καὶ ἐκ τῶν τῆς
ἐλάτης καὶ ἐκ τῶν τῆς πεύκης ἐπὶ πολὺν χρόνον
ὑγρότης καὶ μᾶλλον ἐκ τῶν τῆς ἐλάτης. ἔστι δὲ
καὶ πολύλοπον ἡ ἐλάτη, καθάπερ καὶ τὸ κρόμυον·
ἀεὶ γὰρ ἔχει τινὰ ὑποκάτω τοῦ φαινομένου, καὶ
7 ἐκ τοιούτων ἡ ὅλη. δι' ὃ καὶ τὰς κώπας ξύοντες
ἀφαιρεῖν πειρῶνται καθ' ἕνα καὶ ὁμαλῶς· ἐὰν γὰρ
οὕτως ἀφαιρῶσιν, ἰσχυρὸς ὁ κωπεών, ἐὰν δὲ
παραλλάξωσι καὶ μὴ κατασπῶσιν ὁμοίως, ἀσθε-
νής· πληγὴ γὰρ οὕτως, ἐκείνως δ' ἀφαίρεσις. ἔστι
δὲ καὶ μακρότατον ἡ ἐλάτη καὶ ὀρθοφυέστατον.
δι' ὃ καὶ τὰς κεραίας καὶ τοὺς ἱστοὺς ἐκ ταύτης
ποιοῦσιν. ἔχει δὲ καὶ τὰς φλέβας καὶ τὰς ἶνας
8 ἐμφανεστάτας πάντων. αὐξάνεται δὲ πρῶτον
εἰς μῆκος, ἄχρι οὗ δὴ ἐφίκηται τοῦ ἡλίου· καὶ
οὔτε ὄζος οὐδεὶς οὔτε παραβλάστησις οὔτε πάχος
γίνεται· μετὰ δὲ ταῦτα εἰς βάθος καὶ πάχος·
οὕτως αἱ τῶν ὄζων ἐκφύσεις καὶ παραβλαστήσεις.

---

¹ τὸ μὲν γὰρ ἐνδ. conj. St. from G; ἐνδ. γὰρ Ald.
² cf. 3. 9. 7.
³ cf. 3. 9. 7, μόνον οὐ διαφανεῖς, whence it appears that the
epithet refers to colour.
⁴ Plin. 16. 195.  ⁵ i.e. the annual rings. cf. 1. 5. 2; 5. 5. 3.
⁶ cf. Hom. Od. 12. 172.
⁷ κατασπῶσιν conj. W.; κατὰ πᾶσιν UMV; κατὰ πάντα Ald.
⁸ cf. Plin. l.c.  ⁹ cf. 1. 2. 1.
¹⁰ ἐμφανέστατας conj. W.; εὐγενεστάτας Ald.
¹¹ δὲ conj. Sch.; καὶ UAld.H.

flesh of open texture. Wherefore the timber of the one is heavy, of the other light, the one[1] being resinous, the other without resin; wherefore also it is whiter. Moreover the fir has more branches, but those of the silver-fir are much tougher, or rather they are tougher than those of any other tree; [2] the branches of both however are of close texture, horny,[3] and in colour brown and like resin-glutted wood. [4] When the branches of either tree are cut, sap streams from them for a considerable time, but especially from those of the silver-fir. Moreover the wood of the silver-fir has many layers, like an onion : [5] there is always another beneath that which is visible, and the wood is composed of such layers throughout. Wherefore, when men are shaving this wood to make oars,[6] they endeavour to take off the several coats one by one evenly : for, if they do this, they get a strong spar, while if they do the work irregularly and do not strip[7] off the coats evenly, they get a weak one ; for the process in this case is hacking instead of stripping. The silver-fir also gives timber of the greatest lengths and of the straightest growth ; wherefore yard-arms[8] and masts are made from it. Also the vessels[9] and fibre are more clearly[10] seen in it than in any other tree. At first[11] it grows in height only, until it has reached[12] the sunshine ; and so far there is no branch nor sidegrowth nor density of habit ; but after that the tree proceeds to increase in bulk[13] and density of habit, as[14] the outgrowing branches and sidegrowths develop.

[12] ἄχρι . . . ἐφίκηται conj. Sch.; ἄχρι οὗ δὴ κἀφίκηται U; ἐχρις οὐκ ἀφίκηται MV; ἄχρις οὐ ἀχίκηται Ald. H.
[13] cf. 4. 1. 4.
[14] Lit. 'this being the effect of the outgrowth.' πάχος· ιὕτως Ald.; πάχος, ὅταν conj. W.

9 Ταῦτα μὲν οὖν ἴδια τῆς ἐλάτης, τὰ δὲ κοινὰ καὶ
πεύκης καὶ ἐλάτης καὶ τῶν ἄλλων. ἔστι γὰρ ἡ
μὲν τετράξοος ἡ δὲ δίξοος. καλοῦσι δὲ τετραξόους
μὲν ὅσαις ἐφ' ἑκάτερα τῆς ἐντεριώνης δύο κτη-
δόνες εἰσὶν ἐναντίαν ἔχουσαι τὴν φύσιν· ἔπειτα
καθ' ἑκατέραν τὴν κτηδόνα ποιοῦνται τὴν πελέκησιν ἐναντίας τὰς πληγὰς κατὰ κτηδόνα φέρον-
τες, ὅταν ἐφ' ἑκάτερα τῆς ἐντεριώνης ἡ πελέκησις
ἀναστρέφῃ. τοῦτο γὰρ ἐξ ἀνάγκης συμβαίνει
διὰ τὴν φύσιν τῶν κτηδόνων. τὰς δὲ τοιαύτας
ἐλάτας καὶ πεύκας τετραξόους καλοῦσι. εἰσὶ δὲ
καὶ πρὸς τὰς ἐργασίας αὗται κάλλισται· πυκνότατα γὰρ ἔχουσι τὰ ξύλα καὶ τὰς αἰγίδας αὗται
10 φύουσιν. αἱ δίξοοι δὲ κτηδόνα μὲν ἔχουσι μίαν
ἐφ' ἑκάτερα τῆς ἐντεριώνης, ταύτας δὲ ἐναντίας
ἀλλήλαις, ὥστε καὶ τὴν πελέκησιν εἶναι διπλῆν,
μίαν καθ' ἑκατέραν κτηδόνα ταῖς πληγαῖς ἐναν-
τίαις· ἁπαλώτατα μὲν οὖν ταῦτά φασιν ἔχειν
τὰ ξύλα, χείριστα δὲ πρὸς τὰς ἐργασίας· δια-
στρέφεται γὰρ μάλιστα. μονοξόους δὲ καλοῦσι
τὰς ἐχούσας μίαν μόνον κτηδόνα· τὴν δὲ πελέκησιν αὐτῶν γίνεσθαι τὴν αὐτὴν ἐφ' ἑκάτερα
τῆς ἐντεριώνης· φασὶ δὲ μανότατα μὲν ἔχειν τῇ
φύσει τὰ ξύλα ταῦτα πρὸς δὲ τὰς διαστροφὰς
ἀσφαλέστατα.
11 Διαφορὰς δὲ ἔχουσι τοῖς φλοιοῖς, καθ' ἃς
γνωρίζουσιν ἰδόντες εὐθὺς τὸ δένδρον πεφυκὸς

---

[1] Plin. l.c.

[2] The meaning of 'four-cleft' etc. seems to be this :

4-Cleft: 2-Cleft: 1-Cleft.

These are the characteristics peculiar to the silver-
fir. Others it shares with the fir and the other trees
of this class. [1] For instance, sometimes a tree is
'four-cleft,' sometimes 'two-cleft'; it is called 'four-
cleft' when on either side of the heart-wood there
are two distinct and diverse lines of fissure: in that
case the blows of the axe follow these lines in cases
where the hewing is stopped short on either side of
the heart-wood.[2] For the nature of the lines of fissure
compels the hewing to take this course. Silver-firs
or firs thus formed are said to be 'four-cleft.' And
these are also the fairest trees for carpentry, their
wood being the closest and possessing the *aigis*.[3]
Those which are 'two-cleft' have one single line of
fissure on either side of the heart-wood, and the lines
of fissure do not correspond to each other, so that
the hewing also is performed by cuts which follow
the two lines of fissure, so as to reach the two sides
of the heart-wood at different angles. Now such
wood, they say, is the softest, but the worst for
carpentry, as it warps most easily. Those trees which
have only a single[4] continuous line of fissure are
said to be 'one-cleft,' though here too the cutting
is done from either side of the heart-wood: and such
wood has, they say, an open[5] texture, and yet[6] it is
not at all apt to warp.

[7] There are also differences in the bark, by observation of which they can tell at once what the

---

[3] *cf.* 3. 9. 3.    [4] μίαν conj. W.; μίαν δὲ P₂Ald.
[5] μανότατα conj. W.; μανότητα Ald.
[6] τὰ ξύλα . . . τὰς conj. Sch.; τὰ ξύλα· ταῦτα δὲ πρὸς τὰς
Ald.H.    [7] Plin. 16. 195 and 196.

ποῖόν τί ἐστι· τῶν μὲν γὰρ εὐκτηδόνων καὶ
ἀστραβῶν καὶ ὁ φλοιὸς λεῖος καὶ ὀρθός, τῶν
δ' ἐναντίων τραχύς τε καὶ διεστραμμένος· ὁμοίως
δὲ καὶ ἐπὶ τῶν λοιπῶν. ἀλλ' ἔστι τετράξοα
μὲν ὀλίγα μονόξοα δὲ πλείω τῶν ἄλλων. ἅπασα
δὲ ἡ ὕλη μείζων καὶ ὀρθοτέρα καὶ ἀστραβεστέρα
καὶ στιφροτέρα καὶ ὅλως καλλίων καὶ πλείων
ἡ ἐν τοῖς προσβορείοις, ὥσπερ καὶ πρότερον
ἐλέχθη· καὶ αὐτοῦ τοῦ δένδρου δὲ τὰ πρὸς
βορρᾶν πυκνότερα καὶ νεανικώτερα. ὅσα δὲ
ὑποπαράβορρα καὶ ἐν περίπνῳ, ταῦτα στρέφει
καὶ παραλλάττει παρὰ μικρὸν ὁ βορέας, ὥστε
εἶναι παρεστραμμένην αὐτῶν τὴν μήτραν καὶ
12 οὐ κατ' ὀρθόν. ἔστι δὲ ὅλα μὲν τὰ τοιαῦτα
ἰσχυρὰ τμηθέντα δὲ ἀσθενῆ διὰ τὸ πολλὰς ἔχειν
παραλλαγάς. καλοῦσι δὲ οἱ τέκτονες ἐπίτομα
ταῦτα διὰ τὸ πρὸς τὴν χρείαν οὕτω τέμνειν.
ὅλως δὲ χείρω τὰ ἐκ τῶν ἐφύγρων καὶ εὐ-
διεινῶν καὶ παλισκίων καὶ συνηρεφῶν καὶ πρὸς
τὴν τεκτονικὴν χρείαν καὶ πρὸς τὴν πυρευ-
τικήν. αἱ μὲν οὖν τοιαῦται διαφοραὶ πρὸς τοὺς
τόπους εἰσὶν αὐτῶν τῶν ὁμογενῶν ὥς γε ἁπλῶς
εἰπεῖν.

II. Διαιροῦσι γάρ τινες κατὰ τὰς χώρας, καί
φασιν ἀρίστην μὲν εἶναι τῆς ὕλης πρὸς τὴν
τεκτονικὴν χρείαν τῆς εἰς τὴν Ἑλλάδα παρα-
γινομένης τὴν Μακεδονικήν· λεία τε γάρ ἐστι
καὶ ἀστραβὴς καὶ ἔχουσα θυῖον. δευτέραν δὲ
τὴν Ποντικήν, τρίτην δὲ τὴν ἀπὸ τοῦ Ῥυνδάκου,

---

¹ πεφυκὸς: cf. Xen. Cyr. 4. 3. 5.
² ὑποπαράβορρα conj. St.; ὑπὸ παράβορρα Ald.; ὑπόβορρα ἢ
παράβορρα conj. Sch.

426

timber of the tree is like as it stands.[1] For if the
timber has straight and not crooked lines of fissure,
the bark also is smooth and regular, while if the
timber has the opposite character, the bark is rough
and twisted; and so too is it with other points.
However few trees are 'four-cleft,' and most of
those which are not are 'one-cleft.' All wood, as
was said before, which grows in a position facing
north, is bigger, more erect, of straighter grain,
tougher, and in general fairer and more abundant.
Moreover of an individual tree the wood on the
northward side is closer and more vigorous. But if
a tree stands sideways to the north [2] with a draught
round it, the north wind by degrees twists and con-
torts [3] it, so that its core becomes twisted instead of
running straight. The timber of such a tree while
still in one piece is strong, but, when cut, it is weak,
because the grain slants across the several pieces.
Carpenters call such wood 'short lengths,' because
they thus cut it up for use. Again in general wood
which comes from a moist, sheltered, shady or confined position is inferior both for carpentry and for
fuel. Such are the differences, generally [4] speaking,
between trees of the same kind as they are affected
by situation.

*Of the effects on timber of climate.*

II. [5] Some indeed make a distinction between regions
and say that the best of the timber which comes into
Hellas for the carpenter's purposes is the Macedonian,
for it is smooth and of straight grain, and it contains
resin: second best is that from Pontus, third that

[1] παραλλάττει conj. Dalec.; παραλλάγει U; παραλλήγει Ald.;
παιαλυγίζει conj. H. Steph.
[4] γε conj. Sch.; δὲ Ald.          [5] Plin. 16. 197.

# THEOPHRASTUS

τετάρτην δὲ τὴν Αἰνιανικήν· χειρίστην δὲ τὴν τ‹
Παρνασιακὴν καὶ τὴν Εὐβοϊκήν· καὶ γὰρ ὀζώδει
καὶ τραχείας καὶ ταχὺ σήπεσθαι. περὶ δὲ τῆ
Ἀρκαδικῆς σκεπτέον.

2 Ἰσχυρότατα δὲ τῶν ξύλων ἐστὶ τὰ ἄοζα κα
λεῖα· καὶ τῇ ὄψει δὲ ταῦτα κάλλιστα. ὀζώδι
δὲ γίνεται τὰ κακοτροφηθέντα καὶ ἤτοι χειμὼν
πιεσθέντα ἢ καὶ ἄλλῳ τινὶ τοιούτῳ· τὸ γὰ;
ὅλον τὴν πολυοζίαν εἶναι ἔνδειαν εὐτροφίας
ὅταν δὲ κακοτροφήσαντα ἀναλάβῃ πάλιν καὶ εὐ
σθενήσῃ, συμβαίνει καταπίνεσθαι τοὺς ὄζου‹
ὑπὸ τῆς περιφύσεως· εὐτροφοῦν γὰρ καὶ αὐ
ξανόμενον ἀναλαμβάνει καὶ πολλάκις ἔξωθε‹
μὲν λεῖον τὸ ξύλον διαιρούμενον δὲ ὀζῶδε
ἐφάνη. δι' ὃ καὶ σκοποῦνται τῶν σχιστῶν τὰ‹
μήτρας· ἐὰν γὰρ αὗται ἔχωσιν ὄζους, ὀζώδη κα
τὰ ἐκτός· καὶ οὗτοι χαλεπώτεροι τῶν ἐκτὸς κα
φανεροί.

3 Γίνονται δὲ καὶ αἱ σπεῖραι διὰ χειμῶνας τ‹
καὶ κακοτροφίαν. σπείρας δὲ καλοῦσιν ὅταν ‹
συστροφή τις ἐν αὐτῇ μείζων καὶ κύκλοις περι
εχομένη πλείοσιν οὔθ' ὥσπερ ὁ ὄζος ἁπλῶς οὔθ
ὡς ἡ οὐλότης ἡ ἐν αὐτῷ τῷ ξύλῳ· δι' ὅλου γά;
πως αὕτη καὶ ὁμαλίζουσα· χαλεπώτερον δ‹
τοῦτο πολὺ καὶ δυσεργότερον τῶν ὄζων. ἔοικ‹
δὲ παραπλησίως καὶ ὡς ἐν τοῖς λίθοις ἐγγίνεσθα

---

[1] A river which flows into the Propontis on the Asiatic
side.

[2] Near Mount Oeta. Αἰνιανικήν conj. Palm. from Plin
l.c.; αἰανικὴν P₂Ald.H.

[3] ταῦτα κάλλιστα· ὀζώδη δὲ conj. Scal.; ταῦτα καὶ μάλιστε
ὀζώδη γίν. Ald.H.; ταῦτα μάλιστα· ὀζώδη δὲ γίν. U.

428

from the Rhyndakos,[1] fourth that of the country
of the Ainianes,[2] worst is that of Parnassus and that
of Euboea, for it is full of knots and rough and
quickly rots. As to Arcadian timber the case is
doubtful.

*Of knots and 'coiling' in timber.*

The strongest wood is that which is without knots
and smooth, and it is also the fairest in appearance.[3]
Wood becomes knotty when it has been ill nourished
and has suffered severely whether from winter or
some such cause ; for in general a knotty habit is
supposed to indicate lack of nourishment. When
however, after being ill nourished, the tree recovers
and becomes vigorous, the result is that the knots
are absorbed[4] by the growth which now covers them :
for the tree, being now well fed and growing
vigorously, recovers, and often the wood is smooth
outside, though when split it is seen to have knots.
And this is why they examine the core of wood that
has been split ; for, if this contains knots, the outward[5] parts will also be knotty, and these knots are
harder to deal with than the outer ones, and are
easily recognised.

[6]'Coiling' of the wood is also due to winter or ill
nourishment. Wood is said to 'coil' when there is
in it closer twisting[7] than usual, made up of an
unusual number of rings : this is not quite like a knot,
nor is it like the ordinary curling of the wood, which
runs right through it and is uniform. 'Coiling' is
much more troublesome and difficult to deal with than
knots ; it seems to correspond to the so-called

[4] καταπίνεσθαι : ? καταλαμβάνεσθαι. cf. below, § 3.
[5] i.e. outward in regard to the core.   [6] Plin. 16. 198.
[7] ἢ συστροφή conj. Scal.; ἢ εὐστροφή U; ἢ εὐτραφῇ Ald. etc.

# THEOPHRASTUS

τὰ καλούμενα κέντρα. ὅτι δ' ἡ περίφυσις κατα
λαμβάνει τοὺς ὄζους φανερώτατον ἐξ αὐτῆς τῇ
αἰσθήσεως, οὐ μὴν ἀλλὰ καὶ ἐκ τῶν ἄλλω
4 τῶν ὁμοίων· πολλάκις γὰρ αὐτοῦ τοῦ δένδρο
μέρος τι συνελήφθη ὑπὸ θατέρου συμφυοὺς γενο
μένου· καὶ ἐάν τις ἐκγλύψας θῇ λίθον εἰς τ
δένδρον ἢ καὶ ἄλλο τι τοιοῦτον, κατακρύπτετα
περιληφθὲν ὑπὸ τῆς περιφύσεως· ὅπερ καὶ περ
τὸν κότινον συνέβη τὸν ἐν Μεγάροις τὸν ἐν τ
ἀγορᾷ· οὗ καὶ ἐκκοπέντος λόγιον ἦν ἁλῶναι κα
διαρπασθῆναι τὴν πόλιν· ὅπερ ἐγένετο . . .
Δημήτριος. ἐν τούτῳ γὰρ διασχιζομένῳ κνη
μῖδες εὑρέθησαν καὶ ἄλλ' ἄττα τῆς Ἀττικῇ
ἐργασίας κρεμαστά, τοῦ κοτίνου οὗ ἀνετέθη τ
πρῶτον ἐγκοιλανθέντος. τούτου δ' ἔτι μικρὸ
τὸ λοιπόν. πολλαχοῦ δὲ καὶ ἄλλοθι γίνετα
πλείονα τοιαῦτα. καὶ ταῦτα μέν, ὥσπερ εἴρηται
κοινὰ πλειόνων.

III. Κατὰ δὲ τὰς ἰδίας ἑκάστου φύσεις α
τοιαῦταί εἰσι διαφοραί, οἷον πυκνότης μανότη
βαρύτης κουφότης σκληρότης μαλακότης, ὡσαύ
τως δὲ καὶ εἴ τις ἄλλη τοιαύτη· κοιναὶ δὲ ὁμοίω
αὗται καὶ τῶν ἡμέρων καὶ τῶν ἀγρίων, ὥστε περ
πάντων λεκτέον.

---

[1] ὅτι δ' ἡ conj. W.; ὅτι δὴ UMV; ὅτι δὲ Ald.
[2] cf. καταπίνεσθαι, above, § 2.
[3] Plin. 16. 198 and 199.
[4] ἐκγλύψας θῇ conj. W.; ἐκλύψας θῆι U; ἐκλιθασθῇ Ald. H.
[5] Text defective.
[6] i.e. the bark had grown over these. cf. Plin. l.c.

'centres' which occur in marbles. That [1] vigorous growth covers [2] up the knots is plain from simple observation of the fact and also from other similar instances. [3] For often some part of the tree itself is absorbed by the rest of the tree which has grown into it; and again, if one makes a hole in a tree and puts [4] a stone into it or some other such thing, it becomes buried, being completely enveloped by the wood which grows all round it: this happened with the wild olive in the market-place at Megara: there was an oracle that, if this were cut open, the city would be taken and plundered, which came to pass when Demetrius took it. [5] For, when this tree was split open, there were found greaves and certain other things [6] of Attic workmanship hanging there, the hole [7] in the tree having been made at the place where the things were originally hung on it as offerings. Of this tree a small part still exists, and in many other places further instances have occurred. Moreover, as has been said, such occurrences happen also with various other trees.

*Of differences in the texture of different woods.*

III. [8] Corresponding to the individual characters of the several trees we have the following kinds of differences in the wood:—it differs in closeness, heaviness, hardness or their opposites, and in other similar ways; and these differences are common to cultivated and wild trees. So that we may speak of all trees without distinction.

[1] ἐργασίας κρεμαστὰ τοῦ κοτίνου οὗ I conj. from G and Plin. *l.c.* (certain restoration perhaps impossible); κερμηστι ὅ ἐστιν ἐν κοτίνῳ· οὗ U; Ald. has κερμηστι, M κρεμαστι, V κερμάστων; St. suggested κρεμαστῶν ὅπλων as words of the original text.    [8] Plin. 16. 204–207.

Πυκνότατα μὲν οὖν δοκεῖ καὶ βαρύτατα πύξος εἶναι καὶ ἔβενος· οὐδὲ γὰρ οὐδ' ἐπὶ τοῦ ὕδατος ταῦτ' ἐπινεῖ. καὶ ἡ μὲν πύξος ὅλη, τῆς δὲ ἐβένου ἡ μήτρα, ἐν ᾗ καὶ ἡ τοῦ χρώματός ἐστι μελανία, τῶν δ' ἄλλων ὁ λωτός. πυκνὸν δὲ καὶ ἡ τῆς δρυὸς μήτρα, ἣν καλοῦσι μελάνδρυον· καὶ ἔτι μᾶλλον ἡ τοῦ κυτίσου· παρομοία γὰρ αὕτη δοκεῖ τῇ ἐβένῳ εἶναι.

2  Μέλαν δὲ σφόδρα καὶ πυκνὸν τὸ τῆς τερμίνθου· περὶ γοῦν Συρίαν μελάντερόν φασιν εἶναι τῆς ἐβένου· καὶ ἐκ τούτου γὰρ καὶ τὰς λαβὰς τῶν ἐγχειριδίων ποιεῖσθαι, τορνεύεσθαι δὲ ἐξ αὐτῶν καὶ κύλικας Θηρικλείους, ὥστε μηδένα ἂν διαγνῶναι πρὸς τὰς κεραμέας· λαμβάνειν δὲ τὸ ἐγκάρδιον· δεῖν δὲ ἀλείφειν τὸ ξύλον· οὕτω γὰρ γίνεσθαι καὶ κάλλιον καὶ μελάντερον.

Εἶναι δὲ καὶ ἄλλο τι δένδρον, ὃ ἅμα τῇ μελανίᾳ καὶ ποικιλίαν τινὰ ἔχει ὑπέρυθρον, ὥστε εἶναι τὴν ὄψιν ὡσὰν ἐβένου ποικίλης· ποιεῖσθαι δ' ἐξ αὐτοῦ καὶ κλίνας καὶ δίφρους καὶ τὰ ἄλλα τὰ σπουδαζόμενα. τὸ <δὲ> δένδρον μέγα σφόδρα καὶ καλόφυλλον εἶναι ὅμοιον ταῖς ἀπίοις.

3  Ταῦτα μὲν οὖν ἅμα τῇ μελανίᾳ καὶ πυκνότητα ἔχει. πυκνὸν δὲ καὶ ἡ σφένδαμνος καὶ ἡ ζυγία καὶ ὅλως πάντα τὰ οὖλα· καὶ ἡ ἐλάα δὲ καὶ ὁ κότινος, ἀλλὰ κραῦρα. μανὰ δὲ τῶν μὲν ἀγρίων καὶ ἐρεψίμων τὰ ἐλάτινα μάλιστα,

---

¹ cf. Arist. Meteor. 4. 7 ad fin.
² cf. 1. 6. 1.      ³ cf. 3. 15. 3.
⁴ Probably so called from their resemblance in shape and

Box and ebony seem to have the closest and heaviest wood; for their wood does not even float on water. This applies to the box-tree as a whole, and to the core of the ebony, which contains the black pigment.[1] The nettle-tree also is very close and heavy, and so is the core of the oak, which is called 'heart of oak,' and to a still greater degree this is true of the core of laburnum[2]; for this seems to resemble the ebony.

The wood of the terebinth is also very black and close-grained; at least in Syria[3] they say that it is blacker than ebony, that in fact they use it for making their dagger handles; and by means of the lathe-chisel they also make of it 'Theriklean' cups,[4] so that no one could[5] distinguish these from cups made of pottery; for this purpose they use, it is said, the heart-wood, but the wood has to be oiled, for then it becomes comelier and blacker.

There is also, they say, another tree[6] which, as well as the black colour, has a sort of reddish variegation, so that it looks like variegated ebony, and of it are made beds and couches and other things of superior quality. This tree is very large and has handsome leaves and is like the pear.

These trees then, as well as the black colour, have close wood; so also have maple *zygia* and in general all those that are of compact growth: so also have the olive and the wild olive, but their wood is brittle.[7] Of wild trees which are used for roof-timbers the wood of the silver-fir is the least com-

colour to the cups made by Therikles, a famous Corinthian potter; see reff. to comedy in LS. *s.v.*
[5] μηδένα ἂν conj. W.: μηδ' ἂν ἕνα Ald.
[6] Sissoo wood. See Index App. (21).
[7] ἀλλὰ κραῦρα conj. Sch.; ἀλλὰ καὶ αὖρα MVAld.

THEOPHRASTUS

τῶν δ' ἄλλων τὰ ἄκτινα καὶ τὰ σύκινα καὶ
τὰ τῆς μηλέας καὶ τὰ τῆς δάφνης. σκληρότατα δὲ τὰ δρύϊνα καὶ τὰ ζύγινα καὶ τὰ
τῆς ἀρίας· καὶ γὰρ ὑποβρέχουσι¹ ταῦτα πρὸς
τὴν τρύπησιν μαλάξεως χάριν. μαλακὰ δὲ
καθ' ὅλου μὲν τὰ μανὰ καὶ χαῦνα· τῶν δὲ
σαρκωδῶν μάλιστα φίλυρα. δοκεῖ δὲ καὶ θερ-
μότατον εἶναι τοῦτο· σημεῖον δὲ ὅτι μάλιστα
ἀμβλύνει τὰ σιδήρια· τὴν γὰρ βαφὴν ἀνίησι διὰ
τὴν θερμότητα.

4 Θερμὸν δὲ καὶ κιττὸς καὶ δάφνη καὶ ὅλως
ἐξ ὧν τὰ πυρεῖα γίνεται· Μενέστωρ δέ φησι
καὶ συκάμινον. ψυχρότατα δὲ τὰ ἔνυδρα καὶ
ὑδατώδη. καὶ γλίσχρα δὲ τὰ ἰτέϊνα καὶ ἀμ-
πέλινα, δι' ὃ καὶ τὰς ἀσπίδας ἐκ τούτων ποιοῦσι·
συμμύει γὰρ πληγέντα· κουφότερον δὲ τὸ τῆς
ἰτέας, μανότερον γάρ, δι' ὃ καὶ τούτῳ μᾶλλον
χρῶνται. τὸ δὲ τῆς πλατάνου γλισχρότητα μὲν
ἔχει, φύσει δὲ ὑγρότερον τοῦτο καὶ τὸ τῆς πτελέας. σημεῖον δέ ἐστιν, μετὰ τὴν τομὴν ὀρθὸν
ὅταν σταθῇ, πολὺ ὕδωρ ἀφίησι. τὸ δὲ τῆς συκαμίνου πυκνὸν ἅμα καὶ γλίσχρον.

5 Ἔστι δὲ καὶ ἀστραβέστατον τὸ τῆς πτελέας,
δι' ὃ καὶ τοὺς στροφεῖς τῶν θυρῶν ποιοῦσι
πτελεΐνους· ἐὰν γὰρ οὗτοι μένωσι, καὶ αἱ θύραι
μένουσιν ἀστραβεῖς, εἰ δὲ μή, διαστρέφονται.
ποιοῦσι δ' αὐτοὺς ἔμπαλιν τιθέντες τὰ ξύλα τό
τε ἀπὸ τῆς ῥίζης καὶ τὸ ἀπὸ τοῦ φύλλου·²

¹ ὑποβρέχουσι conj. Harduin from Plin. 16. 207 ; ἀποβρίθουσι
Ald. H. ; ἀποβρέχουσι mBas.
² cf. 5. 5. 1, which, referring to this passage, hardly agrees
with it as now read.

434

pact, and among others that of the elder fig apple
and bay. The hardest woods are those of the oak
*zygia* and *aria* (holm-oak); in fact men wet[1] these
to soften them for boring holes. In general, woods
which are of open porous texture are soft, and of
those of fleshy texture the softest is the lime. The
last-named seems also to be the hottest; the proof
of which is that it blunts iron tools more than any
other; for they lose their edge[2] by reason of its
heat.

Ivy and bay are also hot woods, and so in general
are those used for making fire-sticks; and Menestor[3]
adds the wood of the mulberry. [4]The coldest woods
are those which grow in water and are of succulent
character. The wood again of willow and vine is
tough; wherefore men make their shields of these
woods; for they close up again after a blow; but
that of the willow is lighter, since it is of less compact texture; wherefore they use this for choice.
The wood of the plane is fairly tough, but it is
moister in character, as also is that of the elm. A
proof of this is that, if it is set upright[5] after being
cut, it discharges much water.[6] The wood of the
mulberry is at once of close grain and tough.

[7]The wood of the elm is the least likely to warp;
wherefore they make the 'hinges'[8] of doors out of
elm wood; for, if these hold, the doors also keep in
place; otherwise they get wrenched out of place.
They make the 'hinges' by putting wood from the
root above[9] and wood 'from the foliage' below,[9] thus

---

[3] *cf.* 1. 2. 3 n.      [4] Plin. 16. 209.
[5] ὀρθὸν ὅταν conj. W.; so G; ὀρθὸς ὅταν MV; ὅταν ὀρθὰ Ald.
[6] *cf.* 5. 1. 6.      [7] Plin. 16. 210.
[8] Sc. an arrangement of cylindrical pivot and socket.
[9] i.e. as socket and pivot respectively; *cf.* 5. 5. 4.

καλοῦσι δὲ οἱ τέκτονες τὸ ἀπὸ τοῦ φύλλου τὸ
ἄνω· ἐναρμοσθέντα γὰρ ἀλλήλοις ἑκάτερον κωλύει πρὸς τὴν ὁρμὴν ἐναντίως ἔχον. εἰ δὲ ἔκειτο
κατὰ φύσιν, οὗπερ ἡ ῥοπὴ ἐνταῦθα πάντων ἂν
ἦν ἡ φορά.

Τὰς δὲ θύρας οὐκ εὐθὺς συντελοῦσιν, ἀλλὰ
πήξαντες ἐφιστᾶσι, κἄπειτα ὑστέρῳ οἱ δὲ τῷ
τρίτῳ ἔτει συνετέλεσαν ἐὰν μᾶλλον σπουδάζωσι·
τοῦ μὲν γὰρ θέρους ἀναξηραινομένων διΐστανται,
τοῦ δὲ χειμῶνος συμμύουσιν. αἴτιον δ' ὅτι τῆς
ἐλάτης τὰ μανὰ καὶ σαρκώδη ἕλκει τὸν ἀέρα
ἔνικμον ὄντα.

6    Ὁ δὲ φοῖνιξ κοῦφος καὶ εὔεργος καὶ μαλακός,
ὥσπερ ὁ φελλός, βελτίων δὲ τοῦ φελλοῦ ὅτι γλί-
σχρος· ἐκεῖνο δὲ θραυστόν. διὰ τοῦτο τὰ εἴδωλα
νῦν ἐκ τοῦ τῶν φοινίκων ποιοῦσι, τὸν δὲ φελλὸν
παρήκασι. τὰς ἶνας δὲ οὐ δι' ὅλου ἔχει οὐδ' ἐπὶ
πολὺ καὶ μακρὰς οὐδ' ὡσαύτως τῇ θέσει ἐγκει-
μένας πάσας ἀλλὰ παντοδαπῶς. ἀναξηραίνεται
δὲ καὶ λειαινόμενον καὶ πριόμενον τὸ ξύλον.

7    Τὸ δὲ θύον, οἱ δὲ θύαν καλοῦσι, παρ' Ἄμμωνί
τε γίνεται καὶ ἐν τῇ Κυρηναίᾳ, τὴν μὲν μορφὴν
ὅμοιον κυπαρίττῳ καὶ τοῖς κλάδοις καὶ τοῖς φύλλοις καὶ τῷ στελέχει καὶ τῷ καρπῷ, μᾶλλον δ'
ὥσπερ κυπάριττος ἀγρία· πολὺ μὲν καὶ ὅπου

---

¹ κωλύει : Sch. adds θάτερον from G.
² ἔκειτο conj. W.; ἐκεῖνο Ald.
³ i.e. the 'upper' wood in the upper position.
⁴ πάντων MSS. (?) ; πάντως conj. W.
⁵ i.e. there would be no resistance. ἦν after ἂν add. Sch.

reversing the natural position : (by wood ' from the foliage ' joiners mean the upper wood). For, when these are fitted the one into the other, each counteracts[1] the other, as they naturally tend in opposite directions : whereas, if the wood were set[2] as it grows,[3] all the parts[4] would give where the strain came.[5]

(They do not finish off the doors at once ; but, when they have put them together, stand them up, and then finish them off the next year, or sometimes the next year but one,[6] if they are doing specially good work. For in summer, as the wood dries, the work comes apart, but it closes in winter. The reason is that the open fleshy texture of the wood of the silver-fir[7] drinks in the air, which is full of moisture.)

[8] Palm-wood is light easily worked and soft like cork-oak, but is superior to that wood, as it is tough, while the other is brittle. Wherefore men now make their images of palm-wood and have given up the wood of cork-oak. However the fibres do not run throughout the wood, nor do they run to a good length, nor are they all set symmetrically, but run in every direction. The wood dries while it is being planed and sawn.

[9] *Thyon* (thyine wood), which some call *thya*, grows near the temple of Zeus Ammon and in the district of Cyrene. In appearance the tree is like the cypress alike in its branches, its leaves, its stem, and its fruit ; or rather it is like a wild cypress.[10] There

[6] *cf.* Plin. 16. 215.
[7] Of which the door itself is made.
[8] Plin. 16. 211.    [9] Plin. 13. 100–102.
[10] κυπάριττος ἀγρία conj. Sch.; κυπάρισσον ἀγρίαν M Ald.

νῦν ἡ πόλις ἐστί, καὶ ἔτι διαμνημονεύουσιν ὀροφάς τινας τῶν ἀρχαίων οὔσας. ἀσαπὲς γὰρ ὅλως τὸ ξύλον οὐλότατον δὲ τὴν ῥίζαν ἐστί· καὶ ἐκ ταύτης τὰ σπουδαιότατα ποιεῖται τῶν ἔργων. τὰ δὲ ἀγάλματα γλύφουσιν ἐκ τῶνδε, κέδρων κυπαρίττου λωτοῦ πύξου· τὰ δ' ἐλάττω καὶ ἐκ τῶν ἐλαίνων ῥιζῶν· ἀρραγεῖς γὰρ αὗται καὶ ὁμαλῶς πως σαρκώδεις. ταῦτα μὲν οὖν ἰδιότητά τινα τόπων καὶ φύσεως καὶ χρείας ἀποδηλοῖ.

IV. Βαρέα δὲ καὶ κοῦφα δῆλον ὡς τῇ πυκνότητι καὶ μανότητι καὶ ὑγρότητι καὶ ξηρότητι καὶ τῷ γλοιώδει καὶ σκληρότητι καὶ μαλακότητι ληπτέον. ἔνια μὲν οὖν ἅμα σκληρὰ καὶ βαρέα, καθάπερ πύξος καὶ δρῦς· ὅσα δὲ κραῦρα καὶ τῇ ξηρότητι σκληρότατα, ταῦτ' οὐκ ἔχει βάρος. ἅπαντα δὲ τὰ ἄγρια τῶν ἡμέρων καὶ τὰ ἄρρενα τῶν θηλειῶν πυκνότερά τε καὶ σκληρότερα καὶ βαρύτερα καὶ τὸ ὅλον ἰσχυρότερα, καθάπερ καὶ πρότερον εἴπομεν. ὡς δ' ἐπὶ τὸ πᾶν καὶ τὰ ἀκαρπότερα τῶν καρπίμων καὶ τὰ χείρω τῶν καλλικαρποτέρων· εἰ μή που καρπιμώτερον τὸ ἄρρεν, ὥσπερ ἄλλα τέ φασι καὶ τὴν κυπάριττον καὶ τὴν κράνειαν. ἀλλὰ τῶν γε ἀμπέλων φανερῶς αἱ ὀλιγοκαρπότεραι καὶ πυκνοφθαλμότεραι καὶ στερεώτεραι· καὶ μηλεῶν δὲ καὶ τῶν ἄλλων ἡμέρων.

is abundance of it where now the city stands, and men can still recall that some of the roofs in ancient times were made of it. For the wood is absolutely proof against decay, and the root is of very compact texture, and they make of it the most valuable articles. Images are carved from these woods, prickly cedar cypress nettle-tree box, and the small ones also from the roots of the olive, which are unbreakable and of a more or less uniformly fleshy character. The above facts illustrate certain special features of position, natural character and use.

*Of differences in timber as to hardness and heaviness.*

IV. Difference in weight is clearly to be determined by closeness or openness of texture, dampness or dryness, degree of glutinousness, hardness or softness. Now some woods are both hard and heavy, as box and oak, while those that are brittle and hardest owing to their dryness, are not heavy. [1] All wood of wild trees, as we have said before, is closer harder heavier, and in general stronger than that of the cultivated forms, and there is the same difference between the wood of 'male' and of 'female' trees, and in general between trees which bear no fruit and those which have fruit, and between those which bear inferior fruit and those whose fruit is better; on the other hand occasionally the 'male' tree is the more fruitful, for instance, it is said, the cypress cornelian cherry and others. However of vines it is clear that those which bear less fruit have also more frequent knots and are more solid,[2] and so too with apples and other cultivated trees.

[1] Plin. 16. 211.    [2] *cf. C.P.* 3. 11. 1.

THEOPHRASTUS

2 Ἀσαπῆ δὲ φύσει κυπάριττος κέδρος ἔβενος
λωτός πύξος ἐλάα κότινος πεύκη ἔνδαδος ἀρία
δρῦς καρύα Εὐβοϊκή. τούτων δὲ χρονιώτατα
δοκεῖ τὰ κυπαρίττινα εἶναι· τὰ γοῦν ἐν Ἐφέσῳ,
ἐξ ὧν αἱ θύραι τοῦ νεωστὶ νεώ, τεθησαυρισμένα
τέτταρας ἔκειτο γενεάς. μόνα δὲ καὶ στιλβηδόνα
δέχεται, δι' ὃ καὶ τὰ σπουδαζόμενα τῶν ἔργων ἐκ
τούτων ποιοῦσι. τῶν δὲ ἄλλων ἀσαπέστατον
μετὰ τὰ κυπαρίττινα καὶ τὰ θυώδη τὴν συκάμινον εἶναί φασι, καὶ ἰσχυρὸν ἅμα καὶ εὔεργον τὸ
ξύλον· γίνεται δὲ τὸ ξύλον [καὶ] παλαιούμενον
μέλαν, ὥσπερ λωτός.

3 Ἔτι δὲ ἄλλο πρὸς ἄλλο καὶ ἐν ἄλλῳ ἀσαπές,
οἷον πτελέα μὲν ἐν τῷ ἀέρι, δρῦς δὲ κατορυτ-
τομένη καὶ ἐν τῷ ὕδατι καταβρεχομένη· δοκεῖ
γὰρ ὅλως ἀσαπὲς εἶναι· δι' ὃ καὶ εἰς τοὺς ποταμοὺς καὶ εἰς τὰς λίμνας ἐκ τούτων ναυπηγοῦσιν·
ἐν δὲ τῇ θαλάττῃ σήπεται. τὰ δὲ ἄλλα διαμένει
μᾶλλον, ὅπερ καὶ εὔλογον, ταριχευόμενα τῇ
ἅλμῃ.

4 Δοκεῖ δὲ καὶ ἡ ὀξύη πρὸς τὸ ὕδωρ ἀσαπὴς
εἶναι καὶ βελτίων γίνεσθαι βρεχομένη. καὶ ἡ
καρύα δὲ ἡ Εὐβοϊκὴ ἀσαπής. φασὶ δὲ καὶ τὴν
πεύκην ἐλάτης μᾶλλον ὑπὸ τερηδόνος ἐσθίεσθαι·
τὴν μὲν γὰρ εἶναι ξηράν, τὴν δὲ πεύκην ἔχειν
γλυκύτητα, καὶ ὅσῳ ἐνδαδωτέρα, μᾶλλον· πάντα

---
[1] Plin. 16. 213.
[2] τεθησαυρισμένα . . . ἔκειτο conj. Bentley; τεθησαυρισμέναι
. . . ἔκειντο Ald.H.; P has ἔκειτο.

440

*Of differences in the keeping quality of timber.*

[1] Naturally proof against decay are cypress prickly cedar ebony nettle-tree box olive wild olive resinous fir *aria* (holm-oak) oak sweet chestnut. Of these the wood of the cypress seems to last longest; at least the cypress-wood at Ephesus, of which the doors of the modern temple were made, lay stored up [2] for four generations. And this is the only wood which takes a fine polish, wherefore they make of it valuable articles. Of the others the least liable to decay after the wood of the cypress and thyine-wood is, they say, that of the mulberry, which is also strong and easily worked: when it becomes old, this wood turns black like that of the nettle-tree.

[3] Again whether a given wood is not liable to decay may depend on the purpose to which it is put and the conditions to which it is subjected: thus the elm does not decay if exposed to the air, nor the oak if it is buried or soaked in water; for it appears to be entirely proof against decay: wherefore they build vessels of it for use on rivers and on lakes, but in sea-water it rots, though other woods last all the better; which is natural, as they become seasoned with the brine.

[4] The beech also seems to be proof against decay in water and to be improved by being soaked. The sweet chestnut under like treatment is also proof against decay. They say that the wood of the fir is more liable to be eaten by the *teredon* than that of the silver-fir; for that the latter is dry, while the fir has a sweet taste, and that this is more so, the more the wood is soaked with resin [5]; they go on to

[3] Plin. 16. 218.    [4] Plin. 16. 218 and 219.
[5] *cf.* 3. 9. 4.

441

THEOPHRASTUS

δ' ἐσθίεσθαι τερηδόνι πλὴν κοτίνου καὶ ἐλάας·
τὰ δὲ οὔ, διὰ τὴν πικρότητα. ἐσθίεται δὲ τὰ μὲν
ἐν τῇ θαλάττῃ σηπόμενα ὑπὸ τερηδόνος, τὰ δ' ἐν
τῇ γῇ ὑπὸ σκωλήκων καὶ ὑπὸ θριπῶν· οὐ γὰρ
γίνεται τερηδὼν ἀλλ' ἢ ἐν τῇ θαλάττῃ. ἔστι δὲ
ἡ τερηδὼν τῷ μὲν μεγέθει μικρόν, κεφαλὴν δ' ἔχει
5 μεγάλην καὶ ὀδόντας· οἱ δὲ θρίπες ὅμοιοι τοῖς
σκώληξιν, ὑφ' ὧν τιτραίνεται κατὰ μικρὸν τὰ
ξύλα. καὶ ἔστι ταῦτα εὐίατα· πιττοκοπηθέντα
γὰρ ὅταν εἰς τὴν θάλατταν ἑλκυσθῇ στέγει· τὰ
δὲ ὑπὸ τῶν τερηδόνων ἀνίατα. τῶν δὲ σκωλήκων
τῶν ἐν τοῖς ξύλοις οἱ μέν εἰσιν ἐκ τῆς οἰκείας
σήψεως, οἱ δ' ἐντικτόντων ἑτέρων· ἐντίκτει γάρ,
ὥσπερ καὶ τοῖς δένδροις, ὁ κεράστης καλούμενος,
ὅταν τιτραίνῃ καὶ κοιλάνῃ περιστραφεὶς ὡσπερεὶ
μυοδόχον. φεύγει δὲ τά τε ὀσμώδη καὶ πικρὰ καὶ
σκληρὰ διὰ τὸ μὴ δύνασθαι τιτρᾶναι, καθάπερ
6 τὴν πύξον. φασὶ δὲ καὶ τὴν ἐλάτην φλοισθεῖσαν
ὑπὸ τὴν βλάστησιν ἀσαπῆ διαμένειν ἐν τῷ ὕδατι·
φανερὸν δὲ γενέσθαι ἐν Φενεῷ τῆς Ἀρκαδίας, ὅτε
αὐτοῖς ἐλιμνώθη τὸ πεδίον φραχθέντος τοῦ βερέ-
θρου· τότε γὰρ τὰς γεφύρας ποιοῦντες ἐλατίνας
καί, ὅταν ἐπαναβαίνῃ τὸ ὕδωρ, ἄλλην καὶ ἄλλην
ἐφιστάντες, ὡς ἐρράγη καὶ ἀπῆλθε, πάντα εὑρε-
θῆναι τὰ ξύλα ἀσαπῆ. τοῦτο μὲν οὖν ἐκ συμ-
πτώματος.

---

¹ Plin. 16. 220 and 221.
² τιτραίνεται conj. Scal. from G ; τιτρένεται UVo.; πεπαίνεται
MVAld.    ³ cf 4. 14. 5.
⁴ ὡσπερεὶ μυοδόχον conj. W.; ὥσπερ οἱ μυόχοδοι MSS.; G
omits. The word μυοδόχος does not occur elsewhere as a
subst.

442

say that all woods are eaten by the *teredon* except
the olive, wild or cultivated, and that these woods
escape because of their bitter taste. [1] Now woods
which decay in sea-water are eaten by the *teredon*,
those which decay on land by the *skolex* and *thrips*;
for the *teredon* does not occur except in the sea.
It is a creature small in size, but has a large head
and teeth; the *thrips* resembles the *skolex*, and these
creatures gradually bore through [2] timber. The harm
that these do is easy to remedy: for, if the wood is
smeared with pitch, it does not let in water when it
is dragged down into the sea; but the harm done by
the *teredon* cannot be undone. Of the *skolekes* which
occur in wood some come from the decay of the wood
itself, some from other *skolekes* which engender therein.
For these produce their young in timber, as the worm
called the ' horned worm' [3] does in trees, having bored
and scooped out a sort of mouse-hole [4] by turning
round and round. But it avoids wood which has a
strong smell or is bitter or hard, such as boxwood,
since it is unable to bore through it. They say too
that the wood of the silver-fir, if barked just before
the time of budding, remains in water without de-
caying, and that this was clearly seen at Pheneos
in Arcadia, when their plain was turned into a lake
since the outlet was blocked up.[5] For at that
time they made [6] their bridges of this wood. and,
as the water rose, they placed more and more atop
of them, and, when the water burst its way through
and disappeared, all the wood was found to be
undecayed. This fact then became known by means
of an accident.

[5] *cf.* 3. 1. 2. φραχθέντος conj. Sch.: βραχέντος Ald. H.
[6] ποιοῦντες, ἐφιστάντες nom. pendens.

443

7  Ἐν Τύλῳ δὲ τῇ νήσῳ τῇ περὶ τὴν Ἀραβίαν
εἶναί τί φασι ξύλον ἐξ οὗ τὰ πλοῖα ναυπηγοῦνται·
τοῦτο δὲ ἐν μὲν τῇ θαλάττῃ σχεδὸν ἄσηπτον
εἶναι· διαμένει γὰρ ἔτη πλείω ἢ διακόσια κατα-
βυθιζόμενον· ἐὰν δὲ ἔξω, χρόνιον μὲν θᾶττον δὲ
σήπεται. (θαυμαστὸν δὲ καὶ ἕτερον λέγουσι,
οὐδὲν δὲ πρὸς τὴν σῆψιν. εἶναι γάρ τι δένδρου
ἐξ οὗ τὰς βακτηρίας τέμνεσθαι, καὶ γίνεσθαι
καλὰς σφόδρα ποικιλίαν τινὰ ἐχούσας ὁμοίαν τῷ
τοῦ τίγριος δέρματι· βαρὺ δὲ σφόδρα τὸ ξύλον
τοῦτο· ὅταν δέ τις ῥίψῃ πρὸς στερεώτερον τόπον,
κατάγνυσθαι καθάπερ τὰ κεράμια.)

8  Καὶ τὸ τῆς μυρίκης δὲ ξύλον οὐχ ὥσπερ
ἐνταῦθα ἀσθενές, ἀλλ᾽ ἰσχυρὸν ὥσπερ πρίνινον ἢ
καὶ ἄλλο τι τῶν ἰσχυρῶν. τοῦτο μὲν οὖν ἅμα
μηνύει χώρας τε καὶ ἀέρος διαφορὰς καὶ δυνάμεις.
τῶν δὲ ὁμογενῶν ξύλων, οἷον δρυΐνων πευκίνων,
ὅταν ταριχεύωνται—ταριχεύουσι γὰρ οὐκ ἐν ἴσῳ
βάθει πάντα δύοντες τῆς θαλάττης, ἀλλὰ τὰ μὲν
πρὸς αὐτῇ τῇ γῇ, τὰ δὲ μικρὸν ἀνωτέρω, τὰ δ᾽ ἐν
πλείονι βάθει· πάντων δὲ τὰ πρὸς τὴν ῥίζαν
θᾶττον δύεται καθ᾽ ὕδατος, κἂν ἐπινῇ μᾶλλον
ῥέπει κάτω.

V. Ἔστι δὲ τὰ μὲν εὔεργα τῶν ξύλων, τὰ δὲ
δύσεργα· εὔεργα μὲν τὰ μαλακά, καὶ πάντων

---

¹ Plin. 16. 221 ; cf. 4. 7. 7.
² Teak. See Index App. (22).
³ Calamander-wood. See Index App. (23).

[1] In the island of Tylos off the Arabian coast they say that there is a kind of wood[2] of which they build their ships, and that in sea-water this is almost proof against decay; for it lasts more than 200 years if it is kept under water, while, if it is kept out of water, it decays sooner, though not for some time. They also tell of another strange thing, though it has nothing to do with the question of decay: they say that there is a certain tree,[3] of which they cut their staves, and that these are very handsome, having a variegated appearance like the tiger's skin; and that this wood is exceedingly heavy, yet when one throws it down on hard ground[4] it breaks in pieces like pottery.

Moreover, the wood of the tamarisk[5] is not weak there, as it is in our country, but is as strong as kermes-oak or any other strong wood. Now this illustrates also the difference in properties caused by country and climate. Moreover when wood, such as that of oak or fir, is soaked in brine—not all being soaked at the same depth in the sea, but some of it close to shore, some rather further out, and some at a still greater depth—[6] in all cases the parts of the tree nearest the root (whichever tree it is) sink quicker under water, and even if they float, have a greater tendency to sink.

*Which kinds of wood are easy and which hard to work. Of the core and its effects.*

V. Some wood is easy to work, some difficult. Those woods which are soft are easy, and especially

[4] πρὸς στερ. τόπον can hardly be sound: ? 'on something harder than itself.'
[5] See Index, μυρίκη (2).      [4] Plin. 16. 186.

μάλιστα φίλυρα· δύσεργα δὲ καὶ τὰ σκληρὰ καὶ
τὰ ὀζώδη καὶ οὖλας ἔχοντα συστροφάς· δυσεργό-
τατα δὲ ἀρία καὶ δρῦς, ὡς δὲ κατὰ μέρος ὁ τῆς
πεύκης ὄζος καὶ τῆς ἐλάτης. ἀεὶ δὲ τῶν ὁμογενῶν
τὸ μαλακώτερον τοῦ σκληροτέρου κρεῖττον·
σαρκωδέστερον γάρ· καὶ εὐθὺ σκοποῦνται τὰς
σανίδας οἱ τέκτονες οὕτως. τὰ δὲ μοχθηρὰ
σιδήρια δύναται τέμνειν τὰ σκληρὰ μᾶλλον τῶν
μαλακῶν· ἀνίησι γὰρ ἐν τοῖς μαλακοῖς, ὥσπερ
ἐλέχθη περὶ τῆς φιλύρας, παρακονᾷ δὲ μάλιστα
τὰ σκληρά· δι' ὃ καὶ οἱ σκυτοτόμοι ποιοῦνται
τοὺς πίνακας ἀχράδος.

2 Μήτραν δὲ πάντα μὲν ἔχειν φασὶν οἱ τέκτονες
φανερὰν δ' εἶναι μάλιστα ἐν τῇ ἐλάτῃ· φαίνεσθαι
γὰρ οἷον φλοιώδη τινὰ τὴν σύνθεσιν αὐτῆς τῶν
κύκλων. ἐν ἐλάᾳ δὲ καὶ πύξῳ καὶ τοῖς τοιούτοις
οὐχ ὁμοίως· δι' ὃ καὶ οὔ φασί τινες ἔχειν τῇ
δυνάμει πύξον καὶ ἐλάαν· ἥκιστα γὰρ ἕλκεσθαι
ταῦτα τῶν ξύλων. ἔστι δὲ τὸ ἕλκεσθαι τὸ συμ-
περιΐστασθαι κινουμένης τῆς μήτρας. ζῇ γὰρ
ὡς ἔοικεν ἐπὶ χρόνον πολύν· δι' ὃ πανταχόθεν
μὲν ἅμα μάλιστα δ' ἐκ τῶν θυρωμάτων ἐξαιροῦ-
σιν, ὅπως ἀστραβῆ ᾖ· καὶ διὰ τοῦτο σχίζουσιν.

3 Ἄτοπον δ' ἂν δόξειεν ὅτι ἐν μὲν τοῖς ξύλοις
τοῖς στρογγύλοις ἄλυπος ἡ μήτρα καὶ ἀκίνητος,
ἐν δὲ τοῖς παρακινηθεῖσιν, ἐὰν μὴ ὅλως ἐξαιρεθῇ,

¹ 5. 3. 3.
² τὰ σκληρὰ conj. Sch. from G (?); ταῦτα P₂Ald.H.
³ ἔχειν conj. Sch.; ἔχει ᾖ Ald.H.
⁴ ἐλάαν conj. Scal. from G; ἐλάτην Ald.H.
⁵ i.e. and this happens less in woods which have little
core.    ⁶ ἅμα (? = ὁμοίως) MSS.; αὐτὴν conj. W.

that of the lime; those are difficult which are hard and have many knots and a compact and twisted grain. The most difficult woods are those of *aria* (holm-oak) and oak, and the knotty parts of the fir and silver-fir. The softer part of any given tree is always better than the harder, since it is fleshier: and carpenters can thus at once mark the parts suitable for planks. Inferior iron tools can cut hard wood better than soft: for on soft wood tools lose their edge, as was said [1] in speaking of the lime, while hard woods [2] actually sharpen it: wherefore cobblers make their strops of wild pear.

Carpenters say that all woods have [3] a core, but that it is most plainly seen in the silver-fir, in which one can detect a sort of bark-like character in the rings. In olive box and such woods this is not so obvious; wherefore they say that box and olive [4] lack this tendency; for that these woods are less apt to 'draw' than any others. 'Drawing' is the closing in of the wood as the core is disturbed.[5] For since the core remains alive, it appears, for a long time, it is always removed from any article whatever made of this wood,[6] but especially from doors,[7] so that they may not warp [8]: and that is why the wood is split.[9]

It might seem strange that in 'round' [10] timber the core does no harm and so is left undisturbed, while in wood whose texture has been interfered with,[11] unless it is taken out altogether, it causes

---

[7] θυρωμάτων conj. Sch.; γυρωμάτων Ald. *cf.* 4. 1. 2; Plin. 16. 225, *abietem valvarum paginis aptissimam.*

[3] ἀστραβῆ ἢ conj. Dalec.; ἀστραβῆ UMVAld.

[9] *i.e.* to extract the core.   [10] See below, §5.

[11] παρακινηθεῖσι, *i.e.* by splitting or sawing. πελεκηθεῖσι conj. W.

447

κινεῖ καὶ παραστρέφει· μᾶλλον γὰρ εἰκὸς γυμνωθεῖσαν ἀποθνήσκειν. ὅμως δὲ οἵ γε ἱστοὶ καὶ
αἱ κεραῖαι ἐξαιρεθείσης ἀχρεῖοι. τοῦτο δὲ κατὰ
συμβεβηκός, ὅτι χιτῶνας ἔχει πλείους, ἰσχυρότατον δὲ καὶ λεπτότατον δὲ τὸν ἔσχατον, ξηρότα-
τον γάρ, καὶ τοὺς ἄλλους ἀνὰ λόγον. ὅταν οὖν
4 σχισθῇ, περιαιρεῖται τὰ ξηρότατα. εἰ δ' ἡ μήτρα
διὰ τὸ ξηρὸν σκεπτέον. διαστρέφει δὲ ἑλκομένη
τὰ ξύλα καὶ ἐν τοῖς σχιστοῖς καὶ πριστοῖς, ὅταν
μὴ ὡς δεῖ πρίωσι· δεῖ γὰρ ὀρθὴν τὴν πρίσιν εἶναι
καὶ μὴ πλαγίαν. οἷον οὔσης τῆς μήτρας ἐφ' ἣν
τὸ α, μὴ παρὰ τὴν βγ τέμνειν, ἀλλὰ παρὰ τὴν
βδ. φθείρεσθαι γὰρ οὕτω φασίν, ἐκείνως δὲ ζῆν.
ὅτι δὲ πᾶν ξύλον ἔχει μήτραν ἐκ τούτων οἴονται·
φανερὸν γάρ ἐστι καὶ τὰ μὴ δοκοῦντα πάντ' ἔχειν,
οἷον πύξον λωτὸν πρῖνον. σημεῖον δέ· τοὺς γὰρ
στρόφιγγας τῶν θυρῶν τῶν πολυτελῶν ποιοῦσι
μὲν ἐκ τούτων, συγγράφονται δὲ οἱ ἀρχιτέκτονες
οὕτως <μὴ> ἐκ μήτρας. ταὐτὸ δὲ τοῦτο σημεῖον
καὶ ὅτι πᾶσα μήτρα ἕλκεται, καὶ αἱ τῶν σκληρο-
5 τάτων, ἃς δή τινες καρδίας καλοῦσι. παντὸς δὲ

¹ And so cause no trouble.
² cf. 5. 1. 6. πλείους conj. Sch. from G ; ἄλλους Ald. H.
³ Text probably defective ; ? insert ἐξηρέθη after ξηρόν.
⁴ The figure would seem to be

disturbance and warping: it were rather to be
expected that it would die[1] when exposed. Yet
it is a fact that masts and yard-arms are useless,
if it has been removed from the wood of which
they are made. This is however an accidental exception, because the wood in question has several
coats,[2] of which the strongest and also thinnest is
the outermost, since this is the driest, while
the other coats are strong and thin in proportion
to their nearness to the outermost. If therefore
the wood be split, the driest parts are necessarily
stripped off. Whether however in the other case
the object of removing the core is to secure dryness
is matter for enquiry.[5] However, when the core
'draws,' it twists the wood, whether it has been
split or sawn, if the sawing is improperly performed:
the saw-cut should be made straight and not slantwise. 'Thus, if the core be represented by the
line *A*, the cut must be made along the line *BD*,
and not along the line *BC*: for in that case, they
say, the core will be destroyed, while, if cut in
the other way, it will live. For this reason men
think that every wood has a core: for it is clear
that those which do not seem to possess one nevertheless have it, as box nettle-tree kermes-oak : a proof
of this is the fact that men make of these woods the
pivots[5] of expensive doors, and accordingly[6] the
headcraftsmen specify that wood with a core shall
not[7] be used. This is also a proof that any core
'draws,' even those of the hardest woods, which
some call the heart. In almost every wood, even

---

[5] *cf.* 5. 3. 5. στρόφιγξ here at least probably means 'pivot
and socket.'
[6] οὕτως Ald. H.; αὐτοὺς conj. W.      [7] μὴ add. W.

ὡς εἰπεῖν ξύλου σκληροτάτη καὶ μανοτάτη ἡ
μήτρα, καὶ αὐτῆς τῆς ἐλάτης· μανοτάτη μὲν οὖν,
ὅτι τὰς ἶνας ἔχει καὶ διὰ πολλοῦ καὶ τὸ σαρκῶδες
τὸ ἀνὰ μέσον πολύ· σκληροτάτη δέ, ὅτι καὶ
αἱ ἶνες σκληρόταται καὶ τὸ σαρκῶδες· δι᾽ ὃ καὶ
οἱ ἀρχιτέκτονες συγγράφονται παραιρεῖν τὰ πρὸς
τὴν μήτραν, ὅπως λάβωσι τοῦ ξύλου τὸ πυκνότα-
τον καὶ μαλακώτατον.

8   Τῶν δὲ ξύλων τὰ μὲν σχιστὰ τὰ δὲ πελεκητὰ
τὰ δὲ στρογγύλα· σχιστὰ μέν, ὅσα διαιροῦντες
κατὰ τὸ μέσον πρίζουσι· πελεκητὰ δέ, ὅσων
ἀποπελεκῶσι τὰ ἔξω· στρογγύλα δὲ δῆλον ὅτι
τὰ ὅλως ἄψαυστα. τούτων δὲ τὰ σχιστὰ μὲν
ὅλως ἀρραγῆ διὰ τὸ γυμνωθεῖσαν τὴν μήτραν
ξηραίνεσθαι καὶ ἀποθνήσκειν· τὰ δὲ πελεκητὰ
καὶ τὰ στρογγύλα ῥήγνυται· μᾶλλον δὲ πολὺ
τὰ στρογγύλα διὰ τὸ ἐναπειλῆφθαι τὴν μήτραν·
οὐδὲν γὰρ ὅτι τῶν ἀπάντων οὐ ῥήγνυται. τοῖς
δὲ λωτίνοις καὶ τοῖς ἄλλοις οἷς εἰς τοὺς στρόφιγγας χρῶνται πρὸς τὸ μὴ ῥήγνυσθαι βόλβιτον
περιπλάττουσιν, ὅπως ἀναξηρανθῇ καὶ διαπνευσθῇ
κατὰ μικρὸν ἡ ἐκ τῆς μήτρας ὑγρότης. ἡ μὲν οὖν
μήτρα τοιαύτην ἔχει δύναμιν.

VI. Βάρος δὲ ἐνεγκεῖν ἰσχυρὰ καὶ ἡ ἐλάτη
καὶ ἡ πεύκη πλάγιαι τιθέμεναι· οὐδὲν γὰρ ἐν-

---

¹ ξύλου σκληροτάτη conj. Sch. from G ; ξύλον σκληρότατον
UMV; so Ald. omitting καί.
² ἀποπελεκῶσι conj. Sch.; ἀποπλέκωσι UM ; ἀποπλέκουσι
Ald.; ἀποπελέκουσι mBas.   ³ cf. C.P. 5. 17. 2.

in that of the silver-fir, the core is the hardest part,[1] and the part which has the least fibrous texture :—it is least fibrous because the fibres are far apart and there is a good deal of fleshy matter between them, while it is the hardest part because the fibres and the fleshy substance are the hardest parts. Wherefore the headcraftsmen specify that the core and the parts next it are to be removed, that they may secure the closest and softest part of the wood.

Timber is either 'cleft,' 'hewn,' or 'round': it is called 'cleft,' when in making division they saw it down the middle, 'hewn' when they hew off[2] the outer parts, while 'round' clearly signifies wood which has not been touched at all. Of these, 'cleft' wood[3] is not at all liable to split, because the core when exposed dries and dies : but 'hewn' and 'round' wood are apt to split, and especially 'round' wood, because the core is included in it : no kind of timber indeed is altogether incapable of splitting. The wood of the nettle-tree and other kinds which are used for making pivots for doors are smeared[4] with cow-dung to prevent their splitting : the object being that the moisture due to the core may be gradually dried up[5] and evaporated. Such are the natural properties of the core.

*Which woods can best support weight.*

VI. [6] For bearing weight silver-fir and fir are strong woods, when set slantwise[7] : for they do not give like

[4] περιπλάττουσι conj. Sch. from G ; περιπάττουσιν Ald. H. Plin. 16. 222. [5] ἀναξηρανθῇ conj. Sch.; ἀναξηραίῃ Ald. H.
[6] Plin. 16. 222-224.
[7] e.g. as a strut. πλάγιαι conj. Sch. from Plin. l.c.: ἁπαλαὶ Ald. H.

451

διδόασιν, ὥσπερ ἡ δρῦς καὶ τὰ γεώδη, ἀλλ' ἀντω-
θοῦσι· σημεῖον δὲ ὅτι οὐδέποτε ῥήγνυνται, καθάπερ
ἐλάα καὶ δρῦς, ἀλλὰ πρότερον σήπονται καὶ
ἄλλως ἀπαυδῶσιν. ἰσχυρὸν δὲ καὶ ὁ φοῖνιξ·
ἀνάπαλιν γὰρ ἡ κάμψις ἢ τοῖς ἄλλοις γίνεται·
τὰ μὲν γὰρ εἰς τὰ κάτω κάμπτεται, ὁ δὲ φοῖνιξ
εἰς τὰ ἄνω. φασὶ δὲ καὶ τὴν πεύκην καὶ τὴν
ἐλάτην ἀντωθεῖν. τὸ δὲ τῆς Εὐβοϊκῆς καρύας,
γίνεται γὰρ μέγα καὶ χρῶνται πρὸς τὴν ἔρεψιν,
ὅταν μέλλῃ ῥήγνυσθαι ψοφεῖν ὥστε προαισθάν-
εσθαι πρότερον· ὅπερ καὶ ἐν Ἀντάνδρῳ συνέ-
πεσεν ἐν τῷ βαλανείῳ καὶ πάντες ἐξεπήδησαν.
ἰσχυρὸν δὲ καὶ τὸ τῆς συκῆς πλὴν εἰς ὀρθόν.

2   Ἡ δὲ ἐλάτη μάλιστα ὡς εἰπεῖν ἰσχυρόν. πρὸς
δὲ τὰς τῶν τεκτόνων χρείας ἐχέκολλον μὲν μάλιστα ἡ πεύκη διά τε τὴν μανότητα καὶ τὴν
εὐθυπορίαν· οὐδὲ γὰρ ὅλως οὐδὲ ῥήγνυσθαί φασιν
ἐὰν κολληθῇ. εὐτορνότατον δὲ φιλύκη, καὶ ἡ
λευκότης ὥσπερ ἡ τοῦ κηλάστρου. τῶν δὲ ἄλλων
ἡ φίλυρα· τὸ γὰρ ὅλον εὔεργον, ὥσπερ ἐλέχθη,
διὰ μαλακότητα. εὔκαμπτα δὲ ὡς μὲν ἁπλῶς
εἰπεῖν ὅσα γλίσχρα. διαφέρειν δὲ δοκεῖ συκάμινος καὶ ἐρινεός, δι' ὃ καὶ τὰ ἴκρια καὶ τὰς
στεφάνας καὶ ὅλως ὅσα περὶ τὸν κόσμον ἐκ
τούτων ποιοῦσι.

3   Εὔπριστα δὲ καὶ εὔσχιστα τὰ ἐνικμότερα τῶν

---

[1] i.e. the strut becomes concave or convex respectively.
cf. Xen. Cyr. 7. 5. 11.
[2] i.e. it cannot be used as a strut, or it would 'buckle,'
though it will stand a vertical strain.
[3] Plin. 16. 225.
[4] cf. C.P. 5. 17. 3. εὐθυπορώτατα: εὐθυπορίαν.

oak and other woods which contain mineral matter, but make good resistance. A proof of this is that they never split like olive and oak, but decay first or fail in some other way. Palm-wood is also strong, for it bends the opposite way to other woods : they bend downwards, palm-wood upwards.[1] It is said that fir and silver-fir also have an upward thrust. As to the sweet chestnut, which grows tall and is used for roofing, it is said that when it is about to split, it makes a noise, so that men are forewarned : this occurred once at Antandros at the baths, and all those present rushed out. Fig-wood is also strong, but only when set upright.[2]

*Of the woods best suited for the carpenter's various purposes.*

[3] The wood of the silver-fir may be called the strongest of all. But for the carpenter's purposes fir best takes glue because of its open texture and the straightness of its pores[4]; for they say that it never by any chance comes apart when it is glued. Alaternus[5] is the easiest wood for turning, and its whiteness is like that of the holly. Of the rest lime is the easiest, the whole tree, as was said, being easy to work because of the softness of the wood. In general those woods which are tough are easy to bend. The mulberry and the wild fig seem to be specially so; wherefore they make of these theatre-seats,[6] the hoops of garlands, and, in general, things for ornament.

[7] Woods which have a fair amount of moisture in them are easier to saw or split than those which

[5] *cf.* 5. 7. 7.
[6] Rendering doubtful. ἴκρια has probably here some unknown meaning, on which the sense of κόσμον depends.
[7] Plin. 16. 227.

πάμπαν ξηρῶν· τὰ μὲν γὰρ παύονται, τὰ δὲ
ἵστανται· τὰ δὲ χλωρὰ λίαν συμμύει καὶ ἐνέχε-
ται ἐν τοῖς ὀδοῦσι τὰ πρίσματα καὶ ἐμπλάττει,
δι' ὃ καὶ παραλλάττουσιν ἀλλήλων τοὺς ὀδόντας
ἵνα ἐξάγηται. ἔστι δὲ καὶ δυστρυπητότερα τὰ
λίαν χλωρά· βραδέως γὰρ ἀναφέρεται τὰ ἐκτρυ-
πήματα διὰ τὸ βαρέα εἶναι· τῶν δὲ ξηρῶν ταχέως
καὶ εὐθὺς ὁ ἀὴρ ἀναθερμαινόμενος ἀναδίδωσι·
πάλιν δὲ τὰ λίαν ξηρὰ διὰ τὴν σκληρότητα
δύσπριστα· καθάπερ γὰρ ὄστρακον συμβαίνει
πρίειν, δι' ὃ καὶ τρυπῶντες ἐπιβρέχουσιν.

4 Εὐπελεκητότερα δὲ καὶ εὐτορυότερα καὶ εὐξο-
ώτερα τὰ χλωρά· προσκάθηταί τε γὰρ τὸ τορνευ-
τήριον μᾶλλον καὶ οὐκ ἀποπηδᾷ. καὶ ἡ πελέκησις
τῶν μαλακωτέρων ῥᾴων, καὶ ἡ ξέσις δὲ ὁμοίως καὶ
ἔτι λειοτέρα. ἰσχυρότατον δὲ καὶ ἡ κράνεια, τῶν
δὲ ἄλλων οὐχ ἥκιστα ἡ πτελέα, δι' ὃ καὶ τοὺς
στροφέας, ὥσπερ ἐλέχθη, ταῖς θύραις πτελεΐνους
ποιοῦσιν. ὑγρότατον δὲ μελία καὶ ὀξύη· καὶ γὰρ
τὰ κλινάρια τὰ ἐνδιδόντα ἐκ τούτων.

VII. Ὅλως δὲ πρὸς ποῖα τῆς ὕλης ἑκάστη
χρησίμη καὶ ποῖα ναυπηγήσιμος καὶ οἰκοδομική,
πλείστη γὰρ αὕτη ἡ χρεία καὶ ἐν μεγίστοις,
πειρατέον εἰπεῖν, ἀφορίζοντα καθ' ἕκαστον τὸ
χρήσιμον.

Ἐλάτη μὲν οὖν καὶ πεύκη καὶ κέδρος ὡς ἁπλῶς

---

¹ παύονται can hardly be right : Plin. *l.c.* seems to have
had a fuller text.
² ἐμπλάττει : *cf. de Sens.* 66.

are altogether dry: for the latter give,[1] while the former resist. Wood which is too green closes up again when sawn, and the sawdust catches in the saw's teeth and clogs[2] them; wherefore the teeth of the saw are set alternate ways, to get rid of the sawdust. Wood which is too green is also harder to bore holes in; for the auger's dust is only brought up slowly, because it is heavy; while, if the wood is dry, the air gets warmed by the boring and brings it up readily and at once. On the other hand, wood which is over dry[3] is hard to saw because of its hardness: for it is like sawing through earthenware; wherefore they wet the auger when using it.

However green wood is easier to work with the axe the chisel or the plane; for the chisel gets a better hold and does not slip off. Again softer woods are easier for the axe and for smoothing,[4] and also a better polished surface is obtained. The cornelian cherry is also a very strong wood, and among the rest elm-wood is the strongest; wherefore, as was said,[5] they make the 'hinges' for doors of elm-wood. Manna-ash and beech have very moist wood, for of these they make elastic bedsteads.

*Of the woods used in ship-building.*

VII. Next we must endeavour to say in a general way, distinguishing the several uses, for which purposes each kind of timber is serviceable, which is of use for ship-building, which for house-building: for these uses extend far and are important.

Now silver-fir, fir and Syrian cedar[6] are, generally

[3] τὰ λίαν ξηρὰ conj. St.: λεῖα καὶ ξηρὰ Ald. H.
[4] Sc. with the carpenter's axe.
[5] 5. 3. 5.   [6] See Index.

εἰπεῖν ναυπηγήσιμα· τὰς μὲν γὰρ τριήρεις καὶ τὰ
μακρὰ πλοῖα ἐλάτινα ποιοῦσι διὰ κουφότητα, τὰ
δὲ στρογγύλα πεύκινα διὰ τὸ ἀσαπές· ἔνιοι δὲ καὶ
τὰς τριήρεις διὰ τὸ μὴ εὐπορεῖν ἐλάτης. οἱ δὲ
κατὰ Συρίαν καὶ Φοινίκην ἐκ κέδρου· σπανίζουσι
γὰρ καὶ πεύκης. οἱ δ' ἐν Κύπρῳ πίτυος· ταύτην
γὰρ ἡ νῆσος ἔχει καὶ δοκεῖ κρείττων εἶναι τῆς
2 πεύκης. καὶ τὰ μὲν ἄλλα ἐκ τούτων· τὴν δὲ
τρόπιν τριήρει μὲν δρυΐνην, ἵνα ἀντέχῃ πρὸς τὰς
νεωλκίας, ταῖς δὲ ὁλκάσι πευκίνην· ὑποτιθέασι δ'
ἔτι καὶ δρυΐνην ἐπὰν νεωλκῶσι, ταῖς δ' ἐλάττοσιν
ὀξυΐνην· καὶ ὅλως ἐκ τούτου τὸ χέλυσμα.

Οὐχ ἅπτεται δὲ οὐδὲ κατὰ τὴν κόλλησιν
ὁμοίως τὸ δρύϊνον τῶν πευκίνων καὶ ἐλατίνων· τὰ
μὲν γὰρ πυκνὰ τὰ δὲ μανά, καὶ τὰ μὲν ὅμοια τὰ δ'
οὔ. δεῖ δὲ ὁμοιοπαθῆ εἶναι τὰ μέλλοντα συμφύεσθαι καὶ μὴ ἐναντία, καθαπερανεὶ λίθον καὶ
ξύλον.

3 Ἡ δὲ τορνεία τοῖς μὲν πλοίοις γίνεται συκαμίνου μελίας πτελέας πλατάνου· γλισχρότητα
γὰρ ἔχειν δεῖ καὶ ἰσχύν. χειρίστη δὲ ἡ τῆς
πλατάνου· ταχὺ γὰρ σήπεται. ταῖς δὲ τριήρεσιν
ἔνιοι καὶ πιτυΐνας ποιοῦσι διὰ τὸ ἐλαφρόν. τὸ
δὲ στερέωμα, πρὸς ᾧ τὸ χέλυσμα, καὶ τὰς ἐπω-
τίδας, μελίας καὶ συκαμίνου καὶ πτελέας· ἰσχυρὰ

---

¹ τριήρει conj. W.; τριήρη U; τριήρης MV; τριήρεσι Ald.
² ταῖς δ' ἐλάττοσιν ὀξυΐνην conj. W. (τοῖς Sch.); τοῖς μὲν
ἐλάττοσιν ὀξύῃ Ald. cf. Plin. 16. 226.
³ χέλυσμα, a temporary covering for the bottom : so Poll.
and Hesych. explain.

speaking, useful for ship-building; for triremes and
long ships are made of silver-fir, because of its lightness, and merchant ships of fir, because it does not
decay; while some make triremes of it also because
they are ill provided with silver-fir. The people
of Syria and Phoenicia use Syrian cedar, since they
cannot obtain much fir either; while the people of
Cyprus use Aleppo pine, since their island provides
this and it seems to be superior to their fir. Most
parts are made of these woods; but the keel for a
trireme[1] is made of oak, that it may stand the hauling; and for merchantmen it is made of fir. However they put an oaken keel under this when they
are hauling, or for smaller vessels a keel of beech;[2]
and the sheathing[3] is made entirely of this wood.

[4](However oak-wood does not join well with glue
on to fir or silver-fir; for the one is of close, the
other of open grain, the one is uniform, the other
not so; whereas things which are to be made into
one piece should be of similar character, and not of
opposite character. like wood and stone.)

The work of bentwood[5] for vessels is made of
mulberry manna-ash elm or plane; for it must be
tough and strong. That made of plane-wood is the
worst, since it soon decays. For triremes some make
such parts of Aleppo pine because of its lightness.
The cutwater,[6] to which the sheathing is attached,[7]
and the catheads are made of manna-ash mulberry

[4] This sentence is out of place; its right place is perhaps
at the end of § 4.
[5] τορνεία; but the word is perhaps corrupt: one would
expect the name of some part of the vessel.
[6] στερέωμα: apparently the fore part of the keel; = στεῖρα.
[7] πρὸς ᾧ τὸ χέλυσμα conj. W. after Scal.: πρόσω· τὸ σχέλυσμα
Ald. (σχέλομα M, χέλυσμα U) πρόσω· τὸ δὲ χέλυσμα mBas.

γὰρ δεῖ ταῦτ' εἶναι. ναυπηγήσιμος μὲν οὖν ὕλη
σχεδὸν αὕτη.

4 Οἰκοδομικὴ δὲ πολλῷ πλείων, ἐλάτη τε καὶ
πεύκη καὶ κέδρος, ἔτι κυπάριττος δρῦς καὶ ἄρ-
κευθος· ὡς δ' ἁπλῶς εἰπεῖν πᾶσα χρησίμη πλὴν
εἴ τις ἀσθενὴς πάμπαν· οὐκ εἰς ταὐτὸ γὰρ πᾶσαι,
καθάπερ οὐδ' ἐπὶ τῆς ναυπηγίας. αἱ δ' ἄλλαι
πρὸς τὰ ἴδια τῶν τεχνῶν, οἷον σκεύη καὶ ὄργανα
καὶ εἴ τι τοιοῦτον ἕτερον. πρὸς πλεῖστα δὲ σχεδὸν
ἡ ἐλάτη παρέχεται χρείαν· καὶ γὰρ πρὸς τοὺς
πίνακας τοὺς γραφομένους. τεκτονικῇ μὲν οὖν ἡ
παλαιοτάτη κρατίστη, ἐὰν ᾖ ἀσαπής· εὐθετεῖ γὰρ
ὡς εἰπεῖν πᾶσι χρῆσθαι· ναυπηγικῇ δὲ διὰ τὴν
κάμψιν ἐνικμοτέρᾳ ἀναγκαῖον· ἐπεὶ πρός γε τὴν
κόλλησιν ἡ ξηροτέρα συμφέρει. ἵσταται γὰρ
καινὰ τὰ ναυπηγούμενα καὶ ὅταν συμπαγῇ καθ-
ελκυσθέντα συμμύει καὶ στέγει, πλὴν ἐὰν μὴ
παντάπασιν ἐξικμασθῇ· τότε δὲ οὐ δέχεται κόλλησιν ἢ οὐχ ὁμοίως.

5 Δεῖ δὲ καὶ καθ' ἕκαστον λαμβάνειν εἰς ποῖα
χρήσιμός ἐστιν. ἐλάτη μὲν οὖν καὶ πεύκη,
καθάπερ εἴρηται, καὶ πρὸς ναυπηγίαν καὶ πρὸς

---

[1] ἐλάτη . . . ἄρκευθος conj. W.; ἐλάτη τε καὶ πεύκη καὶ κέδρος
ἔτι κυπάριττος δρῦς πεύκη καὶ κέδρος ἄρκευθος U; ἐλάτη τε καὶ
πεύκη καὶ κέδρος καὶ ἄρκευθος Ald.H.: so also MV, omitting
καὶ before ἄρκ.

[2] ὡς δ' ἁπλῶς conj. Sch.; ἁπλῶς δ' ὡς Ald.

[3] καινὰ conj. Sch.; καὶ νῦν Ald.

[4] συμπαγῇ conj. W., which he renders 'when it has been
glued together'; συμπίῃ Ald. G's reading was evidently
different.

458

and elm; for these parts must be strong.     Such
then is the timber used in ship-building.

*Of the woods used in house-building.*

For house-building a much greater variety is
used, silver-fir fir and prickly cedar; also cypress
oak and Phoenician cedar.[1]  In fact, to speak
generally,[2] any wood is here of service, unless it is
altogether weak : for there are various purposes for
which different woods are serviceable, just as there
are in ship-building.  While other woods are serviceable for special articles belonging to various crafts,
such as furniture tools and the like, the wood of
silver-fir is of use for almost more purposes than any
other wood; for it is even used for painters' tablets.
For carpentry the oldest wood is the best, provided
that it has not decayed ; for it is convenient for
almost anyone to use.  But for ship-building, where
bending is necessary, one must use wood which
contains more moisture (though, where glue is to be
used, drier wood is convenient).  For timber-work
for ships is set to stand when it is newly [3] made :
then, when it has become firmly united,[4] it is
dragged down to the water, and then it closes up
and becomes watertight,—unless [5] all the moisture
has been dried out of it, in which case it will not
take the glue, or will not take it so well.

*Of the uses of the wood of particular trees.*

But we must consider for what purposes [6] each
several wood is serviceable.  Silver-fir and fir, as has
been said, are suitable both for ship-building house-

[5] πλὴν ἐὰν μὴ conj. W.; π. ἐάν τε M ; π. ἐάν γε Ald.
[6] *i.e.* apart from ship-building and house-building, in
which *several* woods are used.

459

οἰκοδομίαν καὶ ἔτι πρὸς ἄλλα τῶν ἔργων, εἰς
πλείω δὲ ἡ ἐλάτη. πίτυϊ δὲ χρῶνται μὲν εἰς
ἄμφω καὶ οὐχ ἧττον εἰς ναυπηγίαν, οὐ μὴν ἀλλὰ
ταχὺ διασήπεται. δρῦς δὲ πρὸς οἰκοδομίαν καὶ
πρὸς ναυπηγίαν ἔτι τε πρὸς τὰ κατὰ γῆς κατορυττόμενα. φίλυρα δὲ πρὸς τὰ σανιδώματα τῶν
μακρῶν πλοίων καὶ πρὸς κιβώτια καὶ πρὸς τὴν
τῶν μέτρων κατασκευήν. ἔχει δὲ καὶ τὸν φλοιὸν
χρήσιμον πρός τε τὰ σχοινία καὶ πρὸς τὰς κίστας·
ποιοῦσι γὰρ ἐξ αὐτῆς.

6 Σφένδαμνός τε καὶ ζυγία πρὸς κλινοπηγίαν
καὶ πρὸς τὰ ζυγὰ τῶν λοφούρων. μίλος δὲ εἰς
παρακολλήματα κιβώτοις καὶ ὑποβάθροις καὶ
ὅλως τοῖς τοιούτοις. πρῖνος δὲ πρὸς ἄξονας ταῖς
μονοστρόφοις ἁμάξαις καὶ εἰς ζυγὰ λύραις καὶ
ψαλτηρίοις. ὀξύη δὲ πρὸς ἁμαξοπηγίαν καὶ
διφροπηγίαν τὴν εὐτελῆ. πτελέα δὲ πρὸς θυρο-
πηγίαν καὶ γαλεάγρας· χρῶνται δὲ καὶ εἰς τὰ
ἁμαξικὰ μετρίως. πηδὸς δὲ εἰς ἄξονάς τε ταῖς
ἁμάξαις καὶ εἰς ἕλκηθρα τοῖς ἀρότροις. ἀνδράχλη
δὲ ταῖς γυναιξὶν εἰς τὰ περὶ τοὺς ἱστούς. ἄρκευθος δὲ εἰς τεκτονίας καὶ εἰς τὰ ὑπαίθρια καὶ
εἰς τὰ κατορυττόμενα κατὰ γῆς διὰ τὸ ἀσαπές.

7 ὡσαύτως δὲ καὶ ἡ Εὐβοϊκὴ καρύα, καὶ πρός γε
τὴν κατόρυξιν ἔτι μᾶλλον ἀσαπής. πύξῳ δὲ
χρῶνται μὲν πρὸς ἔνια, οὐ μὴν ἀλλ' ἥ γε ἐν τῷ
Ὀλύμπῳ γινομένη διὰ τὸ βραχεῖά τε εἶναι καὶ
ὀζώδης ἀχρεῖος. τερμίνθῳ δὲ οὐδὲν χρῶνται

---

¹ κίστας : cf. 3. 13. 1 ; perhaps 'hampers,' cf. 5. 7. 7.
² παρακολλήματα : lit. 'things glued on.'
³ Plin. 16. 229.
⁴ ταῖς μονοστρόφοις ἁμάξαις : or, perhaps, 'the wheels of

building and also for other kinds of work, but silver-
fir is of use for more purposes than fir. Aleppo pine
is used for both kinds of building, but especially for
ship-building, yet it soon rots. Oak is used for
house-building, for ship-building, and also for underground work; lime for the deck-planks of long ships,
for boxes, and for the manufacture of measures; its
bark is also useful for ropes and writing-cases,[1] for
these are sometimes made of it.

Maple and *zygia* are used for making beds
and the yokes of beasts of burden: yew for the
ornamental work attached[2] to chests and footstools
and the like: kermes-oak[3] for the axles of wheel-
barrows[4] and the cross-bars of lyres and psalteries:
beech for making waggons and cheap carts: elm
for making doors and weasel-traps, and to some
extent it is also used for waggon work: *pedos*[5] for
waggon-axles and the stocks of ploughs: andrachne
is used for women for parts of the loom: Phoenician
cedar for carpenters' work[6] and for work which is
either to be exposed to the air or buried underground,
because it does not decay. Similarly the sweet
chestnut is used, and it is even less likely to decay
if it is used for underground work. Box is used for
some purposes; however that which grows on
Mount Olympus[7] is useless, because only short pieces
can be obtained and the wood[8] is full of knots.
Terebinth is not used,[9] except the fruit and the resin.

carts with solid wheels.' ταῖς conj. Sch.; τε καὶ UMV; τε καὶ
ιονοστρόφους ἁμάξας Ald.
[5] πηδὸς (with varying accent) MSS.: probably = πάδος. 4. 1.
3; πύξος Ald., but see §7.
[6] τεκτορίας can hardly be right.        [7] *cf.* 3. 15. 5.
[8] *cf.* 1. 8. 2, of box in general; Plin. 16. 71.
[9] Inconsistent with 5. 3. 2.

πλὴν τῷ καρπῷ καὶ τῇ ῥητίνῃ. οὐδὲ φιλύκῃ
πλὴν τοῖς προβάτοις· ἀεὶ γάρ ἐστι δασεῖα. τῇ
δὲ ἀφάρκῃ εἰς χάρακάς τε καὶ τὸ καίειν. κη-
λιάστρῳ δὲ καὶ σημύδᾳ πρὸς βακτηρίας. ἔνιοι δὲ
καὶ δάφνῃ· τὰς γὰρ γεροντικὰς καὶ κούφας ταύτης
ποιοῦσιν. ἰτέᾳ δὲ πρός τε τὰς ἀσπίδας καὶ
τὰς κίστας καὶ τὰ κανᾶ καὶ τἆλλα. προσανα-
λαβεῖν δέ ἐστι καὶ τῶν ἄλλων ἕκαστον ὁμοίως.

8    Διῄρηται δὲ καὶ πρὸς τὰ τεκτονικὰ τῶν ὀργά-
νων ἕκαστα κατὰ τὴν χρείαν· οἶον σφυρίον μὲν
καὶ τερέτριον ἄριστα μὲν γίνεται κοτίνου· χρῶνται
δὲ καὶ πυξίνοις καὶ πτελεΐνοις καὶ μελεΐνοις· τὰς
δὲ μεγάλας σφύρας πιτυΐνας ποιοῦσιν. ὁμοίως
δὲ καὶ τῶν ἄλλων ἕκαστον ἔχει τινὰ τάξιν. καὶ
ταῦτα μὲν αἱ χρεῖαι διαιροῦσιν.

VIII. Ἑκάστη δὲ τῆς ὕλης, ὥσπερ καὶ πρότερον
ἐλέχθη, διαφέρει κατὰ τοὺς τόπους· ἔνθα μὲν γὰρ
λωτὸς ἔνθα δὲ κέδρος γίνεται θαυμαστή, καθάπερ
καὶ περὶ Συρίαν· ἐν Συρίᾳ γὰρ ἔν τε τοῖς ὄρεσι
διαφέροντα γίνεται τὰ δένδρα τῆς κέδρου καὶ τῷ
ὕψει καὶ τῷ πάχει· τηλικαῦτα γάρ ἐστιν ὥστ᾽
ἔνια μὲν μὴ δύνασθαι τρεῖς ἄνδρας περιλαμβάνειν·
ἔν τε τοῖς παραδείσοις ἔτι μείζω καὶ καλλίω.
φαίνεται δὲ καὶ ἐάν τις ἐᾷ καὶ μὴ τέμνῃ τόπον
οἰκεῖον ἔκαστον ἔχον γίνεσθαι θαυμαστὸν τῷ
μήκει καὶ πάχει. ἐν Κύπρῳ γοῦν οὐκ ἔτεμνον οἱ
βασιλεῖς, ἅμα μὲν τηροῦντες καὶ ταμιευόμενοι, ἅμα

---

¹ Inconsistent with 5. 6. 2.    φιλυρέα conj. Sch.
² καὶ σημύδα conj. Sch.; καὶ μυῖα U ; καὶ μύα Ald.  cf. 3. 14. 4.

[1] Alaternus is only useful for feeding sheep; for it is always leafy. Hybrid arbutus is used for making stakes and for burning: holly and Judas-tree [2] for walking-sticks; some also use bay for these; for of this [3] they make light sticks and sticks for old men. Willow is used for shields hampers baskets and the like. We might in like manner add the several uses of the other woods.

[4] Distinction is also made between woods according as they are serviceable for one or other of the carpenter's tools: thus hammers and gimlets are best made of wild olive, but box elm and manna-ash are also used, while large mallets are made of Aleppo pine. In like manner there is a regular practice about each of the other tools. Such are the differences as to the uses of various woods.

*Of the localities in which the best timber grows.*

VIII. Each kind of timber, as was said before, differs according to the place [5] where it grows; in one place nettle-tree, in another the cedar is remarkably fine, for instance in Syria; for in Syria and on its mountains the cedars grow to a surpassing height and thickness: they are sometimes so large that three men cannot embrace the tree. And in the parks they are even larger and finer. It appears that any tree, if it is left alone in its natural position and not cut down, grows to a remarkable height and thickness. For instance in Cyprus the kings used not to cut the trees, both because they took great care of them and hus-

[3] ταύτης conj. H.; ταύτας UMVAld.
[4] Plin. 16. 230.
[5] τόπους conj. Scal. from G; πόδας Ald.

δὲ καὶ διὰ τὸ δυσκόμιστον εἶναι. μῆκος μὲν ἦν
τῶν εἰς τὴν ἑνδεκήρη τὴν Δημητρίου τμηθέντων
τρισκαιδεκαόργυιον, αὐτὰ δὲ τὰ ξύλα τῷ μήκει
θαυμαστὰ καὶ ἄοζα καὶ λεῖα. μέγιστα δὲ καὶ
παρὰ πολὺ τὰ ἐν τῇ Κύρνῳ φασὶν εἶναι· τῶν
γὰρ ἐν τῇ Λατίνῃ καλῶν γινομένων ὑπερβολῇ
καὶ τῶν ἐλατίνων καὶ τῶν πευκίνων—μείζω γὰρ
ταῦτα καὶ καλλίω τῶν Ἰταλικῶν—οὐδὲν εἶναι
2 πρὸς τὰ ἐν τῇ Κύρνῳ. πλεῦσαι γάρ ποτε τοὺς
Ῥωμαίους βουλομένους κατασκευάσασθαι πόλιν
ἐν τῇ νήσῳ πέντε καὶ εἴκοσι ναυσί, καὶ τηλικοῦτον
εἶναι τὸ μέγεθος τῶν δένδρων ὥστε εἰσπλέοντας
εἰς κόλπους τινὰς καὶ λιμένας διασχισθεῖσι τοῖς
ἱστοῖς ἐπικινδυνεῦσαι. καὶ ὅλως δὲ πᾶσαν τὴν
νῆσον δασεῖαν καὶ ὥσπερ ἠγριωμένην τῇ ὕλῃ·
δι᾿ ὃ καὶ ἀποστῆναι τὴν πόλιν οἰκίζειν· διαβάντας
δέ τινας ἀποτεμέσθαι πάμπολυ πλῆθος ἐκ τόπου
βραχέος, ὥστε τηλικαύτην ποιῆσαι σχεδίαν ἣ
ἐχρήσατο πεντήκοντα ἱστίοις· οὐ μὴν ἀλλὰ
διαπεσεῖν αὐτὴν ἐν τῷ πελάγει. Κύρνος μὲν οὖν
εἴτε διὰ τὴν ἄνεσιν εἴτε καὶ τὸ ἔδαφος καὶ τὸν
ἀέρα πολὺ διαφέρει τῶν ἄλλων.
3    Ἡ δὲ τῶν Λατίνων ἔφυδρος πᾶσα· καὶ ἡ μὲν
πεδεινὴ δάφνην ἔχει καὶ μυρρίνους καὶ ὀξύην
θαυμαστήν· τηλικαῦτα γὰρ τὰ μήκη τέμνουσι
ὥστ᾿ εἶναι διανεκῶς τῶν Τυρρηνίδων ὑπὸ τὴν
τρόπιν· ἡ δὲ ὀρεινὴ πεύκην καὶ ἐλάτην. τὸ δὲ

---

[1] Demetrius Poliorcetes. cf. Plut. Demetr. 43 ; Plin. 16.
203.
[2] ἐπικινδυνεῦσαι conj. W.; ἐπὶ τὸν πύκνον Ald.; so U, but
πυκνον.
[3] i.e. against the overhanging trees. ? ἱστίοις, to which
διασχ. is more appropriate.

banded them, and also because the transport of the
timber was difficult. The timbers cut for Demetrius'[1]
ship of eleven banks of oars were thirteen fathoms
long, and the timbers themselves were without
knots and smooth, as well as of marvellous length.
But largest of all, they say, are the trees of
Corsica; for whereas silver-fir and fir grow in
Latium to a very great size, and are taller and
finer than the silver-firs and firs of South Italy,
these are said to be nothing to the trees of Corsica.
For it is told how the Romans once made an expedition to that island with twenty-five ships, wishing
to found a city there: and so great was the size of
the trees that, as they sailed into certain bays and
creeks, they got into difficulties[2] through breaking
their masts.[3] And in general it is said that the
whole island is thickly wooded and, as it were, one
wild forest: wherefore the Romans gave up the idea
of founding their city: however some of them made
an excursion[4] into the island and cleared away a large
quantity of trees from a small area, enough to make
a raft with fifty sails;[5] but this broke up in the open
sea. Corsica then, whether because of its uncultivated
condition or because of its soil and climate, is very
superior in trees to other countries.

The country of the Latins is all well watered;
the lowland part contains bay, myrtle, and wonderful beech: they cut timbers of it of such a size that
they will run the whole length[6] of the keel of a
Tyrrhenian vessel. The hill country produces fir and
silver-fir. The district called by Circe's name is, it

[4] διαβάντας δέ τινας conj. St. from G; διαβάντα δέ τινα Ald. H.
[5] ἣ ἐχρήσατο πεντ. ἱστ. conj. Sch.; ἣ ἐχρήσαντο οἱ Ald. H.
[6] διατενές conj. Sch.; διὰ νεὼς Ald.

Κιρκαῖον καλούμενον εἶναι μὲν ἄκραν ὑψηλήν, δασεῖαν δὲ σφόδρα καὶ ἔχειν δρῦν καὶ δάφνην πολλὴν καὶ μυρρίνους. λέγειν δὲ τοὺς ἐγχωρίους ὡς ἐνταῦθα ἡ Κίρκη κατῴκει καὶ δεικνύναι τὸν τοῦ Ἐλπήνορος τάφον, ἐξ οὗ φύονται μυρρίναι καθάπερ αἱ στεφανώτιδες τῶν ἄλλων ὄντων μεγάλων μυρρίνων. τὸν δὲ τόπον εἶναι καὶ τοῦτον νέαν πρόσθεσιν, καὶ πρότερον μὲν οὖν νῆσον εἶναι τὸ Κιρκαῖον, νῦν δὲ ὑπὸ ποταμῶν τινων προσκεχῶσθαι καὶ εἶναι ἠιόνα. τῆς δὲ νήσου τὸ μέγεθος περὶ ὀγδοήκοντα σταδίους. καὶ τὰ μὲν τῶν τόπων ἴδια πολλὴν ἔχει διαφοράν, ὥσπερ εἴρηται πολλάκις.

IX. Τὸ δὲ καὶ πρὸς τὴν πύρωσιν πῶς ἑκάστη τῆς ὕλης ἔχει λεκτέον ὁμοίως καὶ πειρατέον λαβεῖν. ἄνθρακες μὲν οὖν ἄριστοι γίνονται τῶν πυκνοτάτων, οἷον ἀρίας δρυὸς κομάρου· στερεώτατοι γάρ, ὥστε πλεῖστον χρόνον ἀντέχουσι καὶ μάλιστα ἰσχύουσι· δι' ὃ καὶ ἐν τοῖς ἀργυρείοις τούτοις χρῶνται πρὸς τὴν πρώτην τούτων ἔψησιν. χείριστοι δὲ τούτων οἱ δρύινοι· γεωδέστατοι γάρ· χείρους δὲ καὶ οἱ τῶν πρεσβυτέρων τῶν νέων, καὶ μάλιστα οἱ τῶν γερανδρύων διὰ ταὐτό· ξηρότατοι γάρ, δι' ὃ καὶ πηδῶσι καιόμενοι· δεῖ δὲ ἔνικμον εἶναι.

2 Βέλτιστοι δὲ οἱ τῶν ἐν ἀκμῇ καὶ μάλιστα οἱ

---

[1] cf. Hom. Od. 10. 552 foll., 11. 51–80, 12. 8–15; Plin. 15. 119.

[2] νέαν πρόσθεσιν conj. Sch.; εἰς ἀνδρὸς θέσιν Ald.

is said, a lofty promontory, but very thickly wooded,
producing oak, bay in abundance, and myrtle. There,
according to the natives, dwelt Circe, and they shew
Elpenor's tomb,[1] on which grow myrtles like those
used for garlands, though other kinds of myrtle are
large trees. Further it is said that the district is a
recent addition [2] to the land, and that once this piece
of land was an island, but now the sea has been
silted up by certain streams and it has become
united to the coast, and the size of the 'island' [3]
is about eighty furlongs in circumference. There
is [4] then much difference in trees, as has been said
repeatedly, which is due to the individual character
of particular districts.

*Of the uses of various woods in making fire: charcoal, fuel,
fire-sticks.*

IX. Next we must state in like manner and
endeavour to determine the properties of each kind
of timber in relation to making fire. The best
charcoal is made from the closest wood, such as
*aria* (holm-oak) oak arbutus ; for these are the most
solid, so that they last longest and are the strongest ;
wherefore these are used in silver-mines for the first
smelting of the ore. Worst of the woods mentioned
is oak, since it contains most mineral matter,[5] and
the wood of older trees is inferior to that of the
younger, and for the same reason that of really old
trees [6] is specially bad. For it is very dry, wherefore
it sputters as it burns; whereas wood for charcoal
should contain sap.

The best charcoal comes from trees in their prime,

---

[2] *cf.* Plin. 3. 57.    [4] ἔχει conj. Sch.; εἶναι Ald.
[5] *i.e.* and so makes much ash.    [6] *cf.* 2. 7. 2.

467

H H 2

τῶν κολοβῶν· συμμέτρως γὰρ ἔχουσι τῷ πυκνῷ
καὶ γεώδει καὶ τῷ ὑγρῷ· βελτίους δὲ καὶ ἐκ τῶν
εὐείλων καὶ ξηρῶν καὶ προσβόρρων ἢ ἐκ τῶν
παλισκίων καὶ ὑγρῶν καὶ πρὸς νότον· καὶ εἰ
ἐνικμοτέρας ὕλης, πυκνῆς· ὑγροτέρα γὰρ ἡ πυκνή.
καὶ ὅλως, ὅσα ἡ φύσει ἢ διὰ [τὸν] τόπον ξηρότερον
πυκνότερα, ἐξ ἁπάντων βελτίω διὰ τὴν αὐτὴν
αἰτίαν. χρεία δὲ ἄλλων ἄλλη· πρὸς ἔνια γὰρ
ζητοῦσι τοὺς μαλακούς, οἷον ἐν τοῖς σιδηρείοις
τοὺς τῆς καρύας τῆς Εὐβοϊκῆς, ὅταν ἤδη κεκαυ-
μένος ᾖ, καὶ ἐν τοῖς ἀργυρείοις τοὺς πιτυΐνους.
3 χρῶνται δὲ καὶ αἱ τέχναι τούτοις. ζητοῦσι δὲ
καὶ οἱ χαλκεῖς τοὺς πευκίνους μᾶλλον ἢ δρυΐνους·
καίτοι ἀσθενέστεροι ἀλλ᾽ εἰς τὴν φύσησιν ἀμεί-
νους ὡς ἧσσον καταμαραινόμενοι· ἔστι δὲ ἡ φλὸξ
ὀξυτέρα τούτων. τὸ δὲ ὅλον ὀξυτέρα φλὸξ καὶ
ἡ τούτων καὶ ἡ τῶν ξύλων τῶν μανῶν καὶ κούφων
καὶ ἡ τῶν αὔων· ἡ δ᾽ ἐκ τῶν πυκνῶν καὶ χλωρῶν
νωθεστέρα καὶ παχυτέρα· πασῶν δὲ ὀξυτάτη ἡ
ἐκ τῶν ὑλημάτων· ἄνθρακες δὲ ὅλως οὐ γίνονται
διὰ τὸ μὴ ἔχειν τὸ σωματῶδες.
4 Τέμνουσι δὲ καὶ ζητοῦσι εἰς τὰς ἀνθρακιὰς τὰ

---

¹ κολοβῶν conj. Palm.; κολλάβων U; κολάβων Ald.
² δὲ καὶ ἐκ τῶν conj. W.; δὲ καὶ οἱ τῶν UMVP; δὲ οἱ τῶν Ald.H.
³ καὶ εἰ ἐνικμοτέρας conj. W.; καὶ οἱ ἐνακμοτέρας U; καὶ ἡ ἐν ἀκμητέρας MV; καὶ οἱ ἐν ἀκμητέρας Ald.Bas.Cam. The sense seems to require ὑγροτέρας for ἐνικμοτέρας and ἐνικμοτέρα for ὑγροτέρα. G seems to have had a fuller text.
⁴ i.e. from growing in a damper place. cf. 5. 9. 4.

and especially from trees which have been topped[1] :
for these contain in the right proportion the qualities
of closeness admixture of mineral matter and moisture.
Again better charcoal comes from trees[2] in a sunny dry
position with a north aspect than from those grown in
a shady damp position facing south. Or, if the wood[3]
used contains a good deal of moisture,[4] it should be
of close texture ; for such wood contains more sap.[5]
And, for the same reason, that which is of closer
texture either from its own natural character or
because it was grown in a drier spot,[6] is, whatever
the kind of tree, better.[7] But different kinds of
charcoal are used for different purposes : for some
uses men require it to be soft; thus in iron-mines
they use that which is made of sweet chestnut
when the iron has been already smelted, and in
silver-mines they use charcoal of pine-wood : and
these kinds are also used by the crafts. Smiths
require charcoal of fir rather than of oak : it is
indeed not so strong, but it blows up better into
a flame, as it is less apt to smoulder : and the flame
from these woods is fiercer. In general the flame is
fiercer not only from these but from any wood which
is of open texture and light, or which is dry : while
that from wood which is of close texture or green is
more sluggish and dull. The fiercest flame of all
is given by brushwood : but charcoal cannot be
made from it at all, since it has not the necessary
substance.

They cut and require for the charcoal-heap straight

[5] cf. § 1 ad fin.
[6] ξηρότερον conj. W.; ξηρότερα UMV; πυκνότερα ξηρότερα
Ald. I have bracketed τὸν.
[7] βελτίω conj. Sch.; βελτίαν UM ; βέλτιον Ald. H.
[8] cf. Plin. 16. 23.

εὐθέα καὶ τὰ λεῖα· δεῖ γὰρ ὡς πυκνότατα συν-
θεῖναι πρὸς τὴν κατάπνιξιν. ὅταν δὲ περι-
αλείψωσι τὴν κάμινον, ἐξάπτουσι παρὰ μέρος
παρακεντοῦντες ὀβελίσκοις. εἰς μὲν τὴν ἀνθρα-
κιὰν τὰ τοιαῦτα ζητοῦσι.

Δύσκαπνα δὲ τῷ γένει μὲν ὅλως τὰ ὑγρά· καὶ
τὰ χλωρὰ διὰ τοῦτο δύσκαπνα. λέγω δὲ τὰ ὑγρὰ
τὰ ἕλεια, οἷον πλάτανον ἰτέαν λεύκην αἴγειρον·
ἐπεὶ καὶ ἡ ἄμπελος ὅτε ὑγρὰ δύσκαπνος. ἐκ δὲ
τῆς ἰδίας φύσεως ὁ φοῖνιξ, ὃν δὴ καὶ μάλιστά
τινες ὑπειλήφασι δύσκαπνον· ὅθεν καὶ Χαιρήμων
ἐποίησε " τοῦ τε δυσκαπνοτάτου φοίνικος ἐκ γῆς
5 ῥιζοφοιτήτους φλέβας." δριμύτατος δὲ ὁ καπνὸς
συκῆς καὶ ἐρινεοῦ καὶ εἴ τι ἄλλο ὀπῶδες· αἰτία
δὲ ἡ ὑγρότης· φλοϊσθέντα δὲ καὶ ἀποβρεχθέντα
ἐν ὕδατι ἐπιρρύτῳ καὶ μετὰ ταῦτα ξηρανθέντα
πάντων ἀκαπνότατα καὶ φλόγα μαλακωτάτην
ἀνίησιν, ἅτε καὶ τῆς οἰκείας ὑγρότητος ἐξῃρημένης.
δριμεῖα δὲ καὶ ἡ τέφρα καὶ ἡ κονία ἡ ἀπ' αὐτῶν.
μάλιστα δέ φασι τὴν ἀπὸ τῆς ἀμυγδαλῆς.

6 Πρὸς δὴ τὰς καμινίας καὶ τὰς ἄλλας τέχνας
ἄλλη ἄλλοις χρησίμη. ἐμπυρεύεσθαι δὲ ἄριστα
συκῆ καὶ ἐλάα· συκῆ μέν, ὅτι γλίσχρον τε καὶ
μανόν, ὥστε ἕλκει τε καὶ οὐ δίεισιν· ἐλάα δέ, ὅτι
πυκνὸν καὶ λιπαρόν.

<hr/>

[1] λεῖα conj. Scal. from G ; νέα Ald.
[2] With sods. cf. Plin., l.c., who seems to have had a fuller text.
[3] An Athenian tragic poet. Scal. restores the quotation

470

smooth[1] billets: for they must be laid as close as possible for the smouldering process. When they have covered[2] the kiln, they kindle the heap by degrees, stirring it with poles. Such is the wood required for the charcoal-heap.

In general damp wood makes an evil smoke, and for this reason green wood does so: I mean the damp woods which grow in marshy ground, such as plane willow abele black poplar: for even vine-wood, when it is damp, gives an evil smoke. So does palm-wood of its own nature, and some have supposed it to give the most evil smoke of all: whence Chaeremon[3] speaks of "Veins issuing underground from roots of palm with its malodorous smoke." Most pungent is the smoke of fig-wood, whether wild or cultivated, and of any tree which has a curdling juice; the reason lies in the sap; when such wood has been barked and soaked in running water and then dried, it gives as little smoke as any other, and sends up a very soft[4] flame, since its natural moisture also has been removed. The cinders and ashes of such wood are also pungent, and especially, they say, those of almond-wood.

For the crafts requiring a furnace and for other crafts various woods are serviceable according to circumstances.[5] For kindling fig and olive are best: fig, because it is tough and of open texture, so that it easily catches fire and does not let it through,[6] olive, because it is of close texture and oily.

thus: τοῦ τε δυσκαπνωτάτου | φοίνικος ἐκ γῆς ῥιζοφοιτήτους φλέβας (ῥιζοφιτύτους conj. Schneidewin).

[4] *i.e.* not sputtering.

[5] καὶ . . . χρησίμη conj. W.; τέχναις ἀλλήλοις χρησίμη U; τ. ἀλλήλας χρ. MV; τέχνη ἄλλη ἐστι χρ. P; τ. ἀλλήλοις ἐστὶ χρησίμη Ald. [6] *i.e.* burn out quickly.

Πυρεῖα δὲ γίνεται μὲν ἐκ πολλῶν, ἄριστα δέ, ὥς φησι Μενέστωρ, ἐκ κιττοῦ· τάχιστα γὰρ καὶ πλεῖστον ἀναπνεῖ. πυρεῖον δέ φασιν ἄριστον μὲν ἐκ τῆς ἀθραγένης καλουμένης ὑπό τινων· τοῦτο δ' ἐστὶ δένδρον ὅμοιον τῇ ἀμπέλῳ καὶ τῇ οἰνάνθῃ τῇ ἀγρίᾳ· ὥσπερ ἐκεῖνα καὶ τοῦτο ἀνα-
7 βαίνει πρὸς τὰ δένδρα. δεῖ δὲ τὴν ἐσχάραν ἐκ τούτων ποιεῖν τὸ δὲ τρύπανον ἐκ δάφνης· οὐ γὰρ ἐκ ταὐτοῦ τὸ ποιοῦν καὶ πάσχον, ἀλλ' ἕτερον εὐθὺ δεῖ κατὰ φύσιν, καὶ τὸ μὲν δεῖ παθητικὸν εἶναι τὸ δὲ ποιητικόν. οὐ μὴν ἀλλὰ καὶ ἐκ τοῦ αὐτοῦ γίνεται καί, ὥς γέ τινες ὑπολαμβάνουσιν, οὐδὲν διαφέρει. γίνεται γὰρ ἐκ ῥάμνου καὶ πρίνου καὶ φιλύρας καὶ σχεδὸν ἐκ τῶν πλείστων πλὴν ἐλάας· ὃ καὶ δοκεῖ ἄτοπον εἶναι· καὶ γὰρ σκληρότερον καὶ λιπαρὸν ἡ ἐλάα· τοῦτο μὲν οὖν ἀσύμμετρον ἔχει δῆλον ὅτι τὴν ὑγρότητα πρὸς τὴν πύρωσιν. ἀγαθὰ δὲ τὰ ἐκ ῥάμνου· ποιεῖ δὲ τοῦτο καὶ τὴν ἐσχάραν χρηστήν· πρὸς γὰρ τῷ ξηρὰν καὶ ἄχυμον εἶναι δεῖ καὶ μανοτέραν, ἵν' ἡ τρίψις ἰσχύῃ, τὸ δὲ τρύπανον ἀπαθέστερον· δι' ὃ τὸ τῆς δάφνης ἄριστον· ἀπαθὲς γὰρ ὂν ἐργάζεται τῇ δριμύτητι. πάντα δὲ τὰ πυρεῖα βορείοις μὲν θᾶττον καὶ μᾶλλον ἐξάπτεται, νοτίοις δὲ ἧττον· καὶ ἐν μὲν τοῖς μετεώροις μᾶλλον, ἐν δὲ τοῖς κοίλοις ἧττον.
8 Ἀνίει δὲ τῶν ξύλων τὰ κέδρινα καὶ ἁπλῶς ὧν

---

¹ π. δὲ γίνεται μὲν conj. Sch.; π. μὲν γίνεται δὲ UMVAld.
² cf. 1. 2. 3 n.
³ κιττοῦ conj. Bod. from de igne 64, Plin. 16. 208 ; καρύου Ald.
⁴ πυρεῖον conj. Salm.; πυροὶ UMVAld.

Fire-sticks are made[1] from many kinds of wood,
but best, according to Menestor,[2] from ivy[3]: for
that flares up most quickly and freely. They
say also that a very good fire-stick[4] is made of
the wood which some call traveller's joy: this is
a tree like the vine or the 'wild vine,' which,
like these, climbs up trees. The stationary piece[5]
should be made of one of these, the drill of bay;
for the active and passive parts of the apparatus
should not be of the same wood, but different in
their natural properties to start with, one being
of active, the other of passive character. Nevertheless they are sometimes made of the same wood,
and some suppose that it makes no difference.
They are made in fact of buckthorn kermes-
oak lime and almost any wood except olive;
which seems surprising, as olive-wood is rather
hard and oily; however it is plainly its moisture
which makes it less suitable for kindling. The
wood of the buckthorn is also good, and it makes
a satisfactory stationary piece; for, besides being
dry and free from sap it is necessary that this
should also be of rather open texture, that the
friction may be effectual; while the drill should
be one which gets little worn by use. And that
is why one made of bay is best; for, as it is not
worn by use, it is effective through its biting
quality. All fire-sticks take fire quicker and better
in a north than in a south wind, and better in an
exposed spot than in one which is shut in.

Some woods, such as prickly cedar, exude[6]
moisture, and, generally speaking, so do those

⁵ *i.e.* the piece of wood to be bored. *cf. de igne, l.c.*
⁶ ἀνίει. ? ἀνιδίει.

ἐλαιώδης ἡ ὑγρότης· δι' ὃ καὶ τὰ ἀγάλματά
φασιν ἰδίειν ἐνίοτε· ποιοῦσι γὰρ ἐκ τούτων. ὃ
δὲ καλοῦσιν οἱ μάντεις Εἰλειθυίας ἄφεδρον, ὑπὲρ
οὗ καὶ ἐκθύονται, πρὸς τοῖς ἐλατίνοις γίνεται
συνισταμένης τινὸς ὑγρότητος, τῷ σχήματι μὲν
στρογγύλον μέγεθος δὲ ἡλίκον ἄπιον ἢ καὶ μικρῷ
μεῖζον ἢ ἔλαττον. ἐκβλαστάνει δὲ μάλιστα τὰ
ἐλάϊνα καὶ ἀργὰ κείμενα καὶ εἰργασμένα πολλάκις, ἐὰν ἰκμάδα λαμβάνῃ καὶ ἔχῃ τόπον νοτερόν·
ὥσπερ ἤδη τις στροφεὺς τῆς θύρας ἐβλάστησε, καὶ
εἰς κυλίκιον πλίνθινον τεθεῖσα κώπη ἐν πήλῳ.

---

[1] cf. C.P. 5. 4. 4. οἱ μάντεις . . . ἐλατίνοις conj. Lobeck.;
οἱ λεῖαν . . . τοῖς ἐκατίνοις U; οἰλείαν . . . τοὺς ἐκματίνοις V; οἱ
λεῖαν τῆς εἰληθήας . . . τοῖς ἐκματίνοις M ; οἱ λεῖαν τῆς ἀληθυίας
ἔφαιδρον . . . τοὺς ἐκατίνους P₂; ἰλεῖαν τῆς εἰληθυίας ἔφυδρον . . .
τοὺς ἐκατίνους Ald.

whose sap is of an oily character; and this is why statues are sometimes said to 'sweat'; for they are made of such woods. That which seers call the *menses* of Eileithuia,'[1] and for the appearance of which they make atonement,[2] forms on the wood of the silver-fir when some moisture gathers on it: the formation is round [3] in shape, and in size about as large as a pear, or a little larger or smaller. Olive-wood is more apt than other woods to produce shoots even when lying idle or made into manufactured articles; this it often does, if it obtains moisture and lies in a damp place; thus the socket of a door-'hinge'[4] has been known to shoot, and also an oar which was standing in damp earth in an earthenware vessel.[5]

[2] *i.e.* as a portent.  *cf. Char.* 16. 2.
[3] στρόγγυλον conj. Sch.; στρογγύλης UMVP₂Ald.
[4] *cf.* 5. 6. 4 ; Plin. 16. 230.
[5] πλινθ. τεθ. κώπη ἐν πήλῳ conj. Spr.; πλίνθινον τεθεὶς τῇ κώπῃ πηλός P₂Ald.H.

PRINTED IN GREAT BRITAIN BY
RICHARD CLAY AND SONS, LIMITED,
BRUNSWICK STREET, STAMFORD STREET, S.E.1
AND BUNGAY, SUFFOLK.

# THE LOEB CLASSICAL LIBRARY.

## VOLUMES ALREADY PUBLISHED.

### Latin Authors.

APULEIUS. The Golden Ass. (Metamorphoses.) Trans. by
W. Adlington (1566). Revised by S. Gaselee. 1 Vol.

CAESAR: CIVIL WARS. Trans. by A. G. Peskett. 1 Vol.

CATULLUS. Trans. by F. W. Cornish ; TIBULLUS.
Trans. by J. P. Postgate ; PERVIGILIUM VENERIS.
Trans. by J. W. Mackail. 1 Vol.

CICERO: DE FINIBUS. Trans. by H. Rackham. 1 Vol.

CICERO: DE OFFICIIS. Trans. by Walter Miller. 1 Vol.

CICERO: LETTERS TO ATTICUS. Trans. by E. O.
Winstedt. Vols I and II.

CONFESSIONS OF ST. AUGUSTINE. Trans. by W. Watts
1631). 2 Vols.

HORACE: ODES AND EPODES. Trans. by C. E. Bennett.
1 Vol.

OVID: HEROIDES AND AMORES. Trans. by Grant
Showerman. 1 Vol.

OVID: METAMORPHOSES. Trans. by F. J. Miller.
2 Vols.

PETRONIUS. Trans. by M. Heseltine ; SENECA : APOCO-
LOCYNTOSIS. Trans. by W. H. D. Rouse. 1 Vol.

PLAUTUS. Trans. by Paul Nixon. Vol. I.

PLINY: LETTERS. Melmoth's Translation revised by
W. M. L. Hutchinson. 2 Vols.

PROPERTIUS. Trans. by H. E. Butler. 1 Vol.

SUETONIUS. Trans. by J. C. Rolfe. 2 Vols.

TACITUS: DIALOGUS. Trans. by Sir Wm. Peterson ;
AGRICOLA AND GERMANIA. Trans. by Maurice
Hutton. 1 Vol.

TERENCE. Trans. by John Sargeaunt. 2 Vols.

## Greek Authors.

APOLLONIUS RHODIUS. Trans. by R. C. Seaton. 1 Vol.

THE APOSTOLIC FATHERS. Trans. by Kirsopp Lake. 2 Vols.

APPIAN'S ROMAN HISTORY. Trans. by Horace White. 4 Vols.

DAPHNIS AND CHLOE. Thornley's Translation revised by J. M. Edmonds; PARTHENIUS. Trans. by S. Gaselee. 1 Vol.

DIO CASSIUS: ROMAN HISTORY. Trans. by E. Cary. Vols. I, II, III, IV, and V.

EURIPIDES. Trans. by A. S. Way. 4 Vols.

THE GREEK ANTHOLOGY. Trans. by W. R. Paton. Vols. I, II, and III.

THE GREEK BUCOLIC POETS (THEOCRITUS, BION, MOSCHUS). Trans. by J. M. Edmonds. 1 Vol.

HESIOD AND THE HOMERIC HYMNS. Trans. by H. G. Evelyn White. 1 Vol.

JULIAN. Trans. by Wilmer Cave Wright. Vols. I and II.

LUCIAN. Trans. by A. M. Harmon. Vols. I and II.

MARCUS AURELIUS. Trans. by C. R. Haines. 1 Vol.

PHILOSTRATUS: THE LIFE OF APOLLONIUS OF TYANA. Trans. by F. C. Conybeare. 2 Vols.

PINDAR. Trans. by Sir J. E. Sandys. 1 Vol.

PLATO: EUTHYPHRO, APOLOGY, CRITO, PHAEDO, PHAEDRUS. Trans. by H. N. Fowler. 1 Vol.

PLUTARCH: THE PARALLEL LIVES. Trans. by B. Perrin. Vols. I, II, III, and IV.

PROCOPIUS. Trans. by H. B. Dewing. Vols. I and II.

QUINTUS SMYRNAEUS. Trans. by A. S. Way. 1 Vol.

SOPHOCLES. Trans. by F. Storr. 2 Vols.

ST. JOHN DAMASCENE: BARLAAM AND IOASAPH. Trans. by the Rev. G. R. Woodward and Harold Mattingly. 1 Vol.

XENOPHON: CYROPAEDIA. Trans. by Walter Miller. 2 Vols.

# IN PREPARATION.

## Greek Authors.

AESCHINES, C. D. Adams, of Dartmouth College.
AESCHYLUS, H. W. Smyth, of Harvard University.
ARISTOPHANES, J. W. White, of Harvard University.
ARISTOTLE, THE NICOMACHEAN ETHICS, Michael
  Heseltine, of New College, Oxford.
ARISTOTLE, THE POLITICS AND ATHENIAN CON-
  STITUTION, Edward Capps, of Princeton University.
ARRIAN, W. K. Prentice, of Princeton University.
ATHENAEUS, C. B. Gulick, of Harvard University.
CALLIMACHUS, A. W. Mair, Professor of Greek in the
  University of Edinburgh; ARATUS, G. R. Mair, of Gonville
  and Caius College, Cambridge.
CLEMENT OF ALEXANDRIA, Rev. G. W. Butterworth,
  of the University of Leeds.
DIO CHRYSOSTOM, W. E. Waters, New York University.
EUSEBIUS, Kirsopp Lake, of Harvard University.
GREEK LYRICS, J. M. Edmonds, of Jesus College, Cam-
  bridge.
HOMER, ILIAD, W. F. Harris, of Harvard University.
HOMER, ODYSSEY, A. T. Murray, of Stanford University.
IAMBIC AND ELEGIAC POETS, E. D. Perry, of Columbia
  University.
ISAEUS, R. J. Bonner, of the University of Chicago.
ISOCRATES, G. Norlin, of the University of Colorado.
MANETHO, S. de Ricci.
MENANDER, F. G. Allinson, of Brown University.
PAUSANIAS, W. H. S. Jones, of St. Catherine's College,
  Cambridge.
PHILOSTRATUS, IMAGINES, Arthur Fairbanks, Boston
  Museum of Fine Arts.
PLATO, LYSIS AND GORGIAS, W. R. Lamb, of Trinity
  College, Cambridge.
PLATO, REPUBLIC, Paul Shorey, University of Chicago.
PLUTARCH, MORALIA, F. C. Babbitt, of Trinity College,
  Hartford.
POLYBIUS, W. R. Paton.
THUCYDIDES, C. F. Smith, of the University of Wisconsin.
XENOPHON, ANABASIS AND HELLENICA, C. W.
  Brownson, of the College of the City of New York.

3

## Latin Authors.

AMMIANUS, C. U. Clark, of Yale University.

AULUS GELLIUS, C. B. Platner, of Western Reserve University.

AUSONIUS, H. G. Evelyn White, of Wadham College, Oxford.

CICERO, AD FAMILIARES, E. O. Winstedt, of Magdalen College, Oxford.

CICERO, DE ORATORE, ORATOR, BRUTUS, Charles Stuttaford.

FRONTINUS, DE AQUIS, C. Herschel, of New York.

FRONTO, C. R. Haines, of St. Catherine's College, Cambridge.

HORACE, EPISTLES AND SATIRES, W. G. Hale, of the University of Chicago, and G. L. Hendrickson, of Yale University.

JUVENAL AND PERSIUS, G. G. Ramsay, of Trinity College, Oxford, and late of Glasgow University.

LIVY, B. O. Foster, of Stanford University.

LUCAN, S. Reinach, Member of the Institute of France.

OVID, TRISTIA AND EX PONTO, A. L. Wheeler, of Bryn Mawr College.

SALLUST, J. C. Rolfe, of the University of Pennsylvania.

SENECA, EPISTULAE MORALES, R. M. Gummere, of Haverford College.

SENECA, MORAL ESSAYS, J. W. Basore, of Princeton University.

TACITUS, ANNALS, John Jackson, of Queen's College, Oxford.

VALERIUS FLACCUS, A. F. Scholfield, of King's College, Cambridge.

VELEIUS PATERCULUS, F. W. Shipley, of Washington University.

VITRUVIUS, F. W. Kelsey, of the University of Michigan.

*DESCRIPTIVE PROSPECTUS ON APPLICATION.*

**London**   =   •   **WILLIAM HEINEMANN**
**New York** =   •   **= G. P. PUTNAM'S SONS**

Lightning Source UK Ltd.
Milton Keynes UK
UKHW011908020323
417947UK00002B/64